Programming
Abstractions in *Java*™

Eric S. Roberts
Stanford University

PEARSON

Boston   Columbus   Indianapolis   New York   San Francisco   Hoboken

Amsterdam   Cape Town   Dubai   London   Madrid   Milan   Munich   Paris   Montreal   Toronto

Delhi   Mexico City   Sao Paulo   Sydney   Hong Kong   Seoul   Singapore   Taipei   Tokyo

Editorial Director, ECS: Marcia Horton
Executive Editor: Tracy Johnson
Developmental and Copy Editor: Lauren Rusk
Editorial Assistants: Kristy Alaura
Executive Marketing Manager: Tim Galligan
Director of Marketing: Christy Lesko
Product Marketing Manager: Bram van Kempen
Field Marketing Manager: Demetrius Hall
Marketing Assistant: Jon Bryant

Team Lead Program and Product Management: Scott Disanno
Program Manager: Carole Snyder
Cover Designer: Joyce Consentino Wells
Manager, Text Permissions: Rachel Youdelman
Text Permission Project Manager: Maya Gomez
Media Project Manager: Renata Butera
Composition and Art: Eric Roberts
Printer/Binder: R. R. Donnelley/Harrisonburg

Credits:
Cover: Polygraphus/DigitalVision Vectors/Getty Images.
Page 45: Ant image. Reprinted with permission © paulrommer | Fotolia.com.
Page 65: Coin images. Reprinted with permission © United States Mint.
Page 181: Dürer's *Melencolia I* (1514). Reprinted with permission © Photoservice Electa/Universal Images Group/SuperStock.
Page 375: Fractal Tree photo. Courtesy of Mark Wallinger. Photograph by Sam Frost/**samfrostphotos.com**.
Page 457: Tortoise and hare images. Reprinted with permission © John T Takai/Shutterstock.

Library of Congress Cataloging-in-Publication Data is available upon request.

10 9 8 7 6 5 4 3 2 1

ISBN 10: 0-13-442118-3
ISBN 13: 978-0-13-442118-6

In loving memory of my mother
Annie Hall Estep Roberts
(1922–2015)

To the Student

Over the last decade, the world of computing has grown vastly more exciting. The networked devices that most of us carry in our pockets have become faster, less expensive, and more powerful. Web-based services like Google and Wikipedia have put much of the world's information at our fingertips. Social networks have connected us with people throughout the world. Streaming technologies and faster hardware have made it possible to download music and video any time we want it.

These technologies, however, don't just happen; someone has to build them. Fortunately—at least for those who study this exciting and dynamic field—people with the necessary software-development skills are in short supply. Here, at the center of the high-tech economy in Silicon Valley, companies cannot find as many talented engineers as they need to turn technological visions into reality. Companies are desperate to find more people who know how to develop and maintain large systems—software developers who understand such issues as data representation, efficiency, security, correctness, and modularity.

Although this book won't teach you everything you need to know about these topics and the broader field of computer science, it will give you a good start. At Stanford, over 1200 students a year take the course that teaches this material. Many of those students find summer internships or industry jobs with no more background than this book provides. An even larger number of students continue on to more advanced courses that prepare them for the seemingly boundless opportunities that exist in this rapidly expanding field.

Beyond the opportunities they offer in the computing industry, the topics in this book are full of intellectual excitement. The algorithms and strategies you learn in this book—some of which were invented in the last decade while others have been around for more than 2000 years—are incredibly clever and stand as monuments to human creativity. They are also eminently practical and will help you become a much more sophisticated programmer.

As you read this book, please keep in mind that programming is always a matter of learning by doing. Reading about an algorithmic technique does not mean that you will be able to apply that algorithm in practice. Your real learning will come from working through the exercises and debugging your early attempts to solve those problems. Although programming can be frustrating at times, the thrill of finding that last bug and watching your program work is so profound that it more than makes up for any difficulties you encounter along the way.

Eric Roberts
Stanford University

To the Instructor

This text is intended for use in the second programming course in a typical college or university curriculum. It covers the material in a traditional CS2 course, as defined in the *Curriculum '78* report prepared by the Association for Computing Machinery (ACM). It therefore includes most of the topics specified for the $CS102_O$ and $CS103_O$ courses, as defined by the *Joint ACM/IEEE-CS Computing Curricula 2001* report and the material in the AL/Fundamental Data Structures and Algorithms unit from *Computer Science Curricula 2013*.

At first glance, the order in which topics appear this book will seem usual. The traditional CS2 curriculum typically consists of a sequential tour of the fundamental data structures. With this model, students learn how to use a particular data structure, how to implement it, and what its performance characteristics are—all at the same time. The primary weakness of this approach is that students are trying to understand how a structure is implemented before they have mastered how one would use that structure in an application. If, for example, students don't know why one would use a map in the first place, it is very hard for them to appreciate why they might prefer one implementation model over another.

At Stanford, we have adopted a different strategy, which we call the ***client-first approach.*** Students begin by learning how to use the full set of collection classes before they are asked to think about any implementation issues. They also have the chance to complete interesting assignments in which they use the collection classes as clients. In the process, those students gain a much better sense of the underlying data model and how each structure can be used. Once students have had time to master the client-side perspective, they are ready to explore the range of possible implementations and their associated computational characteristics.

The client-first approach has proven to be enormously successful in our classes. After we introduced this change in our CS2 course, median scores on the midterm examination increased by approximately 15 percentage points across all instructors. Scores on the final exam rose by more than five percentage points. Course grades and student satisfaction increased along with the improved comprehension. We now teach CS2 to more than 1200 students a year, and we are convinced that the client-first approach has been essential to making that possible.

I wrote this book to enable the many schools that teach CS2 in Java to share in the success that Stanford has experienced. We feel confident that you will be as amazed as we were by the improvement in the level of comprehension and efficacy that your students will achieve.

Supplemental Resources

For students

The following items are available to all readers of this book at the Pearson web site
(`http://www.pearsonhighered.com/ericroberts/`):

- Source code files for each example program in the book
- Full-color PDF versions of sample runs
- Answers to review questions

For instructors

The following items are available to qualified instructors from the Pearson web site
(`http://www.pearsonhighered.com/ericroberts/`):

- Source code files for each example program in the book
- Full-color PDF versions of sample runs
- Answers to review questions
- Solutions to programming exercises
- PowerPoint lecture slides for each of the chapters

Acknowledgments

I want to thank my colleagues at Stanford over the last several years, starting with Julie Zelenski for her pioneering work developing the client-first approach. My colleagues Keith Schwarz, Marty Stepp, Stephen Cooper, Cynthia Lee, Jerry Cain, Chris Piech, and Mehran Sahami have all made valuable contributions to both the pedagogical strategies and the support materials. I also need to express my thanks to several generations of undergraduate section leaders and my many students over the years, all of whom have helped make it so exciting to teach this material.

In addition, I want to express my gratitude to Marcia Horton, Tracy Johnson, and the other members of the team at Pearson for their support on this book as well as its predecessors over the years.

As always, the greatest thanks are due to my wife Lauren Rusk, who has again worked her magic as my developmental editor. Lauren's expertise has added considerable clarity and polish to the text. Without her, nothing would ever come out as well as it should.

Contents

Chapter 1
An Overview of Java

*Out of these various experiments come programs. This is our
experience: programs do not come out of the minds of one person
or two people such as ourselves, but out of day-to-day work.*

— Stokely Carmichael and Charles V. Hamilton,
  Black Power, 1967

In Lewis Carroll's *Alice's Adventures in Wonderland,* the King asks the White Rabbit to "begin at the beginning and go on till you come to the end: then stop." Good advice, but only if you're starting from the beginning. This book is designed for a second course in computer science and therefore assumes that you have already begun your study of programming. At the same time, because first courses vary considerably in what they cover, it is difficult for a textbook author to rely on your having mastered any specific material. Some of you, for example, will already understand Java control structures from prior experience with similar languages. Others will find the structure of Java unfamiliar. Because of this disparity in background, this chapter adopts the King's advice and introduces those parts of the Java language you will need to write simple programs.

1.1 Your first Java program

Java's design draws on several sources, including the programming language C, which appeared in the early 1970s. In the book that serves as C's defining document, *The C Programming Language,* Brian Kernighan and Dennis Ritchie offer the following advice on the very first page:

> The only way to learn a new programming language is by writing programs in it. The first program to write is the same for all languages:
>
> *Print the words*
>   `hello, world`
>
> This is the big hurdle; to leap over it you have to be able to create the program text somewhere, compile it successfully, load it, run it, and find out where the output went. With these mechanical details mastered, everything else is comparatively easy.

If you were to write the simplest possible version of the "Hello World" program in Java, it would end up looking something like the code in Figure 1-1.

FIGURE 1-1 The minimal "Hello World" program

```
/*
 * File: HelloWorld.java
 * ----------------------
 * This file is adapted from the example on page 1 of The C Programming
 * Language by Kernighan and Ritchie.
 */

public class HelloWorld {

    public static void main(String[] args) {
        System.out.println("hello, world");
    }

}
```

At this point, the important thing is not to understand exactly what all the lines in this program mean. There will be plenty of time to master those details later. Your mission—and you *should* decide to accept it—is to get the `Hello.java` program running. Type in the program exactly as it appears in Figure 1-1, and then figure out what you need to do to make it work.

The exact steps you need to follow depend on the programming environment you're using to create and run Java programs. If your computer supports a command-line interface—such as the **Terminal** utility on the Macintosh, the **Console** application on a Windows machine, or any of various shell programs in Linux—you should be able to run the "Hello World" program by typing the following commands in the directory that contains the `HelloWorld.java` file:

```
javac HelloWorld.java
java HelloWorld
```

The first line translates the file `HelloWorld.java` from the human-readable form in Figure 1-1 into a binary file that the computer can execute more efficiently. This process is called *compilation.* The second line runs the Java interpreter on the compiled version of the program.

In a command-line environment, the output from the program appears in the same window as the commands used to compile and run the program. On my Macintosh, for example, the terminal window session looks something like this:

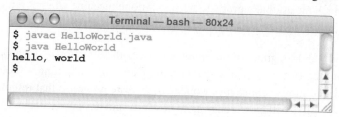

```
$ javac HelloWorld.java
$ java HelloWorld
hello, world
$
```

Although the command-line model gets the job done, professional Java programmers tend to use more sophisticated tools that integrate the process of editing, compiling, running, and debugging programs. Such tools are called *programming environments.* There are many programming environments that support Java, and it is impossible to describe them all in detail. If you are using this book as part of a class, your instructor will presumably provide you with reference material on the programming environments you are expected to use. If you are reading this book on your own, you'll need to refer to the documentation that comes with whatever programming environment you're using.

Even if you are using a professional programming environment, it is still a good idea to start with the "Hello World" program and get it running. Different environments will display the console output in different ways, but you should be able to find your program's cheery "hello, world" greeting. And although it may not be true that "everything else is comparatively easy," you will have passed a significant milestone.

1.2 The history of Java

Although this book is about programming strategies that transcend the details of a particular language, it has to choose some language so that readers can experiment with those techniques. Programming is, after all, a learn-by-doing discipline. You will not become a successful programmer just by reading this book, even if you solve all the exercises on paper. Learning to program is hands-on work that requires you to write and debug programs in a real programming language. Since this book uses the programming language Java, it will probably help to have some understanding of Java's developmental history and the ideas that underlie its design.

Programming languages

In the early days of computing, programs were written in *machine language,* which consists of primitive instructions that the machine can execute directly. Programs written in machine language are difficult to understand, mostly because the structure of machine language reflects the design of the hardware rather than the needs of programmers. Worse still, each type of computing hardware has its own machine language, which means that a program written for one machine will not run on other types of hardware.

In the mid-1950s, a group of programmers under the direction of John Backus at IBM had an idea that profoundly changed the nature of computing. Would it be possible, Backus and his colleagues wondered, to write programs that resembled the mathematical formulas they were trying to compute and have the computer translate those formulas into machine language? In 1955, this team produced the initial version of FORTRAN (whose name is a contraction of *formula translation*), which was the first language that allowed programmers to work with high-level concepts easily understood by people. Such languages are called *higher-level languages.*

Since that time, many new programming languages have been invented, most of which build on previous languages in an evolutionary way. Java represents the joining of two branches in that evolution. One of its ancestors is a language called C, which was designed at Bell Laboratories by Dennis Ritchie in 1972 and then later revised and standardized by the American National Standards Institute (ANSI) in 1989. But Java also descends from a family of languages designed to support a different style of programming—one that has dramatically changed the nature of software development in recent years.

The object-oriented paradigm

Over the last few decades, computer science and programming have gone through something of a revolution. Like most revolutions—whether political upheavals or the conceptual restructurings that Thomas Kuhn describes in his 1962 book *The Structure of Scientific Revolutions*—this change has been driven by the emergence of an idea that challenges an existing orthodoxy. Initially, the two ideas compete, and, at least for a while, the old order maintains its dominance. Over time, however, the strength and popularity of the new idea grows, until it begins to displace the older idea in what Kuhn calls a ***paradigm shift***. In programming, the old order is represented by the ***procedural paradigm,*** in which programs consist of a collection of procedures and functions that operate on data. The new model is called the ***object-oriented paradigm,*** in which programs are viewed instead as a collection of data objects that embody particular characteristics and behavior.

The idea of object-oriented programming is not really all that new. The first object-oriented language was SIMULA, a language for coding simulations that was designed by the Scandinavian computer scientists Ole-Johan Dahl and Kristen Nygaard in 1967. With a design that was far ahead of its time, SIMULA anticipated many of the concepts that later became commonplace in programming, including the concept of abstract data types and the modern object-oriented paradigm. In fact, much of the terminology used to describe object-oriented languages comes from the original 1967 report on SIMULA.

Unfortunately, SIMULA did not generate a great deal of interest in the years after its introduction. The first object-oriented language to gain any significant following within the computing profession was Smalltalk, which was developed at the Xerox Palo Alto Research Center in the late 1970s. The purpose of Smalltalk, which is described in the book *Smalltalk-80: The Language and Its Implementation* by Adele Goldberg and David Robson, was to make programming accessible to a wider audience.

Despite many attractive features and a highly interactive user environment that simplifies the programming process, Smalltalk never achieved much commercial success. The profession as a whole took an interest in object-oriented programming only when the central ideas were incorporated into variants of C, which had already become an industry standard. Although there were several parallel efforts to design an object-oriented language based on C, the most successful such language was C++, designed in the early 1980s by Bjarne Stroustrup at AT&T Bell Laboratories. By making it possible to integrate object-oriented techniques with existing C code, C++ enabled large communities of programmers to adopt the object-oriented paradigm in a gradual, evolutionary way.

Although object-oriented languages have gained some of their popularity at the expense of procedural languages, it would be a mistake to regard the object-oriented and procedural paradigms as mutually exclusive. Programming paradigms are not so much competitive as they are complementary. The object-oriented and the procedural paradigm—along with other important paradigms such as the functional style embodied in the programming language Lisp—all have important applications. Even within the context of a single application, you are likely to find a use for more than one approach. Expert programmers need to master several paradigms, so that they can use the model that is most appropriate to each task.

The Java programming language

Although C++ is still in widespread use, several other programming languages have also sought to incorporate the ideas of object-oriented programming. One of the most successful of these languages is Java, which was developed by a team of programmers at Sun Microsystems led by James Gosling. Today, Java is one of the most widely used programming languages in the computing industry. In particular, Java is the programming language for Google's Android operating system, which is the leading framework for the creation of applications for mobile devices.

When the Java project started in 1991, the goal was to design a language suitable for programming the microprocessors embedded in consumer electronic devices. Had Java retained its original goal, it would probably not have caught on to the extent that it has. As is often the case in computing, the direction of the Java project changed during its developmental phase in response to changing conditions in the industry.

The key factor leading to the change in focus was the phenomenal growth in the Internet that occurred in the early 1990s, particularly after the creation of the World-Wide Web. When interest in the web skyrocketed in 1993, Sun redesigned Java as a tool for writing interactive, web-based applications. That decision proved extremely well-timed. In the years following the release of the language in 1995, Java generated enormous excitement in both the academic and the commercial computing communities. In the process, object-oriented programming has become firmly established as a central paradigm in the computing.

Besides the synergy of its development with that of the web, another factor that has led to Java's success is its portability. For most languages, it is necessary to implement a different compiler for each platform that supports the language. These platforms, after all, have different underlying hardware and therefore use different machine languages. If the compiler has to translate the program files (which are generally referred to as *source files* in this context) into the actual instructions used by the hardware, changing the hardware inevitably requires changing the compiler accordingly.

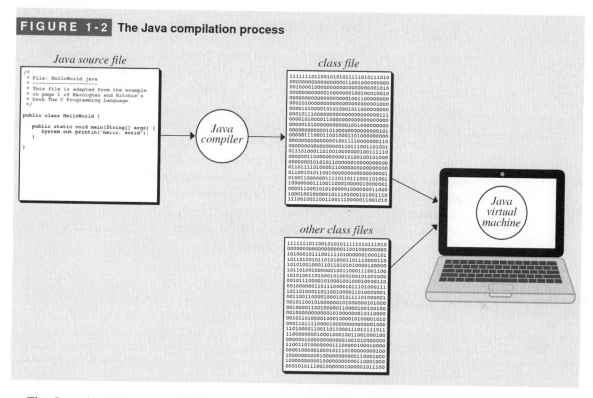

FIGURE 1-2 The Java compilation process

The Java developers pioneered a different approach, which is illustrated in Figure 1-2. The output of the Java compiler is not machine instructions for any existing hardware; the Java compiler instead produces *class files,* each of which contain instructions for an abstract architecture called the *Java virtual machine* or *JVM.* The class files produced by the compiler are then fed into a simulator for the JVM that runs on each platform. Each platform needs its own implementation of the JVM, but that is considerably easier to write than a full compiler.

The evolution of Java

Like human languages, programming languages change over time. Over the years, Java has evolved to meet the changing needs of its user community. New major releases of Java appear roughly every two years. Those releases now come from the Oracle Corporation, which acquired Sun Microsystems in 2010. As of the time of this writing, the most recent version is *Java Standard Edition 8* (usually shortened to *Java 8*), which was released in March 2014. Since new releases take time to make their way into common use, most of the chapters in this book do not depend on the most recent features and should be compatible with any version back to Java 5. Chapter 19 introduces lambda expressions, which are one of the most important new features of Java 8.

1.3 The structure of a Java program

The best way to get a feeling for the Java programming language is to look at some sample programs, even before you understand the details of the language. The **HelloWorld** program is a start, but it is so simple that it doesn't include many of the features you'd expect to see in a program. Since this book is designed for a second course in computer science, you've almost certainly written programs that read input from the user, store values in variables, and use loops to perform repeated calculations. The **HelloWorld** program does none of these things. To illustrate a few more features of Java, Figure 1-3 shows the code for a program called **AddThreeIntegers** that, as its name suggests, reads in three integers from the user, adds them together, and prints the sum. The figure also contains annotations that describe the various components of the program. The sections that follow describe each of those components in more detail.

FIGURE 1-3 Program to add three integers

```java
/*
 * File: AddThreeIntegers.java
 * --------------------------------
 * This program adds three integers and prints their sum.
 */

package edu.stanford.cs.javacs2.ch1;

import java.util.Scanner;

public class AddThreeIntegers {

    public void run() {
        Scanner sysin = new Scanner(System.in);
        System.out.println("This program adds three integers.");
        System.out.print("1st integer: ");
        int n1 = sysin.nextInt();
        System.out.print("2nd integer: ");
        int n2 = sysin.nextInt();
        System.out.print("3rd integer: ");
        int n3 = sysin.nextInt();
        int sum = n1 + n2 + n3;
        System.out.println("The sum is " + sum);
    }

/* Main program */

    public static void main(String[] args) {
        new AddThreeIntegers().run();
    }

}
```

program comments

package declaration

library imports

method containing the actual code

standard boilerplate

Comments

The first section of the **AddThreeIntegers** program in Figure 1-3 consists of an English-language comment. A *comment* is text that is ignored by the compiler but which nonetheless conveys information to other programmers. In Java, a comment is written by enclosing text between the markers **/*** and ***/**, which may continue over several lines. Alternatively, you can also specify single-line comments, which begin with the characters **//** and extend through the end of the line. This book uses the multiline **/* . . . */** comment form except when the comment marks some part of a program that is not yet complete. That strategy makes it easier to find unfinished parts of a program.

It is important to keep in mind that comments are written for human beings, not for the computer. Their primary purpose is to convey information about the program to other programmers. For programs as simple as **AddThreeIntegers**, extensive comments are usually not necessary. As your programs become more complicated, however, you will discover that including useful comments along with the code is one of the best ways to make those programs understandable to someone else—or to figure out what you yourself intended if you return to a program after not looking at it for a while.

Package declarations

The first line after the initial comment is a *package declaration,* which specifies where the compiler should look for the source files used to create this program. In the absence of a package declaration, the compiler looks for files in the current directory. While using the current directory has the advantage of convenience for small programs like **HelloWorld**, that strategy does not scale well when you start to write more sophisticated applications. When you begin working with a larger number of files, it helps to organize those files hierarchically, in much the same way that files are organized into directories.

In **AddThreeIntegers.java**, the package declaration looks like this:

```
package edu.stanford.cs.javacs2.ch1;
```

The package name used in this example conforms to the conventions established by the Java designers. The first three components of the package name come from the Internet domain at which these files are stored, which is **cs.stanford.edu**. The package name reverses the order of these components to preserve the convention of moving to more specific categories as you read from left to right. The component **javacs2** indicates that this package is part of the Java material used in CS2, which is the generic name for a second computer science course. The **ch1** component indicates that these files appear in Chapter 1.

The advantage of this hierarchical naming scheme is that packages can have unique identities throughout the entire Internet, as long as these naming conventions are preserved. When you write your own programs, you should put them into a hierarchy that adheres to these conventions as well.

In Java, source files must be stored in directories whose structure mirrors the package name. In this example, the source file **AddThreeIntegers.java** (along with the other files in Chapter 1) appears in a directory called **ch1**, which in turn appears in a directory called **javacs2**, and so forth back to a directory named **edu**, as illustrated in the following diagram:

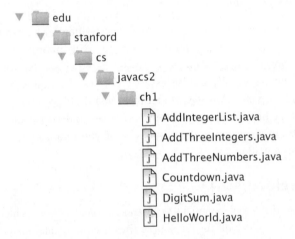

Managing these directories can be something of a bother, but the payoff in terms of organizational clarity more than makes up for the cost. Fortunately, most Java programming environments take care of these details for you. All you need to do is specify the package name, and the programming environment makes sure that the files appear in the right place in the directory hierarchy.

Imports

Programs are rarely written without using *libraries,* which are sets of previously written tools that perform useful operations. Java defines several standard libraries that you will learn about as you make your way through this book. The line

```
import java.util.Scanner;
```

tells the compiler to import the library class called **Scanner** from the **java.util** package, which provides a collection of commonly used utilities. The **Scanner** class simplifies considerably the process of obtaining input from the user, which is otherwise surprisingly complex in Java. Although the **Scanner** class is by no means an ideal facility for reading console input, it is certainly good enough for the examples used in the next few chapters.

Class definitions

The dashed line in Figure 1-3 encloses the definition of the `AddThreeIntegers` class, which begins with the line

```
public class AddThreeIntegers {
```

and ends with the matching closing brace on the last line of the file. Java requires all public classes to be defined in a source file whose name consists of the class name followed by the `.java` suffix. This source file therefore must be named `AddThreeIntegers.java` because it defines the `AddThreeIntegers` class.

The structure of a Java class is much too complicated to introduce in detail this early in the book. The classes in the next few chapters contain—possibly along with definitions of constants as described later in this chapter—one or more *methods,* which are sequences of program steps that have been collected together and given a name. In this respect, methods are similar to what more traditional programming languages call *functions.* The characteristic that sets methods apart from traditional functions in other languages is that methods are always associated with the class in which they are defined. In contrast to many languages, Java supports only methods; free-standing functions are not allowed.

No matter whether you use the term *function* or *method,* having some structure that allows you to invoke an entire sequence of steps under a single name is an absolutely indispensible feature of any programming language. This concept is in fact so important, that this book devotes the entirety of Chapter 2 to the topic. The programs in this chapter, such as the `AddThreeIntegers` example, contain only two methods. The first is a method called `run` that contains the actual code for the program. The second is a method called `main`, which appears in every Java program. Whenever a Java program runs, execution always begins by calling a method with precisely the following header line:

```
public static void main(String[] args)
```

You'll have a chance to learn what each of these keywords means later in the text. For now, however, it is sufficient to think of this line as something of a magic incantation that starts a Java program. Patterns that appear repeatedly in programs but don't require much conscious thought are called *boilerplate.* Whenever you write a new program, you simply write down the boilerplate, and you are set to go.

It is, moreover, helpful to extend this boilerplate to cover the entire definition of `main`, which is really a holdover from the C programming language before the days of object-oriented programming. In this book, all programs (except for the initial `HelloWorld` example) contain a `main` method that fits the following pattern:

```
public static void main(String args) {
    new classname().run();
}
```

This code uses the keyword **new** to invoke a special method that creates a new object of the class that contains the program. These special methods, called **constructors**, are discussed in more detail in Chapter 7. For now, the only thing you have to do to create this boilerplate is fill in the name of the class. In program listings, the definition of **main** is tucked away at the end of the class definition where it doesn't get in the way of understanding the important parts of the program.

The run method

When you follow the conventions described in the preceding section, the code for the actual program appears in a method called **run**, which consists of a series of Java statements. In **AddThreeIntegers**, the **run** method looks like this:

```
void run() {
    Scanner sysin = new Scanner(System.in);
    System.out.println("This program adds three integers.");
    System.out.print("1st integer: ");
    int n1 = sysin.nextInt();
    System.out.print("2nd integer: ");
    int n2 = sysin.nextInt();
    System.out.print("3rd integer: ");
    int n3 = sysin.nextInt();
    int sum = n1 + n2 + n3;
    System.out.println("The sum is " + sum);
}
```

The first line of the **main** method in the **AddThreeIntegers** program is another example of a pattern that will recur in programs that accept user input, which will always appear in exactly this form:

```
Scanner sysin = new Scanner(System.in);
```

This statement creates a new object of the **Scanner** class imported earlier in the program and assigns it a variable named **sysin**, which is short for *system input*. The source of the scanner is the standard input stream **System.in**, which is always available in a Java program, along with the standard output stream **System.out**. Unfortunately, having **System.in** always available does not mean that it is easy to use. As you will learn in Chapter 4, working with Java's standard input streams requires the use of several concepts that are more difficult to understand than any other aspect of the program. The good news is that embedding the **System.in** stream inside a **Scanner** object sidesteps much of this complexity.

The next line in the program is functionally equivalent to the single line in the **HelloWorld** program. The only change is in the string that gets displayed. Here, the string is simply a message that tells the user what the program is doing, at which time the program output looks like this:

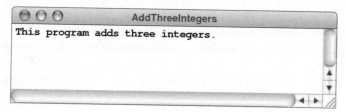

Now that the preliminaries are out of the way, the program can get on with the work of reading in the input values. Reading in each variable requires a pair of statements, which looks like this for the first integer:

```
System.out.print("1st integer: ");
int n1 = sysin.nextInt();
```

The first line is almost the same as the statement that describes the purpose of the program. The only difference is that the code calls the method **print** instead of **println**, which means that the cursor stays on the same line as the text, which is exactly what you want when you ask the user for input. The string inside the call to **print** is called a ***prompt,*** which is a message to the user that indicates what value is expected. At this point, the console output looks like this, where the vertical bar indicates the position of the cursor:

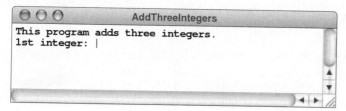

The second line in the input pattern invokes the **nextInt** method on the **Scanner** object to read a value of type **int** into the variable **n1**. If, for example, you type the number 396 and then hit the RETURN key, the variable **n1** will be set to 396, and the console will look like this:

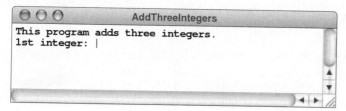

The line

```
int n1 = sysin.nextInt();
```

is an example of a *variable declaration,* which reserves space for a variable used by the program and typically assigns it an initial value. In this case, the statement introduces a new variable named `n1` capable of holding a value of type `int`, the standard type used to represent integers. It also assigns that variable the value that appears on the right side of the equal sign, which is the value entered by the user. The next four lines of the `run` method repeat this process to assign values to the variables `n2` and `n3`.

The next line of the `run` method is

```
int sum = n1 + n2 + n3;
```

This line is also a declaration, which introduces the integer variable `sum`. In this case, the initial value of the variable is given by the expression `n1 + n2 + n3`, which is interpreted as it is in conventional mathematics. The program adds the values in `n1`, `n2`, and `n3` and then stores the result as the initial value of the variable `sum`.

The final statement in the `run` method is

```
System.out.println("The sum is " + sum + ".");
```

which accomplishes the task of displaying the computed result. For the most part, this statement looks like the other statements that call the `System.out.println` method. This time, however, there's a new twist. Instead of taking a single string argument, this statement passes to `println` the argument value

```
"The sum is " + sum + "."
```

As in the `n1 + n2 + n3` expression from the previous statement, this expression uses the `+` operator to combine individual values. In this statement, at least some of the values to which `+` is applied are strings rather than the numeric values for which addition is traditionally defined. In Java, applying the `+` operator to string data reinterprets that operator to mean adding the strings together end to end to combine their characters. This operation is called *concatenation.* If there are any parts of the expression that are not strings, Java converts them into their standard string representation before applying the concatenation operator. The effect of this final statement is to display the value of `sum` after concatenating it with the strings that tell the user what the output value represents. You can see the effect of this statement in the following sample run, in which the user enters the values 396, 183, and 487:

```
┌─────────────────────────────────────────────┐
│ ◯ ◯ ◯          AddThreeIntegers              │
├─────────────────────────────────────────────┤
│ This program adds three integers.           │
│ 1st integer: 396                            │
│ 2nd integer: 183                            │
│ 3rd integer: 487                            │
│ The sum is 1066                             │
│                                             │
└─────────────────────────────────────────────┘
```

Although **AddThreeIntegers** is set up to work only with integers, Java is capable of working with many other types of data as well. You could, for example, change this program so that it added three real numbers simply by changing the types of the variables and the names of the scanner methods, as shown in the following revised implementation of the **run** method:

```java
void run() {
    Scanner sysin = new Scanner(System.in);
    System.out.println("This program adds three numbers.");
    System.out.print("1st number: ");
    double n1 = sysin.nextDouble();
    System.out.print("2nd number: ");
    double n2 = sysin.nextDouble();
    System.out.print("3rd number: ");
    double n3 = sysin.nextDouble();
    double sum = n1 + n2 + n3;
    System.out.println("The sum is " + sum);
}
```

In computer science, numbers that include a decimal fraction, such as 1.5 or 3.14159265, are called *floating-point numbers.* The most common floating-point type in Java is **double**, which is short for *double-precision floating-point.* If you need to store floating-point values in a program, you must declare variables of type **double**, just as you previously had to declare variables of type **int** to write **AddThreeIntegers**. The only other change in the program is that it requests input from the user by calling **nextDouble** instead of **nextInt**. The basic pattern of the program is unchanged.

 ## 1.4 Variables

Data values in a program are usually stored in *variables,* which are named locations in memory capable of holding a particular data type. You have already seen examples of variables in the **AddThreeIntegers** program and are almost certainly familiar with the basic concept from your earlier programming experience. This section outlines the rules for using variables in Java.

Variable declarations

In Java, you must *declare* each variable before you use it. The primary function of declaring a variable is to make an association between the *name* of the variable and the *type* of value that variable contains. The placement of the declaration in a program also determines the *scope* of the variable, which is the region in which that variable is accessible.

The most common syntax for declaring a variable is

type   name = *value;*

where *type* indicates the data type, *name* is the name of the variable, and *value* is the initial value. You can, for example, declare an integer variable named `total` and initialize it to zero using the following line:

```
int total = 0;
```

It is important to remember that both the name and the type of a variable remain fixed throughout its lifetime but that the value of that variable typically changes as the program runs. To emphasize the dynamic nature of the value of a variable, it often helps to diagram variables as boxes in which the name appears outside as a label on the box and the value appears inside. For example, you might diagram the declaration of `total` like this:

```
total
┌─────────┐
│    0    │
└─────────┘
```

Assigning a new value to `total` overwrites any previous contents of the box, but does not change the name or the type.

Naming conventions

The names used for variables, methods, types, constants, and so forth are collectively known as *identifiers.* In Java, the rules for identifier formation are

1. The name must start with a letter or the underscore character (_).

2. All other characters in the name must be letters, digits, or the underscore. No spaces or other special characters are permitted in names.

3. The name must not be one of the reserved keywords listed in Figure 1-4.

Uppercase and lowercase letters appearing in an identifier are considered to be different. Thus, the name `ABC` is not the same as the name `abc`. Identifiers can be of any length, but Java compilers are not required to consider any more than the first 31 characters in determining whether two names are identical.

FIGURE 1-4 Reserved words in Java

abstract	continue	for	new	switch
assert	default	goto	package	synchronized
boolean	do	if	private	this
break	double	implements	protected	throw
byte	else	import	public	throws
case	enum	instanceof	return	transient
catch	extends	int	short	try
char	final	interface	static	void
class	finally	long	strictfp	volatile
const	float	native	super	while

You can improve your programming style by adopting conventions for identifiers that help readers identify their function. In this text, names of variables and methods begin with a lowercase letter, such as `limit` or `raiseToPower`. The names of classes and other programmer-defined data types begin with an uppercase letter, as in `Direction` or `TokenScanner`. Constant values are written entirely in uppercase, as in `PI` or `HALF_DOLLAR`. Whenever an identifier consists of several English words run together, the usual convention is to capitalize the first letter of each word to make the name easier to read. Because that strategy doesn't work for constants, programmers use the underscore character to mark the word boundaries.

Most variables in a Java program are declared within the body of a method. Such variables are called *local variables* because they are defined only within the block in which they are declared. When a method is called, space is allocated for each local variable; when the method returns, all its local variables disappear. Variables, however, can also be declared as part of a class, but outside the body of any of its methods. Such variables are called *instance variables* and will be discussed in detail in Chapter 7.

1.5 Constants

As you write your programs, you will find that you often use the same constant many times in a program. If, for example, you are performing geometrical calculations that involve circles, the constant π comes up frequently. Moreover, if those calculations require high precision, you might actually need all the digits that fit into a value of type `double`, which means you would be working with the value 3.14159265358979323846. Writing that constant over and over again is tedious at best, and likely to introduce errors if you type it in by hand each time instead of cutting and pasting the value. It would be better if you could give this constant a name and then refer to it by that name everywhere in the program. You could, of course, simply declare `pi` as a local variable by writing

```
double pi = 3.14159265358979323846;
```

but you would then be able to use it only within the method in which it was defined. A better strategy is to declare a global constant named `PI` like this:

```
public static final double PI = 3.14159265358979323846;
```

The keyword `public` at the beginning of this declaration indicates that the value is accessible even beyond the confines of this class, which is likely to be useful for a constant like `PI`, which is defined in precisely this fashion in the standard `Math` class. If the constant has no significance outside of the class, however, it is better to declare it using the keyword `private` instead. The keyword `static` indicates that this variable belongs to the class itself and not to each object. The keyword `final` indicates that the value will not change after the variable is initialized, which is what makes it a constant. The rest of the declaration consists of the type, the name, and the value, as before. The only difference is that the name is written entirely in uppercase in accordance with the Java naming conventions for constants.

Using named constants offers several advantages. First, descriptive constant names make the program easier to read. More importantly, using constants can dramatically simplify the problem of maintaining the code for a program as it evolves. Even if the value of `PI` is unlikely to change, some constant definitions specify values that might change as the program evolves, even though they remain constant for a particular version of that program.

The importance of this principle is easiest to illustrate by historical example. Imagine for the moment that you are a programmer in the late 1960s working on the initial design of the *ARPANET,* the first large-scale computer network and the ancestor of today's Internet. Because resource constraints were quite severe at that time, you would need to impose a limit—as the actual designers of the ARPANET did in 1969—on the number of host computers that could be connected. In the early years of the ARPANET, that limit was 127 hosts. If Java had existed in those days, you might have declared a constant that looked like this:

```
static final int MAXIMUM_NUMBER_OF_HOSTS = 127;
```

At some later point, however, the explosive growth of networking would have forced you to raise this bound. That process would be relatively easy if you used named constants in your programs. To raise the limit on the number of hosts to 1023, it might well be sufficient to change this declaration so that it reads

```
static final int MAXIMUM_NUMBER_OF_HOSTS = 1023;
```

If you used `MAXIMUM_NUMBER_OF_HOSTS` everywhere in your program to refer to that maximum value, making this change would automatically propagate to every part of the program in which the constant name appears.

Note that the situation would be entirely different if you had used the numeric constant 127 instead. In that case, you would need to search through the entire program and change all instances of 127 used for this purpose to the larger value. Some instances of 127 might well refer to other things than the limit on the number of hosts, and it would be just as important not to change any of those values. In the likely event that you made a mistake, you would have a very hard time tracking down the bug.

1.6 Data types

Each variable in a Java program contains a value constrained to be of a particular type. You set the type of the variable as part of the declaration. So far, you have seen variables of type **int** and **double**, but these types merely scratch the surface of the types available in Java. Programs today work with many different data types, some of which are built into the language and some of which are defined as part of a particular application. Learning how to manipulate data of various types is an essential part of mastering the basics of any language, including Java.

The concept of a data type

In Java, every data value has an associated data type. From a formal perspective, a *data type* is defined by two properties: a *domain*, which is the set of values that belong to that type, and a *set of operations*, which defines the behavior of that type. For example, the domain of the type **int** includes all integers

$$\ldots -9, -8, -7, -6, -5, -4, -3, -2, -1, 0, 1, 2, 3, 4, 5, 6, 7, 8, 9 \ldots$$

and so on, up to the limits established by the hardware of the machine. The set of operations applicable to values of type **int** includes, for example, the standard arithmetic operations like addition and multiplication. Other types have a different domain and set of operations.

As you will learn in later chapters, much of the power of modern programming languages like Java comes from the fact that you can define new data types from existing ones. To get that process started, Java includes several fundamental types that are defined as part of the language. These types, which act as the building blocks for the type system as a whole, are called *atomic* or *primitive types.* These predefined types are grouped into four categories—integer, floating-point, Boolean, and character—which are discussed in the sections that follow.

Integer types

Although the concept of an integer seems like a simple one, Java actually includes several different data types for representing integer values. In most cases, all you need to know is the type **int**, which corresponds to the standard representation of an integer on the computer system you are using. In certain cases, however, you need to be more careful. Like all data, values of type **int** are stored internally in storage units that have a limited capacity. Those values therefore have a maximum size, which limits the range of integers you can use. To get around this problem, Java defines four integer types—**byte**, **short**, **int**, and **long**—distinguished from each other by the size of their domains. The domains for these four types, along with the other primitive types, are summarized in Figure 1-5.

An integer constant is ordinarily written as a string of decimal digits. If the number begins with the digit 0, however, the compiler interprets the value in base 8, which is called *octal.* Thus, the constant **040** is taken to be in octal and represents the decimal number 32. If you prefix a numeric constant with the characters **0x**, the compiler interprets that number in base 16, or *hexadecimal.* Thus, the constant **0xFF** is equivalent to the decimal constant 255.

Floating-point types

Numbers that include a decimal fraction are called *floating-point numbers,* which are used to approximate real numbers in mathematics. Java defines two different floating-point types: **float** and **double**. Because doing so reduces the need for explicit conversion between these two types, this text avoids using **float** and instead relies on **double** as its standard floating-point type.

FIGURE 1-5 Primitive types in Java

Type	Domain	Common operations
byte	8-bit integers in the range –128 to 127	*The arithmetic operators:* + – * / %
short	16-bit integers in the range –32768 to 32767	*The relational operators:* == != < <= > >=
int	32-bit integers in the range –2147483648 to 2147483647	*The bitwise operators:* & | ~ << >> >>>
long	64-bit integers in the range –9223372036854775808 to 9223372036854775807	
float	32-bit floating point numbers in the range $\pm 1.4 \times 10^{-45}$ to $\pm 3.4028235 \times 10^{-38}$	*The arithmetic operators except* % *The relational operators*
double	64-bit floating point numbers in the range $\pm 4.39 \times 10^{-322}$ to $\pm 1.7976931348623157 \times 10^{-308}$	
char	16-bit characters encoded using Unicode	*The relational operators*
boolean	the values **true** and **false**	*The logical operators:* && || !

Floating-point constants in Java are written with a decimal point. Thus, if **2.0** appears in a program, the number is represented internally as a floating-point value; if the programmer had written **2**, this value would be an integer. Floating-point values can also be written in a special programmer's style of scientific notation, in which the value is represented as a floating-point number multiplied by an integral power of 10. To express a number using this style, you write a floating-point number in standard notation, followed immediately by the letter **E** and an integer exponent, optionally preceded by a + or – sign. For example, the speed of light in meters per second can be written in Java as

    2.9979E+8

where the **E** stands for the words *times 10 to the power.*

Boolean type

In the programs you write, it is often necessary to test a particular condition that affects the subsequent behavior of your code. Typically, that condition is specified using an expression whose value is either true or false. This data type—for which the only legal values are the constants **true** and **false**—is called *Boolean data,* after the mathematician George Boole, who developed an algebraic approach for working with such values.

In Java, the Boolean type is called **boolean**. You can declare variables of type **boolean** and manipulate them in the same way as other data objects. The operations that apply to the type **boolean** are described in detail in the section entitled "Boolean operators" on page 32.

Characters

In the early days, computers were designed to work only with numeric data and were sometimes called *number crunchers* as a result. Modern computers, however, work less with numeric data than they do with text data, that is, any information composed of individual characters that appear on the keyboard and the screen. The ability of modern computers to process text data has led to the development of word processing systems, online reference libraries, electronic mail, social networks, and a seemingly infinite number of exciting applications.

The most primitive elements of text data are individual characters, which are represented in Java using the predefined data type **char**. The domain of type **char** is the set of symbols that can be displayed on the screen or typed on the keyboard: the letters, digits, punctuation marks, space, RETURN, and so forth. The type **char** includes, moreover, symbols from a wide variety of alphabets and special-purpose applications.

Internally, values of type `char` are represented inside the computer by assigning each character a numeric code. In Java, the coding system used to represent characters is called **Unicode,** an international standard derived from an earlier coding scheme called **ASCII,** which stands for the **American Standard Code for Information Interchange.** The Unicode character set includes 15,536 characters, which makes it impossible to list all the character codes in any convenient way. The first 128 characters of Unicode, however, have the same internal values as in the older ASCII code, which appears in Figure 1-6. The numbers at the top of each row and to the left of each column define the numeric code for each character expressed in octal. For example, the letter **J** appears in the row labeled 11x and the column labeled 1. Concatenating these labels shows that the Unicode representation for **J** is 112 in octal, which is equivalent to the decimal value 74 ($1 \times 64 + 1 \times 8 + 2$).

Although it is important to know that characters are represented internally using a numeric code, it is not generally useful to know what numeric value corresponds to a particular character. When you type the letter **J**, the hardware logic built into the keyboard automatically translates that character into the number 74, which is then sent to the computer. Similarly, when the computer sends the Unicode character 74 to the console, the letter **J** appears.

FIGURE 1-6 **The ASCII subset of the Unicode character encoding**

	0	1	2	3	4	5	6	7
0x	\000	\001	\002	\003	\004	\005	\006	\a
1x	\b	\t	\n	\v	\f	\r	\016	\017
2x	\020	\021	\022	\023	\024	\025	\026	\027
3x	\030	\031	\032	\033	\034	\035	\036	\037
4x	space	!	"	#	$	%	&	'
5x	(	)	*	+	,	-	.	/
6x	0	1	2	3	4	5	6	7
7x	8	9	:	;	<	=	>	?
10x	@	A	B	C	D	E	F	G
11x	H	I	J	K	L	M	N	O
12x	P	Q	R	S	T	U	V	W
13x	X	Y	Z	[	\	]	^	_
14x	`	a	b	c	d	e	f	g
15x	h	i	j	k	l	m	n	o
16x	p	q	r	s	t	u	v	w
17x	x	y	z	{	|	}	~	\177

You can write a character constant in Java by enclosing the character in single quotes. Thus, the constant 'J' represents the internal code of the uppercase letter J. In addition to the standard characters, Java allows you to write special characters in a multicharacter form beginning with a backward slash (\). This form is called an *escape sequence.* Figure 1-7 shows the escape sequences that Java supports.

Strings

Characters are most useful when they are collected together into sequential units. In programming, a sequence of characters is called a *string.* So far, the strings you've seen in the **HelloWorld** and **AddThreeIntegers** programs have been used simply to display messages on the screen, but strings have many more applications than that.

You write string constants in Java by enclosing the characters contained within the string in double quotes. As with the data type **char**, Java uses the escape sequences in Figure 1-7 to represent special characters. If a string constant is too long to fit on one program line, you can always use the **+** operator to concatenate two string constants together.

Compound types

The primitives types described in the preceding sections form the basis of a very rich type system that allows you to create new types from existing ones. Learning how to define and manipulate these types is, to a large extent, the theme of this entire book. It therefore does not make sense to squeeze a complete description of these types into Chapter 1. That's what the rest of the chapters are for.

FIGURE 1-7 Java escape sequences	

\b	Backspace
\f	Formfeed (starts a new page)
\n	Newline (moves to the beginning of the next line)
\r	Return (returns to the beginning of the current line without advancing)
\t	Tab (moves horizontally to the next tab stop)
\\	The character \ itself
\'	The character ' (requires the backslash only in character constants)
\"	The character " (requires the backslash only in string constants)
\ddd	The character whose ASCII value is the octal number *ddd*
\uxxxx	The character whose Unicode value is the hexadecimal number *xxxx*

Over many years of teaching this material at Stanford, we have discovered that you are much more likely to master the concepts of object-oriented programming if the details of defining classes and objects are presented *after* you have had a chance to use them in a high-level way. This book adopts that strategy and postpones any discussion of how to define your own objects until Chapter 7, at which point you will have had plenty of time to discover just how useful objects can be.

1.7 Expressions

Whenever you want a program to perform calculations, you need to write an expression that specifies the necessary operations in a form similar to that used for expressions in mathematics. For example, suppose that you wanted to solve the quadratic equation

$$ax^2 + bx + c = 0$$

As you know from high-school mathematics, this equation has two solutions given by the formula

$$x = \frac{-b \pm \sqrt{b^2 - 4ac}}{2a}$$

The first solution is obtained by using + in place of the ± symbol; the second is obtained by using – instead. In Java, you could compute the first of these solutions by writing the following expression:

```
(-b + Math.sqrt(b * b - 4 * a * c)) / (2 * a)
```

There are a few differences in form: multiplication is represented explicitly by a *, division is represented by a /, and the square root operation is represented by the **Math.sqrt** function described in Chapter 2. Even so, the Java form of the expression captures the intent of its mathematical counterpart in a way that is quite readable, particularly if you have prior experience with programming.

In Java, an expression is composed of terms and operators. A *term,* such as the variables **a**, **b**, and **c** or the constants 2 and 4 in the preceding expression, represents a single data value and must be either a constant, a variable, or a method call. An *operator* is a character (or sometimes a short sequence of characters) that denotes a computational operation. A list of the operators available in Java appears in Figure 1-8. The table includes familiar arithmetic operators like + and – along with several others that pertain only to types introduced in later chapters.

FIGURE 1-8 Operators available in Java

Operators organized into precedence groups	Associativity
() [] .	*left*
unary operators: − ++ −− ! ~ *(type)*	*right*
* / %	*left*
+ −	*left*
<< >> >>>	*left*
< <= > >= instanceof	*left*
== !=	*left*
&	*left*
^	*left*
		left
&&	*left*
||	*left*
?:	*right*
= *op=*	*right*

Precedence and associativity

The point of listing all the operators in a single table is to establish how they relate to one another in terms of **precedence,** which is a measure of how tightly an operator binds to its operands in the absence of parentheses. If two operators compete for the same operand, the one that appears higher in the precedence table is applied first. Thus, in the expression

```
(-b + Math.sqrt(b * b - 4 * a * c)) / (2 * a)
```

the multiplications `b * b` and `4 * a * c` are performed before the subtraction because `*` has a higher precedence than `-`. It is, however, important to note that the `-` operator occurs in two forms. Operators that connect two operands are called **binary operators;** operators that take just one operand are called **unary operators.** When a minus sign is written in front of a single operand, as in `-b`, it is interpreted as a unary operator signifying negation. When it appears between two operands, as it does inside the argument to `Math.sqrt`, the minus sign is a binary operator signifying subtraction. The precedence of the unary and binary versions of an operator are different and are listed separately in the precedence table.

If two operators have the same precedence, they are applied in the order specified by their **associativity,** which indicates whether that operator groups to the left or to the right. Most operators in Java are *left-associative,* which means that the leftmost operator is evaluated first. A few operators, such as the assignment operator discussed in its own section later in this chapter, are *right-associative,* which means that they group from right to left. The associativity for each operator appears in the right-hand column of Figure 1-8.

The quadratic formula illustrates the importance of paying attention to precedence and associativity rules. Consider what would happen if you wrote the expression without the parentheses around 2 * a, as follows:

```
(-b + Math.sqrt(b * b - 4 * a * c)) / 2 * a
```

Without the parentheses, the division operator would be performed first, because / and * have the same precedence and associate to the left. This example illustrates the use of the bug icon in this text to mark code that is intentionally incorrect so that you won't copy it into your own programs.

Mixing types in an expression

In Java, you can write an expression that includes values of different numeric types. If Java encounters an operator whose operands are of different types, the compiler automatically converts the operands to a common type as long as the conversion moves along the arrows in the following diagram:

$$\text{byte} \longrightarrow \text{short} \searrow \atop \text{char} \nearrow \text{int} \longrightarrow \text{long} \longrightarrow \text{float} \longrightarrow \text{double}$$

The result of applying the operation is always that of the arguments after any conversions are applied. This convention ensures that the result of the computation is as precise as possible.

As an example, suppose that **n** is declared as an **int**, and **x** is declared as a **double**. The expression

```
n + 1
```

is evaluated using integer arithmetic and produces a result of type **int**. The expression

```
x + 1
```

however, is evaluated by converting the integer 1 to the floating-point value 1.0 and adding the results together using double-precision floating-point arithmetic, which results in a value of type **double**.

Integer division and the remainder operator

The fact that applying an operator to two integer operands generates an integer result leads to an interesting situation with respect to the division operator. If you write an expression like

```
9 / 4
```

Java's rules specify that the result of this operation must be an integer, because both operands are of type `int`. When Java evaluates this expression, it divides 9 by 4 and discards any remainder. Thus, the value of this expression in Java is 2, not 2.25.

If you want to compute the mathematically correct result of 9 divided by 4, at least one of the operands must be a floating-point number. For example, the three expressions

```
9.0 / 4
9 / 4.0
9.0 / 4.0
```

each produce the floating-point value 2.25. The decimal fraction is thrown away only if both operands are of type `int`. The operation of discarding a decimal fraction is called *truncation.*

The `/` operator in Java is closely associated with the `%` operator, which returns the remainder left over when the first operand is divided by the second. For example, the value of

```
9 % 4
```

is 1, since 4 goes into 9 twice, with 1 left over. The following are some other examples of the `%` operator:

```
0 % 4   =   0              19 % 4   =   3
1 % 4   =   1              20 % 4   =   0
4 % 4   =   0            2001 % 4   =   1
```

The `/` and `%` operators are extremely useful in a wide variety of programming applications. You can, for example, use the `%` operator to test whether one number is divisible by another; to determine whether an integer **n** is divisible by 3, you just check whether the result of the expression **n** `%` 3 is 0.

If one or both of the operands to the `%` operator are negative, the Java standard specifies that **x** `%` **y** will always have the same sign as **x**. While the standard means that Java programs will always generate the same result even on different machines, Java's definition is at odds with the mathematical formulation of modular arithmetic. To avoid any possible confusion, it is good programming practice to avoid—as this book does—using the % operator with negative values.

Type casts

In Java, you can convert one type to another by using what is called a *type cast,* which specifies an explicit conversion action. In Java, type casts are usually written by specifying the name of the desired type in parentheses, followed by the value you wish to convert. For example, if **num** and **den** are declared as integers, you can compute the floating-point quotient by writing

```
double quotient = (double) num / den;
```

The first step in evaluating the expression is to convert **num** to a **double**, after which the division is performed using floating-point arithmetic, as described in the section on "Mixing types in an expression" earlier in this chapter.

As long as the conversion follows the arrows in the type-conversion diagram from the preceding section, the conversion involves no loss of information. If, however, you convert a value of a more precise type to a less precise one, some information may be lost. For example, if you use a type cast to convert a value of type **double** to type **int**, any decimal fraction is simply dropped. Thus, the value of the expression

```
(int) 1.9999
```

is the integer 1.

The assignment operator

In Java, assignment of values to variables is built into the structure of the expression. The = operator takes two operands, just like + or *. The left operand must indicate a value that can change, which is typically a variable name. When the assignment operator is executed, the expression on the right-hand side is evaluated, and the resulting value is then stored in the variable that appears on the left-hand side. Thus, if you evaluate an expression like

```
result = 1
```

the effect is that the value 1 is assigned to the variable **result**. In most cases, assignment expressions appear in the context of a simple statement, in which the assignment is followed by a semicolon, as in the line

```
result = 1;
```

Such statements are often called *assignment statements.*

Java allows assignment statements to convert the value on the right-hand side so that it matches the declared type of the variable as long as the conversion involves no loss of accuracy. Thus, if the variable `total` is declared to be of type `double`, and you write the assignment statement

```
total = 0;
```

Java automatically converts the integer 0 into a `double` as part of making the assignment. By contrast, if `n` is declared to be of type `int`, the assignment

```
n = 3.14159265;
```

is illegal in Java, because values of type `double` do not automatically convert to type `int`. If you want Java to perform this conversion, you have to include an explicit type cast, as in

```
n = (int) 3.14159265;
```

which sets the variable `n` to 3.

Even though assignment operators usually occur in the context of simple assignment statements, they can also be incorporated into larger expressions, in which case the result of applying the assignment operator is simply the value assigned. For example, the expression

```
z = (x = 6) + (y = 7)
```

has the effect of setting `x` to 6, `y` to 7, and `z` to 13. The parentheses are required in this example because the `=` operator has a lower precedence than `+`. Assignments that are written as part of larger expressions are called ***embedded assignments.***

Although there are contexts in which embedded assignments are convenient, they often make programs more difficult to read because the assignment is easily overlooked in the middle of a complex expression. For this reason, this text limits the use of embedded assignments to a few special circumstances in which they seem to make the most sense. The most important is when you want to set several variables to the same value. Java's definition of assignment as an operator makes it possible, instead of writing separate assignment statements, to write a single statement like

```
n1 = n2 = n3 = 0;
```

which has the effect of setting all three variables to 0. This statement works because Java evaluates assignment operators from right to left. The entire statement is therefore equivalent to

```
n1 = (n2 = (n3 = 0));
```

Java evaluates the expression **n3 = 0** first, which sets **n3** to 0. It also passes 0 along as the value of the assignment expression, which is then assigned to **n2** and subsequently to **n1**. Statements of this sort are called *multiple assignments.*

As a programming convenience, Java allows you to combine assignment with a binary operator to produce a form called a *shorthand assignment.* For any binary operator *op*, the statement

> *variable op= expression;*

is equivalent to

> *variable = variable op (expression);*

where the parentheses are included to emphasize that the entire expression is evaluated before *op* is applied. Thus, the statement

```
balance += deposit;
```

is shorthand for

```
balance = balance + deposit;
```

which adds **deposit** to **balance**.

Because this same shorthand applies to any binary operator in Java, you can subtract the value of **surcharge** from **balance** by writing

```
balance -= surcharge;
```

Similarly, you can divide the value of **x** by 10 using

```
x /= 10;
```

Increment and decrement operators

Beyond the shorthand assignment operators, Java offers a further level of abbreviation for the particularly common programming operations of adding or subtracting 1 from a variable. Adding 1 to a variable is called *incrementing* it; subtracting 1 is called *decrementing* it. To indicate these operations in an extremely compact form, Java uses the operators **++** and **--**. For example, in Java the statement

```
x++;
```

has the same effect on the variable **x** as

```
x += 1;
```

which is itself short for

```
x = x + 1;
```

Similarly,

```
y--;
```

has the same effect as

```
y -= 1;
```

or

```
y = y - 1;
```

As it happens, these operators are more intricate than the preceding examples would suggest. To begin with, each of these operators can be written in two ways. The operator can come after the operand to which it applies, as in

```
x++
```

or before the operand, as in

```
++x
```

The first form, in which the operator follows the operand, is called the *suffix* form, the second, the *prefix* form.

If all you do is execute the **++** operator in isolation—as you do in the context of a separate statement or the standard **for** loop patterns—the prefix and suffix operators have precisely the same effect. You notice the difference only if you use these operators as part of a larger expression. Then, like all operators, the **++** operator returns a value, but the value depends on where the operator is written relative to the operand. The two cases are as follows:

> **x++** Calculates the value of **x** first, and then increments it. The value returned to the surrounding expression is the original value *before* the increment operation is performed.
>
> **++x** Increments the value of **x** first, and then uses the new value as the value of the **++** operation as a whole.

The **--** operator behaves similarly, except that the value is decremented rather than incremented.

You may wonder why would anyone use such an arcane feature. The ++ and -- operators are certainly not essential. Moreover, there are not many circumstances in which programs that embed these operators in larger expressions are demonstrably better than those that use a simpler approach. On the other hand, ++ and -- are firmly entrenched in the historical tradition shared by the languages C, C++, and Java. Programmers use them so frequently that they have become essential idioms in these languages. In light of their widespread use in programs, you need to understand these operators so that you can make sense of existing code.

Boolean operators

Java defines three classes of operators that manipulate Boolean data: the relational operators, the logical operators, and the ?: operator. The *relational operators* are used to compare two values. Java defines six relational operators, as follows:

==	Equal
!=	Not equal
>	Greater than
<	Less than
>=	Greater than or equal to
<=	Less than or equal to

When you write programs that test for equality, be careful to use the == operator, which is composed of two equal signs. A single equal sign is the assignment operator. Since the double equal sign violates conventional mathematical usage, replacing it with a single equal sign is a particularly common mistake. This mistake can also be very difficult to track down, because the Java compiler does not always catch it as an error. A single equal sign turns the expression into an embedded assignment, which is perfectly legal in Java; it just isn't at all what you want.

The relational operators can be used to compare primitive data values like integers, floating-point numbers, Boolean values, and characters. As you will discover in later chapters, these operators do not work with object types and must instead be implemented using method calls.

In addition to the relational operators, Java defines three *logical operators* that take Boolean operands and combine them to form other Boolean values:

!	Logical *not* (**true** if the following operand is **false**)
&&	Logical *and* (**true** if both operands are **true**)
||	Logical *or* (**true** if either or both operands are **true**)

These operators are listed in decreasing order of precedence.

Although the operators **&&**, **| |**, and **!** closely resemble the English words *and*, *or*, and *not*, it is important to remember that English can be somewhat imprecise when it comes to logic. To avoid that imprecision, it is often helpful to think of these operators in a more formal, mathematical way. Logicians define these operators using **truth tables,** which show how the value of a Boolean expression changes as the values of its operands change. The truth table in Figure 1-9 illustrates the result for each of the logical operators, given all possible values of the variables **p** and **q**.

Whenever a Java program evaluates an expression of the form

      *exp*₁ **&&** *exp*₂

or

      *exp*₁ **| |** *exp*₂

the individual subexpressions are always evaluated from left to right, and evaluation ends as soon as the result is determined. For example, if *exp*₁ is **false** in the expression involving **&&**, there is no need to evaluate *exp*₂, since the final result will always be **false**. Similarly, in the example using **| |**, there is no need to evaluate the second operand if the first operand is **true**. This style of evaluation, which stops as soon as the result is known, is called **short-circuit evaluation.**

The Java programming language includes another Boolean operator called **?:** that can be extremely useful in certain situations. In programming parlance, the name of this operator is always pronounced as *question-mark colon*, even though the two characters do not appear adjacent to each other in the code. Unlike the other operators in Java, **?:** is written in two parts and requires three operands. The general form of the operation is

      (*condition*) **?** *exp*₁ **:** *exp*₂

The parentheses are not technically required, but Java programmers often include them to emphasize the boundaries of the conditional test.

FIGURE 1-9 **Truth table for the logical operators**

p	q	p && q	p || q	!p
false	false	false	false	true
false	true	false	true	true
true	false	false	true	false
true	true	true	true	false

When a Java program encounters the **?:** operator, it first evaluates the condition. If the condition turns out to be **true**, exp_1 is evaluated and used as the value of the entire expression; if the condition is **false**, the value is the result of evaluating exp_2. For example, you can use the **?:** operator to assign to **max** either the value of **x** or the value of **y**, whichever is greater, as follows:

```
max = (x > y) ? x : y;
```

1.8 Statements

Programs in Java are composed of methods, which are made up in turn of statements. As in most languages, statements in Java fall into one of two principal classifications: **simple statements** that perform some action and **control statements** that affect the way in which other statements are executed. The sections that follow review the principal statement forms available in Java, giving you the tools you need to write your own programs.

Simple statements

The most common statement in Java is the simple statement, which consists of an expression—which must be a method call, an assignment, an invocation of the increment or decrement operator, or a declaration—followed by a semicolon:

> *expression;*

The semicolon turns the expression into a simple statement.

Blocks

As Java is defined, control statements typically apply to a single statement. When you are writing a program, you often want a particular control statement to apply to a whole group of statements. To indicate that a sequence of statements is part of a coherent unit, you can assemble those statements into a **block**, which is a collection of statements enclosed in curly braces, as follows:

```
{
    statement₁
    statement₂
    . . .
    statementₙ
}
```

When the Java compiler encounters a block, it treats the entire block as a single statement. Thus, whenever the notation *statement* appears in a pattern for one of the control forms, you can substitute for it either a single statement or a block. Because blocks are statements as far as the compiler is concerned, they are sometimes referred to as **compound statements.** In Java, the statements in any block may be preceded by declarations of variables.

The statements in the interior of a block are usually indented relative to the enclosing context. The compiler ignores the indentation, but the visual effect is extremely helpful to the human reader, because it makes the structure of the program jump out at you from the format of the page. Empirical research has shown that indenting three or four spaces at each new level makes the program structure easiest to see; the programs in this text use three spaces for each new level. Indentation is critical to good programming, so you should strive to develop a consistent indentation style in your programs.

The `if` statement

In writing a program, you will often want to check whether some condition applies and use the result of that check to control the subsequent execution of the program. This type of program control is called **conditional execution.** The easiest way to express conditional execution in Java is by using the `if` statement, which comes in two forms:

> `if` (*condition*) *statement*

> `if` (*condition*) *statement* `else` *statement*

You use the first form of the `if` statement when your solution strategy calls for a set of statements to be executed only if a particular Boolean condition is `true`. If the condition is `false`, the statements that form the body of the `if` statement are simply skipped. You use the second form of the `if` statement for situations in which the program must choose between two independent sets of actions according to the result of a test. This statement form is illustrated by the following code, which reports whether an integer `n` is even or odd:

```
if (n % 2 == 0) {
   System.out.println("That number is even.");
} else {
   System.out.println("That number is odd.");
}
```

As with any control statement, the statements controlled by the `if` statement can be either a single statement or a block. Even if the body of a control form is a single statement, you are free to enclose it in a block if you decide that doing so improves the readability of your code. The programs in this book enclose the body of every control statement in a block unless the entire statement—both the control form and its body—is so short that it fits on a single line.

The switch statement

The **if** statement is ideal for applications in which the program logic calls for a two-way decision point: a condition is either **true** or **false**, and the program acts accordingly. Some applications, however, call for more complicated decision structures involving several mutually exclusive cases: in one case, the program should do *x;* in another case, it should do *y;* in a third, it should do *z;* and so forth. In many applications, the most appropriate statement to use for such situations is the **switch** statement, which has the following syntactic form:

```
switch (e) {
  case c₁:
      statements
     break;
  case c₂:
      statements
     break;
  . . . more case clauses . . .
  default:
      statements
     break;

}
```

The expression *e* is called the ***control expression.*** When the program executes a **switch** statement, it evaluates the control expression and compares it against the values c_1, c_2, and so forth, each of which must be a constant. If one of the constants matches the value of the control expression, the statements in the associated **case** clause are executed. When the program reaches the **break** statement at the end of the clause, the operations specified by that clause are complete, and the program continues with the statement that follows the entire **switch** statement.

The **default** clause is used to specify what action occurs if none of the constants match the value of the control expression. The **default** clause, however, is optional. If none of the cases match and there is no **default** clause, the program simply continues on with the next statement after the **switch** statement without taking any action at all. To avoid the possibility that the program might ignore an unexpected case, it is good programming practice to include a **default** clause in every **switch** statement unless you are certain you have enumerated all the possibilities.

The code pattern I've used to illustrate the syntax of the **switch** statement deliberately suggests that **break** statements are required at the end of each clause. In fact, Java is defined so that if the **break** statement is missing, the program starts executing statements from the next clause after it finishes the selected one. While this design can be useful in some cases, it causes many more problems than it solves. To reinforce the importance of remembering to exit at the end of each **case** clause, the programs in this text include a **break** or **return** statement in all such clauses.

The one exception to this rule is that multiple **case** lines specifying different constants can appear together, one after another, before the same statement group. For example, a **switch** statement might include the following code:

```
case 1:
case 2:
    statements
    break;
```

which indicates that the specified statements should be executed if the **select** expression is either 1 or 2. The Java compiler treats this construction as two **case** clauses, the first of which is empty. Because the empty clause contains no **break** statement, a program that selects the first path simply continues on with the second clause. From a conceptual point of view, however, you are better off if you think of this construction as a single **case** clause representing two possibilities.

The constants in a **switch** statement must be a *scalar type,* which is defined in Java as a type that uses an integer as its underlying representation. In particular, characters are often used as **case** constants, as illustrated by the following code, which tests to see if the value of the character variable **ch** is a vowel:

```
switch (ch) {
  case 'A': case 'E': case 'I': case 'O': case 'U':
  case 'a': case 'e': case 'i': case 'o': case 'u':
    System.out.println(ch + " is a vowel.");
    break;
  default:
    System.out.println(ch + " is not a vowel.");
    break;
}
```

The **while** statement

In addition to the conditional statements **if** and **switch**, Java includes several control statements that allow you to execute some part of the program multiple times to form a loop. Such control statements are called *iterative statements.* The simplest iterative statement in Java is the **while** statement, which executes a statement repeatedly until a conditional expression becomes **false**. The general form for the **while** statement looks like this:

```
while (conditional-expression) {
    statements
}
```

When a program encounters a `while` statement, it first evaluates the conditional expression to see whether it is `true` or `false`. If it is `false`, the loop *terminates* and the program continues with the next statement after the entire loop. If the condition is `true`, the entire body is executed, after which the program goes back to the beginning of the loop to check the condition again. A single pass through the statements in the body constitutes a *cycle* of the loop.

There are two important principles about the operation of a `while` loop:

1. The conditional test is performed before every cycle of the loop, including the first. If the test is `false` initially, the body of the loop is not executed at all.

2. The conditional test is performed only at the *beginning* of a loop cycle. If the condition becomes `false` at some point during the loop, the program won't notice that fact until it completes the entire cycle. At that point, the program evaluates the test condition again. If the condition is still `false`, the loop terminates.

The operation of the `while` loop is illustrated by the `DigitSum` program, which appears in Figure 1-10. The purpose of this program is to calculate the sum of the digits in a positive integer supplied by the user. For example, if you were to enter the integer 1789, the `DigitSum` program should calculate the sum $1+7+8+9$ to generate the answer 25.

The heart of the `DigitSum` program is the following `while` loop:

```
int sum = 0;
while (n > 0) {
    sum += n % 10;
    n /= 10;
}
```

This code depends on the following observations:

*   The expression `n % 10` always returns the last digit in a positive integer `n`.
*   The expression `n / 10` returns a number without its final digit.

The `while` loop is designed for situations in which there is some test condition that can be applied at the beginning of a repeated operation, before any of the statements in the body of the loop are executed. If the problem you are trying to solve fits this structure, the `while` loop is the perfect tool. Unfortunately, many programming problems do not fit easily into the standard `while` loop structure, in

FIGURE 1-10 Program to sum the digits in an integer

```java
/*
 * File: DigitSum.java
 * ---------------------
 * This program adds the digits in a number.
 */

package edu.stanford.cs.javacs2.ch1;

import java.util.Scanner;

public class DigitSum {

   public void run() {
      Scanner sysin = new Scanner(System.in);
      System.out.println("This program sums the digits in an integer.");
      System.out.print("Enter a number: ");
      int n = sysin.nextInt();
      int sum = 0;
      while (n > 0) {
         sum += n % 10;
         n /= 10;
      }
      System.out.println("digitSum(" + n + ") = " + sum);
   }

/* Main program */

   public static void main(String[] args) {
      new DigitSum().run();
   }

}
```

which the test comes at the beginning. Some problems are structured in such a way that the test you want to write to determine whether the loop is complete falls most naturally somewhere in the middle of the loop.

The most common examples of such loops are those that read in data from the user until some special value, or *sentinel,* is entered to signal the end of the input. When expressed in English, the structure of a sentinel-based loop consists of repeating the following steps:

1. Read in a value.
2. If the value is equal to the sentinel, exit from the loop.
3. Perform whatever processing is required for that value.

Unfortunately, there is no test you can perform at the beginning of the loop to determine whether the loop is finished. The termination condition for the loop is reached when the input value is equal to the sentinel; in order to check this condition, the program must first read in some value. If the program has not yet read in a value, the termination condition doesn't make sense.

When some operations must be performed before you can check the termination condition, you have a situation that programmers call the *loop-and-a-half problem.* One strategy for solving the loop-and-a-half problem in Java is to use the **break** statement, which, in addition to its role in the **switch** statement, has the effect of immediately terminating the innermost enclosing loop. If you allow yourself to use the **break** statement, you can code the loop structure in a form that follows the natural structure of the problem, which is called the *read-until-sentinel pattern:*

```
while (true) {
    Prompt user and read in a value.
    if (value == sentinel) break;
    Process the data value.
}
```

Note that the

```
while (true)
```

line itself seems to introduce an infinite loop because the value of the constant **true** can never become **false**. The only way this program can exit from the loop is by executing the **break** statement inside it. The **AddIntegerList** program in Figure 1-11 uses the read-until-sentinel pattern to compute the sum of a list of integers terminated by the sentinel value 0.

There are other strategies for solving the loop-and-a-half problem, most of which involve copying part of the code outside the loop or introducing additional Boolean variables. Empirical studies have demonstrated that students are more likely to write correct programs if they use a **break** statement to exit from the middle of the loop than if they are forced to use some other strategy. This evidence and my own experience have convinced me that using the read-until-sentinel pattern is the best solution to the loop-and-a-half problem.

The `for` statement

One of the most important control statements in Java is the **for** statement, which is used in situations in which you want to repeat an operation a particular number of times. All modern programming languages have a statement that serves that purpose, but the **for** statement in the C family of languages is especially powerful and is useful in a wide variety of applications.

FIGURE 1-11 **Program to add a list of integers**

```
/*
 * File: AddIntegerList.java
 * ---------------------------
 * This program adds a list of integers.  The end of the input is indicated
 * by entering a sentinel value, which is defined by the constant SENTINEL.
 */

package edu.stanford.cs.javacs2.ch1;

import java.util.Scanner;

public class AddIntegerList {

    public void run() {
        Scanner sysin = new Scanner(System.in);
        System.out.println("This program adds a list of integers.");
        System.out.println("Use " + SENTINEL + " to signal the end.");
        int total = 0;
        while (true) {
            System.out.print(" ? ");
            int value = sysin.nextInt();
            if (value == SENTINEL) break;
            total += value;
        }
        System.out.println("The total is " + total);
    }

/* Private constants */

    private static final int SENTINEL = 0;

/* Main program */

    public static void main(String[] args) {
        new AddIntegerList().run();
    }

}
```

Although you will see many other uses of **for** as you make your way through this book, the most common applications of the **for** statement fall into two idiomatic patterns. The first is used when you want to perform an operation a predetermined number of times, represented by *n* in the following pattern:

> **for (int** *var* **= 0;** *var* **<** *n;* *var***++)**

The variable indicated by *var* in this pattern is called an **_index variable._** Although you can use any legal variable name for this purpose, both programmers and mathematicians have a long tradition of using single-letter variable names taken from the middle of the alphabet, such as **i**, **j**, **k**, and so on. Although short variable names are usually poor choices because they convey very little about the purpose of that variable, the fact that this naming convention exists makes such names appropriate in this context. Whenever you see the variable **i** or **j** in a **for** loop, you can be reasonably confident that the variable is counting through a range of values.

The second common pattern appears when you want to count from one value to another. This pattern has the following general form:

```
for (int var = start; var <= finish; var++)
```

In this pattern, the body of the **for** loop is executed with the variable *var* set to each value between *start* and *finish,* inclusive. Thus, you can use a **for** loop to have the variable **i** count from 1 to 100 like this:

```
for (int i = 1; i <= 100; i++)
```

The **for** loop in Java, however, is considerably more general than these common patterns suggest. The general form of the **for** loop in Java looks like this:

```
for (init; test; step) {
    statements
}
```

This code is equivalent to the following **while** statement:

```
init;
while (test) {
    statements
    step;
}
```

The code fragment specified by *init,* which is typically a variable declaration, runs before the loop begins and is most often used to initialize an index variable. For example, if you write

```
for (int i = 0; . . .
```

the loop will begin by setting the index variable **i** to 0. If the loop begins

```
for (int i = -7; . . .
```

the variable **i** will start as −7, and so on.

The *test* expression is a conditional test written just as it is in a **while** statement. As long as the test expression is **true**, the loop continues. Thus, the loop

```
for (int i = 0; i < n; i++)
```

begins with **i** equal to 0 and continues as long as **i** is less than **n**, which turns out to represent a total of **n** cycles, with **i** taking on the values 0, 1, 2, and so on, up to the final value **n−1**. The loop

```
for (int i = 1; i <= n; i++)
```

begins with **i** equal to 1 and continues as long as **i** is less than or equal to **n**. This loop also runs for **n** cycles, with **i** taking on the values 1, 2, and so forth, up to **n**.

The *step* expression indicates how the value of the index variable changes from cycle to cycle. The most common form of step specification is to increment the index variable using the **++** operator, but this is not the only possibility. For example, one can count backward using the **−−** operator, or count by twos using **+= 2** instead of **++**. As an example, in the **Countdown** program included in the programming examples for this chapter, the **for** loop

```
for (int t = 10; t >= 0; t--) {
    System.out.println(t);
}
```

uses the index variable **t** to count backward from 10 to 1, which generates the following sample run:

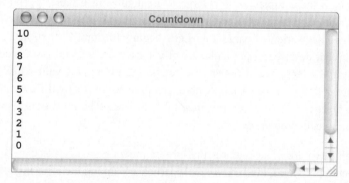

Each of the expressions in a **for** statement is optional, but the semicolons must appear. If *init* is missing, no initialization is performed. If *test* is missing, Java assumes a value of **true**. If *step* is missing, no action occurs between loop cycles.

1.9 Classes, objects, and methods

The concepts of *classes, objects,* and *methods* are essential to programming in Java, and you have already seen examples of these structures in every program in this chapter. Every program is itself a class whose name matches the file in which it was contained. In addition to the program classes, you have also encountered a few classes from the standard Java packages, including the **System** class, which provides the standard input and output streams, and the `Scanner` class used to simplify console input. You have also encountered several objects in the course of these examples. The declaration

```
Scanner sysin = new Scanner(System.in);
```

involves two objects. The expression `System.in` is an object that happens to be an instance of a class called `BufferedInputStream` in the `java.io` package. The keyword `new` invokes the constructor for the `Scanner` class to create an object that reads values of various types from the underlying input stream. You have also had occasion to use methods, which give you access to the operations supported by a class. The `Scanner` class, for example, exports methods named `nextInt` and `nextDouble`, which read the next value of the specified type.

Classes, objects, and methods are all incredibly important topics in Java—so important, in fact, that it is impossible to cover them completely in this chapter, which presents only an overview of these topics. The details come in various places throughout the book. Chapter 2, for example, focuses entirely on methods and fills in most of the missing details. Classes and objects appear not only in Chapter 7, which is named for them, but also in most of the other chapters.

Even though these topics are too large to treat fully in Chapter 1, introducing some vocabulary and high-level concepts at this point can give you a sense of how Java uses the object-oriented paradigm. Let's begin with some definitions. A *class* is a template that describes a particular set of values along with an associated set of operations. In the language of object-oriented programming, the values that belong to a class are called *objects.* A single class can give rise to many different objects; each such object is said to be an *instance* of that class. The operations associated with a class are called *methods.*

Although there are other features that programmers typically associate with the object-oriented paradigm, the following properties are among the most important:

- *Encapsulation.* One of the defining features of a class is that it combines data values and their associated operations into a single, unified whole. In addition, object-oriented languages typically allow the designer of a class to control the level of access that other programs have to those operations and values. If a class defines methods or values that other programmers will need to use, those methods will be marked as `public`. If a class defines methods or values that are relevant only to its own implementation, those methods will be `private`.

- *Inheritance.* Classes in a typical object-oriented language form a hierarchy in which classes inherit behavior from classes at higher levels.

The class structure of an object-oriented language is similar in many ways to the biological classification system developed by the eighteenth-century Swedish botanist Carl Linnaeus as a means of representing the structure of the biological world. In Linnaeus's conception, living things are first subdivided into *kingdoms*. The original system contained only the plant and animal kingdoms, but there are some forms of life—such as fungi and bacteria—that don't fit well in either category and now occupy kingdoms of their own. Each kingdom is further broken down into the hierarchical categories of *phylum, class, order, family, genus,* and *species*. Every living species fits at the bottom of this hierarchy but also belongs to some category at each higher level.

This biological classification system is illustrated in Figure 1-12, which shows the classification of the common black garden ant, whose scientific name,

FIGURE 1-12 Class hierarchies in the biological world

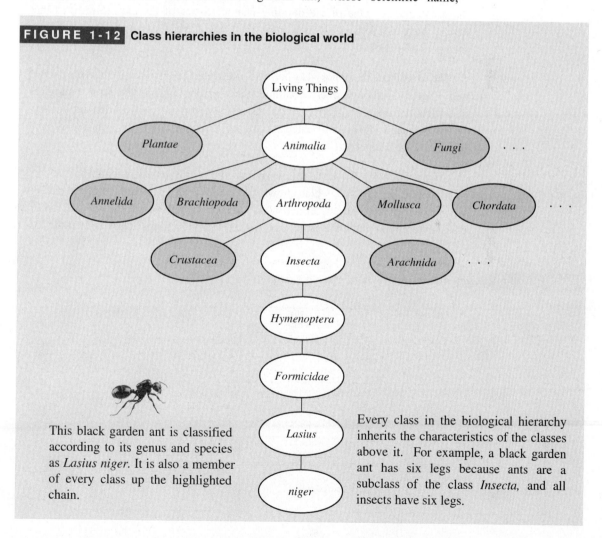

This black garden ant is classified according to its genus and species as *Lasius niger*. It is also a member of every class up the highlighted chain.

Every class in the biological hierarchy inherits the characteristics of the classes above it. For example, a black garden ant has six legs because ants are a subclass of the class *Insecta*, and all insects have six legs.

Lasius niger, corresponds to its genus and species. This species of ant, however, is also part of the family *Formicidae,* which is the classification that actually identifies it as an ant. If you move upward in the hierarchy from there, you discover that *Lasius niger* is also of the order *Hymenoptera* (which includes bees and wasps), the class *Insecta* (which consists of the insects), and the phylum *Arthropoda* (which includes, for example, shellfish and spiders).

One of the properties that makes this biological classification system useful is that all living things belong to a category at every level in the hierarchy. Each individual life form therefore belongs to several categories simultaneously and inherits the properties that are characteristic of each one. The species *Lasius niger,* for example, is an ant, an insect, an arthropod, and an animal—all at the same time. Moreover, each individual ant shares the properties that it inherits from each of those categories. One of the defining characteristics of the class *Insecta* is that insects have six legs. All ants must therefore have six legs because ants are members of that class.

The biological metaphor also helps to illustrate the distinction between classes and objects. Although every common black garden ant has the same biological classification, there are many individuals of the common-black-garden-ant variety. In the language of object-oriented programming, *Lasius niger* is a class and each individual ant is an object.

Class structures in Java follow much the same organizational pattern, as illustrated in Figure 1-13, which shows the relationship between three of the classes you have seen and the predefined class **Object**, which forms the root of Java's class hierarchy in much the same way that the "Living Things" class does at the top

FIGURE 1-13 **A tiny subset of the Java class hierarchy**

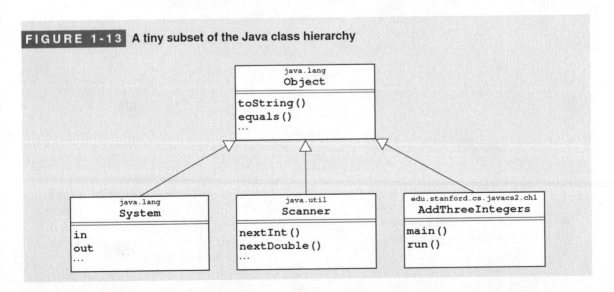

of the biological hierarchy. The diagram in Figure 1-13 adopts parts of a standard methodology for illustrating class hierarchies called the **Universal Modeling Language,** or **UML** for short. In UML, each class appears as a rectangular box whose upper portion contains the name of the class, shown here along with the package that contains it. The methods exported by that class appear in the lower portion. UML diagrams use open arrowheads to point from one class to the class at a higher level of the hierarchy from which it inherits its behavior. The class that appears lower in the hierarchy is a **subclass** of the class to which it points, which is called its **superclass.** In Java, every class except the `Object` class at the top of the hierarchy has a unique superclass.

Given that each of the other classes in Figure 1-13 is a direct subclass of `Object`, this hierarchy is not remotely as sophisticated as the biological hierarchy in the earlier diagram. In subsequent chapters, you will learn about other classes in Java that form more complex hierarchies. As simple as it is, however, the diagram in Figure 1-13 illustrates the fundamental properties of inheritance. The box for the `Object` class shows that it implements the methods `toString` and `equals`, along with an ellipsis to remind you that there are many other methods you have yet to discover. The fact that these methods are defined at the level of the `Object` class means that *every* class in Java has access to these methods, because every Java class is, either directly or indirectly, a descendant of `Object`. These subsidiary classes typically change the implementation of specific methods to make them more appropriate for the new data type, which is called *overriding* the higher-level definition.

 ## Summary

Since this chapter is itself a summary, it is hard to condense into a few central points. Its purpose is to introduce you to the Java programming language and give you a crash course in how to write programs in that language. The chapter focuses on the low-level language structure, concentrating on *expressions* and *statements*.

Important points in the chapter include:

- In the nearly 20 years since its release in 1995, the Java programming language has become one of the most widely used languages in the world.
- A typical Java program consists of comments, a package declaration, a set of imports, and a collection of method definitions. In this chapter, the only methods that appear are one called **run**, which implements the program, and a standardized **main** method that always looks like this:

```
public static void main(String[] args) {
    new classname().run();
}
```

- Variables in a Java program must be declared before they are used. Most variables in Java are *local variables,* which are declared within a method and can only be used inside the body of that method.

- A *data type* is defined by a domain of values and a set of operations. Java includes several *primitive types* that allow programs to store common data values including integers, floating-point numbers, Booleans, and characters. As you will learn in later chapters, Java also allows programmers to define new types from existing ones.

- The easiest way to accept user input in Java is to use the `Scanner` class. To do so, you must first import the `Scanner` class from the `java.util` package by including the following line after the package declaration:

      import java.util.Scanner;

  The next step is to create a `Scanner` object, conventionally called `sysin` in this book, with the following declaration:

      Scanner sysin = new Scanner(System.in);

  Once you have declared the `sysin` variable, you can request data values from the console by invoking the `Scanner` methods `nextInt` or `nextDouble`, depending on the type of value you want the user to enter.

- Expressions in Java are written in a form similar to that in most programming languages, with individual terms connected by operators. A list of the Java operators appears in Figure 1-8 along with their *precedence* and *associativity.*

- Statements in Java fall into two general categories: *simple statements* and *control statements.* A simple statement consists of an expression—typically an assignment or a method call—followed by a semicolon. The control statements described in this chapter are the `if`, `switch`, `while`, and `for` statements. The first two are used to express conditional execution, while the last two are used to specify repetition.

- The concepts of *classes, objects,* and *methods* are critical to programming in Java and come up in all Java programs. These concepts will be discussed in detail in subsequent chapters.

Review questions

1. When you write a Java program, do you prepare a source file or a class file?

2. What characters are used to mark comments in a Java program?

3. What is the significance of each component in the package declaration

    ```
    package edu.stanford.cs.javacs2.ch1;
    ```

4. How would you define a constant called `CENTIMETERS_PER_INCH` with the value 2.54?

5. What is the name of the method that must be defined in every Java program?

6. What is meant by the term *boilerplate?* What is the boilerplate form of the `main` method used throughout this book?

7. Indicate which of the following are legal variable names in Java:

    a. `x`

    b. `formula1`

    c. `average_rainfall`

    d. `%correct`

    e. `short`

    f. `tiny`

    g. `total output`

    h. `aVeryLongVariableName`

    i. `12MonthTotal`

    j. `marginal-cost`

    k. `b4hand`

    l. `_stk_depth`

8. What are the two attributes that define a data type?

9. What sizes does Java assign to the types `byte`, `short`, `int`, and `long`?

10. What coding system does Java use for characters?

11. What does ASCII stand for? What relationship does the ASCII code have to the code used to represent characters in Java?

12. List all possible values of type `boolean`.

13. What statements would you include in a program to read a value from the user and store it in the variable `x`, which is declared as a `double`?

14. Indicate the values and types of the following expressions:

    a. `2 + 3`

    b. `19 / 5`

    c. `19.0 / 5`

    d. `3 * 6.0`

    e. `19 % 5`

    f. `2 % 7`

15. What is the difference between the unary minus and the subtraction operator?

16. Calculate the result of each of the following expressions:

    a. `6 + 5 / 4 - 3`

    b. `2 + 2 * (2 * 2 - 2) % 2 / 2`

    c. `10 + 9 * ((8 + 7) % 6) + 5 * 4 % 3 * 2 + 1`

    d. `1 + 2 + (3 + 4) * ((5 * 6 % 7 * 8) - 9) - 10`

17. What does the term *truncation* mean?

18. What is a *type cast* and how do you indicate one in Java?

19. How do you specify a shorthand assignment operation?

20. What is the difference between the expressions `++x` and `x++`?

21. What is meant by *short-circuit evaluation?*

22. Write out the general syntactic form for each of the following control statements: `if`, `switch`, `while`, and `for`.

23. Describe in English the operation of the `switch` statement, including the role of the `break` statement at the end of each `case` clause.

24. What is a *sentinel?* What is the general form of the *read-until-sentinel* pattern?

25. What `for` loop control line would you use in each of the following situations?

    a.   Counting from 1 to 100
    b.   Counting by sevens starting at 0 until the number has more than two digits
    c.   Counting backward by twos from 100 to 0

26. Define each of the following terms: *class, object, method, instance variable, subclass,* and *superclass.*

27. True or false: In Java, there can be many objects that are instances of a class.

28. In Figure 1-12, what subclasses are shown for the class *Arthropoda?*

29. What two features does this chapter identify as the most important aspects of the object-oriented programming model?

Exercises

1. Rewrite the `HelloWorld` program so that it appears in a package that follows the conventional naming rules and includes both a `run` method and the standard boilerplate version of `main`. Call your new program `HelloWorldWithClass`.

2. Write a program that reads in a temperature in degrees Celsius and displays the corresponding temperature in degrees Fahrenheit. The conversion formula is

$$F = \tfrac{9}{5} C + 32$$

3. Write a program that converts a distance in meters to the corresponding English distance in feet and inches. The conversion factors you need are

    1 inch = 0.0254 meters
    1 foot = 12 inches

4. As mathematical historians have told the story, the German mathematician Carl Friedrich Gauss (1777–1855) began to show his mathematical talent at a very early age. When he was in elementary school, Gauss was asked by his teacher to compute the sum of the numbers between 1 and 100. Gauss is said to have given the answer instantly: 5050. Write a program that computes the answer to the question Gauss's teacher posed.

5. Write a program that reads in a list of integers from the user until the user enters the value 0 as a sentinel. When the sentinel appears, your program should display the largest value in the list, as in the following sample run:

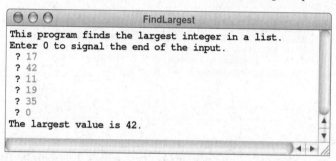

```
This program finds the largest integer in a list.
Enter 0 to signal the end of the input.
 ? 17
 ? 42
 ? 11
 ? 19
 ? 35
 ? 0
The largest value is 42.
```

    Be sure to define the sentinel value as a constant in a way that makes it easy to change. You should also make sure that the program works correctly if all the input values are negative.

6. For a more interesting challenge, write a program that finds both the largest and the second-largest number in a list, prior to the entry of a sentinel. If you once again use 0 as the sentinel, a sample run of the program might look like this:

```
This program finds the two largest integers in a list.
Enter 0 to signal the end of the input.
 ? 223
 ? 251
 ? 317
 ? 636
 ? 766
 ? 607
 ? 607
 ? 0
The largest value is 766.
The second largest value is 636.
```

The values in this sample run are the number of pages in the British hardcover editions of J. K. Rowling's *Harry Potter* series. The output therefore tells us that the longest book (*Harry Potter and the Order of the Phoenix*) has 766 pages and the second-longest book (*Harry Potter and the Goblet of Fire*) weighs in at a mere 636 pages.

7. Using the **AddIntegerList** program from Figure 1-11 as a model, write a program **AverageList** that reads in a list of integers representing exam scores and then prints the average. Because some spectacularly unprepared student might actually get a score of 0, your program should use −1 as the sentinel to mark the end of the input.

8. Using the **digitSum** method from the section entitled "The **while** statement" as a model, write a program that reads in an integer and then displays the number that has the same digits in the reverse order, as illustrated by this sample run:

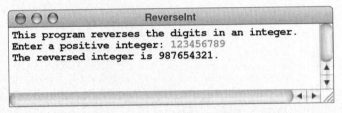

9. Every positive integer greater than 1 can be expressed as a product of prime numbers. This factorization is unique and is called the ***prime factorization.*** For example, the number 60 can be decomposed into the factors 2 × 2 × 3 × 5, each of which is prime. Note that the same prime can appear more than once in the factorization.

    Write a program to display the prime factorization of a number *n,* as illustrated by the following sample run:

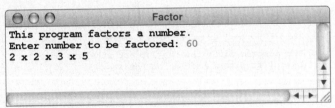

10. In 1979, Douglas Hofstadter, Professor of Cognitive Science at the University of Indiana, wrote *Gödel, Escher, Bach,* which he described as "a metaphorical fugue on minds and machines in the spirit of Lewis Carroll." The book won the Pulitzer Prize for Literature and has over the years become one of the classics of computer science. Much of its charm comes from the mathematical

oddities and puzzles it contains, many of which can be expressed in the form of computer programs. One of the most interesting examples Hofstadter discusses is the sequence of numbers formed by repeatedly executing the following rules for some positive integer n:

- If n is equal to 1, you've reached the end of the sequence and can stop.
- If n is even, divide it by two.
- If n is odd, multiply it by three and add one.

Although it also goes by several other names, this sequence is often called the **hailstone sequence,** because the values tend to go up and down, much as hailstones do in the clouds in which they form.

Write a program that reads in a number from the user and then generates the hailstone sequence from that point, as in the following sample run:

```
● ● ●                    Hailstone
Enter a number: 15
15 is odd, so I multiply by 3 and add 1 to get 46.
46 is even, so I divide it by 2 to get 23.
23 is odd, so I multiply by 3 and add 1 to get 70.
70 is even, so I divide it by 2 to get 35.
35 is odd, so I multiply by 3 and add 1 to get 106.
106 is even, so I divide it by 2 to get 53.
53 is odd, so I multiply by 3 and add 1 to get 160.
160 is even, so I divide it by 2 to get 80.
80 is even, so I divide it by 2 to get 40.
40 is even, so I divide it by 2 to get 20.
20 is even, so I divide it by 2 to get 10.
10 is even, so I divide it by 2 to get 5.
5 is odd, so I multiply by 3 and add 1 to get 16.
16 is even, so I divide it by 2 to get 8.
8 is even, so I divide it by 2 to get 4.
4 is even, so I divide it by 2 to get 2.
2 is even, so I divide it by 2 to get 1.
```

As you can see, this program offers a narrative account of the process as it goes along, in exactly the form Hofstadter presents in his book.

One of the fascinating things about the hailstone sequence is that no one has yet been able to prove that the process always stops. The number of steps in the process can get very large, but somehow it always seems to climb back down to one.

11. The German mathematician Gottfried Wilhelm von Leibniz (1646–1716) discovered the rather remarkable fact that the mathematical constant π can be computed using the following mathematical relationship:

$$\frac{\pi}{4} = 1 - \frac{1}{3} + \frac{1}{5} - \frac{1}{7} + \frac{1}{9} - \cdots$$

The formula to the right of the equal sign represents an infinite series; each fraction represents a term in that series. If you start with 1, subtract one-third, add one-fifth, and so on, for each of the odd integers, you get a number that gets closer and closer to the value of $\pi/4$ as you go along.

Write a program that calculates an approximation of π consisting of the first 10,000 terms in Leibniz's series.

12. You can also compute π by approximating the area bounded by a circular arc. Consider the quarter circle

which has a radius r equal to two inches. From the formula for the area of a circle, you can easily determine that the area of the quarter circle should be π square inches. You can also approximate the area computationally by adding up the areas of a series of rectangles, where each rectangle has a fixed width and the height is chosen so that the circle passes through the midpoint of the top of the rectangle. For example, if you divide the area into 10 rectangles from left to right, you get the following diagram:

The sum of the areas of the rectangles approximates the area of the quarter circle. The more rectangles there are, the closer the approximation.

For each rectangle, the width w is a constant derived by dividing the radius by the number of rectangles. The height h, on the other hand, depends on the position of the rectangle. If the midpoint of the rectangle in the horizontal direction is given by x, the height of the rectangle can be computed using the **sqrt** function to express the distance formula

$$h = \sqrt{r^2 - x^2}$$

The area of each rectangle is then simply $h \times w$.

Write a program to compute the area of the quarter circle by dividing it into 10,000 rectangles.

Chapter 2
Methods

I should not care for my profession, if I did not believe that better methods were to be found and enforced there . . .
— George Eliot, *Middlemarch*, 1871

As you know from the brief discussion in Chapter 1, methods in Java are similar to functions in traditional programming languages; the only difference is that methods belong to a class. That detail, however, doesn't make that much difference in terms of the overall idea. Methods play exactly the same role in Java that functions do in other languages: they make it possible for you to take an arbitrarily large block of code and invoke it with a single name. In this way, methods allow you to ignore the details of the implementation and focus instead on the effect of each method as a whole. By enabling you to hide complexity under the cover of a simple name, methods provide the key to managing the complexity of large programs.

Fortunately, the idea of a method—particularly when you think of it under the more traditional name of *function*—is likely to be familiar from mathematics, so you're not learning a new concept completely from scratch. When you studied algebra in high school, you almost certainly encountered function definitions that looked something like this:

$$f(x) = x^2 + 1$$

which states that the function f transforms a number x into the square of x plus one. For any value of x, you can compute the value of the function simply by evaluating the expression $x^2 + 1$, which is the formula that appears in the definition. Thus, the value of $f(3)$ is $3^2 + 1$, or 10.

Ever since the development of FORTRAN in the 1950s, programming languages have incorporated mathematical functions into their computational framework. In Java, for example, you can implement the function f with the following method:

```
private double f(double x) {
    return x * x + 1;
}
```

This definition includes various bits of syntax that are absent from the mathematical formulation, but the basic idea is the same. The method **f** takes an input value represented by the variable **x** and returns as its output the value of the expression **x * x + 1**.

◼ 2.1 Methods in Java

Although they have similarities, the concept of a function is more general in the programming domain than in mathematics. Like mathematical functions, methods in Java can specify input values but don't need to do so. Similarly, methods in Java aren't required to return results. The essential characteristic of a Java method is that it associates a computational operation—specified by a block of code that forms the *body* of the method—with a particular name. Once a method has been defined, other parts of the program can trigger the associated operations by using only the method name. There is no need to repeat the code for the underlying operation, because the steps required to implement that operation are specified in the body of the method.

This model of methods in the context of programming makes it possible to define several terms that are essential to understanding how methods work in Java. First of all, a ***method*** is a block of code that has been organized into a separate unit and given a name. The act of using the name to invoke that code is known as ***calling*** that method. To specify a method call in Java, you write the name of the method, followed by a list of expressions enclosed in parentheses. These expressions, called ***arguments,*** allow the calling program to pass information to the method. If a method requires no information from its caller, it need not have any arguments, but an empty set of parentheses must appear in both the method definition and any calls to that method.

Once called, the method takes the data supplied as arguments, does its work, and then returns to the point in the code from which the call was made. Remembering what the calling program was doing so that the program can get back to the precise location of the call is one of the essential characteristics of the method-calling mechanism. The operation of going back to the calling program is called ***returning*** from the method. As it returns, a method often passes a value back to its caller. This operation is called ***returning a value.***

The syntactic structure of a Java method

In Java, a method definition has the following syntactic form:

> *modifiers type name*(*parameters*) {
>   . . . *body* . . .
> }

The most common values for the *modifiers* component of this pattern are `public` and `private`, which determine whether the method is visible outside of this class. As with the definitions of constants in Chapter 1, it is good practice to make all method definitions private unless there is a compelling reason to allow external access. In the rest of this pattern, *type* is the type returned by the method, *name* is the method name, and *parameters* is a list of declarations separated by commas, giving the type and name of each parameter to the method. A ***parameter*** is a placeholder for one of the arguments supplied in the method call. In most respects, a parameter acts just like a local variable. The only difference is that each parameter is initialized automatically to hold the value of the corresponding argument. If a method takes no parameters, the entire parameter list in the method header line is empty.

The body of the method is a block consisting of the statements that implement the method, along with the declarations of any local variables the method requires. For methods that return a value to their caller, at least one of the statements must be a **return** statement, which usually has the form

```
return expression;
```

Executing the **return** statement causes the method to return immediately to its caller, passing back the value of the expression as the value of the method.

Methods can return values of any type. The following method, for example, returns a Boolean value indicating whether the argument **n** is an even integer:

```
private boolean isEven(int n) {
    return n % 2 == 0;
}
```

Once you have defined this method, you can use it in an **if** statement, like this:

```
if (isEven(i)) . . .
```

Methods that return Boolean results play an important role in programming and are called *predicate methods.*

Methods do not need to return a value. A method indicates that it does not return a value by using the reserved word **void** as the result type. Such methods ordinarily finish by reaching the end of the statements in the body. You can, however, signal early completion of a **void** method by executing a **return** statement without a value expression, as follows:

```
return;
```

Static methods

Most methods in Java operate on a particular object. Unfortunately, that notion doesn't make much sense until you have a better idea of what an object is. The formal discussion of objects begins in Chapter 3 with the introduction of strings and carries forward through the next several chapters. To support what other languages define as free-standing functions, Java offers *static methods,* which are associated with an entire class rather than a specific object. These methods are identified with the keyword **static**, which appears after the **public** or **private** keyword.

The simplest examples of static methods are associated with the **Math** class, which is Java's mathematical library. Some of the most common entries in the **Math** class appear in Figure 2-1. Along with the constants **PI** and **E**, the **Math** class includes a set of methods, all of which are static.

FIGURE 2-1 Selected entries in the `Math` class

Mathematical constants

`Math.PI`	The mathematical constant π.
`Math.E`	The mathematical constant e, which is the basis for natural logarithms.

General mathematical functions

`Math.abs (x)`	Returns the absolute value of x.
`Math.min (x, y)`	Returns the smaller of x and y.
`Math.max (x, y)`	Returns the larger of x and y.
`Math.sqrt (x)`	Returns the square root of x.
`Math.round (x)`	Returns the closest integer to x. Note: if x is a **double**, the function returns a **long**; you therefore need a type cast to convert the result to an **int**.
`Math.signum (x)`	Returns the sign of x (-1, 0, or $+1$). The result has the same type as x.
`Math.floor (x)`	Returns the largest integer less than or equal to x.
`Math.ceil (x)`	Returns the smallest integer greater than or equal to x.

Logarithmic and exponential functions

`Math.exp (x)`	Returns the exponential function of x (e^x).
`Math.log (x)`	Returns the natural logarithm (base e) of x.
`Math.log10 (x)`	Returns the common logarithm (base 10) of x.
`Math.pow (x, y)`	Returns x^y.

Trigonometric functions

`Math.cos (theta)`	Returns the cosine of the angle *theta*, measured in radians counterclockwise from the $+x$ axis.
`Math.sin (theta)`	Returns the sine of the radian angle *theta*.
`Math.tan (theta)`	Returns the tangent of the radian angle *theta*.
`Math.atan (x)`	Returns the principal arctangent of x. The result is an angle expressed in radians between $-\pi/2$ and $+\pi/2$.
`Math.atan2 (y, x)`	Returns the radian angle formed between the x-axis and the line extending from the origin through the point (x, y).
`Math.hypot (x, y)`	Returns the distance from the origin to the point (x, y).
`Math.toRadians (x)`	Converts the angle x from degrees to radians.
`Math.toDegrees (x)`	Converts the angle x from radians to degrees.

Random number generator

`Math.random ()`	Returns a random number that is at least 0 but strictly less than 1.

In Java, you call a static method by writing the name of the class before the name of the method, separated by a period (.), which is more commonly called a *dot* in this context. For example, you can specify the square root of two in a Java program by writing

```
Math.sqrt(2)
```

The argument to the `Math.sqrt` method can be an arbitrary expression. For example, one possible implementation of the `Math.hypot` method (the name is short for *hypotenuse*) looks like this:

```
public static double hypot(double x, double y) {
    return Math.sqrt(x * x + y * y);
}
```

This method implements the Pythagorean identity that the square of the hypotenuse of a right triangle is equal to the sum of the squares of the other two sides.

Whenever a library class makes some service available to the programs that import it, computer scientists say that the class *exports* that service. The `Math` class, for example, exports the constants `PI` and `E` along with the various methods in Figure 2-1.

One of the design goals of any library is to hide the complexity involved in the underlying implementation. By exporting the `sqrt` method, the designers of the `Math` class made it far easier to write programs that use it. When you call the `sqrt` method, you don't need to have any idea how `sqrt` works internally. Those details are relevant only to the programmers who implement the `Math` class.

Knowing how to call the `sqrt` method and knowing how to implement it are both important skills. It is important to recognize, however, that those two skills—calling a method and implementing one—are to a large extent independent. Successful programmers often use methods that they wouldn't have a clue how to write. Conversely, programmers who implement a library class can never anticipate all the potential uses that class will have.

To emphasize the difference in perspective between programmers who create a library class and those who use it, computer scientists have assigned names to programmers working in each of these roles. Naturally enough, a programmer who implements a class is called an *implementer*. Conversely, a programmer who calls methods provided by a library class is called a *client* of that class. As you go through the chapters in this book, you will have a chance to look at several library classes from both of these perspectives, first as a client and later as an implementer.

Overloading

In Java, it is legal to give the same name to more than one method as long as the pattern of arguments is different. When the compiler encounters a call to a method with that name, it checks to see what arguments have been provided and chooses the version of the method that fits those arguments. Using the same name for more than one version of a method is called *overloading*. The pattern of arguments taken by a method—taking into account only the number and types of the arguments and not the parameter names—is called its *signature*.

As an example of overloading, the `Math` class includes several versions of the method `abs`, one for each of the built-in arithmetic types. For instance, the class includes the method

```
public static int abs(int x) {
    return (x < 0) ? -x : x;
}
```

as well as the identically named method

```
public static double abs(double x) {
    return (x < 0) ? -x : x;
}
```

The only difference between these methods is that the first version takes an `int` as its argument and the second takes a `double`. The compiler chooses which of these versions to invoke by looking at the types of the arguments the caller provides. Thus, if `abs` is called with an `int`, the compiler invokes the integer-valued version of the methods and returns a value of type `int`. If, by contrast, the argument is of type `double`, the compiler chooses the version that takes a `double`.

The primary advantage of using overloading is that doing so makes it easier for you as a programmer to keep track of different function names for the same operation when that function is applied in slightly different contexts. If, for example, you need to call the absolute value function in C, which does not support overloading, you have to remember to call `fabs` for floating-point numbers and `abs` for integers. In C++, all you need to remember is the single function name `abs`.

2.2 Methods and program structure

Methods play several important roles in a programming language. First, defining methods makes it possible to write the code for an operation once but then use it many times. The ability to invoke the same sequence of instructions from many parts of a program can dramatically reduce its size. Having the code for a method appear in just one place also makes a program easier to maintain. When you need to make a change in the way a method operates, it is far easier to do so if the code appears only once than if the same operations are repeated throughout the code.

Defining a method is also valuable even if you use that method only once in a particular program. The most important role that methods play is that they make it possible to divide a large program into smaller, more manageable pieces. This process is called *decomposition.* As you almost certainly know from your prior experience with programming, writing a program as one monolithic block of code is a sure-fire recipe for disaster. Instead, what you want to do is subdivide the high-level problem into a set of lower-level methods, each of which makes sense on its own. Finding the right decomposition, however, turns out to be a challenging task that requires considerable practice. If you choose the individual pieces well, each one will have integrity as a unit and make the program as a whole much simpler to understand. If you choose unwisely, the decomposition can easily get in your way. There are no hard-and-fast rules for selecting a particular decomposition. Programming is an art, and you will learn to choose effective decomposition strategies mostly through experience.

As a general rule, it makes sense to begin the decomposition process starting with the main program. At this level, you think about the problem as a whole and try to identify the major pieces of the entire task. Once you figure out what the big pieces of the program are, you can define them as independent methods. Since some of these methods may themselves be complicated, it is often appropriate to decompose them into still smaller ones. You can continue this process until every piece of the problem is simple enough to be solved on its own. This process is called *top-down design* or *stepwise refinement.*

Methods are also important in programming because they provide a basis for the implementation of *algorithms,* which are precisely specified strategies for solving computational problems. The term comes from the name of the ninth-century Persian mathematician Muḥammad ibn Mūsā al-Khwārizmī, whose treatise on mathematics entitled *Kitab al jabr w'al-muqabala* gave rise to the English word *algebra.* Mathematical algorithms appear much earlier in history, at least as far back as the early Greek, Chinese, and Indian civilizations.

One of the earliest known mathematical procedures worthy of being called an algorithm is named for the Greek mathematician Euclid, who lived in Alexandria during the reign of Ptolemy I (323–283 BCE). In his great mathematical treatise called *Elements,* Euclid outlines a procedure for finding the **greatest common divisor** (or **gcd** for short) of two integers x and y, which is defined to be the largest integer that divides evenly into both. For example, the gcd of 49 and 35 is 7, the gcd of 6 and 18 is 6, and the gcd of 32 and 33 is 1. In modern English, Euclid's algorithm can be described as follows:

1. Divide x by y and compute the remainder; call that remainder r.
2. If r is zero, the algorithm is complete, and the answer is y.
3. If r is not zero, set x to the old value of y, set y equal to r, and repeat the process.

You can easily translate this algorithmic description into the following code in Java:

```java
private int gcd(int x, int y) {
    int r = x % y;
    while (r != 0) {
        x = y;
        y = r;
        r = x % y;
    }
    return y;
}
```

Euclid's algorithm is considerably more efficient than any strategy you would be likely to discover on your own, and is still used today in a variety of practical applications, including the implementation of the cryptographic protocols that enable secure communication on the Internet.

At the same time, it is not easy to see exactly why the algorithm gives the correct result. Fortunately for those who rely on it in modern-day applications, Euclid was able to prove the correctness of his algorithm in *Elements*, Book VII, proposition 2. While it is not always necessary to have formal proofs of the algorithms that drive computer-based applications, such proofs make it possible for you to have more confidence in the correctness of those programs.

2.3 The mechanics of method calls

Although you can certainly get by with an intuitive understanding of how the method-calling process works, it sometimes helps to understand precisely what happens when one method calls another in Java. The sections that follow describe the process in detail and then walk you through a simple example designed to help you visualize exactly what is going on.

The steps in calling a method

Whenever a method call occurs, the Java compiler generates code to implement the following operations:

1. The calling method computes values for each argument using the bindings of local variables in its own context. Because the arguments are expressions, this computation can involve operators and other methods; the calling method evaluates these expressions before execution of the new method begins.

2. The system creates new space for all the local variables required by the new method, including any parameters. These variables are allocated together in a block, which is called a *stack frame.*

3. The value of each argument is copied into the corresponding parameter variable. For methods with more than one argument, these copies occur in order; the first argument is copied into the first parameter, and so forth. If necessary, the compiler generates automatic type conversions between the argument values and the parameter variables, as it does in an assignment statement. For example, if you pass a value of type `int` to a method that expects a parameter of type `double`, the integer is converted into the equivalent floating-point value before it is copied into the parameter variable.

4. The statements in the method body are executed until the program encounters a `return` statement or there are no more statements to execute.

5. The value of the `return` expression, if any, is evaluated and returned as the value of the method. In returning a value, Java applies the same conversion rules that it does for assignment. Thus, you are free to return a value of type `int` from a function that is declared to return a `double`, but not in the opposite direction.

6. The stack frame created for this method call is discarded. In the process, all local variables disappear.

7. The calling program continues, with the returned value substituted in place of the call.

Although this process may seem to make sense, you probably need to work through an example or two before you understand it fully. Reading through the example in the next section will give you some insight into the process, but it is probably even more helpful to take one of your own programs and walk through it at the same level of detail. And while you can trace through a program on paper or a whiteboard, it may be better to get yourself a supply of 3×5 index cards and then use a card to represent each stack frame. The advantage of the index-card model is that you can create a stack of index cards that closely models the operation of the computer. Calling a method adds a card; returning from the method removes it.

The combinations function

The method-calling process is most easily illustrated in the context of a specific example. Suppose that you have a collection of six coins, which in the United

States might be a penny, a nickel, a dime, a quarter, a half-dollar, and a dollar. Given those six coins, how many ways are there to choose two of them? As you can see from the full enumeration of the possibilities in Figure 2-2, the answer is 15. As a computer scientist, you should immediately think about the more general question: given a set containing n distinct elements, how many ways can you choose a subset with k elements? The answer to that question is computed by the **combinations function** $C(n, k)$, which is defined as follows:

$$C(n, k) = \frac{n!}{k! \times (n - k)!}$$

where the exclamation point indicates the **factorial function,** which is simply the product of the integers between 1 and the specified number, inclusive. The code to compute the combinations function in Java appears in Figure 2-3, along with a main program that reads in n and k from the user and then displays the value of $C(n, k)$.

FIGURE 2-2 **Illustration of the combinations function**

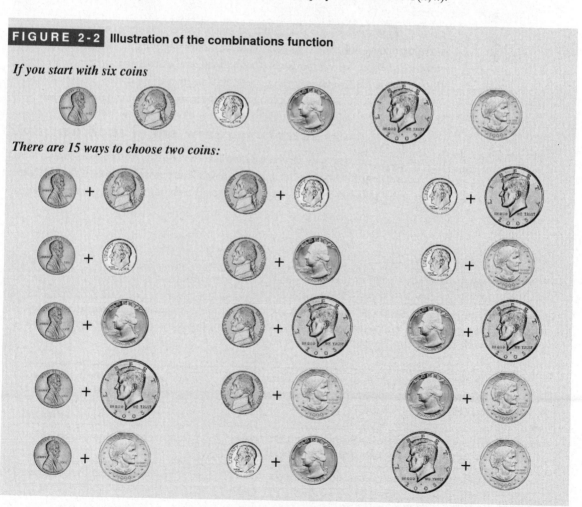

If you start with six coins

There are 15 ways to choose two coins:

FIGURE 2-3 Program to compute the combinations function $C(n, k)$ function

```java
/*
 * File: Combinations.java
 * ---------------------------
 * This program computes the mathematical function C(n, k) from
 * its mathematical definition in terms of factorials.
 */

package edu.stanford.cs.javacs2.ch2;

import java.util.Scanner;

public class Combinations {

    public void run() {
        Scanner sysin = new Scanner(System.in);
        System.out.print("Enter the number of objects (n): ");
        int n = sysin.nextInt();
        System.out.print("Enter the number to be chosen (k): ");
        int k = sysin.nextInt();
        System.out.println("C(n, k) = " + combinations(n, k));
    }

/*
 * Returns the mathematical combinations function C(n, k), which is
 * the number of ways one can choose k elements from a set of size n.
 */

    private int combinations(int n, int k) {
        return fact(n) / (fact(k) * fact(n - k));
    }

/*
 * Returns the factorial of n, which is the product of all the
 * integers between 1 and n, inclusive.
 */

    private int fact(int n) {
        int result = 1;
        for (int i = 1; i <= n; i++) {
            result *= i;
        }
        return result;
    }

/* Main program */

    public static void main(String[] args) {
        new Combinations().run();
    }

}
```

A sample run of the **Combinations** program might look like this:

```
  ⊖ ○ ○                    Combinations
  Enter the number of objects (n) :  6
  Enter the number to be chosen (k) :  2
  C(n, k) = 15
```

As you can see from Figure 2-3, the **Combinations** program is divided into three methods. The **main** method implements the interaction with the user. The **combinations** method computes $C(n, k)$. Finally, the **fact** method computes the factorials required for the computation.

Tracing the combinations function

While the **Combinations** program can be interesting in its own right, the purpose of this example is to illustrate the steps involved in executing methods. In Java, all programs begin by making a call to the static method **main**, which by our convention makes a call on the **run** method for the class, which is where this book begins the tracing process. When it encounters a method call, the Java Virtual Machine creates a new stack frame to keep track of the local variables that method declares. In the **Combinations** program, the **run** method declares two integers, **n** and **k**, so the stack frame must include space for these variables.

In the diagrams in this book, each stack frame appears as a rectangle surrounded by a double line. Each stack-frame diagram shows the code for the method along with a pointing-hand icon that makes it easy to keep track of the current execution point. The frame also contains labeled boxes for each of the local variables. The stack frame for **run** therefore looks like this when execution begins:

```
public void run() {
☞ Scanner sysin = new Scanner(System.in);
    System.out.print("Enter the number of objects (n): ");
    int n = sysin.nextInt();
    System.out.print("Enter the number to be chosen (k): ");
    int k = sysin.nextInt();
    System.out.println("C(n, k) = " + combinations(n, k) );
}

                              k          n
                         ┌──────┐   ┌──────┐
                         └──────┘   └──────┘
```

From this point, the system executes the statements in order, creating the scanner, printing the prompts on the console, reading in the associated values from the user, and storing those values in the variables in that frame. If the user enters the values shown in the earlier sample run, the frame will look like this when it reaches the statement that displays the result:

```
public void run() {
    Scanner sysin = new Scanner(System.in);
    System.out.print("Enter the number of objects (n): ");
    int n = sysin.nextInt();
    System.out.print("Enter the number to be chosen (k): ");
    int k = sysin.nextInt();
☞  System.out.println("C(n, k) = " + combinations(n, k) );
}
```

k	n
2	6

Before the program can complete the output line, it has to evaluate the call to **combinations(n, k)**. At this point, the **run** method calls the **combinations** method, which means that the computer has to go through all the steps that are required in making a method call.

The first step is to evaluate the arguments in the context of the current frame. The variable **n** has the value 6, and the variable **k** has the value 2. These two arguments are then copied into the parameter variables **n** and **k** when the computer creates the **combinations** stack frame. The new frame gets stacked on top of the old one, which allows the computer to remember the values of the local variables in **run**, even though they are not currently accessible. The situation after creating the new frame and initializing the parameter variables looks like this:

```
public void run() {
    private int combinations(int n, int k) {
☞   return fact(n) / ( fact(k) * fact(n - k) );
    }
```

k	n
2	6

To compute the value of the **combinations** method, the program must make three calls to the method **fact**. In Java, those method calls can happen in any order, but it's easiest to process them from left to right. The first call, therefore, is the call to **fact(n)**. To evaluate this method, the system must create yet another stack frame, this time for the method **fact** with an argument value of 6:

```
public void run() {
  private int combinations(int n, int k) {
    private int fact(int n) {
    ☞ int result = 1;
        for (int i = 1; i <= n; i++) {
          result *= i;
        }
        return result;
    }
```

	i	result	n
			6

Unlike the earlier stack frames, the frame for **fact** includes both parameters and local variables. The parameter **n** is initialized to the value of the calling argument and therefore has the value 6. The two local variables, **i** and **result**, have not yet been initialized, but the system nonetheless needs to reserve space in the frame for those variables. Until you assign a new value to those variables, they will contain whatever data happens to be left over in the memory cells assigned to that stack frame, which is completely unpredictable. It is therefore important to initialize all local variables before you use them, ideally as part of the declaration.

The system then executes the statements in the method **fact**. In this instance, the body of the **for** loop is executed six times. On each cycle, the value of **result** is multiplied by the loop index **i**, which means that it will eventually hold the value 720 ($1 \times 2 \times 3 \times 4 \times 5 \times 6$ or 6!). When the program reaches the **return** statement, the stack frame looks like this:

```
public void run() {
  private int combinations(int n, int k) {
    private int fact(int n) {
        int result = 1;
        for (int i = 1; i <= n; i++) {
          result *= i;
        }
    ☞ return result;
    }
```

	i	result	n
		720	6

In this diagram, the box for the variable **i** is empty, because the value of **i** is no longer defined at this point in the program. In Java, index variables declared in a **for** loop header are accessible only inside the loop body. Showing an empty box emphasizes the fact that the value of **i** is no longer available.

Returning from a method involves copying the value of the **return** expression (in this case the local variable **result**), into the point at which the call occurred. The frame for **fact** is then discarded, which leads to the following configuration:

```
public void run() {
   private int combinations(int n, int k) {
      return  fact(n)  / ( fact(k) * fact(n - k) );
   }
                     └─ 720

                                                   k        n
                                                  ┌────┐   ┌────┐
                                                  │ 2  │   │ 6  │
                                                  └────┘   └────┘
```

The next step in the process is to make a second call to **fact**, this time with the argument **k**. In the calling frame, **k** has the value 2. That value is then used to initialize the parameter **n** in the new stack frame, as follows:

```
public void run() {
   private int combinations(int n, int k) {
      private int fact(int n) {
      ☞ int result = 1;
         for (int i = 1; i <= n; i++) {
            result *= i;
         }
         return result;
      }

                         i          result    n
                        ┌────┐      ┌────┐   ┌────┐
                        │    │      │    │   │ 2  │
                        └────┘      └────┘   └────┘
```

The computation of **fact(2)** is a bit easier to perform in one's head than the earlier call to **fact(6)**. This time around, the value of **result** will be 2, which is then returned to the calling frame, like this:

```
public void run() {
   private int combinations(int n, int k) {
      return  fact(n)  / (  fact(k)  * fact(n - k) );
   }
                     └─ 720      └─ 2

                                                   k        n
                                                  ┌────┐   ┌────┐
                                                  │ 2  │   │ 6  │
                                                  └────┘   └────┘
```

The code for **combinations** makes one more call to **fact**, this time with the argument **n - k**. As before, this call creates a new frame with **n** equal to 4:

```
public void run() {
    private int combinations(int n, int k) {
        private int fact(int n) {
        ☞ int result = 1;
            for (int i = 1; i <= n; i++) {
                result *= i;
            }
            return result;
        }
```

i	result	n
		4

The value of **fact(4)** is $1 \times 2 \times 3 \times 4$, or 24. When this call returns, the system is able to fill in the last of the missing values in the calculation, as follows:

```
public void run() {
    private int combinations(int n, int k) {
        return fact(n) / ( fact(k) * fact(n - k) );
    }
            720       2        24
```

k	n
2	6

The computer then divides 720 by the product of 2 and 24 to get the answer 15. This value is then returned to the **run** method, which leads to the following state:

```
public void run() {
    Scanner sysin = new Scanner(System.in);
    System.out.print("Enter the number of objects (n): ");
    int n = sysin.nextInt();
    System.out.print("Enter the number to be chosen (k): ");
    int k = sysin.nextInt();
    System.out.println("C(n, k) = " + combinations(n, k) );
}
                                                    15
```

k	n
2	6

From this point, all that remains is to generate the output line and return from the **run** method, which completes the execution of the program.

2.4 A simple recursive function

The `Combinations` program includes a simple implementation of a method to compute factorials, which looks like this:

```java
private int fact(int n) {
    int result = 1;
    for (int i = 1; i <= n; i++) {
        result *= i;
    }
    return result;
}
```

This implementation uses a **for** loop to cycle through each of the integers between 1 and **n**. Strategies based on looping (typically by using **for** and **while** statements) are said to be *iterative*. Functions like factorial, however, can also be implemented using a distinctly different approach that includes no loops at all. This strategy is called *recursion*, which is the process of solving a problem by breaking it down into simpler problems of the same form. Recursion is an extremely powerful technique that you will have a chance to study in detail beginning in Chapter 8, but it is useful to start with simple mathematical examples in which the recursive nature of the problem is easy to see.

A recursive formulation of `fact`

The iterative implementation of **fact** does not take advantage of an important mathematical property of factorials. Each factorial is related to the factorial of the next smaller integer in the following way:

$$n! = n \times (n-1)!$$

Thus, 4! is $4 \times 3!$, 3! is $3 \times 2!$, and so on. To make sure that this process stops at some point, mathematicians define 0! to be 1. Thus, the conventional mathematical definition of the factorial function looks like this:

$$n! = \begin{cases} 1 & \text{if } n = 0 \\ n \times (n-1)! & \text{otherwise} \end{cases}$$

This definition is recursive, because it defines the factorial of n in terms of a simpler instance of the factorial function: finding the factorial of $n-1$. The new problem has the same form as the original, which is the fundamental characteristic of recursion. You can then use the same process to define $(n-1)!$ in terms of $(n-2)!$. Moreover, you can carry this process forward step by step until the solution is expressed in terms of 0!, which is equal to 1 by definition.

From your perspective as a programmer, the most important consequence of the mathematical definition is that it provides a template for a recursive solution. In Java, you can implement the `fact` method as follows:

```
private int fact(int n) {
    if (n == 0) {
        return 1;
    } else {
        return n * fact(n - 1);
    }
}
```

If `n` is 0, the result of `fact` is 1. If not, the implementation computes the result by calling `fact(n - 1)` and then multiplying the result by `n`. This implementation follows directly from the mathematical definition of the factorial function and has precisely the same recursive structure.

Tracing the recursive process

If you work from the mathematical definition, writing the recursive implementation of `fact` is straightforward. On the other hand, even though the definition is easy to write, the brevity of the solution may seem suspicious. When you are learning about recursion for the first time, the recursive implementation of `fact` seems to leave something out. Even though it clearly reflects the mathematical definition, the recursive formulation makes it hard to identify where the actual computational steps occur. When you call `fact`, for example, you want the computer to give you the answer. In the recursive implementation, all you see is a formula that transforms one call to `fact` into another one. Because the steps in that calculation are not explicit, it seems somewhat magical when the computer gets the right answer.

If you trace through the logic the computer uses to evaluate any method call, however, you discover that no magic is involved. When the computer evaluates a call to the recursive `fact` method, it goes through the same process it uses to evaluate any other method call.

To visualize the process, suppose that you have executed the statement

```
System.out.println("fact(4) = " + fact(4));
```

as part of the method `run`. When `run` calls `fact`, the computer creates a new stack frame and copies the argument value into the formal parameter `n`. The frame for `fact` temporarily supersedes the frame for `run`, as shown in the following diagram:

```
public void run() {

    private int fact(int n) {
    ☞ if (n == 0) {
            return 1;
        } else {
            return n * fact(n - 1);      n
        }                              ┌─────┐
    }                                  │  4  │
}                                      └─────┘
```

The computer now begins to evaluate the body of the method, starting with the
if statement. Because **n** is not equal to 0, control proceeds to the **else** clause,
where the program must evaluate and return the value of the expression

> n * fact(n - 1)

Evaluating this expression requires computing the value of **fact(n - 1)**, which
introduces a recursive call. When that call returns, all the program has to do is
multiply the result by **n**. The current state of the computation can therefore be
diagrammed as follows:

```
public void run() {

    private int fact(int n) {
        if (n == 0) {
            return 1;
        } else {
            return n * fact(n - 1);      n
        }              ‾‾‾‾‾‾‾‾‾‾‾      ┌─────┐
    }                      └─?           │  4  │
}                                        └─────┘
```

The next step in the computation is to evaluate the call to **fact(n - 1)**,
beginning with the argument expression. Because the current value of **n** is 4, the
argument expression **n - 1** has the value 3. The computer then creates a new frame
for **fact** in which the formal parameter is initialized to this value. Thus, the next
frame looks like this:

```
public void run() {

    private int fact(int n) {

        private int fact(int n) {
        ☞ if (n == 0) {
                return 1;
            } else {
                return n * fact(n - 1);      n
            }                              ┌─────┐
        }                                  │  3  │
    }                                      └─────┘
```

There are now two frames labeled **fact**. In the most recent one, the computer is just starting to calculate **fact(3)**. This new frame hides the previous frame for **fact(4)**, which will not reappear until the **fact(3)** computation is complete.

Computing **fact(3)** again begins by testing the value of **n**. Since **n** is still not 0, the **else** clause instructs the computer to evaluate **fact(n - 1)**. As before, this process requires the creation of a new stack frame, as shown:

```
public void run() {
  private int fact(int n) {
    private int fact(int n) {
      private int fact(int n) {
      ☞ if (n == 0) {
           return 1;
        } else {
           return n * fact(n - 1);
        }                          n
      }                          ┌─────┐
                                 │  2  │
                                 └─────┘
```

Following the same logic, the program must now call **fact(1)**, which in turn calls **fact(0)**, creating two new stack frames, as follows:

```
public void run() {
  private int fact(int n) {
    private int fact(int n) {
      private int fact(int n) {
        private int fact(int n) {
          private int fact(int n) {
          ☞ if (n == 0) {
               return 1;
            } else {
               return n * fact(n - 1);
            }                          n
          }                          ┌─────┐
                                     │  0  │
                                     └─────┘
```

At this point, however, the situation changes. Because the value of **n** is 0, the method can return its result immediately by executing the statement

    return 1;

The value 1 is returned to the calling frame, which resumes its position on top of the stack, as shown:

```
public void run() {
  private int fact(int n) {
    private int fact(int n) {
      private int fact(int n) {
        private int fact(int n) {
          if (n == 0) {
            return 1;
          } else {
            return n * fact(n - 1);
          }                          n
        }                      └─1      ┌────┐
      }                                │  1 │
    }                                  └────┘
```

From this point, the computation proceeds back through each of the recursive calls, completing the calculation of the return value at each level. In this frame, for example, the call to **fact(n - 1)** can be replaced by the value 1, as shown in the diagram for the stack frame. In this stack frame, **n** has the value 1, so the result of this call is simply 1. This result gets propagated back to its caller, which is represented by the top frame in the following diagram:

```
public void run() {
  private int fact(int n) {
    private int fact(int n) {
      private int fact(int n) {
        if (n == 0) {
          return 1;
        } else {
          return n * fact(n - 1);
        }                          n
      }                      └─1      ┌────┐
    }                                │  2 │
                                     └────┘
```

Because **n** is now 2, evaluating the **return** statement causes the value 2 to be passed back to the preceding level, as follows:

```
public void run() {
  private int fact(int n) {
    private int fact(int n) {
      if (n == 0) {
        return 1;
      } else {
        return n * fact(n - 1);
      }                          n
    }                      └─2      ┌────┐
  }                                │  3 │
                                   └────┘
```

At this stage, the program returns 3 × 2 to the preceding level, so that the frame for the initial call to **fact** looks like this:

```
public void run() {
    private int fact(int n) {
        if (n == 0) {
            return 1;
        } else {
            return n * fact(n - 1);
        }                            n
    }                     └─ 6      ┌───┐
}                                   │ 4 │
                                    └───┘
```

The final step in the calculation process consists of calculating 4 × 6 and returning the value 24 to the **run** method.

The recursive leap of faith

The point of including the complete trace of the **fact(4)** computation is to convince you that Java treats recursive methods just like all other methods. When you are faced with a recursive method, you can—at least in theory—mimic the operation of the computer and figure out what it will do. By drawing all the frames and keeping track of all the variables, you can duplicate the entire operation and come up with the answer. If you do so, however, you will usually find that the complexity of the process ends up making the computation much harder to follow.

Thus, whenever you try to understand a recursive program, it is useful to put the underlying details aside and focus instead on a single level of the operation. At that level, you are allowed to assume that any recursive call automatically gets the right answer as long as the arguments to that call are in some sense simpler than the original arguments. This psychological strategy—assuming that any simpler recursive call will work correctly—is called the *recursive leap of faith.* Learning to apply this strategy is essential to using recursion in practical applications.

As an example, consider what happens when this implementation is used to compute **fact(n)** with n equal to 4. To do so, the recursive implementation must compute the value of the expression

```
n * fact(n - 1)
```

By substituting the current value of **n** into the expression, you know that the result is

```
4 * fact(3)
```

Stop right there. Computing **fact(3)** is simpler than computing **fact(4)**. Because it is simpler, the recursive leap of faith allows you to assume that it works.

Thus, you should assume that the call to `fact(3)` will correctly compute the value of 3!, which is $3 \times 2 \times 1$, or 6. The result of calling `fact(4)` is therefore 4×6, or 24.

2.5 The Fibonacci function

In a mathematical treatise entitled *Liber Abbaci* published in 1202, the Italian mathematician Leonardo Fibonacci proposed a problem that has had a wide influence on many fields, including computer science. The problem was phrased as an exercise in population biology—a field that has become increasingly important in recent years. Fibonacci's problem concerns how the population of rabbits would grow from generation to generation if the rabbits reproduced according to the following, admittedly fanciful, rules:

- Each pair of fertile rabbits produces a new pair of offspring each month.
- Rabbits become fertile in their second month of life.
- Old rabbits never die.

If a pair of newborn rabbits is introduced in January, how many pairs of rabbits are there at the end of the year?

You can solve Fibonacci's problem simply by keeping a count of the rabbits at each month during the year. At the beginning of January, there are no rabbits, since the first pair is introduced sometime in that month, which leaves one pair of rabbits on February 1st. Since the initial pair of rabbits is newborn, they are not yet fertile in February, which means that the only rabbits on March 1st are the original pair of rabbits. In March, however, the original pair is now of reproductive age, which means that a new pair of rabbits is born. The new pair increases the colony's population—counting by pairs—to two on April 1st. In April, the original pair goes right on reproducing, but the rabbits born in March are as yet too young. Thus, there are three pairs of rabbits at the beginning of May. From here on, with more and more rabbits becoming fertile each month, the rabbit population begins to grow more quickly.

Computing terms in the Fibonacci sequence

At this point, it is useful to record the population data so far as a sequence of terms, indicated by the subscripted value t_i, each of which shows the number of rabbit pairs at the beginning of the ith month from the start of the experiment on January 1st. The sequence itself is called the **Fibonacci sequence** and begins with the following terms, which represent the results of our calculation so far:

t_0	t_1	t_2	t_3	t_4
0	1	1	2	3

You can simplify the computation of further terms in this sequence by making an important observation. Because in this problem pairs of rabbits never die, all the rabbits that were around in the previous month are still around. Moreover, every pair of fertile rabbits has produced a new pair. The number of fertile rabbit pairs capable of reproduction is simply the number of rabbits that were alive in the month before the previous one. The net effect is that each new term in the sequence must simply be the sum of the preceding two. Thus, the next several terms in the Fibonacci sequence look like this:

t_0	t_1	t_2	t_3	t_4	t_5	t_6	t_7	t_8	t_9	t_{10}	t_{11}	t_{12}
0	1	1	2	3	5	8	13	21	34	55	89	144

The number of rabbit pairs at the end of the year is therefore 144.

From a programming perspective, it helps to express the rule for generating new terms in the following more mathematical form:

$$t_n = t_{n-1} + t_{n-2}$$

An expression of this type, in which each element of a sequence is defined in terms of earlier elements, is called a ***recurrence relation.***

The recurrence relation alone is not sufficient to define the Fibonacci sequence. Although the formula makes it easy to calculate new terms in the sequence, the process has to start somewhere. In order to apply the formula, you need to have at least two terms already available, which means that the first two terms in the sequence—t_0 and t_1—must be defined explicitly. The complete specification of the terms in the Fibonacci sequence is therefore

$$t_n = \begin{cases} n & \text{if } n \text{ is 0 or 1} \\ t_{n-1} + t_{n-2} & \text{otherwise} \end{cases}$$

This mathematical formulation is an ideal model for a recursive implementation of a method `fib(n)` that computes the nth term in the Fibonacci sequence. All you need to do is plug the simple cases and the recurrence relation into the standard recursive paradigm. The recursive implementation of `fib(n)` is shown in Figure 2-4, which also includes a test program that displays the terms in the Fibonacci sequence between two specified indices.

FIGURE 2-4 Program to list the Fibonacci series

```
/*
 * File: Fib.java
 * ---------------
 * This program lists the terms in the Fibonacci sequence with
 * indices ranging from LOWER_LIMIT to UPPER_LIMIT.
 */

package edu.stanford.cs.javacs2.ch2;

public class Fib {

   public void run() {
      for (int i = LOWER_LIMIT; i <= UPPER_LIMIT; i++) {
         System.out.println("fib(" + i + ") = " + fib(i));
      }
   }

/*
 * Returns the nth term in the Fibonacci sequence using the
 * following recursive formulation:
 *
 *    fib(0) = 0
 *    fib(1) = 1
 *    fib(n) = fib(n - 1) + fib(n - 2)
 */

   private int fib(int n) {
      if (n < 2) {
         return n;
      } else {
         return fib(n - 1) + fib(n - 2);
      }
   }

/* Private constants */

   private static final int LOWER_LIMIT = 0;
   private static final int UPPER_LIMIT = 20;

/* Main program */

   public static void main(String[] args) {
      new Fib().run();
   }

}
```

Gaining confidence in the recursive implementation

Now that you have a recursive implementation of the method `fib`, how can you go about convincing yourself that it works? You can always begin by tracing through the logic. Consider, for example, what happens if you call `fib(5)`. Because this is not one of the simple cases enumerated in the `if` statement, the implementation computes the result by evaluating the line

```
return fib(n - 1) + fib(n - 2);
```

which in this case is equivalent to

```
return fib(4) + fib(3);
```

At this point, the computer calculates the result of `fib(4)`, adds that to the result of calling `fib(3)`, and returns the sum as the value of `fib(5)`.

But how does the computer evaluate `fib(4)` and `fib(3)`? The answer, of course, is that it uses precisely the same strategy it did to calculate `fib(5)`. The essence of recursion is to break problems down into simpler ones that can be solved by calls to exactly the same method. Those calls get broken down into simpler ones, which in turn get broken down into even simpler ones, until at last the simple cases are reached.

On the other hand, it is best to regard this entire mechanism as irrelevant detail. Instead, just remember the recursive leap of faith. Your job at this level is to understand how the call to `fib(5)` works. In the course of walking though the execution of that method, you have managed to transform the problem into computing the sum of `fib(4)` and `fib(3)`. Because the argument values are smaller, each of these calls represents a simpler case. Applying the recursive leap of faith, you can assume that the program correctly computes each of these values, without going through all the steps yourself. For the purposes of validating the recursive strategy, you can just look the answers up in the table: `fib(4)` is 3 and `fib(3)` is 2. The result of calling `fib(5)` is therefore 3 + 2, or 5, which is indeed the correct answer. Case closed. You don't need to see all the details, which are best left to the computer.

Efficiency of the recursive implementation

However, if you do decide to go through the details of the evaluation of the call to `fib(5)`, you will quickly discover that the calculation is extremely inefficient. The recursive decomposition makes many redundant calls, in which the computer ends up calculating the same term in the Fibonacci sequence several times. This situation is illustrated in Figure 2-5, which shows all the recursive calls required in the calculation of `fib(5)`. As you can see from the diagram, the program ends up

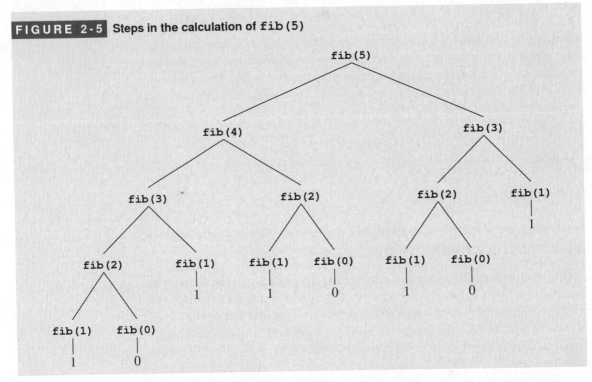

FIGURE 2-5 Steps in the calculation of `fib(5)`

making one call to `fib(4)`, two calls to `fib(3)`, three calls to `fib(2)`, five calls to `fib(1)`, and three calls to `fib(0)`. Given that the Fibonacci function can be implemented efficiently using iteration, the explosion of steps required by the recursive implementation is more than a little disturbing.

Recursion is not to blame

On discovering that the implementation of `fib(n)` given in Figure 2-4 is highly inefficient, many people are tempted to point their finger at recursion as the culprit. The problem in the Fibonacci example, however, has nothing to do with recursion *per se* but rather with the way in which recursion is used. By adopting a different strategy, it is possible to write a recursive implementation of the `fib` method in which the large-scale inefficiencies revealed in Figure 2-5 disappear completely.

As is often the case when using recursion, the key to finding a more efficient solution lies in adopting a more general approach. The Fibonacci sequence is not the only sequence whose terms are defined by the recurrence relation

$$t_n = t_{n-1} + t_{n-2}$$

Depending on how you choose the first two terms, you can generate many different sequences. The traditional Fibonacci sequence

$$0, 1, 1, 2, 3, 5, 8, 13, 21, 34, 55, 89, 144, \ldots$$

comes from defining $t_0 = 0$ and $t_1 = 1$. If, for example, you defined $t_0 = 3$ and $t_1 = 7$, you would get this sequence instead:

$$3, 7, 10, 17, 27, 44, 71, 115, 186, 301, 487, 788, 1275, \ldots$$

Similarly, defining $t_0 = -1$ and $t_1 = 2$ gives rise to the following sequence:

$$-1, 2, 1, 3, 4, 7, 11, 18, 29, 47, 76, 123, 199, \ldots$$

These sequences all use the same recurrence relation, which specifies that each new term is the sum of the preceding two. The only way the sequences differ is in the choice of the first two terms. As a general class, sequences that follow this pattern are called *additive sequences.*

This concept of an additive sequence makes it possible to convert the problem of finding the nth term in the Fibonacci sequence into the more general problem of finding the nth term in an additive sequence whose initial terms are t_0 and t_1. Such a method requires three arguments and might be expressed in Java as a method with the following prototype:

```
private int additiveSequence(int n, int t0, int t1)
```

If you had such a method, it would be easy to implement **fib** using it. All you would need to do is supply the correct values of the first two terms, as follows:

```
private int fib(int n) {
   return additiveSequence(n, 0, 1);
}
```

The body consists of a single line of code that does nothing but call another method, passing along a few extra arguments. Functions of this sort, which simply return the result of another method, often after transforming the arguments in some way, are called *wrapper* methods. Wrapper methods are extremely common in recursive programming. In most cases, a wrapper method is used, as it is here, to supply additional arguments to a subsidiary method that solves a more general problem.

From this point, the one remaining task is to implement **additiveSequence**. If you think about this more general problem for a few minutes, you will discover that additive sequences have an interesting recursive character of their own. The simple case for the recursion consists of the terms t_0 and t_1, whose values are part of the definition of the sequence. In the Java implementation, the values of these terms are passed as arguments. If you need to compute t_0, for example, all you have to do is return the argument **t0**.

But what if you are asked to find a term further down in the sequence? Suppose, for example, that you want to find t_6 in the additive sequence whose initial terms are 3 and 7. By looking at the list of terms in the sequence

t_0	t_1	t_2	t_3	t_4	t_5	t_6	t_7	t_8	t_9	
3	7	10	17	27	44	71	115	186	301	...

you can see that the correct value is 71. The interesting question, however, is how you can use recursion to determine this result.

The key insight you need is that the nth term in any additive sequence is simply the $n-1^{st}$ term in the additive sequence that begins one step further along. For example, t_6 in the sequence shown in the most recent example is simply t_5 in the additive sequence

t_0	t_1	t_2	t_3	t_4	t_5	t_6	t_7	t_8	
7	10	17	27	44	71	115	186	301	...

that begins with 7 and 10.

This insight makes it possible to implement the method **additiveSequence** as follows:

```
private int additiveSequence(int n, int t0, int t1) {
    if (n == 0) return t0;
    if (n == 1) return t1;
    return additiveSequence(n - 1, t1, t0 + t1);
}
```

If you trace through the steps in the calculation of **fib(5)** using this technique, you will discover that the calculation involves none of the redundant computation that made the earlier recursive formulation so inefficient. The steps lead directly to the solution, as shown in the following diagram:

```
fib(5)
  = additiveSequence(5, 0, 1)
    = additiveSequence(4, 1, 1)
      = additiveSequence(3, 1, 2)
        = additiveSequence(2, 2, 3)
          = additiveSequence(1, 3, 5)
            = 5
```

Even though the new implementation is entirely recursive, it is comparable in efficiency to the traditional iterative version of the Fibonacci method. In fact, it is possible to use more sophisticated mathematics to write an entirely recursive implementation of `fib(n)` that is considerably more efficient than the iterative strategy. You will have a chance to code this implementation on your own in the exercises for Chapter 10.

 ## Summary

In this chapter, you learned about *methods*, which enable you to refer to an entire block of code by a simple name. Because they allow the programmer to ignore the internal details and concentrate only on the effect of a method as a whole, methods are an essential tool for reducing the conceptual complexity of programs.

The important points introduced in this chapter include:

- A *method* is a block of code that has been organized into a separate unit and given a name. Other parts of the program can then *call* that method, possibly passing it information in the form of *arguments* and receiving a result *returned* by that method.

- Methods serve several useful purposes in programming. Allowing the same set of instructions to be shared by many parts of a program reduces both its size and its complexity. More importantly, methods make it possible to *decompose* large programs into smaller, more manageable pieces. Methods also serve as the basis for implementing *algorithms,* which are precisely specified strategies for solving computational problems.

- The `Math` library class exports a variety of methods that implement such standard mathematical functions as `sqrt`, `sin`, and `cos`. As a client of the `Math` class, you need to know how to call these methods, but not to know the details of how they work.

- A method that returns a value must have a `return` statement that specifies the result. Methods may return values of any type. Methods that return Boolean values, which are called *predicate methods,* play an important role in programming.

- Java allows you to define several methods with the same name as long as the compiler can use the number and types of the arguments to determine which method is required. This process is called *overloading.* The argument pattern that distinguishes each of the overloaded variants is called a *signature.*

- Variables declared with a method are *local* to that method and cannot be used outside it. Internally, all the variables declared within a method are stored together in a *stack frame.*

- When you call a method, the arguments are evaluated in the context of the caller and then copied into the *parameter variables* specified in the method prototype. The association of arguments and parameters always follows the order in which the variables appear in each of the lists.

- When a method returns, it continues from precisely the point at which the call was made. The computer refers to this point as the *return address* and keeps track of it in the stack frame.

- Solution strategies that proceed by breaking a problem down into simpler problems of the same form are said to be *recursive*. Recursion is an extremely powerful programming technique that you will have a chance to study in more detail in Chapter 8.

- Before you can use recursion effectively, you must learn to limit your analysis to a single level of the recursive decomposition and to rely on the correctness of all simpler recursive calls without tracing through the entire computation. Trusting these simpler calls to work correctly is often called the *recursive leap of faith*.

- Mathematical functions often express their recursive nature in the form of a *recurrence relation*, in which each element of a sequence is defined in terms of earlier elements.

- Although some recursive methods may be less efficient than their iterative counterparts, recursion itself is not the problem. As is typical with all types of algorithms, some recursive strategies are more efficient than others.

- In order to ensure that a recursive decomposition produces subproblems that are identical in form to the original, it is often necessary to generalize the problem. As a result, it is often useful to implement the solution to a specific problem as a simple *wrapper* function whose only purpose is to call a subsidiary function that implements the more general case.

Review questions

1. Explain in your own words the difference between a *method* and a *program*.

2. Define the following terms as they apply to methods: *call*, *argument*, *return*.

3. Can there be more than one **return** statement in the body of a method?

4. What is a *static method?*

5. How would you calculate the trigonometric sine of 45° using the **Math** class?

6. What is a *predicate method?*

7. Describe the difference in role between an *implementer* and a *client.*

8. What is meant by the term *overloading?* How does the Java compiler use *signatures* to implement overloading?

9. What is a *stack frame?*

10. Describe the process by which *arguments* are associated with *parameters.*

11. Variables declared within a method are said to be *local variables.* What is the significance of the word *local* in this context?

12. What is the difference between *iteration* and *recursion?*

13. What is meant by the phrase *recursive leap of faith?* Why is this concept important to you as a programmer?

14. In the section entitled "Tracing the recursive process," the text goes through a long analysis of what happens internally when `fact(4)` is called. Using this section as a model, trace the execution of `fib(3)`, sketching out each stack frame created in the process.

15. What is a *recurrence relation?*

16. Modify Fibonacci's rabbit problem by introducing the additional rule that rabbit pairs stop reproducing after giving birth to *three* litters. How does this assumption change the recurrence relation? What changes do you need to make in the simple cases?

17. How many times is `fib(1)` called when `fib(n)` is calculated using the recursive implementation given in Figure 2-5?

18. What is a *wrapper method?* Why are wrapper methods often useful in writing recursive methods?

19. What would happen if you eliminated the `if (n == 1)` check from the method `additiveSequence`, so that the implementation looked like this:

```
int additiveSequence(int n, int t0, int t1) {
    if (n == 0) return t0;
    return additiveSequence(n - 1, t1, t0 + t1);
}
```

Would the method still work? Why, or why not?

Exercises

1. Rewrite the Celsius-to-Fahrenheit program from exercise 1 in Chapter 1 so that it uses a method to perform the conversion.

2. Write a method `countDigits(n)` that returns the number of digits in the integer **n**, which you may assume is positive. Design a program to test your method. For hints about how to write this method, you might want to look back at the `DigitSum` program in Figure 1-10.

3. Write a program called `PowersOfTwo` that displays the values of 2^k for all values of **k** from 0 to 16, inclusive, as shown in the following sample run:

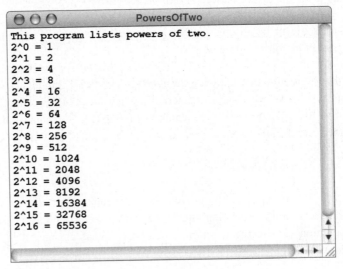

```
This program lists powers of two.
2^0 = 1
2^1 = 2
2^2 = 4
2^3 = 8
2^4 = 16
2^5 = 32
2^6 = 64
2^7 = 128
2^8 = 256
2^9 = 512
2^10 = 1024
2^11 = 2048
2^12 = 4096
2^13 = 8192
2^14 = 16384
2^15 = 32768
2^16 = 65536
```

Your solution should include a method `raiseToPower` that takes two integers, *n* and *k*, and returns n^k.

4. Write overloaded versions of the `raiseToPower` method from exercise 3 that allow the base (represented by the parameter *n*) to be a `long` or a `double` as well as an `int`. Write a program that tests each of these extensions.

5. If you have been outside in cold, windy weather, you know that your perception of the cold depends on the wind speed as well as the temperature. The faster the wind blows, the colder you feel. To quantify how wind affects temperature perception, the National Weather Service reports the **wind chill,** which is illustrated on their website as shown in Figure 2-6.

FIGURE 2-6 Wind chill as a function of temperature and wind speed

	Temperature (°F)																	
Calm	40	35	30	25	20	15	10	5	0	-5	-10	-15	-20	-25	-30	-35	-40	-45
5	36	31	25	19	13	7	1	-5	-11	-16	-22	-28	-34	-40	-46	-52	-57	-63
10	34	27	21	15	9	3	-4	-10	-16	-22	-28	-35	-41	-47	-53	-59	-66	-72
15	32	25	19	13	6	0	-7	-13	-19	-26	-32	-39	-45	-51	-58	-64	-71	-77
20	30	24	17	11	4	-2	-9	-15	-22	-29	-35	-42	-48	-55	-61	-68	-74	-81
25	29	23	16	9	3	-4	-11	-17	-24	-31	-37	-44	-51	-58	-64	-71	-78	-84
30	28	22	15	8	1	-5	-12	-19	-26	-33	-39	-46	-53	-60	-67	-73	-80	-87
35	28	21	14	7	0	-7	-14	-21	-27	-34	-41	-48	-55	-62	-69	-76	-82	-89
40	27	20	13	6	-1	-8	-15	-22	-29	-36	-43	-50	-57	-64	-71	-78	-84	-91
45	26	19	12	5	-2	-9	-16	-23	-30	-37	-44	-51	-58	-65	-72	-79	-86	-93
50	26	19	12	4	-3	-10	-17	-24	-31	-38	-45	-52	-60	-67	-74	-81	-88	-95
55	25	18	11	4	-3	-11	-18	-25	-32	-39	-46	-54	-61	-68	-75	-82	-89	-97
60	25	17	10	3	-4	-11	-19	-26	-33	-40	-48	-55	-62	-69	-76	-84	-91	-98

Wind (mph)

Frostbite Times ▢ 30 minutes ▢ 10 minutes ▢ 5 minutes

Wind Chill (°F) = 35.74 + 0.6215T - 35.75(V$^{0.16}$) + 0.4275T(V$^{0.16}$)

Where, T= Air Temperature (°F) V= Wind Speed (mph)   *Effective 11/01/01*

Source: National Weather Service

As you can see at the bottom of this figure, the National Weather Service calculates wind chill using the formula

$$35.74 + 0.6215\,t - 35.75\,v^{0.16} + 0.4275\,t\,v^{0.16}$$

where *t* is the Fahrenheit temperature and *v* is the wind speed in miles per hour.

Write a method **windChill** that takes the values of *t* and *v* and returns the wind chill. In doing so, your method should take account of two special cases:

- If there is no wind, **windChill** should return the original temperature *t*.

- If the temperature is greater than 40° F, the wind chill is undefined, and your method should return the original temperature in this case as well.

Although it will be easier to write such an application once you learn how to format numeric data in Chapter 4, you already have all the tools you need to align the columns of the wind-chill table as shown in Figure 2-6. If you're up for a challenge, write a main program that uses **windChill** to produce that table.

6. Greek mathematicians took a special interest in numbers that are equal to the sum of their *proper divisors,* which is simply any divisor less than the number itself. They called such numbers *perfect numbers.* For example, 6 is a perfect number because it is the sum of 1, 2, and 3, which are the integers less than 6 that divide evenly into 6. Similarly, 28 is a perfect number because it is the sum of 1, 2, 4, 7, and 14.

    Write a predicate method `isPerfect` that takes an integer `n` and returns `true` if `n` is perfect, and `false` otherwise. Test your implementation by writing a main program that uses the `isPerfect` method to check for perfect numbers in the range 1 to 9999 by testing each number in turn. When a perfect number is found, your program should display it on the screen. The first two lines of output should be 6 and 28. Your program should find two other perfect numbers in the range as well.

7. An integer greater than 1 is said to be *prime* if it has no divisors other than itself and one. The number 17, for example, is prime, because there are no numbers other than 1 and 17 that divide evenly into it. The number 91, however, is not prime because it is divisible by 7 and 13. Write a predicate method `isPrime(n)` that returns `true` if the integer `n` is prime, and `false` otherwise. To test your algorithm, write a main program that lists the prime numbers between 1 and 100.

8. Even though clients of the `Math` class typically don't need to understand how methods like `sqrt` work internally, the implementers of that library have to be able to design an effective algorithm and write the necessary code. If you were asked to implement the `sqrt` method without using the library version, there are many strategies you could adopt. One of the easiest strategies to understand is *successive approximation,* in which you make a guess at the solution and then refine that guess by choosing new values that move closer to the solution.

    You can use successive approximation to determine the square root of *x* by adopting the following strategy:

    1. Begin by guessing that the square root is *x* / 2. Call that guess *g.*

    2. The actual square root must lie between *g* and *x* / *g.* At each step in the successive approximation, generate a new guess by averaging *g* and *x* / *g.*

    3. Repeat step 2 until the values *g* and *x* / *g* are as close together as the precision of the hardware allows. In Java, the best way to check for this condition is to test whether the average is equal to either of the values used to generate it.

    Use this strategy to write your own implementation of the `sqrt` method.

9. In exercise 11 from Chapter 1, you learned that the mathematical constant π can be approximated using the following series developed by Leibniz:

$$\tfrac{\pi}{4} \;=\; 1 - \tfrac{1}{3} + \tfrac{1}{5} - \tfrac{1}{7} + \tfrac{1}{9} - \cdots$$

Unfortunately, this series converges extremely slowly. Even after 10,000 terms, the approximation is correct only to four digits. Using this technique to compute π to the limit of floating-point precision is therefore impractical. The following series converges much more quickly:

$$\tfrac{\pi}{6} \;=\; \tfrac{1}{2} + \left(\tfrac{1}{2}\right)\tfrac{1}{3}\left(\tfrac{1}{2}\right)^3 + \left(\tfrac{1}{2}\times\tfrac{3}{4}\right)\tfrac{1}{5}\left(\tfrac{1}{2}\right)^5 + \left(\tfrac{1}{2}\times\tfrac{3}{4}\times\tfrac{5}{6}\right)\tfrac{1}{7}\left(\tfrac{1}{2}\right)^7 + \cdots$$

Each term can be divided into three parts, as suggested by the parentheses in the formula. Figure out how each part changes from term to term, and use this information to write a program that calculates π to the limit of floating-point accuracy.

10. The library function **Math.exp(x)** returns the value of e^x, which can be computed using the following series:

$$e^x \;=\; \frac{x^0}{0!} + \frac{x^1}{1!} + \frac{x^2}{2!} + \frac{x^3}{3!} + \frac{x^4}{4!} + \frac{x^5}{5!} + \frac{x^6}{6!} + \frac{x^7}{7!} - \cdots$$

Write your own function **exp(x)** that uses this series to approximate the value of e^x. For example, calling **exp(1)** should return the mathematical constant e.

11. Although Euclid's algorithm for calculating the greatest common divisor is one of the oldest to be dignified with that term, there are other algorithms that date back many centuries. In the Middle Ages, one of the problems that required sophisticated algorithmic thinking was determining the date of Easter, which falls on the first Sunday after the first full moon following the vernal equinox. Given this definition, the calculation involves interacting cycles of the day of the week, the orbit of the moon, and the passage of the sun through the zodiac. Early algorithms for solving this problem date back to the third century and are described in the writings of the eighth-century scholar known as the Venerable Bede. In 1800, the German mathematician Carl Friedrich Gauss published an algorithm for determining the date of Easter that was purely computational in the sense that it relied on arithmetic rather than looking up values in tables. His algorithm—translated from the German—appears in Figure 2-7.

  Write a procedure

```
String findEaster(int year)
```

that returns the Easter date for **year** as a string consisting of the month name concatenated with the day, as in **"April 11"**.

FIGURE 2-7	Gauss's algorithm for computing the date of Easter

I.   Divide the number of the year for which one wishes to calculate Easter by 19, by 4, and by 7, and call the remainders of these divisions a, b, and c, respectively. If the division is even, set the remainder to 0; the quotients are not taken into account. Precisely the same is true of the following divisions.

II. Divide the value $19a + 23$ by 30 and call the remainder d.

III. Finally, divide $2b + 4c + 6d + 3$, or $2b + 4c + 6d + 4$, choosing the former for years between 1700 and 1799 and the latter for years between 1800 and 1899, by 7 and call the remainder e.

Then Easter falls on March $22 + d + e$, or when $d + e$ is greater than 9, on April $d + e - 9$.

Translated from Karl Friedrich Gauss, "Berechnung des Osterfestes," August 1800
`http://gdz.sub.uni-goettingen.de/no_cache/dms/load/img/?IDDOC=137484`

Unfortunately, the algorithm in Figure 2-7 only works for years in the 18th and 19th centuries. It is easy, however, to search the web for extensions that work for all years. Once you have completed your implementation of Gauss's algorithm, undertake the necessary research to find a more general approach.

12. The combinations method $C(n, k)$ described in this chapter determines the number of ways you can choose k values from a set of n elements, ignoring the order of the elements. If the order of the value matters—so that, in the case of the coin example, choosing a quarter first and then a dime is seen as distinct from choosing a dime and then a quarter—you need to use a different method, which computes the number of *permutations,* which are all the ways of ordering k elements taken from a collection of size n. This method is denoted as $P(n, k)$, and has the following mathematical formulation:

$$P(n, k) = \frac{n!}{(n - k)!}$$

Although this definition is mathematically correct, it is not well suited to implementation in practice because the factorials involved can get much too large to store in an integer variable, even when the answer is small. For example, if you tried to use this formula to calculate the number of ways to select two cards from a standard 52-card deck, you would end up trying to evaluate the following fraction:

$$\frac{80{,}658{,}175{,}170{,}943{,}878{,}571{,}660{,}636{,}856{,}403{,}766{,}975{,}289{,}505{,}440{,}883{,}277{,}824{,}000{,}000{,}000{,}000}{30{,}414{,}093{,}201{,}713{,}378{,}043{,}612{,}608{,}166{,}064{,}768{,}844{,}377{,}641{,}568{,}960{,}512{,}000{,}000{,}000{,}000}$$

even though the answer is the much more manageable 2652 (52×51).

Write a method **permutations(n, k)** that computes the $P(n, k)$ method without calling the **fact** method. Part of your job in this problem is to figure out how to compute this value efficiently. To do so, you will probably find it useful to play around with some relatively small values to get a sense of how the factorials in the numerator and denominator of the formula behave.

13. One of the most storied mathematical collaborations in history existed between G. H. Hardy and the Indian mathematical prodigy Srinivasa Ramanujan. In his foreword to Hardy's *A Mathematician's Apology*, the British mathematician and novelist C. P. Snow relates the following account of a visit by Hardy to the dying Ramanujan, which has become famous in mathematical lore:

> Hardy, always inept about introducing a conversation, said, probably without a greeting, and certainly as his first remark: "I thought the number of my taxi-cab was 1729. It seemed to me rather a dull number." To which, Ramanujan replied: "No, Hardy! No, Hardy! It is a very interesting number. It is the smallest number expressible as the sum of two cubes in two different ways."
>
> This is the exchange as Hardy recorded it. It must be substantially accurate. He was the most honest of men; and further, no one could possibly have invented it.

Write a Java program that confirms Ramanujan's statement, assuming that only positive numbers are involved.

14. Spherical objects, such as cannonballs, can be stacked to form a pyramid with one cannonball at the top, sitting on top of a square composed of four cannonballs, sitting on top of a square composed of nine cannonballs, and so forth. Write a recursive method `cannonball` that takes as its argument the height of the pyramid and returns the number of cannonballs it contains. Your method must operate recursively and must not use any iterative constructs, such as `while` or `for`.

15. In the 18th century, the astronomer Johann Daniel Titius proposed a rule, later recorded by Johann Elert Bode, for calculating the distance from the sun to each of the planets known at that time. To apply that rule, which is now known as the ***Titius-Bode Law,*** you begin by writing down the sequence

$$b_1 = 1 \quad b_2 = 3 \quad b_3 = 6 \quad b_4 = 12 \quad b_5 = 24 \quad b_6 = 48 \quad \cdots$$

where each subsequent element in the sequence is twice the preceding one. It turns out that an approximate distance to the ith planet can be computed from this series by applying the formula

$$d_i = \frac{4 + b_i}{10}$$

The distance d_i is expressed in ***astronomical units*** (AUs), which correspond to the average distance from the earth to the sun (approximately 93,000,000 miles).   Except for a disconcerting gap between Mars and Jupiter, the Titius-Bode law gives reasonable approximations for the distances to the seven planets known at the time:

Mercury	0.5 AU
Venus	0.7 AU
Earth	1.0 AU
Mars	1.6 AU
?	2.8 AU
Jupiter	5.2 AU
Saturn	10.0 AU
Uranus	19.6 AU

Concern about the gap in the sequence led astronomers to discover the asteroid belt, which they suggested might have been the remains of a planet that had once orbited the sun at the distance specified by the missing entry in the table.

Write a recursive method **getTitiusBodeDistance**(k) that calculates the expected distance between the sun and the kth planet, numbering outward from Mercury starting with 1. Test your method by writing a program that displays the distances to each of these planets in tabular form.

16. Rewrite the **raiseToPower** method from exercise 3 so that it follows the form of this recursive definition:

$$n^k = \begin{cases} 1 & \text{if } k \text{ is } 0 \\ n \times n^{k-1} & \text{otherwise} \end{cases}$$

17. Rewrite the **gcd** function from page 63 so that it computes the greatest common divisor recursively using the following rules:

- If y is zero, then x is the greatest common divisor.

- Otherwise, the greatest common divisor of x and y is always equal to the greatest common divisor of y and the remainder of x divided by y.

18. Write a recursive method **digitSum**(n) that takes a nonnegative integer and returns the sum of its digits. For example, calling **digitSum(1729)** should return $1 + 7 + 2 + 9$, which is 19.

The recursive implementation of **digitSum** depends on the fact that it is easy to break an integer down into two components using division by 10. For example, given the integer 1729, you can divide it into two pieces as follows:

1729

172   9

Each of the resulting integers is strictly smaller than the original and thus represents a simpler case.

19. The *digital root* of an integer n is defined as the result of summing the digits repeatedly until only a single digit remains. For example, the digital root of 1729 can be calculated using the following steps:

Step 1:	$1 + 7 + 2 + 9$	$\rightarrow$	19
Step 2:	$1 + 9$	$\rightarrow$	10
Step 3:	$1 + 0$	$\rightarrow$	1

Write a method `digitalRoot(n)` that returns the digital root of `n`. Part of the challenge of this problem is to write the method recursively without using any explicit loop constructs.

20. Write an iterative implementation of the method `fib(n)`.

21. For each of the two recursive implementations of the method `fib(n)` presented in this chapter, write a recursive method that counts the number of method calls made during the evaluation of the corresponding Fibonacci calculation. Write a program that uses these methods to display a table showing the number of calls made by each algorithm for values of **n** up to some constant limit specified in the program. The first ten terms, for example, look like this:

```
CountFib
 n     fib1    fib2
 --     ----    ----
 0       1       2
 1       1       2
 2       3       3
 3       5       4
 4       9       5
 5      15       6
 6      25       7
 7      41       8
 8      67       9
 9     109      10
```

22. As you know from this chapter, the mathematical combinations method $C(n, k)$ is usually defined in terms of factorials, as follows:

$$C(n, k) = \frac{n!}{k! \times (n - k)!}$$

The values of $C(n, k)$ can also be arranged geometrically to form a triangle in which n increases as you move down the triangle and k increases as you move from left to right. The resulting structure, which is called **Pascal's Triangle** after the French mathematician Blaise Pascal, is arranged like this:

$$C(0, 0)$$
$$C(1, 0) \quad C(1, 1)$$
$$C(2, 0) \quad C(2, 1) \quad C(2, 2)$$
$$C(3, 0) \quad C(3, 1) \quad C(3, 2) \quad C(3, 3)$$
$$C(4, 0) \quad C(4, 1) \quad C(4, 2) \quad C(4, 3) \quad C(4, 4)$$

Pascal's Triangle has the interesting property that every entry is the sum of the two entries above it, except along the left and right edges, where the values are always 1. Consider, for example, the circled entry in the following display of Pascal's Triangle:

$$1$$
$$1 \quad 1$$
$$1 \quad 2 \quad 1$$
$$1 \quad 3 \quad 3 \quad 1$$
$$1 \quad 4 \quad 6 \quad 4 \quad 1$$
$$1 \quad 5 \quad 10 \quad 10 \quad 5 \quad 1$$
$$1 \quad 6 \quad (15) \quad 20 \quad 15 \quad 6 \quad 1$$
$$1 \quad 7 \quad 21 \quad 35 \quad 35 \quad 21 \quad 7 \quad 1$$

This entry, which corresponds to $C(6, 2)$, is the sum of the two entries—5 and 10—that appear above it to either side. Use this relationship between entries in Pascal's Triangle to write a recursive version of `combinations(n, k)` that uses no loops, no multiplication, and no calls to `fact`.

Chapter 3
Strings

Whisper music on those strings.

— T. S. Eliot, *The Waste Land,* 1922

Up to now, most of the programming examples you have seen in this book have used numbers as their basic data type. These days, computers work less with numeric data than with ***text data,*** which is a generic term for information composed of individual characters. The ability of modern computers to process text data has led to the development of text messaging, electronic mail, word processing systems, social networking, and a wide variety of other useful applications.

This chapter introduces the Java `String` class, which provides a convenient abstraction for working with strings. Having this library in your toolbox will make it much easier to write interesting applications. This chapter also begins a multichapter overview of classes and objects, which are central concepts in the object-oriented paradigm. Working with the `String` class in this chapter will increase your understanding of classes and provide the foundation you need to define your own classes in Chapter 7.

■ 3.1 Using strings as abstract values

Conceptually, a ***string*** is simply a sequence of characters. For example, the string `"hello, world"` is a sequence of twelve characters including ten letters, a comma, and a space. In Java, the `String` class and its associated operations are defined in the `java.lang` package, which means that the `String` class is always available even without a specific `import` statement.

In Chapter 1, you learned that data types are defined by two properties: a *domain* and a *set of operations.* For strings, the domain is easy to identify: the domain of type `String` is the set of all sequences of characters. A more interesting problem is to identify the appropriate set of operations. As you have already seen in almost every program, Java defines the + operator for strings to mean ***concatenation,*** which simply means joining two strings together end to end. All other string operations, however, are defined as methods in the `String` class.

For the most part, you can use `String` as a primitive data type in much the same way that you use types like `int` and `double`. You can, for example, declare a variable of type `String` and assign it an initial value, as you would with a numeric variable. When you declare a `String` variable, you typically specify its initial value as a ***string literal,*** which is a sequence of characters enclosed in double quotation marks. For example, the declaration

```
String alphabet = "ABCDEFGHIJKLMNOPQRSTUVWXYZ";
```

sets the variable `alphabet` to a 26-character string containing the uppercase letters.

You can read a string from the user by calling the **nextLine** method in the **Scanner** class, in much the same way that you used **nextInt** and **nextDouble** in the programs in Chapter 1. The **HelloName** program in Figure 3-1 illustrates string input by implementing a personalized version of the **HelloWorld** program that includes the user's name in the output, as shown in the following sample run:

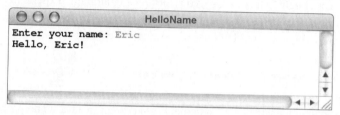

You do, however, have to be careful if you use the **Scanner** to read both numbers and lines of text. If you call **nextInt** or **nextDouble**, the **Scanner** class reads only the number and not the end of line that follows that number. If you then call **nextLine**, you will get the empty line that follows the earlier input value. The simplest strategy for avoiding this problem is to include an extra call to **nextLine** immediately after calls to **nextInt** or **nextDouble**.

FIGURE 3-1   An interactive version of the "Hello World" program

```
/*
 * File: HelloName.java
 * ---------------------------
 * This program reads in a name from the user and then prints that
 * name back as part of a cheery greeting.
 */

package edu.stanford.cs.javacs2.ch3;

import java.util.Scanner;

public class HelloName {

    public void run() {
        Scanner sysin = new Scanner(System.in);
        System.out.print("Enter your name: ");
        String name = sysin.nextLine();
        System.out.println("Hello, " + name + "!");
    }

/* Main program */

    public static void main(String[] args) {
        new HelloName().run();
    }

}
```

◼◼ 3.2 String operations

If you need to perform more complex operations using the **String** class, you will discover that strings in Java don't behave in quite the same way that similar types in other languages do. For one thing, string operations require a different syntactic form than you might expect from your prior programming experience. If, for example, you want to find the number of characters in the **alphabet** variable defined on page 98, you would not use a statement like this:

```
int nLetters = length(alphabet);
```

As the bug icon emphasizes, this statement is incorrect in Java. The problem with this expression is that the data type **String** is not a primitive type but is instead an example of a *class,* which is probably easiest to define informally as a template that describes a set of values together with an associated set of operations. In the language of object-oriented programming, the values that belong to a class are called *objects.* A single class can give rise to many different objects; each such object is said to be an *instance* of that class. Except for static methods that apply to a class as a whole, the methods you define as part of a class are applied to instances.

In the object-oriented paradigm, objects communicate by sending information and requests from one object to another. Collectively, these transmissions are called *messages.* The act of sending a message corresponds to having one object invoke a method that belongs to a different object. For consistency with the conceptual model of sending messages, the object that initiates the method is called the *sender,* and the object that is the target of that transmission is called the *receiver.* In Java, sending a message is specified using the following syntax:

receiver . *name* (*arguments*)

The object-oriented version of the statement that sets **nLetters** to the length of the string variable **alphabet** is therefore

```
int nLetters = alphabet.length();
```

Figure 3-2 lists the most common methods exported by the **String** class, all of which use the receiver syntax. The most important of those methods are then explored in more detail in the sections that follow. As you read through Figure 3-2, it is useful to note that the **String** methods never change the value of the receiver. For example, the **toLowerCase** method doesn't convert the receiver string to lowercase but instead returns an entirely new string with all characters converted to lowercase. To change a string, you need to reassign that value, as in

```
str = str.toLowerCase();
```

| FIGURE 3-2 | Common operations in the `String` class |

String operators

str_1 + str_2	Concatenates str_1 and str_2 end to end and returns a new string containing the combined characters. As long as one operand is a string, Java will convert the other operand to its string form.
str += *suffix*	Appends *suffix* to the end of str.

String methods

str.`length`()	Returns the number of characters in str.
str.`charAt`(k)	Returns the character at index position k in str.
str.`concat`(str_2)	Creates a new string that is the concatenation of str and str_2.
str.`substring`(p_1, p_2) str.`substring`(p_1)	Returns a new string of characters beginning at p_1 in str and extending up to but not including p_2. If p_2 is missing, the new string continues through the end of the original string.
str.`equals`(str_2)	Returns **true** if str and str_2 are equal.
str.`equalsIgnoreCase`(str_2)	Returns **true** if str equals str_2, ignoring differences in case.
str.`compareTo`(str_2)	Compares str with str_2 and returns an integer that is 0 if the two strings are equal, negative if str precedes str_2, in lexicographic order, and positive if str follows str_2.
str.`compareToIgnoreCase`(str_2)	Operates like **compareTo**, ignoring differences in case.
str.`isEmpty`()	Returns **true** if str is the empty string.
str.`startsWith`(*prefix*)	Returns **true** if str starts with the characters in *prefix*.
str.`endsWith`(*suffixr*)	Returns **true** if str ends with the characters in *suffix*.
str.`contains`(*sub*)	Returns **true** if str contains *sub* as a substring.
str.`indexOf`(*pattern*) str.`indexOf`(*pattern*, k)	Searches the string str for *pattern*, which can be either a character or a string. The search starts at the beginning, or at index k, if specified. The function returns the first index at which *pattern* appears, or –1 if it is not found.
str.`lastIndexOf`(*pattern*) str.`lastIndexOf`(*pattern*, k)	Operates like **indexOf**, but searches backward from position k. If k is missing, **lastIndexOf** starts at the end of the string.
str.`replace`(*old*, *new*)	Returns a copy of str after replacing all instances of *old* by *new*. The parameters *old* and *new* can be either strings or characters.
str.`split`(*pattern*)	Splits the string into an array of substrings by dividing it at instances of *pattern*. Arrays are discussed in Chapter 5.
str.`toLowerCase`()	Returns a copy of str converting all characters to lowercase.
str.`toUpperCase`()	Returns a copy of str converting all characters to uppercase.
str.`trim`()	Returns a copy of str after removing whitespace from each end.

Selecting characters from a string

In Java, positions within a string are numbered starting from 0. For example, the characters stored in the string variable **alphabet** are numbered as in the following diagram:

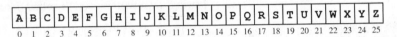

The position number written underneath each character is called its *index.*

In Java, you select a single character from a string by calling the **charAt** method. For example, if **alphabet** has been initialized as shown, the expression

```
alphabet.charAt(0)
```

selects the character **'A'** at the beginning of the string. Since character numbering in Java begins at 0, the last character in a string appears at the index that's one less than the length of the string. Thus, you can select the **'Z'** at the end of **alphabet** with the following expression:

```
alphabet.charAt(alphabet.length() - 1)
```

Extracting parts of a string

While concatenation makes longer strings from shorter pieces, you often need to do the reverse: separate a string into the shorter pieces it contains. A string that is part of a longer string is called a *substring.* The **String** class exports a method called **substring** that takes two parameters: the index of the first character you want to select and the index of the character that immediately follows the desired substring. For example, given the previous definition of **alphabet**, the method call

```
alphabet.substring(1, 4)
```

returns the three-character substring **"BCD"**. Because indices in Java begin at 0, the character at index position 1 is the character **'B'**.

The second argument in the **substring** method is optional. If it is missing, **substring** returns the substring that starts at the specified position and continues through the end of the string. Thus, calling

```
alphabet.substring(23)
```

returns the string **"XYZ"**.

The following method returns the second half of the parameter **str**, which is defined to include the middle character if the length of **str** is odd:

```
private String secondHalf(String str) {
    return str.substring(str.length() / 2);
}
```

Comparing strings

At many times in your programming, you will need to check to see whether two strings have the same value. When you do, you are almost certain to code this test at least once in the following incorrect form:

```
if (s1 == s2) . . .
```

The problem here is that Java defines the relational operators like `==` in the conventional mathematical way only for primitive types like `int` and `char`. In Java, `String` is a class rather than a primitive type. What makes this problem all the more insidious is that the `==` operator does *something* when applied to strings, but not what you'd initially expect. For objects, the `==` operator tests whether the expressions on each side are the same object. What you want in this case, however, is to test whether two different `String` objects have the same value.

To accomplish what you need, the `String` class implements a method called `equals`, which you can use to test two strings for equality. Like the other methods in the `String` class, `equals` is applied to a receiver object, which means that the syntax for an equality test looks like this:

```
if (s1.equals(s2)) . . .
```

There is also a method `equalsIgnoreCase` that checks whether two strings are equal, not counting uppercase/lowercase distinctions.

You will sometimes also find it useful to determine how two strings relate to each other in *lexicographic order,* which is the ordering imposed by the Unicode values of the characters in the string. Lexicographic order differs from traditional alphabetical order in several respects. For example, in an alphabetical index, you will find the entry for *aardvark* before the entry for *Achilles,* because traditional alphabetical ordering ignores case. In lexicographic order, the character `'A'` comes before the character `'a'`, which means that `"Achilles"` comes before `"aardvark"`. As you can see from Figure 3-2, the `String` class includes a method called `compareIgnoreCase`, which considers lowercase and uppercase letters to be the same.

In Java, you call the `compareTo` and `compareIgnoreCase` methods in typical receiver-based fashion, as follows:

```
s1.compareTo(s2)
```

The result of the call is an integer whose sign indicates the relationship between the two strings, as follows:

- If **s1** precedes **s2** in lexicographic order, **compareTo** returns a negative integer.
- If **s1** follows **s2** in lexicographic order, **compareTo** returns a positive integer.
- If the two strings are exactly the same, **compareTo** returns 0.

Thus, if you want to determine whether **s1** comes before **s2** in lexicographic order, you need to write

```
if (s1.compareTo(s2) < 0) . . .
```

Searching within a string

From time to time, you will find it useful to search a string to see whether it contains a particular character or substring. To support such search operations, the **String** class exports a method called **indexOf**, which comes in several forms. The simplest form of the call is

```
str.indexOf(pattern);
```

where *pattern* is the content you're looking for, which can be either a string or a character. When called, the **indexOf** method searches through **str** looking for the first occurrence of the search value. If the search value is found, **indexOf** returns the index position at which the match begins. If the character does not appear before the end of the string, **indexOf** returns −1.

The **indexOf** method takes an optional second argument that indicates the index position at which to start the search. The effect of both styles of the **indexOf** method is illustrated by the following examples, which assume that the variable **str** contains the string **"hello, world"**:

```
str.indexOf('o')       →    4
str.indexOf('o', 5)    →    8
str.indexOf('o', 9)    →   -1
```

The **String** class also exports three predicate methods—**startsWith**, **endsWith**, and **contains**—that turn out to be useful in a variety of contexts. Calls to these methods read almost like English. For example, the expression

```
filename.endsWith(".txt")
```

returns **true** if the string variable **filename** ends with the string **".txt"**.

Iterating through the characters in a string

Even though the methods exported by the **String** class provide the tools you need to implement string applications from scratch, it is usually easier to write programs by adapting existing code patterns that implement particularly common operations. When you work with strings, one of the most important patterns involves iterating through the characters in a string, which requires the following code:

```
for (int i = 0; i < str.length(); i++) {
    . . . body of loop that uses the character str.charAt(i) . . .
}
```

On each loop cycle, the expression **str.charAt(i)** refers to the ith character in the string. Because the purpose of the loop is to process every character, the loop continues as long as **i** is less than the length of the string. Thus, you can count the number of spaces in a string by using the following method:

```
private int countSpaces(String str) {
    int nSpaces = 0;
    for (int i = 0; i < str.length(); i++) {
        if (str.charAt(i) == ' ') nSpaces++;
    }
    return nSpaces;
}
```

For some applications, you will find it useful to iterate through a string in the opposite direction, starting with the last character and continuing backward until you reach the first. This style of iteration uses the following **for** loop:

```
for (int i = str.length() - 1; i >= 0; i--)
```

Here, the index **i** begins at the last index position, which is one less than the length of the string, and then decreases by one on each cycle, down to and including the index position 0.

Assuming that you understood the syntax and semantics of the **for** statement, you could work out these patterns from first principles each time you need them in an application. Doing so, however, would slow you down enormously. These iteration patterns are worth memorizing so that you don't have to waste any time thinking about them. Whenever you recognize that you need to cycle through the characters in a string, some part of your nervous system between your brain and your fingers should be able to translate that idea effortlessly into the following line:

```
for (int i = 0; i < str.length(); i++)
```

Growing a string through concatenation

Another pattern that is important to memorize as you learn how to work with strings is how to create a new string one character at a time. The loop structure itself will depend on the application, but the general pattern for creating a string by concatenation looks like this:

```
String str = "";
for (whatever loop header line fits the application) {
    str += the next substring or character;
}
```

As a simple example, the following method returns a string consisting of n copies of the character ch:

```
private String repeatChar(int n, char ch) {
    String str = "";
    for (int i = 0; i < n; i++) {
        str += ch;
    }
    return str;
}
```

The **repeatChar** method is useful if, for example, you need to generate some kind of section separator in console output. One strategy to accomplish this goal would be to use the statement

```
System.out.println(repeatChar(72, '-'));
```

which prints a line of 72 hyphens.

Many string-processing methods use the iteration and concatenation patterns together. For example, the following method reverses the argument string so that, for example, calling **reverse("stressed")** returns **"desserts"**:

```
private String reverse(String str) {
    String result = "";
    for (int i = str.length() - 1; i >= 0; i--) {
        result += str.charAt(i);
    }
    return result;
}
```

You could also implement **reverse** by running the loop in the forward direction and concatenating each new character to the front of the **result** string, as follows:

```
private String reverse(String str) {
    String result = "";
    for (int i = 0; i < str.length(); i++) {
        result = str.charAt(i) + result;
    }
    return result;
}
```

Using recursion with strings

In addition to the two iterative implementations of **reverse** given at the end of the preceding section, you can also adopt a recursive approach similar to the one used for the **fact** and **fib** functions in Chapter 2. This time, the recursive formulation grows out of the observation that implementing **reverse(str)** can be broken down into two cases, as follows:

1. If **str** is the empty string, **reverse(str)** is also empty.

2. Otherwise, **reverse(str)** is what you get if you reverse all but the first character of **str** and then concatenate the result with the first character.

This case analysis leads directly to a recursive implementation that looks like this:

```
private String reverse(String str) {
    if (str.isEmpty()) {
        return "";
    } else {
        return reverse(str.substring(1)) + str.charAt(0);
    }
}
```

Classifying characters

When you work with individual characters in a string, it is often useful to determine whether those characters fall into particular categories, such as letters or digits. To do so, it is useful to take advantage of the static methods in the **Character** class, the most common of which appear in Figure 3-3. For example, to determine whether the character variable is a letter, all you have to do is call the predicate method

```
Character.isLetter(ch)
```

Similarly, you can check whether **ch** is a *whitespace character* (an "invisible" character such as a space or a tab) by calling

```
Character.isWhitespace(ch)
```

FIGURE 3-3 Selected static methods in the `Character` class

Predicate methods for testing character type

`Character.isDigit`(*ch*)	Returns **true** if *ch* is a digit character.
`Character.isLetter`(*ch*)	Returns **true** if *ch* is a letter.
`Character.isLowerCase`(*ch*)	Returns **true** if *ch* is a lowercase letter.
`Character.isUpperCase`(*ch*)	Returns **true** if *ch* is an uppercase letter.
`Character.isLetterOrDigit`(*ch*)	Returns **true** if *ch* is a letter or a digit. Such characters are said to be *alphanumeric.*
`Character.isWhitespace`(*ch*)	Returns **true** if *ch* is a *whitespace character,* which is an "invisible" character such as a space or a tab.
`Character.isJavaIdentifierStart`(*ch*)	Returns **true** if *ch* can start a Java identifier.
`Character.isJavaIdentifierPart`(*ch*)	Returns **true** if *ch* can be part of a Java identifier.

Methods for case conversion

`Character.toUpperCase`(*ch*)	Returns *ch* converted to uppercase.
`Character.toLowerCase`(*ch*)	Returns *ch* converted to lowercase.

You can use the methods in the **Character** class together with the various string patterns to write your own implementations of several of the methods in the **String** class. For example, you can implement the string method **toUpperCase** using only concatenation, character selection, and the **length** method as follows:

```
private String toUpperCase(String str) {
    String result = "";
    for (int i = 0; i < str.length(); i++) {
        result += Character.toUpperCase(str.charAt(i));
    }
    return result;
}
```

This implementation is not part of the **String** class and therefore cannot use the receiver syntax. It must instead take the string as a parameter in the style of more traditional functions.

Working with strings and characters together is often confusing because they behave so differently. Strings are instances of the predefined **String** class. Characters, by contrast, are represented using the primitive type **char**. Because strings are objects, the operations they support use the receiver syntax; character operations never do. For example, you test whether two characters are equal using the == operator, as in the **if** statement

```
if (c1 == c2) . . .
```

The corresponding statement to test whether two strings are equal looks like this:

```
if (s1.equals(s2)) . . .
```

Similarly, you can convert a character **ch** to its uppercase form using the statement

```
ch = Character.toUpperCase(ch);
```

The corresponding code for strings is

```
str = str.toUpperCase();
```

3.3 Writing string applications

Although they are useful to illustrate how particular string methods work, the string examples you have seen so far are too simple to give you much insight into how to write a significant string-processing application. This section addresses that deficiency by developing two applications that manipulate string data.

Recognizing palindromes

A *palindrome* is a word that reads identically backward and forward, such as *level* or *noon*. The goal of this section is to write a predicate method **isPalindrome** that checks whether a string is a palindrome. Calling **isPalindrome("level")** should return **true**; calling **isPalindrome("xyz")** should return **false**.

As with most programming problems, there are several reasonable strategies for solving this problem. In my experience, the approach that most students are likely to try first uses a **for** loop to run through each index position in the first half of the string. At each position, the code then checks to see whether that character matches the one that appears in the symmetric position relative to the end of the string. Adopting that strategy leads to the following code:

```
private boolean isPalindrome(String str) {
    int n = str.length();
    for (int i = 0; i < n / 2; i++) {
        if (str.charAt(i) != str.charAt(n - i - 1)) {
            return false;
        }
    }
    return true;
}
```

You can also code **isPalindrome** recursively by observing that any string whose length is less than two is automatically a palindrome, and any longer string is a palindrome if its first and last characters match and the substring between them is a palindrome. This algorithm gives rise to the following recursive implementation:

```
private boolean isPalindrome(String str) {
    int n = str.length();
    if (n <= 1) {
        return true;
    } else {
        return str.charAt(0) == str.charAt(n - 1) &&
                isPalindrome(str.substring(1, n - 1));
    }
}
```

Finally, it is useful to note that you can also code **isPalindrome** in a much simpler form by taking advantage of methods that you have already seen, as follows:

```
private boolean isPalindrome(String str) {
    return str.equals(reverse(str));
}
```

Of these three implementations, the first is the most efficient. The other two implementations require either concatenation or the extraction of substrings, both of which require the creation of new strings. The first version doesn't have to create any strings at all. It does its work by selecting and comparing characters, which turn out to be less costly operations.

Despite this difference in efficiency, the third coding has many advantages, particularly as an example for new programmers. For one thing, it takes advantage of existing code by making use of the **reverse** method. For another, it hides the complexity involved in calculating index positions required by the first version. It takes at least a minute or two for most students to figure out why the code includes the selection expression **str.charAt(n - i - 1)** or why it is appropriate to use the < operator in the **for** loop test, as opposed to <=. By contrast, the line

```
return str.equals(reverse(str));
```

reads almost as fluidly as English: a string is a palindrome if it equals the reverse of that same string.

Particularly as you are learning about programming, it is more important to work toward the clarity of the second implementation than the efficiency of the first. Given the speed of modern computers, it is almost always worth sacrificing some efficiency to make a program easier to understand.

Translating English to Pig Latin

To give you more of a sense of how to implement string-processing applications, this section describes a Java program that reads a line of text from the user and then translates each word in that line from English to Pig Latin, a made-up language familiar to most children in the English-speaking world. In Pig Latin, words are formed from their English counterparts by applying the following rules:

1. If the word contains no vowels, no translation is done, which means that the Pig Latin word is the same as the original.

2. If the word begins with a vowel, the Pig Latin translation consists of the original word followed by the suffix *way*.

3. If the word begins with a consonant, the Pig Latin translation is formed by extracting the string of consonants up to the first vowel, moving that collection of consonants to the end of the word, and then adding the suffix *ay*.

As an example, suppose that the English word is *scram*. Because the word begins with a consonant, you divide it into two parts: one consisting of the letters before the first vowel and one consisting of that vowel and the remaining letters:

You then interchange these two parts and add *ay* at the end, as follows:

Thus the Pig Latin word for *scram* is *amscray*. For a word that begins with a vowel, such as *apple,* you simply add *way* to the end, which leaves you with *appleway.*

The code for the **PigLatin** program appears in Figure 3-4. The main program reads a line of text from the user and then calls **lineToPigLatin** to translate that line into Pig Latin. The **lineToPigLatin** method then calls **wordToPigLatin** to convert each word to its Pig Latin equivalent. Characters that are not part of a word are copied directly to the output line so that punctuation and spacing remain unaffected.

A sample run of the program might look like this:

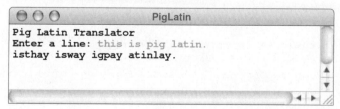

FIGURE 3-4 Program to translate English to Pig Latin

```
/*
 * File: PigLatin.java
 * ---------------------
 * This file takes a line of text and converts each word into Pig Latin.
 * The rules for forming Pig Latin words are as follows:
 *
 * o If the word begins with a vowel, add "way" to the end of the word.
 *
 * o If the word begins with a consonant, extract the set of consonants
 *   up to the first vowel, move that set of consonants to the end of
 *   the word, and add "ay".
 *
 * o If the word contains no vowels, return the original word unchanged.
 */

package edu.stanford.cs.javacs2.ch3;

import java.util.Scanner;

public class PigLatin {

    public void run() {
        Scanner sysin = new Scanner(System.in);
        System.out.println("Pig Latin Translator");
        System.out.print("Enter a line: ");
        String line = sysin.nextLine();
        System.out.println(lineToPigLatin(line));
    }

/*
 * Translates a line to Pig Latin, word by word.
 */

    private String lineToPigLatin(String line) {
        String result = "";
        String word = "";
        for (int i = 0; i < line.length(); i++) {
            char ch = line.charAt(i);
            if (Character.isLetter(ch)) {
                word += ch;
            } else {
                if (!word.isEmpty()) {
                    result += wordToPigLatin(word);
                    word = "";
                }
                result += ch;
            }
        }
        if (!word.isEmpty()) result += wordToPigLatin(word);
        return result;
    }
```

FIGURE 3-4 Program to translate English to Pig Latin (continued)

```java
/*
 * Translates a word to Pig Latin and returns the translated word.
 */

    private String wordToPigLatin(String word) {
        int vp = findFirstVowel(word);
        if (vp == -1) {
            return word;
        } else if (vp == 0) {
            return word + "way";
        } else {
            String head = word.substring(0, vp);
            String tail = word.substring(vp);
            return tail + head + "ay";
        }
    }

/*
 * Returns the index of the first vowel in the word, or -1 if none exist.
 */

    private int findFirstVowel(String word) {
        for (int i = 0; i < word.length(); i++) {
            if (isEnglishVowel(word.charAt(i))) return i;
        }
        return -1;
    }

/*
 * Returns true if the character is a vowel.
 */

    private boolean isEnglishVowel(char ch) {
        switch (ch) {
          case 'A': case 'E': case 'I': case 'O': case 'U':
          case 'a': case 'e': case 'i': case 'o': case 'u':
            return true;
          default:
            return false;
        }
    }

/* Main program */

    public static void main(String[] args) {
        new PigLatin().run();
    }

}
```

It is worth taking a careful look at the implementations of `lineToPigLatin` and `wordToPigLatin` in Figure 3-4. The `lineToPigLatin` method finds the word boundaries in the input, which provides a useful pattern for separating a string into individual words. The `wordToPigLatin` method uses `substring` to extract pieces of the English word and then uses concatenation to put them back together in their Pig Latin form. In Chapter 7, you will learn about a more general facility called a *token scanner* that divides a string into its logically connected parts.

Summary

In this chapter, you have learned how to use the `String` class, which makes it possible to write string-processing methods without worrying about the details of the underlying representation. The important points in this chapter include:

- The `String` class represents an abstract type that is conceptually a sequence of characters. The character positions in a string are assigned index numbers that start at 0 and extend up to one less than the length of the string.

- The most common methods exported by the `String` class appear in Figure 3-2 on page 101. Because `String` is a class, the methods use the *receiver syntax* instead of a more traditional functional form. Thus, to obtain the length of a string stored in the variable `str`, you need to invoke `str.length()`.

- The standard pattern for iterating through the characters in a string is

```
for (int i = 0; i < str.length(); i++) {
    . . . body of loop that manipulates str.charAt(i) . . .
}
```

- The standard pattern for growing a string by concatenation is

```
String str = "";
for (whatever loop control line fits the application) {
    str += the next substring or character;
}
```

- The `Character` class exports several static methods for working with individual characters. The most important of these methods appear in Figure 3-3.

Review questions

1. What is the difference between a *character* and a *string?*

2. True or false: In Java, you can determine the length of the string stored in the variable `str` by calling `length(str)`.

3.   What does it mean to say that the **String** class is *immutable?*

4.   If you call **s1.concat(s2)**, which string is the *receiver?*

5.   What is the effect of the **+** operator when it is used with two string operands? What happens if one operand is a string, but the other is of some numeric type?

6.   True or false: The index positions in a string begin at 0 and extend up to the length of the string minus 1.

7.   What are the arguments to the **substring** method? What happens if you omit the second argument?

8.   What is *lexicographic ordering?*

9.   What happens in Java if you try to use the **==** operator to test whether two strings are equal?

10. Describe how the **compareTo** method uses the return value to indicate the relative ordering of two strings.

11. What value does **indexOf** return if the pattern string does not appear?

12. What is the significance of the optional second argument to **indexOf**?

13. What effect does the following statement have on the value of **str**?

         str.trim()

14. What is the correct way to achieve the effect clearly intended by the expression in the preceding question?

15. Suppose that you have declared and initialized the variable **s** as follows:

         String s = "hello, world";

Given that declaration, what is the value of each of the following calls:

a. s + '!'

b. s.length()

c. s.charAt(5)

d. s.indexOf('l')

e. s.indexOf("l", 5)

f. s.replace('h', 'j')

g. s.substring(0, 3)

h. s.substring(7)

i. s.substring(3, 5)

j. s.substring(3, 3)

16. What is the result of each of the following expressions? (For calls to
`compareTo`, simply indicate the sign of the result.)

a. `"ABC".equals("abc")`   d. `"ABC".compareTo("AB")`
b. `"ABC".equalsIgnoreCase("abc")`   e. `"ABC".compareTo("abc")`
c. `"ABC".compareTo("ABC")`   f. `"ABC".endsWith("c")`

17. What is the pattern for iterating through each character in a string?

18. How does the pattern in question 17 change if you want to iterate through the
characters in reverse order, starting with the last character and ending with the
first?

19. What is the pattern for growing a string through concatenation?

20. What is the result of each of the following calls to the `Character` class:

a. `Character.isDigit(7)`   d. `Character.toUpperCase(7)`
b. `Character.isDigit('7')`   e. `Character.toUpperCase('A')`
c. `Character.isLetter('7')`   f. `Character.toLowerCase('A')`

▕█▌ Exercises

1. Suppose that the `endsWith` method did not exist in the `String` class. How
would you implement your own method `endsWith(str, suffix)` that
performs the same function? As with the reimplementation of `toUpperCase`
on page 108, your implementation should use no string methods other than
`length`, `charAt`, and the concatenation operator.

2. Adhering to the same restrictions as in exercise 1, write your own version of
the `indexOf` method. As in the case of the implementation from the `String`
class, your implementation should overload `indexOf` so that the pattern
argument can be either a string or a character and so that the method takes an
optional second argument that specifies the starting position.

3. In the same fashion as the two previous exercises, write your own version of
`trim(str)`, which returns a new string formed by removing all whitespace
characters from the beginning and end of `str`.

4. Implement a method `capitalize(str)` that returns a string in which the
initial character is capitalized (if it is a letter) and all other letters are converted
to lowercase. Characters other than letters are not affected. For example, both
`capitalize("BOOLEAN")` and `capitalize("boolean")` should return
the string `"Boolean"`.

5. In most word games, each letter in a word is scored according to its point value, which is inversely proportional to its frequency in English words. In Scrabble™, the points are allocated as follows:

Points	Letters
1	A, E, I, L, N, O, R, S, T, U
2	D, G
3	B, C, M, P
4	F, H, V, W, Y
5	K
8	J, X
10	Q, Z

For example, the word `"FARM"` is worth 9 points in Scrabble: 4 for the `F`, 1 each for the `A` and the `R`, and 3 for the `M`. Write a program that reads in words and prints their score in Scrabble, not counting any of the other bonuses that occur in the game. You should ignore any characters other than uppercase letters in computing the score. In particular, lowercase letters are assumed to represent blank tiles, which can stand for any letter but have a score of 0.

6. An *acronym* is a word formed by combining, in order, the initial letters of a series of words. For example, the word *scuba* is an acronym formed from the first letters in *self-contained underwater breathing apparatus.* Similarly, *AIDS* is an acronym for *Acquired Immune Deficiency Syndrome.* Write a method `acronym` that takes a string and returns the acronym formed from that string. To ensure that your method treats hyphenated compounds like *self-contained* as two words, it should define the beginning of a word as any alphabetic character that appears either at the beginning of the string or after a nonalphabetic character.

7. Write a method

```
private String removeCharacters(String str,
                                String remove)
```

that returns a new string consisting of the characters in `str` after removing all instances of the characters in `remove`. For example, if you call

```
removeCharacters("counterrevolutionaries", "aeiou")
```

the method should return `"cntrrvltnrs"`, which is the original string after removing all of its vowels.

8. As in most languages, English includes two types of numbers. The *cardinal numbers* (such as *one, two, three,* and *four*) are used in counting; the *ordinal*

numbers (such as *first, second, third,* and *fourth*) are used to indicate a position in a sequence. In text, ordinals are usually indicated by writing the digits in the number, followed by the last two letters of the English word that names the corresponding ordinal. Thus, the ordinal numbers *first, second, third,* and *fourth* often appear in print as *1st, 2nd, 3rd,* and *4th.* The ordinals for 11, 12, and 13, however, are *11th, 12th,* and *13th.* Devise a rule that determines what suffix should be added to each number, and then use this rule to write a method `createOrdinalForm(n)` that returns the ordinal form of the number **n** as a string.

9.   Write a method `createRegularPlural(word)` that returns the plural of **word** formed by following these standard English rules:

   a.   If the word ends in *s, x, z, ch,* or *sh,* add *es* to the word.

   b.   If the word ends in a *y* preceded by a consonant, change the *y* to *ies.*

   c.   In all other cases, add just an *s.*

Write a test program and design a set of test cases to verify that your program works.

10.   When large numbers are written on paper, it is traditional—at least in the United States—to use commas to separate the digits into groups of three. For example, the number one million is usually written in the following form:

      1,000,000

To make it easier for programmers to display numbers in this fashion, implement a method

      String addCommas(String digits)

that takes a string of decimal digits representing a number and returns the string formed by inserting commas at every third position, starting on the right. For example, if you were to execute the program

```
public void run() {
    Scanner sysin = new Scanner(System.in);
    while (true) {
        System.out.print("Enter a number: ");
        String digits = sysin.nextLine();
        if (digits.isEmpty()) break;
        System.out.println(addCommas(digits));
    }
}
```

your implementation of the **addCommas** method should be able to produce the following sample run:

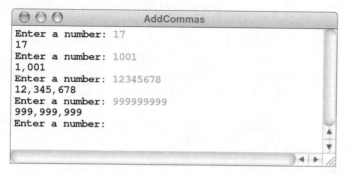

11. The concept of a palindrome is often extended to full sentences by ignoring punctuation and differences in the case of letters. For example, the sentence

Madam, I'm Adam.

is a sentence palindrome, because if you look only at the letters and ignore any distinction between uppercase and lowercase letters, it reads identically backward and forward.

Write a predicate method **isSentencePalindrome(str)** that returns **true** if the string **str** fits this definition of a sentence palindrome. For example, you should be able to use your method to write a main program capable of producing the following sample run:

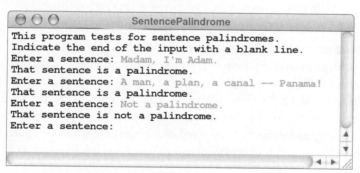

12.   *The waste of time in spelling imaginary sounds and their history (or etymology as it is called) is monstrous in English . . .*

—George Bernard Shaw, 1941

In the early part of the 20th century, there was considerable interest in both England and the United States in simplifying the rules used for spelling English words, which has always been a difficult proposition. One suggestion advanced as part of this movement was to eliminate all doubled letters, so that *bookkeeper* would be written as *bokeper* and *committee* would become *comite*. Write a method `removeDoubledLetters(str)` that returns a new string in which any duplicated characters in `str` have been replaced by a single copy.

13. As written, the `PigLatin` program in Figure 3-4 behaves oddly if you enter a string that includes words beginning with an uppercase letter. For example, if you were to capitalize the first word in the sentence and the name of the Pig Latin language, you would see the following output:

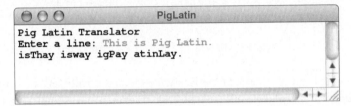

Rewrite the `wordToPigLatin` method so that any word that begins with a capital letter in the English line still begins with a capital letter in Pig Latin. Thus, after you make the necessary changes in the program, the output should look like this:

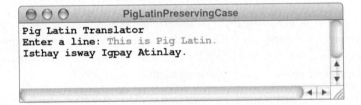

14. Most people in English-speaking countries have played the Pig Latin game at some point in their lives. There are other invented "languages" in which words are created using some simple transformation of English. One such language is called *Obenglobish,* in which words are created by adding the letters *ob* before the vowels (*a, e, i, o,* and *u*) in an English word. For example, under this rule, the word *english* gets the letters *ob* added before the *e* and the *i* to form *obenglobish,* which is how the language got its name.

In official Obenglobish, the *ob* characters are added only before vowels that are pronounced, which means that a word like *game* would become *gobame* rather than *gobamobe* because the final *e* is silent. While it is impossible to implement this rule perfectly, you can do a pretty good job by adopting the rule that the *ob* should be added before every vowel in the English word *except*

- Vowels that follow other vowels

- An *e* that occurs at the end of the word

Write a method **obenglobish** that takes an English word and returns its Obenglobish equivalent, using the translation rule given above. For example, if you used your method with the main program

```
public void run() {
    Scanner sysin = new Scanner(System.in);
    while (true) {
        System.out.println("Enter a word: ");
        String word = sysin.nextLine();
        if (word.isEmpty()) break;
        String trans = obenglobish(word);
        System.out.println(word + " -> " + trans);
    }
}
```

you should be able to generate the following sample run:

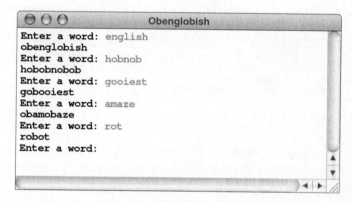

15. If you played around with codes and ciphers as a child, the odds are good that you at some point used a *cyclic cipher*—which is often called a ***Caesar cipher*** because the Roman historian Suetonius records that Julius Caesar used this technique—in which you replace each letter in the original message by the letter that appears a fixed distance ahead in the alphabet. As an example, suppose that you wanted to encode a message by shifting every letter ahead three places. In this cipher, each *A* becomes a *D*, *B* becomes *E*, and so on. If you reach the end of the alphabet, the process cycles around to the beginning, so that *X* becomes *A*, *Y* becomes *B*, and *Z* becomes *C*.

To implement a Caesar cipher, you should first define a method

```
String encodeCaesarCipher(String str, int shift)
```

that returns a new string formed by shifting every letter in **str** forward the number of letters indicated by **shift**, cycling back to the beginning of the alphabet if necessary. After you have implemented **encodeCaesarCipher**, write a program that generates the following sample run:

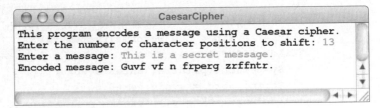

The Caesar cipher transformation applies only to letters; any other characters are copied unchanged to the output. Moreover, the case of letters is unaffected: lowercase letters come out as lowercase, and uppercase letters come out as uppercase. You should also write your program so that a negative value of **shift** means that letters are shifted toward the beginning of the alphabet instead of toward the end, as illustrated by the following sample run:

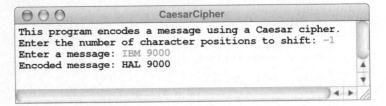

In writing this program, it is important to note that the user input mixes numeric and string input, which means that you need to take account of the fact the numeric input leaves an unread end-of-line character in the input. This issue is discussed in more detail on page 99.

16. Although Caesar ciphers are simple to implement, they are also extremely easy to break. There are, after all, only 25 values for the number of characters to shift. If you want to break a Caesar cipher, all you have to do is try each of the 25 possibilities and see which one translates the original message into something readable. A better scheme is to allow each letter in the original message to be represented by an arbitrary letter instead of one a fixed distance from the original. In this case, the key for the encoding operation is a translation table that shows what each of the 26 letters becomes in the encrypted form. Such a coding scheme is called a *letter-substitution cipher.*

The key in a letter-substitution cipher is a 26-character string that indicates the translation for each character in the alphabet in order. For example, the key "**QWERTYUIOPASDFGHJKLZXCVBNM**" indicates that the encoding process should use the following translation rule:

Write a program that implements encryption using a letter-substitution cipher. Your program should be able to duplicate the following sample run:

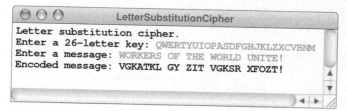

17. Using the definition of keys for letter-substitution ciphers as described in the preceding exercise, write a method **invertKey** that takes an encryption key and returns the 26-letter key necessary to decrypt a message encoded with that encryption key.

18. The genetic code for all living organisms is carried in its DNA—a molecule with the remarkable capacity to replicate its own structure. The DNA molecule itself consists of a long strand of chemical bases wound together with a similar strand in a double helix. DNA's ability to replicate comes from the fact that its four constituent bases—adenosine, cytosine, guanine, and thymine—combine with each other only in the following ways:

- Cytosine on one strand links only with guanine on the other, and vice versa.
- Adenosine links only with thymine, and vice versa.

Biologists abbreviate the names of the bases by writing only the initial letter: **A**, **C**, **G**, or **T**.

Inside the cell, a DNA strand acts as a template to which other DNA strands can attach themselves. As an example, suppose that you have the following DNA strand, in which the position of each base has been numbered as it would be in a Java string:

Your mission in this exercise is to determine at what point a shorter DNA strand can attach itself to the longer one. If, for example, you are trying to find a match for the strand

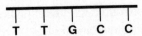

the rules for DNA dictate that this strand can bind to the longer one only at position 1:

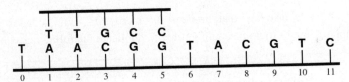

By contrast, the strand

matches at either position 2 or position 7.

Write a method that takes either of the following forms:

```
int findDNAMatch(String s1, String s2)
int findDNAMatch(String s1, String s2, int start)
```

Both methods return the first position at which the DNA strand **s1** can attach to the strand **s2**. As in the **indexOf** method, the optional **start** parameter indicates the index position at which the search should start. If there is no match, **findDNAMatch** should return −1.

Chapter 4
Files

I the heir of all the ages, in the foremost files of time.

— Alfred, Lord Tennyson, *Locksley Hall,* 1842

Programs use variables to store information: input data, calculated results, and any intermediate values generated along the way. The information in variables, however, is ephemeral. When the program stops running, the values of those variables are lost. For many applications, it is important to be able to store data in some more permanent fashion.

Whenever you want to store information on the computer for longer than the running time of a program, the usual approach is to collect the data into a logically cohesive whole and store it on a permanent storage medium as a ***file,*** which is a named collection of data whose lifetime typically extends beyond the execution of a single program. Ordinarily, a file is stored on a hard disk inside the machine, but it can also be stored on a removable medium, such as a CD or flash drive. In either case, the basic principles and modes of operation remain the same. The important point is that the permanent data objects you store on the computer—documents, games, executable programs, source code, and the like—are all stored in the form of files.

4.1 Text files

On most systems, files come in a variety of types. For example, in the Java programming domain, you work with source files, class files, and library archive files, each of which has a distinct representation. When you use a file to store data for use by a program, that file usually consists of text and is therefore called a ***text file.*** You can think of a text file as a sequence of characters stored in a permanent medium and identified by a file name. The name of the file and the characters it contains have the same relationship as the name of a variable and its contents.

As an example, let's suppose that you want to collect a set of your favorite quotations from Shakespeare and have decided to store each quotation in a separate file. You might begin your collection with the following lines from *Hamlet:*

```
Hamlet.txt
To be, or not to be: that is the question.
Whether 'tis nobler in the mind to suffer
The slings and arrows of outrageous fortune,
Or to take arms against a sea of troubles,
And by opposing end them?
```

The diagram shows the name of the file—in this case `Hamlet.txt`—as being external to the file, just as diagrams of variables show the name on the outside and the value on the inside.

For your second quotation, you might choose the following lines from Juliet's balcony scene in *Romeo and Juliet:*

```
Juliet.txt
What's in a name?
That which we call a rose
By any other name would smell as sweet.
```

Your computer can keep the two files separate because they have different names.

When you look at a file, it often makes sense to regard it as a two-dimensional structure—a sequence of lines composed of individual characters. Internally, however, text files are represented as a continuous sequence of characters. In addition to the printing characters you can see, files also contain a special character or character sequence that marks the end of each line. Unfortunately, different operating systems use different character sequences for this purpose. The good news, however, is that Java largely hides these differences, thereby making it much easier to view a text file as a sequence of lines.

In some ways, a text file is similar to a string. Both are ordered sequences of characters. The two critical differences are that

- *The information stored in a file is permanent.* The value of a string variable persists only as long as the variable does. Local variables disappear when the method returns, and instance variables disappear when the object goes away, which typically does not occur until the program exits. Information stored in a file exists until the file is deleted.

- *Files are usually read sequentially.* When you read data from a file, you usually start at the beginning and read the characters in order. Once a character has been read, you go on to the next character until you reach the end of the file.

4.2 Reading text files

The process of reading a file in Java (along with most other languages for that matter) follows a general outline consisting of three steps:

1. *Open the file.* This operation consists of creating an object called a ***reader*** that gives your program access to the data. For text files, you start by calling the constructor for the **FileReader** class, passing in the name of the file. The **FileReader** then manages the process of reading the file data.

2. *Read the data.* Once you have opened the file, you can then read the data by calling the appropriate methods on the **FileReader**. Files can be read character by character or, if you use a more sophisticated reader class called a **BufferedReader**, line by line.

3. *Close the file.* When you are finished reading the data, it is good practice to call the **close** method on the reader, which breaks the association with the file.

Creating the file reader

Opening a file in Java consists of creating an object that is ultimately an instance of the **Reader** class in the **java.io** package. As with most of Java's library classes, the **Reader** class is part of a more elaborate hierarchy that offers a variety of classes for different purposes. Part of the process of opening a file includes choosing the particular subclass of **Reader** that you want.

In reading from a text file, one of the classes you need to use is **FileReader**, which creates a reader by looking up a named file in the file system. You can create a **FileReader** object by calling its constructor, as follows:

```
FileReader rd = new FileReader("Hamlet.txt");
```

This invocation of the **FileReader** constructor asks the file system to open the file named **Hamlet.txt** and then returns a new **FileReader** object that you can use to read data from that file, which is then stored in the variable **rd**.

A **FileReader** object, in and of itself, is not particularly flexible. The **FileReader** class allows you to read characters from a file one at a time, but does not allow you to read data in larger units. In particular, a **FileReader** does not make it easy to read entire lines at once, which is often the most useful operation. For that, you need to turn your **FileReader** into a **BufferedReader**.

The constructor for the **BufferedReader** class takes any kind of reader and creates a new reader with additional capabilities. The new reader and the old one, however, still read data from the same source. Although you can declare separate variables for the **FileReader** and **BufferedReader**, you don't in fact need the **FileReader** value except to create the **BufferedReader**. It is therefore common practice to create both in the same declaration, as follows:

```
BufferedReader rd = new BufferedReader(
                        new FileReader("Hamlet.txt"));
```

Once you have declared and initialized the variable **rd**, you can call methods on that **BufferedReader** to read data from the file. You can read a single character from the file by calling **read**, just as you could with the underlying **FileReader** object. More importantly, the fact that you have a **BufferedReader** allows you to call **readLine**, which reads the entire next line as a string.

Exception handling

Unfortunately, the process of opening a file is not quite as straightforward in Java as the preceding section suggests. Part of the problem is that opening a file is an operation that can sometimes fail. For example, if you request the name of an input file from the user, and the user types the name incorrectly, the **FileReader** constructor will be unable to find the file you requested. To signal a failure of this sort, the methods in Java's libraries respond by ***throwing an exception,*** which is the phrase Java uses to describe the process of reporting an exceptional condition outside the normal program flow.

When a Java method throws an exception, the Java runtime system stops executing code and looks to see whether any method has registered its intent to respond to that exception. Starting with the current method and then proceeding backward through earlier calls, the Java runtime system searches each stack frame until it finds a method that expresses an intention to "catch" such an exception if one is "thrown." If an exception is never caught, the program simply stops running, and the Java runtime system reports the uncaught exception to the user.

Many of the exceptions that occur in Java, such as dividing by 0 and the like, are called ***runtime exceptions*** and can occur at any point in the code. When you write programs, you don't need to declare an interest in runtime exceptions. If your code doesn't catch them, the exception will simply propagate backward on the control stack as described in the preceding paragraph. The situation, however, is different with exception classes that are outside the runtime exception hierarchy. The designers of Java decided that they would *force* clients of the **java.io** package to check for situations like nonexistent input files by requiring clients to catch the exceptions that the methods in the package throw. Thus, the code to open and read a file in Java is not complete unless it explicitly catches exceptions in the **IOException** class. To do so, the code that works with data files must appear inside a **try** statement, which has the following general form:

```
try {
      Block of code in which the exception can be caught.
} catch (type var) {
      Code to respond to an exception of the specified type.
} . . . other catch clauses if necessary . . .
```

In this pattern, *type* refers to the type of exception you are interested in catching, and *var* is a variable that records the details of that exception when it occurs.

In the context of file-processing applications, the **try** statement pattern usually looks like this:

```
try {
      Block of code that works with the file.
} catch (IOException ex) {
      Code to respond to exceptions that occur.
}
```

As an example of how you can use exception handling to check for errors in opening a file, it is useful to write a general method called **openFileReader** that allows the user to select a file by entering its name in response to a prompt. If the file exists, the method returns a **BufferedReader** that can read the contents of the file. If not, the method displays a message indicating that it can't find the specified file and then gives the user another chance to enter the file name. The implementation for that method appears in Figure 4-1.

The **try** statement allows the program to detect whether an **IOException** appears anywhere within the execution of the body, even if that exception occurs in one of the library methods that **openFileReader** calls. In the case of a missing file, that exception is thrown by the constructor for the **FileReader** class, but is caught by the **catch** block in the **try** statement. When that exception occurs, the program reports the error to the user. Moreover, because the assignment to the **rd** variable was never completed, that variable still has the value **null**, which causes the **while** loop to request another file name.

In a context such as the one in **openFileReader**, it is relatively easy to determine what to do when the exception occurs. In that case, the cause of the exception was almost certainly that the user incorrectly entered the name of the file. The problem of responding to an **IOException** is more difficult when the exception occurs on other calls where the most likely cause is an actual error in the file system. Given that there is nothing your program can do to try to fix such an error, the easiest strategy is to abandon any attempt at responding to the exception

---

FIGURE 4-1 Method to open a reader on a user-selected file

```
/*
 * Asks the user for the name of a file and then returns a BufferedReader
 * for that file.  If the file cannot be opened, the method gives the user
 * another chance.  The sysin argument is a Scanner open on the System.in
 * stream.  The prompt gives the user more information about the file.
 */

    private BufferedReader openFileReader(Scanner sysin, String prompt) {
        BufferedReader rd = null;
        while (rd == null) {
            try {
                System.out.print(prompt);
                String name = sysin.nextLine();
                rd = new BufferedReader(new FileReader(name));
            } catch (IOException ex) {
                System.out.println("Can't open that file.");
            }
        }
        return rd;
    }
```

and let the exception handler report that an unrecoverable error has occurred. The usual way to do so is to throw a runtime exception that will propagate back to the operating system. The examples in this book use the following **catch** clause for this purpose:

```
try {
    Block of code that works with the file.
} catch (IOException ex) {
    throw new RuntimeException(ex.toString());
}
```

This code takes the I/O exception, converts it to a string, and then throws a runtime exception with that message.

Reading a file character by character

The most basic strategy for reading data from a text file, which works with either a **FileReader** or a **BufferedReader**, is to read the file one character at a time. If you adopt this approach, you need to call the **read** method on the reader, which returns the next character from the reader. Assuming that the reader is stored in the variable **rd**, the code to read the next character into the variable **ch** looks like this:

```
int ch = rd.read();
```

Although it certainly looks a bit odd, the type declaration in this example is not a typographical error. The **read** method returns an **int** for the simple reason that it has to be able to signal that the reader has reached the end of the file. Given that a file could potentially contain any of the 65,536 characters in Java's Unicode character set, there is no value within the type **char** that can serve as an effective sentinel. By extending the return type to **int**, the designers of the **read** method made it possible to use the value −1, which falls outside the Unicode range, to indicate the end of file.

Figure 4-2 shows the implementation of a **showContentsCharByChar** method that displays the contents of a file using the character-by-character strategy, along with a **run** method that calls **showContentsCharByChar**, passing in the reader produced by **openFileReader**. Note that both of these methods must include a **try** statement to guard against the possibility of an **IOException**. It is also important to note that the integer variable **ch** must be cast to a **char** before printing it on the console.

FIGURE 4-2 Program to display the contents of a file character by character

```
/*
 * This program displays the contents of a text file.
 */
    public void run() {
        Scanner sysin = new Scanner(System.in);
        BufferedReader rd = openFileReader(sysin, "Input file: ");
        showFileCharByChar(rd);
        try {
            rd.close();
        } catch (IOException ex) {
            throw new RuntimeException(ex.toString());
        }
    }

/*
 * Displays the entire contents of the reader on the console.
 */
    private void showFileCharByChar(BufferedReader rd) {
        try {
            while (true) {
                int ch = rd.read();
                if (ch == -1) break;
                System.out.print((char) ch);
            }
        } catch (IOException ex) {
            throw new RuntimeException(ex.toString());
        }
    }
```

To get a better sense of how the code in Figure 4-2 works, imagine for a moment that you are trying to read the file **Antony.txt**, which contains the following excerpt from Marc Antony's funeral oration in *Julius Caesar:*

```
Antony.txt
Friends, Romans, countrymen,
Lend me your ears;
I come to bury Caesar,
Not to praise him.
```

The call to **openFileReader** asks the user for the name of a file and then returns a reader, which is stored in the variable **rd**. To keep track of how far it has progressed in reading the file, the reader maintains an internal file pointer that marks the next character to be read. The diagrams that follow mark the position of the file pointer using a vertical bar, even though that information is stored entirely inside the reader and is not reflected at all in the actual file. When you open a file, the file pointer initially sits before the first character, like this:

```
Friends, Romans, countrymen,
Lend me your ears;
I come to bury Caesar,
Not to praise him.
```

The first call to **rd.read()** reads in the first character as an integer. In this case, that integer has the value 70, which is the Unicode representation of the character **'F'**. In the process, the file pointer moves past the first character, as follows:

```
Friends, Romans, countrymen,
Lend me your ears;
I come to bury Caesar,
Not to praise him.
```

Calling **rd.read()** again reads in the lowercase **'r'** and advances the file pointer one more character position:

```
Friends, Romans, countrymen,
Lend me your ears;
I come to bury Caesar,
Not to praise him.
```

Eventually, this process reaches the end of the line, at which point the file pointer appears in the following position:

```
Friends, Romans, countrymen,
Lend me your ears;
I come to bury Caesar,
Not to praise him.
```

The situation now becomes a little more complicated. Calling **rd.read()** again will read in the end-of-line character that appears in the file. Unfortunately, this character is defined differently on different operating systems and may even consist of two characters. In this application, the fact that the end-of-line sequence varies from platform to platform doesn't cause problems because you are simply copying these characters to the console, which will presumably interpret them correctly given that the console is using the same conventions. For applications in which you care about line boundaries, the lack of standardization is more problematic and represents one of the major disadvantages of reading files one character at a time.

Eventually, the code for **showFileCharByChar** will reach the end of the file, at which point **rd.read()** returns −1. At this point, control passes back to the **run** method, which completes its operation by closing the reader. Combining the code in Figures 4-1 and 4-2 creates a program that can generate the following sample run:

```
ShowFileCharByChar
Input file: Anthony.txt
Can't open that file.
Input file: Antony.txt
Friends, Romans, countrymen,
Lend me your ears;
I come to bury Caesar,
Not to praise him.
```

Note that the user inadvertently misspells Antony's name in the first line and is given a chance to correct the error.

Reading a file line by line

The best way to avoid the problems caused by the lack of standardization of line endings is to read the file a line at a time. Doing so requires a **BufferedReader**, which exports a **readLine** method. The **readLine** method correctly recognizes all end-of-line sequences but deletes them from the result, leaving only the characters on the line itself. Moreover, the fact that **readLine** returns a **String** means that there is an ideal sentinel to mark the end of the file: the special value **null** that Java uses to indicate that an object does not actually exist. The code to show the contents of a file using the line-by-line strategy appears in Figure 4-3.

If you trace the execution of this new implementation, you'll see that the file pointer always advances by an entire line of text. As in the earlier example, the file pointer starts before the first character of the file. Executing the statement

```
String line = rd.readLine();
```

FIGURE 4-3 Code to display the contents of a file line by line

```java
/*
 * Displays the entire contents of the reader on the console.
 */

   private void showFileLineByLine(BufferedReader rd) {
      try {
         while (true) {
            String line = rd.readLine();
            if (line == null) break;
            System.out.println(line);
         }
      } catch (IOException ex) {
         throw new RuntimeException(ex.toString());
      }
   }
```

reads the first line of the file into the variable **line**, leaving out the end-of-line characters (whatever they happen to be). The value of **line** after the first call is therefore the string

```
"Friends, Romans, countrymen,"
```

The file pointer moves to the beginning of the second line, like this:

```
Friends, Romans, countrymen,
|Lend me your ears;
I come to bury Caesar,
Not to praise him.
```

Eventually, after the program has read all four lines, the call to **readLine** returns the sentinel value **null** to indicate that there are no more lines in the file.

4.3 Writing text files

Although reading files is more common, Java also makes it possible to write data files to the file system. As you might expect, writing files requires you to create an object called a *writer* that offers the same functionality for output that readers provide for input. As with readers, writers form a class hierarchy that supports many different kinds of writers, all of which descend from the **Writer** class in the **java.io** package.

Opening a file for output

Opening output files in Java is largely symmetrical to the process of opening input files. When you open a reader on a file, you typically start by constructing a **FileReader** and then increase the efficiency of that reader by enclosing it in a **BufferedReader**. On the output side, you carry this process one step further, creating a **FileWriter**, then a **BufferedWriter**, and finally a **PrintWriter**. For example, the following pattern creates a **PrintWriter** for the output file **Hello.txt** and assigns that writer to the variable **wr**:

```
PrintWriter wr = new PrintWriter(
                new BufferedWriter(
                    new FileWriter("Hello.txt")));
```

Writing output to a file

Once you have opened the writer, you can then write data to the file, usually using the same **print** and **println** calls that you have been using since Chapter 1. The only difference is that these calls take a writer as a receiver, as in the line

```
wr.println("hello, world");
```

which writes a line containing the message **"hello, world"** to the output file. Figure 4-4 shows the complete program necessary to create a file **Hello.txt** containing this message.

As in the case of input files, several of the methods used for output files—most notably the constructors and the **close** method—can throw an **IOException**, which means that you need to catch this condition in your code. For reasons that are partly historical and partly to increase convenience, the **print** and **println** methods never throw this exception, which means that you would not use a **try** statement around a block of code that included only **print** and **println** calls, even if these calls were writing data to a file.

FIGURE 4-4 Program to write the message **"hello, world"** to the file **Hello.txt**

```
/*
 * File: HelloWriter.java
 * ---------------------------
 * This program writes a text file containing the message "hello, world".
 */

package edu.stanford.cs.javacs2.ch4;

import java.io.BufferedWriter;
import java.io.FileWriter;
import java.io.IOException;
import java.io.PrintWriter;

public class HelloWriter {

    public void run() {
        try {
            PrintWriter wr = new PrintWriter(
                            new BufferedWriter(
                                new FileWriter("Hello.txt")));
            wr.println("hello, world");
            wr.close();
        } catch (IOException ex) {
            throw new RuntimeException(ex.toString());
        }
    }

/* Main program */

    public static void main(String[] args) {
        new HelloWriter().run();
    }

}
```

Just as you saw in the case of readers, writers can process their data either character by character or line by line. The following method copies the contents of a reader to a writer using a character-based model:

```
private void copyFileCharByChar(Reader rd, Writer wr) {
    try {
        while (true) {
            int ch = rd.read();
            if (ch == -1) break;
            wr.write(ch);
        }
    } catch (IOException ex) {
        throw new RuntimeException(ex.toString());
    }
}
```

The corresponding line-by-line implementation looks like this:

```
private void copyFileLineByLine(BufferedReader rd,
                                PrintWriter wr) {
    try {
        while (true) {
            String line = rd.readLine();
            if (line == null) break;
            wr.println(line);
        }
    } catch (IOException ex) {
        throw new RuntimeException(ex.toString());
    }
}
```

If you look carefully at the code for the methods `copyFileCharByChar` and `copyFileLineByLine`, you will see that they differ not only in the structure of the `while` loop but also in the header line. The `copyFileCharByChar` declares its parameters as a `Reader` and a `Writer`, which are the most general versions of readers and writers that Java provides. All readers support the `read` method, which reads a single character; similarly, all writers support the `write` method, which writes a single character. It therefore makes sense to define `copyFileCharByChar` so that it takes the most general classes it can support. The `copyFileLineByLine` method, by contrast, calls `readLine` and `println`, which are exported only by the `BufferedReader` and `PrintWriter` classes, respectively.

Like most classes in the Java libraries, the `Reader` and `Writer` classes form hierarchies. The `FileReader` and `BufferedReader` classes are more specialized varieties of the `Reader` class, which is more general. Similarly, `FileWriter`,

BufferedWriter, and **PrintWriter** are all specialized varieties of the **Writer** class. In object-oriented languages, such specialized variants are called **subclasses.** You will have an opportunity to learn more about the structure of class hierarchies in Chapter 8.

4.4 Formatted output

Although the **print** and **println** methods make it possible to display output values on the console or write those values to files, they do not make it easy to control the format of that output. Early versions of Java defined several classes, mostly in a package called **java.text**, to support formatted output in a style that seemed appropriate to an object-oriented language. In recent years, those classes have become much less common because Java 5 introduced a method called **printf** that supports formatted output in the more convenient style supported by the C programming language.

The **printf** function remains one of C's most distinctive features and has been part of the standard library since early in the history of the language. It is used in pretty much every C program, including the version of the "Hello World" program reproduced on the first page of this book. Reintroducing **printf** to Java not only simplified the problem of producing formatted output, but also did it in a way that was familiar to programmers with previous experience in C.

A call to the **printf** method typically has the paradigmatic form

$$wr.\texttt{printf}(\textit{format}, \textit{exp}_1, \textit{exp}_2, \dots);$$

where *wr* is a **PrintWriter** or some other object (most commonly **System.out**) that exports the **printf** method. The number of expressions passed as arguments to **printf** depends on the number of data values that need to be displayed.

At one level, **printf** works very much like the **print** method you have already seen. The **printf** method goes through the format string, character by character, displaying each one on the console. If **printf** encounters a percent sign (**%**), it responds by treating the percent sign and the following letter as a placeholder for a value that should be printed in that position. That value is supplied by the first unused expression in the **printf** argument list. The first percent sign in the format string goes with the argument passed as $\textit{exp}_1$, the second percent sign goes with $\textit{exp}_2$, and so on, until all the arguments and percent signs have been used up. For example, in the statement

```
System.out.printf("%d + %d = %d%n", n1, n2, sum);
```

the first **%d** is used to print the value of **n1**, the second **%d** is used to print the value of **n2**, and the third **%d** is used to print the value of **sum**. The **%n** at the end of the format string tells `printf` to insert the newline sequence appropriate to the current platform, in exactly the same way that `println` does. Thus, if the values of `n1`, `n2`, and `sum` were 2, 3, and 5, respectively, this `printf` statement would generate the following output:

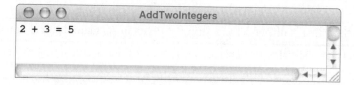

The power of the `printf` method comes from the fact that it can display values in a variety of formats (the `f` at the end of `printf` stands for *formatted*). Each percent sign in the format string is followed—often after a string of options—by a character that specifies the output format. The combination of the percent sign and the key letter is called a *format code*. Figure 4-5 outlines the most useful format codes along with the most important formatting options, which give you control over how the output values appear.

The most common option is the field-width specification, which allows you to align information in columns. Suppose, for example, that you had previously written the following code to test the `fact` method from Chapter 2:

```
for (int n = 0; n <= 12; n++) {
   System.out.println(n + "! = " + fact(n));
}
```

That `for` loop would produce the following output:

```
000                    FactorialTable
0!  = 1
1!  = 1
2!  = 2
3!  = 6
4!  = 24
5!  = 120
6!  = 720
7!  = 5040
8!  = 40320
9!  = 362880
10! = 3628800
11! = 39916800
12! = 479001600
```

If you changed the `println` call in this loop to

```
printf("%2d! = %9d%n", n, fact(n));
```

FIGURE 4-5 Selected format codes for the `printf` method

Conversion codes

`%b`	***Boolean.*** In `%b` format, the value is displayed as either **true** or **false**.
`%c`	***Character.*** In `%c` format, the value is displayed as a single Unicode character.
`%d`	***Decimal.*** In `%d` format, the value is displayed as a string of digits in standard decimal notation.
`%f`	***Floating-point.*** In `%f` format, the value is displayed as a string of digits containing a decimal point.
`%e`	***Exponential.*** In `%e` format, the value is displayed in scientific notation using the standard programming language representation *d.dddddexx*, which corresponds to the mathematical value of *d.ddddd* times 10 to the *xx* power. If you use the format code `%E` instead of `%e`, the letter **E** appears in uppercase in the output.
`%g`	***General.*** In this format, the value is displayed using either `%f` or `%e` format, whichever produces the shorter output. If you use the format code `%G` instead of `%g`, output appearing in scientific notation will use an uppercase **E**.
`%n`	***Newline.*** The `%n` specification is not really a format code but instead calls for the insertion of the newline sequence that is appropriate for the current platform.
`%o`	***Octal.*** In `%o` format, the value is displayed as a string of digits in base-8 (octal) notation.
`%s`	***String.*** In `%s` format, the value is displayed as a string.
`%x`	***Hexadecimal.*** In `%x` format, the value is displayed as a string of digits in base-16 (hexadecimal) notation. If the format `%X` is used, all hexadecimal letters appear in uppercase.
`%%`	***Percent sign.*** The `%%` specification is not really a format but instead provides a way to include a percent sign as part of the output.

Formatting options

–	***Left alignment.*** If the format specification contains a minus sign, fields are aligned on the left instead of the right.
+	***Explicit plus.*** If the format includes a plus sign, all output includes a sign. Without it, only a minus sign appears.
,	***Comma separation.*** If the format includes a comma, numeric output contains commas according to local conventions.
0	***Zero fill.*** If the format specification begins with a zero, leading zeroes are added to fill the field instead of spaces.
w	***Field width.*** If a number appears after the percent sign, it specifies the minimum field width. Values that are shorter than the minimum are aligned within the field, ordinarily on the right.
.d	***Significant digits.*** If the format string contains a decimal point followed by a number, that number controls how many digits are shown. The precise interpretation varies with the format. For `%f` and `%e` formats, this value indicates the number of digits after the decimal point. For `%g` format, it indicates the number of significant digits, not counting leading or trailing zeroes. For `%s` format, it indicates the maximum number of characters to print.

the output would look like this:

```
● ● ●                  FactorialTable
  0! =            1
  1! =            1
  2! =            2
  3! =            6
  4! =           24
  5! =          120
  6! =          720
  7! =         5040
  8! =        40320
  9! =       362880
 10! =      3628800
 11! =     39916800
 12! =    479001600
```

The values of **n** and **fact(n)** appear in fields that are two and nine characters wide, respectively. In this version of the program, the equal signs line up vertically, which makes it easy to see the growth pattern in the factorial values.

The formatting options become even more important when you need to display data in tabular form. Suppose, for example, that you have been commissioned to display a table showing the number of college graduates in the age cohort 24–34, along with the percentage of the total population in that age range, for each of the fifty states. These statistics are readily available from the Department of Education; the problem here is simply to display them in a readable form. Ideally, the first few lines of the table would look something like this:

```
● ● ●           CollegeGraduationRates
Alabama                 189,259   31.5%
Alaska                   31,967   32.9%
Arizona                 283,867   33.0%
Arkansas                105,468   28.6%
California            1,998,766   37.9%
```

Without the **printf** method, producing this output would be difficult. If you instead used **println** to display each value, the lines would appear in a much less readable form, as follows:

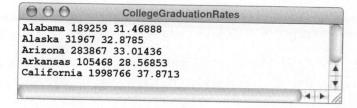

```
● ● ●           CollegeGraduationRates
Alabama 189259 31.46888
Alaska 31967 32.8785
Arizona 283867 33.01436
Arkansas 105468 28.56853
California 1998766 37.8713
```

To generate the formatted table shown in the first sample run, you need to think about how to display each of the values. The field width for the state name has to be large enough to display the longest state name, which is either North Carolina or South Carolina, which have 14 characters each. This field must therefore be at least 14 characters wide, although you may want to use a larger value to increase the spacing between columns. Moreover, the state name needs to be aligned along the left side of the column, which you indicate by preceding the field width by a minus sign. If you decide that 16 characters specify a field whose width seems aesthetically pleasing on the console, you would use a format code of `%-16s` to display the state name.

The second column in the table is the number of graduates in the targeted age range. You want this value (like most numbers) to be aligned on the right. It also helps readability if the output includes commas to divide the digits into groups of three. The format code that produces the desired output in a field of width 12 is `%,12d`.

The third column consists of the graduation rate expressed as a percentage. In this case, it is important to control not only the width of the field but also the precision with which that value is reported. In the second version of the table, the graduation rate appears as 31.46888 percent. While this value is presumably what you get if you divide the number of graduates by the total population in that age group and then multiply by 100, displaying the graduation rate with all those digits is misleading. Given the likely accuracy of the input data, you can have no confidence whatever that the percentage of graduates is 31.46888 rather than 31.46889 or even 31.469. Moreover, even if they were accurate, the last few digits in the percentage are almost certainly not significant in terms of making decisions about educational policy. In the first version of the table, the graduation rate for Alabama is rounded off to 31.5 percent, which is probably as much precision as you need. To display the rate in this format, all you have to do is use a format code like `%7.1f`, which indicates that you want to display the rate in a seven-character field with one digit after the decimal point.

Putting all these format codes together suggests that the `printf` call should look like this:

```
System.out.printf("%-16s%,12d%7.1f%%%n",
                  state, grads, rate);
```

Note that getting an actual percent sign into the output requires using two percent signs in the format string to avoid having the percent sign be interpreted as a format code.

Understanding the details of the precision specification is complicated by the fact that the interpretation depends on the conversion type. For the %f and %e format codes, the precision specification *d* indicates the number of digits to the right of the decimal point. For the %g format code, *d* indicates the number of **significant digits,** which means the number of digits whose value is considered meaningful. Any digits that are necessary to position the decimal point in the correct place appear as zeros. These differences are illustrated by the `FloatingPointFormats` program, which shows how three constants—the mathematical constant π, the speed of light in meters per second, and the fine-structure constant that characterizes the strength of electrical interaction—appear using different format codes and precision specifications. The output of the program appears in Figure 4-6, and the code appears in Figure 4-7 on the next page.

The precision specification also applies to the %s format code, in which case it indicates the maximum number of characters to display from the string (as opposed to the field-width specification, which indicates the *minimum* field width). In the absence of a precision specification, the %s format code always displays the entire string, which can overflow the boundaries of the column.

FIGURE 4-6 Sample run illustrating floating-point formats

```
              FloatingPointFormats
Floating-point format (%f):

 d |      pi     | speed of light | fine structure
---+-------------+----------------+----------------
 1 |        3.1  |   299792458.0  |      0.0
 2 |        3.14 |   299792458.00 |      0.01
 3 |      3.142  |  299792458.000 |      0.007
 4 |     3.1416  | 299792458.0000 |      0.0073

Exponential format (%E):

 d |      pi     | speed of light | fine structure
---+-------------+----------------+----------------
 1 |   3.1E+00   |    3.0E+08     |     7.3E-03
 2 |   3.14E+00  |    3.00E+08    |     7.26E-03
 3 |  3.142E+00  |    2.998E+08   |     7.257E-03
 4 | 3.1416E+00  |    2.9979E+08  |     7.2574E-03

General format (%G):

 d |      pi     | speed of light | fine structure
---+-------------+----------------+----------------
 1 |       3     |     3E+08      |     0.007
 2 |       3.1   |     3.0E+08    |     0.0073
 3 |       3.14  |     3.00E+08   |     0.00726
 4 |       3.142 |     2.998E+08  |     0.007257
```

FIGURE 4-7 Program to test precision in floating-point formats

```
/*
 * File: FloatingPointFormats.java
 * ---------------------------------
 * This program demonstrates various options for floating-point output
 * by displaying three different constants (pi, the speed of light in
 * meters/second, and the fine-structure constant).  These constants
 * are chosen because they illustrate a range of exponent scales.
 */

package edu.stanford.cs.javacs2.ch4;

public class FloatingPointFormats {

   public void run() {
      System.out.printf("Floating-point format (%%f):%n%n");
      showConstants("f");
      System.out.printf("%nExponential format (%%E):%n%n");
      showConstants("E");
      System.out.printf("%nGeneral format (%%G):%n%n");
      showConstants("G");
   }

/*
 * Displays the three constants using the specified format and several
 * different values for the number of digits (d).
 */

   private void showConstants(String format) {
      System.out.println(" d |      pi      | speed of light | fine structure");
      System.out.println("---+-------------+----------------+----------------");
      for (int d = 1; d <= 4; d++) {
         System.out.printf("%2d |", d);
         System.out.printf("%11." + d + format + " |", PI);
         System.out.printf("%15." + d + format + " |", SPEED_OF_LIGHT);
         System.out.printf("%14." + d + format + "%n", FINE_STRUCTURE);
      }
   }

/* Constants */

   private static final double PI = 3.14159265358979323846;
   private static final double SPEED_OF_LIGHT = 2.99792458E+8;
   private static final double FINE_STRUCTURE = 7.2573525E-3;

/* Main program */

   public static void main(String[] args) {
      new FloatingPointFormats().run();
   }

}
```

4.5 Formatted input

While the `readLine` method in the `BufferedReader` class is useful for reading entire lines from a file, it doesn't address the problem of reading other kinds of data. How, for example, would you go about reading files that contain a combination of numeric and string data? In Java, the easiest way to read formatted data is to use the `Scanner` class, which you first encountered in Chapter 1. So far, however, you have only scratched the surface of the capabilities of the `Scanner` class. A more complete list of the methods you can use appears in Figure 4-8.

FIGURE 4-8 Common methods in the `Scanner` class

Constructors

`Scanner` (*reader*)	Constructs a `Scanner` from the specified reader.
`Scanner` (*str*)	Constructs a `Scanner` from the specified string.

Methods for scanning a value

`next ()`	Finds and returns the next complete *token*, which is the longest string of characters not containing the pattern set by `useDelimiter`.
`next` (*pattern*)	Returns the next token if it matches the specified pattern.
`nextBoolean ()`	Scans the next token of the input into a boolean value.
`nextDouble ()`	Scans the next token of the input as a `double`.
`nextInt ()`	Scans the next token of the input as an `int`.
`nextLine ()`	Scans to the end of the current line and returns the contents of that line after removing the end-of-line characters.

Predicate methods for checking whether a value appears

`hasNext ()`	Returns `true` if this scanner has another token in its input.
`hasNext` (*pattern*)	Returns `true` if the next token matches the specified pattern.
`hasNextBoolean ()`	Returns `true` if the scanner can read a boolean value.
`hasNextDouble ()`	Returns `true` if the scanner can read a floating-point value.
`hasNextInt ()`	Returns `true` if the scanner can read an integer value.
`hasNextLine ()`	Returns `true` if there is another line in the input of this scanner.

Miscellaneous methods

`close ()`	Closes this scanner.
`skip` (*pattern*)	Skips input that matches the specified pattern.
`useDelimiter` (*pattern*)	Uses the *pattern* string to set this scanner's **delimiter pattern**, which is the pattern used to separate tokens.

The basic paradigm for using the **Scanner** class is to construct an instance that reads data from a particular source, which is usually a **Reader** or a string. You can then call the various methods beginning with **next** to read data values of specific types. For example, if you want to read a **double** value from the **Scanner**, you can call the **nextDouble** method. That method skips over any whitespace characters and then tries to read the next token as a **double**. If it succeeds, you get the **double** as the return value of the method. If it fails—presumably because the characters that appear at that point in the file do not constitute a legal number—the **nextDouble** method throws an **InputMismatchException**.

Unlike the exceptions in the **java.io** package, **InputMismatchException** is a subclass of **RuntimeException**, which means that you aren't forced to catch it. If such an exception occurs and you haven't taken any steps to catch it, the program will simply stop running because it has encountered an uncaught exception error. One of the advantages of using the **Scanner** class is that it eliminates the need to add a **try** statement to catch the **IOException** condition.

To illustrate the use of the **Scanner** class, it makes sense to return to the program that generated the table of graduation rates by state and think about how you might have read the data from a file. Data files come in many forms, but one of the simplest formats to process is called *comma-separated values* (or *csv*), in which the data values are stored as text, with individual fields separated by commas. If the input data for the program were stored in a **.csv** file, the first few lines would look like this:

```
CollegeGraduationRates.csv
Alabama,189259,31.46888
Alaska,31967,32.8785
Arizona,283867,33.01436
Arkansas,105468,28.56853
California,1998766,37.8713
```

Each line of this file consists of three fields: the name of the state as a string, the number of college graduates in the appropriate age cohort as an integer, and the graduation rate as a floating-point number. These fields—which may contain spaces as in the case of states like New York and South Carolina—are separated by commas, which means that it is appropriate to use a comma rather than whitespace as the scanner's delimited character.

Although you can define the delimiter sequence so that it also matches the end-of-line sequence, it is usually easier (particularly given that the end-of-line sequence varies depending on the platform) to read the file line by line, and then use a scanner to process each line. A complete program that adopts this strategy appears in Figure 4-9.

FIGURE 4-9 Program to produce a report from the data file of college graduation statistics

```java
/*
 * File: CollegeGraduationRates.java
 * ------------------------------------
 * This program produces a formatted table of college graduation rates
 * by state.  It uses a Scanner to read the data from a data file and
 * then prints it on the console.
 */

package edu.stanford.cs.javacs2.ch4;

import java.io.BufferedReader;
import java.io.FileReader;
import java.io.IOException;
import java.util.Scanner;

public class CollegeGraduationRates {

    public void run() {
        try {
            BufferedReader rd = new BufferedReader(new FileReader(DATA_FILE));
            System.out.println("     State          Graduates    Rate");
            System.out.println("------------------ ----------- ------");
            while (true) {
                String line = rd.readLine();
                if (line == null) break;
                Scanner scanner = new Scanner(line);
                scanner.useDelimiter(",");
                String state = scanner.next();
                int grads = scanner.nextInt();
                double rate = scanner.nextDouble();
                System.out.printf("%-16s%,12d%7.1f%%%n", state, grads, rate);
            }
            rd.close();
        } catch (IOException ex) {
            throw new RuntimeException(ex.toString());
        }
    }

/* Constants */

    private static final String DATA_FILE = "CollegeGraduationRates.csv";

/* Main program */

    public static void main(String[] args) {
        new CollegeGraduationRates().run();
    }

}
```

The heart of the data-input section of the `CollegeGraduationRates` program consists of the following lines:

```
Scanner scanner = new Scanner(line);
scanner.useDelimiter(",");
String state = scanner.next();
int grads = scanner.nextInt();
double rate = scanner.nextDouble();
```

The first line creates a `Scanner` object that takes its input from the string stored in `line`. The second line sets the delimiter pattern so that fields are separated by commas, which is, after all, the defining feature of `.csv` files. The last three lines read in the values for the variables `state`, `grads`, and `rate` using the `Scanner` method appropriate to that type. If the file contains errors that prevent any of these method calls from reading a value of the correct type, the `Scanner` implementation will throw an `InputMismatchException`, which will cause the program to fail with an unhandled-exception error.

Several methods in the `Scanner` class take arguments that are indicated by the placeholder *pattern* in Figure 4-8. Such patterns are much more flexible than the strings used in this example. In these methods, each pattern consists of a ***regular expression,*** which is a mathematical formalism that makes it easy to define character patterns. Regular expressions are beyond the scope of this text, but you can consult the documentation for the `java.util.regex.Pattern` class to find out more about them.

▰ 4.6 Using file dialogs

Although being able to enter a file name in a console window might have seemed sufficient a couple of decades ago, few modern applications force the user to enter a file name by hand. What you do instead is use a ***file dialog,*** which is an interactive dialog window that lets you select a file by using the mouse or track pad. The Java libraries include classes that allow you to do exactly that.

Whenever you want to create a file dialog, you need to construct an instance of the `JFileChooser` class, which is part of the `javax.swing` package. The most useful version of the `JFileChooser` constructor takes a directory file as an argument, which ensures that the dialog lists the files in the specified directory. The standard pattern for creating a file dialog in the current directory looks like this:

```
File dir = new File(System.getProperty("user.dir"));
JFileChooser chooser = new JFileChooser(dir);
```

At this point, you have created the chooser object, although nothing appears on the screen as yet. When you need to request an input file from the user, you call the `showOpenDialog` method, which takes a single argument and returns an integer that indicates whether the user confirmed or canceled the dialog. The argument specifies the window in which the dialog should be centered, but you can also use the special value `null` to center the dialog on the screen. A typical call to `showOpenDialog` therefore looks like this:

```
int result = chooser.showOpenDialog(null);
```

As soon as you make this call, a dialog pops up on the screen that looks like the one shown in Figure 4-10. In this example, the user has highlighted the file `Hamlet.txt`. If the user clicks **Open**, the program should open the `Hamlet.txt` file. If the user clicks **Cancel**, the program should not open any file.

Information about the user's selection is provided in two ways. You can tell what button was clicked by checking the result of the `showOpenDialog` call, which is the constant `JFileChooser.APPROVE_OPTION` if the user has clicked **Open** and `JFileChooser.CANCEL_OPTION` if the user has clicked **Cancel**. You can find out what file to open by calling the `getSelectedFile` method of the `JFileChooser` object, which returns the file selected by the user. The result of `getSelectedFile` is a `File` object, as defined in the `java.io` package. Fortunately, the `FileReader` constructor can accept a `File` as well as a `String`.

Figure 4-11 shows how to use these techniques to count the lines in a file selected by the user. The code to open the file chooser is encapsulated in a

---

FIGURE 4-10 **Example of a file dialog**

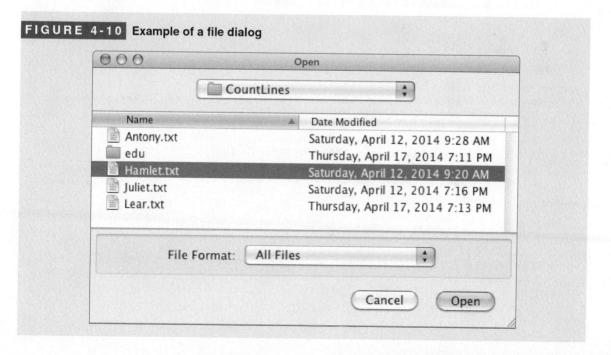

FIGURE 4-11   Program to count the lines in a file chosen using a dialog

```java
/*
 * File: CountLines.java
 * ---------------------
 * This program counts the lines in a file chosen using a file dialog.
 */

package edu.stanford.cs.javacs2.ch4;

import java.io.BufferedReader;
import java.io.File;
import java.io.FileReader;
import java.io.IOException;
import javax.swing.JFileChooser;

public class CountLines {

   public void run() {
      try {
         BufferedReader rd = openFileReaderUsingDialog();
         if (rd != null) {
            int nLines = 0;
            while (rd.readLine() != null) {
               nLines++;
            }
            rd.close();
            System.out.println("That file contains " + nLines + " lines.");
         }
      } catch (IOException ex) {
         throw new RuntimeException(ex.toString());
      }
   }

/*
 * Opens a file reader using the JFileChooser dialog.
 */

   private BufferedReader openFileReaderUsingDialog() throws IOException {
      File dir = new File(System.getProperty("user.dir"));
      JFileChooser chooser = new JFileChooser(dir);
      int result = chooser.showOpenDialog(null);
      if (result == JFileChooser.APPROVE_OPTION) {
         File file = chooser.getSelectedFile();
         return new BufferedReader(new FileReader(file));
      }
      return null;
   }

/* Main program */

   public static void main(String[] args) {
      new CountLines().run();
   }

}
```

method called **openFileReaderUsingDialog**, which returns a **BufferedReader** just like the **openFileReader** method shown in Figure 4-1. The **run** method then takes the reader and counts the lines by calling **readLine** until it reaches the end of the file.

The definition of **openFileReaderUsingDialog** method introduces one new feature of Java that needs some explanation. The calls to the **FileReader** and **BufferedReader** constructors can throw an **IOException** that needs to be caught somewhere. If the method definition does not catch the exception itself, it can pass the exception back to its caller by including a **throws** specification in the method header. Including the notation that the method **throws IOException** keeps the Java compiler happy and allows the **run** method to take control if an exception occurs.

 ## Summary

In this chapter, you have learned how to use Java's library classes to read and write data files. Important points in this chapter include:

- A *text file* is a sequence of characters stored in a permanent medium and identified by a file name.

- The steps involved in reading a file are *opening* the file, *reading* the data, and *closing* the file.

- When you open a text file for reading, the conventional approach is to construct a **FileReader** and then use that result to construct a **BufferedReader**.

- You can process the data in a file character by character using the **read** method that applies to all reader classes. The **read** method returns an **int**, which is either the Unicode value of the next character in the file or the value –1 to indicate the end of the file.

- You can also process the data in a file line by line using the **readLine** method exported by the **BufferedReader** class. The **readLine** method returns the special value **null** to indicate the end of the file.

- The usual approach to writing a file is to construct a **FileWriter**, use it to construct a **BufferedWriter**, and then use that to construct a **PrintWriter**. All writers support the **write** method, which writes a single character expressed as its Unicode value. The **PrintWriter** class supports the **print** and **println** methods that you have used with **System.in** ever since the first program in Chapter 1.

- The easiest way to produce formatted output in Java is to use the **printf** method from the programming language C, which was reintroduced into Java as part of the 5.0 release. The most common format codes and formatting options are described in Figure 4-5.

- The simplest approach to reading formatted data is to use the `Scanner` class from the `java.util` package. The most common methods in the `Scanner` class appear in Figure 4-8.

- Almost all operations in the reader and writer classes throw an `IOException` when they encounter an error condition. When you write file-processing code, Java requires you to catch this exception using a `try` statement.

- The `JFileChooser` class in the `javax.swing` package allows you to open a data file using a standard file dialog.

Review questions

1. What are the principal differences between a *text file* and a *string?*

2. What are the three steps necessary to read the contents of a text file?

3. What is an *exception?*

4. What is the general form of the `try` statement?

5. True or false: Catching the `IOException` raised by the classes in the `java.io` package is optional.

6. Suppose that you have a string variable `filename` that contains the name of a text file. What statements would you write to create a reader variable named `rd` that you could then use to read lines from this file?

7. Why does the `read` method return an `int` rather than a `char`?

8. How do you detect the end of a file if you are using `readLine` to read it line by line?

9. What three writer classes are typically involved in opening a text file for output?

10. True or false: Java 5.0 reintroduced the `printf` method, which was originally designed for the programming language C.

11. What is a *format code?*

12. How do you include a percent sign in a `printf` format string?

13. In your own words, describe the differences between the `%e`, `%f`, and `%g` format codes.

14.   What is the difference in the output produced by the `%e` and `%E` format codes?

15.   The constant `PI` in the `java.lang.Math` class is defined as

```
public static final double PI = 3.141592653589793238;
```

What `printf` format string would you use to produce each line of the following sample run:

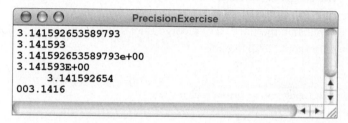

16.   What Java class implements the simplest strategy for reading formatted input?

17.   What do the letters in the file type `.csv` stand for?

18.   What call would you invoke on a `Scanner` object to read `.csv` files?

19.   What Java class makes it possible to open files using an interactive dialog?

20.   What is the purpose of a `throws` clause in a method definition?

Exercises

1.   Write a program that prints the longest line in a file chosen by the user. If several lines are all equally long, your program should print the first such line.

2.   Write a program that reads a file and reports how many lines, words, and characters appear in it. For the purposes of this program, a word consists of a consecutive sequence of any characters except whitespace characters. As an example, suppose that the file `Lear.txt` contains the following passage from Shakespeare's *King Lear:*

```
Lear.txt
Poor naked wretches, wheresoe'er you are,
That bide the pelting of this pitiless storm,
How shall your houseless heads and unfed sides,
Your loop'd and window'd raggedness, defend you
From seasons such as these?  O, I have ta'en
Too little care of this!
```

Your program should be able to generate the following sample run:

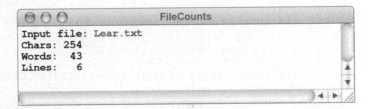

The counts in the output should be displayed in a column that is aligned on the right but nonetheless expands to fit the data. For example, if you have a file containing the full text of George Eliot's *Middlemarch,* the output of your program should look like this:

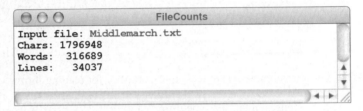

3.   The `printf` method gives programmers considerable control over output format, which makes it easy to create formatted tables. Write a program that displays a table of trigonometric sines and cosines that looks like this:

```
 ● ○ ○                        TrigTable
  theta | sin(theta) | cos(theta) |
 -------+------------+------------+
    -90 | -1.0000000 |  0.0000000 |
    -75 | -0.9659258 |  0.2588190 |
    -60 | -0.8660254 |  0.5000000 |
    -45 | -0.7071068 |  0.7071068 |
    -30 | -0.5000000 |  0.8660254 |
    -15 | -0.2588190 |  0.9659258 |
      0 |  0.0000000 |  1.0000000 |
     15 |  0.2588190 |  0.9659258 |
     30 |  0.5000000 |  0.8660254 |
     45 |  0.7071068 |  0.7071068 |
     60 |  0.8660254 |  0.5000000 |
     75 |  0.9659258 |  0.2588190 |
     90 |  1.0000000 |  0.0000000 |
```

The numeric columns should all be aligned on the right, and the columns containing the trigonometric functions (which are listed here for angles at 15-degree intervals) should all have seven digits after the decimal point.

4.   For exercise 5 in Chapter 2, you wrote a method `windChill` that calculated the wind chill for a given temperature and wind velocity. Write a program that uses this method to display these values in tabular form, as illustrated by the table from the National Weather Service shown in Figure 2-6 on page 89.

5. Even though comments are essential for human readers, the compiler simply ignores them. If you are writing a compiler, you therefore need to be able to recognize and eliminate comments that occur in a source file.

    Write a method

    ```
    public void removeComments(Reader rd, Writer wr)
    ```

    that copies characters from the reader **rd** to the writer **wr**, except for characters that appear inside Java comments. Your implementation should recognize both of Java's comment forms:

    - Any text beginning with **/*** and ending with ***/**, possibly many lines later.
    - Any text beginning with **//** and extending through the end of the line.

    Although the real Java compiler needs to check to make sure that these characters are not contained inside quoted strings, you should feel free to ignore that detail, because the problem is tricky enough as it stands.

6.
    > *Books were bks and Robin Hood was Rbinhd. Little Goody Two Shoes lost her Os and so did Goldilocks, and the former became a whisper, and the latter sounded like a key jiggled in a lck. It was impossible to read "cockadoodledoo" aloud, and parents gave up reading to their children, and some gave up reading altogether. . . .*

    —James Thurber, *The Wonderful O*, 1957

    In James Thurber's children's story *The Wonderful O*, the island of Ooroo is invaded by pirates who set out to banish the letter *O* from the alphabet. Such censorship would be much easier with modern technology. Write a program that asks the user for an input file, an output file, and a string of letters to be eliminated. The program should then copy the input file to the output file, deleting any of the letters that appear in the string of censored letters, no matter whether they appear in uppercase or lowercase form.

    As an example, suppose that you have a file containing the first few lines of Thurber's novel, as follows:

    `TheWonderfulO.txt`

    ```
    Somewhere a ponderous tower clock slowly
    dropped a dozen strokes into the gloom.
    Storm clouds rode low along the horizon,
    and no moon shone.  Only a melancholy
    chorus of frogs broke the soundlessness.
    ```

    If you run your program with the input

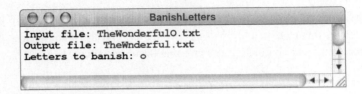

it should write the following file:

TheWnderful.txt

```
Smewhere a pnderus twer clck slwly
drpped a dzen strkes int the glm.
Strm cluds rde lw alng the hrizn,
and n mn shne.  nly a melanchly
chrus f frgs brke the sundlessness.
```

If you tried to get greedy and banish all the vowels by entering **aeiou** in response to the prompt, the contents of the output file would be

```
Smwhr  pndrs twr clck slwly
drppd  dzn strks nt th glm.
Strm clds rd lw lng th hrzn,
nd n mn shn.  nly  mlnchly
chrs f frgs brk th sndlssnss.
```

7. Some files use tab characters to align data into columns. Doing so, however, can cause problems for applications that are unable to work directly with tabs. For these applications, it is useful to have access to a program that replaces tabs in an input file with the number of spaces required to reach the next tab stop. In programming, tab stops are usually set at every eight columns. For example, suppose that the input file contains a line of the form

where the ──┤ symbol represents the space taken up by a tab, which differs depending on where the tab occurs in the line. If the tab stops are set every eight spaces, the first tab character must be replaced by five spaces and the second tab character by three.

Write a program that copies an input file to an output file, replacing all tab characters by the appropriate number of spaces.

Chapter 5
Arrays

Happiness courts thee in her best array.
—William Shakespeare, *Romeo and Juliet,* 1597

Up to now, the programs in this book have worked with individual data items. The real power of computing, however, comes from the ability to work with collections of data. This chapter introduces the idea of an *array,* which is an ordered collection of values of the same type. Arrays are important in programming largely because such collections occur quite often in the real world. Whenever you want to represent a set of values in which it makes sense to think about those values as forming a sequence, arrays are likely to play a role in the solution.

At the same time, arrays, in and of themselves, are becoming less important because Java's library packages include classes that do everything that arrays do and more. Because they represent collections of individual data values, the classes that fill the traditional role of arrays are called *collection classes.* Increasingly, Java programmers rely on these collection classes to represent the kinds of data that would once have been stored in an array. Understanding collection classes, however, is easier if you understand the array model, which forms the conceptual foundation for the various list classes supported by Java's collection framework. This chapter therefore begins with a discussion of arrays as they have been used since the early days of programming. The point, however, is less to ensure that you understand the details of array processing than it is to provide you with the intuition you need to understand Java's collection classes, which are described in detail in Chapter 6.

5.1 Introduction to arrays

An *array* is a collection of individual values with two distinguishing characteristics:

1. *An array is ordered.* You must be able to enumerate the individual values in order: here is the first, here is the second, and so on.

2. *An array is homogeneous.* Every value stored in an array must be of the same type. Thus, you can define an array of integers or an array of floating-point numbers but not an array in which the two types are mixed.

Conceptually, it is easiest to think of an array as a sequence of boxes, with one box for each data value in the array. Each of the values in an array is called an *element.*

Every array has two fundamental properties that apply to the array as a whole:

*   The *element type,* which indicates what values may be stored in the elements
*   The *length,* which is the number of elements the array contains

In Java, it is possible to specify these properties at different times. You define the element type when you declare the array variable; you set the length when you create the initial value. In most cases, however, you specify both properties in the same declaration, as described in the following section.

Array declaration

Like any other variable in Java, an array must be declared before it is used. The most common form for an array declaration uses the following pattern:

type [ ]   *name* = **new** *type* [*size*] ;

For example, the declaration

```
int[] intArray = new int[10];
```

declares an array named **intArray** with 10 elements, each of which is of type **int**. You can represent this declaration graphically by drawing a row of 10 boxes and giving the entire collection the name **intArray**:

intArray

0	0	0	0	0	0	0	0	0	0
0	1	2	3	4	5	6	7	8	9

When Java creates a new array, it initializes each of its elements to the default value for its type. For numbers, that default value is zero, which is why a 0 appears in each element of **intArray**. All other types have a default value as well. For example, the default value for **boolean** is **false**, and the default for objects is the special value **null**.

Each element in the array is identified by a numeric value called its *index*. In Java, the index numbers for an array always begin with 0 and run up to one less than the length of the array. Thus, in an array with 10 elements, the index numbers are 0, 1, 2, 3, 4, 5, 6, 7, 8, and 9, as the preceding diagram shows. In Java, every array has a field called **length** that contains the number of elements. The expression

```
intArray.length
```

has the value 10.

Although it is possible to use integer values—such as the 10 in the preceding example—to specify the length of an array, it is much more common to use constants for this purpose. Suppose, for example, that you have been asked to define an array capable of holding the scores for sports in which scores are assigned by a panel of judges, such as gymnastics or figure skating. Each judge rates the performance on a scale from 0 to 10, with 10 being the highest. Because a score may include a decimal fraction, as in 9.9, each element of the array must be of type **double**. Moreover, because the number of judges might change from application to application, it makes sense to declare the length of the array using a named constant. In this case, the declaration of an array called **scores** might look like this:

```
    private static final int N_JUDGES = 5;

    double[] scores = new double[N_JUDGES];
```

This declaration introduces a new array called **scores** with five elements, as shown in the following diagram:

scores

0.0	0.0	0.0	0.0	0.0
0	1	2	3	4

In Java, the value used to specify the length of an array need not be a constant. If you want to make your sports-scoring program more general, you can read the number of judges from the user, as follows:

```
    System.out.print("Enter number of judges: ");
    int nJudges = sysin.nextDouble();
    double[] scores = new double[nJudges];
```

Array selection

To refer to a specific element within an array, you specify both the array name and the index corresponding to the position of that element within the array. The process of identifying a particular element within an array is called *selection*, and is indicated in Java by writing the name of the array and following it with the index in square brackets. Whenever you select an element from an array, Java checks the value of the index and throws a runtime exception if the index falls outside the array boundaries.

The result of a selection expression is assignable, in the sense that you can use a selection expression on the left side of an assignment statement. For example, if you execute the **for** loop

```
    for (int i = 0; i < intArray.length; i++) {
        intArray[i] = 10 * i;
    }
```

the variable **intArray** will be initialized as follows:

intArray

0	10	20	30	40	50	60	70	80	90
0	1	2	3	4	5	6	7	8	9

You can use array assignment to write a complete program that reads in scores for the gymnastics competition and prints the average score, as shown in Figure 5-1. The **run** method reads in the scores for each judge (adjusting the index in the prompt so that the numbers presented to the user begin with 1 rather than 0) and

FIGURE 5-1 Code for the `GymnasticsJudge` program

```java
/*
 * File: GymnasticsJudge.java
 * ---------------------------
 * This file reads in an array of scores and computes the average.
 */

package edu.stanford.cs.javacs2.ch5;

import java.util.Scanner;

public class GymnasticsJudge {

    public void run() {
        Scanner sysin = new Scanner(System.in);
        System.out.print("Enter number of judges: ");
        int nJudges = sysin.nextInt();
        double[] scores = new double[nJudges];
        for (int i = 0; i < nJudges; i++) {
            System.out.print("Enter score for judge " + (i + 1) + ": ");
            scores[i] = sysin.nextDouble();
        }
        System.out.printf("The average score is %4.2f%n", average(scores));
    }

/*
 * Computes the average of an array of doubles.
 */

    private double average(double[] array) {
        double total = 0;
        for (int i = 0; i < array.length; i++) {
            total += array[i];
        }
        return total / array.length;
    }

/* Main program */

    public static void main(String[] args) {
        new GymnasticsJudge().run();
    }

}
```

then calls a separate **average** method whose code is independent of the specific application and makes no mention of judges or scores. The **average** method takes the array from the caller and computes the average by adding up the values and dividing by the length of the array. A sample run of the **GymnasticsJudge** program might look like this:

```
 _____
|  ⊖ ⊖ ⊙              GymnasticsJudge               |
|---------------------------------------------------|
| Enter number of judges: 5                         |
| Enter score for judge 1: 9.2                      |
| Enter score for judge 2: 9.9                      |
| Enter score for judge 3: 9.7                      |
| Enter score for judge 4: 9.0                      |
| Enter score for judge 5: 9.6                    ▲ |
| The average score is 9.48                        ▼|
|                                          ◄ ►      |
|_____|
```

If you think carefully about this program in light of the rules for parameter passing presented in Chapter 2, you will find yourself faced with an interesting question. In the list of rules presented in the section entitled "The steps in calling a method," rule 3 begins like this:

3. The value of each argument is copied into the corresponding parameter variable.

It is interesting to ask whether this rule is applied when the **run** method calls **average**. Is the **scores** array copied into the parameter variable **array**? In this example, the correctness of the program is unaffected by whether a copy is made or not, but the question nonetheless raises an efficiency concern. Copying an array of five elements presumably doesn't take much time, but what if you were working with an array of 1,000,000 elements or more? Copying a large array imposes unnecessary costs in terms of both memory space and execution time.

Understanding exactly what Java does when it passes an array—or any object for that matter—from one method to another requires knowing something about how arrays and objects are represented inside the memory of the machine. When you pass an array as a parameter, the *elements* of that array are not copied into the frame of the called method. What happens instead is that the parameter-passing process copies a *reference* to the array, which allows the caller and callee to share the actual values. The details of the underlying structure and a more precise definition of the idea of a reference are discussed in the next section.

▆ 5.2 Data representation and memory

Every modern computer contains some amount of high-speed internal memory that is its principal repository for information. In a typical machine, that memory is built out of special integrated-circuit chips called *RAM*, which stands for *random-access memory*. Random-access memory allows the program to use the contents of any memory cell at any time. The technical details of how the RAM chip operates are not important to most programmers. The important thing to understand about memory is its overall organizational structure.

Bits, bytes, and words

Inside the computer, all data values—no matter how complex—are stored as combinations of the fundamental unit of information, which is called a **bit**. Each bit can be in one of two possible states. If you think of the circuitry inside the machine as if it were a tiny light switch, you might label those states as *off* and *on*. If you think of each bit as a Boolean value, you might instead use the labels *false* and *true*. However, because the word *bit* comes originally from a contraction of *binary digit*, it is common to label those states as **0** and **1**, which are the two digits used in the binary number system on which computer arithmetic is based.

Since a single bit holds so little information, individual bits are not the most convenient mechanism for storing data. To make it easier to store such traditional types of information as numbers or characters, computers combine individual bits into larger units that are then treated as integral units of storage. The smallest such combined unit is called a **byte,** which consists of eight bits and is large enough to hold a value of type **char**. Bytes are then assembled into larger structures called **words.** The number of bytes in a word varies depending on the hardware architecture. Today, most computers use words that are either four or eight bytes long (32 or 64 bits).

The amount of memory available to a particular computer varies over a wide range. Early machines supported memories whose size was measured in kilobytes (KB), the machines of the 1980s and '90s had memory sizes measured in megabytes (MB), and today's machines typically have memories measured in gigabytes (GB). In most sciences, the prefixes *kilo, mega,* and *giga* stand for one thousand, one million, and one billion, respectively. In the world of computers, however, those base-10 values do not correspond to the internal structure of the machine. By tradition, therefore, these prefixes are taken to represent the power of two closest to their traditional interpretations. Thus, in programming, the prefixes *kilo, mega,* and *giga* have the following meanings:

$$\text{kilo (K)} \quad = \quad 2^{10} \quad = \quad 1{,}024$$
$$\text{mega (M)} \quad = \quad 2^{20} \quad = \quad 1{,}048{,}576$$
$$\text{giga (G)} \quad = \quad 2^{30} \quad = \quad 1{,}073{,}741{,}824$$

A 64KB computer from the early 1970s would have had 64×1024 or 65,536 bytes of memory. Similarly, a modern 4GB machine would have 4×1,037,741,824 or 4,294,967,296 bytes of memory.

Within the memory system of a typical computer—even the simulated computer of the Java Virtual Machine—every byte is identified by a numeric **address**. The first byte in the computer is numbered 0, the second is numbered 1, and so on, up to the number of bytes in the machine minus one. As an example, the memory addresses in a tiny 64KB computer from decades ago would begin with a byte numbered 0 and end with a byte numbered 65,535. In today's machines, memory addresses might run from 0 up to 4,294,967,295, or even more on a 64-bit machine. As in most languages, Java uses these addresses to serve as shorthand for the data stored in the corresponding region of memory. At the machine-language level, an address used to indicate the contents of memory is called a ***pointer.*** In Java, the conventional term for this concept is a ***reference,*** which helps separate the concept from the underlying details. In general, there is no way in Java to determine the numeric address of a reference. Even so, it is important to keep in mind that values stored in memory have addresses and can therefore be specified by a reference.

Binary and hexadecimal representations

Each of the bytes inside a machine holds data whose meaning depends on how the system interprets the individual bits. Depending on the hardware instructions used to manipulate it, a particular sequence of bits can represent an integer, a character, or a floating-point value, each of which requires some kind of encoding scheme. The easiest encoding scheme to understand is that for unsigned integers. The bits in an unsigned integer are represented using ***binary notation,*** in which the only legal values are **0** and **1**, just as is true for the underlying bits. Binary notation is similar in structure to our more familiar decimal notation, but uses 2 rather than 10 as its base. The contribution that a binary digit makes to the entire number depends on its position within the number as a whole. The rightmost digit represents the units field, and each of the other positions counts for twice as much as the digit to its right.

Consider, for example, the eight-bit byte containing the following binary digits:

0	0	1	0	1	0	1	0

That sequence of bits represents the number 42, which you can verify by calculating the contribution for each of the individual bits, as follows:

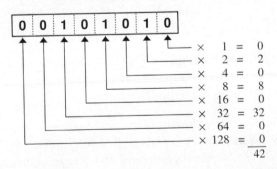

This diagram illustrates how to map an integer into bits using binary notation, but also helps to demonstrate the fact that writing numbers in binary form is terribly inconvenient. Binary numbers are cumbersome, mostly because they tend to be so long. Decimal representations are intuitive and familiar but make it harder to understand how the number translates into bits.

For applications in which it is useful to understand how a number translates into its binary representation without having to work with binary numbers that stretch all the way across the page, computer scientists often use *hexadecimal* (base 16) representation instead. In hexadecimal notation, there are sixteen digits, representing values from 0 to 15. The decimal digits 0 through 9 are perfectly adequate for the first ten digits, but classical arithmetic does not define the extra symbols you need to represent the remaining six. Computer science traditionally uses the letters **A** through **F** for this purpose, where the letters have the following values:

$$\begin{array}{rcl}
\mathbf{A} &=& 10 \\
\mathbf{B} &=& 11 \\
\mathbf{C} &=& 12 \\
\mathbf{D} &=& 13 \\
\mathbf{E} &=& 14 \\
\mathbf{F} &=& 15
\end{array}$$

What makes hexadecimal notation so attractive is that you can instantly convert between hexadecimal values and the underlying binary representation. All you need to do is combine the bits into groups of four. For example, the number forty-two can be converted from binary to hexadecimal notation like this:

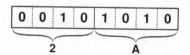

The first four bits represent the number 2, and the next four represent the number 10. Converting each of these to the corresponding hexadecimal digit gives **2A** as the hexadecimal form. You can then verify that this number still has the value 42 by adding up the digit values, as follows:

$$\begin{array}{rcl}
\mathbf{2\ A} & & \\
\quad \times\ 1 &=& 10 \\
\quad \times\ 16 &=& \underline{32} \\
& & 42
\end{array}$$

Java allows you to write integer constants in any of three bases: octal (base 8), decimal (base 10), and hexadecimal (base 16). Decimal constants are written as integers in the standard form. Octal constants are written with a leading **0**, so that the constant **0100**, for example, represents 100 in base 8, or 64. Hexadecimal constants begin with the prefix **0x**, so that the constant **0x2A** represents the decimal number 42.

For readability, this book generally uses decimal notation. If the base is not clear from the context, the text follows the usual strategy of using a subscript to denote the base. Thus, the binary, octal, decimal, and hexadecimal representations of the number 42 look like this:

$$\mathbf{00101010}_2 \ = \ \mathbf{52}_8 \ = \ \mathbf{42}_{10} \ = \ \mathbf{2A}_{16}$$

The key point is that the number itself is always the same; the numeric base affects only the representation. Forty-two has a real-world interpretation that is independent of the base. That real-world interpretation is perhaps easiest to see in the representation an elementary school student might use, which is after all just another way of writing the number down:

$$\cancel{||||}\ \cancel{||||}\ \cancel{||||}\ \cancel{||||}\ \cancel{||||}\ \cancel{||||}\ \cancel{||||}\ \cancel{||||}\ ||$$

The number of line segments in this representation is forty-two. The fact that a number is written in binary, decimal, or any other base is a property of the representation and not of the number itself.

Representing other data types

In many ways, the fundamental idea behind modern computing is that any data value can be represented as a collection of bits. It is easy to see, for example, how to represent a Boolean value in a single bit. All you have to do is assign each of the possible states of a bit to one of the two Boolean values. Conventionally, **0** is interpreted as **false**, and **1** is interpreted as **true**. As the last section makes clear, you can store unsigned integers by interpreting a sequence of bits as a number in binary notation, so that the eight-bit sequence **00101010** represents the number 42. With eight bits, it is possible to represent numbers between 0 and 2^8-1, or 255. Sixteen bits are sufficient to represent numbers between 0 and $2^{16}-1$, or 65,535. Thirty-two bits allow for numbers up to $2^{32}-1$, or 4,294,967,295.

Signed integers can also be stored as bit sequences by making a minor change to the encoding. Primarily because doing so simplifies the hardware design, most computers use a mathematical representation called *two's complement* to represent signed integers. If you want to express a nonnegative value in two's-complement form, you simply use its traditional binary expansion. To represent a negative value, you subtract its absolute value from 2^N, where N is the number of bits used in the representation. For example, the two's complement representation of –1 in a 32-bit word is calculated by performing the following binary subtraction:

```
  1 0 0 0 0 0 0 0 0 0 0 0 0 0 0 0 0 0 0 0 0 0 0 0 0 0 0 0 0 0 0 0 0
 -0 0 0 0 0 0 0 0 0 0 0 0 0 0 0 0 0 0 0 0 0 0 0 0 0 0 0 0 0 0 0 0 1
  1 1 1 1 1 1 1 1 1 1 1 1 1 1 1 1 1 1 1 1 1 1 1 1 1 1 1 1 1 1 1 1 1
```

Floating-point numbers are also represented as fixed-length bit sequences in Java. Although the details of floating-point representation are beyond the scope of this text, it isn't too hard to imagine building hardware that would use some subset of the bits in a word to represent the digits in the floating-point value and some other subset to represent the exponent by which that value is scaled. The important thing to remember is simply that, internally, every data value is stored in the form of bits.

The representation of arrays

In Java, arrays are represented as a reference to a memory structure that contains the length of the array, the data for the elements, and some additional overhead information that is inaccessible (and uninteresting) to clients. The amount of storage required depends on both the length of the array and the memory requirements for the element type. When stored in an array, the eight primitive types in Java require the following amounts of space:

`boolean`	1 bit
`byte`	1 byte
`char`	2 bytes
`short`	2 bytes
`int`	4 bytes
`float`	4 bytes
`long`	8 bytes
`double`	8 bytes

The size of the memory space used to store the elements is simply the product of the length of the array and the size of the element type.

Suppose, for example, that you have declared and initialized the **scores** array by writing

```
double[] scores = new double[nJudges];
```

where **nJudges** has the value 5. The **new** operator allocates memory to store the elements (five elements times eight bytes per element for a total of 40 bytes), an integer value for the length, and some unknown amount of space for the object overhead, which is indicated in memory diagrams by a gray box. The value that is assigned to **scores** is a reference to this memory and not the memory itself. Since the actual addresses are not visible in Java, it is easiest to show a reference value as an arrow that points to the memory space at the specified location. In the sample run from the **GymnasticJudge** program, the internal structure of the **scores** array looks like this after the values have been read in from the user:

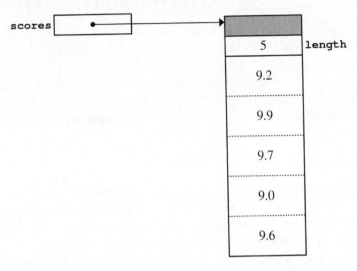

When the **run** method calls **average**, only the reference value is copied so that the **array** variable in the stack frame for **average** looks like this:

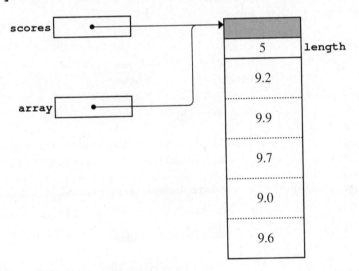

The fact that the variable **scores** in the stack frame for **run** and the variable **array** in the stack frame for **average** contain the same reference means that they share access to the same data. The reference—but not the underlying data—is copied as part of the process of passing parameters to the **average** method. In this way, Java makes it possible to share information between methods and eliminates the need for expensive copying of large arrays and objects.

5.3 Using arrays for tabulation

The data structure of a program is typically designed to reflect the organization of data in the real-world domain of the application. If you are writing a program to solve a problem that involves a list of values, the idea of using an array to represent that list makes intuitive sense. For example, in the **GymnasticsJudge** program shown in Figure 5-1, the problem involves a list of scores—one for each of five judges. Because the individual scores form a list in the conceptual domain of the application, it is not surprising that you would use an array to represent the data in the program. The array elements have a direct correspondence to the individual data items in the list. Thus, **scores[0]** corresponds to the score for judge #0, **scores[1]** to the score for judge #1, and so on.

In general, whenever an application involves data that can be represented in the form of a list like

$$a_0, a_1, a_2, a_3, a_4, \ldots, a_{N-1}$$

an array is the natural choice for the underlying representation. It is also quite common for programmers to refer to the index of an array element as a ***subscript,*** reflecting the fact that arrays are used to hold data that would typically be written with subscripts in mathematics.

There are, however, important uses of arrays in which the relationship between the data in the application domain and the data in the program takes a different form. Instead of storing the data values in successive elements of an array, for some applications it makes more sense to use the data to generate array indices. Those indices are then used to select elements in an array that records some statistical property of the data as a whole.

Understanding how this approach works and appreciating how it differs from more traditional uses of arrays requires looking at a concrete example. Suppose you want to write a program that reads lines of text from the user and keeps track of how often each of the 26 letters appears. When the user types a blank line to signal the end of the input, the program should display a table indicating how many times each letter appears in the input data.

In order to generate this kind of letter-frequency table, the program has to search each line of text character by character. Every time a letter appears, the program must update a running count that keeps track of how often that letter has appeared so far in the input. The interesting part of the problem lies in designing the data structure to maintain a count for each of the 26 letters.

The best strategy for solving this problem is to allocate an array of 26 integers and then to use the character code for the letters in the file to select the appropriate element within the array. Each element in the array contains an integer representing the current count of the letter that corresponds to that index. If you call the array `letterCounts`, you can declare it by writing

```
int[] letterCounts = new int[26];
```

This declaration allocates space for an integer array with 26 elements, as shown in the following diagram:

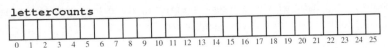

Each time a letter character appears in the input, you need to increment the corresponding element in `letterCounts`. Finding the element to increment is simply a matter of converting the character into an integer in the range 0 to 25 by converting the character to upper case and then subtracting the Unicode value of `'A'`. The code for the **run** method for the **CountLetterFrequencies** program appears in Figure 5-2.

FIGURE 5-2 **Program to count letter frequencies in a file**

```
/*
 * This program opens a file specified by the user and then counts
 * the number of times each of the 26 letters appears, keeping track
 * of those counts in an array with 26 elements.
 */

    public void run() {
        Scanner sysin = new Scanner(System.in);
        int[] letterCounts = new int[26];
        BufferedReader rd = openFileReader(sysin, "Input file: ");
        try {
            while (true) {
                int ch = rd.read();
                if (ch == -1) break;
                if (Character.isLetter(ch)) {
                    letterCounts[Character.toUpperCase(ch) - 'A']++;
                }
            }
            rd.close();
            for (char ch = 'A'; ch <= 'Z'; ch++) {
                System.out.printf("%7d %c\n", letterCounts[ch - 'A'], ch);
            }
        } catch (IOException ex) {
            throw new RuntimeException(ex.getMessage());
        }
    }
```

5.4 Initialization of arrays

In Java, array variables can be given initial values at the time they are declared. In this case, the equal sign specifying the initial value is followed by a list of initializers enclosed in curly braces. For example, the declaration

```
private static final int[] DIGITS = {
   0, 1, 2, 3, 4, 5, 6, 7, 8, 9
};
```

declares a constant array called **DIGITS** in which each of the 10 elements is initialized to its own index number. As you can see from this example, specifying explicit initializers allows you to omit the array size, which is then taken from the number of values.

In the **DIGITS** example, you know that there are 10 digits in the list. In many cases, however, using initializers frees the programmer from having to count the number of elements each time the program is changed. As an example, imagine you're writing a program that requires an array containing the names of all U.S. cities with populations of over 1,000,000. Taking data from the 2010 census, you could declare and initialize **BIG_CITIES** as a constant array using the following declaration:

```
private static final String[] BIG_CITIES = {
   "New York",
   "Los Angeles",
   "Chicago",
   "Houston",
   "Philadelphia",
   "Phoenix",
   "San Antonio",
   "San Diego",
   "Dallas",
};
```

5.5 Multidimensional arrays

In Java, the elements of an array can be of any type. In particular, the elements of an array can themselves be arrays. Arrays of arrays are called *multidimensional arrays*. The most common form of multidimensional array is the two-dimensional array, which is most often used to represent data in which the individual entries form a rectangular structure marked off into rows and columns. This type of two-dimensional structure is often called a *matrix*. Arrays of three or more dimensions are also legal in Java but occur less frequently.

As an example of a two-dimensional array, suppose you wanted to represent a game of tic-tac-toe as part of a program. As you probably know, tic-tac-toe is played on a board consisting of three rows and three columns, as follows:

Players take turns placing the letters *X* and *O* in the empty squares, trying to line up three identical symbols horizontally, vertically, or diagonally.

To represent the tic-tac-toe board, the most natural strategy is to use a two-dimensional array with three rows and three columns. Although you could also define an enumeration type to represent the three possible contents of each square—empty, *X*, and *O*—it is simpler in this case to use **char** as the element type and to represent the three legal states for each square using the characters `' '`, `'X'`, and `'O'`. The declaration for the tic-tac-toe board would then be written as

```
char[][] board = new char[3][3];
```

Given this declaration, you could then refer to the characters in the individual squares by supplying two separate indices, one specifying the row number and another specifying the column number. In this representation, each number varies over the range 0 to 2, and the individual positions in the board have the following names:

board[0][0]	board[0][1]	board[0][2]
board[1][0]	board[1][1]	board[1][2]
board[2][0]	board[2][1]	board[2][2]

Internally, Java represents the variable **board** as an array of three elements, each of which is an array of three characters. By convention, the elements in a multidimensional array are arranged so that the first index value varies less rapidly than the second, and so on. Thus all the elements of **board[0]** appear before any elements of **board[1]**. Because this strategy goes through all the elements on each row before it proceeds to the next one, this ordering is called ***row-major order.***

You can use static initialization with multidimensional arrays just as with single-dimensional arrays. To emphasize the overall structure, the values used to initialize each internal array are usually enclosed in an additional set of curly braces. For example, the declaration

```
public static final double[][] IDENTITY_MATRIX = {
    { 1.0, 0.0, 0.0 },
    { 0.0, 1.0, 0.0 },
    { 0.0, 0.0, 1.0 }
};
```

declares a 3×3 matrix of floating-point numbers and initializes it to contain the following values:

1.0	0.0	0.0
0.0	1.0	0.0
0.0	0.0	1.0

This particular matrix comes up frequently in mathematical applications and is called the *identity matrix.*

5.6 Variadic parameter lists

It is important to learn about arrays in Java not only because they are used so often in existing programs but also because they are integrated into both the language syntax and the structure of its libraries. Unlike the collection classes you will learn about in Chapter 6, arrays have their own selection syntax that uses square brackets to enclose the index. Ever since Java 5, programmers have been able to use arrays to indicate that a method takes a list containing an arbitrary number of values of the same type. The syntax, which applies only to the last parameter in the list, consists of the element type, three consecutive dots, and the parameter name. Parameter lists that use this syntax are said to be *variadic.*

As an example, the following method returns the maximum of any number of integer arguments:

```
private int max(int n1, int... args) {
    int result = n1;
    for (int n : args) {
        if (result < n) result = n;
    }
    return result;
}
```

If you call this method using

```
max(3, 17, 42, 19)
```

the variable **n1** is bound to 3, and the variable **args** is bound to a three-element array containing the integers 17, 42, and 19. The code begins by guessing that the maximum value is the parameter **n1** (which is listed explicitly to ensure that **max** is always called with at least one argument) and then checks that guess against the elements of **args**.

The following particularly useful method creates an array of **int** values from its argument list:

```
private int[] createIntegerArray(int... args) {
    return args;
}
```

Once you have defined this method, you can create an array simply by calling **createIntegerArray** with the desired contents as parameters.

Summary

One of the goals of this book is to encourage you to use high-level structures that allow you to think about data in an abstract way that is independent of the underlying representation. Abstract data types and classes help make it possible to maintain this holistic viewpoint. At the same time, it helps enormously if you have some idea of how data values are represented in memory. In this chapter, you have had a chance to see how data values are stored and to get a sense of what goes on "under the hood" as you write your programs.

The important points introduced in this chapter include:

- Like most languages, Java includes a built-in *array* type for storing an ordered, homogeneous collection of elements. Each element in an array has an integer index that begins with 0.

- The usual syntactic pattern for declaring and initializing an array looks like this:

    type[] *name* = **new** *type*[*size*];

- The number of elements in a Java array is stored in a field called **length**.

- The fundamental unit of information in a modern computer is a *bit,* which can be in one of two possible states. The state of a bit is usually represented in memory diagrams using the binary digits 0 and 1, but it is equally appropriate to think of these values as *off* and *on* or *false* and *true,* depending on the application.

- Sequences of bits are combined inside the hardware to form larger structures, including *bytes,* which are eight bits long, and *words,* which contain either four bytes (32 bits) or eight bytes (64 bits), depending on the machine architecture.

- The internal memory of a computer is arranged into a sequence of bytes in which each byte is identified by its index position in that sequence, which is called its *address.*

- Computer scientists tend to write address values and the contents of memory locations in *hexadecimal* notation (base 16) because doing so makes it easy to identify the individual bits.

- The primitive types in Java require different amounts of memory. A value of type **char** requires two bytes, a value of type **int** requires four, and a value of type **double** requires eight.

- Addresses of data in memory are themselves data values and can be manipulated as such by a program. A data value that is the address of some other piece of data is called a *reference.*

- Arrays in Java are stored as references to the memory containing the values of the array. An important implication of this design is that passing an array as a parameter does not copy the elements. Instead, the method copies the reference value, which specifies the address of the array data. As a result, if a method changes the values of any elements of an array passed as a parameter, those changes will be visible to the caller.

- Arrays can be initialized by listing their values inside curly braces.

- Java supports arrays with any number of dimensions, which are represented as arrays of arrays. A two-dimensional array is often called a *matrix.*

- Methods in Java can take a variable number of parameters. If the last parameter specification consists of a type followed by three consecutive dots, any arguments supplied at and after that position in the argument list will be collected into an array and assigned to the named parameter.

Review questions

1. What are the two characteristic properties of an array?

2. Define the following terms: *element, index, element type, array length,* and *selection.*

3. Write declarations that create and initialize the following array variables:
    a) An array **doubleArray** consisting of 100 values of type **double**
    b) An array **inUse** consisting of 16 values of type **boolean**
    c) An array **lines** consisting of 50 strings

4. How do you determine the length of an array?

5. The code for the **GymnasticsJudge** program uses the following statement to prompt the user to enter each judge's score:

    ```
    System.out.print("Enter score for judge " +
                     (i + 1) + ": ");
    ```

    What is the reason behind adding 1 to the value of **i**?

6. In the code shown for the preceding exercise, are the parentheses around the expression **i + 1** necessary? Why or why not?

7. Define the following terms: *bit, byte,* and *word.*

8. What is the etymology of the word *bit?*

9. How many bytes of memory are there in a 2GB machine?

10. Convert each of the following decimal numbers to its hexadecimal equivalent:

    a) 17   c) 1729
    b) 256   d) 2766

11. Convert each of the following hexadecimal numbers to decimal:

    a) **17**   c) **CC**
    b) **64**   d) **FADE**

12. The first 16 bits of every Java class file have the value **1100101011111110**. What is that value in hexadecimal notation?

13. How many bytes does Java assign to a value of type **char**? How many bytes are required for a **double**?

14. If a machine uses two's complement arithmetic to represent negative numbers, what is the internal representation of −7 in a 32-bit integer format?

15. What is a *reference* in Java?

16. True or false: Arrays violate the following rule for parameter passing, expressed in this sentence from Chapter 2: The value of each argument is copied into the corresponding parameter variable.

17. What is a multidimensional array?

18. How would you write a single declaration that initialized the variable **board** to the two-dimensional array containing the following characters (empty spaces should contain the space character), which corresponds to the starting position of a chessboard:

r	n	b	q	k	b	n	r
P	P	P	P	P	P	P	P
P	P	P	P	P	P	P	P
R	N	B	Q	K	B	N	R

19. What is *row-major order?*

20. What do three consecutive dots signify in a parameter list?

21. True or false: The variadic parameter list syntax applies only to the last parameter.

Exercises

1. Because individual contest judges may have some bias, it is common practice to throw out the highest and lowest score before computing the average. Modify the **GymnasticsJudge** program so that it displays the average of the scores that remain after it discards the highest and lowest values.

2. Implement a method

    ```
    int[] indexArray(int n)
    ```

    that returns an array of **n** values of type **int**, each of which is set to its index in the array. For example, calling **indexArray(10)** should return the array

0	1	2	3	4	5	6	7	8	9
0	1	2	3	4	5	6	7	8	9

3. In statistics, a collection of data values is usually referred to as a ***distribution.*** A primary purpose of statistical analysis is to find ways to compress the complete set of data into summary statistics that express properties of the distribution as a whole. The most common statistical measure is the ***mean,*** which is simply the traditional average, computed by the **average** method in the **GymnasticsJudge** program. In statistics, the mean of a distribution is traditionally represented by the Greek letter μ.

Another common statistical measure is the **standard deviation,** which provides an indication of how much the values in a distribution $x_1, x_2, \ldots, x_n$ differ from the mean. If you are computing the standard deviation of a complete distribution as opposed to a sample, the standard deviation (σ) can be expressed as follows in terms of the mean μ:

$$\sigma = \sqrt{\frac{\sum_{i=1}^{n}(\mu - x_i)^2}{n}}$$

The Greek letter sigma (Σ) indicates a summation of the quantity that follows, which in this case is the square of the difference between the mean and each individual data point. Write a method

```
double stddev(double[] data)
```

that returns the standard deviation of the data distribution.

4. A **histogram** is a graph that displays a set of values by dividing the data into separate ranges and then indicating how many data values fall into each range. For example, given the set of exam scores

$$100, 95, 47, 88, 86, 92, 75, 89, 81, 70, 55, 80$$

a traditional histogram would have the following form:

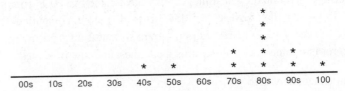

The asterisks in the histogram indicate one score in the 40s, one in the 50s, five in the 80s, and so forth. When you generate histograms using a computer, however, it is easier to display them sideways on the page, like this:

```
○ ○ ○                    Histogram
    0:
   10:
   20:
   30:
   40: *
   50: *
   60:
   70: **
   80: *****
   90: **
  100: *
```

Write a program that reads in an array of integers from a data file and then displays a histogram of those numbers, divided into the ranges 0–9, 10–19, 20–29, and so forth, up to the range containing only the value 100. Your program match the format shown in the sample run as closely as possible.

5. Write the methods

```
String intToString(int value, int base)
```

and

```
int stringToInt(String str, int base)
```

that convert an integer to and from its string equivalent. The second argument indicates the numeric base, which can be any integer in the range 2 through 36 (the 10 digits plus the 26 letters). For example, calling

```
intToString(42, 16)
```

should return the string "**2A**". Similarly, calling

```
stringToInt("111111", 2)
```

should return the integer 63. Your functions should allow for negative numbers and should throw a runtime error if any of the digits in the first argument to **stringToInt** is out of range for the specified base.

6. In exercise 6 from Chapter 2, you wrote a program to find perfect numbers. Rewrite that program so that it displays perfect numbers in binary form. If you're curious as to why all perfect numbers—or at least all even ones—have this distinctive binary form, you can search the web for articles on this topic.

7. In the third century BCE, the Greek astronomer Eratosthenes developed an algorithm for finding all the prime numbers up to some upper limit N. To apply the algorithm, you start by writing down a list of the integers between 2 and N. For example, if N is 20, you begin by writing the following list:

2   3   4   5   6   7   8   9   10   11   12   13   14   15   16   17   18   19   20

You then circle the first number in the list, indicating that you have found a prime. Whenever you mark a number as a prime, you go through the rest of the list and cross off every multiple of that number, since none of those multiples can itself be prime. Thus, after executing the first cycle of the algorithm, you will have circled the number 2 and crossed off every multiple of 2, as follows:

②   3   ✗   5   ✗   7   ✗   9   ✗   11   ✗   13   ✗   15   ✗   17   ✗   19   ✗

To complete the algorithm, you simply repeat the process by circling the first number in the list that is neither crossed off nor circled, and then crossing off its multiples. In this example, you would circle 3 as a prime and cross off all multiples of 3 in the rest of the list, which would result in the following state:

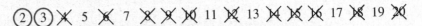

Eventually, every number in the list will either be circled or crossed out, as shown in this diagram:

②③ ✗ ⑤ ✗ ⑦ ✗ ✗ ✗ ⑪ ✗ ⑬ ✗ ✗ ✗ ⑰ ✗ ⑲ ✗

The circled numbers are the primes; the crossed-out numbers are composites. This algorithm is called the ***sieve of Eratosthenes.*** Write a program that uses the sieve of Eratosthenes to generate and display a list of the primes between 2 and 1000.

8. A ***magic square*** is a two-dimensional array of integers in which the rows, columns, and diagonals all add up to the same value. One of the most famous magic squares appears in the 1514 engraving *Melencolia I* by Albrecht Dürer shown in Figure 5-3, in which a 4×4 magic square appears at the upper right, just under the bell. In Dürer's square, which can be read more easily in the magnified inset shown at the right of the figure, all four rows, all four columns, and both diagonals add up to 34. A more familiar example is the following 3×3 magic square in which each of the rows, columns, and diagonals add up to 15, as shown:

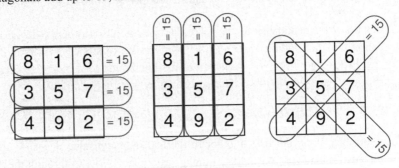

Implement a method

```
boolean isMagicSquare(int[][] square)
```

that tests to see whether **square** is a magic square. Your method should work for matrices of any size. If you call **isMagicSquare** with an array with a different number of rows and columns, the method should return **false**.

FIGURE 5-3 Magic square in Albrecht Dürer's *Melencolia I* (1514)

16	3	2	13
5	10	11	8
9	6	7	12
4	15	14	1

9. In the game of Minesweeper, a player searches for hidden mines on a rectangular grid that might—for a very small board—look like this:

One way to represent that grid in Java is to use an array of Boolean values marking mine locations, where **true** indicates the location of a mine. In

Boolean form, the two-dimensional array for the sample board therefore looks like this:

T	F	F	F	F	T
F	F	F	F	F	T
T	T	F	T	F	T
T	F	F	F	F	F
F	F	T	F	F	F
F	F	F	F	F	F

Given a two-dimensional array of mine locations, write a method

```
int[][] countMines(boolean[][] mines)
```

that goes through the array of mines and returns a new array with the same dimensions in which each element indicates how many mines are in the neighborhood of that element's location. For the purposes of this problem, you should define the neighborhood to include the location itself and any of the eight adjacent locations that are inside the boundaries of the array. For example, if **mineLocations** contains the Boolean matrix shown at the bottom of the previous page, the code

```
int[][] mineCounts = countMines(mineLocations)
```

should initialize **mineCounts** as follows:

1	1	0	0	2	2
3	3	2	1	4	3
3	3	2	1	3	2
3	4	3	2	2	1
1	2	1	1	0	0
0	1	1	1	0	0

10. In the last several years, a new logic puzzle called *Sudoku* has become quite popular throughout the world. In Sudoku, you start with a 9×9 array of integers in which some of the cells have been filled with a digit between 1 and 9. Your job in the puzzle is to fill each of the empty spaces with a digit between 1 and 9 so that each digit appears exactly once in each row, each column, and each of the smaller 3×3 squares. Each Sudoku puzzle is carefully constructed so that there is only one solution. For example, Figure 5-4 shows a typical Sudoku puzzle on the left and its unique solution on the right.

FIGURE 5-4 Typical Sudoku puzzle and its solution

		2	4		5	8		
	4	1	8				2	
6				7			3	9
2				3			9	6
		9	6		7	1		
1	7			5				3
9	6			8				1
	2				9	5	6	
		8	3		6	9		

3	9	2	4	6	5	8	1	7
7	4	1	8	9	3	6	2	5
6	8	5	2	7	1	4	3	9
2	5	4	1	3	8	7	9	6
8	3	9	6	2	7	1	5	4
1	7	6	9	5	4	2	8	3
9	6	7	5	8	2	3	4	1
4	2	3	7	1	9	5	6	8
5	1	8	3	4	6	9	7	2

Although you won't discover the algorithmic strategies you need to solve Sudoku puzzles until Chapter 9, you can easily write a method that checks to see whether a proposed solution follows the Sudoku rules against duplicating values in a row, column, or outlined 3×3 square. Write a method

```
boolean checkSudokuSolution(int[][] puzzle)
```

that performs this check and returns **true** if **puzzle** is a valid solution. Your program should check to make sure that the dimensions of the **puzzle** matrix are indeed 9×9 and should throw a runtime error if this is not the case.

11. The mechanism depicted in the following diagram—which has sometimes been marketed by toy stores as a "probability board"—can be used to demonstrate important properties of random processes.

The mechanism works as follows. You start by dropping a marble in the hole at the top. The marble falls down and hits the uppermost peg, indicated by the topmost small circle in the diagram. The marble bounces off the peg and falls, with equal probability, to the left or right. Whichever way it goes, it then hits a peg on the second level and bounces again, one direction or the other. The process continues until the marble passes all the pegs and drops into one of the channels at the bottom. For example, the dotted line in the following diagram shows one possible path for the first marble:

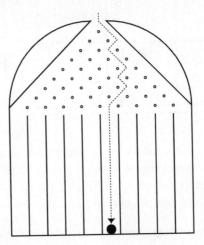

Write a program that simulates the operation of dropping 50 marbles into a probability board with 10 channels along the bottom and then displays the number in each column. Part of the point of this exercise is to show that the columns near the center tend to get more marbles, as in the following diagram:

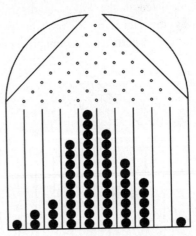

12. Write a method **sum** that takes any number of arguments of type **double** and returns their sum.

Chapter 6
Collections

In this way I have made quite a valuable collection.

— Mark Twain, *A Tramp Abroad,* 1880

As you know from your programming experience, data structures can be assembled to form hierarchies. The atomic data types like `int`, `char`, `double` are the basic building blocks of those hierarchies. To represent more complex information, you combine the atomic types to form larger structures. These larger structures can then be assembled into even larger ones in an open-ended process. Collectively, these assemblages are called *data structures.*

As you learn more about programming, you will discover that particular data structures are so useful that they are worth studying in their own right. Moreover, it is usually far more important to know how to use those structures effectively than it is to understand their underlying representation. For example, even though a string might be represented inside the machine as an array of characters, it also has an abstract behavior that transcends its representation. A type defined in terms of its behavior rather than its representation is called an *abstract data type,* which is often abbreviated to *ADT.* Abstract data types are central to the object-oriented style of programming, which encourages programmers to think about data structures in a holistic way.

The purpose of this chapter is to introduce several essential library classes from the `java.util` package, each of which maintains a collection of values of some simpler type. These classes are part of a suite of abstract data types called the *Java Collections Framework* or, more simply, Java's *collection classes.* For the moment, you don't need to understand how these classes are implemented, because your primary focus is on learning how to use these classes as a client. In later chapters, you'll have a chance to explore a variety of implementation strategies and learn about the algorithms and data structures needed to make the implementations efficient.

Separating the behavior of a class from its underlying implementation is a fundamental technique of object-oriented programming. As a design strategy, maintaining that separation offers the following advantages:

- *Simplicity.* Hiding the internal representation from the client means that there are fewer details for the client to understand.

- *Flexibility.* Because a class is defined in terms of its public behavior, the programmer who implements a class is free to change its underlying private representation. As with any abstraction, it is appropriate to change the implementation as long as the interface remains the same.

- *Security.* The interface boundary acts as a wall that protects the implementation and the client from each other. If a client program has access to the representation, it can change the values in the underlying data structure in unexpected ways. Keeping the representation private prevents the client from making such changes.

6.1 The `ArrayList` class

One of the most valuable collection classes is the `ArrayList` class, which provides a facility similar to the arrays described in Chapter 5. Arrays in Java, however, are not as flexible as one might like, primarily because their size is fixed when they are created. The `ArrayList` class eliminates that restriction by reimplementing the array concept in the form of an abstract data type.

As you will discover in Chapter 13, the `ArrayList` class is implemented using arrays in its underlying structure. As a client of the `ArrayList` class, however, you are not interested in the underlying structure and can leave the details to the programmers who implement the abstract data type. As a client, you are concerned with a different set of issues and need to answer the following questions:

1. How is it possible to specify the type of object contained in an `ArrayList`?

2. How does one create an object that is an instance of the `ArrayList` class?

3. What methods exist in the `ArrayList` class to implement its abstract behavior?

The next three sections explore the answers to each of these questions in turn.

Specifying the element type of an `ArrayList`

In Java, collection classes specify the type of object they contain by including the class name of the element in angle brackets following the name of the collection class. For example, the class `ArrayList<String>` represents an `ArrayList` whose elements are strings. The class name enclosed within the angle brackets is called the *element type* for the collection. Classes that include an element-type specification are called *parameterized classes.*

Declaring an `ArrayList` object

One of the philosophical principles behind abstract data types is that clients should be able to think of them as if they were built-in primitive types. Thus, just as you would declare an integer variable by writing a declaration such as

```
int n;
```

it ought to be possible to declare a new `ArrayList` of strings by writing

```
ArrayList<String> list;
```

In Java, that is precisely what you do. That declaration introduces a new variable named `lines`, which is—as the type specification in angle brackets indicates—an `ArrayList` whose element type is `String`.

Just as with the declaration of a local variable, however, it is customary to initialize the variable as part of the declaration. The usual technique for doing so is to use the name of the collection class—including the type parameter—as a constructor that creates an empty object from that collection. Thus, the usual pattern for declaring an **ArrayList** of strings looks like this:

```
ArrayList<String> list = new ArrayList<String>();
```

Repeating the name of the type on both sides of the declaration seems redundant at first, but it is wise to get used to this syntactic pattern. You will see it over and over again as you use collection classes.

ArrayList operations

When you use the initialization pattern from the preceding section, the variable **list** starts out as an *empty* **ArrayList,** which means that it contains no elements. Since an empty **ArrayList** is not that useful on its own, one of the first things you need to learn is how to add new elements to an **ArrayList** object. The usual approach is to invoke the **add** method, which adds a new element at the end of the existing ones. For example, if **list** is an empty **ArrayList** of strings as declared in the preceding section, executing the code

```
list.add("alpha");
list.add("beta");
list.add("gamma");
list.add("delta");
list.add("epsilon");
```

changes **list** into a five-element **ArrayList** containing the English names of the first five letters in the Greek alphabet. As with the elements of an array, Java numbers the elements of an **ArrayList** starting at 0, which means that you could diagram the contents of **list** as follows:

list

alpha	beta	gamma	delta	epsilon
0	1	2	3	4

Unlike the primitive array type introduced in Chapter 5, the size of an **ArrayList** is not fixed, which means that you can add additional elements at any time. Later in the program, for example, you could call

```
list.add("zeta");
```

which would add the string **"zeta"** to the end of the **ArrayList**, like this:

```
list
```

alpha	beta	gamma	delta	epsilon	zeta
0	1	2	3	4	5

The **ArrayList** class, however, supports several methods other than **add**. You can set and retrieve the elements of an **ArrayList** by index number, insert new elements anywhere in the list, remove existing elements, or search for an existing value. The most useful methods exported by the **ArrayList** class appear in Figure 6-1.

A simple application of the ArrayList class

The **ReverseFile** program in Figure 6-2 shows a complete Java program that uses the **ArrayList** class to display the lines from a file in reverse order. You will find that the **readEntireFile** method will often come in handy and will be worth keeping around for use in other applications.

FIGURE 6-1 Selected methods in the **ArrayList** class

Constructor	
new ArrayList<_type_**>()**	Creates an empty **ArrayList** of the specified type.

Methods	
size()	Returns the number of elements in the **ArrayList**.
isEmpty()	Returns **true** if the **ArrayList** is empty.
get(_index_**)**	Returns the element at the specified index position. If the index is out of bounds, **get** throws a runtime exception.
set(_index, value_**)**	Sets the element at the specified index to the new value. If the index is out of bounds, **set** throws a runtime exception.
add(_value_**)**	Adds a new element at the end of the **ArrayList**.
add(_index, value_**)**	Inserts the new value before the specified index position.
remove(_index_**)**	Removes the element at the specified index position.
remove(_value_**)**	Removes the first instance of the specified value.
clear()	Removes all elements from the **ArrayList**.
contains(_value_**)**	Returns **true** if the **ArrayList** contains the specified value.
indexOf(_value_**)**	Returns the first index in the **ArrayList** containing the specified value, or –1 if it does not appear.
lastIndexOf(_value_**)**	Returns the last index in the **ArrayList** containing the specified value, or –1 if it does not appear.

FIGURE 6-2 Program to print the lines of a file in reverse order

```java
/*
 * File: ReverseFile.java
 * -----------------------
 * This program displays the lines of an input file in reverse order.
 */

package edu.stanford.cs.javacs2.ch6;

import java.io.BufferedReader;
import java.io.FileReader;
import java.io.IOException;
import java.util.ArrayList;
import java.util.Scanner;

public class ReverseFile {

    public void run() {
        Scanner sysin = new Scanner(System.in);
        try {
            BufferedReader rd = openFileReader(sysin, "Input file: ");
            ArrayList<String> lines = readEntireFile(rd);
            rd.close();
            for (int i = lines.size() - 1; i >= 0; i--) {
                System.out.println(lines.get(i));
            }
        } catch (IOException ex) {
            throw new RuntimeException(ex.toString());
        }
    }

/* Reads the entire contents of a file from a reader into an ArrayList */

    private ArrayList<String> readEntireFile(BufferedReader rd) {
        try {
            ArrayList<String> lines = new ArrayList<String>();
            while (true) {
                String line = rd.readLine();
                if (line == null) break;
                lines.add(line);
            }
            return lines;
        } catch (IOException ex) {
            throw new RuntimeException(ex.toString());
        }
    }

/* The code for openFileReader appears in Chapter 3 */

    public static void main(String[] args) {
        new ReverseFile().run();
    }

}
```

6.2 Wrapper classes

Although the **ArrayList** class described in section 6.1 is ideal for storing values of type **String** or any other Java class, it cannot be used directly with the primitive types such as **int** and **double**. As with the other collection classes that you will learn about in Chapter 6, the values in an **ArrayList** must be objects. The Java primitive types are not objects and therefore cannot be used in conjunction with these marvelously convenient classes.

To get around this limitation, Java defines a class to go along with each of the eight primitive types, as follows:

Primitive type	Wrapper class
boolean	Boolean
byte	Byte
char	Character
double	Double
float	Float
int	Integer
long	Long
short	Short

These classes are defined in the **java.lang** package, which means that you can use them without an **import** statement. Programmers often refer to these classes as *wrapper classes* because they "wrap" a primitive value inside an object.

Creating objects from primitive types

Each of the wrapper classes has a constructor that creates a new object from the corresponding primitive type. For example, if **n** is an **int**, the declaration

```
Integer nAsObject = new Integer(n);
```

creates a new **Integer** object whose internal value is **n** and assigns it to the variable **nAsObject**. Each of the wrapper classes also defines a method to retrieve the underlying value. The name of that method is always the name of the primitive type followed by the suffix **Value**. Thus, once you have initialized the variable **nAsObject**, you can get back the value stored inside it by writing

```
nAsObject.intValue()
```

Because **nAsObject** is a legitimate object, you can store it in an **ArrayList** or any of the other collection classes. All you need to do is use the name of the wrapper class as the type parameter. Thus, you will often see declarations like

```
ArrayList<Integer> intList;
```

but never declarations like

```
ArrayList<int> intList;
```

Autoboxing

If you had to worry about calling the correct constructors for the wrapper classes and converting the values back to primitive types, using the collection classes with primitive values would get tedious very quickly. Fortunately, the Java compiler does the necessary work for you by performing automatic conversions between primitive types and their associated wrapper classes. Thus, instead of forcing you to write a declaration like

```
Integer nAsObject = new Integer(n);
```

Java now allows you to simplify the declaration to

```
Integer nAsObject = n;
```

When the Java compiler discovers that you are trying to assign a value of type `int` to a variable declared as type `Integer`, it automatically creates an `Integer` object with the appropriate value before performing the assignment. Conversely, if you use the variable `nAsObject` in a context in which Java expects a value of type `int`, the compiler automatically performs the necessary conversion in that direction as well. This process of adding or removing the wrapper classes as needed is called *automatic boxing* and *unboxing,* or *autoboxing* for short.

The primary advantage of autoboxing is that it leads to more readable code. The constructors that create the wrapper classes and the methods that select the primitive contents from a wrapper object disappear completely. The improvement in readability that comes from this technique is so significant that you should certainly use it in your own programs. At the same time, it is important to keep in mind that primitive values and their wrapped object counterparts behave differently in certain cases. In particular, applying the `==` and `!=` operators to objects checks whether both sides of the comparison refer to the same object, not whether those objects have the same value. This difference is illustrated by the following code:

```
public void run() {
    Integer x = 5;
    Integer y = new Integer(x);
    System.out.println("x == y -> " + (x == y));
    System.out.println("x < y  -> " + (x < y));
    System.out.println("x > y  -> " + (x > y));
}
```

The statements in this method create two values of type **Integer**, both of which have the value 5. The value assigned to **x** is created by autoboxing; the value assigned to **y** is a newly constructed **Integer** whose initial value comes from unboxing the contents of **x**. The next three lines display the values of the relational expressions **x == y**, **x < y**, and **x > y**, respectively.

If you compile and run this program, the output at first seems rather surprising:

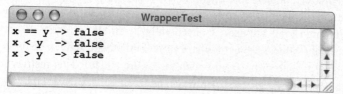

According to the rules of mathematics, exactly one of the expressions should be true, no matter what values have been assigned to **x** and **y**. The reason that all three comparisons are **false** is that unboxing of the objects occurs only with the < and > operators; the equality operator == has a well-defined interpretation when applied to objects of type **Integer**, which means that Java does not try to convert them into primitive values. When applied to objects, the equality operator returns **true** only if the values on each side of the == are the same object.

Static methods in the wrapper classes

The wrapper classes also include several static methods that you are likely to find useful. You've already learned in Chapter 3 about the methods in the **Character** class that are used to check for specific character types. Figure 6-3 lists a few of the

---

FIGURE 6-3 Selected static methods in the wrapper classes

Integer methods

`Integer.parseInt`(*string*) `Integer.parseInt`(*string*, *base*)	Converts the string to its integer form. If *base* is supplied, the conversion uses that value as the numeric base. If the string is not a legal integer, this method throws a runtime exception.
`Integer.toString`(*number*) `Integer.toString`(*number*, *base*)	Converts the number to its integer form. If *base* is supplied, the conversion uses that value as the numeric base.

Double class

`Double.parseDouble`(*string*)	Converts the string to its floating-point value. If the string is not a legal number, this method throws a runtime exception.
`Double.toString`(*number*)	Converts the number to its string representation.

most important static methods for the classes **Integer** and **Double**. For example, you can convert the integer 50 into a hexadecimal string by calling

```
Integer.toString(50, 16)
```

6.3 The stack abstraction

When measured in terms of the operations it supports, the simplest collection class is the **Stack** class, which—despite its simplicity—turns out to be useful in a variety of programming applications. Conceptually, a *stack* provides storage for a collection of data values, subject to the restriction that values must be removed from a stack in the opposite order from which they were added. This restriction implies that the last item added to a stack is always the first item that gets removed.

In light of their importance in computer science, stacks have a terminology of their own. Adding a new value to a stack is called *pushing* that value; removing the most recent item from a stack is called *popping* the stack. Moreover, the order in which stacks are processed is sometimes called *LIFO,* which stands for "last in, first out."

A common (but possibly apocryphal) explanation for the words *stack, push,* and *pop* is that the stack model is derived from the way plates are stored in a cafeteria. Particularly, if you are at a cafeteria in which customers pick up their own plates at the beginning of a buffet line, those plates are placed in spring-loaded columns that make it easy for people in line to take the top plate, as illustrated in the following diagram:

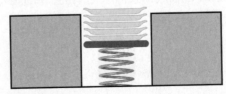

When a dishwasher adds a new plate, it goes on the top of the stack, pushing the others down slightly as the spring is compressed, as shown:

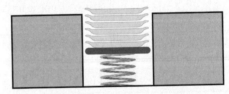

Customers can take plates only from the top of the stack. When they do, the remaining plates pop back up. The last plate added to the stack is the first one a customer takes.

The primary reason that stacks are important in programming is that nested function calls behave in a stack-oriented fashion. For example, if the main program calls a function named **f**, a stack frame for **f** gets pushed on top of the stack frame for **main**, as illustrated by the following diagram:

```
int main() {
   void f() {
      ☞ cout << "This is the function f" << endl;
         g();
   }
```

If **f** calls **g**, a new stack frame for **g** is pushed on top of the frame for **f**, as follows:

```
int main() {
   void f() {
      void g() {
         ☞ cout << "This is the function g" << endl;
      }
```

When **g** returns, its frame is popped off the stack, restoring **f** to the top of the stack as shown in the original diagram.

The structure of the Stack class

A list of the most important methods exported by the **Stack** class appears in Figure 6-4. Like **ArrayList**, **Stack** is a collection class that requires you to

FIGURE 6-4 Methods exported by the **Stack** class

Constructor	
`new Stack<`*type*`>()`	Creates an empty stack capable of holding values of the specified type.

Methods	
`size()`	Returns the number of elements currently on the stack.
`isEmpty()`	Returns **true** if the stack is empty.
`push(`*value*`)`	Pushes *value* on the stack so that it becomes the topmost element.
`pop()`	Pops the topmost value from the stack and returns it to the caller. Calling **pop** on an empty stack throws a runtime error.
`peek()`	Returns the topmost value on the stack without removing it. Calling **peek** on an empty stack throws a runtime error.
`clear()`	Removes all the elements from a stack.

specify the element type. For example, `Stack<Integer>` represents a stack whose elements are integers, and `Stack<String>` represents one in which the elements are strings. Similarly, if you define the classes `Plate` and `Frame`, you can create stacks of these objects using the classes `Stack<Plate>` and `Stack<Frame>`.

Stacks and pocket calculators

One interesting application of stacks is in electronic calculators, where stacks are used to store intermediate results. Although stacks play a central role in the operation of most calculators, that role is easiest to see in early scientific calculators that required users to enter expressions in *reverse Polish notation,* or *RPN.*

In reverse Polish notation, operators are entered after the operands to which they apply. For example, to compute the result of the expression

$$8.5 * 4.4 + 6.9 / 1.5$$

on an RPN calculator, you would enter the operations in the following order:

8.5   (ENTER)   4.4   (*)   6.9   (ENTER)   1.5   (/)   (+)

When the **ENTER** button is pressed, the calculator takes the previous value and pushes it on a stack. When an operator button is pressed, the calculator first checks whether the user has just entered a value and, if so, automatically pushes it on the stack. It then computes the result of applying the operator by

- Popping the top two values from the stack
- Applying the arithmetic operation indicated by the button to these values
- Pushing the result back on the stack

Except when the user is actually typing in a number, the calculator display shows the value at the top of the stack. Thus, at each point in the operation, the calculator display and stack contain the values shown in Figure 6-5.

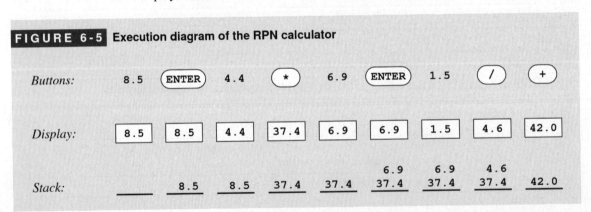

FIGURE 6-5   Execution diagram of the RPN calculator

Buttons:	8.5 (ENTER) 4.4 (*) 6.9 (ENTER) 1.5 (/) (+)							
Display:	8.5	8.5	4.4	37.4	6.9	6.9	1.5	4.6	42.0
Stack:	___	8.5	8.5	37.4	37.4	6.9 37.4	6.9 37.4	4.6 37.4	42.0

Implementing the RPN calculator in Java requires making some changes in the user-interface design. In a real calculator, the digits and operations appear on a keypad. In this implementation, it is easier to imagine that the user enters lines on the console, where those lines take one of the following forms:

- A floating-point number

- An arithmetic operator chosen from the set +, -, *, and /

- The letter Q, which causes the program to quit

- The letter H, which prints a help message

- The letter C, which clears any values left on the stack

A sample run of the calculator program might therefore look like this:

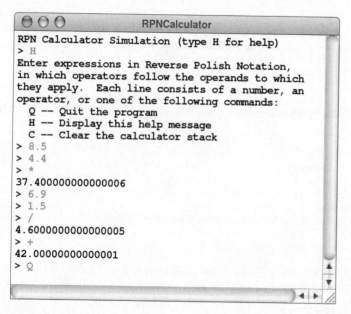

```
RPNCalculator

RPN Calculator Simulation (type H for help)
> H
Enter expressions in Reverse Polish Notation,
in which operators follow the operands to which
they apply.  Each line consists of a number, an
operator, or one of the following commands:
  Q -- Quit the program
  H -- Display this help message
  C -- Clear the calculator stack
> 8.5
> 4.4
> *
37.400000000000006
> 6.9
> 1.5
> /
4.6000000000000005
> +
42.00000000000001
> Q
```

Because the user enters each number on a separate line terminated with the RETURN key, there is no need for any counterpart to the calculator's ENTER button, which really serves only to indicate that a number is complete. The calculator program can simply push the numbers on the stack as the user enters them. When the calculator reads an operator, it pops the top two elements from the stack, applies the operator, displays the result, and then pushes the result back on the stack.

The complete implementation of the calculator application appears in Figure 6-6, which continues over the next two pages.

FIGURE 6-6 Program to implement a simple RPN calculator

```java
/*
 * File: RPNCalculator.java
 * ---------------------------
 * This program simulates an electronic calculator that uses
 * reverse Polish notation, in which the operators come after
 * the operands to which they apply.  Information for users
 * of this application appears in the helpCommand function.
 */

package edu.stanford.cs.javacs2.ch6;

import java.util.Scanner;
import java.util.Stack;

public class RPNCalculator {

    public void run() {
        Scanner sysin = new Scanner(System.in);
        System.out.println("RPN Calculator Simulation (type H for help)");
        Stack<Double> operandStack = new Stack<Double>();
        while (true) {
            System.out.print("> ");
            String line = sysin.nextLine();
            char ch = Character.toUpperCase(line.charAt(0));
            if (ch == 'Q') {
                break;
            } else if (ch == 'C') {
                operandStack.clear();
            } else if (ch == 'H') {
                helpCommand();
            } else if (Character.isDigit(ch)) {
                operandStack.push(Double.parseDouble(line));
            } else if (ch == '+' || ch == '-' || ch == '*' || ch == '/') {
                applyOperator(ch, operandStack);
            } else {
                System.out.println("Unrecognized command " + ch);
            }
        }
    }

/**
 * Generates a help message for the user.
 */

    private void helpCommand() {
        System.out.println("Enter expressions in Reverse Polish Notation,");
        System.out.println("in which operators follow the operands to which");
        System.out.println("they apply.  Each line consists of a number, an");
        System.out.println("operator, or one of the following commands:");
        System.out.println("  Q -- Quit the program");
        System.out.println("  H -- Display this help message");
        System.out.println("  C -- Clear the calculator stack");
    }
```

FIGURE 6-6   **Program to implement a simple RPN calculator (continued)**

```
/**
 * Applies the operator to the top two elements on the operand stack.
 */

    private void applyOperator(char op, Stack<Double> operandStack) {
        double result;
        double rhs = operandStack.pop();
        double lhs = operandStack.pop();
        switch (op) {
          case '+': result = lhs + rhs; break;
          case '-': result = lhs - rhs; break;
          case '*': result = lhs * rhs; break;
          case '/': result = lhs / rhs; break;
          default: throw new RuntimeException("Undefined operator " + op);
        }
        System.out.println(result);
        operandStack.push(result);
    }

/* Main program */

    public static void main(String[] args) {
        new RPNCalculator().run();
    }

}
```

6.4 The queue abstraction

As you learned in section 6.3, the defining feature of a stack is that the last item pushed is always the first item popped. As noted in the introduction to that section, this behavior is often referred to in computer science as *LIFO,* which is an acronym for the phrase "last in, first out." The LIFO discipline is useful in programming contexts because it reflects the operation of function calls; the most recently called function is the first to return. Relatively few real-world situations, however, follow this "last in, first out" model. Indeed, in human society, our collective notion of fairness assigns some priority to being first, as expressed in the maxim "first come, first served." In programming, the usual phrasing of this ordering strategy is "first in, first out," which is traditionally abbreviated as *FIFO.*

A data structure that stores items using a FIFO discipline is called a *queue.* In Java, the fundamental operations on a queue—which are analogous to the **push** and **pop** operations for stacks—are called **add** and **remove**. The **add** operation adds a new element to the end of the queue, which is traditionally called its *tail.* The **remove** operation removes the element at the beginning of the queue, which is called its *head.*

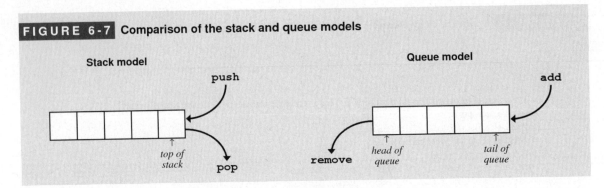

FIGURE 6-7 Comparison of the stack and queue models

Stack model

push

top of stack

pop

Queue model

add

remove

head of queue

tail of queue

The conceptual difference between these structures can be illustrated most easily with a diagram. In a stack, the client must add and remove elements from the same end of the internal data structure, as shown in Figure 6-7.

Given the similarities in the structure, you would certainly expect that the **Stack** and **Queue** models would be similar in Java. Although these models do have many similarities, there are also some unexpected differences that come from Java's history. The **Stack** class dates all the way back to Java 1.0, which predates the rest of the Java Collections Framework. When queues were added to the library, they were included in a way that is more consistent with the collection classes as a whole.

The biggest difference in the model Java uses for these abstractions is that **Stack** is a class and **Queue** is what Java calls an *interface,* which is a data structure definition that outlines a set of operations without providing an underlying representation. An interface *specifies* the behavior for other classes that *implement* that interface. As you will see in later chapters, a class definition can implement several different interfaces even though it has only one superclass.

Figure 6-8 shows that the methods specified by the **Queue** interface are indeed similar to those defined by the **Stack** class. The primary difference is in how one constructs a new queue. Because **Queue** is an interface, it is not legal in Java to construct a **Queue** using a declaration like

```
Queue<String> queue = new Queue<String>();
```

What you have to do instead is choose a concrete class that implements the **Queue** interface. There are several such classes, of which the most common are **ArrayDeque** (which stands for *array double-ended queue* and is pronounced like *array-deck*) and **LinkedList**. From the client perspective, these two classes behave the same way; the differences are limited to the implementation. You will have a chance to explore these two implementations in Chapter 13.

FIGURE 6-8 Methods specified by the Queue interface

`size()`	Returns the number of elements currently on the queue.
`isEmpty()`	Returns **true** if the queue is empty.
`add(value)`	Adds *value* to the tail of the queue.
`remove()`	Removes the value at the head of the queue and returns it to the caller. Calling **remove** on an empty queue throws a runtime error.
`peek()`	Returns the value at the head of the queue without removing it. Calling **peek** on an empty queue throws a runtime error.
`clear()`	Removes all the elements from a queue.

You can use the Universal Modeling Language introduced in Chapter 1 to describe the relationship between classes and interfaces. In UML, you indicate that a class implements an interface by using a dashed arrow instead of the solid arrow used to model the subclass relation. UML diagrams also mark Java interfaces by including the keyword «**interface**» above the interface name. The structure of the **Queue** interface and its implementing classes can be diagrammed as follows:

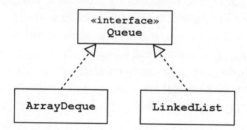

Queue applications

The queue data structure has many applications in programming. Not surprisingly, queues turn up in many situations in which it is important to maintain a first-in/first-out discipline in order to ensure that service requests are treated fairly. For example, if you are working in an environment in which a single printer is shared among several computers, the printing software is usually designed so that all print requests are entered in a queue. Thus, if several users decide to enter print requests, the queue structure ensures that each user's request is processed in the order received.

Queues are also common in programs that simulate the behavior of waiting lines. For example, if you wanted to decide how many cashiers you needed in a supermarket, it might be worth writing a program that could simulate the behavior of customers in the store. Such a program would almost certainly involve queues, because a checkout line operates in a first-in/first-out way. Customers who have completed their purchases arrive in the checkout line and wait for their turn to pay. Each customer eventually reaches the front of the line, at which point the cashier totals up the purchases and collects the money. Because simulations of this sort represent an important class of application programs, it is worth spending a little time understanding how such simulations work.

Simulations and models

Beyond the world of programming, there are many real-world events and processes that—although they are undeniably important—are nonetheless too complicated to understand completely. For example, it would be very useful to know how various pollutants affect the ozone layer and how the resulting changes in the ozone layer affect the global climate. Similarly, if economists and political leaders had a more complete understanding of exactly how the national economy works, it would be possible to evaluate precisely how much a tax cut would add to the economy and how much that cut would exacerbate the existing disparities of wealth and income.

When faced with such large-scale problems, it is usually necessary to come up with an idealized *model,* which is a simplified representation of a process. Most real-world problems are far too complex to allow for a complete understanding. There are just too many details. The reason to build a model is that, despite the complexity of a particular problem, it is often possible to make certain assumptions that allow you to simplify a complicated process without affecting its fundamental character. If you can come up with a reasonable model for a process, you can often translate the dynamics of the model into a program that captures the behavior of that model. Such a program is called a *simulation.*

It is important to remember that creating a simulation is usually a two-step process. The first step consists of designing a conceptual model for the real-world behavior you are trying to simulate. The second consists of writing a program that implements the conceptual model. Because errors can occur in both steps of the process, maintaining a certain skepticism about simulations and their applicability to the real world is probably wise. In a society conditioned to believe the "answers" delivered by computers, it is critical to recognize that the simulations can never be better than the models on which they are based.

The waiting-line model

Suppose that you want to design a simulation that models the behavior of a supermarket waiting line. By simulating the waiting line, you can determine some useful properties of waiting lines that might help a company make decisions such as how many cashiers are needed, how much space needs to be reserved for the line itself, and so forth.

The first step in the process of writing a checkout-line simulation is to develop a model for the waiting line, in which you identify any simplifying assumptions. For example, to make the initial implementation of the simulation as simple as possible, you might begin by assuming that there is one cashier who serves customers from a single queue. You might then assume that customers arrive with a random probability and enter the queue at the end of the line. Whenever the cashier is free and someone is waiting in line, the cashier begins to serve that customer. After an appropriate service period—which you must also model in some way—the cashier completes the transaction with the current customer and is then free to serve the next customer in the queue.

Discrete time

Another assumption often required in a model is some limitation on the level of accuracy. In the context of the checkout-line simulation, the time a customer spends being served by the cashier will clearly vary within some limits. One customer might spend 30 seconds; another might spend five minutes. It is important, however, to consider whether measuring time in minutes allows the simulation to be sufficiently precise. If you had a sufficiently accurate stopwatch, you might discover that a customer actually spent 3.14159265 minutes. The question you need to resolve is how precise you have to be.

For most models, and particularly for those intended for simulation, it is useful to introduce the simplifying assumption that all events within the model happen in discrete integral time units. Using discrete time assumes that you can find a time unit that—for the purpose of the model—you can treat as indivisible. In general, the time units used in a simulation must be small enough that the probability of more than one event occurring during a single time unit is negligible. In the checkout-line simulation, for example, minutes may not be accurate enough; two customers could easily arrive in the same minute. The sections that follow use seconds as the time step to avoid multiple events occurring in the same interval.

Events in simulated time

One of the advantages of using discrete time units is that doing so makes it possible to work with variables of type **int** instead of the less efficient type **double**. A more important advantage of discrete time is that it allows you to structure the simulation as a loop in which each time unit represents a single cycle. When you approach the problem in this way, a simulation program has the following form:

```
for (int time = 0; time < SIMULATION_TIME; time++) {
    Execute one cycle of the simulation.
}
```

Within the body of the loop, the program performs the operations necessary to advance through one unit of simulated time.

Think for a moment about what events might occur during each time unit of the checkout-line simulation. One possibility is that a new customer might arrive. Another is that the cashier might finish with the current customer and go on to serve the next person in line. These events raise some interesting issues. To complete the model, you need to say something about how often customers arrive and how much time they spend at the cash register. You could (and probably should) gather approximate data by watching a real checkout line in a store. Even if you collected that information, however, you would need to simplify it to a form that (1) captures enough of the real-world behavior to be useful and (2) is easy to understand in terms of the model. For example, your surveys might show that customers arrive at the line on average once every 200 seconds. This average arrival rate is certainly useful input to the model. On the other hand, you would not have much confidence in a simulation in which customers arrived exactly once every 200 seconds. Such an implementation would violate the real-world condition that customer arrivals have some random variability and that they sometimes bunch together.

For this reason, the arrival process is usually modeled by specifying the probability that an arrival takes place in any discrete time unit instead of specifying the average time between arrivals. For example, if your studies indicated that a customer arrived once every 200 seconds, the average probability of a customer arriving in any particular second would be 1/200 or 0.005. If you assume that arrivals occur randomly with an equal probability in each unit of time, the arrival process forms a pattern that mathematicians call a *Poisson distribution* after the French mathematician Siméon Poisson (1781–1840). The simulation also assumes that the service time required for each customer is uniformly distributed within a certain range.

Implementing the simulation

Even though it is longer than the other programs in this chapter, the code for the simulation program is easy to write. The code for the **CheckoutLine** program appears in Figure 6-9. The core of the simulation is a loop that runs for the number of seconds indicated by the parameter **SIMULATION_TIME**. In each second, the simulation performs the following operations:

1. Check whether a customer has arrived and, if so, add that person to the queue.

2. If the cashier is busy, note that the cashier has spent another second with the current customer. Eventually, the required service time will be complete, which will free the cashier.

3. If the cashier is free, serve the next customer in line.

FIGURE 6-9 Program to simulate a checkout line

```java
/*
 * File: CheckoutLine.java
 * -------------------------
 * This program simulates a checkout line, such as one you might encounter
 * in a supermarket.  Customers arrive at the checkout stand and get in
 * line.  Those customers wait until the cashier is free, at which point
 * they occupy the cashier for some period of time.  After the service time
 * is complete, the cashier is free to serve the next customer.
 *
 * In each second, the simulation performs the following operations:
 *
 * 1. Determine whether a new customer has arrived.  New customers arrive
 *    randomly, with a probability given by the constant ARRIVAL_PROBABILITY.
 *
 * 2. If the cashier is busy, subtract one second from the time remaining.
 *    When that count reaches zero, the current customer is finished.
 *
 * 3. If the cashier is free, serve the next customer.  The service time
 *    is uniformly distributed between MIN_SERVICE_TIME and MAX_SERVICE_TIME.
 *
 * At the end of the simulation, the program displays the simulation
 * parameters along with the results of the simulation.
 */

package edu.stanford.cs.javacs2.ch6;

import java.util.ArrayDeque;
import java.util.Queue;

public class CheckoutLine {

   public void run() {
      Queue<Integer> queue = new ArrayDeque<Integer>();
      int timeRemaining = 0;
      int nServed = 0;
      double totalWait = 0;
      double totalLength = 0;
      for (int t = 0; t < SIMULATION_TIME; t++) {
         if (randomBoolean(ARRIVAL_PROBABILITY)) {
            queue.add(t);
         }
         if (timeRemaining > 0) {
            timeRemaining--;
         } else if (!queue.isEmpty()) {
            totalWait += t - queue.remove();
            nServed++;
            timeRemaining = randomInt(MIN_SERVICE_TIME, MAX_SERVICE_TIME);
         }
         totalLength += queue.size();
      }
      printReport(nServed, totalWait / nServed, totalLength / SIMULATION_TIME);
   }
```

FIGURE 6-9 Program to simulate a checkout line (continued)

```
/*
 * Reports the results of the simulation in tabular format.
 */

   private void printReport(int nServed, double avgWait, double avgLength) {
      System.out.printf("Simulation results given the following constants:%n");
      System.out.printf("  SIMULATION_TIME:     %5d min%n",
                        (int) Math.round(SIMULATION_TIME / MINUTES));
      System.out.printf("  MIN_SERVICE_TIME:    %5d sec%n", MIN_SERVICE_TIME);
      System.out.printf("  MAX_SERVICE_TIME:    %5d sec%n", MAX_SERVICE_TIME);
      System.out.printf("  ARRIVAL_PROBABILITY: %5.3f%n", ARRIVAL_PROBABILITY);
      System.out.println();
      System.out.printf("Customers served:      %5d%n", nServed);
      System.out.printf("Average waiting time:  %5.2f min%n",
                        avgWait / MINUTES);
      System.out.printf("Average queue length:  %5.2f%n", avgLength);
   }

/*
 * Returns a random integer between low and high, inclusive.
 */

   private int randomInt(int low, int high) {
      return (int) Math.floor(low + ((double) high - low + 1) * Math.random());
   }

/*
 * Returns true with probability p, which is a floating-point number
 * between 0 (impossible) and 1 (certain).
 */

   private boolean randomBoolean(double p) {
      return Math.random() < p;
   }

/* Constants */

   private static final int SECONDS = 1;
   private static final int MINUTES = 60;
   public static final double ARRIVAL_PROBABILITY = 0.005;
   public static final int MIN_SERVICE_TIME = 30 * SECONDS;
   public static final int MAX_SERVICE_TIME = 5 * MINUTES;
   public static final int SIMULATION_TIME = 500 * MINUTES;

/* Main program */

   public static void main(String[] args) {
      new CheckoutLine().run();
   }

}
```

The waiting line itself is represented, naturally enough, as a queue. The value stored in the queue is the time at which that customer arrived in the queue, which makes it possible to determine how many seconds that customer spent in line before reaching the head of the queue.

The simulation is controlled by the following constants:

- `SIMULATION_TIME`—This constant specifies the duration of the simulation.

- `ARRIVAL_PROBABILITY`—This constant indicates the probability that a new customer will arrive at the checkout line during a single unit of time. The probability is expressed as a real number between 0 and 1.

- `MIN_SERVICE_TIME`, `MAX_SERVICE_TIME`—These constants define the legal range of customer service time. For any particular customer, the amount of time spent with the cashier is determined by picking a random integer in this range.

When the simulation is complete, the program reports the simulation constants along with the number of customers served, the average amount of time customers spent in the waiting line, and the average length of the waiting line.

For example, the following sample run shows the results of the simulation for the indicated constant values:

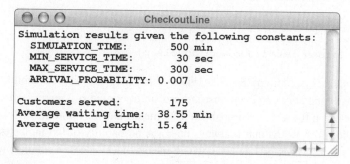

```
                        CheckoutLine
Simulation results given the following constants:
   SIMULATION_TIME:        500 min
   MIN_SERVICE_TIME:        30 sec
   MAX_SERVICE_TIME:       300 sec
   ARRIVAL_PROBABILITY:  0.007

Customers served:         175
Average waiting time:   38.55 min
Average queue length:   15.64
```

The behavior of the simulation depends significantly on the values of the constants used to control it. Suppose, for example, that the probability of a customer arriving increases from 0.005 to 0.010. Running the simulation with these parameters gives the following results:

```
                        CheckoutLine
Simulation results given the following constants:
   SIMULATION_TIME:        500 min
   MIN_SERVICE_TIME:        30 sec
   MAX_SERVICE_TIME:       300 sec
   ARRIVAL_PROBABILITY:  0.007

Customers served:         175
Average waiting time:   38.55 min
Average queue length:   15.64
```

As you can see, even a slight increase in the probability of arrival from 0.005 to 0.007 causes the average waiting time to grow from under four minutes to more than half an hour, which is obviously a dramatic increase. The reason for the poor performance is that the arrival rate in the second run of the simulation means that new customers arrive at approximately the same rate at which they are served. When this threshold is reached, the length of the queue and the average waiting time both begin to grow very quickly. Simulations of this sort make it possible to experiment with different parameter values. Those experiments, in turn, make it possible to identify potential sources of trouble in the corresponding real-world systems.

Random numbers

The simulation program from Figure 6-9 includes two methods for generating random numbers that will come in handy in a variety of applications. The first is

```
double randomInt(int low, int high)
```

which returns a new random integer in the range between **low** and **high**, inclusive. You can, for example, generate a random die roll by calling

```
nextRandomInt(1, 6)
```

The second method is

```
boolean randomBoolean(double p)
```

which generates a random Boolean value that is **true** with probability **p**. In keeping with statistical conventions, the probability value **p** is expressed as a real number between 0 and 1. A probability of 0 means that an event never occurs, and a probability of 1 means that it always does. A probability of 0.5 indicates that an event occurs 50 percent of the time, which means that you could simulate tossing a coin with the following code:

```
randomBoolean(0.5) ? "Heads" : "Tails"
```

Each of these methods is implemented using the library method **Math.random**, which returns a random **double** that is greater than or equal to 0 but strictly less than 1. The implementation of **randomBoolean** simply checks whether the result of **Math.random** is less than the desired probability **p**. The implementation of the **randomInt** method consists of the following steps:

1. Use **Math.random** to generate a floating-point number d in the range $0 \le d < 1$.

2. Scale the value d by multiplying it by the size of the desired range, so that it spans the correct number of integers.

3. Translate the value by adding in the lower bound so that the range begins at the desired point.

4. Convert the number to an integer by calling the function **Math.floor**, which returns the floating-point representation of the largest integer that is smaller than its argument, and then casting that result to an integer.

The methods **randomInt** and **randomBoolean** are sufficiently useful that it makes sense to include them in a library. You will have a chance to do just that in the exercises for Chapter 7.

▉ 6.5 The map abstraction

This section introduces another abstract collection called a *map*, which is conceptually similar to a dictionary. A dictionary allows you to look up a word to find its meaning. A map is a generalization of this idea that provides an association between an identifying tag called a *key* and an associated *value*, which is often a much larger and more complicated structure. In the dictionary example, the key is the word you're looking up, and the value is its definition.

Maps have many applications in programming. For example, an interpreter for a programming language needs to be able to assign values to variables, which can then be referenced by name. A map makes it easy to maintain the association between the name of a variable and its corresponding value.

In the Java Collections Framework, **Map** is an interface that must be constructed using a concrete class that implements the **Map** interface. The collection class library includes two such classes: **HashMap** and **TreeMap**. The **HashMap** class is slightly more efficient, but less convenient to use for applications that require processing keys in order. You'll have a chance to learn about the differences between these implementations of the map concept in Chapters 14 and 15.

The structure of the Map interface

As with the collection classes introduced earlier in this chapter, **Map** requires type parameters that specify both the key type and the value type. For example, if you wanted to simulate a dictionary in which individual words are associated with their definitions, you might begin by declaring a **dict** variable as follows:

```
Map<String,String> dict = new TreeMap<String,String>();
```

Similarly, if you were implementing a programming language, you could use a **Map** to store the values of floating-point variables, as follows:

```
Map<String,Double> varTable = new HashMap<String,Double>();
```

These definitions create empty maps that contain no keys and values. In either case, you would subsequently need to add key/value pairs to the map. In the case of the dictionary, you could read the contents from a data file. For the symbol table, you would add new associations whenever an assignment statement appeared.

The most common methods specified by the **Map** interface appear in Figure 6-10. Of these methods, the ones that implement the fundamental behavior of the map concept are **put** and **get**. The **put** method creates an association between a key and a value. Its operation is analogous to assigning a value to a variable in Java: if there is a value already associated with the key, the old value is replaced by the new one. The **get** method retrieves the value most recently associated with a particular key and therefore corresponds to the act of using a variable name to retrieve its value. If no value appears in the map for a particular key, calling **get** with that key returns the default value for the value type. You can check whether a key exists in a map by calling the **containsKey** method, which returns **true** or **false** depending on whether the specified key has been defined.

A few diagrams may help to illustrate the operation of the **Map** abstraction. Suppose that you have declared **varTable** as a **Map<String,Double>** and then initialized it to be a **HashMap** as shown earlier in this section. That declaration creates an empty map, as represented by the following diagram:

varTable

FIGURE 6-10 Methods specified by the **Map** interface

size()	Returns the number of key/value pairs contained in the map.
isEmpty()	Returns **true** if the map is empty.
put(*key, value*)	Associates the specified key and value in the map. If *key* has no previous definition, a new entry is added; if a previous association exists, the old value is discarded and replaced by the new one.
get(*key*)	Returns the value currently associated with *key* in the map. If *key* is not defined, **get** returns **null**.
remove(*key*)	Removes *key* from the map along with any associated value. If *key* does not exist, this call leaves the map unchanged.
containsKey(*key*)	Returns **true** if *key* is associated with a value.
clear()	Removes all the key/value pairs from the map.
keySet()	Returns a set of all the keys in the map.

Once you have the map, you can use **put** to establish new associations. For example, if you called

        varTable.put("pi", 3.14159);

the conceptual effect would be to add an association between the key **"pi"** and the value 3.14159, as follows:

                    varTable
                    | pi = 3.14159 |

Similarly, calling

        varTable.put("e", 2.71828);

would add a new association between the key **"e"** and the value 2.71828, like this:

                    varTable
                    | pi = 3.14159 |
                    | e = 2.71828 |

You could then use **get** to retrieve these values. Calling **varTable.get("e")** would return the value 2.71828, and calling **varTable.get("pi")** would return 3.14159.

Although it hardly makes sense in the case of mathematical constants, you could change the values in the map by making additional calls to **put**. You could, for example, reset the value associated with **"pi"** (as an 1897 bill before the Indiana State General Assembly sought to do) by calling

        varTable.put("pi", 3.0);

which would lead to the following state:

                    varTable
                    | pi = 3.0 |
                    | e = 2.71828 |

You can remove a key entirely by calling **remove**. For example, you can delete the erroneous value of **pi** by calling **varTable.delete("pi")**, which would leave the map looking like this:

                    varTable
                    | e = 2.71828 |

Using maps in an application

If you fly at all frequently, you quickly learn that every airport in the world has a three-letter code assigned by the International Air Transport Association (IATA). For example, the John F. Kennedy airport in New York City is assigned the three-letter code JFK. Other codes, however, are considerably harder to recognize. Most web-based travel systems offer some means of looking up these codes as a service to their customers.

Suppose that you have been asked to write a simple Java program that reads a three-letter airport code from the user and responds with the location of that airport. The data you need is in the form of a text file called **AirportCodes.txt**, which contains a list of the several thousand airport codes that IATA has assigned. Each line of the file consists of a three-letter code, an equal sign, and the location of the airport. If the file were sorted in descending order by passenger traffic in 2009, as compiled by Airports Council International, the file would begin with the lines in Figure 6-11.

The existence of the map abstraction makes this application very easy to write. The entire application fits on a single page, as shown in Figure 6-12.

FIGURE 6-11 Beginning of a data file containing airport codes and locations

```
AirportCodes.txt
ATL=Atlanta, GA, USA
ORD=Chicago, IL, USA
LHR=London, England, United Kingdom
HND=Tokyo, Japan
LAX=Los Angeles, CA, USA
CDG=Paris, France
DFW=Dallas/Ft Worth, TX, USA
FRA=Frankfurt, Germany
PEK=Beijing, China
MAD=Madrid, Spain
DEN=Denver, CO, USA
AMS=Amsterdam, Netherlands
JFK=New York, NY, USA
HKG=Hong Kong, Hong Kong
LAS=Las Vegas, NV, USA
IAH=Houston, TX, USA
PHX=Phoenix, AZ, USA
BKK=Bangkok, Thailand
SIN=Singapore, Singapore
MCO=Orlando, FL, USA
     .
     .
     .
```

FIGURE 6-12 Program to look up three-letter airport codes

```java
/*
 * File: AirportCodes.java
 * ------------------------
 * This program looks up a three-letter airport code in a Map.
 */

package edu.stanford.cs.javacs2.ch6;

import java.io.BufferedReader;
import java.io.FileReader;
import java.io.IOException;
import java.util.Map;
import java.util.Scanner;
import java.util.TreeMap;

public class AirportCodes {

    public void run() {
        Scanner sysin = new Scanner(System.in);
        Map<String,String> airportCodes = readCodeFile("AirportCodes.txt");
        while (true) {
            System.out.print("Airport code: ");
            String code = sysin.nextLine().toUpperCase();
            if (code.equals("")) break;
            if (airportCodes.containsKey(code)) {
                System.out.println(code + " is in " + airportCodes.get(code));
            } else {
                System.out.println("There is no such airport code");
            }
        }
    }

    private Map<String,String> readCodeFile(String filename) {
        Map<String,String> map = new TreeMap<String,String>();
        try {
            BufferedReader rd = new BufferedReader(new FileReader(filename));
            while (true) {
                String line = rd.readLine();
                if (line == null) break;
                String code = line.substring(0, 3).toUpperCase();
                String city = line.substring(4);
                map.put(code, city);
            }
            rd.close();
        } catch (IOException ex) {
            throw new RuntimeException(ex.getMessage());
        }
        return map;
    }

    public static void main(String[] args) {
        new AirportCodes().run();
    }
}
```

The main program in the **AirportCodes** application reads in three-letter codes, looks up the corresponding location, and then prints the location on the console, as shown in the following sample run:

6.6 The set abstraction

One of the most useful abstractions in the Java Collections Framework is the **Set** interface, which specifies the methods shown in Figure 6-13. This class is used to model the mathematical abstraction of a *set,* which is a collection in which the elements are unordered and in which each value appears only once. Sets turn out to be extremely useful in many algorithmic applications and are therefore worth a chapter of their own. Even before you have a chance to read the more detailed account in Chapter 16, it is worth considering a few examples of sets so you can get a better sense of how sets work and how they might be useful in applications.

As with the **Map** interface, the **Set** interface has two concrete implementations: **HashSet** and **TreeSet**. The fact that these names follow the same pattern as the concrete implementations of **Map** is not an accident. The **HashMap** and **HashSet** classes use the same underlying representation, which is called a *hash table.* Similarly, the **TreeMap** and **TreeSet** classes share a common representation based on a structure called a *binary search tree.* You will have a chance to learn about these structures in Chapters 14, 15, and 16.

FIGURE 6-13 Methods specified by the Set interface

`size()`	Returns the number of elements in the set.
`isEmpty()`	Returns **true** if the set is empty.
`add(`*value*`)`	Adds the value to the set. If the value is already in the set, no error is generated, and the set remains unchanged.
`remove(`*value*`)`	Removes the value from the set. If the value is not present, no error is generated, and the set remains unchanged.
`contains(`*value*`)`	Returns **true** if the value is in the set.
`clear()`	Removes all elements from the set.

In the discussion of the **Map** abstraction earlier in the chapter, one of the examples used to explain the underlying concept is that of a dictionary in which the keys are individual words and the corresponding values are the definitions. In some applications, such as a spelling checker or a program that plays Scrabble, you don't need to know the definition of a word. All you need to know is whether a particular combination of letters is a legal word. For such applications, the **Set** class is an ideal tool. Instead of a map containing both words and definitions, all you need is a **Set<String>** whose elements are the legal words. A word is legal if it is contained in the set, and illegal if it is not.

A set of words with no associated definitions is called a *lexicon*. If you have a text file named **EnglishWords.txt** containing all the words in English, one word per line, you can create a lexicon named **english** using the following code:

```
Set<String> english = new TreeSet<String>();
try {
   BufferedReader rd =
      new BufferedReader(new FileReader(filename));
   while (true) {
      String line = rd.readLine();
      if (line == null) break;
      english.add(line);
   }
   rd.close();
} catch (IOException ex) {
   throw new RuntimeException(ex.toString());
}
```

You can then use this lexicon to produce what every Scrabble player needs: a list of the valid two-letter words. One approach to doing so is shown in Figure 6-14, in which the program produces a list of the two-letter words by generating every possible combination of two letters and then looking up each one to see whether that two-letter string appears in the lexicon of English words.

6.7 Iterating over a collection

Although the **TwoLetterWords** program in Figure 6-14 uses a reasonably efficient strategy to produce the list of the two-letter words, that strategy is far less attractive if you are trying to produce a list of all seven-letter words, which is also useful for Scrabble players. If you adopt the generate-all-possible-strings approach used in Figure 6-14, the **SevenLetterWords** program requires seven nested loops. The body of the inner loop would run through 26^7 iterations, which is more than eight billion cycles. Surely there must be a better way.

FIGURE 6-14 Program to generate a list of all two-letter English words

```java
/*
 * File: TwoLetterWords.java
 * ---------------------------
 * This program generates a list of the two-letter words by creating every
 * possible two-letter combination and checking whether it is a legal word.
 */

package edu.stanford.cs.javacs2.ch6;

import java.io.BufferedReader;
import java.io.FileReader;
import java.io.IOException;
import java.util.Set;
import java.util.TreeSet;

public class TwoLetterWords {

    public void run() {
        Set<String> english = readWordList("EnglishWords.txt");
        for (char c1 = 'a'; c1 <= 'z'; c1++) {
            for (char c2 = 'a'; c2 <= 'z'; c2++) {
                String word = "" + c1 + c2;
                if (english.contains(word)) System.out.println(word);
            }
        }
    }

/*
 * Reads in a lexicon set from the specified file.
 */

    private Set<String> readWordList(String filename) {
        try {
            Set<String> lexicon = new TreeSet<String>();
            BufferedReader rd = new BufferedReader(new FileReader(filename));
            while (true) {
                String line = rd.readLine();
                if (line == null) break;
                lexicon.add(line);
            }
            rd.close();
            return lexicon;
        } catch (IOException ex) {
            throw new RuntimeException(ex.toString());
        }
    }

/* Main program */

    public static void main(String[] args) {
        new TwoLetterWords().run();
    }

}
```

A more natural strategy for solving the problem of listing all seven-letter words is to go through every word in the lexicon and display the words whose length is equal to 7. To do so, all you need is some way of stepping through the contents of a set, one element at a time.

Using iterators

Iterating through the elements is a fundamental operation for any collection class. Moreover, if the package of collection classes is well designed, clients should be able to use the same strategy to perform that operation, no matter whether they are cycling through all elements in an **ArrayList**, a **Set**, or even a Java array. The Java Collections Framework offers a powerful mechanism called an *iterator* for doing just that. The even better news is that iterators are so important in Java that they are now included in the language in an extension to the **for** statement that has the following general form:

```
for (type variable : collection) {
      body of the loop
}
```

For example, if you want to iterate through all the words in the English lexicon and select only those containing seven letters, you can use the following **for** loop:

```
for (String word : english) {
   if (word.length() == 7) {
      System.out.println(word);
   }
}
```

This code is both compact and expressive. As soon as you become familiar with the syntactic pattern, you can translate this program almost directly into English, as follows:

> *For each word in the English lexicon*
> *If the length of that word is seven*
> *Print that word on the console.*

Iteration order

When you use the **for** loop to iterate over a collection, it is useful to understand the order in which it processes the individual values. There is no universal rule. Each collection class defines its own policy about iteration order, usually based on considerations of efficiency. The classes you've already seen make the following guarantees about the order of values:

- When you iterate through the elements of an array or an `ArrayList`, the `for` loop delivers the elements in order by index position, so that the element in position 0 comes first, followed by the element in position 1, and so on, up to the end of the array or `ArrayList`. The iteration order is therefore the same as that produced by the traditional `for` loop pattern:

```
for (int i = 0; i < array.length; i++) {
    code to process array[i]
}
```

- When you iterate through the elements of a `HashSet`, the elements appear in an order that is determined by the underlying representation but which seems totally random to clients.

- When you iterate through the elements of a `TreeSet`, the elements appear in the natural order defined by the element type. For example, if you iterate over a `TreeSet<Integer>`, the elements will be produced in numeric order. If you instead iterate over a `TreeSet<String>`, the elements will be produced in the lexicographic order defined by the underlying character codes.

- Java does not allow you to iterate over the keys in a map directly. The `Map` interface specifies a method called `keySet`, which returns a set of the keys in the map. Calling `keySet` on a `HashMap` returns a `HashSet`; calling `keySet` on a `TreeMap` returns a `TreeSet`. When you iterate over the key set, you get the iteration order appropriate to the set.

- This book avoids using iterators with the `Stack` and `Queue` classes. Allowing unrestricted access to these structures violates the principle that only one element (the element at the top of a stack or the one at the head of a queue) is visible at a particular time.

Computing word frequencies

Iteration comes up in a wide variety of applications, such as the `WordFrequency` program in Figure 6-15, which counts the number of times each word appears in an input file. Given the tools you have at your disposal from earlier examples, the necessary code is quite straightforward. The strategy for dividing a line into words is similar to what you have already seen in the `PigLatin` program from Chapter 3. For tracking the number of times each word appears, a `Map<String,Integer>` is precisely what you need. Any kind of map works for most of the code. If you want the words to appear in alphabetical order, you need to construct a `TreeMap`. The first time a word appears, the code for the `incrementCount` method sets its value in the map to 1; if the word appears again, `incrementCount` adds one to the previous value.

FIGURE 6-15   **Program to compute word frequencies**

```
/*
 * File: WordFrequency.java
 * ----------------------------
 * This program computes the frequency of words in a text file.
 */

package edu.stanford.cs.javacs2.ch6;

import java.io.BufferedReader;
import java.io.FileReader;
import java.io.IOException;
import java.util.Map;
import java.util.Scanner;
import java.util.TreeMap;

public class WordFrequency {

    public void run() {
        Scanner sysin = new Scanner(System.in);
        try {
            BufferedReader rd = openFileReader(sysin, "Input file: ");
            Map<String,Integer> wordCounts = new TreeMap<String,Integer>();
            while (true) {
                String line = rd.readLine();
                if (line == null) break;
                countWords(line, wordCounts);
            }
            rd.close();
            displayCounts(wordCounts);
        } catch (IOException ex) {
            throw new RuntimeException(ex.toString());
        }
    }

/*
 * Breaks a line into words, updating the word counts.
 */

    private void countWords(String line, Map<String,Integer> wordCounts) {
        String word = "";
        for (int i = 0; i < line.length(); i++) {
            char ch = line.charAt(i);
            if (Character.isLetter(ch)) {
                word += Character.toLowerCase(ch);
            } else {
                if (!word.isEmpty()) {
                    incrementCount(word, wordCounts);
                    word = "";
                }
            }
        }
        if (!word.isEmpty()) incrementCount(word, wordCounts);
    }
```

☞

FIGURE 6-15 **Program to compute word frequencies (continued)**

```java
/*
 * Increments the count for word in the map.
 */

   private void incrementCount(String word, Map<String,Integer> wordCounts) {
      if (wordCounts.containsKey(word)) {
         wordCounts.put(word, wordCounts.get(word) + 1);
      } else {
         wordCounts.put(word, 1);
      }
   }

/*
 * Displays the word count along with the word.
 */

   private void displayCounts(Map<String,Integer> wordCounts) {
      for (String word : wordCounts.keySet()) {
         System.out.printf("%4d  %s%n", wordCounts.get(word), word);
      }
   }

/*
 * Asks the user for the name of a file and then returns a BufferedReader
 * for that file.  If the file cannot be opened, the method gives the user
 * another chance.  The sysin argument is a Scanner open on the System.in
 * stream.  The prompt gives the user more information about the file.
 */

   private BufferedReader openFileReader(Scanner sysin, String prompt) {
      BufferedReader rd = null;
      while (rd == null) {
         try {
            System.out.print(prompt);
            String name = sysin.nextLine();
            rd = new BufferedReader(new FileReader(name));
         } catch (IOException ex) {
            System.out.println("Can't open that file.");
         }
      }
      return rd;
   }

/* Main program */

   public static void main(String[] args) {
      new WordFrequency().run();
   }

}
```

Computing word frequencies turns out to be valuable for applications in which the use of such modern tools might at first seem surprising. For example, over the last few decades, computer analysis has become central to resolving questions of disputed authorship. There are several plays from the Elizabethan era that might have been written by Shakespeare, even though they are not part of the traditional canon. Conversely, several Shakespearean plays that are attributed to Shakespeare have parts that don't sound like his other works and may have in fact been written by someone else. To resolve such questions, Shakespearean scholars often compute the frequency of particular words that appear in the text and see whether those frequencies match what we expect to find according to an analysis of Shakespeare's known works.

Suppose, for example, that you have a text file containing a passage from Shakespeare, such as the following well-known lines from Act 5 of *Macbeth:*

Macbeth.txt

```
Tomorrow, and tomorrow, and tomorrow
Creeps in this petty pace from day to day
```

If you are trying to determine the relative frequency of words in Shakespeare's writing, you can use the **WordFrequency** program to count how many times each word appears in the data file. Thus, given the file **Macbeth.txt**, you would like your program to produce something like the following output:

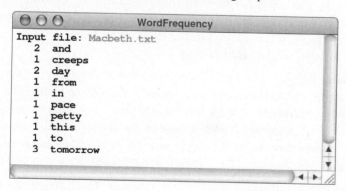

```
WordFrequency
Input file: Macbeth.txt
   2   and
   1   creeps
   2   day
   1   from
   1   in
   1   pace
   1   petty
   1   this
   1   to
   3   tomorrow
```

Summary

This chapter introduced the Java classes **ArrayList**, **Stack**, **Queue**, **Map**, and **Set**, which together constitute a powerful framework for storing collections. For the moment, you have looked at these classes only as a client. In later chapters, you will have a chance to learn more about how they are implemented.

Important points in this chapter include:

- Data structures defined in terms of their behavior rather than their representation are called *abstract data types*. Abstract data types have several important advantages over more primitive data structures. These advantages include simplicity, flexibility, and security.

- Classes that contain other objects as elements of an integral collection are called *collection classes*. In Java, collection classes are defined as *parameterized types,* in which the type name of the element appears in angle brackets after the name of the collection class. For example, the class `ArrayList<String>` signifies an `ArrayList` containing values of type `String`.

- The parameterized type facility in Java can be used only with classes, and not with primitive types. This limitation is not particularly onerous in practice because Java defines *wrapper classes* for each of the primitive types and offers automatic boxing and unboxing of primitive values and their corresponding wrapper classes. Thus, you can create an `ArrayList<Integer>` that functions as an array of integer values.

- The `ArrayList` class is an abstract data type that behaves in much the same fashion as a one-dimensional array but is much more powerful. Unlike an array, an `ArrayList` can grow dynamically as elements are added and removed.

- The `Stack` class represents a collection of objects whose behavior is defined by the property that items are removed from a stack in the opposite order from which they were added: last in, first out (LIFO). The fundamental operations on a stack are `push`, which adds a value to the stack, and `pop`, which removes and returns the value most recently pushed.

- The `Queue` interface specifies an abstraction that is similar to the `Stack` class except for the fact that elements are removed from a queue in the same order in which they were added: first in, first out (FIFO). The fundamental operations on a queue are `add`, which adds a value to the end of a queue, and `remove`, which removes and returns the value from the front. The `Queue` interface is implemented by the classes `ArrayDeque` and `LinkedList`.

- The `Map` interface makes it possible to associate *keys* with *values* in a way that enables clients to retrieve those associations efficiently. The fundamental operations on a map are `put`, which adds a key/value pair; `get`, which returns the value associated with a particular key; and `containsKey`, which checks whether a key is defined. The `Map` interface is implemented by the classes `HashMap` and `TreeMap`.

- The `Set` interface represents a collection in which the elements are unordered and in which each value appears only once, as with sets in mathematics. The fundamental operations on a set include `add`, which stores a new element in the set, and **contains**, which checks to see whether an element is in the set.   The **Map** interface is implemented by the classes **HashSet** and **TreeSet**.

- Java makes it easy to iterate through the elements of an array, an **ArrayList**, or a **Set** using the following extended **for** loop syntax:

```
for (type variable : collection) {
      body of the loop
   }
```

Each collection defines its own iteration order, as described in the section on "Iteration order" on page 217.

Review questions

1.   True or false: An abstract data type is one defined in terms of its behavior rather than its representation.

2.   What three advantages does this chapter cite for separating the behavior of a class from its underlying implementation?

3.   What is the Java Collections Framework?

4.   If you want to use the **ArrayList** class in a program, what **import** line do you need to add to your source file?

5.   What advantages does the **ArrayList** class offer over Java arrays?

6.   What is a *parameterized type?*

7.   What type name would you use to store an **ArrayList** of Boolean values?

8.   Is it legal in Java to declare an **ArrayList<int>**?

9.   What is a *wrapper class?*

10.   What method do you call to determine the number of elements in an **ArrayList**?

11.   If an **ArrayList** object has N elements, what is the legal range of values for the first argument to **add**? What about for the argument to **remove**?

12.   What do the acronyms *LIFO* and *FIFO* stand for? How do these terms apply to stacks and queues?

13.   What are the names of the two fundamental operations for a stack?

14.   What are the names for the corresponding operations for a queue?

15. What does the **peek** operation do in each of the stack and queue abstractions?

16. What are the two concrete types that implement the **Queue** interface?

17. What are the two type parameters used with the **Map** interface?

18. What happens if you call **get** for a key that doesn't exist in a map?

19. What difference between the **HashSet** class and the **TreeSet** class is most visible to clients?

20. What is the general form of the **for** loop pattern when you iterate over a collection?

21. How do you iterate over the keys in a map?

22. Describe the order in which the range-based **for** loop processes elements for each of the collection classes introduced in this chapter.

Exercises

1. Write a program that uses a stack to reverse a sequence of integers read from the console one number per line, as shown in the following sample run:

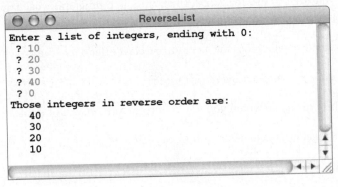

2. Write a program that checks whether the bracketing operators (parentheses, brackets, and curly braces) in a string are properly matched. As an example of proper matching, consider the string

```
{ s = 2 * (a[2] + 3); x = (1 + (2)); }
```

If you go through the string carefully, you will discover that all the bracketing operators are correctly nested, with each open parenthesis matched by a close parenthesis, each open bracket matched by a close bracket, and so on. On the other hand, the following strings are all unbalanced for the reasons indicated:

(([ ])   *The line is missing a close parenthesis.*
) (*The close parenthesis comes before the open parenthesis.*
{ (})   *The bracketing operators are improperly nested.*

3. The figures in this book are created using PostScript®, a powerful graphics language developed by the Adobe Corporation in the early 1980s. PostScript programs store their data on a stack. Many of the operators available in the PostScript language have the effect of manipulating the stack in some way. You can, for example, invoke the **pop** operator, which pops the top element off the stack, or the **exch** operator, which swaps the top two elements.

One of the most interesting (and surprisingly useful) PostScript operators is the **roll** operator, which takes two arguments, *n* and *k*. The effect of applying **roll** (*n*, *k*) is to rotate the top *n* elements of a stack by *k* positions, where the general direction of the rotation is toward the top of the stack. More specifically, **roll** (*n*, *k*) has the effect of removing the top *n* elements, cycling the top element to the last position *k* times, and then replacing the reordered elements on the stack. Figure 6-16 shows before and after pictures for three different examples of **roll**.

Write a function

```
void roll(Stack<char> & stack, int n, int k)
```

that implements the **roll** (*n*, *k*) operation on the specified stack. Your implementation should check that **n** and **k** are both nonnegative and that **n** is not larger than the stack size; if either of these conditions is violated, your implementation should throw a runtime exception with the message

```
roll: argument out of range
```

FIGURE 6-16 **Examples of the roll function for stacks**

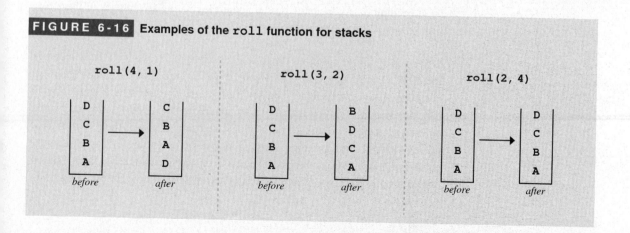

Note, however, that **k** can be larger than **n**, in which case the **roll** operation continues through more than a complete cycle. This case is illustrated by the final example in Figure 6-16, in which the top two elements on the stack are rolled four times, leaving the stack exactly as it started.

4.
> *And the first one now*
> *Will later be last*
> *For the times they are a-changin'.*
> —Bob Dylan, "The Times They Are a-Changin'," 1963

Following the inspiration from Bob Dylan's song (which is itself inspired by Matthew 19:30), write a function

```
void reverseQueue(Queue<String> queue)
```

that reverses the elements in the queue. Remember that you have no access to the internal representation of the queue and must therefore come up with an algorithm—presumably involving other structures—that accomplishes the task.

5.   You can extend the checkout-line simulation in Figure 6-9 to investigate important practical questions about how waiting lines behave. As a first step, rewrite the simulation so that there are several independent queues, as is usually the case in supermarkets. A customer arriving at the checkout area finds the shortest checkout line and enters that queue. Your revised simulation should report the same results as the simulation in the chapter.

6.   As a second extension to the checkout-line simulation, change the program from the preceding exercise so that there is a single waiting line served by multiple cashiers—a practice that has become more common in recent years. In each cycle of the simulation, any cashier who becomes idle serves the next customer in the queue. If you compare the data produced by this exercise and the preceding one, what can you say about the relative advantages of these two strategies for organizing a checkout line?

7.   Write a program to simulate the following experiment, which was included in the 1957 Disney film *Our Friend the Atom,* to illustrate the chain reactions involved in nuclear fission. The setting for the experiment is a large cubical box, the bottom of which is completely covered with 625 mousetraps arranged to form a square grid with 25 mousetraps on a side. Each of the mousetraps is initially loaded with two ping-pong balls. At the beginning of the simulation, an additional ping-pong ball is released from the top of the box and falls on one of the mousetraps. That mousetrap springs and shoots its two ping-pong

balls into the air. The ping-pong balls bounce around the sides of the box and eventually land on the floor, where they are likely to set off more mousetraps.

In writing this simulation, you should make the following simplifying assumptions:

- Every ping-pong ball that falls always lands on a mousetrap, chosen randomly by selecting a random row and column in the grid. If the trap is loaded, its balls are released into the air. If the trap has already been sprung, having a ball fall on it has no effect.

- Once a ball falls on a mousetrap—whether or not the trap is sprung—that ball stops and takes no further role in the simulation.

- Balls launched from a mousetrap bounce around the room and land again after a random number of simulation cycles have gone by. That random interval is chosen independently for each ball and is always between one and four cycles.

Your simulation should run until there are no balls in the air. At that point, your program should report how many time units have elapsed since the beginning, what percentage of the traps have been sprung, and the maximum number of balls in the air at any time in the simulation.

8. In May of 1844, Samuel F. B. Morse sent the message "What hath God wrought!" by telegraph from Washington to Baltimore, heralding the beginning of the age of electronic communication. To make it possible to communicate information using only the presence or absence of a single tone, Morse designed a coding system in which letters and other symbols are represented as coded sequences of short and long tones, traditionally called *dots* and *dashes*. In Morse code, the 26 letters of the alphabet are represented by the codes shown in Figure 6-17.

Write a program that reads in lines from the user and translates each line either to or from Morse code, depending on the first character of the line:

- If the line starts with a letter, you want to translate it to Morse code. Any characters other than the 26 letters should simply be ignored.

- If the line starts with a period (dot) or a hyphen (dash), it should be read as a series of Morse code characters that you need to translate back to letters. You may assume that each sequence of dots and dashes in the input string will be separated by spaces, and you are free to ignore any other characters that appear. Because there is no encoding for the space between words, the characters of the translated message will be run together when your program translates in this direction.

FIGURE 6-17 Morse code

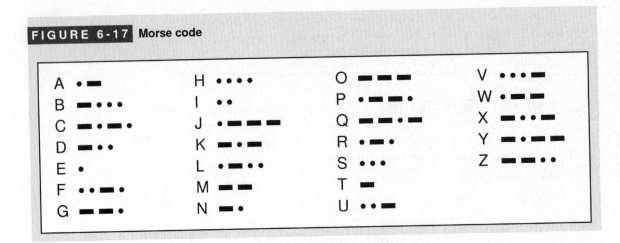

The program should end when the user enters a blank line. A sample run of this program (taken from the messages between the Titanic and the Carpathia in 1912) might look like this:

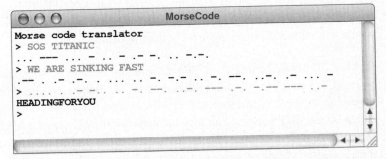

9. Telephone numbers in the United States and Canada are organized into various three-digit *area codes*. A single state or province often has many area codes, but a single area code never crosses a state or provincial boundary. This rule makes it possible to list the geographical locations of each area code in a data file. For this problem, assume that you have access to the file **AreaCodes.txt**, which lists all the area codes paired with their locations, as illustrated by the first few lines of that file:

AreaCodes.txt

```
201-New Jersey
202-District of Columbia
203-Connecticut
204-Manitoba
205-Alabama
206-Washington
```

Using the **AirportCodes** program from Figure 6-12 as a model, write the code necessary to read this file into a **Map<Integer,String>**, where the key is the area code and the value is the location. Once you've read in the data, write a main program that repeatedly asks the user for an area code and then looks up the corresponding location, as illustrated in the following sample run:

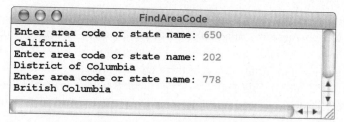

As the prompt suggests, however, your program should also allow users to enter the name of a state or province and have the program list all the area codes that serve that area, as illustrated by the following sample run:

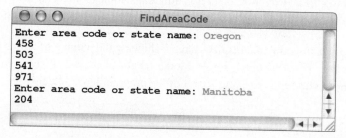

10. When you wrote the **FindAreaCode** program for the preceding exercise, it is likely that you generated the list of area codes for a state by looping through the entire map and printing any area codes that mapped to that state. Although this strategy is fine for small maps like that in the area code example, efficiency becomes an issue in working with much larger data maps.

    An alternative approach is to *invert* the map so that you can perform lookup operations in either direction. You can't, however, declare the inverted map as a **Map<String,Integer>**, because there is often more than one area code associated with a state. What you need to do instead is to make the inverted map a **Map< String,ArrayList<Integer> >** that maps each state name to an **ArrayList** of the area codes that serve that state. Rewrite the **FindAreaCode** program so that it creates an inverted map after reading in the data file and then uses that map to list the area codes for a state.

11. Section 3.6 defines the function **isPalindrome** that checks whether a word reads identically forward and backward. Use that function together with the English lexicon to display a list of all words that are palindromes.

12. In Scrabble, knowing the two-letter word list is important because those short words make it easy to "hook" a new word into tiles already on the board. Another list that Scrabble experts memorize is the list of three-letter words that can be formed by adding a letter to the front or back of a two-letter word. Write a program that generates this list.

13. One of the most important strategic principles in Scrabble is to conserve your **S** tiles, because the rules for English plurals mean that many words take an **S**-hook at the end. Some words, of course, allow an **S** tile to be added at the beginning, but it turns out that there are 680 words—including, for example, both the words *cold* and *hot*—that allow **S**-hooks on either end. Write a program that uses the English lexicon to make a list of all such words.

14. When you convert English to Pig Latin, most words turn into something that sounds vaguely Latinate but different from conventional English. There are, however, a few words whose Pig Latin equivalents just happen to be English words. For example, the Pig Latin translation of *trash* is *ashtray,* and the translation for *entry* is *entryway.* Write a program that lists all such words.

15. Write a program that displays a table showing the number of words that appear in the English lexicon, sorted by the length of the word. For the lexicon in **EnglishWords.txt**, the output of the program looks like this:

	WordCountsByLength
1	3
2	94
3	962
4	3862
5	8548
6	14383
7	21729
8	26448
9	18844
10	12308
11	7850
12	5194
13	3275
14	1775
15	954
16	495
17	251
18	89
19	48
20	21
21	6
22	3
24	1
28	1
29	1

Chapter 7
Classes and Objects

My object all sublime . . .

— William S. Gilbert, *The Mikado,* 1885

Although you have been using classes extensively throughout this book, you have not yet had the chance to define classes of your own besides the classes that implement programs. The purpose of this chapter is to fill that gap by giving you the tools to implement new classes that you can then use as tools for building applications. This chapter covers the fundamental mechanics of class design, stopping just short of the idea of inheritance, which is the focus of Chapter 8.

7.1 Classes and object-oriented design

Classes lie at the heart of Java's implementation of the object-oriented paradigm. As you know from the brief discussion in Chapter 1, classes constitute templates for creating objects. There may be many objects that are instances of a single class, but each of those objects is a primary instance of exactly one class. Classes also form hierarchies in which subclasses inherit behavior from their superclasses. In Java, every class has a unique superclass, which ensures that classes form an inheritance hierarchy. For every Java class, the inheritance hierarchy extends all the way up the superclass chain to `Object`, which represents the root of the class hierarchy.

Even without inheritance, classes offer the following advantages:

- *Classes combine independent data values into an integrated whole.* In this respect, classes offer a facility similar to records or structures in more traditional programming languages. The variables within a class that store this information are called *instance variables* because they are associated with each instance of a class. Instance variables are also sometimes called *fields.*

- *Classes associate behavior with the data stored in the object.* In addition to the instance variables, classes typically include method definitions that define the behavior of the class.

- *Classes form an abstraction barrier between the client and the implementation.* The implementer of a class can control the client's access to instance variables and methods, thereby making it possible to hide the underlying complexity. This abstraction barrier also protects the integrity of the data structures in the implementation from inadvertent or malicious manipulation by the client.

7.2 Defining a simple `Point` class

As a simple example of how classes work in Java, suppose that you are working with coordinates in an *x-y* grid in which the coordinates are always integers. Although it is possible to work with the *x* and *y* values independently, it is more convenient to define an abstract data type that combines an *x* and a *y* value. Since this unified pair of coordinate values is called a *point* in geometry, it makes sense to use the name `Point` for the corresponding type.

Java offers several strategies for defining a `Point` type, ranging in sophistication from simple structure types that have always been available in the C family of languages to more powerful structures that use a modern object-oriented style. The sections that follow explore these strategies, beginning with the structure-based model and then moving on to the class-based form.

Defining a point as a record type

In your past experience with programming, you have almost certainly encountered types that are defined by combining values of simpler types that already exist. Such types are called *records.* If you chose to adopt this simple approach—despite the fact that Java offers many better alternatives—you could define the `PointRecord` class as follows:

```
public class PointRecord {
    public int x;
    public int y;
};
```

This code defines the class `PointRecord` as a traditional record with two public instance variables named `x` and `y`, both of which are of type `int`.

When you work with classes in Java, it is important to keep in mind that the definition introduces a new type and does not in itself declare any variables. Once you have the definition, you can then use the type name to declare variables, just as you would with any other type. For example, if you include the local variable declaration

```
PointRecord p;
```

in a method, the compiler will reserve space for a variable of type `PointRecord` named `p`, just as the declaration

```
int n;
```

reserves space for a variable of type `int` named `n`. The variable `p`, however, does not include the space for the `x` and `y` components. In Java, objects are always stored as references, which means that the variable `p` is assigned only enough space to hold the address of a `PointRecord` object. To reserve space for the `x` and `y` components, you need to use the `new` operator to allocate a new object, much as you did for arrays in Chapter 5.

In most cases, it makes sense to allocate an object as part of the declaration. In this case, for example, you would like the declaration of the `PointRecord p` to include the code to create the underlying object.

In Java, you create new objects by writing the keyword **new**, followed by the name of the class and a parenthesized list of any arguments needed to create the new object. The **PointRecord** class defines no constructor methods, so the initialization of **p** will use an empty parameter list, as follows:

```
PointRecord p = new PointRecord();
```

This declaration gives rise to the following diagram:

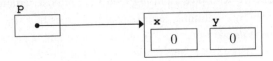

The important thing to notice in this diagram is that the value stored in **p** is a *reference* to the data structure in memory and not the structure itself, in exactly the same way that the value of an array is a reference, as discussed in Chapter 5. In Java, objects are *always* stored as references.

Given an object, you can select its fields using the **dot operator,** which is written in the form

   var . name

where *var* is the variable containing the object reference and *name* specifies the desired field. For example, you can use the expressions **p.x** and **p.y** to select the individual coordinate value of the **PointRecord** object whose address is stored in the variable **p**. Selection expressions are assignable, so you can initialize the fields of **p** to represent the point (2, 3) using the code

```
p.x = 2;
p.y = 3;
```

which leads to the state shown in the following diagram:

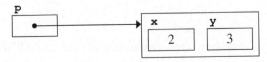

As noted in the first paragraph of this section, defining a class as a record is not the ideal approach. In this text, no public classes will include only public instance variables without any associated methods. At the same time, many applications later in this text will use this record-like model to define classes that are accessible only within the body of some other class. Such classes are called **inner classes.** Inner classes are important tools for expert Java programmers that are used in this text primarily to hide the class definition from clients. You will see examples of inner classes beginning in section 7.5.

Including methods in a Point class

The **java.awt** package defines a class called **Point** that stores a pair of x and y coordinates as a single object. One of the fundamental characteristics of any object is that it can be viewed both as a collection of individual fields and as a single value. At the lower levels of the implementation, the values stored in the individual fields are likely to be important. At higher levels of detail, it makes sense to focus on the value as an integral unit. Given a **Point** value, for example, you can assign that value to a variable, pass it as a parameter to a method, return it as a result, or convert it to a string. You can select the **x** and **y** fields if you need to look at the components individually, but you can also work with the value as a whole.

A simplified implementation of the library **Point** class appears in Figure 7-1 on the next page. As in the **PointRecord** definition, the **Point** class declares public instance variables **x** and **y**, which are directly visible to clients. The new features are two versions of a constructor to create new **Point** values and a new definition of the **toString** method that converts a **Point** value to a string.

The first version of the constructor takes no arguments and simply sets the values of the instance variables **x** and **y** to 0 using the multiple assignment pattern. In Java, a constructor that takes no arguments is called the ***default constructor*** for that class. Java automatically creates a default constructor with an empty body for any class in which you don't define any other constructors. The **Point** class, however, defines an explicit constructor that takes coordinate values for the x and y components. To export a constructor for the **Point** class that takes no arguments, the code must define that constructor explicitly.

The second version of the constructor has the following definition:

```
public Point(int x, int y) {
    this.x = x;
    this.y = y;
}
```

The effect of this constructor is to initialize the instance variable **x** to the value of the parameter **x** and the instance variable **y** to the value of the parameter **y**. The syntax, however, will seem confusing at first because of the appearance of the keyword **this**, which indicates a reference to the current object. The selection expression **this.x** indicates the instance variable **x** in the current object, which avoids confusion with the identically named parameter variable. When a local variable (including a parameter) has the same name as an instance variable, the compiler assumes that the name refers to the local copy unless you specify the keyword **this**. This process of hiding an instance variable with a local variable is called ***shadowing***.

FIGURE 7-1 Simplified version of the `Point` class

```
/*
 * File: Point.java
 * -----------------
 * This file exports a simplified version of the java.awt.Point class.
 */

package edu.stanford.cs.javacs2.ch7;

/**
 * This class combines a pair of <i>x</i> and <i>y</i> coordinates.
 */

public class Point {

/**
 * The <i>x</i> coordinate of this point.
 */

   public int x;

/**
 * The <i>y</i> coordinate of this point.
 */

   public int y;

/**
 * Constructs a new point at the origin (0, 0).
 */

   public Point() {
      x = y = 0;
   }

/**
 * Constructs a new point with the specified coordinates.
 *
 * @param x The <i>x</i> coordinate of the point
 * @param y The <i>y</i> coordinate of the point
 */

   public Point(int x, int y) {
      this.x = x;
      this.y = y;
   }

/**
 * Converts this point to its string representation.
 *
 * @return A string representation of this point
 */

   @Override
   public String toString() {
      return "(" + x + ", " + y + ")";
   }

}
```

The only other method in the definition of the `Point` class besides the two constructors is the `toString` method. The `toString` method is defined as part of the `Object` class, which means that every Java object has a `toString` method. When you define a new class, it is good practice to define an implementation of `toString` that performs the conversion in a way that is appropriate to the data type. The `toString` method for `Point` uses the concatenation operator to create a string that consists of the two components enclosed in parentheses and separated by a comma, as specified by the following code:

```
public String toString() {
    return "(" + x + ", " + y + ")";
}
```

Whenever a method in one class duplicates the name and parameter structure of a method in a superclass, the local definition *overrides* the definition from the superclass. To indicate that the decision to replace the definition of an existing method with a new one was intentional, it is now conventional in Java to specify that you are supplying a new implementation of an existing method by writing `@Override` before the new definition, as follows:

```
@Override
public String toString()
```

The `@Override` syntax is an example of what Java calls an ***annotation.*** Like comments, annotations provide documentation about the code even though those annotations have no effect when the program runs. Unlike comments, however, annotations are read by the compiler, which can then use the information to improve its operation. In the case of the `@Override` annotation, for example, the compiler checks to ensure that the method does indeed override a method from its superclass.

Although there is widespread agreement that it is good programming practice to use the `@Override` annotation, doing so can sometimes clutter a program listing so that it becomes harder to read. Although the source files supplied with this book include the `@Override` specification whenever it applies, the figures sometimes omit the `@Override` marker to save space and improve readability.

Javadoc comments

The code in Figure 7-1 also introduces an important set of conventions for writing comments for the public instance variables and methods in your classes. As you can see from the code, the comments that precede each of the definitions include a second asterisk in their opening line and begin with the character `/**`. Such comments are called *javadoc comments* because they are interpreted by the javadoc application that Java uses to prepare online documentation for each class. Inside a javadoc comment, you write comments that tell clients what they need to know to use the class, just as you would for traditional comments. These comments, however, can include HTML tags to improve formatting, as shown in the use of notations like `<i>x</i>`, which requests that x be set in italics. Most javadoc comments also include annotations called *tags,* of which the most common are `@param` and `@return`. The `@param` tag generates notes about method parameters, and the `@return` tag describes method results. The beginning of the javadoc page for the `Point` class appears in Figure 7-2.

FIGURE 7-2 Screen shot of the javadoc file for the simplified `Point` class

Package **Class** **Tree** **Deprecated** **Index** **Help**

PREV CLASS   NEXT CLASS   FRAMES   NO FRAMES
SUMMARY: NESTED | FIELD | CONSTR | METHOD   DETAIL: FIELD | CONSTR | METHOD

---

edu.stanford.cs.javacs2.ch7

Class Point

```
java.lang.Object
   └ edu.stanford.cs.javacs2.ch7.Point
```

```
public class Point
extends java.lang.Object
```

This class combines a pair of x and y coordinates.

Field Summary

int	x
	The x coordinate of this point.
int	y
	The y coordinate of this point.

Constructor Summary

Point()
    Constructs a new point at the origin (0, 0).

Point(int x, int y)
    Constructs a new point with the specified coordinates.

Method Summary

java.lang.String	**toString**()
	Converts this point to its string representation.

Including complete javadoc comments in every class is a useful habit to learn, but in a textbook can get in the way of understanding program listings, mostly because the HTML tags are hard to read and the added length increases the likelihood that a figure will extend across multiple pages. Thus, most of the figures in this book use traditional comments, although the source files supplied with this book that are intended to be used as tools for other applications include the full javadoc annotations.

Keeping instance variables private

The **Point** class in the **java.awt** package dates back to the first version of Java, and its design in some way betrays its age. Exporting public instance variables—as the **Point** class does with **x** and **y**—compromises the integrity of the class and violates the principle of encapsulation that is such an important part of modern object-oriented design. The public classes in this book never declare **public** instance variables, which prevents unauthorized clients from seeing those variables. Those classes instead mediate the client's access to the underlying instance variables through methods, thereby maintaining consistency with the principles of modern object-oriented design.

Figure 7-3 illustrates this technique by defining a **GPoint** class that is part of the simple graphics library you will have a chance to build in Chapter 8. In contrast to the **Point** class described in the preceding section, **GPoint** uses double-precision values for the x and y components. The corresponding instance variables are therefore declared to be of type **double**. More importantly, those variables are declared as **private** instead of **public**. The **GPoint** class provides access to these variables through the methods **getX** and **getY**. In computer science, methods that retrieve the values of instance variables are formally called *accessors,* but are more often known as *getters.* By convention, the name of a getter method begins with the prefix **get** followed by the name of the field, rewritten so that the first letter is capitalized. The getters for the **Point** class follow this convention.

In some cases, classes export methods that allow clients to change the value of the instance variables. Such methods are called *mutators* or, more informally, *setters.* It is, however, a bit unsatisfying to think about adding setter methods to a class so soon after deciding that it was important to make its instance variables private. After all, part of the reason for making instance variables private is to ensure that clients don't have unrestricted access to them. Including setter methods circumvents those restrictions and eliminates the advantages one might have obtained by making the variables private in the first place. In general, it is considerably safer to allow clients to *read* the values of the instance variables than it is to have clients *change* those values. As a result, setter methods are far less common than getters in object-oriented design.

FIGURE 7-3   Implementation of the GPoint class

```java
/*
 * File: GPoint.java
 * ------------------
 * This file exports a double-precision version of the Point class.
 */

package edu.stanford.cs.javacs2.ch8;

public class GPoint {

/*
 * Constructs a new GPoint at the origin (0, 0).
 */

   public GPoint() {
      x = y = 0.0;
   }

/*
 * Constructs a new GPoint with the specified coordinates.
 */

   public GPoint(double x, double y) {
      this.x = x;
      this.y = y;
   }

/*
 * Returns the x coordinate of this GPoint.
 */

   public double getX() {
      return x;
   }

/*
 * Returns the y coordinate of this GPoint.
 */

   public double getY() {
      return y;
   }

/*
 * Converts this GPoint to its string representation.
 */

   @Override
   public String toString() {
      return "(" + x + ", " + y + ")";
   }

/* Private instance variables */

   private double x;
   private double y;

}
```

In fact, many programmers take the recommendation against allowing change to an even higher level by making it impossible to change the values of any instance variables after an object has been created. Classes designed in this way are said to be *immutable.* The `GPoint` class is immutable, as are many of the library classes you have already seen, including the `String` described in Chapter 3 and the various wrapper classes introduced in Chapter 6. Immutable classes have many advantages that will become more evident later in this text.

◼ 7.3 Rational numbers

Although the `Point` and `GPoint` classes from section 7.2 illustrate the basic syntactic rules for defining new classes, developing a solid understanding of the topic requires you to consider more sophisticated examples. This section walks you through the design of a class to represent *rational numbers,* which are numbers that can be expressed as the quotient of two integers. In elementary school, you probably called these numbers *fractions.*

In some respects, rational numbers are similar to the floating-point numbers you have been using since Chapter 1. Both types of numbers can represent fractional values, such as 1.5, which is the rational number 3/2. The difference is that rational numbers are exact, while floating-point numbers are approximations limited by the precision of the hardware.

To get a sense of why this distinction might be important, consider the arithmetic problem of adding together the following fractions:

$$\frac{1}{2} + \frac{1}{3} + \frac{1}{6}$$

Basic arithmetic—or even a little intuition—makes it clear that the mathematically precise answer is 1, but that answer is difficult to get if you use the type `double`. The following program, which uses double-precision arithmetic to compute the sum of these three fractions, illustrates the problem:

```
public void run() {
    double a = 1.0 / 2.0;
    double b = 1.0 / 3.0;
    double c = 1.0 / 6.0;
    double sum = a + b + c;
    System.out.println("1/2 + 1/3 + 1/6 = " + sum);
}
```

If you run this program, you get the following result:

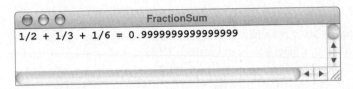

The problem is that the memory cells used to store numbers inside a computer have a limited storage capacity, which in turn restricts the precision they can offer. Within the limits of double-precision arithmetic, the sum of one-half plus one-third plus one-sixth is closer to 0.9999999999999999 than it is to 1.0. Worse still, the calculated value of the sum really is less than 1 and would show up as such if you were to test it in your program. At the end of the run, the value of the expression `sum < 1` would be **true**, and the value of `sum == 1` would be **false**. That result is all rather unsettling from a mathematical point of view.

By contrast, rational numbers are not subject to rounding errors because no approximations are involved. What's more, rational numbers obey well-defined arithmetic rules, which are summarized in Figure 7-4. Java, however, does not include rational numbers among its predefined types. If you want to use rational numbers in Java, you have to define a class to represent them.

A strategy for defining new classes

When you work in object-oriented languages, designing new classes is the most important skill you need to master. As with much of programming, designing a new class is as much an art as it is a science. Developing effective class designs requires a strong sense of aesthetics and sensitivity to the needs and desires of clients who will use those classes as tools. Experience and practice are the best teachers, but following a general design framework can help get you started along this path.

In my experience, I've found that the following step-by-step approach is often helpful:

1. *Think generally about how clients are likely to use the class.* From the very beginning of the process, it is essential to remember that library classes are

---

FIGURE 7-4 **Rules for rational arithmetic**

Addition

$$\frac{a}{b} + \frac{c}{d} = \frac{ad + bc}{bd}$$

Multiplication

$$\frac{a}{b} \times \frac{c}{d} = \frac{ac}{bd}$$

Subtraction

$$\frac{a}{b} - \frac{c}{d} = \frac{ad - bc}{bd}$$

Division

$$\frac{a}{b} \div \frac{c}{d} = \frac{ad}{bc}$$

designed to meet the needs of clients and not to make things convenient for the implementer. In a professional context, the most effective way to ensure that a new class meets their needs is to involve clients in the design process. At a minimum, however, you need to put yourself in the client role as you sketch the outlines of the class design.

2. *Determine what information belongs in the private state of each object.* Although the private section is conceptually part of the implementation of a class, it simplifies the later design phases if you have at least an intuitive sense of what information objects of this class contain. In many cases, you can immediately write down the instance variables that go into the private section. Although such precise details are not essential at this point, having a feeling for the inner structure makes it easier to define the constructors and methods.

3. *Define a set of constructors to create new objects.* Since classes often define more than one overloaded form of the constructor, it is useful to think from the client's point of view about the types of objects that will need to be created and what information the client will have on hand at that time. Typically, every class exports a default constructor, which makes it possible for clients to declare variables of that class and initialize them later on. During this phase, it is also useful for you to consider whether the constructors need to apply any restrictions to ensure that the resulting objects are valid.

4. *Enumerate the operations that will become the public methods of the class.* In this phase, the goal is to write the prototypes for the exported methods, thereby adding specificity to the general outline you developed at the beginning of the process.

5. *Code and test the implementation.* Once you have the interface specification, you need to write the code that implements it. Writing the implementation is not only essential to having a working program but also offers validation for the design. As you write the implementation, it is sometimes necessary to revisit the interface design if, for example, you discover that a particular feature is difficult to implement at an acceptable level of efficiency. As the implementer, you also have a responsibility to test your implementation to ensure that the class delivers the functionality it advertises in the interface.

The sections that follow carry out these steps for the `Rational` class.

Adopting the client perspective

As a first step toward the design of the `Rational` class, you need to think about what features your clients are likely to need. In a large company, you might have various implementation teams that would need to use rational numbers and could give you a good sense of what they needed. In that setting, it would be useful to work together with those clients to agree on a set of design goals.

Since this example is a textbook scenario, however, it isn't possible for you to schedule meetings with prospective clients. The primary purpose of the example is to illustrate the structure of class definitions in Java. Given these limitations and the need to manage the complexity of the example, it makes sense to limit the design goals so that the **Rational** class implements only the arithmetic operations defined in Figure 7-4.

Specifying the private state of the Rational class

For the **Rational** class, the private state is easy to specify. A rational number is defined as the quotient of two integers. Each rational object must therefore keep track of these two values. The declarations of the instance variables will therefore look something like this:

```
private int num;
private int den;
```

The names for these variables are shortened versions of the mathematical terms *numerator* and *denominator,* which refer to the upper and lower parts of a fraction.

It is interesting to note that the instance variables of the **Point** class and the **Rational** class are the same except for the variable names. The values maintained by each of these classes consist of a pair of integers. What makes these classes different is the interpretation of those integers, which is reflected in the operations each class supports.

Defining constructors for the Rational class

Given that a rational number represents the quotient of two integers, one of the constructors will presumably take two integers representing the components of the fraction. Having such a constructor makes it possible, for example, to define the rational number one-third by calling **new Rational(1, 3)**.

Although it isn't necessary to think about the implementation at this stage in the process, keeping implementation issues in the back of your mind can sometimes save you headaches later on. In this case, it is worth recognizing that it isn't appropriate to implement this constructor in the following form:

```
public Rational(int x, int y) {
    num = x;
    den = y;
}
```

The problem with this implementation is that the rules of arithmetic place constraints on the values of the numerator and denominator—constraints that need to be incorporated into the constructor. The most obvious constraint is that the value of the denominator cannot be zero. The constructor should check for this case and throw an exception if it occurs. There is, however, a more subtle issue. If the client is given unconstrained choice for the numerator and denominator, there will be many different ways to represent the same rational number. For example, the rational number one-third can be written as a fraction in any of the following ways:

$$\frac{1}{3} \qquad \frac{2}{6} \qquad \frac{100}{300} \qquad \frac{-1}{-3}$$

Given that these fractions all represent the same rational number, it is inelegant to allow arbitrary combinations of numerator and denominator values in a **Rational** object. It simplifies the implementation if every rational number has a consistent, unique representation.

Mathematicians achieve this goal by insisting on the following rules:

- The fraction is always expressed in lowest terms, which means that any common factors are eliminated from the numerator and the denominator. In practice, the easiest way to reduce a fraction to lowest terms is to divide both the numerator and the denominator by their greatest common divisor, which you already know how to compute using the **gcd** method presented on page 63.

- The denominator is always positive, which means that the sign of the value is stored with the numerator.

- The rational number 0 is always represented as the fraction 0/1.

Implementing these rules results in the following code for the constructor:

```
public Rational(int x, int y) {
   if (y == 0) {
      throw new RuntimeException("Division by zero");
   }
   if (x == 0) {
      num = 0;
      den = 1;
   } else {
      int g = gcd(abs(x), abs(y));
      num = x / g;
      den = abs(y) / g;
      if (y < 0) num = -num;
   }
}
```

You might, however, want to include other forms of the constructor as well. In particular, you might want clients to be able to write

```
Rational wholeNumber = new Rational(n);
```

to create a new **Rational** number from the integer **n**. It is also conventional to define a *default constructor* that takes no arguments and sets the value of the object to some reasonable default, which for numeric values is presumably 0. Thus, it should also be possible to write the following declaration:

```
Rational zero = new Rational();
```

Although it would be easy enough in this example to write these new constructors from scratch, it is often easier to pass the job along to other forms of the overloaded constructor. In Java, you indicate a call to another constructor in the same class by using the keyword **this** as if it were a method, as illustrated in the following definitions:

```
public Rational() {
   this(0);
}

public Rational(int n) {
   this(n, 1);
}
```

Defining methods for the `Rational` class

In light of the earlier decision to limit the functionality of the **Rational** class to the arithmetic operations **+**, **-**, *****, and **/**, the decision about what methods to export has in some sense already been made. Since Java does not allow you to assign new meanings to the standard operators, you need to define methods that implement these operations, presumably named **add**, **subtract**, **multiply**, and **divide**. Like all operations on objects, these methods use the receiver syntax. Thus, instead of writing the intuitively satisfying declaration

```
Rational sum = a + b + c;
```

Java requires you to write

```
Rational sum = a.add(b).add(c);
```

Although there are many other methods and operators that would make sense in a professional implementation of the **Rational** class, the only additional facilities included in this example are a **toString** method that converts a **Rational** number to a string. As noted earlier in the chapter, it is good practice to override **toString** in the classes you design because doing so enables you to display those values in a human-readable form, which is useful for both testing and debugging.

Implementing the Rational class

The complete implementation of the **Rational** class appears in Figure 7-5. Since the only complex part of the implementation is the constructor for which you have already seen the necessary code, the contents of **Rational.java** are reasonably straightforward. The definitions of the arithmetic methods follow directly from the mathematical definitions in Figure 7-4. For example, the implementation of **multiply**

```
public Rational multiply(Rational r2) {
    return new Rational(this.num * r2.num,
                        this.den * r2.den);
}
```

is a direct translation of the rules for multiplying rational numbers **r1** and **r2**, as long as you keep in mind that **r1** is the current object:

$$r1 \cdot r2 = \frac{r1_{num}\ r2_{num}}{r1_{den}\ r2_{den}}$$

The use of the keyword **this** to indicate the first rational number is in some sense optional, because the instance variable names **num** and **den** would automatically refer to the current object. Particularly when more than one object of the current class is involved, including an explicit reference to **this** emphasizes the connection to the current object.

Once you have completed the code for the **Rational** class, the program

```
public void run() {
    Rational a = new Rational(1, 2);
    Rational b = new Rational(1, 3);
    Rational c = new Rational(1, 6);
    Rational sum = a.add(b).add(c);;
    System.out.println("1/2 + 1/3 + 1/6 = " + sum);
}
```

produces the following sample run:

```
RationalSum
1/2 + 1/3 + 1/6 = 1
```

which is mathematically more reassuring than the answer 0.9999999999999999 shown in the sample run of the **FractionSum** program on page 242.

FIGURE 7-5 Simple definition of the `Rational` class

```
/*
 * File: Rational.java
 * --------------------
 * This file defines a simple class for representing rational numbers.
 */

package edu.stanford.cs.javacs2.ch7;

/**
 * This class represents a rational number (the quotient of two integers).
 */

public class Rational {

/**
 * Creates a new Rational initialized to zero.
 */

   public Rational() {
      this(0);
   }

/**
 * Creates a new Rational from the integer argument.
 *
 * @param n The initial value
 */

   public Rational(int n) {
      this(n, 1);
   }

/**
 * Creates a new Rational with the value x / y.
 *
 * @param x The numerator of the rational number
 * @param y The denominator of the rational number
 */

   public Rational(int x, int y) {
      if (y == 0) throw new RuntimeException("Division by zero");
      if (x == 0) {
         num = 0;
         den = 1;
      } else {
         int g = gcd(Math.abs(x), Math.abs(y));
         num = x / g;
         den = Math.abs(y) / g;
         if (y < 0) num = -num;
      }
   }
```

FIGURE 7-5 Simple definition of the `Rational` class (continued)

```java
/**
 * Adds the current number (r1) to the rational number r2 and returns the sum.
 *
 * @param r2 The rational number to be added
 * @return The sum of the current number and r2
 */

   public Rational add(Rational r2) {
      return new Rational(this.num * r2.den + r2.num * this.den,
                          this.den * r2.den);
   }

/**
 * Subtracts the rational number r2 from this one (r1).
 *
 * @param r2 The rational number to be subtracted
 * @return The result of subtracting r2 from the current number
 */

   public Rational subtract(Rational r2) {
      return new Rational(this.num * r2.den - r2.num * this.den,
                          this.den * r2.den);
   }

/**
 * Multiplies this number (r1) by the rational number r2.
 *
 * @param r2 The rational number used as a multiplier
 * @return The result of multiplying the current number by r2
 */

   public Rational multiply(Rational r2) {
      return new Rational(this.num * r2.num, this.den * r2.den);
   }

/**
 * Divides this number (r1) by the rational number r2.
 *
 * @param r2 The rational number used as a divisor
 * @return The result of dividing the current number by r2
 */

   public Rational divide(Rational r2) {
      return new Rational(this.num * r2.den, this.den * r2.num);
   }
```

FIGURE 7-5 **Simple definition of the Rational class (continued)**

```
/**
 * Creates a string representation of this rational number.
 *
 * @return The string representation of this rational number
 */

   @Override
   public String toString() {
      if (den == 1) {
         return "" + num;
      } else {
         return num + "/" + den;
      }
   }

/**
 * Calculates the greatest common divisor using Euclid's algorithm.
 *
 * @param x First integer
 * @param y Second integer
 * @return The greatest common divisor of x and y
 */

   private int gcd(int x, int y) {
      int r = x % y;
      while (r != 0) {
         x = y;
         y = r;
         r = x % y;
      }
      return y;
   }

/* Private instance variables */

   private int num;      /* The numerator of this Rational   */
   private int den;      /* The denominator of this Rational */

}
```

7.4 Designing a token scanner class

In Chapter 3, the most sophisticated example of string processing is the Pig Latin translator. As it appears in Figure 3-4, the **PigLatin** program decomposes the problem into two phases: the **lineToPigLatin** method divides the input line into words and then calls **wordToPigLatin** to convert each word to its Pig Latin form. The first phase of this decomposition, however, is not at all specific to the Pig Latin domain. Many applications need to divide a string into words, or more generally, into logical units that may be larger than a single character. In computer science, such units are typically called *tokens.*

Since the problem of dividing a string into individual tokens comes up frequently in applications, it is useful to build a library package that takes care of that task. This section introduces a **TokenScanner** class designed for that purpose. The primary goal of the **TokenScanner** design is to offer a package that is both simple to use and flexible enough to meet the needs of a variety of clients.

What clients want from a token scanner

As always, the best way to begin the design of the **TokenScanner** class is to look at the problem from the client perspective. Every client that wants to use a scanner starts with a source of tokens, which might be a string but might also be an input stream for applications that read data from files. In either case, what the client needs is some way to retrieve individual tokens from that source.

There are several strategies for designing a **TokenScanner** class that offers the necessary functionality. You could, for example, have the token scanner return a vector containing the entire list of tokens. That strategy, however, isn't appropriate for applications that work with large input file, because the scanner has to create a single vector containing the entire list of tokens. A more space-efficient approach is to have the scanner deliver its tokens one at a time. When you use this design, the process of reading tokens from a scanner has the following pseudocode form:

> *Set the input for the token scanner to be some string or input stream.*
> **while** (*more tokens are available*) {
>   *Read the next token.*
> }

This pseudocode structure immediately suggests the sort of methods that the **TokenScanner** class will need to support. From this example, you would expect **TokenScanner** to export the following methods:

- A **setInput** method that allows clients to specify the token source. Ideally, this method should be overloaded to take either a string or an input stream.

- A **hasMoreTokens** method that tests whether the token scanner has any tokens left to process.

- A **nextToken** method that scans and returns the next token.

These methods define the operational structure of a token scanner and are largely independent of the specifics of the applications. Different applications, however, define tokens in all sorts of different ways, which means that the **TokenScanner** class must give the client some control over what types of tokens are recognized.

The need to recognize different types of tokens is easiest to illustrate by offering a few examples. As a starting point, it is instructive to revisit the problem of translating English into Pig Latin. If you rewrite the **PigLatin** program to use the token scanner, you can't ignore the spaces and punctuation marks, because those characters need to be part of the output. In the context of the Pig Latin problem, tokens fall into one of two categories:

1. A string of consecutive alphanumeric characters representing a word

2. A single-character string consisting of a space or punctuation mark

If you gave the token scanner the input

```
This is Pig Latin.
```

calling **nextToken** repeatedly would return the following sequence of eight tokens:

| This | | is | | Pig | | Latin | . |

Other applications, by contrast, are likely to define tokens in different ways. Your Java compiler, for example, uses a token scanner to break programs into tokens that make sense in the programming context, including identifiers, constants, operators, and other symbols that define the syntactic structure of the language. For example, if you give the compiler's token scanner the line

```
double area = Math.PI * r * r;
```

you would like it to deliver up the following sequence of tokens:

| double | area | = | Math | . | PI | * | r | * | r | ; |

These two applications differ somewhat in the definition of a token. In the Pig Latin translator, anything that's not a sequence of alphanumeric characters is returned as a single-character token, including the spaces. By contrast, token scanners for programming languages usually ignore whitespace characters.

As you will learn if you go on to take a course on compilers, it is possible to build a token scanner that allows the client to specify what constitutes a legal token, typically by supplying a precise set of rules. That design offers the greatest possible generality. Generality, however, sometimes comes at the expense of simplicity. If you force clients to specify the rules for token formation, they need to learn how to write those rules, which is similar in many respects to learning a new language. Worse still, the rules for token formation are often difficult for clients to get right, particularly if they need to recognize a complex pattern, such as the one that compilers use to recognize floating-point numbers.

If your goal in the interface is to maximize simplicity, it is probably better to design the **TokenScanner** class so that clients can enable specific options that allow the token scanner to recognize specific token types in particular application contexts. If all you want is a token scanner that collects consecutive alphanumeric characters into words, you use the `TokenScanner` class in its simplest possible configuration. If you instead want the `TokenScanner` class to identify the units in a Java program, you can enable options that tell the scanner, for instance, to ignore whitespace characters, to treat quoted strings as single units, and to recognize particular combinations of punctuation marks as multicharacter operators.

The `TokenScanner` class

The `edu.stanford.cs.javacs2.tokenscanner` package exports a class called `TokenScanner` that offers considerable flexibility without sacrificing simplicity. The methods exported by the complete version of `TokenScanner` appear in Figure 7-6. The standard pattern for using the `TokenScanner` class is to create a token scanner for a particular input string and then to call `nextToken` repeatedly until `hasNextToken` returns `false`. If, for instance, the input for the scanner comes from the string `line`, you could use the following code to print all the tokens in the line:

```
TokenScanner scanner = new TokenScanner(line);
while (scanner.hasMoreTokens()) {
   System.out.println(scanner.nextToken());
}
```

The default behavior for a `TokenScanner` object is to return all tokens, including those composed of a single whitespace character. If you were building a programming-language application, you might want to tell the scanner to ignore those tokens by calling

```
scanner.ignoreWhitespace();
```

The full version of the `TokenScanner` class contains several other options, such as the ability to read floating-point numbers, quoted strings, and multicharacter operators. These options are shown in the list of `TokenScanner` methods in Figure 7-6. The list of available methods also includes several other useful facilities, such as scanning tokens from a reader instead of a string, determining the type of a token, and saving previously read tokens so that they can be read again at a later time.

The code for the complete `TokenScanner` class is too long to present in this book, but Figure 7-7 implements several of the more important methods and gives you a good sense of how the `TokenScanner` class works.

FIGURE 7-6 Methods exported by the full version of the `TokenScanner` class

Constructors

`TokenScanner()`
`TokenScanner(`*str*`)`
`TokenScanner(`*infile*`)`
	Initializes a scanner object. The source for the tokens is initialized from the specified string or input file. If no token source is provided, the client must call `setInput` before reading tokens from the scanner.

Methods for reading tokens

`hasMoreTokens()`	Returns `true` if there are more tokens to read from the input source.
`nextToken()`	Returns the next token from this scanner. If `nextToken` is called when no tokens are available, it returns the empty string.
`saveToken(token)`	Saves the specified token as part of this scanner's internal state so that it will be returned on the next call to `nextToken`. The library implementation allows clients to save any number of tokens, which are then delivered in a stack-like fashion.

Methods for controlling scanner options

`ignoreWhitespace()`	Tells the scanner to ignore whitespace characters.
`ignoreComments()`	Tells the scanner to ignore comments, which can be in either the slash-star or slash-slash form.
`scanNumbers()`	Tells the scanner to recognize any legal number as a single token. The syntax for numbers is the same as that used in Java.
`scanStrings()`	Tells the scanner to return a string enclosed in quotation marks as a single token. The quotation marks (which may be either single or double quotes) are included in the scanned token so that clients can differentiate strings from other token types.
`addWordCharacters(`*str*`)`	Adds the characters in `str` to the set of characters legal in a word.
`addOperator(`*op*`)`	Defines a new multicharacter operator. The scanner will return the longest defined operator, but will always return at least one character.

Miscellaneous methods

`setInput(`*str*`)` `setInput(`*infile*`)`	Sets the input source for this scanner to the specified string or input stream. Any tokens remaining in the previous source are lost.
`getPosition()`	Returns the current position of the scanner in the input stream.
`isWordCharacter(`*ch*`)`	Returns `true` if the character *ch* is valid in a word.
`verifyToken(`*expected*`)`	Reads the next token and makes sure it matches the string *expected*.
`getTokenType(`*token*`)`	Returns the type of the token, which must be one of the following constants: `EOF`, `SEPARATOR`, `WORD`, `NUMBER`, `STRING`, `OPERATOR`.

FIGURE 7-7 Simplified implementation of the `TokenScanner` class

```
/*
 * File: TokenScanner.java
 * ------------------------
 * This file exports a simplified version of the TokenScanner class.
 */

package edu.stanford.cs.javacs2.ch7;

/**
 * This class provides an abstract data type for dividing a string
 * into tokens, which are strings of consecutive characters that form
 * logical units.  In this simplified version of the TokenScanner class,
 * there are just two types of tokens:
 *
 * 1. Word -- A string of consecutive letters and digits
 * 2. Operator -- A single character string
 *
 * To use this class, you must first create a TokenScanner instance using
 * the declaration
 *
 *     TokenScanner scanner = new TokenScanner(str);
 *
 * Once you have initialized the scanner, you can retrieve the next token
 * from the token stream by calling
 *
 *     token = scanner.nextToken();
 *
 * To determine whether any tokens remain to be read, you can either
 * call the predicate method scanner.hasMoreTokens() or check to see
 * whether nextToken returns the empty string.
 *
 * The following code fragment serves as a pattern for processing
 * each token in the string inputString:
 *
 *     TokenScanner scanner < new TokenScanner(inputString);
 *     while (scanner.hasMoreTokens()) {
 *         String token < scanner.nextToken();
 *         . . . code to process the token . . .
 *     }
 *
 * By default, TokenScanner treats whitespace characters as operators.
 * You can ignore these characters, by calling scanner.ignoreWhitespace();
 */

public class TokenScanner {

/**
 * Initializes a new TokenScanner object.
 */

   public TokenScanner() {
      ignoreWhitespaceFlag = false;
      setInput("");
   }
```

FIGURE 7-7 Simplified implementation of the TokenScanner class (continued)

```java
/**
 * Initializes a new TokenScanner object that reads tokens from the
 * specified string.
 */

   public TokenScanner(String str) {
       this();
       setInput(str);
   }

/**
 * Sets this scanner input to the specified string.  Any previous input
 * string is discarded.
 */

   public void setInput(String str) {
       input = str;
       savedToken = null;
       cp = 0;
   }

/**
 * Returns the next token from this scanner.  If it is called when no
 * tokens are available, nextToken returns the empty string.
 */

   public String nextToken() {
       String token = savedToken;
       savedToken = null;
       if (token == null) {
           token = "";
           if (ignoreWhitespaceFlag) skipWhitespace();
           if (cp == input.length()) return "";
           char ch = input.charAt(cp++);
           token += ch;
           if (Character.isLetterOrDigit(ch)) {
               while (cp < input.length() &&
                       Character.isLetterOrDigit(input.charAt(cp))) {
                   token += input.charAt(cp++);
               }
           }
       }
       return token;
   }

/**
 * Saves one token to reread later.
 */

   public void saveToken(String token) {
       savedToken = token;
   }
```

FIGURE 7-7 Simplified implementation of the TokenScanner class (continued)

```java
/**
 * Returns true if there are more tokens for this scanner to read.
 */

   public boolean hasMoreTokens() {
      if (ignoreWhitespaceFlag) skipWhitespace();
      return cp < input.length();
   }

/**
 * Causes the scanner to ignore whitespace characters.
 */

   public void ignoreWhitespace() {
      ignoreWhitespaceFlag = true;
   }

/**
 * Skips over any whitespace characters before the next token.
 */

   private void skipWhitespace() {
      while (cp < input.length() && Character.isWhitespace(input.charAt(cp))) {
         cp++;
      }
   }

/* Private instance variables */

   private String input;
   private String savedToken;
   private int cp;
   private boolean ignoreWhitespaceFlag;

}
```

The `TokenScanner` class makes it easier to write many applications. You can, for example, simplify `PigLatin.java` by rewriting `lineToPigLatin` like this:

```java
   private String lineToPigLatin(String line) {
      TokenScanner scanner = new TokenScanner(line);
      String result = "";
      while (scanner.hasMoreTokens()) {
         String word = scanner.nextToken();
         if (Character.isLetter(word.charAt(0))) {
            word = wordToPigLatin(word);
         }
         result += word;
      }
      return result;
   }
```

While the new version of **wordToPigLatin** is shorter than the original implementation, the real simplification is conceptual. The original code had to operate at the level of individual characters; the new version gets to work with complete words, because the **TokenScanner** class takes care of the low-level details.

7.5 Linking objects together

In Java, all objects are stored as references, which means that the value recorded in a variable of any object type is always simply an address. This fact makes it possible to record connections among different values in a larger data structure. When one data structure contains a reference to another, those structures are said to be *linked.* In later chapters, you will see many examples of linked structures. To give you a preview of those coming attractions and to provide more examples of the use of object references, the next two sections introduce a fundamental data structure called a *linked list* in which the references connect individual data values in a single linear chain.

The Beacons of Gondor

My favorite example of a linked list takes its inspiration from the following passage in *The Return of the King* by J. R. R. Tolkien:

> For answer Gandalf cried aloud to his horse. "On, Shadowfax! We must hasten. Time is short. See! The beacons of Gondor are alight, calling for aid. War is kindled. See, there is the fire on Amon Dîn, and flame on Eilenach; and there they go speeding west: Nardol, Erelas, Min-Rimmon, Calenhad, and the Halifirien on the borders of Rohan."

In adapting this scene for the concluding episode in his *Lord of the Rings* film trilogy, Peter Jackson produced an evocative interpretation of this scene. After the first beacon is lit in the towers of Minas Tirith, we see the signal pass from mountaintop to mountaintop as the keepers of each signal tower, ever vigilant, light their own fires when they see the triggering fire at the preceding station. The message of Gondor's danger thus passes quickly over the many leagues that separate it from Rohan, as illustrated in Figure 7-8.

FIGURE 7-8 Schematic diagram of Tolkien's Beacons of Gondor

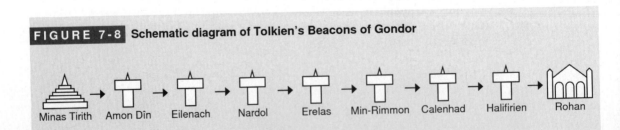

To simulate the Beacons of Gondor in Java, you need to use an object to represent each of the towers in the chain. Those objects are instances of a `Tower` class that contains the name of the tower along with a reference to the next tower in the chain. Thus, the structure representing Minas Tirith contains a reference to the one used for Amon Dîn, which in turn contains a reference to the structure for Eilenach, and so on, up to a `null` reference that marks the end of the chain.

If you adopt this approach, the definition of the `Tower` class looks like this:

```
private static class Tower {
    String name;
    Tower link;
};
```

This class has much the same form as the `PointRecord` class at the beginning of the chapter. It contains only instance variable declarations and therefore acts as a record class containing two fields: the `name` field holds the name of the tower and the `link` field points to the next tower in the chain. The `Tower` class, however, is defined *inside* the definition of `BeaconsOfGondor` and is therefore what Java calls an *inner class.* The `private` keyword ensures that the `Tower` class can be used only within `BeaconsOfGondor`. The `static` keyword indicates that the `Tower` class does not need access to the instance variables in the enclosing class.

Figure 7-9 illustrates how these structures appear in memory in the completed linked list. Each of the individual `Tower` structures represents a *cell* in the linked list, and the internal pointers are called *links.* The cells may appear anywhere in memory; the order is determined by the links that connect each cell to its successor.

The program in Figure 7-10 simulates the process of lighting the Beacons of Gondor. The program begins by creating the linked list using a series of calls to the `createTower` method, which allocates space for a new `Tower` value and then fills in the `name` and `link` fields from the arguments. The `run` method assembles the list in reverse order, starting with Rohan and continuing backward, one tower at a time, until it reaches Minas Tirith.

FIGURE 7-9 **Linked list representing the Beacons of Gondor**

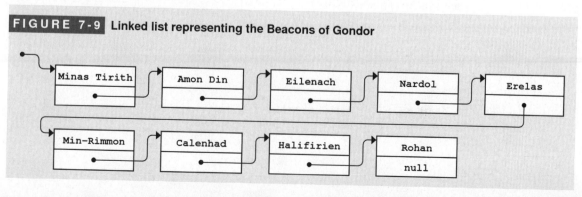

FIGURE 7-10   Program to simulate the Beacons of Gondor

```
/*
 * File: BeaconsOfGondor.java
 * ---------------------------
 * This program illustrates the concept of a linked list by simulating the
 * Beacons of Gondor story from J. R. R. Tolkien's Return of the King.
 */

package edu.stanford.cs.javacs2.ch7;

public class BeaconsOfGondor {

    public void run() {
        Tower rohan = createTower("Rohan", null);
        Tower halifirien = createTower("Halifirien", rohan);
        Tower calenhad = createTower("Calenhad", halifirien);
        Tower minRimmon = createTower("Min-Rimmon", calenhad);
        Tower erelas = createTower("Erelas", minRimmon);
        Tower nardol = createTower("Nardol", erelas);
        Tower eilenach = createTower("Eilenach", nardol);
        Tower amonDin = createTower("Amon Din", eilenach);
        Tower minasTirith = createTower("Minas Tirith", amonDin);
        signal(minasTirith);
    }

/* Creates a new Tower object from its name and link fields */

    private Tower createTower(String name, Tower link) {
        Tower t = new Tower();
        t.name = name;
        t.link = link;
        return t;
    }

/* Generates a signal starting at start and propagating down the chain */

    private void signal(Tower start) {
        for (Tower cp = start; cp != null; cp = cp.link) {
            System.out.println("Lighting " + cp.name);
        }
    }

/* Defines an inner class named Tower that acts as a cell in a linked list */

    private static class Tower {
        String name;         /* The name of this tower                 */
        Tower link;          /* Link to the next tower in the chain    */
    }

/* Main program */

    public static void main(String[] args) {
        new BeaconsOfGondor().run();
    }

}
```

After the linked list has been initialized, the main program calls `signal` to display the names of the towers, as follows:

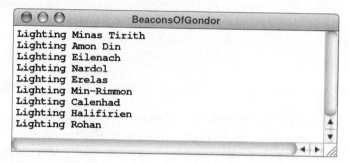

Iteration in linked lists

The code for `signal` illustrates one of the fundamental programming patterns for linked lists, which is embodied in the `for` loop

```
for (Tower cp = start; cp != null; cp = cp.link)
```

The effect of the `for` loop pattern in the `signal` function is to cycle through each element in the linked list in much the same way as the classic `for` loop pattern cycles through the elements in an array. The initialization expression declares the variable `cp` and initializes it so that it indicates the first tower in the list. The test expression ensures that the loop continues as long as the `cp` variable is not `null`, which is the value that marks the end. The step expression in the `for` loop is

```
cp = cp.link;
```

which changes the value of `cp` to the `link` field of the current `Tower`, thereby advancing `cp` to the next tower in the list.

7.6 Enumerated types

As you learned from the discussion of the Unicode character set in Chapter 1, computers store characters in integer form by assigning a numeric representation to each character. This strategy of encoding data as integers by numbering the elements of the domain in fact represents a more general principle. Like most modern languages, Java allows you to define new types by listing the elements in their domain. Such types are called ***enumerated types.***

In its simplest form, the syntax for defining an enumerated type in Java is

```
enum typename { namelist }
```

where *typename* is the name of the new type and *namelist* is a list of the values in the domain, separated by commas. Each value in the list must be a legal identifier; moreover, given that the names assigned to these values never change, those names are conventionally written entirely in uppercase, as is true for other constants. For example, the following definition introduces a new `Suit` type whose values consist of the four suit names in a standard deck of playing cards:

```
public enum Suit { CLUBS, DIAMONDS, HEARTS, SPADES }
```

When the Java compiler encounters this definition, it assigns values to the constant names by numbering them consecutively starting with 0. Thus, `CLUBS` is assigned the value 0, `DIAMONDS` is assigned the value 2, `HEARTS` is assigned the value 3, and `SPADES` is assigned the value 3. These values, however, are not typically important for you to know, just as you rarely need to know the Unicode value of a character.

Whenever you use an enumerated constant name in your code, you ordinarily include the type name, as in `Suit.HEARTS`. The one case in which the names appear without the type qualifier is in the `case` clauses of a `switch` statement. For example, the following method returns the color of a suit:

```
private String getColor(Suit s) {
    switch (s) {
      case CLUBS: case SPADES: return "BLACK";
      case DIAMONDS: case HEARTS: return "RED";
    }
    throw new RuntimeException("Illegal suit");
}
```

The presence of the `throw` statement at the end of this method may at first seem odd. The `switch` statement appears to have taken care of all four possible values of the argument, which is declared to be of the enumerated type `Suit`, in which case the compiler should be clever enough to know that the `switch` statement will always hit one of the `return` statements. That reasoning, however, fails to take account of the fact that enumerated types in Java are implemented as classes, which means that `null` is also a legal value. If `s` is `null`, the code for `getColor` would indeed reach the `throw` statement, at which point it is appropriate to report an error.

The fact that enumerated types are implemented as classes means that they turn out to be much more flexible and powerful in Java than they are in most other languages. Enumerated types can declare their own methods and instance variables, just as classes do. When these definitions appear, they must follow the list of values, which must be terminated with a semicolon. This facility is illustrated in Figure 7-11, which defines an enumerated type called `Direction` whose values consist of the four principal compass directions.

FIGURE 7-11 Implementation of the `Direction` class

```
/*
 * File: Direction.java
 * ------------------------
 * This file defines an enumerated type called Direction whose values are
 * the four major compass points: NORTH, EAST, SOUTH, and WEST.
 */

package edu.stanford.cs.javacs2.ch7;

/**
 * This enumerated type represents a direction which must be one of the
 * four major compass points (NORTH, EAST, SOUTH, WEST).
 */

public enum Direction {
    NORTH, EAST, SOUTH, WEST;

/**
 * Returns the direction that is 90 degrees to the left of this one.
 *
 * @return The direction 90 degrees to the left
 */

    public Direction turnLeft() {
        switch (this) {
          case NORTH: return WEST;
          case EAST: return NORTH;
          case SOUTH: return EAST;
          case WEST: return SOUTH;
        }
        throw new RuntimeException("Illegal direction");
    }

/**
 * Returns the direction that is 90 degrees to the right of this one.
 *
 * @return The direction 90 degrees to the right
 */

    public Direction turnRight() {
        switch (this) {
          case NORTH: return EAST;
          case EAST: return SOUTH;
          case SOUTH: return WEST;
          case WEST: return NORTH;
        }
        throw new RuntimeException("Illegal direction");
    }

}
```

In addition to the constants **NORTH**, **EAST**, **SOUTH**, and **WEST**, the **Direction** class in Figure 7-11 exports the methods **turnLeft** and **turnRight**. Given a value of type **Direction**, these methods return the direction 90 degrees to the left and 90 degrees to the right, respectively.

In Java, every enumerated type automatically implements a few useful methods. Every enumerated type, for example, automatically overrides the **toString** method so that values of that type can be displayed by name. In addition, every enumerated type also exports a method called **values**, which returns an array of the values of that type, in the order determined by the definition. Both of these features are illustrated in the following code, which tests **turnLeft** and **turnRight** for each of the four directions:

```
public void run() {
    for (Direction dir : Direction.values()) {
        System.out.println(dir.turnLeft() +
                    " <- " + dir + " -> " +
                    dir.turnRight());
    }
}
```

This code produces the following sample run:

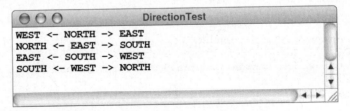

```
                    DirectionTest
WEST <- NORTH -> EAST
NORTH <- EAST -> SOUTH
EAST <- SOUTH -> WEST
SOUTH <- WEST -> NORTH
```

7.7 Unit testing

Even though the title bar of the last sample run indicates that the name of the program is called **DirectionTest**, it hardly constitutes an adequate test of the **Direction** class. Whenever you define a new class for clients to use, it is essential to test your implementation as thoroughly as you can. Untested code is almost always buggy, and it is your responsibility as a programmer to find and fix as many of those bugs as you can.

Although testing is certainly important at the level of a complete application, it is often important to test individual classes independently. If you design your test programs so that they depend on several classes functioning correctly, it is harder to find the errors when something goes wrong. The strategy of checking each class separately is called ***unit testing.***

Several tools exist to help you write unit tests in Java. One of the most popular tools is **JUnit**, which is an open-source package designed for this purpose. The web site at **junit.org**, however, defines **JUnit** as a "work in progress," which makes it harder to include it in a published textbook because of the likelihood of change. This book therefore defines its own unit-testing framework in a way that is compatible with **JUnit**, at least as it exists during the writing of this book. That framework is exported by the **UnitTest** class, which is contained in the **edu.stanford.cs.javacs2.unittest** package.

The methods exported by the **UnitTest** package appear in Figure 7-12. Each of the methods makes an assertion about some property specified by the arguments. If that assertion is true, everything continues normally. If that assertion is false, the implementation of the **UnitTest** class prints an error message indicating the source of the failure. Each of the methods allows the client to substitute a specific failure message for the standard one created by the **UnitTest** class, which prints the values involved in the failing test.

For a wide variety of applications, the only method you need from **UnitTest** is **assertEquals**, which tests whether its two arguments are equal, as defined by the **equals** method for the first value in the comparison. The **equals** method is defined in the **Object** class and is therefore available in all classes, although it doesn't necessarily provide a useful answer unless the class overrides **equals** to

FIGURE 7-12 Methods exported by the **UnitTest** class, which is adapted from **JUnit**

assertTrue (*exp*) **assertTrue** (*msg*, *exp*)	Checks that the boolean expression is **true**. In each method, *msg* indicates what to print if the assertion fails.
assertFalse (*exp*) **assertFalse** (*msg*, *exp*)	Checks that the boolean expression is **false**.
assertNull (*exp*) **assertNull** (*msg*, *exp*)	Checks that the value of the expression is **null**.
assertNotNull (*exp*) **assertNotNull** (*msg*, *exp*)	Checks that the value of the expression is not **null**.
assertEquals (exp_1, exp_2) **assertEquals** (*msg*, exp_1, exp_2)	Checks that the two expressions are equal, which is determined by calling the **equals** method of exp_1.
assertNotEquals (exp_1, exp_2) **assertNotEquals** (*msg*, exp_1, exp_2)	Checks that the two expressions are not equal.
assertSame (exp_1, exp_2) **assertSame** (*msg*, exp_1, exp_2)	Checks that the expressions exp_1 and exp_2 are the same object.
assertNotSame (exp_1, exp_2) **assertNotSame** (*msg*, exp_1, exp_2)	Checks that the expressions exp_1 and exp_2 are not the same object.

return an answer appropriate to that type. Unfortunately, overriding **equals** turns out to be tricky in Java for reasons that won't make sense until Chapter 14. To avoid the danger of encouraging bad programming habits, none of the classes you have seen so far override **equals**, even when doing so would make sense. That limitation might seem to rule out using **assertEquals** for classes like **Rational**, where it would be useful in checking whether the result of some computation was equal to the expected value.

Fortunately, this problem has a simple fix. Java's **String** class correctly overrides **equals**, and the **Rational** class defines a **toString** method. You can therefore use **assertEquals** and **toString** together to check that a computation produces the expected string. This strategy has the additional advantage of making it possible to catch errors in the internal representation. If the **Rational** class failed to reduce the result of some computation to lowest terms, that result would still be equal to the intended result in a mathematical sense. By comparing the string representations, the test suite can detect that a **Rational** number stored as 3/6 is not correctly represented, because its string value is not equal to "1/2".

The code in Figure 7-13 demonstrates the use of **assertEquals** and **toString** to implement a unit test of the **Rational** class. For clarity, the test program is divided into several private methods that test the constructors and the four arithmetic operations supported by the **Rational** class. The individual assertions all look more or less like the following line from the **addTest** method, which asserts that the constant **ONE** plus the constant **ONE** prints as the string "2":

```
UnitTest.assertEquals(ONE.add(ONE).toString(), "2");
```

If you try to read through the code in Figure 7-13—and especially if you need to write a similar unit test for some other class—the seemingly endless repetition of the **UnitTest** class name quickly becomes tiresome. Java makes it possible to shorten the method name to **assertEquals** by changing the **import** line to

```
import static edu.stanford.cs.javacs2.unittest.UnitTest.
                                               assertEquals;
```

which doesn't quite fit within the margins of the page. The inclusion of the **static** keyword turns this declaration into a *static import,* which imports the named static method into the current compilation so that you don't need to specify the **UnitTest** class name. For example, in a mathematically intensive program that used lots of sines and cosines, you could add the static import lines

```
import static java.lang.Math.sin;
import static java.lang.Math.cos;
```

and then call **sin** and **cos** without specifying the **Math** qualifier.

FIGURE 7-13 Unit test for the Rational class

```
/*
 * File: RationalUnitTest.java
 * -------------------------------
 * This program implements a unit test for the Rational class.
 */

package edu.stanford.cs.javacs2.ch7;

import edu.stanford.cs.unittest.UnitTest;

public class RationalUnitTest {

   public void run() {
      testConstructor();
      testAdd();
      testSubtract();
      testMultiply();
      testDivide();
   }

/* Test the three forms of the Rational constructor */

   private void testConstructor() {
      UnitTest.assertEquals(new Rational().toString(), "0");
      UnitTest.assertEquals(new Rational(42).toString(), "42");
      UnitTest.assertEquals(new Rational(-17).toString(), "-17");
      UnitTest.assertEquals(new Rational(3, 1).toString(), "3");
      UnitTest.assertEquals(new Rational(1, 3).toString(), "1/3");
      UnitTest.assertEquals(new Rational(2, 6).toString(), "1/3");
      UnitTest.assertEquals(new Rational(-1, 3).toString(), "-1/3");
      UnitTest.assertEquals(new Rational(1, -3).toString(), "-1/3");
      UnitTest.assertEquals(new Rational(0, 2).toString(), "0");
   }

/* Test the add method */

   private void testAdd() {
      UnitTest.assertEquals(ONE.add(ONE).toString(), "2");
      UnitTest.assertEquals(ONE_HALF.add(ONE_THIRD).toString(), "5/6");
      UnitTest.assertEquals(ONE.add(MINUS_ONE).toString(), "0");
      UnitTest.assertEquals(MINUS_ONE.add(ONE).toString(), "0");
   }

/* Test the subtract method */

   private void testSubtract() {
      UnitTest.assertEquals(ONE.subtract(ONE).toString(), "0");
      UnitTest.assertEquals(ONE_HALF.subtract(ONE_THIRD).toString(), "1/6");
      UnitTest.assertEquals(ONE.subtract(MINUS_ONE).toString(), "2");
      UnitTest.assertEquals(MINUS_ONE.subtract(ONE).toString(), "-2");
   }
```

FIGURE 7-13 Unit test for the `Rational` class (continued)

```
/* Test the multiply method */

    private void testMultiply() {
        UnitTest.assertEquals(ZERO.multiply(TWO).toString(), "0");
        UnitTest.assertEquals(ONE_HALF.multiply(ONE_THIRD).toString(), "1/6");
        UnitTest.assertEquals(MINUS_ONE.multiply(ONE_THIRD).toString(), "-1/3");
        UnitTest.assertEquals(MINUS_ONE.multiply(MINUS_ONE).toString(), "1");
    }

/* Test the divide method, including the division-by-zero exception */

    private void testDivide() {
        UnitTest.assertEquals(ZERO.divide(TWO).toString(), "0");
        UnitTest.assertEquals(ONE.divide(TWO).toString(), "1/2");
        UnitTest.assertEquals(TWO_THIRDS.divide(ONE_THIRD).toString(), "2");
        UnitTest.assertEquals(TWO.divide(MINUS_ONE).toString(), "-2");
        try {
            TWO.divide(ZERO);
            System.err.println("Failure: Zero divide");
        } catch (RuntimeException ex) {
            /* OK */
        }
    }

/* Constants */

    private static final Rational ZERO = new Rational(0);
    private static final Rational ONE = new Rational(1);
    private static final Rational TWO = new Rational(2);
    private static final Rational ONE_HALF = new Rational(1, 2);
    private static final Rational ONE_THIRD = new Rational(1, 3);
    private static final Rational TWO_THIRDS = new Rational(2, 3);
    private static final Rational MINUS_ONE = new Rational(-1);

/* Main program */

    public static void main(String[] args) {
        new RationalUnitTest().run();
    }

}
```

Static imports, however, can easily be overused. Oracle's Java tutorial warns:

> So when should you use static import? **Very sparingly!** . . . If you overuse the static import feature, it can make your program unreadable and unmaintainable, polluting its namespace with all the static members you import. Readers of your code (including you, a few months after you wrote it) will not know which class a static member comes from.

This book finesses the issue by avoiding static imports altogether.

Although testing is essential to software development, it does not eliminate the need for careful implementation. The number of ways clients will find to use a library package is just too large. The late Edsger W. Dijkstra defined the essential problem of testing in a 1972 monograph entitled *Notes on Structured Programming:*

> Program testing can be used to show the presence of bugs, but never to show their absence!

As an implementer, you need to employ many different techniques to reduce the number of errors. Careful design helps to simplify the overall structure, making it much easier to find where things go awry. Tracing your code by hand can often reveal bugs before the formal testing phase even begins. In many cases, having other programmers look over your code is one of the best ways to find problems you have managed to overlook. In the industry, this process is often formalized in a series of ***code reviews*** scheduled during the software development cycle.

Summary

The primary purpose of this chapter has been to give you the tools you need to design and implement classes on your own. The examples in this chapter have focused on classes that encapsulate data and operations into a coherent whole, deferring the issue of inheritance to Chapter 8.

Important points covered in this chapter include:

- In many applications, it is useful to combine several independent data values into a single abstract data type along with methods that define the behavior of that class. In this book, all instance variables in public classes are declared as `private` to protect the integrity of the data.

- Given an object, you can select an instance variable using the *dot operator.* External clients cannot see private instance variables, but the implementation of a class has access to the private members of all objects of that class.

- Class definitions typically export one or more *constructors* that are responsible for initializing objects of that class. In general, all class definitions include a *default constructor* that takes no arguments.

- Methods that give clients access to the values of the instance variables are called *getters;* methods that allow clients to change the value of an instance variable are called *setters.* A class that gives the client no opportunity to change the value of an object after it is created is said to be *immutable.*

- Class definitions typically override the definition of `toString` so that it produces a human-readable version of the object. This method is particularly useful for testing and debugging.

- Designing a new class is as much an art as a science. Although the chapter offers some general guidelines to guide you in this process, experience and practice are the best teachers.

- The `edu.stanford.cs.javacs2.tokenscanner` package exports a class called `TokenScanner` that supports the process of breaking input text into individual units called *tokens*. The complete version of the `TokenScanner` class supports a variety of options that make this package useful in a wide range of applications.

- You can indicate the order of elements in a sequence by storing a pointer with each value linking it to the one that follows it. In programming, structures designed in this way are called *linked lists*. The pointers that connect one value to the next are called *links,* and the individual records used to store the values and link fields together are called *cells*.

- The conventional way to mark the end of a linked list is to store the pointer constant `null` in the link field of the last cell.

- You can iterate through the cells of a linked list by using the following idiom, where *type* is the name of the cell type:

```
for (type cp = start; cp != null; cp = cp.link) {
    . . . code using cp . . .
}
```

- In Java, you can define a new type consisting of a set of constant values by using the `enum` keyword to produce an *enumerated type*. Java's enumerated types are much more powerful than their counterparts in other languages and can include constructors and methods along with the list of values.

- Whenever you implement a class for others to use, you have a responsibility to test that package as thoroughly as possible. One useful technique is to write a program that automatically tests every method in that class independently of any other modules in an application. Such test programs are called *unit tests* and are an essential part of good software engineering practice.

Review questions

1. Define each of the following terms: *object, structure, class, instance variable, method.*

2. What operator does Java use to select an instance variable from an object?

3. What is the syntax for a Java constructor?

4. How many arguments are passed to the *default constructor?*

5.   How can you invoke a different overloaded form of a constructor from inside another constructor?

6.   What reasons does this chapter offer for declaring all instance variables in public classes as **private**?

7.   What are *getters* and *setters?*

8.   What does it mean for a class to be *immutable?*

9.   What are the five steps suggested in this chapter as guidelines for designing a class?

10.   What is a *rational number?*

11.   What restrictions does the **Rational** constructor place on the stored values of the **num** and **den** variables?

12.   The code for the **Rational** constructor on page 248 includes an explicit check to see whether **x** is zero. Would the **Rational** class still work the same way if this check were eliminated?

13.   What is a *token?*

14.   What is the standard pattern for reading all tokens from a string?

15.   How do you construct a **TokenScanner** that ignores whitespace characters in the input?

16.   What is a *linked list?*

17.   What is the standard pattern for iterating through the cells in a linked list?

18.   What is an *enumerated type?*

19.   True or false: In Java, the body of every **enum** definition consists of a list of the constant values for that type and nothing more.

20.   How would you define an enumerated type called **Weekday** whose elements were the names of the seven days of the week?

21.   What method does Java include with all enumerated types that returns an array consisting of all values of that type?

22.   What is the implication of the word *unit* in the phrase *unit test?*

23. What reason does Oracle's Java tutorial offer for avoiding static imports?

24. What advice did the computer scientist Edsger W. Dijkstra offer about the value of testing?

Exercises

1. The game of *dominos* is played using pieces that are usually black rectangles with some number of white dots on each side. For example, the domino

is called the 4-1 domino, with four dots on its left side and one on its right.

Define a simple **Domino** class that represents a traditional domino. Your class should export the following entries:

- A default constructor that creates the 0-0 domino

- A constructor that takes the number of dots on each side

- A **toString** method that creates a string representation of the domino

- Two getter methods named **getLeftDots** and **getRightDots**

Test your implementation of the **Domino** class by writing a program that creates a full set of dominos from 0-0 to 6-6 and then displays those dominos on the console. A full set of dominos contains one copy of each possible domino in that range, disallowing duplicates that result from flipping a domino over. Thus, a domino set has a 4-1 domino but not a separate 1-4 domino.

2. Define a **Card** class suitable for representing a standard playing card, which is identified by two components: a *rank* and a *suit*. The rank is stored as an integer between 1 and 13 in which an ace is a 1, a jack is an 11, a queen is a 12, and a king is a 13. The suit is represented using the **Suit** enumeration type defined on page 262. Your class should export the following methods:

- A default constructor that creates a card that can later be assigned a value

- A constructor that takes a short string name like **"10S"** or **"JD"**

- A constructor that takes separate values for the rank and the suit

- A **toString** method that returns the short string representation of the card

- The getter methods **getRank** and **getSuit**

- The constants **ACE**, **JACK**, **QUEEN**, and **KING**, which are bound to the integers 1, 11, 12, and 13, respectively

Test your implementation with the **run** method

```
public void run() {
    for (Suit suit : Suit.values()) {
        for (int rank = Card.ACE; rank <= Card.KING;
                                    rank++) {
            System.out.print(" " + new Card(rank, suit));
        }
        System.out.println();
    }
}
```

which should produce the following sample run:

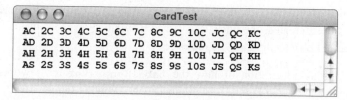

3. Implement an enumerated type called **Month** whose elements are the English names of the months (**JANUARY**, **FEBRUARY**, and so on).

4. Implement a **Date** class that exports the following methods:

- A default constructor that sets the date to January 1, 1900.

- A constructor that takes a month (as defined in exercise 3), day, and year and initializes the **Date** accordingly, as in the declaration

    Date moonLanding = new Date(Month.JULY, 20, 1969);

- An overloaded version of the constructor that takes the first two parameters in the opposite order, for the benefit of clients outside the United States. This change allows the declaration of **moonLanding** to be written as

    Date moonLanding = new Date(20, Month.JULY, 1969);

- The getter methods **getDay**, **getMonth**, and **getYear**.

- A **toString** method that returns the date in the form *dd-mmm-yyyy*, where *dd* is a one- or two-digit date, *mmm* is the three-letter English abbreviation for the month, and *yyyy* is the four-digit year. Thus, calling **toString(moonLanding)** should return the string **"20-Jul-1969"**.

5. For certain applications, it is useful to be able to generate a series of names that form a sequential pattern. For example, if you were writing a program to number figures in a paper, having some mechanism to return the sequence of strings **"Figure 1"**, **"Figure 2"**, **"Figure 3"**, and so on, would be very

handy. However, you might also need to label points in a geometric diagram, in which case you would want a similar but independent set of labels for points such as `"P0"`, `"P1"`, `"P2"`, and so forth.

If you think about this problem more generally, the tool you need is a label generator that allows the client to define arbitrary sequences of labels, each of which consists of a prefix string (`"Figure "` or `"P"` for the examples in the preceding paragraph) coupled with an integer used as a sequence number. Because the client may want different sequences to be active simultaneously, it makes sense to define the label generator as a **LabelGenerator** class. To initialize a new generator, the client provides the prefix string and the initial index as arguments to the **LabelGenerator** constructor. Once the generator has been created, the client can return new labels in the sequence by calling **nextLabel** on the **LabelGenerator**.

As an illustration of how the **LabelGenerator** class works, the **run** method shown in Figure 7-14 produces the following sample run:

```
●○○                    LabelGeneratorTest
Figure numbers: Figure 1, Figure 2, Figure 3
Point numbers:  P0, P1, P2, P3, P4
More figures:   Figure 4, Figure 5, Figure 6
```

FIGURE 7-14 Program to test the label generator

```java
public void run() {
    LabelGenerator figureNumbers = new LabelGenerator("Figure ", 1);
    LabelGenerator pointNumbers = new LabelGenerator("P", 0);
    System.out.print("Figure numbers: ");
    for (int i = 0; i < 3; i++) {
        if (i > 0) System.out.print(", ");
        System.out.print(figureNumbers.nextLabel());
    }
    System.out.println();
    System.out.print("Point numbers:  ");
    for (int i = 0; i < 5; i++) {
        if (i > 0) System.out.print(", ");
        System.out.print(pointNumbers.nextLabel());
    }
    System.out.println();
    System.out.print("More figures:   ");
    for (int i = 0; i < 3; i++) {
        if (i > 0) System.out.print(", ");
        System.out.print(figureNumbers.nextLabel());
    }
    System.out.println();
}
```

6. The checkout-line simulation from Chapter 6 included implementations of two methods for generating random values that are natural candidates for inclusion in a library class. Define a class called `RandomLib` that exports the static methods `nextInt` and `nextChance` (it seems appropriate to shorten the method names, given that the idea of randomness is clear from the class name), along with a static method called `nextDouble` that produces a random floating-point number in a range specified by the client.

7.
> *I shall never believe that God plays dice with the world.*
>
> —Albert Einstein, 1947

Despite Einstein's metaphysical objections, the current models of physics, and particularly of quantum theory, are based on the idea that nature does indeed involve random processes. A radioactive atom, for example, does not decay for any specific reason that we mortals understand. Instead, that atom has a random probability of decaying within a particular period of time. Sometimes it does, sometimes it doesn't, and there is no way to know for sure.

Because physicists consider radioactive decay a random process, it is not surprising that random numbers can be used to simulate it. Suppose you start with a collection of atoms, each of which has a certain probability of decaying in any unit of time. You can then approximate the decay process by taking each atom in turn and deciding randomly whether it decays.

Use the `RandomLib` class you created for exercise 6 to write a program that simulates the decay of a sample that contains 5000 atoms of radioactive material, where each atom has a 50 percent chance of decaying in a year. The output of your program should show the number of atoms remaining at the end of each year, which might look something like this:

```
 ● ○ ○              RadioactiveDecay
There are 5000 atoms initially.
There are 2470 atoms at the end of year 1.
There are 1246 atoms at the end of year 2.
There are 623 atoms at the end of year 3.
There are 323 atoms at the end of year 4.
There are 156 atoms at the end of year 5.
There are 86 atoms at the end of year 6.
There are 38 atoms at the end of year 7.
There are 10 atoms at the end of year 8.
There are 5 atoms at the end of year 9.
There are 2 atoms at the end of year 10.
There are 0 atoms at the end of year 11.
```

As the numbers indicate, roughly half the atoms in the sample decay each year. In physics, the conventional way to express this observation is to say that the sample has a ***half-life*** of one year.

8.   Random numbers offer yet another strategy for approximating the value of π. Imagine that you have a dartboard hanging on your wall that consists of a circle painted on a square backdrop, as in the following diagram:

What happens if you throw a whole bunch of darts completely randomly, ignoring any darts that miss the board altogether? Some of the darts will fall inside the gray circle, but some will be outside the circle in the white corners of the square. If the throws are random, the ratio of the number of darts landing inside the circle to the total number of darts hitting the square should be approximately equal to the ratio between the two areas. The ratio of the areas is independent of the size of the dartboard, as illustrated by the formula

$$\frac{darts\ falling\ inside\ the\ circle}{darts\ falling\ inside\ the\ square} \cong \frac{area\ inside\ the\ circle}{area\ inside\ the\ square} = \frac{\pi r^2}{4r^2} = \frac{\pi}{4}$$

To simulate this process in a program, imagine that the dartboard is drawn on the standard Cartesian coordinate plane with its center at the origin and a radius of 1 unit. The process of throwing a dart randomly at the square can be modeled by generating two random numbers, x and y, each of which lies between −1 and +1. This (x, y) point always lies somewhere inside the square. The point (x, y) lies inside the circle if

$$\sqrt{x^2 + y^2} < 1$$

This condition, however, can be simplified considerably by squaring each side of the inequality, which yields the following more efficient test:

$$x^2 + y^2 < 1$$

If you perform this simulation many times and compute what fraction of the darts fall inside the circle, the result will be an approximation of π/4.

Write a program that simulates throwing 10,000 darts and then uses the simulation technique described in this exercise to generate and display an approximate value of π. Don't worry if your answer is correct only in the first few digits. The strategy used in this problem is not particularly accurate, even though it occasionally proves useful as an approximation technique. In mathematics, this technique is called **Monte Carlo integration**, after the capital city of Monaco, famous for its casinos.

9. *Heads. . . .*
    Heads. . . .
    Heads. . . .
    A weaker man might be moved to re-examine his faith, if in
    nothing else at least in the law of probability.

    —Tom Stoppard, *Rosencrantz and Guildenstern Are Dead,* 1967

    Write a program that simulates flipping a coin repeatedly and continues until
    three consecutive heads have been tossed. At that point, your program should
    display the total number of coin flips that were made. The following is one
    possible sample run of the program:

    ```
    ○ ○ ○            ConsecutiveHeads
    tails
    tails
    heads
    heads
    tails
    heads
    heads
    heads
    It took 8 flips to get 3 consecutive heads.
    ```

10. Reimplement the RPN calculator from Figure 6-6 so that it performs its
    internal calculations using rational instead of floating-point numbers. For
    example, your program should be able to produce the following sample run
    (which demonstrates that rational arithmetic is always exact):

    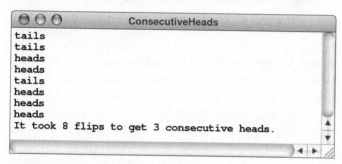

    ```
    ○ ○ ○            RationalRPNCalculator
    RPN Calculator Simulation (type H for help)
    > 1
    > 2
    > /
    1/2
    > 1
    > 3
    > /
    1/3
    > 1
    > 6
    > /
    1/6
    > +
    1/2
    > +
    1
    > Q
    ```

11. Write a program that checks the spelling of all words in a file. Your program
    should use the **TokenScanner** class to read tokens from an input file and then
    look up each word in the set of words stored in the file **EnglishWords.txt**

as discussed in Chapter 6. If some word in the input file does not appear in the set of English words, your program should print a message to that effect. If, for example, you ran the program on a file containing the text of this paragraph, the **SpellCheck** program would produce the following output:

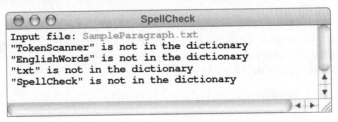

12§. Implement **saveToken** for the **TokenScanner** class. This method saves the specified token so that subsequent calls to **nextToken** return the saved token without consuming any additional characters from the input. Note: The § following the exercise number indicates that the solution to this exercise is available in the code distributed with this book, even though the code is not included in the text. Exercises that are marked in this way are excellent self-tests, because you can compare your answer to the published solution.

13§. Implement the **scanStrings** method for the **TokenScanner** class. When **scanStrings** is in effect, the token scanner should return quoted strings as single tokens. The strings may use either single or double quotation marks and should include the quotation marks in the string that **nextToken** returns.

14§. Implement the **scanNumbers** method for the **TokenScanner** class, which causes the token scanner to read any valid Java number as a single token. The difficult part of this extension lies in understanding the rules for what constitutes a valid numeric string and then finding a way to implement those rules efficiently. The easiest way to specify those rules is in a form that computer scientists call a *finite-state machine,* which is usually represented diagrammatically as a collection of circles representing the possible states of the machine. The circles are then connected by a set of labeled arcs that indicate how the process moves from one state to another. A finite-state machine for scanning a real number appears in Figure 7-15.

When you use a finite-state machine, you start in state s_0 and then follow the labeled arcs for each character in the input until there is no arc that matches the current character. If you end up in a state marked by a double circle, you have successfully scanned a number. These states that indicate successful scanning of a token are called *final states.* Figure 7-15 includes three examples that show how the finite-state machine scans numbers of various kinds.

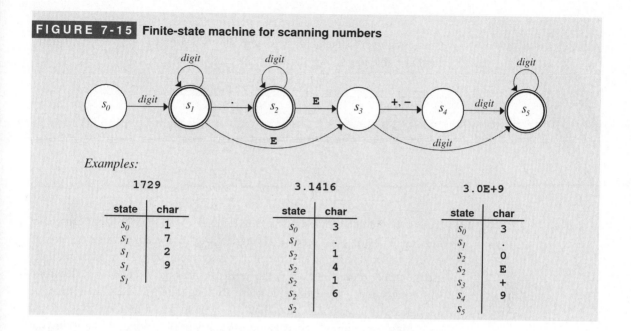

FIGURE 7-15 Finite-state machine for scanning numbers

Examples:

	1729			3.1416			3.0E+9	
state	**char**		**state**	**char**		**state**	**char**	
s_0	1		s_0	3		s_0	3	
s_1	7		s_1	.		s_1	.	
s_1	2		s_2	1		s_2	0	
s_1	9		s_2	4		s_2	E	
s_1			s_2	1		s_3	+	
			s_2	6		s_4	9	
			s_2			s_5		

15. Write a program that implements a simple arithmetic calculator. Input to the calculator consists of lines composed of integers combined using the standard arithmetic operators +, -, *, and /. For each line of input, your program should display the result of applying the operators from left to right. You should use the token scanner to read the terms and operators and set up the scanner so that it ignores all whitespace characters. Your program should exit when the user enters a blank line. A sample run of your program might look like this:

```
●  ○  ○            ExpressionCalculator
> 2 + 2
4
> 6 * 7
42
> 35500000 / 113
314159
> 4+9-2*16+1/3*6-67+8*2-3+26-1/34+3/7+2-5
0
>
```

The last line in this sample run is the arithmetic problem the Mathemagician gives to Milo in Norton Juster's children's story, *The Phantom Tollbooth*.

16. Extend the program you wrote for the preceding exercise so that the terms in the expressions can also be variable names assigned earlier in the session

using assignment statements that store the values in a map. Your program should be able to generate the following sample run:

```
●  ●  ●           ExpressionCalculatorWithVariables
> n1 = 17
> n2 = 36
> n3 = 73
> ave = n1 + n2 + n3 / 3
> ave
42
>
```

17§. Extend the implementation of the **TokenScanner** so that the input can come from either a string or a reader. The easiest way to implement this extension is to rewrite the scanner so that the input always comes from a reader and then use the **StringReader** class in the **java.io** package to create a reader from any string values provided by the user. Although the **StringReader** class is not discussed in this book, you should be able to figure out how to use it by consulting the online documentation. While you're looking on the web, you might check out the documentation for the **PushbackReader** class, which may also prove useful in this problem.

18. The names of the towers in the **BeaconsOfGondor** program from Figure 7-10 are listed explicitly in the **run** method. One way to provide more flexibility would be to read the names of the beacons from a data file instead. Modify the **BeaconsOfGondor** program so that the main program calls a method

    private Tower readBeaconsFromFile(String filename)

    that reads in the list of beacon towers from the specified file. For example, if the file **BeaconsOfGondor.txt** contains the following text, your program should produce the same sample run as shown in the chapter:

```
Minas Tirith
Amon Din
Eilenach
Nardol
Erelas
Min-Rimmon
Calenhad
Halifirien
Rohan
```

19. Implement a unit test for the simplified version of the **TokenScanner** class as it appears in Figure 7-7. If you're up for a real challenge, you could extend this program so that it serves as a unit test for the complete **TokenScanner** abstraction defined in Figure 7-6.

Chapter 8
Inheritance

Even in the angels there is the subordination of one hierarchy to another . . .

— Saint Ignatius, letter on obedience, 1553

As you know from the brief discussion of classes in Chapter 1, one of the defining properties of object-oriented languages like Java is that they allow you to define hierarchical relationships among classes. Whenever you have a class that provides some of the functionality you need for a particular application, you can define new subclasses that are derived from the original class, but which specialize its behavior in some way. Each subclass inherits behavior from its superclass, which in turn inherits the behavior of its superclasses, all the way up to the **Object** class that forms the root of the class hierarchy. The discussion of classes in Chapter 7 stopped short of discussing inheritance. This chapter completes that discussion by building several class hierarchies—including one to support simple graphical displays—in which inheritance plays a central role.

8.1 Simple examples of inheritance

Before moving on to consider more sophisticated applications of inheritance, it makes sense to begin with a few simple examples. In its most basic form, the definition of a subclass in Java looks like this:

```
class subclass extends superclass {
    new entries for the subclass
};
```

In this pattern, *subclass* inherits all the public entries in *superclass*. The entries in the private section of *superclass* remain private. Subclasses therefore have no direct access to the private methods and instance variables of their superclasses.

Specifying types in a parameterized class

In Java, it is possible to create useful subclasses that contain no code other than the class header, particularly if the superclass is a template class. For example, you can define a **StringMap** class that maps strings to strings by writing the following definition:

```
public class StringMap extends TreeMap<String,String> {
    /* No additional code is required */
}
```

Using the simple type name **StringMap** makes programs shorter and more readable because it is no longer necessary to write out the type parameters in every reference to that class.

In most cases, however, the body of a subclass definition will add new methods and instance variables to the facilities provided by the superclass. Figure 8-1, for example, shows the definition of a class called **IntegerList** that extends **ArrayList<Integer>** so that it includes a constructor that supports creating a

FIGURE 8-1 The `IntegerList` class

```
/*
 * File: IntegerList.java
 * ------------------------
 * This file exports the IntegerList class, which extends the parameterized
 * class ArrayList<Integer>.  It inherits all the methods from ArrayList
 * but also defines a new constructor that takes its values from the
 * parameter list and a new toString method that overrides its superclass.
 */

package edu.stanford.cs.javacs2.ch8;

import java.util.ArrayList;

public class IntegerList extends ArrayList<Integer> {

/**
 * Constructs a new IntegerList from the parameters.
 *
 * @param args A list of the integers used to initialize the IntegerList
 */

   public IntegerList(int... args) {
      for (int k : args) {
         add(k);
      }
   }

/**
 * Converts this IntegerList to a string consisting of the elements
 * enclosed in square brackets and separated by commas.
 *
 * @return The string representation of this list
 */

   public String toString() {
      String str = "";
      for (int k : this) {
         if (!str.isEmpty()) str += ", ";
         str += k;
      }
      return "[" + str + "]";
   }

}
```

new **IntegerList** object by listing its elements. In this example, the usual rule that would require inclusion of an explicit constructor does not apply. The variadic constructor will accept an empty list of arguments, which means that the zero-argument constructor comes for free. The implementation of **toString** creates a new string by concatenating together all the elements of the list.

Rules for calling inherited methods

When you first encounter the concepts of inheritance and overriding, it is easy to get confused as to which version of a method should be called for a particular object. In Java, the rule is that the method that gets executed is the one that is closest in the inheritance hierarchy to the actual class of the object. Thus, given a method call to an object of class `IntegerList`, for example, the Java compiler will first look for a method with the appropriate name and argument structure in the `IntegerList` class itself. If the method is defined there, the compiler will use that version. If not, it will look for the method in the `ArrayList` class, which is the next class in the chain. The compiler continues in this way until it finds an appropriate definition or discovers that no such method exists.

The point that can be confusing is that Java always makes this decision on the basis of what the object actually *is* rather than on what you have declared it to be at that particular point in the program. Suppose, for example, that you were to declare a variable of type `IntegerList` as follows:

```
IntegerList primes = new IntegerList(2, 3, 5, 7);
```

calling `primes.toString()` would clearly invoke the `toString` method shown in Figure 8-1. But what would happen if you then executed the following lines?

```
Object obj = primes;
System.out.println(obj);
```

It is certainly legal to assign `primes` to the variable `obj` because every Java class is a subclass of `Object`. The question now is which version of the `toString` method will be called when Java evaluates the argument to `println`. The `Object` class has its own definition of `toString`. Given that the code is now declaring the value to be an `Object` rather than an `IntegerList`, will Java go back to using the `Object` version of `toString`? The answer is no. The value stored in the variable `obj` is still an `IntegerList`, and the Java runtime system will correctly invoke the version of `toString` defined for that class.

Although the ability to override methods provides considerable flexibility and power, it also carries with it a certain amount of risk. Suppose, for example, that you are designing a class in which one of your public methods calls another public method in the class. At the time that you write the code, you assume that the method you're calling has the particular effect that you designed. Unfortunately, if someone else declares a subclass of your class, they can invalidate that assumption by overriding the method on which your code depends. This situation can quickly become a maintenance nightmare. Worse still, if the problem occurs in privileged classes that perform operations unavailable to clients, the ability of other programmers to substitute one piece of code for another can become a security loophole.

As a general principle, it is best to use overriding sparingly and to limit your use of it to cases in which the designer of the original class has clearly allowed for that possibility. Class designers issue such invitations all the time. The comments for the **toString** method in the **Object** class, for example, begin as follows:

```
/**
 * Returns a string representation of the object. In
 * general, the toString method returns a string that
 * "textually represents" this object. The result
 * should be a concise but informative representation
 * that is easy for a person to read. It is recommended
 * that all subclasses override this method.
 */
```

The designers of the **Object** class don't merely invite you to override the **toString** method but actively recommend that you do so.

On some occasions, it is useful to be able to invoke the original definition of a method from inside the code that overrides it. This situation arises, for example, when a class defines an **init** method that performs initialization operations that are separate from those defined by the constructor. Subclasses may want to add additional initialization code, but must also ensure that any initialization code in the superclass remains in effect. In Java, you can invoke the behavior of your superclass by using the keyword **super** as if it were the receiver of the method. Thus, if you needed to write an extension of the **init** method provided by your superclass, you could do so by writing

```
public void init() {
    super.init();
    Code to perform any further initialization goes here.
}
```

The first line makes sure that all the initializations required for the superclass are complete, after which the method can perform any additional initialization operations required at this level.

Rules for calling inherited constructors

Although they have much in common with methods, constructors in Java are somewhat more subtle. The reason for this subtlety comes from the fact that classes form hierarchies. Instances of the **IntegerList** class defined in the preceding section are also instances of **ArrayList<Integer>**, along with every class in the inheritance hierarchy for `ArrayList` up to and including the `Object` class at the top. To ensure that a new `IntegerList` object is correctly initialized, Java must make sure that the constructor for each of these classes is invoked during the construction process. The first step consists of initializing the data associated with every `Object` by calling the `Object` constructor. From there, Java must call the constructor at each subclass level, moving downward through the inheritance chain until it reaches `ArrayList<Integer>` and `IntegerList` at the bottom.

Java makes sure that each superclass is correctly initialized by calling its default constructor automatically. When you define a class, however, you can choose to call a specific variant of the superclass constructor by including the line

> `super`(*args*) ;

as the first line of a constructor for the subclass, where *args* are the arguments necessary to select the desired version of the superclass constructor.

Every constructor in a Java class will invoke the superclass constructor in one of three ways:

1. Classes that begin with an explicit call to `this` invoke one of the other constructors for this class, delegating to that constructor the responsibility for making sure that the superclass constructor gets called.

2. Classes that begin with an explicit call to `super` invoke the constructor in the superclass that matches the argument list provided.

3. Classes that begin without a call to either `super` or `this` invoke the default superclass constructor with no arguments.

Controlling access to the contents of a class

So far, every method or instance variable in the text has been marked as either `public` or `private`. Java offers two more possibilities, both of which are offer levels of access that are intermediate between these two extremes. The `protected` keyword indicates an entry that is available only to subclasses of the current class or any class defined in the same package. If none of these keywords appear in a declaration, that entry is defined to be *package-private,* which means that it is visible to other classes in the same package, but not to classes defined in other packages, even if those classes are subclasses of the one defining those entries.

Most of the entries in this book specify either `public` or `private` visibility, but there are some occasions in which the other storage classes arise. All inner classes in this book, for example, are defined with package-private visibility for both the class itself and the entries it defines. For example, the definition of the `Tower` class in Figure 7-10 is

```
    private static class Tower
        String name;
        Tower link;
    }
```

As noted in Chapter 7, the **private** keyword ensures that the class name **Tower** and its instance variables are not visible outside the defining class. The **static** keyword tells the compiler that the **Tower** class needs no access to the instance variables of the class in which the definition of **Tower** appears.

Alternatives to inheritance

Inheritance can easily be overused in object-oriented languages. In many cases, extending an existing class to include new operations is less appropriate than the alternative strategy of embedding an object inside a new class that exports the desired set of operations and then implements those operations by applying the appropriate methods to the embedded value.

As an example, consider the idea of a lexicon as described in Chapter 6. That chapter included several applications that created a lexicon by reading the file **EnglishWords.txt**. The words in the lexicon were stored in a **TreeSet** because doing so guarantees that the words appear in alphabetical order. Using a **TreeSet** for that purpose made sense at the time, particularly because sets were the focus of that section. From the perspective of a client writing an application, however, the idea of a lexicon is far easier to understand than that of a **TreeSet**, which is really just a detail of a particular implementation strategy. One way to reduce the conceptual complexity for the client is to define a **Lexicon** class that hides those details inside the implementation.

In an object-oriented language, one of the simplest ways to define a **Lexicon** class is to have it extend **TreeSet<String>**, which automatically provides the new **Lexicon** class with methods like **add**, **contains**, **size**, **isEmpty**, and **clear**, all of which make sense in the context of a word list. The **TreeSet** class, however, defines other methods—mostly outside of the ones presented in Chapter 6—that are appropriate for sets but are less relevant to lexicons. If you define **Lexicon** as an extension of **TreeSet<String>**, the **Lexicon** class inherits these methods as well, even if they are of questionable utility in that context.

You may also want to define a lexicon in ways that make it incompatible with the standard **TreeSet** class. Lexicons, for example, typically ignore case. If you added the word **"hello"** to a lexicon, you would expect that lexicon to identify **"Hello"** as a legal word. Although you could achieve that effect by overriding methods so that they converted all strings to lower case, the idea of defining **Lexicon** as a subclass of **TreeSet<String>** becomes less attractive.

FIGURE 8-2 The methods exported by the `Lexicon` class

Constructors

`new Lexicon ()`	Creates an empty lexicon.
`new Lexicon` (*filename*)	Creates a lexicon by reading lines from the specified text file.

Methods

`size ()`	Returns the number of words in the lexicon.
`isEmpty ()`	Returns `true` if the lexicon is empty.
`add` (*word*)	Adds a new word to the lexicon, if that word is not already present. All words in a lexicon are stored in lower case.
`contains` (*word*)	Returns `true` if *word* is in the lexicon.
`containsPrefix` (*prefix*)	Returns `true` if any of the words in the lexicon start with the specified prefix.
`clear ()`	Removes all the words from the lexicon.

A better strategy is to define the `Lexicon` class without specifying a superclass and then use a `TreeSet<String>` to implement it. By choosing this strategy, you give yourself full control over the methods that the `Lexicon` class exports. Suppose, for example, that you want your `Lexicon` class to export the methods shown in Figure 8-2. You can then write a `Lexicon` class that exports precisely those methods, as shown in Figure 8-3 on the next two pages. The constructor creates a `TreeSet<String>` and stores it in the instance variable `set`. The other methods generally pass the job along to the corresponding method in the `TreeSet` class. This strategy is called *forwarding.*

The code in Figure 8-3 does introduce a couple of new features that have not yet been described in this book. For a start, the implementation of `containsPrefix` calls a method named `ceiling`, which was not included among the common methods from the set abstraction in Figure 6-13. The `ceiling` method in the `TreeSet` class takes a value of the set's element type and returns either that value, if that value is indeed a member of the set, or the next larger value in the set. A string value is the prefix of some word in the lexicon if `ceiling` returns a non-`null` value that starts with the string `prefix`.

The second new feature in the implementation of the `Lexicon` class is the `iterator` method, which makes it possible to use the `for` statement to cycle through all the words of a lexicon in order. In this implementation, the code for `iterator` simply forwards that request on to the underlying `TreeSet` object. You will have the chance to learn more about the `iterator` method in Chapter 13.

FIGURE 8-3 Implementation of the `Lexicon` class

```java
/*
 * File: Lexicon.java
 * -------------------
 * This file implements the Lexicon class by embedding a TreeSet object
 * in the private data and forwarding the necessary operations to it.
 */

package edu.stanford.cs.javacs2.ch8;

import java.io.BufferedReader;
import java.io.FileReader;
import java.io.IOException;
import java.util.Iterator;
import java.util.TreeSet;

public class Lexicon implements Iterable<String> {

    public Lexicon(String filename) {
        set = new TreeSet<String>();
        try {
            BufferedReader rd = new BufferedReader(new FileReader(filename));
            while (true) {
                String line = rd.readLine();
                if (line == null) break;
                add(line);
            }
        } catch (IOException ex) {
            throw new RuntimeException(ex.toString());
        }
    }

/**
 * Returns the number of words in the lexicon.
 *
 * @return The number of words in the lexicon
 */

    public int size() {
        return set.size();
    }

/**
 * Returns true if the lexicon is empty.
 *
 * @return The constant true if the lexicon is empty
 */

    public boolean isEmpty() {
        return set.isEmpty();
    }
```

FIGURE 8-3 Implementation of the Lexicon class (continued)

```java
/**
 * Removes all words from the lexicon.
 */

   public void clear() {
      set.clear();
   }

/**
 * Adds a word to the lexicon.
 *
 * @param word The word being added
 */

   public void add(String word) {
      set.add(word.toLowerCase());
   }

/**
 * Returns true if the specified string is a valid word in the lexicon.
 *
 * @param word The word being tested
 * @return The value true if the string exists in the lexicon
 */

   public boolean contains(String word) {
      return set.contains(word.toLowerCase());
   }

/**
 * Returns true if the specified string is a valid prefix of some word
 * in the lexicon.
 *
 * @param prefix The prefix string being tested
 * @return The value true if the string is a valid prefix
 */

   public boolean containsPrefix(String prefix) {
      prefix = prefix.toLowerCase();
      String next = set.ceiling(prefix);
      return next != null && next.startsWith(prefix);
   }

/**
 * Returns an iterator for the lexicon.
 */

   public Iterator<String> iterator() {
      return set.iterator();
   }

/* Private instance variables */

   private TreeSet<String> set;

}
```

8.2 Defining an Employee class

Suppose that you have been given the task of designing an object-oriented payroll system for a company. You might begin by defining a general class called **Employee** that encapsulates the information about an individual worker along with methods that implement operations required for the payroll system. These operations might include simple methods like **getName**, which returns the name of an employee, along with more complicated methods like **getPay**, which calculates the pay for an employee according to data stored within each **Employee** object. In many companies, however, employees fall into several different classes that are similar in certain respects but different in others. For example, a company might have hourly, commissioned, and salaried employees on the same payroll. In such companies, it might make sense to define subclasses for each employee category as illustrated by the UML diagram in Figure 8-4.

The root of this hierarchy is the **Employee** class, which defines the methods that are common to all employees. The **Employee** class therefore exports methods like **getName**, which the other classes simply inherit. All employees, after all, have a name. On the other hand, it is almost certainly necessary to write separate **getPay** methods for each of the subclasses, because the computation is different in each case. The pay of an hourly employee depends on the hourly rate and the number of hours worked. For a commissioned employee, the pay is typically the sum of some base salary plus a commission on the sales volume for which that employee is responsible. At the same time, it is important to note that every employee has a **getPay** method, even though its implementation differs for each of the subclasses. It therefore makes sense to *specify* that method at the level of the **Employee** class and then to *override* that definition in each of the subclasses.

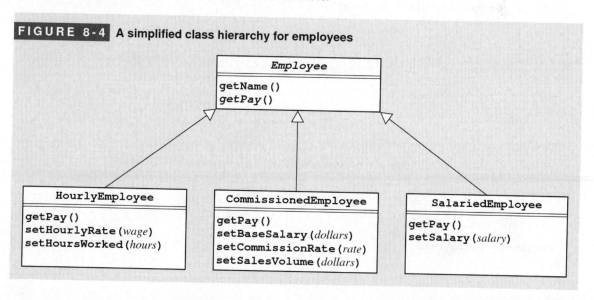

FIGURE 8-4 A simplified class hierarchy for employees

If you look closely at the typography in Figure 8-4, you'll notice that the name of the `Employee` class and its `getPay` method appear in italics. In UML, italic type is used to specify that a class or method is *abstract,* which indicates that definitions at this level of the hierarchy provide only a specification for definitions that appear in the subclasses. There are, for example, no objects whose primary type is `Employee`. Every `Employee` must instead be constructed as an `HourlyEmployee`, a `CommissionedEmployee`, or a `SalariedEmployee`. Any object belonging to one of these subclasses is still an `Employee` and therefore inherits the `getName` method along with the prototype for the virtual method `getPay`.

Figure 8-5 defines a very simple version of the `Employee` class that begins with a constructor marked with the `protected` keyword, which means that it is visible

FIGURE 8-5 Minimal definition of the `Employee` class

```
/*
 * File: Employee.java
 * --------------------
 * This file defines the abstract class Employee, which forms the root of
 * the Employee hierarchy.
 */

package edu.stanford.cs.javacs2.ch8;

public abstract class Employee {

/**
 * Constructs a new Employee object with the specified name.
 */

   protected Employee(String name) {
      this.name = name;
   }

/**
 * Returns the name of this employee.
 */

   public String getName() {
      return name;
   }

/**
 * Specifies the prototype of the abstract getPay method.
 */

   public abstract double getPay();

/* Private instance variables */

   private String name;

}
```

only within this package and to its subclasses. Subclasses of `Employee` will invoke this constructor automatically, but it is not legal to construct a value of type `Employee` on its own. The `Employee` class also declares two methods: a `getName` method that returns a `String` and an abstract `getPay` method that returns a `double`. The definition of `getName` looks just like any other getter method. The declaration of the `getPay` method, however, has the following form

```
public abstract double getPay();
```

This keyword `abstract` marks this method as one that is supplied only by the concrete subclasses of `Employee`. Since the `Employee` class doesn't implement this method, the body of the method definition is replaced with a semicolon.

Although the code for the `Employee` class in Figure 8-5 doesn't supply a definition for `getPay`, there is nothing that prevents it from doing so. In many hierarchies, the base class provides a default definition, which is then overridden only in those subclasses that need to change it. You will see several examples of that technique later in this text.

The class definitions for the three subclasses of `Employee` each have a common form. The class header indicates the subclass relationship by indicating that these new classes extend `Employee`. Those subclasses then go on to define the specific behavior and data required for that subclass. For example, assuming that the relevant information has already been stored in `hoursWorked` and `hourlyRate`, the `HourlyEmployee` class would calculate the employee's pay using a method like this:

```
public double getPay() {
    return hoursWorked * hourlyRate;
}
```

The `CommissionedEmployee` class, by contrast, would override this method differently, presumably with a definition like this:

```
public double getPay() {
    return baseSalary + commissionRate * salesVolume;
}
```

The `SalariedEmployee` class would use the following simpler calculation:

```
public double getPay() {
    return salary;
}
```

Figure 8-6 shows a definition of the `HourlyEmployee` subclass. The implementations of the other two subclasses are left to you as an exercise.

FIGURE 8-6   Minimal definition of the `HourlyEmployee` class

```java
/*
 * File: HourlyEmployee.java
 * --------------------------
 * This file defines the concrete class HourlyEmployee, whose pay is
 * computed as the number of hours worked times the hourly rate.
 */

package edu.stanford.cs.javacs2.ch8;

public class HourlyEmployee extends Employee {

/**
 * Constructs a new HourlyEmployee object with the specified name.
 */

   public HourlyEmployee(String name) {
      super(name);
   }

/**
 * Sets the hourly wage for this worker.
 */

   public void setHourlyRate(double wage) {
      hourlyRate = wage;
   }

/**
 * Sets the number of hours worked.
 */

   public void setHoursWorked(double hours) {
      hoursWorked = hours;
   }

/**
 * Computes the pay for an hourly employee.
 */

   @Override
   public double getPay() {
      return hoursWorked * hourlyRate;
   }

/* Private instance variables */

   private double hourlyRate;
   private double hoursWorked;

}
```

8.3 A brief overview of Java graphics

One of the contexts in which inheritance hierarchies are worth the added complexity is the design of graphical interfaces. Graphical user interfaces are ubiquitous in systems today and typically rely on inheritance hierarchies to define the associated *application programming interface* (or *API* for short) that implementers use to write the necessary code. The Java libraries include an extremely rich graphical API that contains more than 2000 classes distributed across several packages. Figure 8-7 shows a few of the more common classes in Java's graphics framework. The diagram includes, for example, the `JFileChooser` and `Point` classes you have already seen, along with classes describing windows and a variety of tools for creating user interfaces, such as buttons, check boxes, and scroll bars. Since the

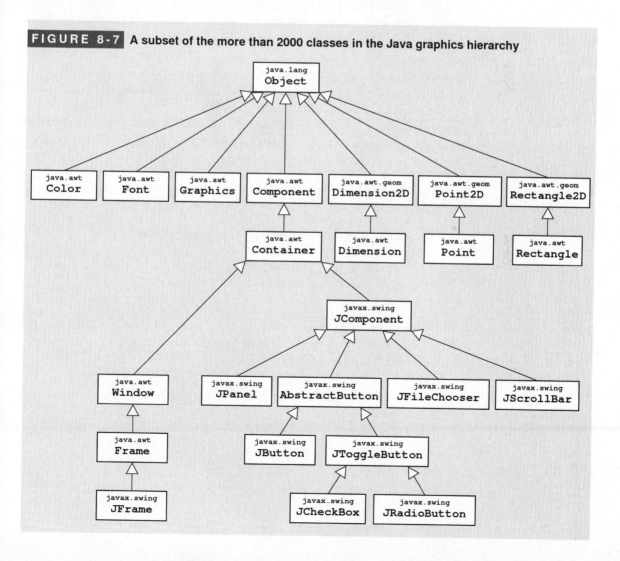

FIGURE 8-7 A subset of the more than 2000 classes in the Java graphics hierarchy

focus of this chapter is on inheritance hierarchies rather than the details of Java graphics, you won't have to learn more than a few of the classes in Figure 8-7, but it is still nice to see how those classes fit into the hierarchy as a whole.

Putting a window on the screen

Just as when you were getting started with the **HelloWorld** program in Chapter 1, the best way to begin working with the graphics library is to write the simplest possible program that makes something appear on the screen. The class that is most important for this purpose is the **JFrame** class in the lower left corner of Figure 8-7. As you can see from the diagram, the **JFrame** class is deeply nested in the inheritance hierarchy, which starts with **Object**, as all Java classes do. The next class in the inheritance chain is **Component**, which represents any graphical object that can appear on the screen. The **Container** class restricts the **Component** class to those that can contain other components. The **Window** class then specializes this idea to components that are managed by the window system. From there, the **Frame** class specializes the concept of a **Window** by adding borders, titles, and menu bars. Finally, the **JFrame** class takes the concept of a **Frame** and integrates it into the graphics package called *Swing,* which is now part of the standard Java libraries in a package called **javax.swing**. As with any class in a hierarchy, the **JFrame** class belongs to all the classes above it in the hierarchy. Thus, a **JFrame** is a **Frame**, a **Window**, a **Container**, a **Component**, and ultimately an **Object**.

The simplest program to create and display a **JFrame** looks something like this:

```
public void run() {
    JFrame frame = new JFrame("EmptyJFrame");
    frame.setSize(400, 225);
    frame.setBackground(Color.WHITE);
    frame.setVisible(true);
}
```

This program creates a **JFrame** with the title **"EmptyJFrame"**, sets its size to 400×225 screen units, selects white as its background color, and then makes that **JFrame** visible, creating the following window:

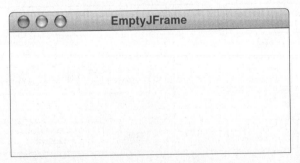

The numbers 400 and 225 in the `setSize` call are measured in units called *pixels,* which are the individual dots that cover the surface of the display screen. The argument to the `setBackground` method is an object from the `Color` class in the `java.awt` package. Although you can work with a wide variety of colors in Java, you can usually get by with the following predefined ones:

```
Color.BLACK            Color.RED          Color.BLUE
Color.DARK_GRAY        Color.YELLOW       Color.MAGENTA
Color.GRAY             Color.GREEN        Color.ORANGE
Color.LIGHT_GRAY       Color.CYAN         Color.PINK
Color.WHITE
```

Adding graphics to the window

The empty `JFrame` displayed in the preceding section is certainly a start, but it is not very interesting on its own. In Java, the standard way to add graphical content to a window is to add a `JComponent` object—or, more accurately, an instance of some subclass of `JComponent` that you have defined—to the `JFrame` and then let that subclass take responsibilty for updating the screen. The `JComponent` class defines a default version of a method called `paintComponent` that has no effect, at least in the `JComponent` class. Your subclass then overrides the `paintComponent` method so that it produces the desired graphical display.

The `paintComponent` method takes one argument, conventionally named `g`, of type `Graphics`, which exports the methods shown in Figure 8-8. The first two

FIGURE 8-8 Selected methods in the `Graphics` class

`drawRect` (*x, y, width, height*)	Draws the outline of a rectangle whose upper left corner is the point (x, y) with the specified width and height.
`fillRect` (*x, y, width, height*)	Fills the interior of the specified rectangle.
`drawOval` (*x, y, width, height*)	Draws the outline of the oval that fits just inside the bounding rectangle as specified in the description of `drawRect`.
`fillOval` (*x, y, width, height*)	Fills the interior of the oval specified by the bounding rectangle.
`drawLine` (*x_1, y_1, x_2, y_2*)	Draws a line from the point (x_1, y_1) to the point (x_2, y_2).
`drawString` (*str, x, y*)	Draws a string so that the baseline origin of the first character appears at the point (x, y).
`setColor` (*color*)	Sets the color for all drawing operations.
`getColor` ()	Returns the current color.
`setFont` (*font*)	Sets the font for drawing strings.
`getFont` ()	Returns the current font.

methods, for example, are **drawRect**, which draws the outline of a rectangle, and **fillRect**, which draws a rectangle filled with a solid color. Both methods take the same four arguments: *x*, *y*, *width*, and *height*. The *x* and *y* coordinate values specify the point at the upper left corner of the rectangle, and *width* and *height* specify its dimensions. The rectangle is drawn or filled in the current color maintained by the **Graphics** object, which you can change by calling **setColor**.

This approach is illustrated in Figure 8-9, which contains a program to draw a blue rectangle on the screen. The code that is responsible for the actual drawing is

FIGURE 8-9   Program to draw a blue rectangle on the screen

```
/*
 * File: BlueRectangle.java
 * ---------------------------------
 * This program creates a JFrame that defines a JComponent subclass to
 * draw a blue rectangle on the screen.
 */

package edu.stanford.cs.javacs2.ch8;

import java.awt.Color;
import java.awt.Graphics;
import javax.swing.JComponent;
import javax.swing.JFrame;

public class BlueRectangle {

    public void run() {
        JFrame frame = new JFrame("BlueRectangle");
        frame.add(new BlueRectangleCanvas());
        frame.setBackground(Color.WHITE);
        frame.setSize(400, 225);
        frame.setVisible(true);
    }

/* Inner class that draws a blue rectangle */

    private static class BlueRectangleCanvas extends JComponent {

        @Override
        public void paintComponent(Graphics g) {
            g.setColor(Color.BLUE);
            g.fillRect(100, 50, 200, 100);
        }

    }

/* Main program */

    public static void main(String[] args) {
        new BlueRectangle().run();
    }

}
```

the `paintComponent` method in the **BlueRectangleCanvas** class, which extends `JComponent` and then overrides the default definition of `paintComponent` with the following definition:

```
public void paintComponent(Graphics g) {
    g.setColor(Color.BLUE);
    g.fillRect(100, 50, 200, 100);
}
```

The first line sets the current color of **g** to blue, and the second draws a filled rectangle starting at the point (100, 50), with a width of 200 pixels and a height of 100 pixels.

In Java's graphics library, the *x* and *y* parameters represent the distance in that dimension from the *origin,* which is the point (0, 0) in the upper left corner of the window. As in traditional Cartesian coordinates, the value for *x* increases as you move rightward across the window. Having the location of the origin in the upper left corner, however, means that the *y* value increases as you move downward, which is precisely opposite to the convention used in the standard Cartesian plane. Computer-based graphics packages invert the *y* coordinate because doing so is more natural for text. If *y* values increase downward, successive lines of text appear at increasing values of *y*. The structure of Java's coordinate system is illustrated in Figure 8-10, which shows how the coordinate values in the **BlueRectangle** program map to screen coordinates.

FIGURE 8-10 The Java coordinate system

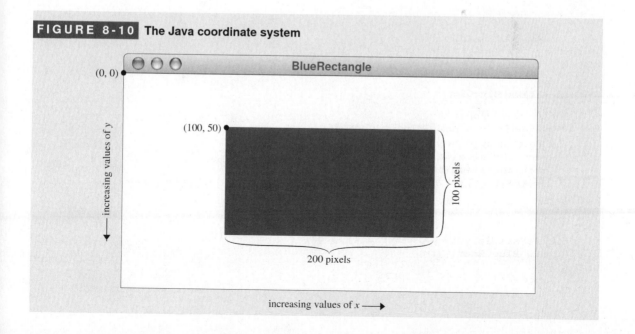

8.4 A hierarchy of graphical objects

Although you can use the facilities provided by the **Graphics** class to create much more sophisticated pictures than the blue rectangle, it is worth taking a step back and looking at the design of the **Graphics** class. In contrast to the rich hierarchy that exists for graphical components as illustrated in Figure 8-7, the structure of the **Graphics** class itself does not use an object-oriented design. The methods exported by the **Graphics** class are all imperative: draw this rectangle, draw this line, set the current color, and so on. When you are using Java's graphics model, there is no object that corresponds to a rectangle or a line displayed on the screen, which is what you would expect in an object-oriented approach. In that more modern style, you would create graphical objects and add them to a canvas embedded in a **JFrame**. Those objects would maintain their own state and take care of the details of painting themselves on the screen.

Figure 8-11 shows how the program to draw a blue rectangle changes if you move to an object-oriented design. The program begins by creating a **GWindow** object of the desired size and then sets its title to the name of the program class. The rest of the program then creates a **GRect** object with the same dimensions as in

---

FIGURE 8-11 Program to draw a blue GRect object on the screen

```
/*
 * File: BlueGRect.java
 * ------------------------
 * This program uses the object-oriented graphics model to draw a
 * blue rectangle on the screen.
 */

package edu.stanford.cs.javacs2.ch8;

import java.awt.Color;

public class BlueGRect {

    public void run() {
        GWindow gw = new GWindow(400, 200);
        GRect rect = new GRect(100, 50, 200, 100);
        rect.setColor(Color.BLUE);
        rect.setFilled(true);
        gw.add(rect);
    }

/* Main program */

    public static void main(String[] args) {
        new BlueGRect().run();
    }
}
```

the original program, calls **setFilled(true)** to specify that the **GRect** should be filled in rather than outlined, and then calls **setColor(Color.BLUE)** to set its color to blue. The last statement in the **run** method simply adds the **GRect** object to a list maintained as part of the **GWindow** class. Whenever the window is painted, the implementation of **GWindow** goes through every graphical object in its list and asks that object to repaint itself. The resulting program is significantly shorter and less complex, which is precisely what you hope to achieve when you adopt object-oriented designs.

Creating an object-oriented graphics package

A decade ago, the Association for Computing Machinery (ACM) established the Java Task Force (JTF) with the goal of creating new libraries to make Java easier to teach. One of the libraries the JTF produced was the **acm.graphics** package, which exports a powerful set of graphics classes that uses the object-oriented style described in the preceding section. The classes in that package are distributed with this text in the **edu.stanford.cs.javacs2.graphics** package along with the associated javadoc pages.

As with the **TokenScanner** class in Chapter 7, the graphics package is too large to show its full implementation. The rest of this chapter walks through a simpler version of the package containing only the classes shown in Figure 8-12.

FIGURE 8-12 **Class structure of the simplified graphics package**

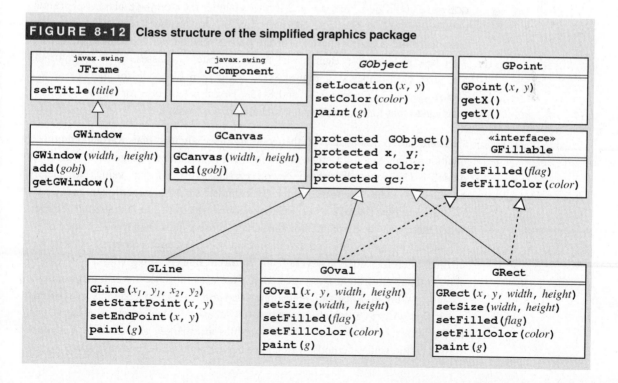

To convince you that nothing critical is being hidden away, the examples in this book restrict themselves to the classes and methods shown in Figure 8-12, which means that you will see the implementation of everything you need for this book. The more advanced features of the complete graphics library are available in case you get excited about the possibilities they offer, but those advanced features are not used in any of the program examples.

The root of the hierarchical part of the graphics library is the GObject class, which extends the universal Object class. The GObject class is abstract, which means that you will never construct a GObject directly, but will instead construct one of the three concrete subclasses that extend GObject: GLine, GOval, and GRect. The GObject class defines methods that are common to all GObject values. For example, since every GObject has a location and a color, it makes sense to define the setLocation, move, and setColor methods in the GObject class itself. By contrast, it doesn't make sense to fill a line segment, so the setFilled and setFillColor methods are defined only in the GOval and GRect subclasses, which support that operation. To ensure that GOval and GRect implement the same model for filling, both classes implement the GFillable interface, which specifies the two methods that every fillable class must support.

There is one more method that shows up in the UML diagram for the GObject class and all three of its subclasses, which is the method paint(g). Since a GObject could be a line, an oval, or a rectangle, the GObject class itself cannot possibly know how to create the necessary picture on the screen. The GObject class therefore specifies the form of the paint method but does not implement it. That task is left up to each of the three concrete subclasses. The code for the GObject class appears in Figure 8-13, along with the code for the GLine and GRect classes in Figures 8-14 and 8-15. Because the code for GOval is almost identical to that for GRect, it is not included in this book.

There are a few parts of the code in these figures that warrant additional mention. The first is a slight but nonetheless important change in the graphics model. The methods in the Graphics class use integer values to specify coordinates. The GObject model, by contrast, stores all coordinate and length values using type double to avoid having rounding errors spoil the graphical effect. When these objects are painted on the screen, those values need to be rounded off to the nearest integer before you call the methods in the Graphics class. The paint methods therefore contain several calls to Math.round, along with a type cast to convert the result from a long to an int. Another point that is worth mentioning is the fact that the instance variables in the GObject class are declared as protected rather than private, which means that the subclasses have access to these values. In the library implementation, these variables are marked as private, but those classes define getter methods, which have been eliminated here to save space.

FIGURE 8-13 Implementation of the GObject class

```java
/*
 * File: GObject.java
 * --------------------
 * This file exports the GObject class at the top of the graphics hierarchy.
 */

package edu.stanford.cs.javacs2.ch8;

import java.awt.Color;
import java.awt.Graphics;

public abstract class GObject {

/* Initializes the color of this object to BLACK */

    protected GObject() {
        color = Color.BLACK;
    }

/* Paints the object using the specified graphics context */

    public abstract void paint(Graphics g);

/* Sets the location of this object to the point (x, y) */

    public void setLocation(double x, double y) {
        this.x = x;
        this.y = y;
        repaint();
    }

/* Sets the color used to display this object */

    public void setColor(Color color) {
        this.color = color;
        repaint();
    }

/* Signals that the object needs to be repainted */

    protected void repaint() {
        if (gc != null) gc.repaint();
    }

/* Helper method used by subclasses to round a double to an int */

    protected int round(double x) {
        return (int) Math.round(x);
    }

/* Protected instance variables */

    protected double x;
    protected double y;
    protected Color color;
    protected GCanvas gc;

}
```

FIGURE 8-14   Implementation of the GLine class

```java
/*
 * File: GLine.java
 * ------------------
 * This file exports a GObject subclass that displays a line segment.
 */

package edu.stanford.cs.javacs2.ch8;

import java.awt.Graphics;

public class GLine extends GObject {

/* Constructs a line segment from its endpoints */

    public GLine(double x1, double y1, double x2, double y2) {
        setLocation(x1, y1);
        dx = x2 - x1;
        dy = y2 - y1;
    }

/* Sets the start point without changing the end point */

    public void setStartPoint(double x, double y) {
        dx = x - this.x;
        dy = y - this.y;
        repaint();
    }

/* Sets the end point without changing the start point */

    public void setEndPoint(double x, double y) {
        dx += this.x - x;
        dy += this.y - y;
        setLocation(x, y);
    }

/* Implements the paint operation for this graphical object */

    public void paint(Graphics g) {
        g.setColor(color);
        g.drawLine(round(x), round(y), round(x + dx), round(y + dy));
    }

/* Private instance variables */

    private double dx;
    private double dy;

}
```

FIGURE 8-15   Implementation of the GRect class

```
/*
 * File: GRect.java
 * ----------------
 * This class exports a GObject subclass that displays a rectangle.
 */

package edu.stanford.cs.javacs2.ch8;

import java.awt.Color;
import java.awt.Graphics;

public class GRect extends GObject implements GFillable {

/* Constructs a new rectangle with the specified bounds */

    public GRect(double x, double y, double width, double height) {
        setLocation(x, y);
        setSize(width, height);
    }

/* Changes the width and height of this rectangle */

    public void setSize(double width, double height) {
        this.width = width;
        this.height = height;
    }

/* Sets whether this object is filled */

    public void setFilled(boolean fill) {
        isFilled = fill;
        repaint();
    }

/* Sets the color used to fill this object */

    public void setFillColor(Color color) {
        fillColor = color;
        repaint();
    }

/* Implements the paint operation for this graphical object */

    public void paint(Graphics g) {
        if (isFilled) {
            g.setColor((fillColor == null) ? color : fillColor);
            g.fillRect(round(x), round(y), round(width), round(height));
        }
        g.setColor(color);
        g.drawRect(round(x), round(y), round(width), round(height));
    }

/* Private instance variables */

    private double width, height;
    private boolean isFilled;
    private Color fillColor;

}
```

The implementations of the GRect and GOval classes are longer than that of the GLine class because these classes implement the GFillable interface. The GFillable interface itself, which appears in Figure 8-16, is very short, because it includes only the prototypes for the setFilled and setFillColor methods, and not the code that implements them. That code must be repeated, with minor modifications, in each of the GRect and GOval classes.

Implementing the GWindow and GCanvas classes

The two classes left to implement in the stripped-down version of the graphics package are the GWindow class, which extends JFrame to create a window that maintains a list of the GObject instances that appear in the graphical display, and the GCanvas class, which is a JComponent that lives inside the GWindow and is responsible for painting the objects. The code for the GWindow class appears in Figure 8-17 on the next page. The GWindow class creates a GCanvas and then forwards operations to it. The code for the GCanvas class appears in Figure 8-18. The GCanvas stores the list of GObject instances in an ArrayList<GObject> called contents. The add method adds the GObject to contents and also sets the gw instance variable in the GObject to ensure that changes trigger repainting. The paintComponent method iterates over the elements of contents, invoking the paint method appropriate to that type of GObject.

FIGURE 8-16   Code for the GFillable interface

```
/*
 * File: GFillable.java
 * ----------------------
 * This file exports the GFillable interface that marks objects as fillable.
 */

package edu.stanford.cs.javacs2.ch8;

import java.awt.Color;

public interface GFillable {

/**
 * Sets whether this object is filled.
 */

   public void setFilled(boolean fill);

/**
 * Sets the color used to display the filled region of this object.
 */

   public void setFillColor(Color color);

}
```

FIGURE 8-17 Code for the `GWindow` class

```java
/*
 * File: GWindow.java
 * --------------------
 * This file exports the GWindow class, which is a JFrame containing GObjects.
 */

package edu.stanford.cs.javacs2.ch8;

import java.awt.Color;
import javax.swing.JFrame;

public class GWindow extends JFrame {

/* Creates a new GWindow containing a GCanvas with no preferred size */

    public GWindow() {
       this(new GCanvas());
    }

/* Creates a new GWindow containing a GCanvas with a preferred size */

    public GWindow(double width, double height) {
       this(new GCanvas(width, height));
    }

/* Creates a new GWindow containing a GCanvas object */

    public GWindow(GCanvas gc) {
       String title = System.getProperty("sun.java.command");
       setTitle((title == null) ? "Graphics Window" :
                                   title.substring(title.lastIndexOf('.') + 1));
       setBackground(Color.WHITE);
       this.gc = gc;
       add(gc);
       pack();
       setDefaultCloseOperation(JFrame.EXIT_ON_CLOSE);
       setVisible(true);
    }

/* Adds the graphical object to this canvas */

    public void add(GObject gobj) {
       gc.add(gobj);
    }

/* Returns the GCanvas embedded in this GWindow */

    public GCanvas getGCanvas() {
       return gc;
    }

/* Private instance variables */

    private GCanvas gc;

}
```

FIGURE 8-18 Code for the GCanvas class

```java
/*
 * File: GCanvas.java
 * ------------------
 * This file exports the GCanvas class, which is a graphical component
 * capable of containing GObjects.
 */

package edu.stanford.cs.javacs2.ch8;

import java.awt.Graphics;
import java.util.ArrayList;
import javax.swing.JComponent;

public class GCanvas extends JComponent {

/* Creates a new GCanvas with no preferred size */

    public GCanvas() {
        contents = new ArrayList<GObject>();
    }

/* Creates a new GCanvas with the specified preferred size */

    public GCanvas(double width, double height) {
        this();
        setSize((int) Math.round(width), (int) Math.round(height));
        setPreferredSize(getSize());
    }

/* Adds the graphical object to this canvas */

    public void add(GObject gobj) {
        synchronized (contents) {
            contents.add(gobj);
            gobj.gc = this;
        }
        repaint();
    }

/* Paints the contents of the GCanvas */

    @Override
    public void paintComponent(Graphics g) {
        synchronized (contents) {
            for (GObject gobj : contents) {
                gobj.paint(g);
            }
        }
    }

/* Private instance variables */

    private ArrayList<GObject> contents;

}
```

In both of these cases, the operations on the **contents** list are nested inside the body of a Java statement called **synchronized**, which you have not yet seen. The **add** method contains the code

```
synchronized (contents) {
   contents.add(gobj);
   gobj.gc = this;
}
```

Similarly, the code for **paintComponent** in the **GCanvas** class includes the lines

```
synchronized (contents) {
   for (GObject gobj : contents) {
      gobj.paint(g);
   }
}
```

Java allows several independent activities to run concurrently in a single program. Those activities are called **threads.** The purpose of the **synchronized** statement is to ensure that two threads do not try to execute the same code simultaneously. When a thread encounters a **synchronized** statement, it acquires exclusive access to the object that appears inside the parentheses. If some other thread executes a **synchronized** statement that refers to the same object, the second thread waits until the first one reaches the end of the code controlled by the **synchronized** statement. The second thread then can then proceed.

The **synchronized** statement is required in this application because the thread that runs the application is independent of the thread that repaints the components on the screen. Without the **synchronized** statement, it is possible—but by no means inevitable—that the application tries to add a **GObject** to **contents** while the repainting thread is going through its elements. If the internal structure of the **ArrayList** happened to be in an inconsistent intermediate state, this simultaneous access might cause the program to fail. Because such failures are intermittent and depend on the timing of the two threads, they tend to be difficult to debug. In general, concurrency is a difficult topic with subtleties that are well beyond the level of a second course in computer science.

The code for the **add** method in the **GWindow** class also sets an instance variable called **gc** in the **GObject** that gives the object a reference to the **GCanvas** that contains it. That reference is necessary to ensure that changes to any of the **GObject** instances correctly trigger a repaint of the **GCanvas**.

The **GWindow** and **GCanvas** constructors also divide the responsibility for setting the size of the frame. Instead of setting the size of the **JFrame** explicitly, the **GWindow** constructor passes **width** and **height** parameters to the **GCanvas** constructor, which uses these values to set both the current and preferred size of the **GCanvas** object. After adding the canvas to the window, the **GWindow** constructor calls **pack** to set the size of the frame so that the internal components fit exactly within it.

The only other new features in **GWindow.java** are the calls to **getProperty**, which returns the name of the program, and to **setDefaultCloseOperation**, which ensures that the application exits properly if the user closes the window. In the absence of the **setDefaultCloseOperation** call, the program keeps running even after the user clicks the close box.

Illustrating the GObject classes

The **BlueGRect** program uses only the **GRect** class, which is hardly a proper illustration of the **GObject** hierarchy. The code in Figure 8-19 uses all three of the **GObject** subclasses to create a diamond shape that exactly fills the graphics window and then inscribes within that diamond a blue rectangle and a gray oval, producing the following display on the screen:

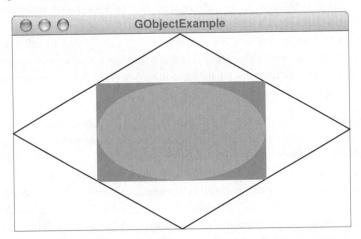

The output of this program illustrates another feature of the **GObject** model. The fact that the **add** method adds each **GObject** to the end of the **ArrayList** means that objects added later appear to be nearer to the top of this diagram and overwrite parts of the display that were drawn earlier. The complete version of the graphics library allows you to change the order in which objects are stored in the **ArrayList**, which is then reflected in the way those objects appear in the window. This order is called the *stacking order* or sometimes the *z-ordering*, which reflects the convention that the axis perpendicular to the Cartesian *x-y* plane is traditionally called the *z-axis*. The complete version of the graphics library includes the methods **sendToBack**, **sendToFront**, **sendBackward**, and **sendForward**. You will have a chance to implement these methods in the exercises.

FIGURE 8-19 Code for the `GObjectExample` program

```
/*
 * File: GObjectExample.java
 * ---------------------------
 * This program illustrates the use of each of the GObject classes.
 */

package edu.stanford.cs.javacs2.ch8;

import java.awt.Color;

public class GObjectExample {

   public void run() {
      GWindow gw = new GWindow(WIDTH, HEIGHT);
      addDiamond(gw);
      addRectangleAndOval(gw);
   }

/* Adds a diamond connecting the midpoints of the window edges */

   private void addDiamond(GWindow gw) {
      gw.add(new GLine(0, HEIGHT / 2, WIDTH / 2, 0));
      gw.add(new GLine(WIDTH / 2, 0, WIDTH, HEIGHT / 2));
      gw.add(new GLine(WIDTH, HEIGHT / 2, WIDTH / 2, HEIGHT));
      gw.add(new GLine(WIDTH / 2, HEIGHT, 0, HEIGHT / 2));
   }

/* Adds a blue rectangle and a gray oval inscribed in the diamond */

   private void addRectangleAndOval(GWindow gw) {
      GRect rect = new GRect(WIDTH / 4, HEIGHT / 4, WIDTH / 2, HEIGHT / 2);
      rect.setFilled(true);
      rect.setColor(Color.BLUE);
      gw.add(rect);
      GOval oval = new GOval(WIDTH / 4, HEIGHT / 4, WIDTH / 2, HEIGHT / 2);
      oval.setFilled(true);
      oval.setColor(Color.GRAY);
      gw.add(oval);
   }

/* Constants */

   private static final double WIDTH = 500;
   private static final double HEIGHT = 300;

/* Main program */

   public static void main(String[] args) {
      new GObjectExample().run();
   }

}
```

Creating simple animations

In the `GObject` model, objects are responsible for painting themselves on the graphics window, which is in turn repainted whenever any `GObject` changes. By changing the position of a `GObject` a little bit at a time and then delaying the process long enough to complete the repainting of the window, you can create simple animations in which an object moves around the window. The code in Figure 8-20, for example, animates a ball bouncing off the borders of the window.

In the `BouncingBall` program, the location of the center of the ball is stored in the variables `x` and `y`. The `GOval` class, however, uses the upper left corner of the bounding rectangle as its reference point, which means that the location of the `GOval` is at $(x - r, y - r)$, where `r` is the radius of the ball. The variables `vx` and `vy` store the velocity of the ball along each of the coordinate axes. In each time step, the `x` and `y` coordinates are adjusted by `vx` and `vy`, and the position of the ball is updated to reflect the new location.

Implementing the bounces is simply a matter of checking to see if the `x` and `y` coordinates, adjusted to include the radius of the ball, have moved outside the boundaries of the window. If so, a bounce simply changes the sign of the velocity component corresponding to the out-of-range coordinate. The `BouncingBall` program implements this operation using the following lines:

```
if (x < r || x > WIDTH - r) vx = -vx;
if (y < r || y > HEIGHT - r) vy = -vy;
```

Modern computers run so quickly that it is necessary to slow the animation down to the human scale by inserting a delay in each cycle of the loop. The delay is implemented by calling the static method `Thread.sleep`, which delays the calling thread by the specified number of milliseconds. This method can throw an `InterruptedException`, which means that the code must enclose it in a `try` statement, as shown in the following implementation of the `pause` method, which will prove useful in other animations:

```
private void pause(int milliseconds) {
   try {
      Thread.sleep(milliseconds);
   } catch (InterruptedException ex) {
      /* Ignore the exception */
   }
}
```

You can change the speed by adjusting the `PAUSE_TIME` constant or by changing the initial values of `dx` and `dy`.

FIGURE 8-20 Code for the `BouncingBall` program

```java
/*
 * File: BouncingBall.java
 * --------------------------
 * This program displays a ball bouncing off the walls of the window.
 */

package edu.stanford.cs.javacs2.ch8;

public class BouncingBall {

    public void run() {
        GWindow gw = new GWindow(WIDTH, HEIGHT);
        double r = BALL_RADIUS;
        double x = WIDTH / 2;
        double y = HEIGHT / 2;
        double vx = 2;
        double vy = -2;
        GOval ball = new GOval(x - r, y - r, 2 * r, 2 * r);
        ball.setFilled(true);
        gw.add(ball);
        while (true) {
            x += vx;
            y += vy;
            ball.setLocation(x - r, y - r);
            if (x < r || x > WIDTH - r) vx = -vx;
            if (y < r || y > HEIGHT - r) vy = -vy;
            pause(PAUSE_TIME);
        }
    }

/* Pauses for the specified number of milliseconds */

    private void pause(int milliseconds) {
        try {
            Thread.sleep(milliseconds);
        } catch (InterruptedException ex) {
            /* Ignore the exception */
        }
    }

/* Constants */

    private static final int WIDTH = 500;
    private static final int HEIGHT = 300;
    private static final int BALL_RADIUS = 9;
    private static final int PAUSE_TIME = 10;

/* Main program */

    public static void main(String[] args) {
        new BouncingBall().run();
    }

}
```

◼◼ 8.5 Defining a Console interface

Ever since Chapter 1, the programs in this book have used the **Scanner** class from **java.util** to read input values from the user. While that strategy makes it easier to write your first few programs, using the **Scanner** class has some serious disadvantages. For one thing, the **Scanner** class doesn't give the user the opportunity to correct input errors. If you are trying to enter an integer and type some incorrect character by mistake, the **Scanner** class throws an exception that terminates the entire program. Perhaps more subtly, using **Scanner** makes it difficult to mix numeric and string input. Reading a number typically leaves the scanner just before the end of the line the user entered, which means that the **nextLine** method will read an empty line. It's time to adopt a better strategy.

Conceptually, the **System.out** and **System.in** streams define a bidirectional channel for communication with the user reminiscent of early computer consoles. The **System.out** stream is so simple that you've been using it since the very first program. By contrast, reading data using **System.in** is so complex that it makes sense to define a new abstraction that hides the unnecessary detail.

The goal of this section is to define and implement a **Console** interface that provides input and output operations that are easy to use. The methods supported by a console simply combine the ones you've been using all along for **System.out** and **Scanner**, joining them to produce a single abstraction. For output, a **Console** supplies the methods **print**, **println**, and **printf**. For input, a **Console** supplies the methods **nextInt**, **nextDouble**, and **nextLine**.

Although it would be easy enough to define and implement a class that exports these methods, the idea behind this example is a little more ambitious. In a modern window system, using the **System.out** and **System.in** streams is a bit of a throwback to the early days of computing. It would be nice if it were possible to implement the console model in a window that supports such advanced features as cutting and pasting, changing the font and point size of the text, and displaying user input in color, just as all the sample runs do. At the same time, it is important for this more sophisticated console to implement the same operations as the traditional one. If the operations stay the same, you should be able to substitute a console window for the more traditional model based on the standard system streams.

The **Console** interface in Figure 8-21 specifies the prototypes for each of the methods that any console must implement but does not specify any particular implementation. The details are left to concrete implementations, such as the **SystemConsole** class in Figure 8-22, which implements the **Console** methods using the **System.out** and **System.in** streams.

FIGURE 8-21 The Console interface

```
/*
 * File: Console.java
 * --------------------
 * This interface defines the behavior of a console that can communicate
 * with the user.  Two concrete implementations are provided:
 * SystemConsole, which uses the System.in and System.out streams, and
 * ConsoleWindow, which creates a new console window.
 */

package edu.stanford.cs.console;

/**
 * The Console interface defines the input and output methods supported by
 * an interactive console.
 */

public interface Console {

/**
 * Prints the argument value, allowing for the possibility of more output
 * on the same line.
 *
 * @param value The value to be displayed
 */

   public void print(Object value);

/**
 * Prints the end-of-line sequence to move to the next line.
 */

   public void println();

/**
 * Prints the value and then moves to the next line.
 *
 * @param value The value to be displayed
 */

   public void println(Object value);

/**
 * Formats and prints the argument values as specified by the format
 * string. The printf formats are described in the java.util.Formatter
 * class.
 *
 * @param format The format string
 * @param args The list of arguments to be formatted
 */

   public void printf(String format, Object... args);
```

FIGURE 8-21 The Console interface (continued)

```
/**
 * Reads and returns a line of input, without including the end-of-line
 * characters that terminate the input.
 *
 * @return The next line of input as a String
 */

   public String nextLine();

/**
 * Prompts the user to enter a line of text, which is then returned as the
 * value of this method.
 *
 * @param prompt The prompt string to display to the user
 * @return The next line of input as a String
 */

   public String nextLine(String prompt);

/**
 * Reads and returns an integer value from the user.
 *
 * @return The value of the input interpreted as a decimal integer
 */

   public int nextInt();

/**
 * Prompts the user to enter an integer.
 *
 * @param prompt The prompt string to display to the user
 * @return The value of the input interpreted as a decimal integer
 */

   public int nextInt(String prompt);

/**
 * Reads and returns a double-precision value from the user.
 *
 * @return The value of the input interpreted as a double
 */

   public double nextDouble();

/**
 * Prompts the user to enter an double-precision number.
 *
 * @param prompt The prompt string to display to the user
 * @return The value of the input interpreted as a double
 */

   public double nextDouble(String prompt);

}
```

FIGURE 8-22 The SystemConsole class

```java
/*
 * File: SystemConsole.java
 * --------------------------
 * This file implements the Console interface using the standard streams.
 */

package edu.stanford.cs.console;

import java.io.IOException;

/**
 * This class implements Console using System.in and System.out.
 */

public class SystemConsole implements Console {

/* These methods simply forward the request to System.out */

    public void print(Object value) {
        System.out.print(value);
    }

    public void println() {
        System.out.println();
    }

    public void println(Object value) {
        System.out.println(value);
    }

    public void printf(String format, Object... args) {
        System.out.printf(format, args);
    }

/* This method reads characters until it finds an end-of-line sequence */

    public String nextLine() {
        try {
            String line = "";
            while (true) {
                int ch = System.in.read();
                if (ch == -1) return null;
                if (ch == '\r' || ch == '\n') break;
                line += (char) ch;
            }
            return line;
        } catch (IOException ex) {
            throw new RuntimeException(ex.toString());
        }
    }

    public String nextLine(String prompt) {
        if (prompt != null) print(prompt);
        return nextLine();
    }
```

FIGURE 8-22   The SystemConsole class (continued)

```
/*
 * Implementation notes: nextInt and nextDouble
 * ---------------------------------------------
 * These methods use a try statement to catch errors in numeric formatting.
 * If an error occurs, the user is given another chance to enter the data.
 */

   public int nextInt() {
      return nextInt(null);
   }

   public int nextInt(String prompt) {
      while (true) {
         String line = nextLine(prompt);
         try {
            return Integer.parseInt(line);
         } catch (NumberFormatException ex) {
            println("Illegal integer format");
            if (prompt == null) prompt = "Retry: ";
         }
      }
   }

   public double nextDouble() {
      return nextDouble(null);
   }

   public double nextDouble(String prompt) {
      while (true) {
         String line = nextLine(prompt);
         try {
            return Double.parseDouble(line);
         } catch (NumberFormatException ex) {
            println("Illegal floating-point format");
            if (prompt == null) prompt = "Retry: ";
         }
      }
   }

}
```

Each of the input methods in the Console interface exists in two forms: one that takes a prompt string and one that assumes that the calling program has already printed the prompt. Taking the prompt as a parameter has the following advantages:

- The variable declaration, prompt, and input operation all fit on a single line.

- The implementation of the input method can reprint the prompt if the user enters an illegal value.

You can use the **SystemConsole** class with any of the programs from earlier in the book to ensure that those programs recover gracefully from errors in user input. Figure 8-23, for example, contains an updated version of the **AddIntegerList**

FIGURE 8-23 Program to add a list of integers using the SystemConsole class

```java
/*
 * File: AddListWithSystemConsole.java
 * ----------------------------------------
 * This program adds a list of integers.  The end of the input is indicated
 * by entering a sentinel value, which is defined by the constant SENTINEL.
 * This version uses a Console object for input and output.  The console is
 * created using a factory method, which makes it easy for subclasses to
 * substitute a different implementation.
 */

package edu.stanford.cs.javacs2.ch8;

import edu.stanford.cs.console.Console;
import edu.stanford.cs.console.SystemConsole;

public class AddListWithSystemConsole {

   public void run() {
      Console console = createConsole();
      console.println("This program adds a list of integers.");
      console.println("Use " + SENTINEL + " to signal the end.");
      int total = 0;
      while (true) {
         int value = console.nextInt(" ? ");
         if (value == SENTINEL) break;
         total += value;
      }
      console.println("The total is " + total);
   }

/* Factory method to create the console */

   public Console createConsole() {
      return new SystemConsole();
   }

/* Private constants */

   private static final int SENTINEL = 0;

/* Main program */

   public static void main(String[] args) {
      new AddListWithSystemConsole().run();
   }

}
```

program from Chapter 1. The updated version allows the user to correct input errors, as shown in the following sample run:

```
○ ○ ○          AddListWithSystemConsole
This program adds a list of integers.
Use 0 to signal the end.
 ? 17.0
Illegal integer format
 ? 17
 ? 11
 ? 14
 ? 0
The total is 42
```

The code for **AddListWithSystemConsole** creates the **Console** object using a method called **createConsole**, which in this example has the following form:

```
public Console createConsole() {
    return new SystemConsole();
}
```

Methods that create an object for use by a class are called *factory methods.* In the typical case, a factory method creates an object of a specific subclass but declares its result type to be a more general class.

The advantage of this design is that subclasses can override the definition of the factory method to create a different instance. As an example, you can easily create a new application whose only definition is

```
@Override
public Console createConsole() {
    return new ConsoleWindow();
}
```

The **ConsoleWindow** class in the **edu.stanford.cs.java.console** package implements the **Console** interface in a **JFrame** that lives in the window system, just as the **GWindow** class does. In addition, the **ConsoleWindow** class uses the expanded capabilities of the Java graphics model to display user input in a different color from that of the output generated by the program. Even though the implementation of **ConsoleWindow** is beyond the scope of this book, you are free to use it if you want your programs to look more like the sample runs.

The code in the rest of this book uses the **Console** model for user input. For the most part, those programs continue to use **System.out** for output, primarily because it is more conventional. If you want your applications to support either a system console or a console window, you should use the factory-method strategy.

Summary

In this chapter, you have learned how to use inheritance in Java and have seen a few practical applications of the concept. You have also learned how to use inheritance to create an object-oriented graphics library.

Important points in this chapter include:

- Java allows subclasses to inherit the public behavior of the superclasses. In its simplest form, the Java syntax for defining a subclass looks like this:

```
public class subclass extends superclass {
      new entries for the subclass
};
```

- Methods that are implemented only by subclasses are said to be *abstract*. Such methods are marked in the superclass with the **abstract** keyword.

- Java classes support two levels of access control beyond **public** and **private**. Declarations marked as **protected** are available to subclasses but inaccessible to classes outside the defining package. Declarations that include no keyword are *package-private* and are visible only within the defining package.

- Calling the constructor for a subclass always invokes a constructor for its superclass. In the absence of any other specification, Java invokes the default constructor although clients can use the **super** keyword to call a different one.

- Inheritance is often overused. In many situations, it is better to embed an existing object inside a new class and then use forwarding to implement the desired operations.

- The **GObject** hierarchy defined in this chapter includes the concrete subclasses **GRect**, **GOval**, and **GLine**, which are sufficient for creating any of the graphical examples used in this book. These classes form a subset of the **acm.graphics** package, which is exported from **edu.stanford.cs.javacs2.graphics**.

- Operations that apply to every graphical object are defined in the **GObject** class. Operations that are specific to individual subclasses must be defined in those subclasses. If several classes share a common structure, it is good practice to specify that common behavior using an interface.

- Java uses a coordinate system in which the *origin* is in the upper left corner of the graphics window and the values of the y coordinate increase as you move downward. All coordinates and distances are expressed in terms of *pixels,* which are the individual dots that fill the surface of the screen.

- The **edu.stanford.cs.java.console** package includes two implementations of the **Console** interface. The **SystemConsole** class uses the **System.out** and **System.in** streams; the **ConsoleWindow** class creates a new window.

Review questions

1. In Java, what header line would you use to define a class named **Sub** that inherited the public behavior from a class named **Super**?

2. True or false: The superclass specification in a new class definition may not be a parameterized class with specific instantiation of the types.

3. True or false: A new definition of a method in a Java subclass automatically overrides the definition of that method in its superclass.

4. What is an *abstract class?* Is it possible for an abstract class to provide its own implementation of its exported methods?

5. What two levels of access control does Java offer beyond **public** and **private**?

6. A constructor for a subclass always calls a constructor for its superclass. How do you specify that you would like to call some constructor that is not the default constructor?

7. What strategy is suggested in the chapter as an alternative to inheritance?

8. What are the three concrete **GObject** subclasses implemented in this chapter?

9. Which of these subclasses respond to the method **setFilled**? Which respond to the method **setColor**? In which classes are these two methods defined?

10. In what ways does Java's coordinate system differ from the traditional Cartesian coordinate system?

11. What classes exist in the superclass chain for **GWindow**, going all the way back to **Object**?

12. What is the purpose of the **synchronized** statement in the implementation of the **GWindow** class?

Exercises

1. Complete the implementation of the **Employee** class hierarchy by defining the **SalariedEmployee** and **CommissionedEmployee** classes. Design a simple program to test your code.

2. Define a **StringSet** class that extends **TreeSet** so that its elements are always strings. Include a new constructor in the class that allows you to create a **StringSet** by listing its elements.

3. Use Java's standard graphics library to write a program that displays the string
    `"hello, world"` at the center of a `JFrame`. If you set the font to Lucida
    Blackletter and use a point size of 18, you get a display that looks like this:

    This chapter doesn't explain how to create a font or how to determine how
    much space a letter occupies in a particular font. You will need to explore the
    web to find the answers to these questions.

4. Rewrite the `GObjectExample` program from Figure 8-18 so that it uses the
    standard graphics library to produce the same graphical display inside a
    `JFrame`.

5. Use the `GObject` hierarchy to draw a pyramid consisting of bricks arranged in
    horizontal rows, as shown in the following sample run:

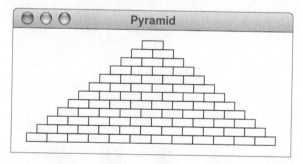

    As you can see from the diagram, the number of bricks in each row decreases
    by one as you move up the pyramid. Your program should center the drawing
    in the graphics window and should use the following constants to control the
    dimensions of the pyramid:

```
private static final int WIDTH = 500;
private static final int HEIGHT = 300;
private static final int BRICK_WIDTH = 30;
private static final int BRICK_HEIGHT = 14;
private static final int BRICKS_IN_BASE = 15;
```

    Changing any of these parameters should change the display accordingly.

6. Use the **GObject** hierarchy to draw a rainbow that looks something like this:

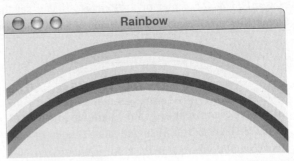

Starting at the top, the six bands in the rainbow are red, orange, yellow, green, blue, and magenta, respectively; cyan makes a lovely color for the sky. Remember that this chapter defines only the **GLine**, **GRect**, and **GOval** classes and does not include a graphical object that represents an arc. It will help to think outside the box, in a more literal sense than usual.

7. Use the graphics library to write a program that draws a checkerboard on the graphics window. Your picture should include the red and black pieces, as they exist at the beginning of the game, like this:

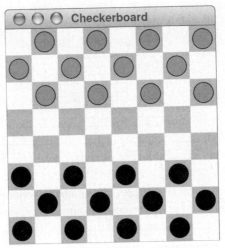

8. It is possible to make amazing images using only lines. Imagine that you start with a rectangular board and then arrange pegs around the edges so that they are evenly spaced along all four edges, with **N_ACROSS** pegs along the top and bottom and **N_DOWN** pegs along the left and right edges. To model this process using the **GObject** hierarchy, you start by creating an **ArrayList<GPoint>** that holds the coordinates of each of these pegs, which are inserted into the list

starting at the upper left and then proceeding clockwise around the edges of the rectangle, as follows:

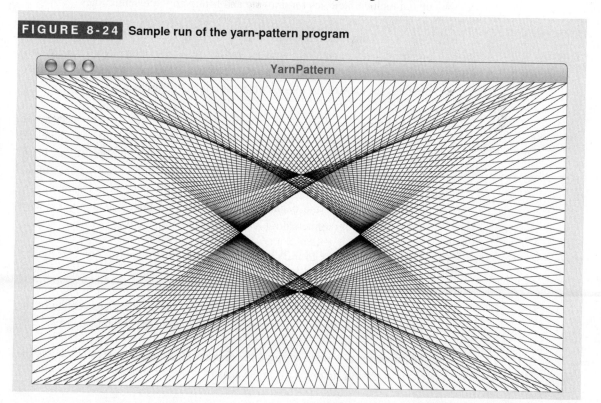

From here, you create a figure by winding a single piece of yarn through the pegs, starting at peg 0 and then moving ahead a fixed number of spaces on each cycle, as specified by the constant **DELTA**. For example, if **DELTA** is 11, the yarn goes from peg 0 to peg 11, then from peg 11 to peg 22, and then (counting past the beginning) from peg 22 to peg 5. The process continues until the yarn returns to peg 0. On the screen, each segment of the yarn pattern is represented by a **GLine** object.

Write a program that simulates this process on the graphics window using larger values for **N_ACROSS** and **N_DOWN**. As an example, Figure 8-24 shows

FIGURE 8-24   Sample run of the yarn-pattern program

the output of the program with **N_ACROSS** equal to 50, **N_DOWN** equal to 30, and **DELTA** equal to 67. By changing those constants, you can create other wonderful patterns composed entirely of straight lines.

9. One of the principles that defines Taoist philosophy is that dichotomies do not have rigid boundaries, and that there is mixing even between categories that most people see as opposites. This idea is captured in the Yin-Yang symbol, in which each region contains a bit of the other color:

Write a graphics program to draw this symbol at the center of an empty graphics window. The challenge is to decompose the drawing in such a way that you can create it using only the classes and methods in Figure 8-12, which do not include facilities for drawing and filling arcs and semicircles.

10§. One of the obvious omissions in the **GObject** hierarchy is that there are no getter methods to go along with the various setter methods like **setLocation**, **setColor**, **setFilled**, and **setFillColor**. Design and implement these methods for each of the classes in the **GObject** hierarchy.

11§. The **GObject** class in the full version of the graphics package specifies an abstract method called **contains** that takes an *x* and a *y* coordinate value and returns **true** if the point (*x*, *y*) is inside the object. For the **GLine** class, **contains** should return **true** if the point is within half a pixel distance of the line. If you are unsure of how to determine whether a point is inside an oval or how to calculate the distance from a point to a line, you should do what professional programmers do: look the answer up on the web.

12§. Add a **GLabel** class to the **GObject** hierarchy that displays a text string at a given location on the screen. Your **GLabel** class should allow clients to set the font for the **GLabel**. If you're feeling ambitious, you can implement the other methods of the **GLabel** class that appear in the complete version of the graphics library, all of which are described in the online documentation.

13§. Add a **remove** method to the **GWindow** and **GCanvas** classes that allows the client to remove an object from the canvas.

FIGURE 8-25	Methods to add vertices to a GPolygon object

addVertex (x, y)	Adds a new vertex at the point (x, y), where the point is expressed relative to the location of the GPolygon itself. By defining vertex coordinates in this way, moving the GPolygon preserves its shape.
addEdge (dx, dy)	Adds a new vertex at the end of an edge that is dx and dy pixels away from the previous vertex along the two coordinate axes.
addPolarEdge (r, $theta$)	Adds a new vertex whose coordinates are computed from the previous one by moving r units in the direction specified by $theta$, which is measured in degrees counterclockwise from the +x axis.

14§. The full version of the **GObject** hierarchy also includes a class called **GPolygon** that displays a polygon on the screen. Unlike the other **GObject** subclasses, the **GPolygon** class is not created entirely by the constructor. The constructor instead creates an empty polygon to which you can later add vertices. The library version of the **GPolygon** class allows you to add new vertices in any of three ways, as shown in Figure 8-25. The first vertex is always added using **addVertex**, but it is often easier to add the remaining vertices using **addEdge** or **addPolarEdge**.

As an example of how you might use the **GPolygon** class, the following **run** method draws an outlined hexagon at the center of the graphics window, where **WIDTH** and **HEIGHT** are constants that determine the size of the GWindow and where **EDGE** is the edge length of the hexagon:

```
public void run() {
    GWindow gw = new GWindow(WIDTH, HEIGHT);
    gw.setTitle("DrawHexagon");
    GPolygon hexagon = new GPolygon();
    hexagon.addVertex(-EDGE, 0);
    for (int theta = -60; theta <= 235; theta += 60) {
        hexagon.addPolarEdge(EDGE, theta);
    }
    hexagon.setLocation(WIDTH / 2, HEIGHT / 2);
    gw.add(hexagon);
}
```

The **GPolygon** class should implement the **GFillable** interface, so that the polygon can be filled in exactly the same way as a **GRect** or **GOval**. Fortunately, the **Graphics** class in the **java.awt** package exports both a **drawPolygon** and a **fillPolygon** method, although you will need to look up the details.

15§. One of the most useful classes in the complete graphics library is **GCompound**, which is a **GObject** that contains other **GObject** instances, in much the same way that the **GWindow** class does. Like **GWindow**, the **GCompound** class will need to maintain an **ArrayList** containing the objects in that compound. It will, moreover, need to use a **synchronized** statement to prevent concurrent access to the list. The figures included in the **GCompound** should be drawn relative to the location of the **GCompound** itself. To make that model work in the context of the **GCompound** class, the easiest approach is to use the **create** method in the **Graphics** class to create a new **Graphics** object that is translated by the **GCompound** location.

The **GCompound** class becomes even more useful if you also implement the methods **sendToBack**, **sendToFront**, **sendBackward**, and **sendForward**, which change the position of the objects in the stacking order. If you add these methods, both **GCompound** and **GCanvas** need to implement this feature. Given that two classes implement the same behavior, it makes sense to define a **GContainer** interface to specify the common methods. Stacking order is easier to control if you add methods with the same names to the **GObject** class, where they take no arguments and forward the request to their container.

16. The **Console** class makes it easy to interleave numeric and string input, which was tricky using the **Scanner** class. Reimplement the Caesar-cipher program described in exercise 15 from Chapter 3, which needs to read both an integer and a string. Make sure that your solution uses a factory method to create the console so that you can easily substitute a **ConsoleWindow** for the default **SystemConsole**.

Chapter 9
Recursive Strategies

Tactics without strategy is the noise before defeat.

— Sun Tzu, ~5th Century BCE

When a recursive decomposition follows directly from a mathematical definition, as it does in the case of the **fact** and **fib** methods in Chapter 2, applying recursion is not particularly hard. In most cases, you can translate the mathematical definition directly into a recursive implementation by plugging the appropriate expressions into the standard recursive paradigm. The situation changes, however, as you begin to solve more complex problems.

This chapter introduces several programming problems that seem—at least on the surface—much more difficult than the simple recursive examples you have seen so far. In fact, if you try to solve these problems without using recursion, relying instead on more familiar iterative techniques, you will find them quite difficult. By contrast, each of the problems has a recursive solution that is surprisingly short. If you exploit the power of recursion, a few lines of code are sufficient for each task.

The brevity of these solutions, however, gives them a deceptive aura of simplicity. The hard part of solving these problems has nothing to do with the length of the code. What makes the programming difficult is finding the recursive decomposition in the first place. Doing so can require some cleverness, but what you really need is practice.

9.1 Thinking recursively

In my experience, the key to writing programs that use recursion is learning to think about those programs in a new way. When you were first learning to program, it's likely that you focused much of your attention on the details of the solution. Particularly when those details are new and unfamiliar, putting your energy into working them out makes a great deal of sense. When faced with a recursive problem, it is important to ignore the details and think instead about the big picture. What you need to do is think about the problem as a whole and determine whether there is any way to divide it into problems of the same form that are easier to solve. Because recursive techniques invariably involve dividing a hard problem into simpler pieces and then solving those subproblems using the same approach, recursive solutions are often called *divide-and-conquer* algorithms.

A simple example of a divide-and-conquer algorithm

To get a sense of how divide-and-conquer strategies might apply in the real world, imagine for the moment that you have been appointed as the funding coordinator for a large charitable organization that is long on volunteers but short on cash. Your job is to raise $1,000,000 in contributions so the organization can meet its expenses.

If you know someone who is willing to write a check for the entire $1,000,000, your job is easy. On the other hand, you may not be lucky enough to have friends who are generous millionaires. In that case, you must raise the $1,000,000 in smaller amounts. If the average contribution to your organization is $100, you might choose a different tack: call 10,000 friends and ask each of them for $100. But then again, you probably don't have 10,000 friends. So what can you do?

As is often the case when you are faced with a task that exceeds your own capacity, the answer lies in delegating part of the work to others. Your organization has a reasonable supply of volunteers. If you could find 10 dedicated supporters in different parts of the country and appoint them as regional coordinators, each of those 10 people could then take responsibility for raising $100,000.

Raising $100,000 is simpler than raising $1,000,000, but it hardly qualifies as easy. What should your regional coordinators do? If they adopt the same strategy, they will in turn delegate parts of the job. If they each recruit 10 fundraising volunteers, those people will only have to raise $10,000 each. The delegation process can continue until the volunteers are able to raise the money on their own; because the average contribution is $100, the volunteer fundraisers can probably raise $100 from a single donor, which eliminates the need for further delegation.

If you express this fundraising strategy in pseudocode, it has the following structure:

```
void collectContributions(int n) {
    if (n <= 100) {
        Collect the money from a single donor.
    } else {
        Find 10 volunteers.
        Get each volunteer to collect n/10 dollars.
        Combine the money raised by the volunteers.
    }
}
```

The most important thing to notice about this pseudocode translation is that the line

> Get each volunteer to collect **n/10** dollars.

is simply the original problem reproduced at a smaller scale. The basic character of the task—raise n dollars—remains exactly the same; the only difference is that n has a smaller value. Moreover, because the problem is the same, you can solve it by calling the original method. Thus, the preceding line of pseudocode would eventually be replaced with the following line:

```
collectContributions(n / 10);
```

It's important to note that the `collectContributions` method ends up calling itself if the contribution level is greater than $100. In the context of programming, having a method call itself is the defining characteristic of recursion.

The structure of the `collectContributions` method is typical of recursive methods. In general, the body of a recursive method has the following form:

```
if (test for simple case) {
    Compute a simple solution without using recursion.
} else {
    Break the problem down into subproblems of the same form.
    Solve each of the subproblems by calling this method recursively.
    Reassemble the subproblem solutions into a solution for the whole.
}
```

This structure provides a template for writing recursive methods and is therefore called the ***recursive paradigm.*** You can apply this technique to programming problems as long as they meet the following conditions:

1. You must be able to identify ***simple cases*** for which the answer is easily determined.

2. You must be able to identify a ***recursive decomposition*** that allows you to break any complex instance of the problem into simpler problems of the same form.

The `collectContributions` example illustrates the power of recursion. As with any recursive technique, the original problem is solved by breaking it down into smaller subproblems that differ from the original only in their scale. Here, the original problem is to raise $1,000,000. At the first level of decomposition, each subproblem is to raise $100,000. These problems are then subdivided in turn to create smaller problems until the problems are simple enough to be solved immediately without recourse to further subdivision.

Understanding a recursive example like the `collectContributions` method turns out to be much easier than learning to apply recursive techniques yourself. The key to success lies in developing the right frame of mind—in learning how to think recursively. The next several sections offer some tidbits of advice designed to help you achieve that goal.

Maintaining a holistic perspective

When you are learning to program, I think it helps enormously to keep in mind the philosophical concepts of holism and reductionism. Simply stated, ***reductionism*** is the belief that the whole of an object can be understood merely by understanding the parts that make it up. Its antithesis is **holism,** the position that the whole is often greater than the sum of its parts. As you learn about programming, it helps to be able to interleave these two perspectives, sometimes focusing on the behavior of a program as a whole, and at other times delving into the details of its execution. When you try to learn about recursion, however, this balance seems to change. Thinking recursively requires you to think holistically. In the recursive domain, reductionism is the enemy of understanding and almost always gets in the way.

To maintain the holistic perspective, you must become comfortable adopting the recursive leap of faith, which was introduced in Chapter 2. Whenever you are writing a recursive program or trying to understand the behavior of one, you must get to the point where you ignore the details of the individual recursive calls. As long as you have chosen the right decomposition, identified the appropriate simple cases, and implemented your strategy correctly, those recursive calls will simply work. You don't need to think about them.

Unfortunately, until you have had extensive experience working with recursive methods, applying the recursive leap of faith does not come easily. The problem is that doing so requires to suspend your disbelief and to make assumptions about the correctness of your programs that fly in the face of your experience. After all, when you write a program, the odds are good—even if you are an experienced programmer—that your program won't work the first time. In fact, it is quite likely that you have chosen the wrong decomposition, messed up the definition of the simple cases, or somehow gotten things muddled as you tried to implement your strategy. If you have done any of these things, your recursive calls won't work.

When things go wrong—as they inevitably will—you have to remember to look for the error in the right place. The problem lies somewhere in your recursive implementation, not in the recursive mechanism itself. If there is a problem, you should be able to find it by looking at a single level of the recursive hierarchy. Looking down through additional levels of recursive calls is not going to help. If the simple cases work and the recursive decomposition is correct, the subsidiary calls will work correctly. If they don't, the problem must lie in your formulation of the recursive decomposition.

Avoiding the common pitfalls

As you gain experience with recursion, the process of writing and debugging recursive programs will become more natural. At the beginning, however, finding out what you need to fix in a recursive program can be difficult. The following checklist will help you identify the most common sources of error.

- *Does your recursive implementation begin by checking for simple cases?* Before you attempt to solve a problem by transforming it into a recursive subproblem, you must first check to see if the problem is so simple that such decomposition is unnecessary. In almost all cases, recursive methods begin with the keyword `if`. If your method doesn't, you should look carefully at your program and make sure that you know what you're doing.

- *Have you solved the simple cases correctly?* A surprising number of bugs in recursive programs arise from having incorrect solutions to the simple cases. If the simple cases are wrong, the recursive solutions to more complicated problems will inherit the same mistake. For example, if you had mistakenly defined `fact(0)` as 0 instead of 1, calling `fact` on any argument would end up returning 0.

- *Does your recursive decomposition make the problem simpler?* For recursion to work, the problems have to get simpler as you go along. More formally, there must be some *metric*—a standard of measurement that assigns a numeric difficulty rating to the problem—that gets smaller as the computation proceeds. For mathematical functions like `fact` and `fib`, the value of the integer argument serves as a metric. On each recursive call, the value of the argument gets smaller. For the `isPalindrome` method in Chapter 3, the appropriate metric is the length of the argument string, because the string gets shorter on each recursive call. If the problem instances do not get simpler, the decomposition process will just keep making more and more calls, giving rise to the recursive analogue of the infinite loop, which is called ***nonterminating recursion.***

- *Does the simplification process eventually reach the simple cases, or have you left out some of the possibilities?* A common source of error is failing to include simple case tests for all the cases that can arise as the result of the recursive decomposition. For example, in the `isPalindrome` implementation on page 110, it is critically important to check for the zero-character case as well as the one-character case, even if the client never intends to call `isPalindrome` on the empty string. As the recursive decomposition proceeds, the string arguments get shorter by two characters at each level of the recursive call. If the length of the original argument string is even, the recursive decomposition will never get to the one-character case.

- *Do the recursive calls in your method represent subproblems that are truly identical in form to the original?* When you use recursion to break down a problem, it is essential that the subproblems be of the same form. If the recursive calls change the nature of the problem or violate one of the initial assumptions, the entire process can break down. As several of the examples in this chapter illustrate, it is often useful to define the publicly exported method as a simple wrapper that calls a more general recursive method that is private to the implementation. Because the private method has a more general form, it is usually easier to decompose the original problem in such a way that it still fits within the recursive structure.

- *When you apply the recursive leap of faith, do the solutions to the recursive subproblems provide a complete solution to the original problem?* Breaking a problem down into recursive subinstances is only part of the recursive process. Once you get the solutions, you must also be able to reassemble them to generate the complete solution. The way to check whether this process in fact generates the solution is to walk through the decomposition, religiously applying the recursive leap of faith. Work through all the steps in the current method call, but assume that every recursive call generates the correct answer. If following this process yields the right solution, your program should work.

9.2 The Towers of Hanoi

The classic example of recursion comes from a simple puzzle that has come to be known as the ***Towers of Hanoi.*** Invented by French mathematician Édouard Lucas in the 1880s, the Towers of Hanoi puzzle quickly became popular in Europe. Its success was due in part to the legend that grew up around the puzzle, which was described as follows in *La Nature* by the French mathematician Henri de Parville (as translated by the mathematical historian W. W. R. Ball):

> In the great temple at Benares beneath the dome which marks the center of the world, rests a brass plate in which are fixed three diamond needles, each a cubit high and as thick as the body of a bee. On one of these needles, at the creation, God placed sixty-four disks of pure gold, the largest disk resting on the brass plate and the others getting smaller and smaller up to the top one. This is the Tower of Brahma. Day and night unceasingly, the priests transfer the disks from one diamond needle to another according to the fixed and immutable laws of Brahma, which require that the priest on duty must not move more than one disk at a time and that he must place this disk on a needle so that there is no smaller disk below it. When all the sixty-four disks shall have been thus transferred from the needle on which at the creation God placed them to one of the other needles, tower, temple and Brahmins alike will crumble into dust, and with a thunderclap the world will vanish.

Over the years, the setting has shifted from India to Vietnam, but the puzzle and its legend remain the same.

As far as I know, the Towers of Hanoi puzzle has no practical use except one: teaching recursion to computer science students. In that domain, it has tremendous value because the solution involves nothing other than recursion. In contrast to most recursive algorithms that arise in response to real-world problems, the Towers of Hanoi problem has no extraneous complications that might interfere with your understanding and keep you from seeing how the recursive solution works. Because it works so well as an example, the Towers of Hanoi is included in most textbooks that treat recursion and has become—much like the "hello, world" program in Chapter 1—part of the cultural heritage that computer scientists share.

In commercial versions of the puzzle, the 64 golden disks of legend are replaced with eight wooden or plastic ones, which makes the puzzle considerably easier to solve (not to mention less expensive). The initial state of the puzzle looks like this:

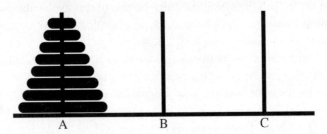

At the beginning, all eight disks are on spire A. Your goal is to move the eight disks from spire A to spire B, while adhering to the following rules:

- You can only move one disk at a time.

- You are not allowed to move a larger disk on top of a smaller one.

Framing the problem

In order to apply recursion to the Towers of Hanoi problem, you must first frame the problem in more general terms. Although the ultimate goal is to move eight disks from A to B, the recursive decomposition of the problem will involve moving smaller subtowers from spire to spire in various configurations. In the more general case, the problem you need to solve is moving a tower of a given height from one spire to another, using the third spire as a temporary repository. To ensure that all subproblems fit the original form, your recursive procedure must therefore take the following arguments:

1. The number of disks to move

2. The name of the spire where the disks start out

3. The name of the spire where the disks should finish

4. The name of the spire used for temporary storage

The number of disks to move is clearly an integer, and the fact that the spires are labeled with the letters *A, B,* and *C* suggests the use of type **char** to indicate which spire is involved. Knowing the types allows you to write a prototype for the operation that moves a tower, as follows:

```
void moveTower(int n, char start, char finish, char tmp);
```

To move the eight disks in the example, the initial call is

```
moveTower(8, 'A', 'B', 'C');
```

This method call corresponds to the English command "Move a tower of size 8 from spire A to spire B using spire C as a temporary repository." As the recursive decomposition proceeds, `moveTower` will be called with different arguments that move smaller towers in various configurations.

Finding a recursive strategy

Now that you have a more general definition of the problem, you can return to the problem of finding a strategy for moving a large tower. To apply recursion, you must first make sure that the problem meets the following conditions:

1. *There must be a simple case.* In this problem, the simple case occurs when **n** is equal to 1, which means that there is only a single disk to move. As long as you don't violate the rules by placing a larger disk on top of a smaller one, you can move a single disk in a single operation.

2. *There must be a recursive decomposition.* In order to implement a recursive solution, it must be possible to break the problem down into simpler problems in the same form as the original. This part of the problem is harder and will require closer examination.

To see how solving a simpler subproblem helps solve a larger problem, it helps to go back and consider the original example with eight disks.

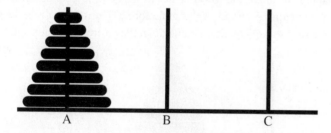

The goal here is to move eight disks from spire A to spire B. You need to ask yourself how it would help if you could solve the same problem for a smaller number of disks. In particular, you should think about how being able to move a stack of seven disks would help you to solve the eight-disk case.

If you think about the problem for a few moments, it becomes clear that you can solve the problem by dividing it into these three steps:

1. Move the entire stack consisting of the top seven disks from spire A to spire C.
2. Move the bottom disk from spire A to spire B.
3. Move the stack of seven disks from spire C to spire B.

Executing the first step takes you to the following position:

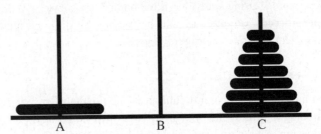

Once you have gotten rid of the seven disks on top of the largest disk, the second step is simply to move that disk from spire A to spire B, which results in the following configuration:

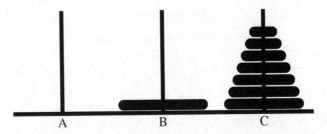

All that remains is to move the tower of seven disks back from spire C to spire B, which is again a smaller problem of the same form. This operation is the third step in the recursive strategy and leaves the puzzle in the desired final configuration:

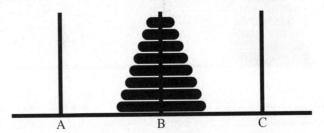

That's it! You're finished. You've reduced the problem of moving a tower of size eight to one of moving a tower of size seven. More importantly, this recursive strategy generalizes to towers of size N, as follows:

1. Move the top $N - 1$ disks from the start spire to the temporary spire.

2. Move a single disk from the start spire to the finish spire.

3. Move the stack of $N - 1$ disks from the temporary spire back to the finish spire.

At this point, it is hard to avoid saying to yourself, "Okay, I can reduce the problem to moving a tower of size $N-1$, but how do I accomplish that?" The answer, of course, is that you move a tower of size $N-1$ in precisely the same way. You break that problem down into one that requires moving a tower of size $N-2$, which further breaks down into moving a tower of size $N-3$, and so forth, until there is just one disk to move. Psychologically, however, the important thing is to avoid asking that question altogether. The recursive leap of faith should be sufficient. You've reduced the scale of the problem without changing its form. That's the hard work. All the rest is bookkeeping, and it's best to let the computer take care of that.

Once you have identified the simple cases and the recursive decomposition, all you need to do is plug them into the standard recursive paradigm, which results in the following pseudocode procedure:

```
void moveTower(int n, char start, char finish, char tmp) {
    if (n == 1) {
        Move a single disk from start to finish.
    } else {
        Move a tower of size n - 1 from start to tmp.
        Move a single disk from start to finish.
        Move a tower of size n - 1 from tmp to finish.
    }
}
```

Validating the strategy

Although the pseudocode strategy is in fact correct, the derivation up to this point has been a little careless. Whenever you use recursion to decompose a problem, you must make sure that the new problems are identical in form to the original. The task of moving $N-1$ disks from one spire to another certainly sounds like an instance of the same problem and fits the **moveTower** prototype. Even so, there is a subtle but important difference. In the original problem, the destination and temporary spires are empty. When you move a tower of size $N-1$ to the temporary spire as part of the recursive strategy, you've left a disk behind on the starting spire. Does the presence of that disk change the nature of the problem and thus invalidate the recursive solution?

To answer this question, you need to think about the subproblem in light of the rules of the game. If the recursive decomposition doesn't end up violating the rules, everything should be okay. The first rule—that only one disk can be moved at a time—is not an issue. If there is more than a single disk, the recursive decomposition breaks the problem down to generate a simpler case. The steps in the pseudocode that actually transfer disks move only one disk at a time. The second rule—that you are not allowed to place a larger disk on top of a smaller one—is the critical one. You need to convince yourself that you will not violate this rule in the recursive decomposition.

The important observation to make is that, as you move a subtower from one spire to the other, the disk you leave behind on the original spire—and indeed any disk left behind at any previous stage in the operation—must be larger than anything in the current subtower. Thus, as you move those disks among the spires, the only disks below them will be larger in size, which is consistent with the rules.

Coding the solution

To complete the Towers of Hanoi solution, the only remaining step is to substitute method calls for the remaining pseudocode. The task of moving a complete tower requires a recursive call to the **moveTower** method. The only other operation is moving a single disk from one spire to another. For the purposes of writing a test program that displays the steps in the solution, all you need is a method that records its operation on the console. For example, you can implement the method **moveSingleDisk** as follows:

```
void moveSingleDisk(char start, char finish) {
   System.out.println(start + " -> " + finish);
}
```

The **moveTower** code itself looks like this:

```
void moveTower(int n, char start, char finish, char tmp) {
   if (n == 1) {
      moveSingleDisk(start, finish);
   } else {
      moveTower(n - 1, start, tmp, finish);
      moveSingleDisk(start, finish);
      moveTower(n - 1, tmp, finish, start);
   }
}
```

The complete implementation appears in Figure 9-1.

Tracing the recursive process

The only problem with this implementation of **moveTower** is that it seems like magic. If you're like most students learning about recursion for the first time, the solution seems so short that you feel sure there must be something missing. Where is the strategy? How can the computer know which disk to move first and where it should go?

FIGURE 9-1 Program to solve the Towers of Hanoi puzzle

```java
/*
 * File: Hanoi.java
 * ----------------
 * This program solves the Towers of Hanoi puzzle.
 */

package edu.stanford.cs.javacs2.ch9;

import edu.stanford.cs.console.Console;
import edu.stanford.cs.console.SystemConsole;

public class Hanoi {

   public void run() {
      Console console = new SystemConsole();
      int n = console.nextInt("Enter number of disks: ");
      moveTower(n, 'A', 'B', 'C');
   }

/**
 * Moves a tower of size n from the start spire to the finish
 * spire using the tmp spire as the temporary repository.
 */

   private void moveTower(int n, char start, char finish, char tmp) {
      if (n == 1) {
         moveSingleDisk(start, finish);
      } else {
         moveTower(n - 1, start, tmp, finish);
         moveSingleDisk(start, finish);
         moveTower(n - 1, tmp, finish, start);
      }
   }

/**
 * Executes the transfer of a single disk from the start spire to the
 * finish spire.  In this implementation, the move is simply displayed
 * on the console; in a graphical implementation, the code would update
 * the graphics window to show the new arrangement.
 */

   private void moveSingleDisk(char start, char finish) {
      System.out.println(start + " -> " + finish);
   }

/* Main program */

   public static void main(String[] args) {
      new Hanoi().run();
   }

}
```

The answer is that the recursive process—breaking a problem down into smaller subproblems of the same form and then providing solutions for the simple cases—is all you need to solve the problem. If you take the recursive leap of faith, you're done. You can skip this section of the book and go on to the next. If, on the other hand, you're still suspicious, it may be necessary for you to go through the steps in the complete process and watch what happens.

To make the problem more manageable, consider what happens if there are only three disks in the original tower. The main program call is therefore

```
moveTower(3, 'A', 'B', 'C');
```

To trace how this call computes the steps necessary to transfer a tower of size 3, all you need to do is keep track of the operation of the program, using precisely the same strategy as in the factorial example from Chapter 2. For each new method call, you introduce a stack frame that shows the values of the parameters for that call. The initial call to **moveTower**, for example, creates the following stack frame:

```
public int run() {

  void moveTower(int n, char start, char finish, char tmp) {
☞   if (n == 1) {
        moveSingleDisk(start, finish);
    } else {
        moveTower(n - 1, start, tmp, finish);
        moveSingleDisk(start, finish);
        moveTower(n - 1, tmp, finish, start);
    }
  }
}
```

n	start	finish	tmp
3	'A'	'B'	'C'

As the current location marker in the code indicates, the method has just been called, so execution begins with the first statement in the method body. The current value of **n** is not equal to 1, which means that the program skips ahead to the **else** clause and executes the statement

```
moveTower(n - 1, start, tmp, finish);
```

As with any method call, you begin by evaluating the arguments. To do so, you need to determine the values of the variables **n**, **start**, **tmp**, and **finish**. Whenever you need to find the value of a variable, you use the value as it is defined in the current stack frame. Thus, the **moveTower** call is equivalent to

```
moveTower(2, 'A', 'C', 'B');
```

This operation, however, requires making another method call, which means that the current operation is suspended until the new method call is complete. To trace the operation of the new method call, you need to generate a new stack frame and repeat the process. As always, the parameters in the new stack frame are copied from the calling arguments in the order in which they appear. Thus, the new stack frame looks like this:

```
public int run() {
  void moveTower(int n, char start, char finish, char tmp) {
    void moveTower(int n, char start, char finish, char tmp) {
      ☞ if (n == 1) {
          moveSingleDisk(start, finish);
        } else {
          moveTower(n - 1, start, tmp, finish);
          moveSingleDisk(start, finish);
          moveTower(n - 1, tmp, finish, start);
        }
    }
  }
}
```

n	start	finish	tmp
2	'A'	'C'	'B'

As the diagram illustrates, the new stack frame has its own set of variables, which temporarily supersede the variables in frames that are further down on the stack. Thus, as long as the program is executing in this stack frame, **n** will have the value 2, **start** will be **'A'**, **finish** will be **'C'**, and **tmp** will be **'B'**. The old values in the previous frame will not reappear until this call to **moveTower** returns.

The evaluation of the recursive call to **moveTower** proceeds exactly like that of the original one. Once again, **n** is not 1, which requires another call of the form

```
moveTower(n - 1, start, tmp, finish);
```

Because this call comes from a different stack frame, however, the values of the individual variables are different from those in the original call. If you evaluate the arguments in the context of the current stack frame, you discover that this method call is equivalent to

```
moveTower(1, 'A', 'B', 'C');
```

The effect of making this call is to introduce yet another stack frame for the **moveTower** method, as follows:

```
public int run() {
  void moveTower(int n, char start, char finish, char tmp) {
    void moveTower(int n, char start, char finish, char tmp) {
      void moveTower(int n, char start, char finish, char tmp) {
        ☞ if (n == 1) {
            moveSingleDisk(start, finish);
          } else {
            moveTower(n - 1, start, tmp, finish);
            moveSingleDisk(start, finish);
            moveTower(n - 1, tmp, finish, start);
          }
      }
    }
  }
}
```

n	start	finish	tmp
1	'A'	'B'	'C'

This call to **moveTower**, however, does represent the simple case. Since **n** is 1, the program calls the **moveSingleDisk** method to move a disk from A to B, leaving the puzzle in the following configuration:

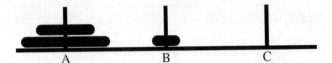

At this point, the most recent call to **moveTower** is complete, and the method returns. In the process, its stack frame is discarded, which brings the execution back to the preceding stack frame. Execution in that frame continues from the point after the just-completed call, as indicated in the following diagram:

```
public int run() {
   void moveTower(int n, char start, char finish, char tmp) {
      void moveTower(int n, char start, char finish, char tmp) {
         if (n == 1) {
            moveSingleDisk(start, finish);
         } else {
            moveTower(n - 1, start, tmp, finish);
         ☞ moveSingleDisk(start, finish);
            moveTower(n - 1, tmp, finish, start);
         }
      }                                  n        start    finish   tmp
   }                                   ┌─────┐  ┌─────┐  ┌─────┐  ┌─────┐
}                                      │  2  │  │ 'A' │  │ 'C' │  │ 'B' │
                                       └─────┘  └─────┘  └─────┘  └─────┘
```

The call to **moveSingleDisk** again represents a simple operation, which leaves the puzzle in the following state:

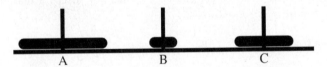

With the **moveSingleDisk** operation completed, the only remaining step required to finish the current call to **moveTower** is the last statement in the method:

```
moveTower(n - 1, tmp, finish, start);
```

Evaluating these arguments in the context of the current frame reveals that this call is equivalent to

```
moveTower(1, 'B', 'C', 'A');
```

Once again, this call requires the creation of a new stack frame. By this point in the process, however, you should be able to see that the effect of this call is simply to move a tower of size 1 from B to C, using A as a temporary repository. Internally, the method determines that **n** is 1 and then calls **moveSingleDisk** to reach the following configuration:

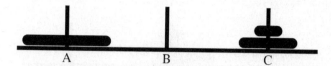

This operation again completes a call to **moveTower**, allowing it to return to its caller having completed the subtask of moving a tower of size 2 from A to C. Discarding the stack frame from the just-completed subtask reveals the stack frame for the original call to **moveTower**, which is now in the following state:

```
public int run() {

   void moveTower(int n, char start, char finish, char tmp) {
      if (n == 1) {
         moveSingleDisk(start, finish);
      } else {
         moveTower(n - 1, start, tmp, finish);
    ☞  moveSingleDisk(start, finish);
         moveTower(n - 1, tmp, finish, start);
      }
   }
```

n	start	finish	tmp
3	'A'	'B'	'C'

The next step is to call **moveSingleDisk** to move the largest disk from A to B, which results in the following position:

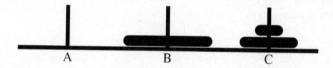

The only operation that remains is to call

```
moveTower(n - 1, tmp, finish, start);
```

with the arguments from the current stack frame, which are

```
moveTower(2, 'C', 'B', 'A');
```

If you're still suspicious of the recursive process, you can draw the stack frame created by this method call and continue tracing the process to its ultimate conclusion. At some point, however, it is essential that you trust the recursive process enough to see that method call as a single operation that has the effect of the following command in English:

Move a tower of size 2 from C to B, using A as a temporary repository.

If you think about the process in this holistic form, you can immediately see that completion of this step will move the tower of two disks back from C to B, leaving the desired final configuration:

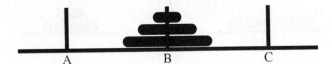

9.3 The subset-sum problem

Although the Towers of Hanoi problem offers a wonderful illustration of the power of recursion, its effectiveness as an example is compromised by its lack of any practical application. Many people are drawn to programming because it enables them to solve practical problems. If all examples of recursion were like the Towers of Hanoi, it would be easy to conclude that recursion is useful only for solving abstract puzzles. Nothing could be further from the truth. Recursive strategies give rise to extremely efficient solutions to practical problems—most notably the problem of sorting introduced in Chapter 12—that are hard to solve in other ways.

The problem addressed in this section is the *subset-sum problem,* which can be defined as follows:

> Given a set of integers and a target value, determine whether it is possible to find a subset of those integers whose sum is equal to the specified target.

For example, given the set { −2, 1, 3, 8 } and the target value 7, the answer to the subset-sum question is yes, because the subset { −2, 1, 8 } adds up to 7. If the target value were 5, however, the answer would be no, because there is no way to choose a subset of the integers in { −2, 1, 3, 8 } that adds up to 5.

It is easy to translate the idea of the subset-sum problem into Java. The concrete goal is to write a predicate method

```
boolean subsetSumExists(TreeSet<int> set, int target);
```

that takes the required information and returns **true** if it is possible to generate the value **target** by adding together some combination of elements chosen from **set**.

Even though the subset-sum problem might at first seem just as esoteric as the Towers of Hanoi, it is important in both the theory and the practice of computer science. As you will discover in Chapter 11, the subset-sum problem is an instance of an important class of computational problems that are hard to solve efficiently. That very fact, however, makes problems like subset-sum useful in applications where the goal is to keep information secret. The first implementation of public-key cryptography, for example, used a variant of the subset-sum problem as its mathematical foundation. Modern encryption strategies base their operation on problems that are provably hard, which makes such codes very difficult to break.

The search for a recursive solution

The subset-sum problem is difficult to solve using a traditional iterative approach. To make any headway, you need to think recursively. As always, you therefore need to identify a simple case and a recursive decomposition. In applications that work with sets, the simple case almost always occurs when the set is empty. There is no way that you can add elements to an empty set in order to produce a target value unless the target is zero. That discovery suggests that the code for `subsetSumExists` will start off like this:

```
boolean subsetSumExists(TreeSet<int> set, int target) {
   if (set.isEmpty()) {
      return target == 0;
   } else {
      Find a recursive decomposition that simplifies the problem.
   }
}
```

In this problem, the hard part is finding that recursive decomposition.

When you are seeking a recursive decomposition, you need to be on the lookout for some value in the inputs—which are conveyed as arguments in the Java formulation of the problem—that you can make smaller. In this case, you need to make the set smaller, because what you're trying to do is move toward the simple case that occurs when the set is empty. If you take an element out of the set, what's left over is smaller by one element. The operations exported by the **TreeSet** class make it easy to choose an element from a set and then determine what remains. All you need is the following code:

```
int element = set.first();
TreeSet<int> rest = new TreeSet(set);
rest.remove(element);
```

The **first** method returns the element of the set that appears first in its iteration order. The next two statements create a new **TreeSet** called **rest** that contains every element in **set** except the value of **element**. The fact that **element** is first in iteration order is not important here. All you really need is some way to choose an element and then create a smaller set by removing the element you selected from the original set.

Making the set smaller, however, is not enough to solve this problem. In terms of structure, you know that `subsetSumExists` must call itself recursively on the smaller set now stored in the variable `rest`. What you haven't yet determined is how the solution to these recursive subproblems will help to solve the original. The strategy you need to do so, which is described in the following section, illustrates a general programming pattern that will prove useful in many applications.

The inclusion/exclusion pattern

The key insight you need to complete the implementation of `subsetSumExists` is that there are two ways you might be able to produce the desired target sum after you have identified a particular element. One possibility is that the subset you're looking for *includes* that element. In that case, it must be possible to take the rest of the set and produce the value `target - element`. The other possibility is that the subset you're looking for *excludes* that element, in which case it must be possible to generate the value `target` using only the leftover set of elements. This insight is enough to complete the implementation of `subsetSumExists`, as follows:

```
boolean subsetSumExists(TreeSet<int> set, int target) {
    if (set.isEmpty()) {
        return target == 0;
    } else {
        int element = set.first();
        TreeSet<Integer> rest = new TreeSet<Integer>(set);
        rest.remove(element);
        return subsetSumExists(rest, target)
            || subsetSumExists(rest, target - element);
    }
}
```

Because the recursive strategy subdivides the general case into one branch that includes a particular element and another that excludes it, this strategy is sometimes called the *inclusion/exclusion pattern.* As you work through the exercises in this chapter as well as several subsequent ones, you will find that this strategy, with slight variations, comes up in many different contexts. Although the pattern is easiest to recognize when you are working with sets, it also arises in applications involving vectors and strings, and you should be on the lookout for it in those situations as well.

▇ 9.4 Generating permutations

Many word games and puzzles require the ability to rearrange a set of letters to form a word. Thus, if you wanted to write a Scrabble program, it would be useful to have a facility for generating all possible arrangements of a particular set of tiles. In word games, such arrangements are generally called **anagrams.** In mathematics, they are known as **permutations.**

Let's suppose you want to write a method

```
TreeSet<String> generatePermutations(String str)
```

that returns a set containing all permutations of the string. For example, if you call

```
generatePermutations("ABC")
```

the method should return a set containing the following elements:

{ "ABC", "ACB", "BAC", "BCA", "CAB", "CBA" }

How might you go about implementing the `generatePermutations` method? If you are limited to iterative control structures, finding a general solution that works for strings of any length is difficult. Thinking about the problem recursively, on the other hand, leads to a relatively straightforward solution.

As is usually the case with recursive programs, the hard part of the solution process is figuring out how to divide the original problem into simpler instances of the same problem. In this case, to generate all permutations of a string, you need to discover how being able to generate all permutations of a shorter string might contribute to the solution.

Before you turn the page and look at the solution, stop and think about this problem for a few minutes. When you are first learning about recursion, it is easy to look at a recursive solution and believe that you could have generated it on your own. Without trying it first, however, it is hard to know whether you would have come up with the necessary recursive insight.

To give yourself more of a feel for the problem, it helps to consider a concrete case. Suppose you want to generate all permutations of a five-character string, such as "ABCDE". In your solution, you can apply the recursive leap of faith to generate all permutations of any shorter string. Just assume that the recursive calls work and be done with it. Once again, the critical question is how being able to permute shorter strings helps you solve the problem of permuting the original five-character string.

If you focus on breaking the five-character permutation problem down into some number of instances of the permutation problem involving four-character strings, you will soon discover that the permutations of the five-character string "ABCDE" consist of the following strings:

- The character `'A'` followed by every possible permutation of `"BCDE"`
- The character `'B'` followed by every possible permutation of `"ACDE"`
- The character `'C'` followed by every possible permutation of `"ABDE"`
- The character `'D'` followed by every possible permutation of `"ABCE"`
- The character `'E'` followed by every possible permutation of `"ABCD"`

More generally, you can construct the set of all permutations of a string of length n by selecting each character in turn and then, for each of those n possible first characters, concatenating the selected character on to the front of every possible permutation of the remaining $n - 1$ characters. The problem of generating all permutations of $n - 1$ characters is a smaller instance of the same problem and can therefore be solved recursively.

As always, you also need to define a simple case. One possibility is to check whether the string contains a single character. Computing all the permutations of a single-character string is easy, because there is only one possible ordering. In string processing, however, the best choice for the simple case is rarely a one-character string, because there is in fact an even simpler alternative: the empty string containing no characters at all. Just as there is only one ordering for a single-character string, there is only one way to write the empty string. If you call `generatePermutations("")`, you should get back a set containing a single element, which is the empty string.

Once you have both the simple case and the recursive insight, writing the code for `generatePermutations` becomes reasonably straightforward. The code for `generatePermutations` appears in Figure 9-2, along with a simple test program that asks the user for a string and then prints every possible permutation of the characters in that string.

If you run the `Permutations` program and enter the string `"ABC"`, you see the following output:

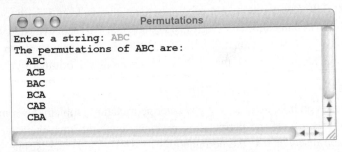

FIGURE 9-2 Program to generate all permutations of a string

```
/*
 * File: Permutations.java
 * -------------------------
 * This file generates all permutations of an input string.
 */

package edu.stanford.cs.javacs2.ch9;

import edu.stanford.cs.console.Console;
import edu.stanford.cs.console.SystemConsole;
import java.util.TreeSet;

public class Permutations {

   public void run() {
      Console console = new SystemConsole();
      String str = console.nextLine("Enter a string: ");
      System.out.println("The permutations of " + str + " are:");
      for (String s : generatePermutations(str)) {
         System.out.println("   " + s);
      }
   }

/*
 * Returns a set consisting of all permutations of the specified string.
 * This implementation uses the recursive insight that you can generate
 * all permutations of a string by selecting each character, generating
 * all permutations of the string without that character, and then
 * concatenating the selected character on the front of each string.
 */

   private TreeSet<String> generatePermutations(String str) {
      TreeSet<String> result = new TreeSet<String>();
      if (str.equals("")) {
         result.add("");
      } else {
         for (int i = 0; i < str.length(); i++) {
            char ch = str.charAt(i);
            String rest = str.substring(0, i) + str.substring(i + 1);
            for (String s : generatePermutations(rest)) {
               result.add(ch + s);
            }
         }
      }
      return result;
   }

/* Main program */

   public static void main(String[] args) {
      new Permutations().run();
   }
}
```

The use of sets in this application ensures that the program generates permutations in alphabetical order and that each distinct ordering of the characters appears exactly once, even if there are repeated letters in the input string. For example, if you enter the string **AABB** in response to the prompt, the program produces only six permutations, as follows:

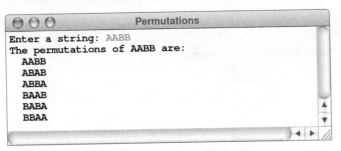

The recursive process calls the **add** method 24 (4!) times, but the implementation of the **TreeSet** class ensures that no duplicate values appear.

You can use the **generatePermutations** method to generate all anagrams of a word by changing the main program from Figure 9-2 so that it checks each string against the English lexicon. If you enter the string **"aeinrst"**, you get the following output—a list that serious Scrabble players will recognize instantly:

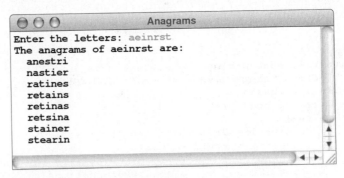

▮▮ 9.5 Graphical recursion

Some of the most exciting applications of recursion use graphics to create intricate pictures in which a particular motif is repeated at many different scales. The remainder of this chapter offers a few examples of graphical recursion that make use of the **GWindow** class introduced in Chapter 8. This material is not essential to learning about recursion, and you can skip it if you are unfamiliar with the graphics library. On the other hand, working through these examples will make recursion seem a lot more powerful, not to mention more fun.

An example from computer art

In the early part of the twentieth century, a controversial artistic movement arose in Paris, largely under the influence of Pablo Picasso and Georges Braque. The Cubists—as they were called by their critics—rejected classical artistic notions of perspective and representationalism and instead produced highly fragmented works based on simple geometrical forms. Strongly influenced by Cubism, the Dutch painter Piet Mondrian (1872–1944) produced a series of compositions based on horizontal and vertical lines. The recursive structure of those paintings make them ideal candidates for computer simulation.

Suppose, for example, that you wanted to generate a Mondrian-like composition such as the following:

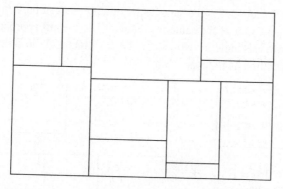

How would you go about designing a general strategy to create such a figure?

To understand how a program might produce such a figure, it helps to think about the process as one of successive decomposition. At the beginning, the canvas was simply an empty rectangle that looked like this:

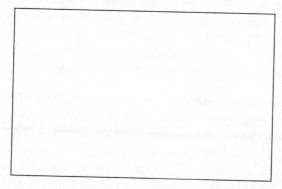

If you want to subdivide the canvas using a series of horizontal and vertical lines, the easiest way to start is by drawing a randomly chosen line that divides the rectangle in two:

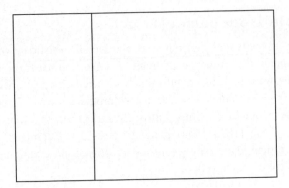

If you're thinking recursively, the thing to notice at this point is that you now have two empty rectangular canvases, each of which is smaller in size. The task of subdividing these rectangles is the same as before, so you can perform it by using a recursive implementation of the same procedure. The overall approach is therefore to divide the entire rectangle in two, subdivide each rectangle in turn, and then put the two pieces together, as follows:

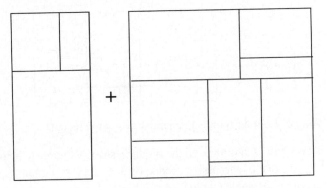

The only thing you need to complete the recursive strategy is a simple case. The process of dividing up rectangles should not go on indefinitely. As the rectangles get smaller and smaller, you have to stop the process at some point. One approach is to look at the area of each rectangle before you start. Once the area of a rectangle falls below some threshold, you needn't bother to subdivide it any further.

The **Mondrian.java** program in Figure 9-3 implements this recursive strategy, starting with the entire graphics canvas. In this program, the **subdivideCanvas** method does all the work. The arguments give the position and dimensions of the current rectangle on the canvas. At each step in the decomposition, the method checks whether that rectangle is large enough to split. If so, the method checks to see which dimension—width or height—is larger and then divides the rectangle with a vertical or horizontal line. In each case, the method draws only a single line; all remaining lines in the figure are drawn by subsequent recursive calls.

FIGURE 9-3 Program to subdivide the plane in a Mondrian-like style

```
/*
 * File: Mondrian.java
 * ---------------------
 * This program draws a recursive Mondrian style picture by recursively
 * subdividing the plane.
 */

package edu.stanford.cs.javacs2.ch9;

import edu.stanford.cs.javacs2.ch8.GLine;
import edu.stanford.cs.javacs2.ch8.GWindow;

public class Mondrian {

   public void run() {
      GWindow gw = new GWindow(WIDTH, HEIGHT);
      subdivideCanvas(gw, 0, 0, WIDTH, HEIGHT);
   }

/*
 * At each level, subdivideCanvas first checks for the simple case, which
 * is when the size of the rectangular canvas is too small to subdivide
 * (i.e., when the area is less than MINIMUM_AREA).  In the simple case,
 * the method does nothing.  In the recursive case, the method splits the
 * canvas along its longest dimension by choosing a random dividing line
 * that leaves at least MINIMUM_EDGE on each side.  The program then uses
 * a divide-and-conquer strategy to subdivide the two new rectangles.
 */

   private void subdivideCanvas(GWindow gw, double x, double y,
                                           double width, double height) {
      if (width * height >= MINIMUM_AREA) {
         if (width > height) {
            double dx = randomReal(MINIMUM_EDGE, width - MINIMUM_EDGE);
            gw.add(new GLine(x + dx, y, x + dx, y + height));
            subdivideCanvas(gw, x, y, dx, height);
            subdivideCanvas(gw, x + dx, y, width - dx, height);
         } else {
            double dy = randomReal(MINIMUM_EDGE, height - MINIMUM_EDGE);
            gw.add(new GLine(x, y + dy, x + width, y + dy));
            subdivideCanvas(gw, x, y, width, dy);
            subdivideCanvas(gw, x, y + dy, width, height - dy);
         }
      }
   }
}
```

FIGURE 9-3 Program to subdivide the plane in a Mondrian-like style (continued)

```
/**
 * Returns a random real number in the specified range.
 */

   private double randomReal(double low, double high) {
      return low + Math.random() * (high - low);
   }

/* Private constants */

   private static final int WIDTH = 700;
   private static final int HEIGHT = 400;
   private static final double MINIMUM_AREA = 4000;
   private static final double MINIMUM_EDGE = 10;

/* Main program */

   public static void main(String[] args) {
      new Mondrian().run();
   }

}
```

Fractals

In the late 1970s, a researcher at IBM named Benoit Mandelbrot (1924–2010) generated a great deal of excitement by publishing a book on *fractals,* which are geometrical structures in which the same pattern is repeated at many different scales. Although mathematicians have known about fractals for a long time, there was a resurgence of interest in the subject during the 1980s, partly because the development of computers made it possible to do so much more with fractals than had ever been possible before.

One of the earliest examples of fractal figures is called the *Koch snowflake* after its inventor, Helge von Koch (1870–1924). The Koch snowflake begins with an equilateral triangle like this:

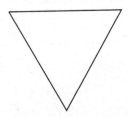

This triangle, in which the sides are straight lines, is called the Koch snowflake of order 0. The figure is then revised in stages to generate fractals of successively higher orders. At each stage, every straight-line segment in the figure is replaced by one in which the middle third consists of an equilateral triangular bump protruding outward from the figure. Thus, the first step is to replace each line segment in the triangle with a line that looks like this:

Applying this transformation to each of the three sides of the original triangle generates the Koch snowflake of order 1, as follows:

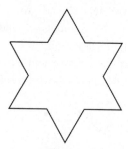

If you then replace each line segment in this figure with a new line that again includes a triangular wedge, you create the following order-2 Koch snowflake:

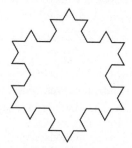

Replacing each of these line segments gives the order-3 fractal shown in the following diagram, which now looks even more like a snowflake:

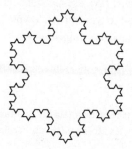

Because figures like the Koch snowflake are much easier to draw by computer than by hand, it makes sense to write a program that uses the graphical facilities introduced in Chapter 8 to generate this design. Each of the line segments in these figures is an instance of a **GLine**, and the process of drawing the snowflake is simply a matter of computing the endpoints of each segment.

As it is defined in Chapter 8, the constructor for the **GLine** class requires you to know the x and y coordinates of both endpoints of the line. In drawing the Koch snowflake, it is easier to write the code if you keep track of the current point in the figure and then specify each additional line segment in terms of its length and a direction. In mathematics, the length and direction of a line segment are conventionally represented by the symbols r and θ, which are called its *polar coordinates.* The use of polar coordinates is illustrated by the following diagram, in which the solid line has length r and extends from its starting point at the angle θ measured in degrees counterclockwise from the x-axis:

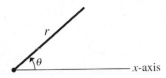

In mathematics, the x and y displacements of a line specified in polar coordinates can be computed using the following formulae:

$$dx = r \cos \theta$$
$$dy = r \sin \theta$$

Translating these formulae into code, however, requires you to take account of two special considerations of the **Math** class and the Java graphics model:

1. The **Math.cos** and **Math.sin** methods expect their arguments in radians rather than degrees, which means that you need to convert these values to the appropriate units before calling the **Math** methods.

2. Like most modern languages, Java uses a coordinate system in which the values of the y coordinate increase as you move downward. As a result, the value of the y displacement needs a negative sign.

If you take these considerations into account, you can compute the displacements for each line segment using the following code:

```
double dx = r * Math.cos(Math.toRadians(theta));
double dy = -r * Math.sin(Math.toRadians(theta));
```

You can further encapsulate the mathematical complexity involved in drawing the line by defining a method `addPolarLine`, which adds a `GLine` segment to the canvas from the current point, as follows:

```
void addPolarLine(double r, double theta) {
    double dx = r * Math.cos(Math.toRadians(theta));
    double dy = -r * Math.sin(Math.toRadians(theta));
    gw.add(new GLine(cx, cy, cx + dx, cy + dy));
    cx += dx;
    cy += dy;
}
```

In this design, the graphics window (`gw`) and the current position (`cx` and `cy`) are part of the program state and must therefore be stored in instance variables.

The design of `addPolarLine` makes it easy to chain consecutive line segments together. For example, the following code draws a downward-pointing equilateral triangle whose upper left corner is at the original value of the point (`cx`, `cy`):

```
addPolarLine(size, 0);
addPolarLine(size, -120);
addPolarLine(size, +120);
```

This code creates the snowflake fractal of order 0. To generalize it so that it creates higher-order fractals, all you need to do is replace the calls to `addPolarLine` with a new method called `addFractalLine` that takes a third parameter indicating the order of the fractal line, as follows:

```
addFractalLine(size, 0, order);
addFractalLine(size, -120, order);
addFractalLine(size, +120, order);
```

The only remaining task is to implement `addFractalLine`, which is easy if you think about it recursively. The simple case for `addFractalLine` occurs when `order` is 0, in which case the method simply draws a straight line with the specified length and direction. If `order` is greater than 0, the fractal line is broken down into four components, each of which is a fractal line of the next lower order. The complete implementation of the `Snowflake` program, which includes the finished code for `addFractalLine`, appears in Figure 9-4.

Besides the calculation of the `dx` and `dy` displacements, the only other part of Figure 9-4 that requires further explanation is the calculation of the initial values of `cx` and `cy`. The formulas that set these values use the geometry of equilateral triangles to find the point in the upper left corner of the order-0 fractal that centers the fractal on the canvas.

FIGURE 9-4 Program to draw the Koch fractal snowflake

```
/*
 * File: Snowflake.java
 * ----------------------
 * This program draws a recursive fractal snowflake using GLine segments.
 */

package edu.stanford.cs.javacs2.ch9;

import edu.stanford.cs.javacs2.ch8.GLine;
import edu.stanford.cs.javacs2.ch8.GWindow;

public class Snowflake {

    public void run() {
        gw = new GWindow(WIDTH, HEIGHT);
        cx = WIDTH / 2 - EDGE / 2;
        cy = HEIGHT / 2 - EDGE / (2 * Math.sqrt(3));
        addFractalLine(EDGE, 0, ORDER);
        addFractalLine(EDGE, -120, ORDER);
        addFractalLine(EDGE, +120, ORDER);
    }

/*
 * Adds a fractal line to the GCanvas with the specified radial length,
 * starting angle, and fractal order.
 */

    private void addFractalLine(double r, double theta, int order) {
        if (order == 0) {
            addPolarLine(r, theta);
        } else {
            addFractalLine(r / 3, theta, order - 1);
            addFractalLine(r / 3, theta + 60, order - 1);
            addFractalLine(r / 3, theta - 60, order - 1);
            addFractalLine(r / 3, theta, order - 1);
        }
    }
```

> **FIGURE 9-4** **Program to draw the Koch fractal snowflake (continued)**
>
> ```java
> /*
>  * Adds a line segment to the GCanvas with the specified radial length
>  * and starting angle.
>  */
>
>     private void addPolarLine(double r, double theta) {
>         double dx = r * Math.cos(Math.toRadians(theta));
>         double dy = -r * Math.sin(Math.toRadians(theta));
>         gw.add(new GLine(cx, cy, cx + dx, cy + dy));
>         cx += dx;
>         cy += dy;
>     }
>
> /* Constants */
>
>     private static final int WIDTH = 400;
>     private static final int HEIGHT = 400;
>     private static final int EDGE = 300;
>     private static final int ORDER = 4;
>
> /* Private instance variables */
>
>     private GWindow gw;           /* The graphics window      */
>     private double cx;            /* The current x coordinate */
>     private double cy;            /* The current y coordinate */
>
> /* Main program */
>
>     public static void main(String[] args) {
>         new Snowflake().run();
>     }
>
> }
> ```

Summary

Although you have seen simple applications of recursion ever since Chapter 2, the primary purpose of this chapter is to explore more sophisticated examples of recursion that are difficult to solve in any other way. Given this increase in sophistication, most students find these problems harder to comprehend than those in the preceding chapters. They are indeed more difficult, but recursion is a tool for solving hard problems. To master it, you need to practice with problems at this level of complexity.

The important points in this chapter include:

- Whenever you want to apply recursion to a programming problem, you have to devise a strategy that transforms the problem into simpler instances of the same problem. Until you find an insight that leads to the recursive strategy, there is no way to apply recursive techniques.

- Once you identify a recursive approach, it is important for you to check your strategy to ensure that it does not violate any conditions imposed by the problem.

- When the problems you are trying to solve increase in complexity, the importance of accepting the recursive leap of faith increases.

- Recursion is not magical. If you need to do so, you can simulate the operation of the computer yourself by drawing the stack frames for every procedure that is called in the course of the solution. On the other hand, it is critical to get beyond the skepticism that forces you to look at all the underlying details.

Review questions

1. In your own words, describe the recursive insight necessary to solve the Towers of Hanoi puzzle.

2. The following strategy for solving the Towers of Hanoi puzzle is structurally similar to the strategy used in the text:

    1. Move the top disk from the start spire to the temporary spire.

    2. Move a stack of $N-1$ disks from the start spire to the finish spire.

    3. Move the top disk now on the temporary spire back to the finish spire.

    Why does this strategy fail?

3. If you call

    ```
    moveTower(16, 'A', 'B', 'C')
    ```

    what line is displayed by **moveSingleDisk** as the first step in the solution? What is the last step in the solution?

4. What is a *permutation?*

5. In your own words, explain the recursive insight necessary to enumerate the permutations of the characters in a string.

6. How many permutations are there of the string **"WXYZ"**?

7. What simple case is used to terminate the recursion in **Mondrian.java**?

8. Draw a picture of the order-1 fractal snowflake.

9. How many line segments appear in the order-2 fractal snowflake?

Exercises

1. Following the logic of the **moveTower** method, write a recursive method **countHanoiMoves(n)** that computes the number of moves required to solve the Towers of Hanoi puzzle for **n** disks.

2. To make the operation of the program somewhat easier to explain, the implementation of **moveTower** in this chapter uses

    ```
    if (n == 1)
    ```

    as its simple case test. Whenever you see a recursive program use 1 as its simple case, it pays to be a little skeptical; in most applications, 0 is a more appropriate choice. Rewrite the Towers of Hanoi program so that the **moveTower** method checks whether **n** is 0 instead.

3. Rewrite the Towers of Hanoi program so that it uses an explicit stack of pending tasks instead of recursion. In this context, a task can be represented most easily as a structure containing the number of disks to move and the names of the spires used for the start, finish, and temporary repositories. At the beginning of the process, you push onto your stack a single task that describes the process of moving the entire tower. The program then repeatedly pops the stack and executes the task found there until no tasks are left. Except for the simple cases, the process of executing a task results in the creation of more tasks that get pushed onto the stack for later execution.

4. As you know from Chapter 5, integers are represented inside the computer as a sequence of bits, each of which is a single digit in the binary number system and can therefore have only the value 0 or 1. With N bits, you can represent 2^N distinct integers. For example, three bits are sufficient to represent the eight (2^3) integers between 0 and 7, as follows:

    000 $\rightarrow$ 0
    001 $\rightarrow$ 1
    010 $\rightarrow$ 2
    011 $\rightarrow$ 3
    100 $\rightarrow$ 4
    101 $\rightarrow$ 5
    110 $\rightarrow$ 6
    111 $\rightarrow$ 7

    The bit patterns for these integers follow a recursive pattern. The binary numbers with N bits consist of the following two sets in order:

    - All binary numbers with $N-1$ bits preceded by a **0**
    - All binary numbers with $N-1$ bits preceded by a **1**

Write a recursive function

```
void generateBinaryCode(int nBits)
```

that generates the bit patterns for the binary representation of all integers that can be represented using the specified number of bits. For example, calling **generateBinaryCode(3)** should produce the following output:

```
         ⊖ ○ ○            GenerateBinaryCode
        000
        001
        010
        011
        100
        101
        110
        111
```

5. Although the binary coding used in exercise 4 is good for most applications, it has certain drawbacks. As you count in standard binary notation, there are some points in the sequence at which several bits change at the same time. For example, in the three-bit binary code, the value of every bit changes as you move from 3 (**011**) to 4 (**100**).

In some applications, this instability in the bit patterns used to represent adjacent numbers can lead to problems. Suppose, for example, that you are using a hardware measurement device containing a three-bit value that varies between 3 and 4. Sometimes, the device will register **011** to indicate the value 3; at other times, it will register **100** to indicate 4. For this device to work correctly, the bit transitions must occur simultaneously. If the first bit changes more quickly than the others, for example, there may be an intermediate state in which the device reads **111**, which would be a highly inaccurate reading.

You can avoid this problem simply by assigning three-bit values to the numbers 0 through 7 so that only one bit changes in the representation when you move between adjacent integers. Such an encoding is called a *Gray code* (after its inventor, the mathematician Frank Gray) and looks like this:

$$\begin{array}{ccc}
\mathbf{000} & \rightarrow & 0 \\
\mathbf{001} & \rightarrow & 1 \\
\mathbf{011} & \rightarrow & 2 \\
\mathbf{010} & \rightarrow & 3 \\
\mathbf{110} & \rightarrow & 4 \\
\mathbf{111} & \rightarrow & 5 \\
\mathbf{101} & \rightarrow & 6 \\
\mathbf{100} & \rightarrow & 7
\end{array}$$

The recursive insight that you need to create a Gray code of N bits is summarized in the following informal procedure:

1. Write down the Gray code for $N-1$ bits.

2. Copy that same list *in reverse order* below the original one.

3. Add a **0** bit in front of the encodings in the original half of the list and a **1** bit in front of those in the reversed copy.

This procedure is illustrated in the following derivation of the Gray code for three bits:

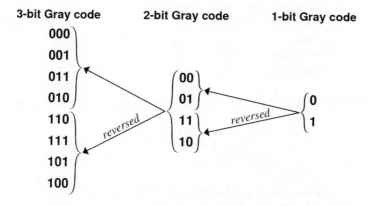

Write a recursive function **generateGrayCode(nBits)** that generates the Gray code patterns for the specified number of bits. For example, if you call the function

        generateGrayCode(3)

the program should produce the following output:

```
000
001
011
010
110
111
101
100
```

6.   In the subset-sum problem introduced in section 9.2, there are often several ways to generate the desired target number. For example, given the set { 1, 3, 4, 5 }, there are two different ways to produce the target value 5: you

can select the 1 and the 4 or, alternatively, select just the 5. By contrast, there is no way to partition the set { 1, 3, 4, 5 } to get 11.

Write a method

```
int subsetSumWays(TreeSet<Integer> set, int target)
```

that returns the number of ways in which you can produce the target value by choosing a subset of the specified set. For example, suppose that `sampleSet` has been initialized as follows:

```
TreeSet<Integer> sampleSet;
sampleSet.add(1);
sampleSet.add(3);
sampleSet.add(4);
sampleSet.add(5);
```

Given this definition of `sampleSet`, calling

```
subsetSumWays(sampleSet, 5);
```

should return 2 (there are two ways to make 5), and calling

```
subsetSumWays(sampleSet, 11)
```

should return 0 (there are no ways to make 11).

7. Write a program `EmbeddedWords` that finds all English words that can be formed by taking some subset of letters in order from a given starting word. For example, given the starting word *happy,* you can certainly produce the words *a, ha, hap,* and *happy,* in which the letters appear consecutively. You can also produce the words *hay* and *ay,* because those letters appear in *happy* in the correct left-to-right order. You cannot, however, produce the words *pa* or *pap* because the letters—even though they appear in the word—don't appear in the correct order. A sample run of the program might look like this:

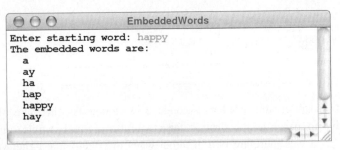

8.   *I am the only child of parents who weighed, measured, and*
      priced everything; for whom what could not be weighed,
      measured, and priced had no existence.

                              —Charles Dickens, *Little Dorrit,* 1857

In Dickens's time, merchants measured many commodities using weights and
a two-pan balance—a practice that continues in many parts of the world today.
If you are using a limited set of weights, however, you can measure only
certain quantities. For example, suppose that you have only two weights: a
1-ounce weight and a 3-ounce weight. With these weights you can easily
measure 4 ounces, as shown:

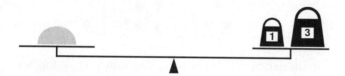

It is somewhat more interesting to discover that you can also measure 2 ounces
by shifting the 1-ounce weight to the other side, as follows:

Write a recursive method

```
boolean isMeasurable(int target, IntegerList weights)
```

that determines whether it is possible to measure the desired target amount
with a given set of weights, which is stored in the parameter **weights**, which
is declared to be an **IntegerList** as defined in Figure 8-1 on page 283.

For example, suppose that **sampleWeights** has been initialized like this:

```
IntegerList sampleWeights = new IntegerList(1, 3);
```

Given these values, the method call

```
isMeasurable(2, sampleWeights)
```

should return **true** because it is possible to measure 2 ounces using the
sample weight set as illustrated in the preceding diagram. On the other hand,
calling

```
isMeasurable(5, sampleWeights)
```

should return **false** because it is impossible to use the 1- and 3-ounce weights to measure 5 ounces.

9. In the card game called Cribbage, part of the game consists of adding up the score from a set of five playing cards. One of the components of the score is the number of distinct card combinations whose values add up to 15, with aces counting as 1 and all face cards (jacks, queens, and kings) counting as 10. Consider, for example, the following cards:

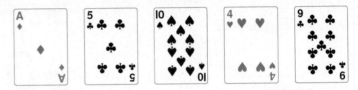

There are three different combinations that sum to 15, as follows:

$$AD + 10S + 4H \qquad AD + 5C + 9C \qquad 5C + 10S$$

As a second example, the cards

contain the following eight different combinations that add up to 15:

5C + JC	5D + JC	5H + JC	5S + JC
5C + 5D + 5H	5C + 5D + 5S	5C + 5H + 5S	5D + 5H + 5S

Write a method

```
private int countFifteens(Card[] cards)
```

that takes an array of **Card** values (as defined in Chapter 7, exercise 2) and returns the number of ways you can make 15 from that set of cards. You don't need to know much about the **Card** class to solve this problem. The only thing you need is the **getRank** method, which returns the rank of the card as an integer. You may assume that the **Card** class exports the constant names **ACE**, **JACK**, **QUEEN**, and **KING** with the values 1, 11, 12, and 13, respectively.

10. The recursive decomposition presented in section 9.3 is not the only effective strategy for generating permutations. Another way of implementing the recursive case looks like this:

    1. Remove the first character from the string and store it in the variable **ch**.

    2. Generate the set containing all permutations of the remaining characters.

    3. Form a new set by inserting **ch** in every possible position in each of those permutations.

    Rewrite the **Permutations** program so that it uses this new strategy.

11. The strategy used to implement the **Permutations** program in the text is designed to emphasize its recursive character. The resulting code is not particularly efficient, mostly because it ends up generating sets that are later discarded and because it applies methods like **substring** that require copying the characters in a string. It is possible to eliminate those inefficiencies by converting the string into a character array—the **String** class includes a **toCharArray** method that does just that—and then applying the following recursive strategy:

    1. At each level, pass the character array along with an index that indicates where the permutation process starts. Characters in the string before this index stay where they are.

    2. The simple case occurs when the index reaches the end of the array.

    3. The recursive case operates by swapping the character at the index position with every other character in the array and then generating every permutation starting with the next higher index. You then need to swap the characters back to ensure that the original order is restored.

    Use this strategy to implement a method

    ```
    void listPermutations(String str)
    ```

    that lists all permutations of the string **str** without generating any sets at all. The **listPermutations** method itself must be a wrapper method for a second method that includes the index.

    This method is relatively easy to implement if you don't try to take account of duplicated letters in the string. The interesting challenge arises only when you change the structure of the algorithm so that it lists each unique permutation exactly once without using sets to accomplish that task. You should not, however, worry about the order in which **listPermutations** delivers its output.

12. On a telephone keypad, the digits are mapped onto the alphabet as shown in the following diagram:

In order to make their phone numbers more memorable, service providers like to find numbers that spell out some word (called a *mnemonic*) appropriate to their business that makes that phone number easier to remember.

Write a method **listMnemonics** that generates all possible letter combinations that correspond to a given number, represented as a string of digits. For example, the call

```
listMnemonics("723")
```

should list the following 36 possible letter combinations that correspond to that prefix:

```
PAD  PBD  PCD  QAD  QBD  QCD  RAD  RBD  RCD  SAD  SBD  SCD
PAE  PBE  PCE  QAE  QBE  QCE  RAE  RBE  RCE  SAE  SBE  SCE
PAF  PBF  PCF  QAF  QBF  QCF  RAF  RBF  RCF  SAF  SBF  SCF
```

13. Rewrite the program from exercise 12 so that it lists only those mnemonics that are valid English words, as defined in the **EnglishWords.txt** file introduced in Chapter 6.

14. These days, the letters on a telephone keypad are not used for mnemonics as much as they are for texting. Entering text using a keypad is problematic, because there are fewer keys than there are letters in the alphabet. Some older cell phones use a "multi-tap" user interface, in which you tap the 2 key once for **a**, twice for **b**, and three times for **c**, which can get tedious. A streamlined alternative is to use a predictive strategy in which the cell phone guesses which of the possible letters you intended, based on the sequence so far and its possible completions.

For example, if you type the digit sequence 72, there are 12 possibilities: **pa**, **pb**, **pc**, **qa**, **qb**, **qc**, **ra**, **rb**, **rc**, **sa**, **sb**, and **sc**. Only four of these letter pairs—**pa**, **ra**, **sa**, and **sc**—seem promising because they are prefixes of common English words like **party**, **radio**, **sandwich**, and **scanner**. The others can be ignored because there are no common words that begin with those sequences of letters. If the user enters 9956, there are 144 (4 x 4 x 3 x 3) possible letter sequences, but you can be assured the user meant **xylo** since that is the only sequence that is a prefix of any English words.

Write a method

```
void listCompletions(String digits, Lexicon lex)
```

that prints all words from the lexicon that can be formed by extending the given digit sequence. For example, calling

```
listCompletions("72547", english)
```

should generate the following sample run:

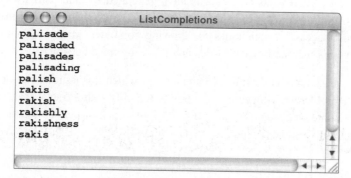

If your only concern is getting the answer, the easiest way to solve this problem is to iterate through the words in the lexicon and print each word that matches the specified digit string. That solution requires no recursion and very little thinking. Your managers, however, believe that looking through every word in the dictionary is slow and insist that your code use the lexicon only to test whether a given string is a word or a prefix of an English word. With that restriction, you need to figure out how to generate all possible letter sequences from the string of digits. That task is easiest to solve recursively.

15. Many of Mondrian's geometrical paintings fill in the rectangular regions with some color. Extend the **Mondrian** program from the text so that it fills with randomly chosen colors some fraction of the rectangular regions it creates.

16. In countries like the United States that still use the traditional English system of measurement, each inch on a ruler is marked off into fractions using tick marks that look like this:

The longest tick mark falls at the half-inch position, two smaller tick marks indicate the quarter inches, and even smaller ones are used to mark the eighths and sixteenths. Write a recursive program that draws a line 100 pixels long at the center of the graphics window and then draws the tick marks shown in the diagram. Assume that the length of the tick mark indicating the half-inch position is given by the constant definition

```
private static final double HALF_INCH_TICK = 20;
```

and that each smaller tick mark is half the size of the next larger one.

17. One of the reasons that fractals have generated so much interest is that they turn out to be useful in some surprising practical contexts. For instance, the most successful techniques for drawing computer images of mountains and certain other landscape features involve using fractal geometry.

As a simple example of a situation in which this issue comes up, consider the problem of connecting two points A and B with a fractal that looks like a coastline on a map. The simplest possible strategy would be to draw a straight line between the two points:

This is the order-0 coastline and represents the base case of the recursion.

Of course, an actual coastline will have small peninsulas or inlets somewhere along its length, so you would expect a more realistic drawing of a coastline to jut in or out occasionally. As a first approximation, you could replace the straight line with the same fractal line used to create the snowflake fractal, as follows:

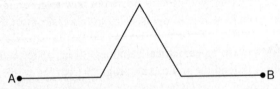

This process creates the order-1 coastline. The jags in coastlines, however, don't always point in the same direction. The triangular wedges should therefore point up and down with equal probability.

If you then replace each of the straight-line segments in the order-1 fractal with a fractal line in a random direction, you get the order-2 coastline, which might look like this:

A●   ●B

Continuing this process eventually results in a drawing that conveys a remarkably realistic sense, as in this order-5 coastline:

A●   ●B

Write a program to draw a fractal coastline on the graphics window.

18. If you search the web for fractal designs, you will find many intricate wonders beyond the Koch snowflake illustrated in this chapter. One is the **H-*fractal*,** in which the repeated pattern is shaped like an elongated letter **H** that fits inside a square. Thus, the order-0 H-fractal looks like this:

To create the order-1 fractal, all you do is add four new H-fractals—each half the original size—at each open end of the order-0 fractal, like this:

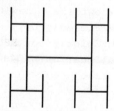

To create the order-2 fractal, you just add even smaller H-fractals (again half the size of the fractal to which they connect) to each of the open endpoints.

Write a recursive method

```
drawHFractal(GWindow gw, double x, double y,
             double size, int order)
```

where **gw** is the graphics window, **x** and **y** are the coordinates of the center of the H-fractal, **size** specifies the width and the height, and **order** indicates the order of the fractal. As an example, the main program

```
public void run() {
    GWindow gw = new GWindow(WIDTH, HEIGHT);
    drawHFractal(gw, WIDTH / 2, HEIGHT / 2, 100, 3);
}
```

would draw an order-3 H-fractal at the center of the graphics window, like this:

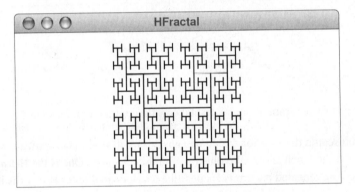

19. If you have implemented the **GPolygon** class described in exercise 14 in Chapter 8, define a **GSnowflake** class that extends **GPolygon** and draws a snowflake fractal. The size and order of the fractal should be parameters to the **GSnowflake** constructor. For example, the following program should draw a filled, red, order-3 snowflake of size 200 at the center of the window:

```
public void run() {
    GWindow gw = new GWindow(WIDTH, HEIGHT);
    GSnowflake snowflake = new GSnowflake(200, 3);
    snowflake.setFilled(true);
    snowflake.setColor(Color.RED);
    snowflake.setLocation(WIDTH / 2, HEIGHT / 2);
    gw.add(snowflake);
}
```

20. To celebrate its 550th anniversary in 2008, Magdalen College at Oxford University commissioned the English artist Mark Wallinger to create a sculpture called Y that has a decidedly recursive structure. A photograph of

FIGURE 9-5 Installation view of Mark Wallinger's Y, 2008, in Bat Willow Meadow, Magdalen College, Oxford

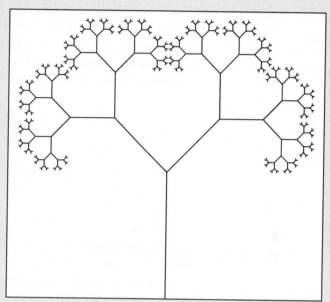

the sculpture appears at the left of Figure 9-5 and a diagram illustrating its fractal design appears at the right. Given its branching structure, the underlying pattern in Wallinger's sculpture is called a *fractal tree.* The tree begins as a simple trunk indicated by a straight vertical line, as follows:

The trunk branches at the top to form two lines that veer off at an angle, as shown:

These branches themselves split to form new branches, which split to form new ones, and so on.

Write a program that uses the graphics library to draw the fractal tree in Wallinger's sculpture. If you carry this process on to the eighth-order fractal, you get the image on the right of Figure 9-5.

21. Another interesting fractal is the ***Sierpinski Triangle,*** named after its inventor, the Polish mathematician Wacław Sierpiński (1882–1969). The order-0 Sierpinski Triangle is simply an equilateral triangle. To create an order-N Sierpinski Triangle, you draw three Sierpinski Triangles of order $N-1$, each of which has half the edge length of the original. Those three triangles are placed in the corners of the larger triangle, which means that the order-1 Sierpinski Triangle looks like this:

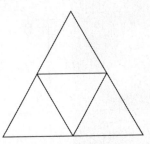

The downward-pointing triangle in the middle of this figure is not drawn explicitly, but is instead formed by the sides of the other three triangles. That area, moreover, is not recursively subdivided and will remain unchanged at every level of the fractal decomposition. Thus, the order-2 Sierpinski Triangle has the same open area in the middle:

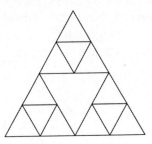

If you continue this process through three more recursive levels, you get the order-5 Sierpinski Triangle, which looks like this:

Write a program that asks the user for an edge length and a fractal order and draws a Sierpinski Triangle at the center of the graphics window.

Chapter 10
Backtracking Algorithms

Threads snap. You would lose your way in the labyrinth.

— Oscar Wilde, *The Picture of Dorian Gray,* 1890

For many real-world problems, the solution process consists of working your way through a sequence of decision points in which each choice leads you further along some path. If you make the correct set of choices, you end up at the solution. On the other hand, if you reach a dead end or otherwise discover that you have made an incorrect choice somewhere along the way, you have to backtrack to a previous decision point and try a different path. Algorithms that take this approach are called *backtracking algorithms.*

If you think about a backtracking algorithm as the process of repeatedly exploring paths until you encounter the solution, the process appears to have an iterative character. As it happens, however, most problems of this form are easier to solve recursively. The fundamental recursive insight is simply this: a backtracking problem has a solution if and only if at least one of the smaller backtracking problems that result from making each possible initial choice has a solution. The examples in this chapter are designed to illustrate this process and demonstrate the power of recursion in this domain.

▨ 10.1 Recursive backtracking in a maze

Once upon a time, in the days of Greek mythology, the Mediterranean island of Crete was ruled by a tyrannical king named Minos. From time to time, Minos demanded tribute from the city of Athens in the form of young men and women, whom he would sacrifice to the Minotaur, a fearsome beast with the head of a bull and the body of a man. To house this deadly creature, Minos forced his servant Daedalus (the engineering genius who later escaped by constructing a set of wings) to build a vast underground labyrinth at Knossos. The victims would be led into the labyrinth, where they would be eaten by the Minotaur before they could find their way out. This tragedy continued until Theseus volunteered to be one of the sacrifices. Following the advice of Minos's daughter Ariadne, Theseus entered the labyrinth with a sword and a ball of string. After slaying the monster, Theseus was able to find his way back to the exit by unwinding the string as he went along.

The right-hand rule

Ariadne's strategy is an algorithm for escaping from a maze, but not everyone trapped in a maze is lucky enough to have a ball of string. Fortunately, there are other strategies for solving a maze. Of these strategies, the best known is called the *right-hand rule,* which can be expressed in the following pseudocode form:

> *Put your right hand against a wall.*
> **while** (*you have not yet escaped from the maze*) {
> *Walk forward keeping your right hand on a wall.*
> }

To visualize the operation of the right-hand rule, imagine that Theseus has successfully dispatched the Minotaur and is now standing in the position marked by the first character in Theseus's name, the Greek letter theta (Θ):

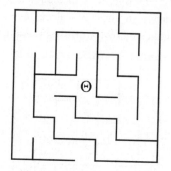

If Theseus puts his right hand on the wall and then follows the right-hand rule from there, he will trace out the path shown by the dashed line in this diagram:

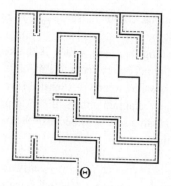

Unfortunately, the right-hand rule does not work in every maze. If there is a loop that surrounds the starting position, Theseus can get trapped in an infinite loop, as illustrated by the following simple maze:

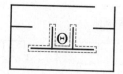

Finding a recursive approach

As the `while` loop in its pseudocode form makes clear, the right-hand rule is an *iterative* strategy. You can, however, also think about the process of solving a maze from a *recursive* perspective. To do so, you must adopt a different mental strategy. You no longer consider the problem in terms of finding a complete path. Instead, your goal is to find a recursive insight that simplifies the problem, one step at a time. Once you have made the simplification, you use the same process to solve each of the resulting subproblems.

Let's go back to the initial configuration of the maze shown in the illustration of the right-hand rule. Put yourself in Theseus's place. From the initial configuration, you have three choices, as indicated by the arrows in the following diagram:

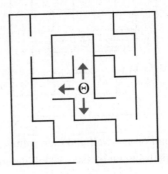

The exit, if any, must lie along one of those paths. Moreover, if you choose the correct direction, you will be one step closer to the solution. The maze has therefore become simpler along that path, which is the key to a recursive solution. This observation suggests the necessary recursive insight. The original maze has a solution if and only if it is possible to solve at least one of the new mazes shown in Figure 10-1. The × in each diagram marks the original starting square and is off-limits for any of the recursive solutions because the optimal solution will never have to backtrack through this square.

If you look at the mazes in Figure 10-1, it is easy to see—at least from your global vantage point—that the submazes labeled (a) and (c) represent dead-end paths and that the only solution begins in the direction shown in the submaze (b). If you are thinking recursively, however, you don't need to proceed with the analysis

FIGURE 10-1   **Recursive decomposition of a maze**

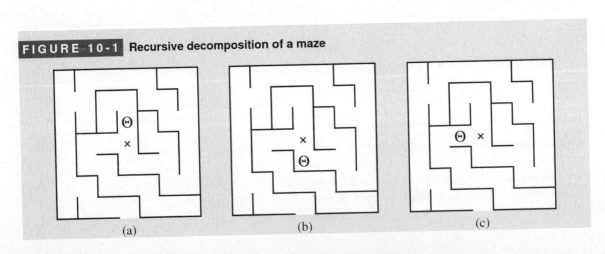

all the way to the solution. You have already decomposed the problem into simpler instances. All you need to do is rely on the power of recursion to solve the individual subproblems, and you're home free. You still have to identify a set of simple cases so that the recursion can terminate, but the hard work has been done.

Identifying the simple cases

What constitutes the simple case for a maze? One possibility is that you might already be standing outside the maze. If so, you're finished. Clearly, this situation represents one simple case. There is, however, another possibility. You might also reach a blind alley where you've run out of places to move. For example, if you try to solve the sample maze by moving north and then continue to make recursive calls along that path, you will eventually be in the position of trying to solve the following maze:

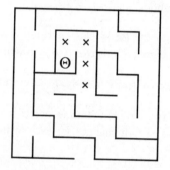

At this point, you've run out of room to maneuver. Every path from the new position is either marked or blocked by a wall, which makes it clear that the maze has no solution from this point. Thus, the maze problem has a second simple case in which every direction from the current square is blocked by either a wall or a marked square.

It is easier to code the recursive algorithm if, instead of checking for marked squares as you consider the possible directions of motion, you go ahead and make the recursive calls on those squares. If you check at the beginning of the procedure to see whether the current square is marked, you can terminate the recursion at that point. After all, if you find yourself positioned on a marked square, you must be retracing your path, which means that the optimal solution must lie in some other direction.

Thus, the two simple cases for this problem are as follows:

1. If the current square is outside the maze, the maze is solved.

2. If the current square is marked, the maze is unsolvable, at least along the path you've chosen so far.

Coding the maze-solving algorithm

Although the recursive insight and the simple cases are all you need to solve the problem on a conceptual level, writing a complete program to navigate a maze requires you to consider a number of implementation details as well. For example, you need to decide on a representation for the maze that allows you to figure out where the walls are, keep track of the current position, indicate that a particular square is marked, and determine whether you have escaped from the maze. While designing an appropriate data structure for the maze is an interesting programming challenge in its own right, it has very little to do with understanding the recursive algorithm, which is the focus of this discussion. If anything, the details of the data structure are likely to get in the way and make it more difficult for you to understand the algorithmic strategy as a whole. Fortunately, it is possible to set those details aside by introducing a new class called `Maze` that hides some of the complexity. The public methods in the `Maze` class appear in Figure 10-2.

Once you have access to the `Maze` class, writing a program to solve a maze becomes much simpler. The goal of this exercise is to write a method

```
boolean solveMaze(Maze maze, Point pt)
```

The arguments to `solveMaze` are (1) the `Maze` object that holds the data structure and (2) the starting position, which changes for each of the recursive subproblems.

FIGURE 10-2 Public methods in the Maze class

`public Maze(String filename)` Creates a new maze by reading in the specified file.
`public Maze(String filename, GWindow gw)` Creates a new maze from the specified file and displays it on the graphics window.
`public Point getStartPosition()` Returns the starting position in the maze as a `Point`.
`public boolean isOutside(Point pt)` Returns `true` if the point is outside the maze.
`public boolean wallExists(Point pt, Direction dir)` Returns `true` if there is a wall in the indicated direction.
`public void markSquare(Point pt)` Marks the square at `pt`.
`public void unmarkSquare(Point pt)` Unmarks the square at `pt`.
`public boolean isMarked(Point pt)` Returns `true` if the square at `pt` is marked.

To ensure that the recursion can terminate when a solution is found, the `solveMaze` method returns `true` if a solution has been found, and `false` otherwise. The code for the `run` method looks like this:

```
public void run() {
    GWindow gw = new GWindow();
    Maze maze = new Maze("SampleMaze.txt", gw);
    if (!solveMaze(maze, maze.getStartPosition())) {
        System.out.println("No solution exists.");
    }
}
```

The code for the `solveMaze` method appears in Figure 10-3.

FIGURE 10-3 Implementation of the `solveMaze` method

```
/*
 * Attempts to generate a solution to the current maze from the specified
 * start point.  The method returns true if the maze has a solution.
 */

    private boolean solveMaze(Maze maze, Point start) {
        if (maze.isOutside(start)) return true;
        if (maze.isMarked(start)) return false;
        maze.markSquare(start);
        for (Direction dir : Direction.values()) {
            if (!maze.wallExists(start, dir)) {
                if (solveMaze(maze, takeOneStep(start, dir))) {
                    return true;
                }
            }
        }
        maze.unmarkSquare(start);
        return false;
    }

/*
 * Returns the point that is one step from pt in the specified direction.
 */

    private Point takeOneStep(Point pt, Direction dir) {
        switch (dir) {
          case NORTH: return new Point(pt.x, pt.y - 1);
          case EAST: return new Point(pt.x + 1, pt.y);
          case SOUTH: return new Point(pt.x, pt.y + 1);
          case WEST: return new Point(pt.x - 1, pt.y);
        }
        throw new RuntimeException("Illegal direction");
    }
```

Convincing yourself that the solution works

In order to use recursion effectively, at some point you must be able to look at a recursive method like the `solveMaze` example in Figure 10-3 and say to yourself something like this: "I understand how this works. The problem is getting simpler because more squares are marked each time. The simple cases are clearly correct. This code must do the job." For most of you, however, that confidence in the power of recursion will not come easily. Your natural skepticism makes you want to see the steps in the solution. The problem is that, even for a maze as simple as the one shown earlier in this chapter, the complete history of the steps involved in the solution is far too large to think about comfortably. Solving that maze, for example, requires 66 calls to `solveMaze` that are nested 27 levels deep when the solution is finally discovered. If you attempt to trace the code in detail, you will almost certainly get lost.

If you are not yet ready to adopt the recursive leap of faith, the best you can do is track the operation of the code in a more general sense. You know that the program first tries to solve the maze by moving one square to the north, because the `for` loop goes through the directions in the order defined by the `Direction` enumeration. Thus, the first step in the solution process is to make a recursive call that starts in the following position:

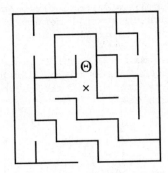

At this point, the entire process repeats. The program again tries to move north and makes a new recursive call in this position:

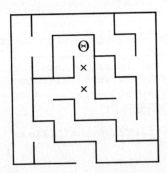

At this level of the recursion, moving north is no longer possible, so the `for` loop cycles through the other directions. After a brief excursion southward, upon which the program encounters a marked square, the program finds the opening to the west and proceeds to generate a new recursive call. The same process occurs in this new square, which in turn leads to the following configuration:

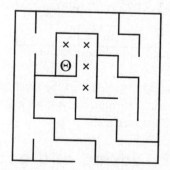

In this position, none of the directions in the `for` loop do any good; every square is either blocked by a wall or already marked. Thus, when the `for` loop at this level exits at the bottom, it unmarks the current square and returns to the previous level. It turns out that all the paths have been explored in this position as well, so the program once again unmarks the square and returns to the next higher level in the recursion. Eventually, the program backtracks all the way to the initial call, having completely exhausted the possibilities that begin by moving north. The `for` loop then tries the eastward direction, finds it blocked, and continues on to explore the southern corridor, beginning with a recursive call in this configuration:

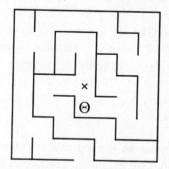

From here, the algorithm follows exactly the same process. The recursion systematically explores every corridor along this path, backing up through the stack of recursive calls whenever it reaches a dead end. The only difference along this route is that eventually—after descending through an additional recursive level for every step on the path—the program makes a recursive call in the following position:

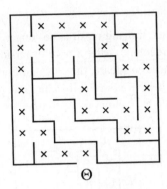

At this point, Theseus is outside the maze, so the simple case kicks in and returns **true** to its caller. This value is then propagated back through all 27 levels of the recursion, eventually returning to the main program.

◼︎ 10.2 Backtracking and games

Although backtracking is easiest to illustrate in the context of a maze, the strategy is considerably more general. For example, you can apply backtracking to most two-player strategy games. Initially, the first player has several choices for a move. Depending on which move is chosen, the second player then has a particular set of available responses. Each of these responses leads in turn to new options for the first player, and this process continues until the end of the game. The different possible positions at each turn in the game form a branching structure in which each option opens up more and more possibilities.

If you want to program a computer to take one side of a two-player game, one approach is to have the computer follow all the branches in the list of possibilities. Before making its first move, the computer would try every possible choice. For each of these choices, it would then try to determine what its opponent's response would be. To do so, it would follow the same logic: try every possibility and evaluate the possible counterplays. If the computer can look far enough ahead to discover that some move would leave its opponent in a hopeless position, it should make that move.

In theory, this strategy can be applied to any two-player strategy game. In practice, the process of looking at all the possible moves, potential responses, responses to those responses, and so on requires too much time and memory, even for modern computers. There are several games, however, that are simple enough to play optimally by looking at all the possibilities, yet complex enough so that the solution is not immediately obvious to the human player.

The game of Nim

To see how recursive backtracking applies to two-player games, it helps to consider a simple example such as the game of *Nim,* which is the generic name for an entire class of games in which players take turns removing objects from some initial configuration. In this particular version, the game begins with a pile of 13 coins. On each turn, a player takes either one, two, or three coins from the pile and puts them aside. The object of the game is to avoid being forced to take the last coin. Figure 10-4 shows a sample game between the computer and a human player.

How would you go about writing a program to play a winning game of Nim? The mechanical aspects of the game—keeping track of the number of coins, asking the player for a move, determining the end of the game, and so forth—constitute a straightforward programming task. The interesting part of the program consists of figuring out how to give the computer a strategy for playing the best possible game.

Finding a successful strategy for Nim is not particularly hard, especially if you work backward from the end of the game. The rules of Nim indicate that the loser is the player who takes the last coin. Thus, if you ever find yourself with just one coin on the table, you're in a bad position: you have to take that coin and lose. On the other hand, things look good if you find yourself with two, three, or four coins. In any of these cases, you can always take all but one of the remaining coins, leaving your opponent in the unenviable position of being stuck with just one coin.

FIGURE 10-4 **Sample run of the Nim game**

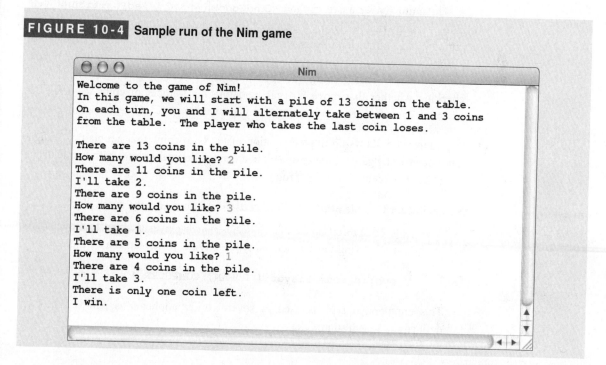

But what if there are five coins on the table? What can you do then? After a bit of thought, it's easy to see that you're also doomed if you're left with five coins. No matter what you do, you have to leave your opponent with two, three, or four coins—situations that you've just discovered represent good positions from your opponent's perspective. If your opponent is playing intelligently, you will surely be left with a single coin on your next turn. Since you have no good moves, being left with five coins is clearly a bad position.

This informal analysis reveals an important insight about the game of Nim. On each turn, you are looking for a good move. A good move is one that leaves your opponent in a bad position. But what is a bad position? A bad position is one in which there is no good move.

Even though these definitions of *good move* and *bad position* are circular, they nonetheless constitute a complete strategy for playing a perfect game of Nim. You just have to rely on the power of recursion. If you have a method **findGoodMove** that takes the number of coins as its argument, all it has to do is try every possibility, looking for one that leaves a bad position for the opponent. You can then assign the job of determining whether a particular position is bad to the predicate method **isBadPosition**, which calls **findGoodMove** to see if there is one. The two methods call each other back and forth, evaluating all possible branches as the game proceeds.

The mutually recursive methods **findGoodMove** and **isBadPosition** provide all the strategy that the Nim program needs to play a perfect game. To complete the program, all you need to do is write the code that takes care of the mechanics of playing Nim with a human player. This code is responsible for setting up the game, printing instructions, keeping track of whose turn it is, asking the user for a move, checking whether that move is legal, updating the number of coins, figuring out when the game is over, and letting the user know who won.

Figure 10-5 shows an implementation of the Nim game that adopts this design. The code for the game is encapsulated in a class called **Nim**, along with two instance variables that keep track of the progress of play:

- An integer variable **nCoins** that records the number of coins in the pile.
- A variable **currentPlayer** that indicates which player is about to move. This value is stored using the enumerated type **Player**, which has the definition

```
public enum Player { HUMAN, COMPUTER }
```

This enumerated type is used in several other applications and is therefore defined in its own source file.

FIGURE 10-5 A simple implementation of the Nim game

```
/*
 * File: Nim.java
 * ---------------
 * This program simulates a simple variant of the game of Nim.  In this
 * version, the game starts with a pile of 13 coins on a table.  Players
 * then take turns removing 1, 2, or 3 coins from the pile.  The player
 * who takes the last coin loses.
 */

package edu.stanford.cs.javacs2.ch10;

import edu.stanford.cs.console.Console;
import edu.stanford.cs.console.SystemConsole;

public class Nim {

    public void run() {
        console = new SystemConsole();
        printInstructions();
        nCoins = STARTING_COINS;
        currentPlayer = STARTING_PLAYER;
        while (nCoins > 1) {
            System.out.println("There are " + nCoins + " coins in the pile.");
            if (currentPlayer == Player.HUMAN) {
                nCoins -= getUserMove();
            } else {
                int nTaken = getComputerMove();
                System.out.println("I'll take " + nTaken + ".");
                nCoins -= nTaken;
            }
            switchPlayer();
        }
        announceResult();
    }

/**
 * Asks the user to enter a move and returns the number of coins taken.
 * If the move is not legal, the user is asked to reenter a valid move.
 */

    private int getUserMove() {
        int limit = (nCoins < MAX_MOVE) ? nCoins : MAX_MOVE;
        while (true) {
            int nTaken = console.nextInt("How many would you like? ");
            if (nTaken > 0 && nTaken <= limit) return nTaken;
            System.out.println("That's cheating!  Please choose " +
                               "between 1 and " + limit + ".");
            System.out.println("There are " + nCoins + " coins in the pile.");
        }
    }
```

FIGURE 10-5 A simple implementation of the Nim game (continued)

```
/**
 * Figures out what move is best for the computer player and returns
 * the number of coins taken.  The method first calls findGoodMove
 * to see if a winning move exists.  If none does, the program takes
 * only one coin to give the human player more chances to make a mistake.
 */

   private int getComputerMove() {
      int nTaken = findGoodMove(nCoins);
      return (nTaken == NO_GOOD_MOVE) ? 1 : nTaken;
   }

/**
 * Looks for a winning move, given the specified number of coins.  If
 * there is a winning move, the method returns that value; if not, the
 * method returns the constant NO_GOOD_MOVE.  The recursive insight is
 * that a good move is one that leaves your opponent in a bad position
 * and a bad position is one that offers no good moves.
 */

   private int findGoodMove(int nCoins) {
      int limit = (nCoins < MAX_MOVE) ? nCoins : MAX_MOVE;
      for (int nTaken = 1; nTaken <= limit; nTaken++) {
         if (isBadPosition(nCoins - nTaken)) return nTaken;
      }
      return NO_GOOD_MOVE;
   }

/**
 * Returns true if nCoins represents a bad position.  Since being left
 * with a single coin is clearly a bad position, having nCoins be equal
 * to 1 represents the simple case of the recursion.
 */

   private boolean isBadPosition(int nCoins) {
      if (nCoins == 1) return true;
      return findGoodMove(nCoins) == NO_GOOD_MOVE;
   }

/**
 * Switches between the human and computer player.
 */

   private void switchPlayer() {
      currentPlayer = (currentPlayer == Player.HUMAN) ? Player.COMPUTER
                                                      : Player.HUMAN;
   }
```

FIGURE 10-5   A simple implementation of the Nim game (continued)

```java
/**
 * Explains the rules of the game to the user.
 */

   private void printInstructions() {
      System.out.println("Welcome to the game of Nim!");
      System.out.println("In this game, we will start with a pile of " +
                          STARTING_COINS + " coins on the table.");
      System.out.println("On each turn, you and I will alternately take " +
                          "between 1 and " + MAX_MOVE + " coins");
      System.out.println("from the table.  The player who takes the " +
                          "last coin loses.");
      System.out.println();
   }

/**
 * Announces the final result of the game.
 */

   private void announceResult() {
      if (nCoins == 0) {
         System.out.println("You took the last coin.  You lose.");
      } else {
         System.out.println("There is only one coin left.");
         if (currentPlayer == Player.HUMAN) {
            System.out.println("I win.");
         } else {
            System.out.println("I lose.");
         }
      }
   }

/* Private constants */

   private static final int MAX_MOVE = 3;
   private static final int NO_GOOD_MOVE = -1;
   private static final int STARTING_COINS = 13;
   private static final Player STARTING_PLAYER = Player.HUMAN;

/* Private instance variables */

   private Console console;         /* Console for user interaction   */
   private int nCoins;              /* Number of coins left on the table */
   private Player currentPlayer;    /* Indicates whose turn it is     */

/* Main program */

   public static void main(String[] args) {
      new Nim().run();
   }

}
```

A generalized program for two-player games

The code in Figure 10-5 is highly specific to Nim. The **run** method, for example, is directly responsible for setting up the **nCoins** variable and updating it after each player moves. The general structure of a two-player game, however, is more widely applicable. Many games can be solved using the same overall strategy, even though different games will require different implementations to get the details right.

One of the key concepts in this text is the notion of *abstraction,* which is the process of separating out the general aspects of a problem so that they are no longer obscured by the details of a specific domain. You may not be terribly interested in a program that plays Nim; after all, Nim is rather boring once you figure it out. What you would probably enjoy more is a program that is general enough to be adapted to play Nim, tic-tac-toe, or any other two-player strategy game you choose.

The possibility of creating such a generalization arises from the fact that most games share a few fundamental concepts. The first such concept is that of *state.* For any game, there are data values that define exactly what is happening at any point. In the Nim game, for example, the state consists of the values of its two instance variables, **nCoins** and **currentPlayer**. For a game like chess, the state would need to include what pieces are currently placed on which squares, although it would presumably also include the **currentPlayer** variable, or something that fulfills the same function. For any two-player game, however, it should be possible to store the relevant data in the instance variables of the class that implements the game.

The second important concept is that of a *move.* In Nim, a move consists of an integer representing the number of coins taken away. In chess, a move might consist of a pair indicating the starting and ending coordinates of the piece that is moving, although this approach is in fact complicated by the need to represent such esoteric moves as castling or the promotion of a pawn. For any game, however, it is possible to define a **Move** class that encapsulates whatever information is necessary to represent a move in that game. In the case of Nim, for example, you could define **Move** as the following inner class:

```
class Move {
    int nTaken;
}
```

Once you have defined the **Move** class, it is then straighforward to define a few additional helper methods that allow you to rewrite the **run** method as follows:

```
public void run() {
    initGame();
    printInstructions();
    while (!gameIsOver()) {
        displayGame();
        if (currentPlayer == Player.HUMAN) {
            makeMove(getUserMove());
        } else {
            Move move = getComputerMove();
            displayMove(move);
            makeMove(move);
        }
    }
    announceResult();
}
```

The most important thing to notice about the revised implementation of the **run** method is that the code gives no indication of what game is being played. It might be Nim, but it could just as easily be some other game. Every game requires its own definition for the **Move** type, along with specialized implementations of the various game-specific methods such as **initGame** and **makeMove**, which in the general case incorporates the call to **switchPlayer**. The code for the **run** method itself is general enough to work for many different two-player games.

The **run** method, however, is not the most exciting aspects of writing a program for a two-player game. The algorithmically interesting part is embedded inside the method **getComputerMove**, which is responsible for choosing the best move for the computer. The version of Nim in Figure 10-5 implements this strategy using the mutually recursive methods **findGoodMove** and **isBadPosition**, which search through all possible choices to find a winning move in the current position. Since that strategy is also independent of the details of any particular game, it ought to be possible to write these methods in a more general way. Before continuing down that path, however, it helps to generalize the problem further, which will make the solution strategy applicable to a wider variety of games.

10.3 The minimax algorithm

The techniques described in the preceding section work well for simple, completely solvable games like Nim. As games become more complex, though, it quickly becomes impossible to examine every possible outcome. If you tried to go through every possible game of chess, for example, the process could take billions of years, even at the speed of modern computers. Yet somehow, in spite of this limitation, computers are very good at chess. In 1997, IBM's "Deep Blue" supercomputer beat the reigning world champion at that time, Garry Kasparov. Deep Blue did not win by conducting an exhaustive analysis of all possible games; it instead looked ahead only for a restricted number of moves, much as humans do.

Even with games for which it is computationally infeasible to work through every possible sequence of moves, the recursive concepts of good moves and bad positions from the Nim game still come in handy. Although it may not be possible to identify a move as a surefire winner, it is still true that the best move in any position is the one that leaves your opponent in the worst position. Similarly, the worst position is the one that offers your opponent the weakest best move. This strategy—which consists of finding the position that leaves your opponent with the worst possible best move—is called the **minimax** algorithm because the goal is to find the move that minimizes your opponent's maximum opportunity.

Game trees

The best way to visualize the operation of the minimax strategy is to think about the possible future moves in a game as forming a branching diagram that expands at each turn. Because of this branching structure, such diagrams are called *game trees*. The initial state is represented by a dot at the top of the game tree. If there are, for example, three possible moves from this position, there will be three lines emanating downward from the current state to three new states that represent the results of these moves, as shown in the following diagram:

From each of the new positions, your opponent also has options. If each position again has three options, the next generation of the game tree looks like this:

Which move do you choose in the initial position? Clearly, your goal is to achieve the best outcome. Unfortunately, you only get to control half of the game. If you were able to select your opponent's move as well as your own, you could select the path to the state two turns away that left you in the best position. Given that your opponent is also trying to win, the best thing you can do is choose the initial move that leaves your opponent with as few winning chances as possible.

Rating positions and moves

In order to get a sense of how you can find the optimal move from a particular position, it helps to add some quantitative data to the analysis. Deciding whether one move is better than another is much easier if you assign a numeric score to each possible move. The higher the numeric score, the better the move. Thus, a move that has a score of +7, for example, is better than a move with a rating of –4. In addition to rating each possible move, it makes sense to assign a similar numeric rating to each position in the game. Thus, one position might have a rating of +9 and would therefore be better than a position with a score of only +2.

Both positions and moves are rated from the perspective of the player making the move. Moreover, the rating system is designed to be symmetric around 0, in the sense that a position that has a score of +9 for the current player would have a score of –9 from the opponent's point of view. This interpretation of rating numbers captures the idea that a position that is good for one player is bad for the other, as was true in the case of the game of Nim. More importantly, defining the rating system in this way makes it easy to express the relationship between the scores for moves and positions. The rating for any move is simply the negative of the rating for the resulting position when evaluated by your opponent. Similarly, the rating of any position can be defined as the rating of its best move.

To make this discussion more concrete, it helps to consider a simple example. Suppose that you have looked two steps ahead in the game, anticipating one move by you and the possible responses from your opponent. In computer science, a single move for a single player is called a *ply* to avoid the ambiguity associated with the words *move* and *turn,* which sometimes suggest that both players have a chance to play. If you rated the positions at the conclusion of your two-ply analysis, the game tree might look like this:

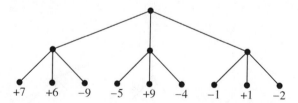

Because the positions at the bottom of this tree are again positions in which—as at the top of the tree—you have to move, the rating numbers in those positions are assigned from your perspective. Given these ratings of the potential positions, what move should you make from the original configuration?

At first glance, you might be attracted by the fact that the center branch contains a path that leads to a +9, which is an excellent outcome for you. Unfortunately, the fact that the center branch offers such a wonderful outcome doesn't really matter. If your opponent is playing rationally, there is no way that the game can reach the +9 position. Suppose, for example, that you do choose the center branch. Given the options available, your opponent will select the leftmost branch, as illustrated by the highlighted path in the following game tree:

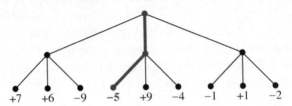

Your initial choice thus leaves you in a position that—from your point of view—has a rating of −5. You would do better to choose the rightmost branch, from which your opponent's best strategy leaves you in a position with a −2 rating:

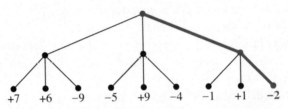

As noted earlier in this section, the rating of a move is the negative of the rating of the resulting position when evaluated from the opponent's perspective. The rating of the last move in the highlighted line of the game tree is +2 because it leads to a position with a −2 rating. The negative sign indicates the shift in perspective. Moves that lead to positions that are bad for your opponent are good for you, and vice versa. The rating of each position is simply the rating of the best move it offers. The ratings for the positions and moves along the highlighted path in the game tree therefore look like this:

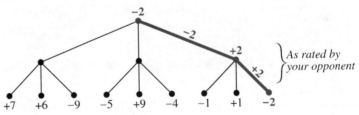

The rating of the starting position is therefore −2. While this position is hardly ideal, it is better for you than the other possible outcomes, assuming that your opponent is playing rationally.

In the implementation of the minimax application outlined later in this chapter, the values used as ratings are integers that must fall between the limits defined by the following constants:

```
public static final int WINNING_POSITION = 1000;
public static final int LOSING_POSITION = -1000;
```

At the end of a game, the rating of a position can be determined by checking to see who has won. The rating of any position for which the outcome is not yet determined must be an integer somewhere between these extremes.

Limiting the depth of the recursive search

If you could search an entire game tree from the beginning of a game through to every possible conclusion, you could implement the minimax algorithm using pretty much the same structure as in the earlier Nim example. All you would need are two mutually recursive methods, one that finds the best move and one that evaluates positions. For games that involve a significant level of complexity, it is impossible to search the entire game tree in a reasonable amount of time. A practical implementation of the minimax algorithm must therefore include a provision for cutting off the search at a certain point.

The usual strategy for limiting the search is to set some maximum value for the depth of the recursion. You could, for example, allow the recursion to continue until each player has made five moves, for a total of ten ply. If the game ends before that limit is reached, you can evaluate the final position by checking to see who won the game and then returning **WINNING_POSITION** or **LOSING_POSITION**, as appropriate.

But what happens if you hit the recursion limit before the outcome of the game is decided? At that point, you need to evaluate the position in some other way that does not involve making additional recursive calls. Given that this kind of analysis depends only on the state of the game as it stands, it is usually called *static analysis.* In chess-playing programs, for example, static analysis usually performs some simple calculation based on the values of the pieces each side has on the board. If the player to move is ahead in that calculation, the position has a positive rating; if not, the rating is negative.

Although any simple calculation is sure to overlook some important factor, it is important to remember that static analysis applies only after the recursion limit has been reached. If, for example, there is some line of play that will force a win in the game in the next few moves, the quality of the static analysis is irrelevant, because the recursive evaluation will find that winning line of play before getting to the static-analysis phase.

The easiest way to add a depth limit to the minimax implementation is to have each of the recursive methods take a parameter named **depth** that records how many levels have already been analyzed and add one to that value before trying to rate the next position. If that parameter exceeds a defined constant **MAX_DEPTH**, any further evaluations must be performed using static analysis.

Implementing the minimax algorithm

The minimax algorithm can be implemented using the mutually recursive methods **findBestMove** and **evaluatePosition**, which appear in Figure 10-6. The **findBestMove** method tries every possible move and calls **evaluatePosition** on the resulting positions, looking for the position with the lowest rating when evaluated from the opponent's perspective. The **evaluatePosition** method uses **findBestMove** to determine the best move, stopping the mutual recursion only at the end of the game or when the search has reached the maximum allowable depth.

FIGURE 10-6 Generalized implementation of the minimax algorithm

```
/**
 * Finds and returns the best move for the current player.  The depth
 * parameter is used to limit the number of moves in the search.
 */

   public Move findBestMove(int depth) {
      ArrayList<Move> moveList = generateLegalMoves();
      Move bestMove = null;
      int minRating = WINNING_POSITION + 1;
      for (Move move : moveList) {
         makeMove(move);
         int moveRating = evaluatePosition(depth + 1);
         if (moveRating < minRating) {
            bestMove = move;
            minRating = moveRating;
         }
         retractMove(move);
      }
      if (bestMove != null) bestMove.setRating(-minRating);
      return bestMove;
   }

/**
 * Evaluates a position by returning the rating of the best move.
 */

   public int evaluatePosition(int depth) {
      if (gameIsOver() || depth >= MAX_DEPTH) {
         return evaluateStaticPosition();
      }
      return findBestMove(depth).getRating();
   }
```

The code in Figure 10-6 depends on an extension to the **Move** class that supports associating a rating with each move. This extension is common to all two-player games, independent of their specific characteristics. It therefore makes sense to define an abstract **Move** class that specific implementations can extend to include the additional information required for that game. The code for the abstract **Move** class appears in Figure 10-7.

FIGURE 10-7 The abstract Move class

```
/*
 * File: Move.java
 * ------------------
 * This class represents the superclass for all moves in two-player games.
 */

package edu.stanford.cs.javacs2.ch10;

/**
 * This class represents the common superclass for moves in a two-player
 * game.  At this level, the class exports getters and setters for the
 * rating of the move.  Clients should extend this class to include
 * whatever fields are necessary to define a move in a particular game.
 */

public abstract class Move {

/**
 * Gets the rating for this move, as previously set by setRating.
 *
 * @return The rating for this move
 */

   public int getRating() {
      return rating;
   }

/**
 * Sets the rating for this move.
 *
 * @param rating The rating for this move
 */

   public void setRating(int rating) {
      this.rating = rating;
   }

/* Private instance variables */

   private int rating;

}
```

The implementation of **findBestMove** and **evaluatePosition** in Figure 10-6 also depends on several additional methods, each of which is coded independently for a particular game:

- The **generateLegalMoves** method returns an **ArrayList<Move>** containing a list of the legal moves available in the current state.

- The methods **makeMove** and **retractMove** have the effect of making and taking back a particular move. These methods call **switchPlayer** internally to record the fact that the player changes after each move.

- The **evaluateStaticPosition** method evaluates a particular state in the game without making any further recursive calls.

Summary

In this chapter, you have learned to solve problems that require making a sequence of choices as you search for a goal, as illustrated by finding a path through a maze or a winning strategy in a two-player game. The basic strategy is to write programs that can backtrack to previous decision points if the choices lead to dead ends. By exploiting the power of recursion, however, you can avoid coding the details of the backtracking process and develop general solution strategies that apply to a wide variety of problem domains.

Important points in this chapter include:

- You can solve most problems that require backtracking by adopting the following recursive approach:

    > *If you are already at a solution, report success.*
    > **for** (*every possible choice in the current position*) {
    >   *Make that choice and take one step along the path.*
    >   *Use recursion to solve the problem from the new position.*
    >   *If the recursive call succeeds, report the success to the next higher level.*
    >   *If not, back out of the current choice to restore the previous state.*
    > }
    > *Report failure.*

- The complete history of recursive calls in a backtracking problem is usually too complex to understand in detail. For problems that involve any significant amount of backtracking, it is essential to accept the recursive leap of faith.

- You can often find a winning strategy for two-player games by adopting a recursive-backtracking approach. Because the goal in such games involves minimizing the winning chances for your opponent, the conventional strategic approach is called the *minimax algorithm*.

▉▉ Review questions

1. What is the principal characteristic of a backtracking algorithm?

2. Using your own words, state the right-hand rule for escaping from a maze. In what cases can the right-hand rule fail?

3. What is the insight that makes it possible to solve a maze by recursive backtracking?

4. What are the simple cases that apply in the recursive implementation of `solveMaze`?

5. Why is it important to mark squares as you proceed through the maze? What would happen in the `solveMaze` method if you never marked any squares?

6. What is the purpose of the `unmarkSquare` call at the end of the `for` loop in the `solveMaze` implementation? Is this statement essential to the algorithm?

7. What is the purpose of the Boolean result returned by `solveMaze`?

8. In your own words, explain how the backtracking process actually takes place in the recursive implementation of `solveMaze`.

9. In the simple Nim game, the human player plays first and begins with a pile of 13 coins. Is this a good or a bad position? Why?

10. Write a simple Java expression based on the value of `nCoins` that has the value `true` if the position is good for the current player and `false` otherwise.

11. What is the minimax algorithm? What does its name signify?

12. Why is it useful to develop an abstract implementation of the minimax algorithm that does not depend on the details of a particular game?

13. What is the role of the `depth` argument in the methods `findBestMove` and `evaluatePosition`?

14. Explain the role of the `evaluateStaticPosition` method in the minimax implementation.

15. Suppose that you are in a position in which the analysis for the next two moves shows the following outcomes, rated from your perspective:

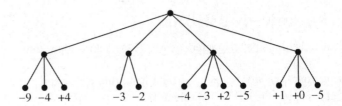

If you adopt the minimax strategy, what is the best move to make in this position? What is the rating of that move from your perspective?

Exercises

1. Change the definition of the **SolveMaze** program so that it implements the right-hand rule instead of the recursive strategy. Your implementation will no longer be recursive and may fail to terminate in some cases, but it will give you practice working with the **Maze** class.

2. In many mazes, there are multiple paths. For example, Figure 10-8 shows three solutions for the same maze. None of these solutions, however, is optimal. The shortest path through the maze has a path length of 11:

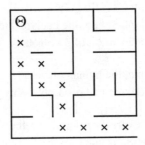

Write a method

```
int shortestPathLength(Maze maze, Point start)
```

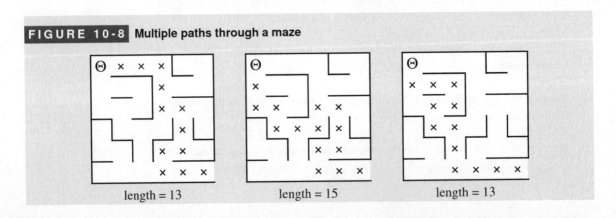

FIGURE 10-8 Multiple paths through a maze

length = 13   length = 15   length = 13

that returns the length of the shortest path in the maze from the specified position to any exit. If there is no solution, `shortestPathLength` should return −1.

3. As implemented in Figure 10-3, the `solveMaze` method unmarks each square as it discovers that there are no solutions from that point. Although this design strategy has the advantage that the final configuration of the maze shows the solution path as a series of marked squares, the decision to unmark squares as you backtrack has a cost in terms of the overall efficiency of the algorithm. If you've marked a square and then backtracked through it, you've already explored the possibilities leading from that square. If you come back to it by some other path, you might as well rely on your earlier analysis instead of exploring the same options again.

    To give yourself a sense of how much these unmarking operations cost in terms of efficiency, extend the `solveMaze` program so that it records the number of recursive calls as it proceeds. Use this program to calculate how many recursive calls are required to solve the following maze if the call to `unmarkSquare` remains part of the program:

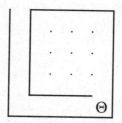

    Run your program again, this time without the call to `unmarkSquare`. What happens to the number of recursive calls?

4. As the result of the preceding exercise makes clear, the idea of keeping track of the path through a maze by using the `markSquare` facility in the `Maze` class has a substantial cost. A more practical approach is to change the definition of the recursive method so that it keeps track of the current path as it goes. Following the logic of `solveMaze`, write a method

```
ArrayList<Point> findSolutionPath(Maze maze,
                                  Point start)
```

    that returns an `ArrayList` of the points in some solution path or the value `null` if the maze is unsolvable.

5.   Most drawing programs for personal computers make it possible to fill an enclosed region on the screen with a solid color. Typically, you invoke this operation by selecting a "paint bucket" tool and then clicking the mouse, with the cursor somewhere in your drawing. When you do, the paint spreads to every part of the picture it can reach without going through a line.

For example, suppose you have drawn the following picture of a house:

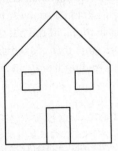

If you select the paint bucket and click inside the door, the drawing program fills the area bounded by the doorframe as shown at the left side of the following diagram. If you instead click somewhere on the front wall of the house, the program fills the entire wall space except for the windows and doors, as shown on the right:

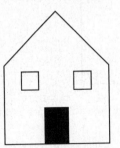   

In order to understand how this process works, it is important to understand that the screen of the computer is broken down into an array of tiny dots called *pixels.* On a monochrome display, pixels can be either white or black. The paint-fill operation consists of painting in black the starting pixel (i.e., the pixel you click while using the paint-bucket tool) along with any pixels connected to that starting point by an unbroken chain of white pixels. Thus, the patterns of pixels on the screen representing the preceding two diagrams would look like this:

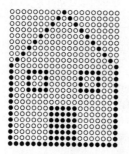
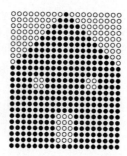

It is easy to represent a pixel grid using a two-dimensional array of Boolean values. White pixels in the grid have the value **false**, and black pixels have the value **true**. Given this representation, write a method

```
void fillRegion(boolean[][] pixels, int row, int col)
```

that simulates the operation of the paint-bucket tool by painting in black all white pixels reachable from the specified row and column without crossing an existing black pixel.

6. The most powerful piece in the game of chess is the queen, which can move any number of squares in any direction, horizontally, vertically, or diagonally. For example, the queen shown in this chessboard can move to any of the marked squares:

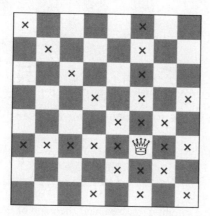

Even though the queen can cover a large number of squares, it is possible to place eight queens on an 8×8 chessboard so that none of them attacks any of the others, as shown in the following diagram:

Write a program that solves the more general problem of whether it is possible to place N queens on an $N \times N$ chessboard so that none of them can move to a square occupied by any of the others in a single turn. Your program should either display a solution if it finds one or report that no solutions exist.

7. In chess, a knight moves in an L-shaped pattern: two squares in one direction horizontally or vertically, and then one square at right angles to that motion. For example, the white knight in the following diagram can move to any of the eight squares marked with an **×**:

The mobility of a knight decreases near the edge of the board, as illustrated by the black knight in the corner, which can reach only the two squares marked with an **O**.

It turns out that a knight can visit all 64 squares on a chessboard without ever moving to the same square twice. A path for the knight that moves through all the squares without repeating a square is called a **knight's tour.**

One such tour is shown in the following diagram, in which the numbers in the squares indicate the order in which they were visited:

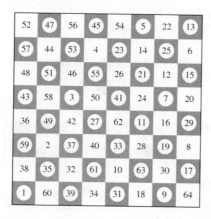

Write a program that uses backtracking recursion to find a knight's tour.

8. In the 1960s, a puzzle called *Instant Insanity* was popular for some years before it faded from view. The puzzle consisted of four cubes whose faces were each painted with one of the colors red, blue, green, and white, represented in the rest of this problem by their initial letter. The goal of the puzzle was to arrange the cubes into a line so that if you looked at the line from any of its edges, you would see no duplicated colors.

    Cubes are hard to draw in two dimensions, but the following diagram shows what the cubes would look like if you unfolded them and placed them flat on the page:

Write a program that uses backtracking to solve the Instant Insanity puzzle.

9. In theory, the recursive backtracking strategy described in this chapter should be sufficient to solve puzzles that involve performing a sequence of moves until the puzzle reaches some goal state. In practice, however, many of those

puzzles are too complex to solve in a reasonable amount of time. One puzzle that is just at the limit of what recursive backtracking can accomplish without some additional cleverness is the *peg solitaire* puzzle, which dates from the 17th century. Peg solitaire is usually played on a board that looks like this:

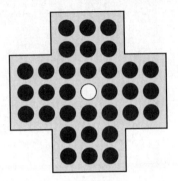

The black dots in the diagram are pegs, which fill the board except for the center hole. On a turn, you are allowed to jump over and remove a peg, as illustrated in the following diagram, in which the colored peg jumps into the vacant center hole and the peg in the middle is removed:

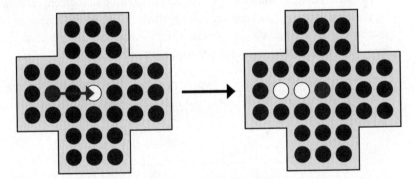

The object of the game is to perform a series of jumps that leaves only one peg in the center hole. Write a program to solve this puzzle.

10. The game of dominos is played with rectangular pieces composed of two connected squares, each of which is marked with a certain number of dots. For example, each of the following four rectangles represents a domino:

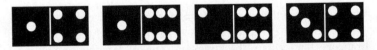

Dominos can be connected end-to-end to form chains, subject to the condition that two dominos can be linked together only if the numbers match where the dominos touch. For example, you can form a chain consisting of these four dominos by connecting them in the following order:

In the traditional game, dominos can be rotated by 180° so that their numbers are reversed. In this chain, for example, the 1–6 and 3–4 dominos have been "turned around" so that they fit into the chain.

Suppose that you have access to a **Domino** class (as described in exercise 1 from Chapter 7) that exports the methods **getLeftDots** and **getRightDots**. Given this class, write a recursive method

```
boolean formsDominoChain(ArrayList<Domino> dominos)
```

that returns **true** if it is possible to build a chain consisting of every domino in the list.

11. Suppose that you have been assigned the job of buying the plumbing pipes for a construction project. Your supervisor gives you a list of the varying lengths of pipe needed, but the distributor sells stock pipe only in one fixed size. Even though the stock pipes are all one size, you can cut each stock pipe to get any smaller size you need. Your job is to figure out the minimum number of stock pipes required to satisfy the list of requests, thereby saving money and minimizing waste.

Write a recursive method

```
int cutStock(int[] requests, int stockLength)
```

that takes two arguments—an array of the lengths needed and the length of stock pipe that the distributor sells—and returns the minimum number of stock pipes required to service all requests in the array. For example, if the array contains [4, 3, 4, 1, 7, 8] and the stock pipe length is 10, you can purchase three stock pipes and divide them as follows:

> Pipe 1: 4, 4, 1
> Pipe 2: 3, 7
> Pipe 3: 8

Doing so leaves you with two small remnants left over. There are other possible arrangements that use three stock pipes, but the task cannot be done with fewer.

12. Most operating systems and many applications that allow users to work with files support **wildcard patterns,** in which special characters are used to create filename patterns that can match many different files. The most common special characters used in wildcard matching are `?`, which matches any single character, and `*`, which matches any sequence of characters. Other characters in a filename pattern must match the corresponding character in a filename. For example, the pattern `*.*` matches any filename that contains a period, such as `EnglishWords.dat` or `HelloWorld.java`, but does not match filenames that do not contain a period. Similarly, the pattern `test.?` matches any filename that consists of the name `test`, a period, and a single character; thus, `test.?` matches `test.c` but not `test.java`. These patterns can be combined in any way you like. For example, the pattern `??*` matches any filename containing at least two characters.

Write a method

```
boolean wildcardMatch(String name, String pattern)
```

that takes two strings, representing a filename and a wildcard pattern, and returns **true** if that filename matches the pattern. Thus,

`wildcardMatch("US.txt", "*.*")`	*returns* **true**
`wildcardMatch("test", "*.*")`	*returns* **false**
`wildcardMatch("test.c", "test.?")`	*returns* **true**
`wildcardMatch("test.java", "test.?")`	*returns* **false**
`wildcardMatch("x", "??*")`	*returns* **false**
`wildcardMatch("yy", "??*")`	*returns* **true**
`wildcardMatch("zzz", "??*")`	*returns* **true**

13. Rewrite the simple Nim game so that it uses the generalized minimax algorithm presented in Figure 10-6. Your program should not change the code for **findBestMove** or **evaluatePosition**. Your job is to come up with an appropriate definition of the **Move** type and the various game-specific methods so that the program still plays a perfect game of Nim.

14. Modify the code for the simple Nim game you wrote for exercise 13 so that it plays a different variant of Nim. In this version, the pile begins with 17 coins. On each turn, players alternate taking one, two, three, or four coins from the pile. In the simple Nim game, the coins the players took away were simply ignored; in this game, the coins go into a pile for each player. The player whose pile contains an even number of coins after the last coin is taken wins the game.

15. In the most common variant of Nim, the coins are not combined into a single pile but are instead arranged in three rows like this:

A move in this game consists of taking any number of coins, subject to the condition that all the coins must come from the same row. The player who takes the last coin loses.

Write a program that uses the minimax algorithm to play a perfect game of three-pile Nim. The starting configuration shown here is a typical one, but your program should be general enough so that you can easily change either the number of rows or the number of coins in each row.

16. The game of *tic-tac-toe* (or ***naughts and crosses***) is played by two players who take turns placing **X**s and **O**s in a 3×3 grid that looks like this:

The object of the game is to line up three of your own symbols in a row, horizontally, vertically, or diagonally. In the following game, for example, **X** has won the game by completing three in a row across the top:

If the board fills up without either player completing a row, the game is a draw, which is called a ***cat's game*** in tic-tac-toe.

Write a program that uses the minimax algorithm to play a perfect game of tic-tac-toe. Figure 10-9 shows a sample run against an especially inept player.

FIGURE 10-9 Sample run of the tic-tac-toe game

```
⬤⬤⬤                        TicTacToe
Welcome to TicTacToe, the game of three in a row.
I'll be X, and you'll be O.
The squares are numbered like this:

 1 | 2 | 3
---+---+---
 4 | 5 | 6
---+---+---
 7 | 8 | 9

I'll move to 1.
The game now looks like this:

 X |   |
---+---+---
   |   |
---+---+---
   |   |

Your move.
What square? 5
The game now looks like this:

 X |   |
---+---+---
   | O |
---+---+---
   |   |

I'll move to 2.
The game now looks like this:

 X | X |
---+---+---
   | O |
---+---+---
   |   |

Your move.
What square? 7
The game now looks like this:

 X | X |
---+---+---
   | O |
---+---+---
 O |   |

I'll move to 3.
The final position looks like this:

 X | X | X
---+---+---
   | O |
---+---+---
 O |   |

I win.
```

17. Just so we have a name for the concept, let's say that an English word is *reducible* if it is possible to cross out each of its letters, one at a time, and always have an English word all the way down to a single letter. For example, the word *cats* is reducible because you can cross out first the *s*, then the *c*, and then the *t*, leaving the words *cat*, *at*, and *a*, in order. The longest reducible word in the `EnglishWords.txt` file is *complecting* (the process of joining by weaving or binding together), which survives the following chain of deletions:

> *complecting*
> *completing*
> *competing*
> *compting*
> *comping*
> *coping*
> *oping*
> *ping*
> *pig*
> *pi*
> *i*

Write a function `isReducible` that takes a word and determines whether the word is reducible.

18. The game of Boggle is played with a 4×4 array of cubes, each of which shows a letter on its face. The goal is to form as many words of four or more letters as possible, moving only between letter cubes that are adjacent—horizontally, vertically, or diagonally—without ever using any cube more than once. Figure 10-10 shows a possible Boggle layout along with all the English words

FIGURE 10-10   Sample configuration in the Boggle® game and the words it contains

ager	agog	agon	agonic	algor
ammino	ammo	ammonic	among	argon
cion	egal	emic	ergo	gammer
gamming	gammon	gamp	gear	gemma
glamor	glare	gnome	gnomic	going
gomeral	gong	gorp	gram	gramme
gramp	lager	lamming	lamp	large
largo	mage	malgre	mare	marge
meal	mice	minor	mome	momi
nice	nicer	noma	nome	norm
normal	ogam	ogre	omega	omer
plage	prog	program	programming	prom
prong	rage	ramming	ramp	real
realm	ream	regal	regma	remix
roger	romp	zoic		

that you can find in that layout. As an example, you can form the word *programming* using the following sequence of cubes:

Write a method

```
ArrayList<String> findBoggleWords(char[][] board,
                                  Lexicon english)
```

that returns a list of all the legal words on the board that appear in the **english** lexicon.

Chapter 11
Algorithmic Analysis

Without analysis, no synthesis.

— Friedrich Engels, *Herr Eugen Dühring's Revolution in Science*, 1878

In Chapter 2, you were introduced to two different recursive implementations of the function `fib(n)`, which computes the nth Fibonacci number. The first, which is based directly on the mathematical definition

$$\text{fib(n)} = \begin{cases} n & \text{if } n \text{ is } 0 \text{ or } 1 \\ \text{fib(n - 1) + fib(n - 2)} & \text{otherwise} \end{cases}$$

turns out to be wildly inefficient. The second implementation, which uses the notion of additive sequences to produce a version of `fib(n)` that is comparable in efficiency to traditional iterative approaches, demonstrates that recursion itself is not the cause of the problem. Even so, examples like the first version of the Fibonacci function have such high execution costs that recursion sometimes gets a bad name as a result.

As you will see in this chapter, the ability to think recursively about a problem often leads to new strategies that are considerably *more* efficient than anything that would come out of an iterative design process. The enormous power of divide-and-conquer algorithms has a profound impact on many problems that arise in practice. By using recursive algorithms of this form, it is possible to achieve dramatic increases in efficiency that can cut the solution times, not by factors of two or three, but by factors of a thousand or more.

Before looking at these algorithms, however, it is important to ask a few questions. What does the term *efficiency* mean in an algorithmic context? How would you go about measuring that efficiency? These questions form the foundation for the subfield of computer science known as ***analysis of algorithms.*** Although a detailed understanding of algorithmic analysis requires a reasonable facility with mathematics and a lot of careful thought, you can get a sense of how it works by investigating the performance of a few simple algorithms.

11.1 The sorting problem

The best way to appreciate the importance of algorithmic analysis is to consider a problem domain in which different algorithms vary widely in their performance. Of these, one of the most interesting problems is that of **sorting,** which consists of rearranging the elements in an array so that they appear in some defined order. For example, suppose you have stored the following integers in the variable **array**, which is an integer array:

array

56	25	37	58	95	19	73	30
0	1	2	3	4	5	6	7

Your mission is to write a method **sort(array)** that rearranges the elements into ascending order, like this:

19	25	30	37	56	58	73	95
0	1	2	3	4	5	6	7

The selection sort algorithm

There are many algorithms you could choose to sort an array of integers into ascending order. One of the simplest is called *selection sort,* which is implemented in Figure 11-1. Given an array of size *N*, the selection sort algorithm goes through each element position and finds the value that should occupy that position in the sorted array. When it finds the appropriate element, the algorithm exchanges that

FIGURE 11-1 **Implementation of the selection sort algorithm**

```
/**
 * Sorts an array of integers into ascending order.
 */

   public void sort(int[] array) {
      for (int lh = 0; lh < array.length - 1; lh++) {
         int rh = findSmallest(array, lh);
         swapArrayElements(array, lh, rh);
      }
   }

/**
 * Returns the index of the smallest element in the array between the
 * specified start position and the end of the array.
 */

   private int findSmallest(int[] array, int start) {
      int rh = start;
      for (int i = start + 1; i < array.length; i++) {
         if (array[i] < array[rh]) {
            rh = i;
         }
      }
      return rh;
   }

/**
 * Exchanges the array elements at index positions p1 and p2.
 */

   private void swapArrayElements(int[] array, int p1, int p2) {
      int tmp = array[p1];
      array[p1] = array[p2];
      array[p2] = tmp;
   }
```

element with the value that previously occupied the desired position to ensure that no elements are lost. Thus, on the first cycle, the algorithm finds the smallest element and swaps it with the first element, which appears at index position 0 in Java. On the second cycle, it finds the smallest remaining element and swaps it with the second element. Thereafter, the algorithm continues this strategy until all positions in the array are correctly ordered.

For example, if the initial contents of the array are

56	25	37	58	95	19	73	30
0	1	2	3	4	5	6	7

the first cycle through the outer **for** loop identifies the 19 in index position 5 as the smallest value in the entire array and then swaps it with the 56 in index position 0 to leave the following configuration:

19	25	37	58	95	56	73	30
0	1	2	3	4	5	6	7

On the second cycle, the algorithm finds the smallest element between positions 1 and 7, which turns out to be the 25 in position 1. The program goes ahead and performs the exchange operation, leaving the array unchanged from that in the preceding diagram. On each subsequent cycle, the algorithm performs a swap operation to move the next smallest value into its appropriate final position. When the **for** loop is complete, the entire array is sorted.

Empirical measurement of performance

How efficient is the selection sort algorithm as a strategy for sorting? To answer questions of this kind, it helps to collect empirical data about how long it takes the computer to complete a task for problems of varying size. When I ran the selection sort algorithm on my MacBook Pro laptop, for example, I observed the following running times, where N represents the number of elements in the array:

N	Running time
10	0.00000018 sec
100	0.0000132 sec
1000	0.00126 sec
10,000	0.1258 sec
100,000	12.522 sec
1,000,000	1251.9 sec

For an array of 10 integers, the selection sort algorithm completes its work in a fraction of a microsecond. Even for 10,000 integers, this implementation of **sort** takes less than a second, which certainly seems fast enough in terms of our human sense of time. As the array sizes get larger, however, the performance of selection sort begins to go downhill. For an array of 100,000 integers, the algorithm requires more than 12 seconds. If you're sitting in front of your computer waiting for it to reply, that seems a long time. But that number pales into insignificance when you compare it to the time required to sort 1,000,000 integers, which takes more than 20 minutes.

The performance of selection sort rapidly gets worse as the array size increases. As you can see from the timing data, every time you multiply the number of values by 10, the time required to sort the array goes up a hundredfold. Sorting a list of ten million numbers would therefore take somewhere around 2000 minutes, which is approximately 33 hours. If your business required sorting arrays on this scale, you would have no choice but to find a more efficient approach.

Analyzing the performance of selection sort

What makes selection sort perform so badly as the number of values to be sorted becomes large? To answer this question, it helps to think about what the algorithm has to do on each cycle of the outer loop. To correctly determine the first value in the array, the selection sort algorithm must consider all N elements as it searches for the smallest value. Thus, the time required on the first cycle of the loop is presumably proportional to N. For each of the other elements in the array, the algorithm performs the same basic steps but looks at a smaller number of elements each time. It looks at $N-1$ elements on the second cycle, $N-2$ on the third, and so on, so the total running time is roughly proportional to

$$N + N-1 + N-2 + \ldots + 3 + 2 + 1$$

Because it is difficult to work with an expression in this expanded form, it is useful to simplify it by applying a bit of mathematics. As you may have learned in an algebra course, the sum of the first N integers is given by the formula

$$\frac{N \times (N+1)}{2}$$

or, after evaluating the multiplication sign in the numerator,

$$\frac{N^2 + N}{2}$$

You will learn how to prove that this formula is correct in the section on "Mathematical induction" later in this chapter. For the moment, all you need to know is that the sum of the first N integers can be expressed in this more compact form.

If you write out the values of the function

$$\frac{N^2 + N}{2}$$

for various values of N, you get a table that looks like this:

N	$\dfrac{N^2 + N}{2}$
10	55
100	5050
1000	500,500
10,000	50,005,000
100,000	5,000,050,000
1,000,000	500,000,500,000

Because the running time of the selection sort algorithm is presumably related to the amount of work the algorithm needs to do, the values in this table should be roughly proportional to the observed execution time of the algorithm, which turns out to be true. If you look at the measured timing data for selection sort in Figure 11-2, for example, you discover that the algorithm requires 12.522 seconds to sort 100,000 numbers. In that time, the selection sort algorithm has to perform 50,005,000 operations in its innermost loop. Assuming that there is indeed a proportionality relationship between these two values, dividing the time by the number of operations gives the following estimate of the proportionality constant:

$$\frac{12.522 \text{ seconds}}{5,000,050,000} \approx 2.5 \times 10^{-9} \text{ seconds}$$

If you apply this same proportionality constant to the other entries in the table, you discover that the formula

$$2.5 \times 10^{-9} \text{ seconds} \times \frac{N^2 + N}{2}$$

offers a reasonable approximation of the running time, at least for large values of N. The observed times and the estimates calculated using this formula appear in Figure 11-2, along with the relative error between the two.

▮ 11.2 Computational complexity

The problem with carrying out a detailed analysis like the one shown in Figure 11-2 is that you end up with too much information. Although it is occasionally useful to have a formula for predicting exactly how long a program will take, you can usually get away with more qualitative measures. The reason that selection sort is impractical for large values of N has little to do with the precise timing characteristics of a particular implementation running on the laptop I happen to have

FIGURE 11-2 Observed and estimated times for selection sort

N	Observed time	Estimated time	Error
10	0.00000018 sec	0.00000014 sec	24%
100	0.0000132 sec	0.0000126 sec	4%
1000	0.00126 sec	0.00125 sec	< 1%
10,000	0.1258 sec	0.125 sec	< 1%
100,000	12.522 sec	12.5 sec	< 1%
1,000,000	1251.9 sec	1250.0 sec	< 1%

at the moment. The problem is simpler and more fundamental. At its essence, the problem with selection sort is that doubling the size of the input array increases the running time of the selection sort algorithm by a factor of four, which means that the running time grows more quickly than the number of elements in the array.

The most valuable qualitative insights you can obtain about algorithmic efficiency are usually those that help you understand how the performance of an algorithm responds to changes in problem size. Problem size is usually easy to quantify. For algorithms that operate on numbers, it generally makes sense to let the numbers themselves represent the problem size. For most algorithms that operate on arrays, you can use the number of elements. When evaluating algorithmic efficiency, computer scientists traditionally use the letter N to indicate the size of the problem, no matter how it is calculated. The relationship between N and the performance of an algorithm as N becomes large is called the *computational complexity* of that algorithm. In general, the most important measure of performance is execution time, although it is also possible to apply complexity analysis to other concerns, such as the amount of memory space required. Unless otherwise stated, all assessments of complexity used in this text refer to execution time.

Big-O notation

Computer scientists use a special shorthand called *big-O notation* to denote the computational complexity of algorithms. Big-O notation was introduced by the German mathematician Paul Bachmann in 1892—long before the development of computers. The notation itself is very simple and consists of the letter O, followed by a formula enclosed in parentheses. When it is used to specify computational complexity, the formula is usually a simple function involving the problem size N. For example, in this chapter you will soon encounter the big-O expression

$$O(N^2)$$

which reads aloud as "big-oh of N squared."

Big-O notation is used to specify qualitative approximations and is therefore ideal for expressing the computational complexity of an algorithm. Coming as it does from mathematics, big-O notation has a precise definition, which appears later in this chapter in the section entitled "A formal definition of big-O." At this point, however, it is far more important for you—no matter whether you think of yourself as a programmer or a computer scientist—to understand what big-O means from a more intuitive point of view.

Standard simplifications of big-O

When you use big-O notation to estimate the computational complexity of an algorithm, the goal is to provide a *qualitative* insight as to how changes in N affect the algorithmic performance as N becomes large. Because big-O notation is not intended to be a quantitative measure, it is not only appropriate but desirable to reduce the formula inside the parentheses so that it captures the qualitative behavior of the algorithm in the simplest possible form. The most common simplifications that you can make when using big-O notation to express computational complexity are as follows:

1. *Eliminate any term whose contribution to the total ceases to be significant as N becomes large.* When a formula involves several terms added together, one of the terms often grows much faster than the others and ends up dominating the entire expression as N becomes large. For large values of N, this term alone will control the running time of the algorithm, and you can ignore the other terms in the formula entirely.

2. *Eliminate any constant factors.* When you calculate computational complexity, your main concern is how running time changes as a function of the problem size N. Constant factors have no effect on the overall pattern. If you bought a machine that was twice as fast as your old one, any algorithm that you executed on your machine would run twice as fast as before for every value of N. The growth pattern, however, would remain exactly the same. Thus, you can ignore constant factors when you use big-O notation.

The computational complexity of selection sort

You can apply the simplification rules from the preceding section to derive a big-O expression for the computational complexity of selection sort. From the analysis in the section "Analyzing the performance of selection sort" earlier in the chapter, you know that the running time of the selection sort algorithm for an array of N elements is proportional to

$$\frac{N^2 + N}{2}$$

Although it would be mathematically correct to use this formula directly in the big-O expression

$$O\left(\frac{N^2 + N}{2}\right)$$

you would never do so in practice because the formula inside the parentheses is not expressed in the simplest form.

The first step toward simplifying this relationship is to recognize that the formula is actually the sum of two terms, as follows:

$$\frac{N^2}{2} + \frac{N}{2}$$

You then need to consider the contribution of each of these terms to the total formula as N increases in size, which is illustrated by the following table:

N	$\dfrac{N^2}{2}$	$\dfrac{N}{2}$	$\dfrac{N^2 + N}{2}$
10	50	5	55
100	5000	50	5050
1000	500,000	500	500,500
10,000	50,000,000	5000	50,005,000
100,000	5,000,000,000	50,000	5,000,050,000

As N increases, the term involving N^2 quickly dominates the term involving N. As a result, the simplification rule allows you to eliminate the smaller term from the expression. Even so, you would not write that the computational complexity of selection sort is

$$O\left(\frac{N^2}{2}\right)$$

because you can eliminate the constant factor. The simplest expression you can use to indicate the complexity of selection sort is

$$O(N^2)$$

This expression captures the essence of the performance of selection sort. As the size of the problem increases, the running time tends to grow by the square of that increase. Thus, if you double the size of the array, the running time goes up by a factor of four. If you instead multiply the number of input values by 10, the running time explodes by a factor of 100.

Deducing computational complexity from code

It is often possible to determine the computational complexity of a method simply by looking at the code, as in the following method that computes the average of the elements in an array:

```
double average(double[] array) {
    int n = array.length;
    double total = 0;
    for (int i = 0; i < n; i++) {
        total += array[i];
    }
    return total / n;
}
```

When you call this method, some parts of the code are executed only once, such as the initialization of **total** to 0 and the division operation in the **return** statement. These computations take a certain amount of time, but that time is constant in the sense that it doesn't depend on the size of the array. Code whose execution time does not depend on the problem size is said to run in *constant time,* which is expressed in big-O notation as $O(1)$.

The designation $O(1)$ can seem confusing, because the expression inside the parentheses does not depend on N. In fact, this lack of any dependency on N is the whole point of the $O(1)$ notation. As you increase the size of the problem, the time required to execute code whose running time is $O(1)$ increases in exactly the same way that 1 increases; in other words, the running time does not increase at all.

There are, however, other parts of the **average** method that are executed exactly **n** times, once for each cycle of the **for** loop. These components include the expression **i++** in the **for** loop and the statement

```
total += array[i];
```

that constitutes the loop body. Although any single execution of this part of the computation takes a fixed amount of time, the fact that these statements are executed **n** times means that their total execution time is directly proportional to the array size. The computational complexity of this part of the **average** method is $O(N)$, which is commonly called *linear time.*

The total running time for **average** is therefore the sum of the times required for the constant parts and the linear parts of the algorithm. As the size of the problem increases, however, the constant term becomes less and less relevant. By exploiting the simplification rule that allows you to ignore terms that become insignificant as N gets large, you can assert that the **average** method as a whole runs in $O(N)$ time.

You could also predict this result just by looking at the loop structure of the code. For the most part, the individual expressions and statements—unless they involve method calls that must be accounted separately—run in constant time. What matters in terms of computational complexity is how often those statements are executed. For many programs, you can determine the computational complexity simply by finding the piece of the code that is executed most often and determining how many times it runs as a function of N. In the case of the **average** method, the body of the loop is executed **n** times. Because no part of the code is executed more often than this, you can predict that the computational complexity will be $O(N)$.

The selection sort method can be analyzed in a similar way. The most frequently executed part of the code is the comparison in the statement

```
if (array[i] < array[rh]) rh = i;
```

That statement is nested inside two **for** loops whose limits depend on the value of N. The inner loop runs N times as often as the outer loop, which implies that the inner loop body is executed $O(N^2)$ times. Algorithms like selection sort that exhibit $O(N^2)$ performance are said to run in *quadratic time.*

Worst-case versus average-case complexity

In some cases, the running time of an algorithm depends not only on the size of the problem but also on the specific characteristics of the data. For example, consider the method

```
int linearSearch(int key, int[] array) {
   int n = array.length;
   for (int i = 0; i < n; i++) {
      if (key == array[i]) return i;
   }
   return -1;
}
```

which returns the first index position in **array** at which the value **key** appears, or the sentinel value −1 if the value **key** does not appear anywhere in the array. Because the **for** loop in the implementation executes **n** times, you expect the performance of **linearSearch**, as its name implies, to be $O(N)$.

On the other hand, some calls to **linearSearch** can be executed very quickly. Suppose, for example, that the key element you are searching for happens to be in the first position in the array. In that case, the body of the **for** loop will run only once. If you're lucky enough to search for a value that always occurs at the beginning of the array, `linearSearch` will run in constant time.

When you analyze the computational complexity of a program, you're usually not interested in the minimum possible time. In general, computer scientists tend to be concerned about analyzing the following two types of complexity:

- *Worst-case complexity.* The most common type of complexity analysis consists of determining the performance of an algorithm in the worst possible case. Such an analysis is useful because it allows you to set an upper bound on the computational complexity. If you analyze for the worst case, you can guarantee that the performance of the algorithm will be at least as good as your analysis indicates. You might sometimes get lucky, but you can be confident that the performance will not get any worse.

- *Average-case complexity.* From a practical point of view, it is often useful to consider how well an algorithm performs if you average its behavior over all possible sets of input data. Particularly if you have no reason to assume that the specific input to your problem is in any way atypical, the average-case analysis provides the best statistical estimate of actual performance. The problem, however, is that average-case analysis is usually much more difficult to carry out and typically requires considerable mathematical sophistication.

The worst case for the `linearSearch` method occurs when the key is not in the array at all. When the key is not there, the method must complete all **n** cycles of the `for` loop, which means that its performance is $O(N)$. If the key is known to be in the array, the `for` loop will be executed about half as many times on average, which implies that average-case performance is also $O(N)$. As you will discover in the section on "The Quicksort algorithm" later in this chapter, the average-case and worst-case performances of an algorithm sometimes differ in qualitative ways, which means that in practice it is often important to take both performance characteristics into consideration.

A formal definition of big-O

Because understanding big-O notation is critical to modern computer science, it is important to offer a more formal definition to help you understand why the intuitive model of big-O works and why the suggested simplifications of big-O formulas are in fact justified. Doing so, however, inevitably requires some mathematics. If mathematics scares you, try not to worry. It is much more important for you to understand what big-O means in practice than it is to follow all the steps presented in this section.

In computer science, big-O notation is used to express the relationship between two functions, typically in an expression like this:

$$t(N) = O(f(N))$$

The formal meaning of this expression is that $f(N)$ is an approximation of $t(N)$ with the following characteristic: it must be possible to find a constant N_0 and a positive constant C so that for every value of $N \geq N_0$ the following condition holds:

$$t(N) \leq C \times f(N)$$

In other words, as long as N is sufficiently large, the function $t(N)$ is always bounded by a constant multiple of the function $f(N)$.

When it is used to express computational complexity, the function $t(N)$ represents the actual running time of the algorithm, which is usually difficult to compute. The function $f(N)$ is a much simpler formula that nonetheless provides a reasonable qualitative estimate of how the running time changes as a function of N, because the condition expressed in the mathematical definition of big-O ensures that the actual running time cannot grow faster than $f(N)$.

To see how the formal definition applies, it is useful to return to the selection sort example. Analyzing the loop structure of selection sort showed that the operations in the innermost loop were executed

$$\frac{N^2 + N}{2}$$

times and that the running time was presumably roughly proportional to this formula. When this complexity was expressed in terms of big-O notation, the constants and low-order terms were eliminated, leaving only the assertion that the execution time was $O(N^2)$, which is in fact an assertion that

$$\frac{N^2 + N}{2} = O(N^2)$$

To show that this expression is indeed true under the formal definition of big-O, all you need to do is come up with values for the constants C and N_0 such that

$$\frac{N^2 + N}{2} \leq C \times N^2$$

for all values of $N \geq N_0$. This particular example is extremely simple, since the inequality always holds if you set the constants C and N_0 both to 1. After all, as long as N is no smaller than 1, you know that $N^2 \geq N$. It must therefore be the case that

$$\frac{N^2 + N}{2} \leq \frac{N^2 + N^2}{2}$$

But the right side of this inequality is simply N^2, which means that

$$\frac{N^2 + N}{2} \leq N^2$$

for all values of $N \geq 1$, as required by the definition.

You can use a similar argument to show that any polynomial of degree k, which can be expressed in general terms as

$$a_k N^k + a_{k-1} N^{k-1} + a_{k-2} N^{k-2} + \ldots + a_2 N^2 + a_1 N + a_0$$

is $O(N^k)$. Once again, your goal is to find constants C and N_0 such that

$$a_k N^k + a_{k-1} N^{k-1} + a_{k-2} N^{k-2} + \ldots + a_2 N^2 + a_1 N + a_0 \leq C \times N^k$$

for all values of $N \geq N_0$. As in the preceding example, you can start by choosing 1 for the value of the constant N_0. For all values of $N \geq 1$, each successive power of N is at least as large as its predecessor, so

$$N^k \geq N^{k-1} \geq N^{k-2} \geq \ldots \geq N \geq 1$$

This property in turn implies that

$$a_k N^k + a_{k-1} N^{k-1} + a_{k-2} N^{k-2} + \ldots + a_1 N + a_0$$
$$\leq |a_k| N^k + |a_{k-1}| N^k + |a_{k-2}| N^k + \ldots + |a_1| N^k + |a_0| N^k$$

where the vertical bars surrounding the coefficients on the right side of the equation indicate absolute value. By factoring out N^k, you can simplify the right side of this inequality to

$$(|a_k| + |a_{k-1}| + |a_{k-2}| + \ldots + |a_1| + |a_0|) N^k$$

Thus, if you define the constant C to be

$$|a_k| + |a_{k-1}| + |a_{k-2}| + \ldots + |a_1| + |a_0|$$

you have established that

$$a_k N^k + a_{k-1} N^{k-1} + a_{k-2} N^{k-2} + \ldots + a_2 N^2 + a_1 N + a_0 \leq C \times N^k$$

This result proves that the entire polynomial is $O(N^k)$.

11.3 Recursion to the rescue

At this point, you know considerably more about complexity analysis than you did when you started the chapter. However, you are no closer to solving the practical problem of how to write a sorting algorithm that is more efficient for large arrays. The selection sort algorithm is clearly not up to the task, because the running time increases in proportion to the square of the input size. The same is true for most sorting algorithms that process the elements of an array in a linear order. To develop a better sorting algorithm, you need to adopt a qualitatively different approach.

The power of divide-and-conquer strategies

Oddly enough, the key to finding a better sorting strategy lies in recognizing that the quadratic behavior of algorithms like selection sort has a hidden virtue. The basic characteristic of quadratic complexity is that, as the size of a problem doubles, the running time increases by a factor of four. The reverse, however, is also true. If you divide the size of a quadratic problem by two, you decrease the running time by that same factor of four. This fact suggests that dividing an array in half and then applying a recursive divide-and-conquer approach might reduce the required sorting time.

To make this idea more concrete, suppose you have a large array that you need to sort. What happens if you divide the array into two halves and then use the selection sort algorithm to sort each of those pieces? Because selection sort is quadratic, each of the smaller arrays requires one quarter of the original time. You need to sort both halves, of course, but the total time required to sort the two smaller arrays is still only half the time that would have been required to sort the original array. If it turns out that sorting two halves of an array simplifies the problem of sorting the complete array, you will be able to reduce the total time substantially. More importantly, once you discover how to improve performance at one level, you can use the same algorithm recursively to sort each half.

To determine whether a divide-and-conquer strategy is applicable to the sorting problem, you need to answer the question of whether dividing an array into two smaller arrays and then sorting each one helps to solve the general problem. As a way to gain some insight into this question, suppose that you start with an array containing the following eight elements:

`array`

56	25	37	58	95	19	73	30
0	1	2	3	4	5	6	7

If you divide the array of eight elements into two arrays of length four and then sort each of those smaller arrays—keep in mind that the recursive leap of faith means you can assume that the recursive calls work correctly—you get the following situation in which each of the smaller arrays is sorted:

a1

25	37	56	58
0	1	2	3

a2

19	30	73	95
0	1	2	3

How useful is this decomposition? Remember that your goal is to take the values out of these smaller arrays and put them back into the original array in the correct order. How does having these smaller sorted arrays help you accomplish that goal?

Merging two arrays

As it happens, reconstructing the complete array from the smaller sorted arrays is a much simpler problem than sorting itself. The required technique, called **merging,** depends on the fact that the first element in the complete ordering must be either the first element in **a1** or the first element in **a2**, whichever is smaller. In this example, the first element you want in the new array is the 19 in **a2**. If you add that element to an empty array **array** and, in effect, cross it out of **a2**, you get the following configuration:

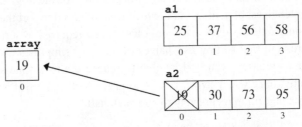

Once again, the next element can only be the first unused element in one of the two smaller arrays. This time, you compare the 25 from **a1** against the 30 in **a2** and choose the former:

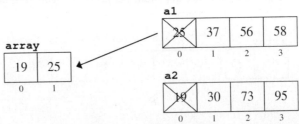

You can easily continue this process of choosing the smaller value from **a1** or **a2** until you have reconstructed the entire array.

The merge sort algorithm

The merge operation, combined with recursive decomposition, gives rise to a sorting algorithm called **_merge sort,_** which turns out to be much more efficient than selection sort. The basic outline of the merge sort algorithm looks like this:

1. Check to see if the array is empty or has only one element. If so, it must already be sorted. This condition defines the simple case for the recursion.
2. Divide the array into two smaller arrays, each of which is half the size.
3. Sort each of the smaller arrays recursively.
4. Merge the two sorted arrays back into the original one.

The code for the merge sort algorithm, shown in Figure 11-3, divides neatly into two methods: **sort** and **merge**. The code for **sort** follows directly from the outline of the algorithm. After checking for the special case, the algorithm divides the original array into two smaller ones, **a1** and **a2**, sorts these arrays recursively, and then calls **merge** to reassemble the complete solution.

Most of the work is done by the **merge** method, which takes the destination array along with the smaller arrays **a1** and **a2**. The heart of the **merge** method is the following loop:

```
for (int i = 0; i < array.length; i++) {
    if (p2 == n2 || (p1 < n1 && a1[p1] < a2[p2])) {
        array[i] = a1[p1++];
    } else {
        array[i] = a2[p2++];
    }
}
```

The indices **p1** and **p2** mark the progress through each of the subsidiary arrays. On each cycle of the loop, the method selects the smaller element from **a1** or **a2** (after first checking whether any elements are left) and adds that value to the next free slot in **array**.

The computational complexity of merge sort

You now have an implementation of the **sort** method based on the strategy of divide-and-conquer. How efficient is it? You can measure its efficiency by sorting arrays of numbers and timing the result, but it is helpful to start by thinking about the algorithm in terms of its computational complexity.

FIGURE 11-3 Implementation of the merge sort algorithm

```
/**
 * Sorts an array of integers into ascending order.
 */

   public void sort(int[] array) {
      if (array.length > 1) {
         int half = array.length / 2;
         int[] a1 = subarray(array, 0, half);
         int[] a2 = subarray(array, half, array.length);
         sort(a1);
         sort(a2);
         merge(array, a1, a2);
      }
   }

/**
 * Merges the two sorted arrays a1 and a2 into the array storage passed
 * as the first parameter.
 */

   private void merge(int[] array, int[] a1, int[] a2) {
      int n1 = a1.length;
      int n2 = a2.length;
      int p1 = 0;
      int p2 = 0;
      for (int i = 0; i < array.length; i++) {
         if (p2 == n2 || (p1 < n1 && a1[p1] < a2[p2])) {
            array[i] = a1[p1++];
         } else {
            array[i] = a2[p2++];
         }
      }
   }

/**
 * Creates a new array that contains the elements from array starting
 * at p1 and continuing up to but not including p2.
 */

   private int[] subarray(int[] array, int p1, int p2) {
      int[] result = new int[p2 - p1];
      for (int i = p1; i < p2; i++) {
         result[i - p1] = array[i];
      }
      return result;
   }
```

When you call the merge sort implementation of **sort** on a list of N numbers, the running time can be divided into two components:

1. The amount of time required to execute the operations at the current level of the recursive decomposition

2. The time required to execute the recursive calls

At the top level of the recursive decomposition, the cost of performing the nonrecursive operations is proportional to N. The loop to fill the subsidiary arrays accounts for N cycles, and the call to **merge** has the effect of refilling the original N positions in the array. If you add these operations and ignore the constant factor, you discover that the complexity of any single call to **sort**—not counting the recursive calls within it—requires $O(N)$ operations.

But what about the cost of the recursive operations? To sort an array of size N, you must recursively sort two arrays of size $N / 2$. Each of these operations requires some amount of time. If you apply the same logic, you quickly determine that sorting each of these smaller arrays requires time proportional to $N / 2$ at that level of the recursive decomposition, plus whatever time is required by any further recursive calls. The same process then continues until you reach the simple case in which the arrays consist of a single element or no elements at all.

The total time required to solve the problem is the sum of the time required at each level of the recursive decomposition. In general, the decomposition has the structure shown in Figure 11-4. As you move down through the recursive

FIGURE 11-4 **Recursive decomposition of merge sort**

Sorting an array of size N

N operations

requires sorting two arrays of size N / 2

$2 \times N/2$ operations

requires sorting four arrays of size N / 4

$4 \times N/4$ operations

requires sorting eight arrays of size N / 8

$8 \times N/8$ operations

and so on.

hierarchy, the arrays get smaller, but more numerous. The amount of work done at each level, however, is always directly proportional to N. Determining the total amount of work is thus a question of finding out how many levels there will be.

At each level of the hierarchy, the value of N is divided by 2. The total number of levels is therefore equal to the number of times you can divide N by 2 before you get down to 1. Rephrasing this problem in mathematical terms, you need to find a value of k such that

$$N = 2^k$$

Solving the equation for k gives you

$$k = \log_2 N$$

Because the number of levels is $\log_2 N$ and the amount of work done at each level is proportional to N, the total amount of work is proportional to $N \log_2 N$.

Unlike other scientific disciplines, in which logarithms are expressed in terms of powers of 10 (common logarithms) or the mathematical constant e (natural logarithms), computer science tends to use **binary logarithms,** which are based on powers of 2. Logarithms computed using different bases differ only by a constant factor, and it is therefore traditional to omit the logarithmic base when you talk about computational complexity. Thus, the computational complexity of merge sort is usually written as

$$O(N \log N)$$

Comparing N^2 and $N \log N$ performance

But how much better is an algorithm that runs in $O(N \log N)$ time than one that requires $O(N^2)$? One way to assess the level of improvement is to look at empirical data to get a sense of how the running times of the selection and merge sort algorithms compare. That timing information appears in Figure 11-5. For 10 items,

---

FIGURE 11-5 Empirical comparison of selection and merge sorts

N	Selection sort	Merge sort
10	0.00000018 sec	0.00000102 sec
100	0.0000132 sec	0.000011 sec
1000	0.00126 sec	0.00012 sec
10,000	0.1258 sec	0.0023 sec
100,000	12.522 sec	0.0235 sec
1,000,000	1251.9 sec	0.297 sec

this implementation of merge sort is more than five times slower than selection sort. At 100 items, selection sort is slightly slower than merge sort. By the time you get up to 100,000 items, merge sort is almost 500 times faster than selection sort. On my computer, the selection sort algorithm requires more than twenty minutes to sort 1,000,000 items while merge sort completes the job in less than half a second. For large arrays, merge sort clearly represents a significant improvement.

You can get much the same information by comparing the computational complexity formulas for the two algorithms, as follows:

N	N^2	$N \log N$
10	100	33
100	10,000	664
1000	1,000,000	9965
10,000	100,000,000	132,877

The numbers in both columns grow as N becomes larger, but the N^2 column grows much faster than the $N \log N$ column. Sorting algorithms based on an $N \log N$ algorithm will therefore be useful over a much larger range of array sizes.

11.4 Standard complexity classes

In programming, most algorithms fall into one of several common complexity classes. The most important complexity classes are shown in Figure 11-6, which gives the common name of the class along with the corresponding big-O expression and a representative algorithm in that class.

The classes in Figure 11-6 are presented in strictly increasing order of complexity. If you have a choice between one algorithm that requires $O(\log N)$ time and another that requires $O(N)$ time, the first will always outperform the second as N grows large. For small values of N, terms that are discounted in the big-O calculation may allow a theoretically less efficient algorithm to outperform

FIGURE 11-6 Standard complexity classes

Constant	$O(1)$	Returning the first element in an array
Logarithmic	$O(\log N)$	Binary search in a sorted array
Linear	$O(N)$	Linear search in an array
$N \log N$	$O(N \log N)$	Merge sort
Quadratic	$O(N^2)$	Selection sort
Cubic	$O(N^3)$	Conventional algorithms for matrix multiplication
Exponential	$O(2^N)$	Tower of Hanoi

one that has a lower computational complexity. On the other hand, as N grows larger, there will always be a point at which the theoretical difference in efficiency becomes the deciding factor.

The differences in efficiency between these classes are in fact profound. You can begin to get a sense of how the different complexity functions stand in relation to one another by looking at the graph in Figure 11-7, which plots these complexity functions on a traditional linear scale. Unfortunately, this graph tells an incomplete and somewhat misleading part of the story, because the values of N are all very small. Complexity analysis, after all, is primarily relevant as the values of N become large. Figure 11-8 shows the same data plotted on a logarithmic scale, which gives you a better sense of how these functions grow over a more extensive range of values.

Algorithms that fall into the constant, linear, quadratic, and cubic complexity classes are all part of a more general family called **polynomial algorithms,** which execute in time N^k for some constant k. One of the useful properties of the logarithmic plot shown in Figure 11-8 is that the graph of any function N^k always comes out as a straight line whose slope is proportional to k. If you look at the

FIGURE 11-7 **Growth characteristics of the standard complexity classes: linear plot**

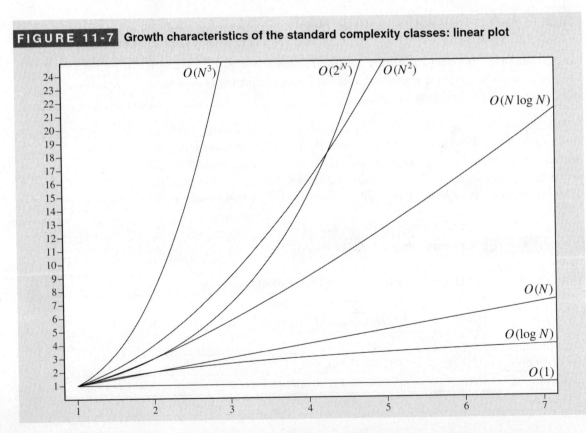

figure, it is clear that the function N^k—no matter how big k happens to be—invariably grows more slowly than the exponential function represented by 2^N, which continues to curve upward as the value of N increases. This property has important implications in terms of finding practical algorithms for real-world problems. Even though the selection sort example demonstrates that quadratic algorithms have substantial performance problems for large values of N, algorithms whose complexity is $O(2^N)$ are considerably less efficient. As a general rule of thumb, computer scientists classify problems that can be solved using algorithms that run in polynomial time as *tractable,* in the sense that they are amenable to implementation on a computer. Problems for which no polynomial-time algorithm exists are regarded as *intractable.*

Unfortunately, there are many commercially important problems for which all known algorithms require exponential time. One of those is the subset-sum problem introduced in Chapter 8, which arises in several practical contexts. Another is the *traveling salesman problem,* which consists of finding the shortest route by which one can visit a set of N cities connected by some transportation system and then return to the starting point. As far as anyone knows, it is not

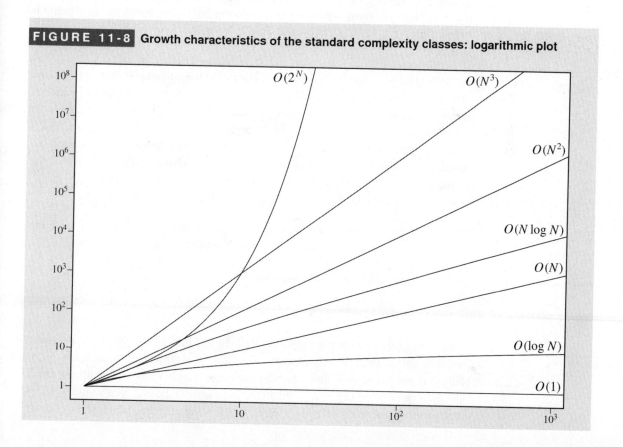

FIGURE 11-8 Growth characteristics of the standard complexity classes: logarithmic plot

possible to solve either the subset-sum problem or the traveling salesman problem in polynomial time. The best-known approaches all have exponential performance in the worst case and are equivalent in efficiency to generating all possible routings and comparing the cost. At least for the moment, the optimal solution to each of these problems is to try every possibility, which requires exponential time. On the other hand, no one has been able to prove conclusively that no polynomial-time algorithm for this problem exists. There might be some clever algorithm that would make these problems tractable. If so, many problems currently believed to be difficult would move into the tractable range as well.

The question of whether problems like subset-sum or the traveling salesman problem can be solved in polynomial time is one of the most important open questions in computer science and indeed in mathematics. This question is known as the **P = NP problem** and carries a million dollar prize for its solution.

11.5 The Quicksort algorithm

Even though the merge sort algorithm presented earlier in this chapter performs well in theory and has a worst-case complexity of $O(N \log N)$, it is not used much in practice. Instead, most sorting programs in use today are based on an algorithm called Quicksort, developed by the British computer scientist C. A. R. (Tony) Hoare.

Both Quicksort and merge sort employ a divide-and-conquer strategy. In the merge sort algorithm, the original array is divided into two halves, each of which is sorted independently. The resulting sorted arrays are then merged together to complete the sort operation for the entire array. Suppose, however, that you took a different approach to dividing up the array. What would happen if you started the process by making an initial pass through the array, changing the positions of the elements so that "small" values come at the beginning of the array and "large" values come at the end, for some definition of the words *large* and *small?*

For example, suppose that the original array you wanted to sort was the following one, presented earlier in the discussion of merge sort:

array

56	25	37	58	95	19	73	30
0	1	2	3	4	5	6	7

Since half of these elements are larger than 50 and half are smaller, it might make sense to define *small* in this case as being less than 50 and *large* as being 50 or more. If you could then find a way to rearrange the elements so that all the small elements came at the beginning and all the large ones at the end, you would wind up with an array that looks something like the following diagram, which shows one of many possible orderings in which the small and large elements appear on opposite sides of the boundary:

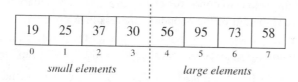

small elements   large elements

When the elements are divided into parts in this fashion, all that remains to be done is to sort each of the parts, using a recursive call to the method that does the sorting. Since all the elements on the left side of the boundary line are smaller than all those on the right, the final result will be a completely sorted array:

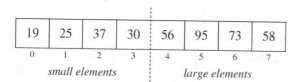

small elements   large elements

If you could always choose the optimal boundary between the small and large elements on each cycle, this algorithm would divide the array in half each time and end up demonstrating the same qualitative characteristics as merge sort. In practice, the Quicksort algorithm selects some existing element in the array and uses that value to represent the dividing line between the small and large elements. Although you will have a chance to explore more effective strategies in the exercises, one strategy is to pick the first element (56 in the original array) and use that to represent the boundary value. When the array is reordered, the boundary will fall at a particular index position rather than between two positions, as follows:

19	25	37	30	56	95	73	58
0	1	2	3	4	5	6	7

From this point, the recursive calls must sort the array between positions 0 and 3 and the array between positions 5 and 7, leaving index position 4 right where it is.

As in merge sort, the simple case of the Quicksort algorithm is an array of size 0 or 1, which must already be sorted. The recursive part of the Quicksort algorithm consists of the following steps:

1. *Choose an element to serve as the boundary between the small and large elements.* This element is called the **pivot.** For the moment, it is sufficient to choose any element for this purpose, and the simplest strategy is to select the first element in the array.

2. *Rearrange the elements in the array so that large elements are moved toward the end of the array and small elements toward the beginning.* More formally, the goal of this step is to divide the elements around a boundary position so that all elements to the left of the boundary are less than the pivot and all elements to the right are greater than or possibly equal to the pivot. This processing is called *partitioning* the array and is discussed in detail in the next section.

3. *Sort the elements in each of the partial arrays.* Because all elements to the left of the pivot boundary are strictly less than all those to the right, sorting each of the arrays must leave the entire array in sorted order. Moreover, since the algorithm uses a divide-and-conquer strategy, these smaller arrays can be sorted using a recursive application of Quicksort.

Partitioning the array

In the partition step of the Quicksort algorithm, the goal is to rearrange the elements so that they are divided into three classes: those that are smaller than the pivot; the pivot element itself, which is situated at the boundary position; and those elements that are at least as large as the pivot. The tricky part about partitioning is to rearrange the elements without using any extra storage, which is typically done by swapping pairs of elements.

Tony Hoare's original approach to partitioning is fairly easy to explain in English. As in the preceding section, the discussion that follows assumes that the pivot is stored in the initial element position. Because the pivot value has already been selected when you start the partitioning phase of the algorithm, you can tell immediately whether a value is large or small relative to that pivot. Hoare's partitioning algorithm then proceeds as follows:

1. For the moment, ignore the pivot element at index position 0 and concentrate on the remaining elements. Use two index values, `lh` and `rh`, to record the index positions of the first and last elements in the rest of the array, as shown:

56	25	37	58	95	19	73	30
0	1	2	3	4	5	6	7

`lh` points to position 1, `rh` points to position 7.

2. Move the `rh` index to the left until it either coincides with `lh` or points to an element containing a value that is small with respect to the pivot. In this example, the value 30 in position 7 is already a small value, so the `rh` index does not need to move.

3. Move the `lh` index to the right until it coincides with `rh` or points to an element containing a value that is larger than or equal to the pivot. In this example, the

lh index must move to the right until it points to an element larger than 56, which leads to the following configuration:

56	25	37	58	95	19	73	30
0	1	2	3	4	5	6	7

lh   rh

4. If the **lh** and **rh** index values have not yet reached the same position, exchange the elements in the **lh** and **rh** positions, which leaves the array looking like this:

56	25	37	30	95	19	73	58
0	1	2	3	4	5	6	7

lh   rh

5. Repeat steps 2 through 4 until the **lh** and **rh** positions coincide. On the next pass, for example, the exchange operation in step 4 swaps the 19 and the 95. As soon as that happens, the next execution of step 2 moves the **rh** index to the left, where it ends up matching the **lh**, as follows:

56	25	37	30	19	95	73	58
0	1	2	3	4	5	6	7

lh+rh

6. Unless the chosen pivot just happened to be the smallest element in the entire array (and the code includes a special check for this case), the point at which the **lh** and **rh** index positions coincide will be the small value that is furthest to the right in the array. The only remaining step is to exchange that value with the pivot element at the beginning of the array, as shown:

19	25	37	30	56	95	73	58
0	1	2	3	4	5	6	7

boundary

Note that this configuration meets the requirements of the partitioning step. The pivot value is at the marked boundary position, with every element to the left being smaller and every element to the right being at least as large.

An implementation of **sort** using the Quicksort algorithm is shown in Figure 11-9.

FIGURE 11-9 Implementation of the Quicksort algorithm

```
/**
 * Sorts an array of integers into ascending order.
 */

   public void sort(int[] array) {
      quicksort(array, 0, array.length);
   }

/**
 * Applies the Quicksort algorithm to the elements in the subarray
 * starting at p1 and continuing up to but not including p2.
 */

   private void quicksort(int[] array, int p1, int p2) {
      if (p2 - 1 <= p1) return;
      int boundary = partition(array, p1, p2);
      quicksort(array, p1, boundary);
      quicksort(array, boundary + 1, p2);
   }

/**
 * Rearranges the elements of the subarray delimited by the indices
 * p1 and p2 so that "small" elements are grouped at the left end
 * of the array and "large" elements are grouped at the right end.
 * The distinction between small and large is made by comparing each
 * element to the "pivot" value, which initially appears in array[start].
 * When the partitioning is done, the function returns a boundary index
 * such that array[i] < pivot for all i < boundary, array[i] == pivot
 * for i == boundary, and array[i] >= pivot for all i > boundary.
 */

   private int partition(int[] array, int p1, int p2) {
      int pivot = array[p1];
      int lh = p1 + 1;
      int rh = p2 - 1;
      while (true) {
         while (lh < rh && array[rh] >= pivot) rh--;
         while (lh < rh && array[lh] < pivot) lh++;
         if (lh == rh) break;
         int tmp = array[lh];
         array[lh] = array[rh];
         array[rh] = tmp;
      }
      if (array[lh] >= pivot) return p1;
      array[p1] = array[lh];
      array[lh] = pivot;
      return lh;
   }
```

Analyzing the performance of Quicksort

A head-to-head comparison of the actual running times for the merge sort and Quicksort algorithms appears in Figure 11-10. As you can see, this implementation of Quicksort tends to run slightly faster than the implementation of merge sort given in Figure 11-3, which is one of the reasons why programmers use it more frequently in practice. Moreover, the running times for both algorithms appear to grow in roughly the same way.

The empirical results presented in Figure 11-10, however, obscure an important point. As long as the Quicksort algorithm chooses a pivot that is close to the median value in the array, the partition step will divide the array into roughly equal parts. If the pivot value does not actually fall near the middle of the range of values, one of the two partial arrays may be much larger than the other, which defeats the purpose of the divide-and-conquer strategy. In an array with randomly chosen elements, Quicksort tends to perform well, with an average-case complexity of $O(N \log N)$. In the worst case—which paradoxically consists of an array that is already sorted—the performance degenerates to $O(N^2)$. Despite this inferior behavior in the worst case, Quicksort is so much faster in practice than most other algorithms that it has become the standard choice for general sorting procedures.

There are several strategies you can use to increase the likelihood that the pivot is in fact close to the median value in the array. One simple approach is to have the Quicksort implementation choose the pivot element at random. Although it is still possible that the random process will choose a poor pivot value, it is unlikely that it would make the same mistake repeatedly at each level of the recursive decomposition. Moreover, there is no distribution of the original array that is always bad. Given any input, choosing the pivot randomly ensures that the average-case performance for that array will be $O(N \log N)$. Another possibility, which you can explore in more detail in exercise 6, is to select a few values, typically three or five, from the array and choose the median of those values as the pivot.

FIGURE 11-10   **Empirical comparison of merge sort and Quicksort**

N	Merge sort	Quicksort
10	0.00000102 sec	0.00000029 sec
100	0.000011 sec	0.0000046 sec
1000	0.00012 sec	0.000104 sec
10,000	0.0023 sec	0.0013 sec
100,000	0.0235 sec	0.0168 sec
1,000,000	0.297 sec	0.207 sec

You do have to be somewhat careful as you try to improve the algorithm in this way. Picking a good pivot improves performance, but also costs some time. If the algorithm spends more time choosing the pivot than it gets back from making a good choice, you will end up slowing down the implementation rather than speeding it up.

11.6 Mathematical induction

Earlier in the chapter, I asked you to rely on the fact that the sum

$$N + N{-}1 + N{-}2 + \ldots + 3 + 2 + 1$$

could be simplified to the more manageable formula

$$\frac{N^2 + N}{2}$$

If you were skeptical about this simplification, how would you go about proving that the simplified formula is indeed correct?

There are, in fact, several different proof techniques you could try. One possibility is to represent the original extended sum in a geometric form. Suppose, for example, that N is 5. If you then represent each term in the summation with a row of dots, those dots form the following triangle:

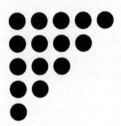

If you make a copy of this triangle and flip it upside down, the two triangles fit together to form a rectangle, shown here with the lower triangle in gray:

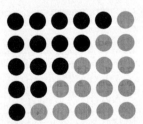

Since the pattern is now rectangular, the total number of dots—both black and gray—is easy to compute. In this picture, there are five rows of six dots each, so the total collection of dots, counting both colors, is 5×6, or 30. Since the two triangles are identical, exactly half of these dots are black; thus the number of black dots is 30 / 2, or 15. In the more general case, there are N rows containing $N+1$ dots each, and the number of black dots from the original triangle is therefore

$$\frac{N \times (N+1)}{2}$$

Proving that a formula is correct in this fashion has some potential drawbacks, however. For one thing, geometrical arguments presented in this style are not as formal as many computer scientists would like. More to the point, constructing this type of argument requires that you come up with the right geometrical insight, which is different for each problem. It would be better to adopt a more general proof strategy that would apply to many different problems.

The technique that computer scientists generally use to prove propositions like

$$N + N\text{–}1 + N\text{–}2 + \cdots + 3 + 2 + 1 = \frac{N \times (N+1)}{2}$$

is called **mathematical induction.** Mathematical induction applies when you want to show that a proposition is true for all values of an integer N beginning at some initial starting point. This starting point is called the **basis** of the induction and is typically 0 or 1. The process consists of the following steps:

- *Prove the base case.* The first step is to establish that the proposition holds true when N has the basis value. In most cases, this step is a simple matter of plugging the basis value into a formula and showing that the desired relationship holds.

- *Prove the inductive case.* The second step is to demonstrate that, if you assume the proposition to be true for N, it must also be true for $N+1$.

As an example, here is how you can use mathematical induction to prove the proposition that

$$N + N\text{–}1 + N\text{–}2 + \cdots + 3 + 2 + 1 = \frac{N \times (N+1)}{2}$$

is indeed true for all N greater than or equal to 1. The first step is to prove the base case, in which N is equal to 1. That part is easy. All you have to do is substitute 1 for N in both halves of the formula to determine that

$$1 = \frac{1 \times (1+1)}{2} = \frac{2}{2} = 1$$

To prove the inductive case, you begin by assuming that the proposition

$$N + N\text{--}1 + N\text{--}2 + \cdots + 3 + 2 + 1 = \frac{N \times (N + 1)}{2}$$

is indeed true for N. This assumption is called the ***inductive hypothesis.*** Your goal is now to verify that the same relationship holds for $N+1$. In other words, what you need to do to establish the truth of the current formula is show that

$$N+1 + N + N\text{--}1 + N\text{--}2 + \cdots + 3 + 2 + 1 = \frac{(N + 1) \times (N + 2)}{2}$$

If you look at the left side of the equation, you should notice that the sequence of terms beginning with N is exactly the same as the sequence of terms on the left side of your inductive hypothesis. Since you have assumed that the inductive hypothesis is true, you can substitute the equivalent closed-form expression, so that the left side of the proposition you're trying to prove looks like this:

$$N+1 + \frac{N \times (N + 1)}{2}$$

From here on, the rest of the proof is simple algebra:

$$N+1 + \frac{N \times (N + 1)}{2}$$

$$= \frac{2N + 2}{2} + \frac{N^2 + N}{2}$$

$$= \frac{N^2 + 3N + 2}{2}$$

$$= \frac{(N + 1) \times (N + 2)}{2}$$

The last line in this derivation is precisely the result you were looking for and therefore completes the proof.

Many students need time to get used to the idea of mathematical induction. At first glance, the inductive hypothesis seems to be "cheating" in some sense; after all, you get to assume precisely the proposition that you are trying to prove. In fact, the process of mathematical induction is nothing more than an infinite family of proofs, each of which proceeds by the same logic. The base case in a typical example establishes that the proposition is true for $N = 1$. Once you have proved the base case, you can adopt the following chain of reasoning:

Now that I know the proposition is true for $N = 1$, I can prove it is true for $N = 2$.
Now that I know the proposition is true for $N = 2$, I can prove it is true for $N = 3$.
Now that I know the proposition is true for $N = 3$, I can prove it is true for $N = 4$.
Now that I know the proposition is true for $N = 4$, I can prove it is true for $N = 5$.
And so on. . . .

At each step in this process, you could write out a complete proof by applying the logic you used to establish the inductive case. The power of mathematical induction comes from the fact that you don't actually need to write out the details of each step individually.

In a way, the process of mathematical induction is like the process of recursion viewed from the opposite direction. If you try to explain a typical recursive decomposition in detail, the process usually sounds something like this:

> To calculate this function for $N = 5$, I need to know its value for $N = 4$.
> To calculate this function for $N = 4$, I need to know its value for $N = 3$.
> To calculate this function for $N = 3$, I need to know its value for $N = 2$.
> To calculate this function for $N = 2$, I need to know its value for $N = 1$.
> The value $N = 1$ represents a simple case, so I can return the result immediately.

Both induction and recursion require you to make a leap of faith. When you write a recursive method, this leap consists of believing that all simpler instances of the method call will work without your paying any attention to the details. Making the inductive hypothesis requires much the same mental discipline. In both cases, you have to restrict your thinking to one level of the solution and not get sidetracked by trying to follow the details all the way to the end.

Summary

The most valuable concept to take with you from this chapter is that algorithms for solving a problem can vary widely in their performance characteristics. Choosing an algorithm that has better computational properties can often reduce the time required to solve a problem by many orders of magnitude. The difference in behavior is illustrated dramatically by the tables presented in this chapter that give the actual running times for various sorting algorithms. When sorting an array of 10,000 integers, for example, the Quicksort algorithm outperforms selection sort by a factor of almost 100; as the array sizes get larger, the difference in efficiency between these algorithms becomes even more pronounced.

Other important points in this chapter include:

- Most algorithmic problems can be characterized by an integer N that represents the size of the problem. For algorithms that operate on large integers, the size of the integer provides an effective measure of problem size; for algorithms that operate on arrays, it usually makes sense to define the problem size as the number of elements.

- The most useful qualitative measure of efficiency is *computational complexity*, which is defined as the relationship between problem size and algorithmic performance as the problem size becomes large.

- *Big-O notation* provides an intuitive way of expressing computational complexity because it allows you to highlight the most important aspects of the complexity relationship in the simplest possible form.

- When you use big-O notation, you can simplify the formula by eliminating any term in the formula that becomes insignificant as N becomes large, along with any constant factors.

- You can often predict the computational complexity of a program by looking at the nesting structure of the loops it contains.

- Two useful measures of complexity are *worst-case* and *average-case* analysis. Average-case analysis is usually much more difficult to conduct.

- Divide-and-conquer strategies make it possible to reduce the complexity of sorting algorithms from $O(N^2)$ to $O(N \log N)$, which is a significant reduction.

- Most algorithms fall into one of several common *complexity classes*, which include the *constant, logarithmic, linear, N log N, quadratic, cubic,* and *exponential* classes. Algorithms whose complexity class appears earlier in this list are more efficient than those that come later, at least when the problems being considered are sufficiently large.

- Problems that can be solved in *polynomial time,* which is defined to be $O(N^k)$ for some constant value k, are considered to be *tractable*. Problems for which no polynomial-time algorithm exists are considered *intractable* because solving such problems requires prohibitive amounts of time, even for problems of relatively modest size.

- Because it tends to perform extremely well in practice, most sorting programs are based on the *Quicksort algorithm,* developed by Tony Hoare, even though its worst-case complexity is $O(N^2)$.

- Mathematical induction provides a general technique for proving that a property holds for all values of N greater than or equal to some *base* value. When you apply this technique, your first step is to demonstrate that the property holds in the base case. In the second step, you must prove that, if the formula holds for a specific value N, then it must also hold for $N+1$.

Review questions

1. The simplest recursive implementation of the Fibonacci function is considerably less efficient than the iterative version. Does this fact allow you to make any general conclusions about the relative efficiency of recursive and iterative solutions?

2. What is the sorting problem?

3. The implementation of **sort** shown in Figure 11-1 runs through the code to exchange the values at positions **lh** and **rh** even if these values happen to be the same. If you change the program so that it checks to make sure **lh** and **rh** are different before making the exchange, it is likely to run more slowly than the original algorithm. Why might this be so?

4. Suppose that you are using the selection sort algorithm to sort an array of 250 values and you find that it takes 50 milliseconds to complete the operation. What would you expect the running time to be if you used the same algorithm to sort an array of 1000 values on the same machine?

5. What is the closed-form expression that computes the sum of the series

$$N + N{-}1 + N{-}2 + \cdots + 3 + 2 + 1$$

6. In your own words, define the concept of computational complexity.

7. True or false: Big-O notation was invented as a means of expressing computational complexity.

8. What are the two rules given in this chapter for simplifying big-O notation?

9. Is it technically correct to say that selection sort runs in

$$O\left(\frac{N^2 + N}{2}\right)$$

time? What, if anything, is wrong with expressing computational complexity in this form?

10. Is it technically correct to say that selection sort runs in $O(N^3)$ time? Again, what, if anything, is wrong with characterizing selection sort in this way?

11. What is the computational complexity of the following method:

```
int mystery1(int n) {
    int sum = 0;
    for (int i = 0; i < n; i++) {
        for (int j = 0; j < i; j++) {
            sum += i * j;
        }
    }
    return sum;
}
```

12. What is the computational complexity of this method:

```
int mystery2(int n) {
    int sum = 0;
    for (int i = 0; i < 10; i++) {
        for (int j = 0; j < i; j++) {
            sum += j * n;
        }
    }
    return sum;
}
```

13. Why is it customary to omit the base of the logarithm in big-O expressions such as $O(N \log N)$?

14. Explain the difference between worst-case and average-case complexity. In general, which of these measures is harder to compute?

15. Explain the roles of the constants C and N_0 in the formal definition of big-O.

16. In your own words, explain why the **merge** method runs in linear time.

17. Explain each of the lines in the following loop from the **merge** method:

```
for (int i = 0; i < array.length; i++) {
    if (p2 == n2 || (p1 < n1 && a1[p1] < a2[p2])) {
        array[i] = a1[p1++];
    } else {
        array[i] = a2[p2++];
    }
}
```

18. What are the seven complexity classes identified in this chapter as the most common classes encountered in practice?

19. What does the term *polynomial algorithm* mean?

20. What is the difference between a *tractable* and an *intractable* problem?

21. In Quicksort, what conditions must be true at the end of the partitioning step?

22. What are the worst- and average-case complexities for Quicksort?

23. Describe the two steps involved in a proof by mathematical induction.

24. In your own words, describe the relationship between recursion and mathematical induction.

Exercises

1. It is easy to write a recursive method

    ```
    double raiseToPower(double x, int n)
    ```

    that calculates x^n, by relying on the recursive insight that

    $$x^n = x \times x^{n-1}$$

    Such a strategy leads to an implementation that runs in linear time. You can, however, adopt a recursive divide-and-conquer strategy which takes advantage of the fact that

    $$x^{2n} = x^n \times x^n$$

    Use this fact to write a recursive version of **raiseToPower** that runs in $O(\log N)$ time.

2. There are several other sorting algorithms that exhibit the $O(N^2)$ behavior of selection sort. Of these, one of the most important is **insertion sort,** which operates as follows. You go through each element in the array in turn, as with the selection sort algorithm. At each step in the process, however, the goal is not to find the smallest remaining value and switch it into its correct position, but rather to ensure that the values considered so far are correctly ordered with respect to each other. Although these values may shift as more elements are processed, they form an ordered sequence in and of themselves.

    For example, if you consider again the data used in the sorting examples from this chapter, the first cycle of the insertion sort algorithm requires no work, because an array of one element is always sorted:

    in order

56	25	37	58	95	19	73	30
0	1	2	3	4	5	6	7

    On the next cycle, you need to put 25 in the correct position with respect to the elements you have already seen, which means that you need to exchange the 56 and 25 to reach the following configuration:

    in order

25	56	37	58	95	19	73	30
0	1	2	3	4	5	6	7

    On the third cycle, you need to find where the value 37 should go. To do so, you must move backward through the earlier elements—which you know are in order with respect to each other—looking for the position where 37 belongs. As you go, you need to shift each of the larger elements one position to the right, which eventually makes room for the value you're trying to insert. In this case, the 56 gets shifted by one position, and the 37 winds up in position 1. Thus, the configuration after the third cycle looks like this:

in order

25	37	56	58	95	19	73	30
0	1	2	3	4	5	6	7

After each cycle, the initial portion of the array is always sorted, which implies that cycling through all the positions in this way will sort the entire array.

The insertion sort algorithm is important in practice because it runs in linear time if the array is already more or less in the correct order. It therefore makes sense to use insertion sort to restore order to a large array in which only a few elements are out of sequence.

Write an implementation of **sort** that uses the insertion sort algorithm. Construct an informal argument to show that the worst-case behavior of insertion sort is $O(N^2)$.

3. Write a method that keeps track of the elapsed time as it executes the **sort** procedure on a randomly chosen array. Use that method to write a program that produces a table of the observed running times for a predefined set of sizes, as shown in the following sample run:

```
●○○                       SortTimer
   N    |    Time (sec)
--------+----------------
     10 |    0.00000078
    100 |    0.00000880
   1000 |    0.00012000
  10000 |    0.00170000
 100000 |    0.02440000
1000000 |    0.20900000
```

The best way to measure elapsed system time for programs of this sort is to call the standard method **System.currentTimeMillis()**, which returns the current time expressed as the number of milliseconds that have elapsed since midnight on January 1, 1970. If you record the starting and finishing times in the variables **start** and **finish**, you can use the following code to compute the elapsed time in seconds required by a calculation:

```
double start = System.currentTimeMillis();
. . . Perform some calculation . . .
double finish = System.currentTimeMillis();
double elapsed = (finish - start) / 1000;
```

Unfortunately, calculating the time requirements for a program that runs quickly requires some subtlety because there is no guarantee that the system clock unit is precise enough to measure the elapsed time. For example, if you used this strategy to time the process of sorting 10 integers, the odds are good that the value of **elapsed** at the end of the code fragment would be 0. The reason is that the processing unit on most machines can execute many instructions in the space of a single clock tick—almost certainly enough to get the entire sorting process done for an array of 10 elements. Because the system's internal clock may not tick in the interim, the values recorded for **start** and **finish** are likely to be the same.

The best way to get around this problem is to repeat the calculation many times between the two calls to **currentTimeMillis**. For example, if you want to determine how long it takes to sort 10 numbers, you can perform the sort-10-numbers experiment 1000 times in a row and then divide the total elapsed time by 1000. This strategy gives you a timing measurement that is much more accurate.

4. Suppose you know that all the values in an integer array fall into the range 0 to 9999. Show that it is possible to write a $O(N)$ algorithm to sort arrays with this restriction. Implement your algorithm and evaluate its performance by taking empirical measurements using the strategy outlined in exercise 3. Explain why the algorithm is less efficient than selection sort for small values of N.

5. Write a program that generates a table comparing the performance of two algorithms—linear and binary search—when used to find a randomly chosen integer key in a sorted array of integers. The linear search algorithm simply goes through each element of the array in turn until it finds the desired one or determines that the key does not appear. The binary search algorithm, which is implemented for string arrays in Figure 7-5, uses a divide-and-conquer strategy by checking the middle element of the array and then deciding which half of the remaining elements to search.

The table you generate in this problem, rather than computing the time as in exercise 3, should instead calculate the number of comparisons made against elements of the array. To ensure that the results are not completely random, your program should average the results over several independent trials. A sample run of the program might look like this:

```
  ● ● ●                    SearchComparison
      N    |   Linear   |   Binary
  ---------+------------+----------
     10    |     6.6    |    2.6
     50    |    30.9    |    4.5
    100    |    63.0    |    5.4
    500    |   316.9    |    7.6
   1000    |   572.0    |    8.7
   5000    |  3222.9    |   11.1
  10000    |  5272.9    |   12.0
  50000    | 34917.2    |   14.6
 100000    | 68825.9    |   15.6
```

6. Change the implementation of the Quicksort algorithm so that, instead of picking the first element in the array as the pivot, the **partition** method chooses the median of the first, middle, and last elements.

7. Although $O(N \log N)$ sorting algorithms are clearly more efficient than $O(N^2)$ algorithms for large arrays, the simplicity of quadratic algorithms like selection sort often means that they perform better for small values of N. This fact raises the possibility of developing a strategy that combines the two algorithms, using Quicksort for large arrays but selection sort whenever the size of the arrays becomes less than some threshold called the ***crossover point***. Approaches that combine two different algorithms to exploit the best features of each are called ***hybrid strategies.***

    Reimplement **sort** using a hybrid of the Quicksort and selection sort strategies. Experiment with different values of the crossover point below which the implementation chooses to use selection sort, and determine what value gives the best performance. The value of the crossover point depends on the specific timing characteristics of your computer and will change from system to system.

8. Another interesting hybrid strategy for the sorting problem is to start with a recursive implementation of Quicksort that simply returns when the size of the array falls below a certain threshold. When this method returns, the array is not sorted, but all the elements are relatively close to their final positions. At this point, you can use the insertion sort algorithm presented in exercise 2 on the entire array to fix any remaining problems. Because insertion sort runs in linear time on arrays that are mostly sorted, this two-step process may run more quickly than either algorithm alone. Write an implementation of the **sort** method that uses this hybrid approach.

9. Suppose you have two functions, f and g, for which $f(N)$ is less than $g(N)$ for all values of N. Use the formal definition of big-O to prove that

$$15f(N) + 6g(N)$$

is $O(g(N))$.

10. Use the formal definition of big-O to prove that N^2 is $O(2^N)$.

11. Use mathematical induction to prove that the following properties hold for all positive values of N.

a) $1 + 3 + 5 + 7 + \cdots + 2N{-}1 = N^2$

b) $1_2 + 2_2 + 3_2 + 4_2 + \cdots + N_2 = \dfrac{N \times (N+1) \times (2N+1)}{6}$

c) $1^3 + 2^3 + 3^3 + 4^3 + \ldots + N^3 = (1 + 2 + 3 + 4 + \ldots + N)^2$

d) $2^0 + 2^1 + 2^2 + 2^3 + \ldots + 2^N = 2^{N+1} - 1$

12. Exercise 1 shows that it is possible to compute x^n in $O(\log N)$ time. This fact in turn makes it possible to write an implementation of the `fib(n)` method that also runs in $O(\log N)$ time, which is much faster than the traditional iterative version. To do so, you need to rely on the somewhat surprising fact that the Fibonacci function is closely related to a value called the ***golden ratio,*** which has been known since the days of ancient Greek mathematics. The golden ratio, which is usually designated by the Greek letter phi (φ), is defined to be the value that satisfies the equation

$$\varphi^2 - \varphi - 1 = 0$$

Because this is a quadratic equation, it actually has two roots. If you apply the quadratic formula, you will discover that these roots are

$$\varphi = \frac{1 + \sqrt{5}}{2}$$

$$\phi = \frac{1 - \sqrt{5}}{2}$$

In 1718, the French mathematician Abraham de Moivre discovered that the nth Fibonacci number can be represented in closed form as

$$\frac{\varphi^n - \phi^n}{\sqrt{5}}$$

Moreover, because ϕ^n is always very small, the formula can be simplified to

$$\frac{\varphi^n}{\sqrt{5}}$$

rounded to the nearest integer.

Use this formula and the `raiseToPower` method from exercise 1 to write an implementation of `fib(n)` that runs in $O(\log N)$ time. Once you have verified empirically that the formula seems to work for the first several terms in the sequence, use mathematical induction to prove that the formula

$$\frac{\varphi^n - \phi^n}{\sqrt{5}}$$

actually computes the nth Fibonacci number.

13. In a properly formed linked list, the cells in the list form a chain that ends with a `null` reference, like this:

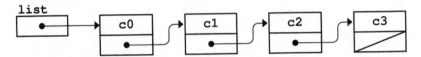

Unfortunately, because the links in the cell structures are references, it's possible that a buggy program might cause the link field in the final cell to point back to some earlier cell in the chain, as shown in the following diagram:

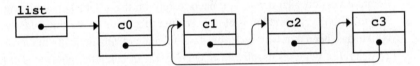

If you tried to iterate through the cells in this diagram, your program would go into an infinite loop, cycling endlessly through the cells `c1`, `c2`, and `c3`.

To avoid such situations, it would be useful to have a function to check whether a linked list contains a loop or whether it is properly terminated with a `null` reference at the end of the chain. In the 1960s, a computer science professor at Stanford, the late Robert W. Floyd, found a beautiful algorithm for detecting loops in a linked list without having to keep track of all the cells you've visited. The algorithm begins by assigning two references—a "slow pointer" and a "fast pointer"—to the beginning of the chain. On each cycle of the loop, you advance the slow pointer one step along the chain and the fast pointer two steps. If the fast pointer ever hits a `null` link, it has reached the end of the list and therefore knows that there are no loops in the chain. If, however, the slow and fast pointers ever again point to the same cell, the linked list must contain a cycle. This algorithm is illustrated in Figure 11-11.

Using the linked-list structure from Figure 8-10, write a function

```
boolean isLooped(Cell list)
```

that takes a reference to a linked-list cell and applies Floyd's algorithm to determine whether a loop exists in the chain.

FIGURE 11-11   **Robert Floyd's algorithm for detecting loops in a linked list**

Floyd's algorithm is often called the "Tortoise and Hare" algorithm because the two pointers race through the list at different speeds. The slower tortoise starts at the beginning and moves one step at a time. The faster hare starts at the same place but advances two cells for each cycle in the loop. The diagrams on this page use this tortoise-and-hare metaphor to show how the algorithm works.

Cycle 0: At the beginning, both pointers are on the first cell in the list:

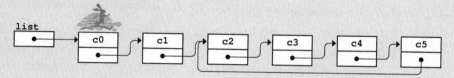

Cycle 1: After the first cycle, the tortoise and hare are on the cells containing c_1 and c_2, respectively:

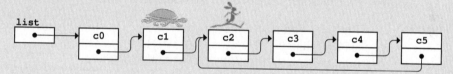

Cycle 2: On the next cycle, both pointers advance at the appropriate speed:

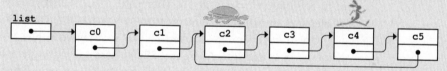

Cycle 3: On the third cycle, moving the hare two steps forward brings it around the loop so that it is now in some sense behind the tortoise:

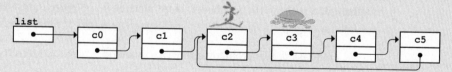

Cycle 4: On the last cycle, the hare catches up to the tortoise, which means that the list must contain a loop:

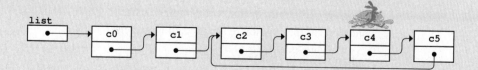

14. If you're ready for a real algorithmic challenge, write the method

    ```
    int findMajorityElement(int[] array)
    ```

    that takes an array of nonnegative integers and returns the *majority element,* which is defined to be a value that occurs in an absolute majority (at least 50 percent plus one) of the element positions. If no majority element exists, the method should return -1 to signal that fact. Your method must also meet the following conditions:

    - It must run in $O(N)$ time.

    - It must use $O(1)$ additional space. In other words, it may use individual temporary variables but may not allocate any additional array storage. Moreover, this condition rules out recursive solutions, because the space required for stack frames grows with the depth of the recursion.

    - It must not change any of the values in the array.

    The hard part about this problem is coming up with the algorithm, not implementing it. Play with some sample arrays and see if you can come up with an effective strategy that satisfies the conditions.

15. If you enjoyed the previous problem, here's an even more challenging one that used to be an interview question at Microsoft. Suppose that you have an array of N elements, in which each element has a value in the inclusive range 1 to $N-1$. Given that there are N elements in the array and only $N-1$ possible values to store in each slot, there must be at least one value that is duplicated in the array. There may, of course, be many duplicated values, but you know that there must be at least one by virtue of what mathematicians call the *pigeonhole principle:* if you have more items to put into a set of pigeonholes than the number of pigeonholes, there must be some pigeonhole that ends up with more than one item.

    Your task in this problem is to write a method

    ```
    int findDuplicate(int[] array)
    ```

    that takes an array whose values are constrained to be in the 1 to $N-1$ range and returns one of the duplicated values. The hard part of this problem is to design an algorithm so that your implementation adheres to the same set of conditions as the solution to the preceding exercise:

    - It must run in $O(N)$ time.

    - It must use $O(1)$ additional space.

    - It must not change any of the values in the array.

Chapter 12
Efficiency and Representation

The object of the engine is in fact to give the utmost practical efficiency to the resources of numerical interpretations of the higher science of analysis.

— Ada Augusta Lovelace, notes accompanying
Sketch of the Analytical Engine, 1842

This chapter brings together two ideas that might at first seem to have little to do with each other: the design of data structures and the concept of algorithmic efficiency. Up to now, discussions of efficiency have focused on the algorithms. If you choose a more efficient algorithm, you can reduce the running time of a program substantially, particularly if the new algorithm is in a different complexity class. In some cases, however, choosing a different underlying representation for a class can have an equally dramatic effect. To illustrate that idea, this chapter looks at a specific class that can be represented in several different ways and contrasts the efficiency of those representations.

▰ 12.1 Software patterns for editing text

In this age in which most people carry cell phones, texting has become one of the most popular forms of communication. You create a message on the keypad of your phone and send it off to one or more friends who then read it on their own phones. Modern cell phones require an enormous amount of software, typically involving several million lines of code. To manage that level of complexity, it is essential to decompose the implementation into separate modules that can be developed and managed independently. It is helpful, moreover, to make use of well-established software patterns to simplify the implementation process.

To get a sense of what patterns might be useful, it helps to think about what happens when you compose a text message on your phone. You enter the characters on a keypad, which also includes keys for editing. Depending on the type of phone, that keypad might take different forms. On older phones, it usually consists of a numeric keypad in which you use a series of clicks to generate each letter. A smart phone may not have a physical keypad at all but may rely instead on images of keys displayed on a touch-sensitive screen. In either case, there is a conceptual keypad that allows you to compose and edit the message. A cell phone also has a display that lets you see the message as you write it. In any modern design, however, there is a third component that is invisible to you as a user. Between the keypad and the display is an abstract data structure that records the current contents of the message. The keypad updates the contents of that data structure, which in turn provides the information you see on the display.

The tripartite decomposition described in the preceding paragraph is an example of an important design strategy called the ***model-view-controller pattern,*** or ***MVC*** for short. In the case of the cell phone, the keypad represents the controller, the display represents the view, and the underlying data structure represents the model. The application of this pattern to the cell phone example is illustrated in Figure 12-1, which traces the flow of information among the different modules.

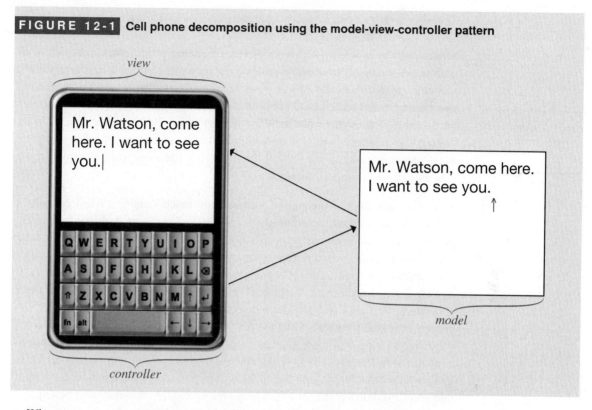

FIGURE 12-1 Cell phone decomposition using the model-view-controller pattern

When you use your cell phone to send a text message as pictured in Figure 12-1, you are using an *editor,* which is a software module that supports the creation and manipulation of text data. Editors show up in many different applications. When you enter information on a web-based form or compose a Java program in your development environment, you are using an editor. Most editors today are designed using the model-view-controller pattern. Inside the model, an editor maintains a sequence of characters, which is usually called a *buffer.* The controller allows users to perform various operations on the contents of the buffer, many of which are limited to the current location in the buffer. This location is marked on the screen by a symbol called a *cursor,* which typically appears in the view as a vertical line between two characters.

Although the controller and the view components of the editor application present interesting programming challenges, the focus of this chapter is on the editor buffer that constitutes the model. The efficiency of the editor application as a whole is extremely sensitive to the data structures you choose to represent the buffer. This chapter implements the editor buffer abstraction using three different underlying representations—a character array, a pair of character stacks, and a linked list of characters—and evaluates their advantages and disadvantages.

12.2 Designing a simple text editor

Modern editors provide a highly sophisticated editing environment, complete with such features as using a mouse to position the cursor or commands that search for a particular text string. Moreover, they tend to show the results of all editing operations precisely as they are performed. Editors that display the current contents of the buffer throughout the editing process are called **wysiwyg** (pronounced "wizzy-wig") editors, which is an acronym for "what you see is what you get." Such editors are easy to use, but all those advanced features make it harder to see how an editor works on the inside.

In the early days of computing, editors were much simpler. When computers had no mouse or sophisticated graphics displays, editors were designed to respond to commands entered on the keyboard. For example, with a typical keyboard-based editor, you insert new text by typing the command letter **I**, followed by a sequence of characters. Additional commands perform other editing functions, such as moving the cursor around in the buffer. By entering the right combinations of these commands, you can make any desired set of changes. Given that the focus of this chapter is on the representation of the editor buffer and not on the advanced features necessary to support a more sophisticated editing environment, it makes sense to explore the buffer abstraction in the context of this command-driven style. Once you've finished implementing the editor buffer, you can go back and incorporate it into a more sophisticated application based on the model-view-controller pattern.

Editor commands

The next few sections walk through the development of an extremely simple editor that can execute the commands shown in Figure 12-2. Except for the **I** command,

FIGURE 12-2   **Commands available in a simple command-based editor**

F	Moves the editing cursor forward one character position.
B	Moves the editing cursor backward one character position.
J	Jumps to the beginning of the buffer.
E	Moves the cursor to the end of the buffer.
I*xxx*	Inserts the characters *xxx* at the current cursor position.
D	Deletes the character just after the current cursor position.
H	Prints a help message listing the commands.
Q	Quits the editor program.

which also includes the characters to be inserted, every editor command consists of a single letter read in on a line.

The following sample run illustrates the operation of the command-based editor, along with annotations that describe each action. In this session, the user first inserts the characters **axc** and then corrects the contents of the buffer to **abc**.

The editor program displays the state of the buffer after each command. As you can see in the sample run, the program marks the position of the cursor with a caret symbol (^) on the next line. That behavior is not what you would expect in a real editor, but makes it easy to see exactly what is going on.

In Java, it makes sense to define the editor buffer as an interface because doing so allows you to separate the specification of behavior and representation. Because you understand the operations to which it must respond, you already know how an editor buffer behaves. The **EditorBuffer** interface defines the required set of operations, which can then be implemented by different concrete classes. Clients work entirely with **EditorBuffer** objects through the methods in the interface without any access to the underlying data representation. That fact, in turn, leaves you free to change that representation simply by changing the name of the concrete class.

At a minimum, the **EditorBuffer** interface must define methods for each of the six editor commands. In addition, the editor application program must be able to display the contents of the buffer, including the position of the cursor. To make these operations possible, the **EditorBuffer** interface defines the methods **getText** and **getCursor**, which return the text stored in the buffer and the position of the cursor as an integer in which 0 signifies the beginning of the buffer. The complete **EditorBuffer** interface appears in Figure 12-3.

FIGURE 12-3 Interface for the editor buffer abstraction

```java
/*
 * File: EditorBuffer.java
 * -------------------------
 * This file defines the interface for the editor buffer abstraction.
 */

package edu.stanford.cs.javacs2.ch12;

public interface EditorBuffer {

/**
 * Moves the cursor forward one character, if it is not at the end.
 */

   public void moveCursorForward();

/**
 * Moves the cursor backward one character, if it is not at the beginning.
 */

   public void moveCursorBackward();

/**
 * Moves the cursor to the start of this buffer.
 */

   public void moveCursorToStart();

/**
 * Moves the cursor to the end of this buffer.
 */

   public void moveCursorToEnd();

/**
 * Inserts the character ch, leaving the cursor after the inserted character.
 */

   public void insertCharacter(char ch);

/**
 * Deletes the character immediately after the cursor, if any.
 */

   public void deleteCharacter();

/**
 * Returns the contents of the buffer as a string.
 */

   public String getText();

/**
 * Returns the index of the cursor.
 */

   public int getCursor();

}
```

Thinking about the underlying representation

Even at this early stage, you probably have some ideas about what internal data structures might be appropriate. Because the buffer contains an ordered sequence of characters, one seemingly obvious choice is to use a **String** or an **ArrayList** of characters as the underlying representation. As long as these classes are available, either would be an appropriate choice. The goal of this chapter, however, is to investigate how the choice of representation affects the efficiency of applications. That point is harder to understand if the program uses higher-level structures like **String** and **ArrayList**, because the inner workings of those classes are not visible to clients. If you choose instead to limit your implementation to simpler structures, every operation becomes visible, and it is therefore easier to determine the relative efficiency of various competing designs. That logic suggests using a character array as the underlying representation, because array operations have no hidden costs.

Although using an array to represent the buffer is certainly a reasonable approach, there are other representations that offer interesting possibilities. The fundamental lesson in this chapter—and indeed in much of this book—is that you should not choose a particular representation hastily. In the case of the editor buffer, arrays are only one of several options, each of which has certain advantages and disadvantages. After evaluating the tradeoffs, you may decide to use one strategy in a certain set of circumstances and a different strategy in another. At the same time, it is important to note that, no matter what representation you choose, the editor must always be able to perform the same set of commands. Thus, the external behavior of an editor buffer must remain the same even if the underlying representation changes.

Coding the editor application

Once you have defined the public interface, you are free to go back and write the editor application, even though you have not yet implemented the buffer class or settled on an appropriate internal representation. When you're writing the editor application, the only important consideration is what each of the operations does. At this level, the details of the implementation are unimportant.

As long as you limit yourself to the commands in Figure 12-2, writing the editor program is relatively simple. The program runs as a loop in which it reads a series of editor commands from the console. Whenever the user enters a command, the program looks at the first character and then performs the requested operation by calling the appropriate method on the buffer. The code for the command-based editor appears in Figure 12-4. The **SimpleTextEditor** class does not construct the editor buffer itself, but relies instead on the calling program to construct an instance of any concrete class that implements the **EditorBuffer** interface.

FIGURE 12-4 Simple text editor to test the `EditorBuffer` abstraction

```
/*
 * File: SimpleTextEditor.java
 * ------------------------------
 * This file implements a simple command-based text editor.
 */

package edu.stanford.cs.javacs2.ch12;

import edu.stanford.cs.console.Console;
import edu.stanford.cs.console.SystemConsole;

public abstract class SimpleTextEditor {

/* Defines the method that clients must implement to create the buffer */

    public abstract EditorBuffer createEditorBuffer();

/* Runs the text editor */

    public void run() {
        Console console = new SystemConsole();
        EditorBuffer buffer = createEditorBuffer();
        while (true) {
            String cmd = console.nextLine("*");
            if (!cmd.equals("")) executeCommand(buffer, cmd);
        }
    }

/* Executes the command on the editor buffer */

    private void executeCommand(EditorBuffer buffer, String cmd) {
        switch (Character.toUpperCase(cmd.charAt(0))) {
          case 'I': for (int i = 1; i < cmd.length(); i++) {
                        buffer.insertCharacter(cmd.charAt(i));
                    }
                    displayBuffer(buffer);
                    break;
          case 'D': buffer.deleteCharacter(); displayBuffer(buffer); break;
          case 'F': buffer.moveCursorForward(); displayBuffer(buffer); break;
          case 'B': buffer.moveCursorBackward(); displayBuffer(buffer); break;
          case 'J': buffer.moveCursorToStart(); displayBuffer(buffer); break;
          case 'E': buffer.moveCursorToEnd(); displayBuffer(buffer); break;
          case 'H': printHelpText(); break;
          case 'Q': System.exit(0);
          default:  System.out.println("Illegal command"); break;
        }
```

FIGURE 12-4 Simple text editor to test the `EditorBuffer` class (continued)

```
/* Displays the state of the buffer including the position of the cursor */

    private void displayBuffer(EditorBuffer buffer) {
        String str = buffer.getText();
        for (int i = 0; i < str.length(); i++) {
            System.out.print(" " + str.charAt(i));
        }
        System.out.println();
        int cursor = buffer.getCursor();
        for (int i = 0; i < cursor; i++) {
            System.out.print("  ");
        }
        System.out.println("^");
    }

/* Displays a message showing the legal commands */

    private void printHelpText() {
        System.out.println("Editor commands:");
        System.out.println("  Iabc   Inserts abc at the cursor position");
        System.out.println("  F      Moves the cursor forward one character");
        System.out.println("  B      Moves the cursor backward one character");
        System.out.println("  D      Deletes the character after the cursor");
        System.out.println("  J      Jumps to the beginning of the buffer");
        System.out.println("  E      Jumps to the end of the buffer");
        System.out.println("  H      Prints this message");
        System.out.println("  Q      Exits from the editor program");
    }

}
```

The `SimpleTextEditor` class is abstract and requires each subclass to define a `createEditorBuffer` method appropriate to the representation strategy. The `ArrayEditor` application, for example, will use this method to create an `ArrayBuffer` object that implements the `EditorBuffer` interface.

The one method call in the `SimpleTextEditor` implementation that you have not yet seen is the call to `System.exit` in the code to implement the `Q` command. The `System.exit` method exits from the Java interpreter, passing along an integer that serves as a status indicator, which should be 0 for normal exit conditions.

12.3 An array-based implementation

As noted earlier in the section on "Thinking about the underlying representation," one of the possible representations for the buffer is an array of characters. Although this design is not the only option for representing the editor buffer, it is nonetheless a useful starting point. After all, the characters in the buffer form an ordered, homogeneous sequence, which is precisely the context in which one traditionally uses arrays. The array used to implement the buffer, however, cannot be of a fixed size, since the number of characters in the buffer changes over time. Unfortunately, the size of a Java array doesn't change once it has been allocated, so the representation for the buffer will have to use a more convoluted strategy.

The usual approach in such cases is to allocate an array that contains more space than you currently need. As long as the inserted characters fit within the existing capacity, everything is fine. If there is no longer room to insert a new character, you can expand the buffer capacity by allocating an entirely new array of a larger size and then copying the old array into the new one. When you create the buffer, you can allocate some number of array elements to get things started. In the code for the array-based buffer, the initial size of the array is determined by the following constant:

```
private static final int INITIAL_CAPACITY = 10;
```

When space runs out, the code increases the size by doubling the current capacity. That strategy is not as arbitrary as it might sound. As you will learn in Chapter 13, this doubling strategy helps to reduce the average execution cost of operations that might require expanding the buffer capacity.

Defining the private data structure

You can use this strategy to create a class called **ArrayBuffer** that implements the **EditorBuffer** interface using a character array. The **ArrayBuffer** class requires three instance variables: the array of characters contained in the buffer, the number of array positions that are actually in use, and the current position of the cursor. These instance variables have the following declarations:

```
private char[] array;
private int count;
private int cursor;
```

The constructor for the **ArrayBuffer** class simply initializes these variables, as follows:

```
public ArrayBuffer() {
    array = new char[INITIAL_CAPACITY];
    count = 0;
    cursor = 0;
}
```

After calling this constructor, the empty buffer looks like this:

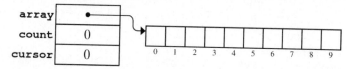

A buffer containing

H E L L O
    ^

with the cursor between the two **L** characters has the following structure:

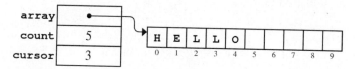

Implementing the buffer operations

Most of the editor operations for the array-based editor are easy to implement. Each of the four operations that move the cursor can be implemented by assigning a new value to the contents of the **cursor** field. Moving to the beginning of the buffer, for example, requires nothing more than assigning the value 0 to **cursor**; moving to the end is simply a matter of copying the **count** field into the **cursor** field. Similarly, moving forward and backward is a simple matter of incrementing or decrementing the **cursor** field, although it is important to make sure that the value of **cursor** doesn't go outside the legal range. You can see the code for these methods in the implementation of the **ArrayBuffer** class shown in Figure 12-5.

The only operations in Figure 12-5 that require any additional discussion are the **insertCharacter** and **deleteCharacter** methods. Because these methods might seem a little tricky, particularly to someone encountering them for the first time, it is worth including comments that document their operation. The code in Figure 12-5, for example, offers additional documentation for these particular methods in comments labeled "Implementation notes"; the simple methods that implement cursor motion are not documented individually.

The **insertCharacter** and **deleteCharacter** methods are interesting because each of them requires shifting characters in the array, either to make room for a character you want to insert or to close up space left by a deleted character. Suppose, for example, that you want to insert the character **X** at the cursor position in the buffer containing

H E L L O
    ^

FIGURE 12-5 **Array-based implementation of the editor buffer**

```
/*
 * File: ArrayBuffer.java
 * ------------------------
 * This file implements the EditorBuffer abstraction using an array of
 * characters as the underlying storage model.
 */

package edu.stanford.cs.javacs2.ch12;

/*
 * Implementation notes: ArrayBuffer
 * -----------------------------------
 * This class implements the EditorBuffer abstraction using an array of
 * characters.  In addition to the array, the structure keeps track of
 * the actual number of characters in the buffer (which is typically less
 * than the length of the array) and the current position of the cursor.
 */

public class ArrayBuffer implements EditorBuffer {

    public ArrayBuffer() {
        array = new char[INITIAL_CAPACITY];
        count = 0;
        cursor = 0;
    }

/*
 * Implementation notes: moveCursor methods
 * -----------------------------------------
 * The four moveCursor methods simply adjust the value of cursor.
 */

    public void moveCursorForward() {
        if (cursor < count) cursor++;
    }

    public void moveCursorBackward() {
        if (cursor > 0) cursor--;
    }

    public void moveCursorToStart() {
        cursor = 0;
    }

    public void moveCursorToEnd() {
        cursor = count;
    }
```

FIGURE 12-5 **Array-based implementation of the editor buffer (continued)**

```
/*
 * Implementation notes: character insertion and deletion
 * ------------------------------------------------------
 * Each of the functions that inserts or deletes characters must shift
 * all subsequent characters in the array, either to make room for new
 * insertions or to close up space left by deletions.
 */

   public void insertCharacter(char ch) {
      if (count == array.length) expandCapacity();
      for (int i = count; i > cursor; i--) {
         array[i] = array[i - 1];
      }
      array[cursor] = ch;
      count++;
      cursor++;
   }

   public void deleteCharacter() {
      if (cursor < count) {
         for (int i = cursor+1; i < count; i++) {
            array[i - 1] = array[i];
         }
         count--;
      }
   }

/* Simple getter methods: getText, getCursor */

   public String getText() {
      return new String(array, 0, count);
   }

   public int getCursor() {
      return cursor;
   }

/*
 * Implementation notes: expandCapacity
 * ------------------------------------
 * This private method doubles the size of the array whenever the old one
 * runs out of space.  To do so, expandCapacity allocates a new array,
 * copies the old characters to the new array, and then replaces the old
 * array with the new one.
 */

   private void expandCapacity() {
      char[] newArray = new char[2 * array.length];
      for (int i = 0; i < count; i++) {
         newArray[i] = array[i];
      }
      array = newArray;
   }
```

FIGURE 12-5 Array-based implementation of the editor buffer (continued)

```
/* Constants */

   private static final int INITIAL_CAPACITY = 10;

/* Private instance variables */

   private char[] array;      /* Allocated array of characters    */
   private int count;         /* Actual number of character in use */
   private int cursor;        /* Index of character after cursor   */

}
```

To do so in the array representation of the buffer, you first need to make sure that there is room in the array. If the **count** field is equal to the length of the array, there is no more room in the currently allocated array to accommodate the new character. In that case, it is necessary to expand the array capacity, which is accomplished by the private **expandCapacity** method, which looks like this:

```
private void expandCapacity() {
    char[] newArray = new char[2 * array.length];
    for (int i = 0; i < count; i++) {
        newArray[i] = array[i];
    }
    array = newArray;
}
```

The first line allocates a new array with twice the number of elements, the **for** loop copies the old array into the new one, and the last line of the method replaces the instance variable **array** with the new array. The memory space used for the old array is eventually reclaimed by the garbage collector.

Even if you don't have to expand the array capacity, you still have to take account of the fact that the extra space in the array is always at the end. To insert a character in the middle of the existing ones, you need to make room for that character at the current position of the cursor. The only way to get that space is to shift the remaining characters one position to the right, leaving the buffer structure in the following state:

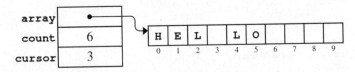

The resulting gap in the array gives you the space you need to insert the **x**, after which the cursor advances so that it follows the newly inserted character, leaving the following configuration:

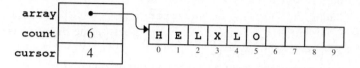

The **deleteCharacter** operation is similar in that it requires a loop to close the gap left by the deleted character.

Computational complexity of the array-based editor

In order to establish a baseline for comparison with other representations, it is useful to determine the computational complexity of the **ArrayBuffer** implementation of the editor. As usual, the goal of the complexity analysis is to understand how the execution time required for the editing operations varies qualitatively as a function of the problem size. In the editor example, the number of characters in the buffer is the best measure of problem size. For the editor buffer, you therefore need to determine how the number of characters in the buffer affects the running time of each of the editing operations.

For the array-based implementation, the easiest operations to understand are the ones that move the cursor. As an example, the method **moveCursorForward** has the following implementation:

```
public void moveCursorForward() {
    if (cursor < count) cursor++;
}
```

Even though the method includes a reference to the instance variable **count**, its execution time is independent of the buffer length. This method executes precisely the same operations no matter how long the buffer is: there is one test and, in almost all cases, one increment operation. Because the execution time is independent of *N*, the **moveCursorForward** operation runs in $O(1)$ time. The same analysis holds for the other operations that move the cursor, none of which involve any operations that depend on the length of the buffer.

But what about **insertCharacter**? In the **ArrayBuffer** implementation, the **insertCharacter** method contains the **for** loop

```
for (int i = count; i > cursor; i--) {
    array[i] = array[i - 1];
}
```

If you insert a character at the end of the buffer, this method runs pretty quickly, because there is no need to shift characters to make room for the new one. On the other hand, if you insert a character at the beginning of the buffer, every character in the buffer must be shifted one position rightward in the array. Thus, in the worst case, the running time for `insertCharacter` is proportional to the number of characters in the buffer and is therefore $O(N)$. Because the `deleteCharacter` operation has a similar structure, its complexity is also $O(N)$. The computational complexities for each of the editor operations appear in Figure 12-6.

The fact that the last two operations in the table require linear time has important performance implications for the editor program. If an editor uses arrays to represent its internal buffer, it will start to run more slowly as the number of characters in the buffer becomes large. Because this problem seems serious, it makes sense to explore other representational possibilities.

12.4 A stack-based implementation

The problem with the array implementation of the editor buffer is that insertions and deletions run slowly when they occur near the beginning of the buffer. When those same operations are applied at the end of the buffer, they run relatively quickly because there is no need to shift the characters in the internal array. This property suggests an approach to making things faster: force all insertions and deletions to occur at the end of the buffer. While this approach is completely impractical from the user's point of view, it does contain the seed of a workable idea.

The key insight necessary to make insertions and deletions faster is that you can divide the buffer at the cursor boundary and store the characters before and after the cursor in separate structures. Because all changes to the buffer occur at the cursor position, each of those structures behaves like a stack and can be represented using the `Stack<Character>` class from Chapter 6. The characters that precede the cursor are pushed on one stack so that the beginning of the buffer is at the base and

| FIGURE 12-6 | Computational complexity of the array-based buffer |

Operation	Array
`moveCursorForward`	$O(1)$
`moveCursorBackward`	$O(1)$
`moveCursorToStart`	$O(1)$
`moveCursorToEnd`	$O(1)$
`insertCharacter`	$O(N)$
`deleteCharacter`	$O(N)$

the character just before the cursor is at the top. The characters after the cursor are stored in the opposite direction, with the end of the buffer at the base of the stack and the character just after the cursor at the top.

The best way to illustrate this structure is with a diagram. If the buffer contains

$$H\ E\ L\underset{\wedge}{L}\ O$$

the two-stack representation of the buffer looks like this:

```
  L
  E      L
  H      O
before   after
```

To read the contents of the buffer, it is necessary to read up through the characters in the **before** stack and then down the **after** stack, as indicated by the arrow.

Defining the private data structure

If you implement the buffer using this strategy, the only instance variables you need are a pair of stacks, one to hold the characters before the cursor and another to hold the ones that come after it. For the stack-based buffer, the class declares only the following two instance variables:

```
private Stack<Character> before;
private Stack<Character> after;
```

It is important to note that the cursor is not explicitly represented in this model but is instead simply the boundary between the two stacks.

Implementing the buffer operations

In the stack model, implementing most of the operations for the editor is surprisingly easy. For example, moving backward consists of popping a character from the **before** stack and pushing it back on the **after** stack. Moving forward is entirely symmetrical. Inserting a character consists of pushing that character on the **before** stack. Deleting a character consists of popping a character from the **after** stack and throwing it away.

This conceptual outline makes it easy to write the code for the stack-based editor, which appears in Figure 12-7. Four of the commands—**insertCharacter**, **deleteCharacter**, **moveCursorForward**, and **moveCursorBackward**—run in constant time because the stack operations they call are themselves $O(1)$ operations.

FIGURE 12-7 Stack-based implementation of the editor buffer

```java
/*
 * File: StackBuffer.java
 * ------------------------
 * This file implements the EditorBuffer abstraction using a pair of stacks.
 */

package edu.stanford.cs.javacs2.ch12;

import java.util.Stack;

/*
 * Implementation notes: StackBuffer
 * ---------------------------------
 * This class implements the EditorBuffer abstraction using a pair of stacks.
 * Characters before the cursor are stored in a stack named "before"; those
 * after the cursor are stored in a stack named "after".  In each case, the
 * characters closest to the cursor are closer to the top of the stack.
 */

public class StackBuffer implements EditorBuffer {

    public StackBuffer() {
        before = new Stack<Character>();
        after = new Stack<Character>();
    }

/*
 * Implementation notes: moveCursor methods
 * ----------------------------------------
 * These methods use push and pop to transfer values between the two stacks.
 */

    public void moveCursorForward() {
        if (!after.isEmpty()) {
            before.push(after.pop());
        }
    }

    public void moveCursorBackward() {
        if (!before.isEmpty()) {
            after.push(before.pop());
        }
    }

    public void moveCursorToStart() {
        while (!before.isEmpty()) {
            after.push(before.pop());
        }
    }

    public void moveCursorToEnd() {
        while (!after.isEmpty()) {
            before.push(after.pop());
        }
    }
```

☞

FIGURE 12-7 Stack-based implementation of the editor buffer (continued)

```
/*
 * Implementation notes: character insertion and deletion
 * -------------------------------------------------------
 * Each of the functions that inserts or deletes characters can do so
 * with a single push or pop operation.
 */

   public void insertCharacter(char ch) {
      before.push(ch);
   }

   public void deleteCharacter() {
      if (!after.isEmpty()) {
         after.pop();
      }
   }

/*
 * Implementation notes: getText and getCursor
 * --------------------------------------------
 * This implementation of getText uses only the push, pop, size, and isEmpty
 * methods, which are fundamental primitives for the stack abstraction.  The
 * code must restore the contents of the stacks after creating the string.
 */

   public String getText() {
      int nBefore = before.size();
      int nAfter = after.size();
      String str = "";
      while (!before.isEmpty()) {
         str = before.pop() + str;
      }
      while (!after.isEmpty()) {
         str += after.pop();
      }
      for (int i = 0; i < nBefore; i++) {
         before.push(str.charAt(i));
      }
      for (int i = nBefore + nAfter - 1; i >= nBefore; i--) {
         after.push(str.charAt(i));
      }
      return str;
   }

   public int getCursor() {
      return before.size();
   }

/* Private instance variables */

   private Stack<Character> before;    /* Characters before the cursor */
   private Stack<Character> after;     /* Characters after the cursor  */
}
```

But what about the two remaining operations? The `moveCursorToStart` and `moveCursorToEnd` methods each require the program to transfer the entire contents of one of the stacks to the other. Given the operations provided by the `CharStack` class, the only way to accomplish this operation is to pop values from one stack and push them back on the other stack, one value at a time, until the original stack is empty. For example, the `moveCursorToEnd` operation has the following implementation:

```
void moveCursorToEnd() {
    while (!after.isEmpty()) {
        before.push(after.pop());
    }
}
```

These implementations have the desired effect, but require $O(N)$ time in the worst case.

Comparing computational complexities

Figure 12-8 shows the computational complexity of the editor operations for both the array- and the stack-based versions of the editor. Which implementation is better? Without some knowledge of the usage pattern, it is impossible to answer this question. Knowing a little about the way people use editors, however, suggests that the stack-based strategy is likely to be more efficient because the slow operations for the array implementation (insertion and deletion) are used much more frequently than the slow operations for the stack implementation (moving the cursor a long distance).

While this tradeoff seems reasonable given the relative frequency of the operations involved, it makes sense to ask whether it is possible to do even better. After all, it is now true that each of the six fundamental editing operations runs in constant time in at least one of the two editor implementations. Insertion is slow in

---

FIGURE 12-8 Computational complexity of the array- and stack-based buffers

Operation	Array	Stack
moveCursorForward	$O(1)$	$O(1)$
moveCursorBackward	$O(1)$	$O(1)$
moveCursorToStart	$O(1)$	$O(N)$
moveCursorToEnd	$O(1)$	$O(N)$
insertCharacter	$O(N)$	$O(1)$
deleteCharacter	$O(N)$	$O(1)$

the array implementation but fast when the implementation uses the stack approach. By contrast, moving to the front of the buffer is fast in the array case but slow in the stack case. None of the operations, however, seems to be *fundamentally* slow, since there is always some implementation that makes that operation fast. Is it possible to develop an implementation in which all the operations are fast? The answer to this question turns out to be "yes," but discovering the key to the puzzle will require you to learn a new approach to representing ordering relationships in a data structure.

12.5 A list-based implementation

As an initial step toward finding a more efficient representation for the editor buffer, it makes sense to examine why the previous approaches have failed to provide efficient service for certain operations. In the case of the array implementation, the answer is obvious: the problem comes from the fact that you have to move a large number of characters whenever you need to insert some new text near the beginning of the buffer. For example, suppose that you were trying to enter the alphabet and instead typed

```
A  C  D  E  F  G  H  I  J  K  L  M  N  O  P  Q  R  S  T  U  V  W  X  Y  Z
```

When you discovered that you'd left out the letter **B**, you would have to shift each of the next 24 characters one position to the right in order to make room for the missing letter. A modern computer could handle this shifting operation relatively quickly as long as the buffer did not grow too large; even so, the delay would eventually become noticeable for such an operation if the number of characters in the buffer became sufficiently large.

Let's suppose, however, that you were writing before the invention of modern computers. Imagine for the moment that you are Thomas Jefferson, busily at work drafting the Declaration of Independence. In the list of grievances against King George, you carefully pen the following text:

Our repeated Petitions have been answered by repeated injury.

Unfortunately, just at the last minute, someone decides that this sentence needs the word *only* before the phrase *by repeated injury*. After contesting the issue for a while, you might decide—as someone clearly did in the actual text of the Declaration—to take out your pen and add the missing word like this:

Our repeated Petitions have been answered by repeated injury.

If you applied the same strategy to the alphabet with the missing letter, you might simply make the following edit:

$$\overset{\text{B}}{\underset{\wedge}{\text{A}}}\text{ C D E F G H I J K L M N O P Q R S T U V W X Y Z}$$

The result is perhaps a trifle inelegant, but nonetheless acceptable in such desperate circumstances.

The advantage of this age-old editing strategy is that it allows you to suspend the rule that says all letters are arranged in sequence in precisely the form in which they appear on the printed page. The caret symbol below the line tells your eyes that, after reading the **A**, you have to then move up, read the **B**, come back down, read the **C**, and then continue with the sequence. It is also important to notice another advantage of using this insertion strategy. No matter how long the line is, all you have to draw is the new character and the caret symbol. When you use pencil and paper, insertion runs in constant time.

A linked list allows you to achieve much the same effect. If the characters are stored in a linked list rather than a character array, all you need to do to insert a missing character is change a couple of pointers. If the original contents of the buffer were stored as the linked list

$$\text{A→C→D→E→F→G→H→I→J→K→L→M→N→O→P→Q→R→S→T→U→V→W→X→Y→Z}$$

all you would need to do is (1) write the **B** down somewhere, (2) draw an arrow from **B** to the letter to which **A** is pointing (which is currently the **C**), and (3) change the arrow pointing from the **A** so that it now points to the **B**, as follows:

$$\overset{\leftarrow\text{B}}{\text{A}}\text{→C→D→E→F→G→H→I→J→K→L→M→N→O→P→Q→R→S→T→U→V→W→X→Y→Z}$$

This structure has much the same form as the linked-list example from Chapter 8. In this case, the definition of the inner class `Cell` has the following form:

```
private static class Cell {
    char ch;
    Cell link;
};
```

To represent the chain of characters, all you need to do is store the characters in the cells of a linked list. The list for the characters **ABC**, for example, looks like this:

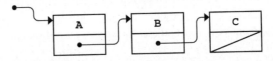

At first glance, it might seem that the linked list is all you need to represent the contents of the buffer. The only problem is that you also need to represent the cursor. If you store the cursor as an integer, finding the current position will require counting through the cells in the list until you reach the desired index. That strategy requires linear time. A better approach is to define the **ListBuffer** class so that it maintains two references to **Cell** objects, one that points to the start of the list and another that marks the cursor's current position.

This design seems reasonable until you try to figure out how the cursor reference works in detail. If you have a buffer containing three characters, your first reaction is almost certain to be that you using a linked list with three cells. Unfortunately, there's a bit of a problem. In a buffer containing three characters, there are *four* possible positions for the cursor, as follows:

A B C   A B C   A B C   A B C
^   ^   ^   ^

If there are only three cells to which the **cursor** field can point, it is not clear how you could represent each of the possible cursor locations.

There are many tactical approaches to solving this problem, but the one that often turns out to be the best is to allocate an extra cell so that the list contains one cell for each possible insertion point. Typically, this cell goes at the beginning of the list and is called a ***dummy cell***. The value of the **ch** field in the dummy cell is irrelevant and is indicated in diagrams by filling that field with a gray background.

When you use the dummy cell approach, the **cursor** field points to the cell immediately before the logical insertion point. For example, a buffer containing **ABC** with the cursor at the beginning of the buffer would look like this:

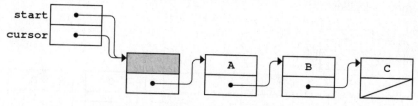

Both **start** and **cursor** point to the dummy cell, and insertions occur immediately after this cell. If the **cursor** field instead indicates the end of the buffer, the diagram looks like this:

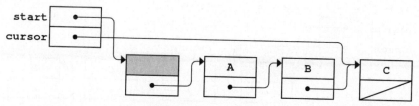

The only instance variables you need in the **ListBuffer** class are the **start** and **cursor** references. Even though the rest of this structure is not formally part of the object, it will help programmers who later have to work with this structure if you document the design of the data structure somewhere in the code.

Insertion into a linked-list buffer

No matter where the cursor is positioned, the insertion operation for a linked list consists of the following steps:

1. Allocate space for a new **Cell** object, and store the reference to this cell in the temporary variable **cp**.

2. Copy the character to be inserted into the **ch** field of the new cell.

3. Go to the cell indicated by the **cursor** field of the buffer and copy its link field to the **link** field of the new cell. This operation makes sure that you don't lose the characters that lie beyond the current cursor position.

4. Change the **link** field in the cell addressed by the cursor so that it points to the new cell.

5. Change the **cursor** field in the buffer so that it also points to the new cell. This operation ensures that the next character will be inserted after this one in repeated insertion operations.

To illustrate this process, suppose that you want to insert the letter **B** into a buffer that currently contains

A C D
^

with the cursor between the **A** and the **C** as shown. The situation prior to the insertion looks like this:

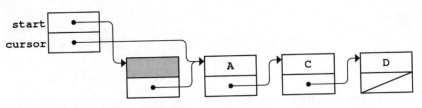

Step 1 in the insertion strategy consists of allocating a new cell and storing a reference to it in the variable **cp**, as shown:

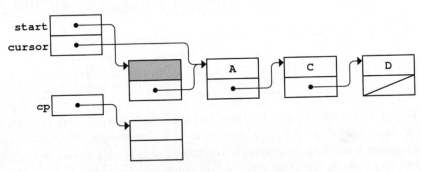

In step 2, you store the character **B** into the **ch** field of the new cell, which leaves the following configuration:

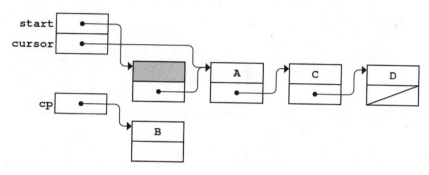

In step 3, you copy the **link** field from the cell whose address appears in the **cursor** field into the **link** field of the new cell. That **link** field points to the cell containing **C**, so the resulting diagram looks like this:

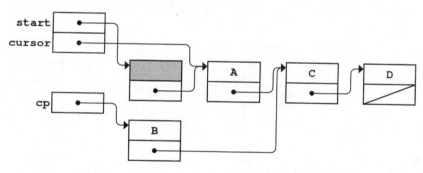

In step 4, you change the **link** field in the current cell addressed by the cursor so that it points to the newly allocated cell, as follows:

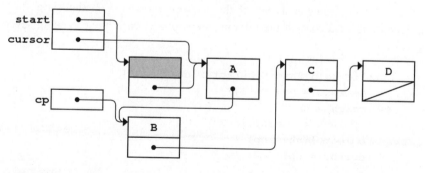

The buffer now has the correct contents. If you follow the arrows from the dummy cell at the beginning of the buffer, you encounter the cells containing **A**, **B**, **C**, and **D**, in order along the path.

The final step consists of changing the **cursor** field in the buffer structure so that it also points to the new cell, which results in this configuration:

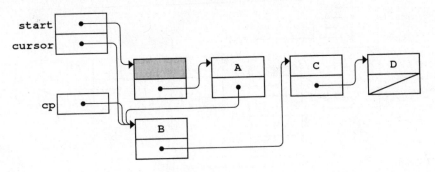

When the program returns from the **insertCharacter** method, the temporary variable **cp** is released, which produces the following final buffer state:

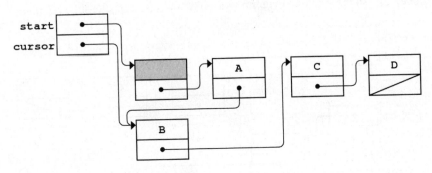

which represents the buffer contents

A B C D
  ^

The following implementation of the **insertCharacter** method is a simple translation into Java code of the informal steps illustrated in the preceding several diagrams:

```java
public void insertCharacter(char ch) {
    Cell cp = new Cell();
    cp.ch = ch;
    cp.link = cursor.link;
    cursor.link = cp;
    cursor = cp;
}
```

Because there are no loops inside this method, the **insertCharacter** method now runs in constant time.

Deletion in a linked-list buffer

To delete a cell in a linked list, all you have to do is remove it from the reference chain. Let's assume that the current contents of the buffer are

A B C
  ^

which has the following graphical representation:

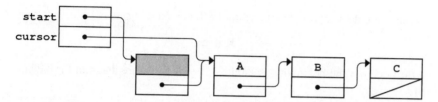

Deleting the character after the cursor requires you to eliminate the cell containing the **B** by changing the `link` field of the cell containing **A** so that it points to the next character further on. To find that character, you need to follow the `link` field from the current cell and continue on to the following `link` field. The necessary statement is therefore

```
cursor.link = cursor.link.link;
```

Executing this statement leaves the buffer in the following state:

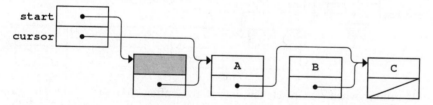

The code for **deleteCharacter** therefore looks like this:

```
public void deleteCharacter() {
   if (cursor.link != null) {
      cursor.link = cursor.link.link;
   }
}
```

The cell containing **B** is no longer accessible and will eventually be reclaimed by the garbage collector.

Cursor motion in the linked-list representation

The remaining operations in the **ListBuffer** class simply move the cursor. How would you go about implementing these operations in the linked-list buffer? Two of these operations—**moveCursorForward** and **moveCursorToStart**—are easy to perform in the linked-list model. To move the cursor forward, for example, all you have to do is pick up the **link** field from the current cell and make that reference be the new current cell by storing it in the **cursor** field of the buffer. The statement necessary to accomplish this operation is simply

```
cursor = cursor.link;
```

As an example, suppose that the editor buffer contains

A B C
^

with the cursor at the beginning as shown. The list structure diagram for the buffer is then

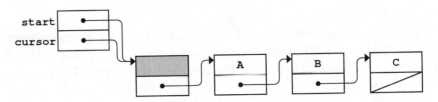

and the result of executing the **moveCursorForward** operation is

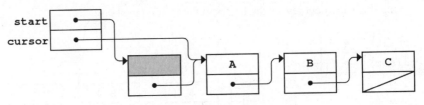

Of course, when you reach the end of the buffer, you can no longer move forward. Since the implementation of **moveCursorForward** must check for this case, the complete method definition looks like this:

```
public void moveCursorForward() {
    if (cursor.link != null) {
        cursor = cursor.link;
    }
}
```

Moving the cursor to the beginning of the buffer is equally easy. No matter where the cursor is, you can always restore it to the beginning of the buffer by copying the **start** field into the **cursor** field. Thus, the implementation of **moveCursorToStart** is simply

```
public void moveCursorToStart() {
    cursor = start;
}
```

The operations **moveCursorBackward** and **moveCursorToEnd**, however, are more complicated. Suppose, for example, that the cursor is sitting at the end of a buffer containing the characters **ABC** and that you want to move it back one position. In its graphical representation, the buffer looks like this:

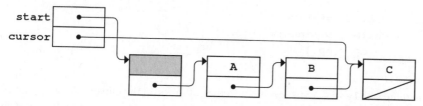

Given the structure used by the **ListBuffer** class, there is no constant-time strategy for backing up the cursor. The problem is that you have no straightforward way—given the information you can see—to find out what cell precedes the current one. Linked lists allow you to follow a chain from one **link** field to the object it points to, but there is no way to reverse the direction. Given only a reference to a cell, it is impossible to find out what cells point to it. With respect to the diagrams, the effect of this restriction is that you can move from the dot at the base of an arrow to the cell to which the arrow points, but you can never go from an arrowhead back to its base.

In the list-structure representation of the buffer, you have to implement every operation in terms of the data that you can see from the buffer structure itself, which contains the **start** and the **cursor** references. Looking at just the **cursor** field and following the links that are accessible from that position does not seem promising, because the only cell reachable on that chain is the very last cell in the buffer. The **start** reference, however, gives you access to the entire linked-list chain. At the same time, you clearly need to consider the value of the **cursor** field, because you have to back up from that position.

Before abandoning hope, you need to recognize that it is possible to find the cell that precedes the current cell. It is just not possible to do so in constant time. If you start at the beginning of the buffer and follow the links through all its cells, you will eventually find a cell whose **link** field points to the same cell as the **cursor** field in the **EditorBuffer** itself. This cell must be the preceding cell in the list. Once you find it, you can simply change the **cursor** field in the **EditorBuffer** to point to that cell, which has the effect of moving the cursor backward.

You can write the code to find the cursor position using the traditional **for** loop idiom for linked lists introduced in Chapter 7. There are, however, two problems with this approach. First, you need to use the value of the index variable after the loop is finished, which means that you need to declare it outside the loop. Second, if you do use the standard **for** loop idiom, you'll discover that there is absolutely nothing to do in the body, since all you care about is the final value of the pointer. Control structures with empty bodies give readers the impression that there is something missing and can make the code harder to read.

For these reasons, it is easier to code this loop using a **while** statement, like this:

```
Cell cp = start;
while (cp.link != cursor) {
   cp = cp.link;
}
```

When the **while** loop exits, **cp** is set to the cell prior to the cursor. As with moving forward, you need to protect this loop against trying to move past the limits of the buffer, so the complete code for **moveCursorBackward** would be

```
public void moveCursorBackward() {
   if (cursor != start) {
      Cell cp = start;
      while (cp.link != cursor) {
         cp = cp.link;
      }
      cursor = cp;
   }
}
```

For the same reasons, you can implement **moveCursorToEnd** only by moving the cursor forward until it finds the **null** in the last cell in the chain, as follows:

```
public void moveCursorToEnd() {
   while (cursor.link != null) {
      cursor = cursor.link;
   }
}
```

Completing the buffer implementation

The full definition of the **ListBuffer** class includes several methods that have yet to be implemented: the constructor and the methods **getText** and **getCursor**. In the constructor, the only wrinkle is that you need to remember the existence of the dummy cell. The code must allocate the dummy cell that is present even in the empty buffer. Once you remember this detail, however, the code is fairly straightforward. The complete implementation of the **ListBuffer** class appears in Figure 12-9.

FIGURE 12-9 List-based implementation of the editor ListBuffer

```
/*
 * File: ListBuffer.java
 * -----------------------
 * This file implements the EditorBuffer abstraction using a linked
 * list as the underlying storage model.
 */

package edu.stanford.cs.javacs2.ch12;

/*
 * Implementation notes: ListBuffer
 * ------------------------------------
 * This class implements the EditorBuffer abstraction using a linked list.
 * In the linked-list model, the characters in the buffer are stored in a
 * list of Cell structures, each of which contains a character and a
 * reference to the next cell in the chain.  To simplify the code used to
 * maintain the cursor, this implementation adds an extra "dummy cell" at
 * the beginning of the list.  The character in this cell is not used, but
 * having it in the data structure simplifies the code.
 *
 * The following diagram shows the structure of the list-based buffer
 * containing "ABC" with the cursor at the beginning:
 *
 *        +-----+       +-----+       +-----+       +-----+       +-----+
 *  start | o---+--==>|     |   -->|  A  |   -->|  B  |   -->|  C  |
 *        +-----+  /   +-----+  /   +-----+  /   +-----+  /   +-----+
 * cursor | o---+--    | o---+--    | o---+--    | o---+--    |  /  |
 *        +-----+       +-----+       +-----+       +-----+       +-----+
 */

public class ListBuffer implements EditorBuffer {

/* Cell structure */

   private static class Cell {
      char ch;                /* The character in the cell                */
      Cell link;              /* A reference to the next cell in the chain */
   }

/* Constructor */

   public ListBuffer() {
      start = cursor = new Cell();
      start.link = null;
   }
```

FIGURE 12-9 List-based implementation of the editor buffer (continued)

```
/*
 * Implementation notes: moveCursor methods
 * -----------------------------------------------
 * The four methods that move the cursor have different time complexities
 * because the structure of a linked list is asymmetrical with respect to
 * moving backward and forward.  The moveCursorForward and moveCursorToStart
 * methods operate in constant time.  By contrast, the moveCursorBackward
 * and moveCursorToEnd methods each require a loop that runs in linear time.
 */

   public void moveCursorForward() {
      if (cursor.link != null) {
         cursor = cursor.link;
      }
   }

   public void moveCursorBackward() {
      if (cursor != start) {
         Cell cp = start;
         while (cp.link != cursor) {
            cp = cp.link;
         }
         cursor = cp;
      }
   }

   public void moveCursorToStart() {
      cursor = start;
   }

   public void moveCursorToEnd() {
      while (cursor.link != null) {
         cursor = cursor.link;
      }
   }

/*
 * Implementation notes: insertCharacter
 * -----------------------------------------------
 * The steps required to insert a new character are:
 *
 * 1. Create a new cell and put the new character in it.
 * 2. Copy the reference indicating the rest of the list into the link.
 * 3. Update the link in the current cell to point to the new one.
 * 4. Move the cursor forward over the inserted character.
 */

   public void insertCharacter(char ch) {
      Cell cp = new Cell();
      cp.ch = ch;
      cp.link = cursor.link;
      cursor.link = cp;
      cursor = cp;
   }
```

FIGURE 12-9 List-based implementation of the editor buffer (continued)

```
/*
 * Implementation notes: deleteCharacter
 * --------------------------------------------
 * Deletion of the character requires removing the next cell from the
 * chain by changing the link field so that it points to the following
 * cell.
 */

   public void deleteCharacter() {
      if (cursor.link != null) {
         cursor.link = cursor.link.link;
      }
   }

/*
 * Implementation notes: getText and getCursor
 * --------------------------------------------
 * The getText method uses the standard linked-list pattern to loop
 * through the cells in the linked list.  The getCursor method counts
 * the characters in the list until it reaches the cursor.
 */

   public String getText() {
      String str = "";
      for (Cell cp = start.link; cp != null; cp = cp.link) {
         str += cp.ch;
      }
      return str;
   }

   public int getCursor() {
      int nChars = 0;
      for (Cell cp = start; cp != cursor; cp = cp.link) {
         nChars++;
      }
      return nChars;
   }

/* Private instance variables */

   private Cell start;      /* Reference to the dummy cell               */
   private Cell cursor;     /* Reference to the cell before the cursor */

}
```

| FIGURE 12-10 | Computational complexity of the three buffer models | | | |

Operation	Array	Stack	List
moveCursorForward	$O(1)$	$O(1)$	$O(1)$
moveCursorBackward	$O(1)$	$O(1)$	$O(N)$
moveCursorToStart	$O(1)$	$O(N)$	$O(1)$
moveCursorToEnd	$O(1)$	$O(N)$	$O(N)$
insertCharacter	$O(N)$	$O(1)$	$O(1)$
deleteCharacter	$O(N)$	$O(1)$	$O(1)$

Computational complexity of the linked-list buffer

From the discussion in the preceding section, it is easy to add another column to the complexity table showing the cost of the fundamental editing operations as a function of the number of characters in the buffer. The new table, which includes the data for all three implementations, appears in Figure 12-10.

Unfortunately, the table for the list structure representation still contains two $O(N)$ operations, **moveCursorBackward** and **moveCursorToEnd**. The problem with this representation is that the link pointers impose a preferred direction on the implementation: moving forward is easy because the pointers move in the forward direction.

Doubly linked lists

The good news is that this problem is easy to solve. To get around the problem that the links run in only one direction, all you need to do is make the pointers symmetrical. In addition to having a pointer from each cell that indicates the next one, you can also include a pointer to the previous cell. The resulting structure is called a *doubly linked list.*

Each cell in the doubly linked list has two link fields, a **prev** field that points to the previous cell and a **next** field that points to the next one. For reasons that will become clear when you implement the primitive operations, it simplifies the manipulation of the structure if the **prev** field of the dummy cell points to the end of the buffer and the **next** field of the last cell points back to the dummy cell.

If you use this design, the doubly linked representation of the buffer containing

A B C

looks like this:

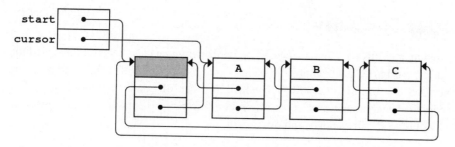

There are quite a few pointers in this diagram, which makes it is easy to get confused. On the other hand, the structure has all the information you need to implement each of the fundamental editing operations in constant time. The actual implementation, however, is left as an exercise so that you can refine your understanding of linked lists.

Time-space tradeoffs

The fact that you can implement the **EditorBuffer** interface so that the standard editing operations all run in constant time is an important theoretical result. Unfortunately, that result may not in fact be so useful in practice, at least in the context of the editor application. By the time you get around to adding the **prev** field to each cell for the doubly linked list, you will end up using at least nine bytes of memory to represent each character. You may be able to perform editing operations very quickly, but you will use up memory at an extravagant rate. At this point, you face what computer scientists call a ***time-space tradeoff.*** You can improve the computational efficiency of your algorithm, but waste space in doing so. Wasting this space could matter a lot, if, for example, it meant that the maximum size of the file you could edit on your machine were only a tenth what it would have been if you had chosen the array representation.

When such situations arise in practice, it is usually possible to develop a hybrid strategy that allows you to select a point somewhere in the middle of the time-space tradeoff curve. For example, you could combine the array and linked-list strategies by representing the buffer as a doubly linked list of lines, where each line was represented using the array form. In this case, insertion at the beginning of a line would be a little slower, but only in proportion to the length of the line and not to the length of the entire buffer. On the other hand, this strategy requires link pointers for each line rather than for each character. Since a line typically contains many characters, using this representation would reduce the storage overhead considerably. Getting the details right on hybrid strategies can be a challenge, but it is important to know that such strategies exist and that there are ways to take advantage of algorithmic time improvements that are not prohibitively expensive in terms of their storage requirements.

Summary

Even though this chapter has focused on implementing a class representing an editor buffer, the buffer itself is not the main point. Text buffers that maintain a cursor position are useful in a relatively small number of application domains. The individual techniques used to improve the buffer representation are fundamental ideas that you will use over and over again.

Important points in this chapter include:

- The strategy used to represent a class can have a significant effect on the computational complexity of its operations.

- Although an array provides a workable representation for an editor buffer, you can improve its performance by using other representation strategies. Using a pair of stacks, for example, reduces the cost of insertion and deletion but makes it harder to move the cursor a long distance.

- If you are inserting and deleting values from a linked list, it is often convenient to allocate an extra dummy cell at the beginning of the list. The advantage of this technique is that the existence of the dummy cell reduces the number of special cases you need to consider in your code.

- Insertions and deletions at specified points in a linked list are constant-time operations.

- Doubly linked lists make it possible to traverse a list efficiently in both directions.

- Linked lists tend to be efficient in execution time but inefficient in their use of memory. In some cases, you may be able to design a hybrid strategy that allows you to combine the execution efficiency of linked lists with the space advantages of arrays.

 Review questions

1. True or false: The computational complexity of a program depends only on its algorithmic structure, not on the structures used to represent the data.

2. What does *wysiwyg* stand for?

3. In your own words, describe the purpose of the buffer abstraction used in this chapter.

4. What are the six commands implemented by the editor application? What are the corresponding public methods in the `EditorBuffer` interface?

5.   In addition to the methods that correspond to the editor commands, what other public operations are specified by the **EditorBuffer** interface?

6.   Which editor operations require linear time in the array representation of the editor buffer? What makes those operations slow?

7.   Draw a diagram showing the contents of the **before** and **after** stack in the two-stack representation of a buffer that contains the following text, with the cursor positioned as shown:

A B C D E F G H I J

8.   How is the cursor position indicated in the two-stack representation of the editor buffer?

9.   Which editor operations require linear time in the two-stack representation?

10. What is the purpose of the dummy cell in a linked list used to represent the editor buffer?

11. Does the dummy cell go at the beginning or the end of a linked list? Why?

12. What are the five steps required to insert a new character into the linked-list buffer?

13. Draw a diagram showing all the cells in the linked-list representation of a buffer that contains the following text, with the cursor positioned as shown:

H E L L O

14. Modify the diagram you drew in the preceding exercise to show what happens if you insert the character **X** at the cursor position.

15. Which editor operations require linear time in the linked-list representation of the editor buffer? What makes those operations slow?

16. What is a *time-space tradeoff?*

17. What modification can you make to the linked-list structure so that all six of the editor operations run in constant time?

18. What is the major drawback to the solution you offered in your answer to question 17? What might you do to improve the situation?

Exercises

1. Although the **SimpleTextEditor** application is useful for demonstrating the workings of the editor, it is not ideal as a test program, mostly because it relies on explicit input from the user. Design and implement a unit test for the **EditorBuffer** interface that exercises the methods comprehensively enough to uncover likely errors in the implementation.

2. Even though the stacks in the two-stack implementation of the **EditorBuffer** interface expand dynamically, the amount of character space required in the stacks is likely to be twice as large as that required in the corresponding array implementation. The problem is that each stack must be able to accommodate all the characters in the buffer. Suppose, for example, that you are working with a buffer containing N characters. If you're at the beginning of the buffer, those N characters are in the **after** stack; if you move to the end of the buffer, those N characters move to the **before** stack. As a result, each of the stacks must have a capacity of N characters.

    You can reduce the storage requirement in the two-stack implementation of the buffer by storing the two stacks at opposite ends of the same internal array. The **before** stack starts at the beginning of the array, while the **after** stack starts at the end. The two stacks then grow toward each other as indicated by the arrows in the following diagram:

    Reimplement the **EditorBuffer** interface using this representation (which is, in fact, the design strategy used in many editors today). Make sure that your program continues to have the same computational efficiency as the two-stack implementation in the text and that the buffer space expands dynamically as needed.

3. If you were using a real editor application, you would probably want the program to display the contents of the buffer on request rather than after every command. Change the implementation of the **SimpleTextEditor** application so that it no longer displays the buffer after every command and instead offers a **T** command that prints the contents. In contrast to the **displayBuffer** method included in Figure 12-4, the **T** command should simply print the contents of the buffer as a string, without showing the cursor position. A sample run of your new editor might look like this:

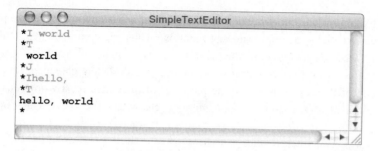

4. One of the serious limitations of the **SimpleTextEditor** application is that it offers no way to insert a newline character into the buffer, which makes it impossible to enter more than one line of data. Starting with the editor application from exercise 3, add an **A** command that reads text on subsequent lines, and ends when the user enters a line consisting of a single period (as in the **ed** editor on Unix systems). A sample run of this version of the editor might look like this:

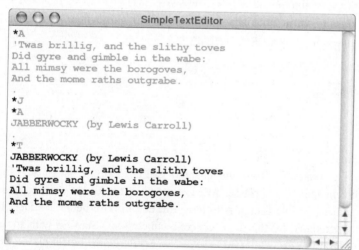

5. Rewrite the editor application given in Figure 12-4 so that the **F**, **B**, and **D** commands take a repetition count specified by a string of digits before the command letter. Thus, the command **17F** would move the cursor forward 17 character positions.

6. Add the methods **characterBeforeCursor** and **characterAfterCursor** to the **EditorBuffer** interface. As their names suggest, these methods return the character immediately before and after the cursor, or the null character if that character position would be outside the buffer boundaries. Implement these methods for each of the three buffer implementations, making sure that each method runs in constant time.

7. Extend the editor application so that the **F**, **B**, and **D** commands can be preceded with the letter **W** to indicate word motion. Thus, the command **WF** should move forward to the end of the next word, **WB** should move backward to the beginning of the preceding word, and **WD** should delete characters through the end of the next word. For the purposes of this exercise, a word consists of a consecutive sequence of alphanumeric characters (i.e., letters or digits) and includes any adjacent nonalphanumeric characters between the cursor and the word. This interpretation is easiest to see in the context of an example (which, for clarity, returns to the model of displaying the buffer after each command):

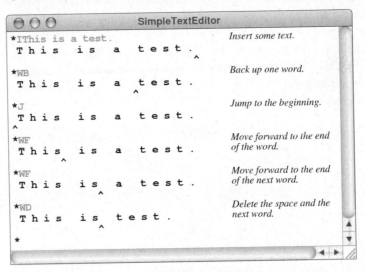

8. In the examples from the chapter, **EditorBuffer** is an interface that is implemented by the classes **ArrayBuffer**, **StackBuffer**, and **ListBuffer**. Another possible design is to have **EditorBuffer** be an abstract class that is then extended by the three concrete subclasses. Starting with the version of **EditorBuffer** you wrote for exercise 6, rewrite the buffer classes so that they use this new design.

9. The strategy of using an abstract class is most appropriate if you want to implement some methods at the level of the abstract class. For example, you can easily implement a cut/copy/paste facility at the level of the buffer without knowing the representation details just by making calls to **getText** and **getCursor** and then selecting the appropriate text. Implement this feature by adding the following methods to the abstract-class version of **EditorBuffer**:

```
public void cut(int n)
public void copy(int n)
public void paste()
```

Calling **cut** deletes the next **n** characters after the cursor but saves the deleted text in an internal buffer. Calling **copy** stores the characters without deleting them. Calling **paste** inserts the saved text at the cursor position.

Test your implementation by adding the commands **X**, **C**, and **V** to the editor application that call the **cut**, **copy**, and **paste** methods, respectively. The **X** and **C** commands should take a numeric argument to specify the number of characters using the technique described in exercise 5.

10. Extend the **EditorBuffer** class so that it exports a method

    ```
    public boolean search(String str)
    ```

    that searches the buffer starting at the current cursor position, looking for the next occurrence of the string **str**. If **str** exists in the buffer, **search** should leave the cursor after the last character in **str** and return the value **true**. If **str** does not occur between the cursor and the end of the buffer, then **search** should leave the cursor unchanged and return **false**. Add an **S** command to the editor that invokes the search operation, as shown in the following sample run:

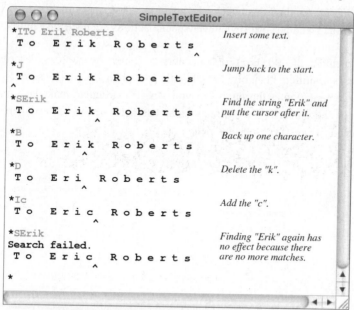

11. Without making any changes to the **EditorBuffer** interface, add an **R** command to the editor application that replaces the next occurrence of a pattern string with some other string, where the pattern and replacement strings appear after the **R** command, with the two strings separated by a slash, as shown:

```
┌─────────────────────────────────────────────────────────────┐
│  ○ ○ ○                    SimpleTextEditor                   │
├─────────────────────────────────────────────────────────────┤
│ *ITo Erik Roberts                                           │
│   To   Erik   Roberts                                       │
│                         ^                                   │
│                                                             │
│ *J                                                          │
│   To   Erik   Roberts                                       │
│   ^                                                         │
│                                                             │
│ *RErik/Eric                                                 │
│   To   Eric   Roberts                                       │
│                ^                                            │
│                                                             │
│ *                                                           │
└─────────────────────────────────────────────────────────────┘
```

12. The dummy cell strategy described in the text is useful because it reduces the number of special cases in the code, but it is not strictly necessary. Write a new implementation of the **ListBuffer** class in which you make the following changes:

   - The linked list contains no dummy cell—just a cell for every character.

   - A buffer in which the cursor occurs before the first character is indicated by storing **null** in the **cursor** field.

   - Every method that checks the position of the cursor makes a special test for **null** and performs whatever special actions are necessary in that case.

13. Implement the **EditorBuffer** interface using the strategy described in the section entitled "Doubly linked lists" on page 492. Be sure to test your implementation as thoroughly as you can. In particular, make sure that you can move the cursor in both directions across parts of the buffer where you have recently made insertions and deletions.

Chapter 13
Linear Structures

It does not come to me in quite so direct a line as that; it takes a bend or two, but nothing of consequence.

— Jane Austen, *Persuasion,* 1818

The **Stack**, **Queue**, and **ArrayList** classes introduced in Chapter 6 are examples of a general category of abstract data types called *linear structures,* in which the elements are arranged in a linear order. This chapter looks at several possible representations for these types and considers how the choice of representation affects efficiency.

Because the elements in a linear structure are arranged in an array-like order, using arrays to represent them seems like an obvious choice. As you saw in Chapter 12, other representations may have advantages over arrays, depending on the application. In this chapter, you will have a chance to see how each of these three abstractions—stacks, queues, and lists—can be implemented using either arrays or linked lists as their underlying representation.

This chapter has another purpose as well. As you know from Chapter 6, Java's collection classes—unlike the **EditorBuffer** class from Chapter 12—aren't limited to a single data type. The actual **Stack** class allows the client to specify the type of value by providing a type parameter, as in **Stack<Character>** or **Stack<Point>**. So far, however, you have only had a chance to use generic types as a client. In this chapter, you will learn how to implement them.

◼️ 13.1 Generic types

In computer science, being able to use the same code for more than one data type is called *polymorphism.* Programming languages implement polymorphism in a variety of ways. Java uses a model called *generic typing,* in which clients can supply type parameters to a general implementation of a class so that the compiler can check that the types are consistent. Java's collection classes all use generic typing, which means that you need to understand how that process works before you can implement similar classes on your own.

The implementation of generic types in Java

You have been using generic types as a client ever since you started using the **ArrayList** class in Chapter 5, so you should be feeling comfortable with the idea by now. For example, if you need a stack containing rational numbers as defined in Chapter 7, you would use the type **Stack<Rational>**. Similarly, if you need a map that associates strings and integers, you would presumably use some concrete subclass of **Map<String,Integer>**, such as **HashMap<String,Integer>**.

At one level, implementing your own generic types is surprisingly easy in Java, particularly in comparison to the much more complex process required for many other languages. All you have to do is add type parameters to the name of the class, just as you do as a client. This approach is illustrated in Figure 13-1, which defines a generic type for storing key-value pairs of the sort you find in a map.

FIGURE 13-1 Generic class to support key-value pairs

```java
/*
 * File: KeyValuePair.java
 * -------------------------
 * This file exports a generic class that stores an arbitrary key-value pair.
 */

package edu.stanford.cs.javacs2.ch13;

/**
 * This class stores an encapsulated key-value pair.
 */

public class KeyValuePair<K,V> {

/**
 * Creates a new key-value pair.
 */

   public KeyValuePair(K key, V value) {
      this.key = key;
      this.value = value;
   }

/**
 * Retrieves the key component of a key-value pair.
 */

   public K getKey() {
      return key;
   }

/**
 * Retrieves the value component of a key-value pair.
 */

   public V getValue() {
      return value;
   }

/**
 * Converts a key-value pair to a readable string representation.
 */

   @Override
   public String toString() {
      return "<" + key + ", " + value + ">";
   }

/* Private instance variables */

   private K key;
   private V value;

}
```

The class definition includes two type parameters, one for the key type and one for the value type, as follows:

```
public class KeyValuePair<K,V>
```

In keeping with Java's naming conventions, type parameters are designated using a single uppercase letter that suggests its role, as the **K** and **V** do in this example. Everywhere else in the class definition, these type parameters refer to the actual types used when the client supplies these parameters. The instance variables for the class are therefore declared as follows:

```
private K key;
private V value;
```

If the client then constructs a **KeyValuePair<String,Integer>**, these variables act as if they had been declared like this:

```
private String key;
private Integer value;
```

The constructor for **KeyValuePair** takes parameters of type **K** and **V**, which again stand as placeholders for the client-supplied types. For example, if you declare the variable **kvp** as

```
KeyValuePair<String,Integer> kvp =
    new KeyValuePair<String,Integer>("one", 1);
```

that variable is bound to an object that conceptually looks like this:

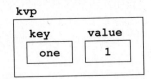

As in all collection classes, the **value** component is an **Integer** wrapper object rather than an **int**, but Java's strategy of boxing and unboxing allows you to ignore the distinction most of the time.

Restrictions on generic types

Although generic types in Java often appear simple to both the client and the implementer, they create a great deal of internal complexity. When Java was first released in 1995, there were no generic types. The elements of the various collection classes were all declared to be of type **Object**, which is the most general class in the Java hierarchy. Since every value in Java (other than the primitive types like `int` and `double`) is ultimately an `Object`, Java's early design made it possible to store any value in a collection.

Java's original design, however, created lots of problems. Most importantly, having every collection element be a general `Object` violated the principle of strong typing. Since there was no way for the programmer to specify the element type of an `ArrayList`, there was no way for the compiler to check that the values stored in that `ArrayList` had the correct type, or even that all the types in an `ArrayList` would be the same. Programmers who had used conceptually similar polymorphic features in other languages, most notably the template facility in C++, found Java's lack of type safety unacceptable and lobbied hard to include generic types in the language structure.

Unfortunately, it is extremely difficult to make significant changes in an existing programming language after it has been released. By the time generic types were added in Java 5.0, programmers had been using Java for almost a decade. The designers of the new generic features had to maintain *backward compatibility,* which is a fancy way of saying that Java programs written under the old assumptions had to work correctly after the new features were introduced. In the case of generic types, maintaining backward compatibility was a challenging requirement that took considerable resourcefulness on the part of the developers.

In the end, the generic types introduced with Java 5 vastly improved the language, but there are nonetheless some areas where the transition was not smooth. In particular, Java imposes the following restrictions on generic types, even though there is no reason other than backward compatibility to enforce these limitations:

- You can't use a primitive type as the value of a type parameter but must instead use the appropriate wrapper class.

- You can't use the type parameter name as a constructor to create new objects of that type.

- You can't declare static fields of a parameterized type.

- You can't embed parameterized types inside exceptions.

- You can't define more than one method that uses the same parameterized type.

- You can't create arrays of a parameterized type.

Most of these restrictions are of little consequence, because programmers have little reason to use the prohibited operations. The only one that matters a lot in practice is the last one in the list, which rules out creating arrays of parameterized types. This restriction is particularly important in this chapter, because arrays are in some sense the most natural model for linear structures. It is therefore necessary to develop a workaround, which is described in the following section.

The GenericArray class

As part of their strategy for maintaining backward compatibility, the designers of the generic type mechanism in Java 5.0 decided to retain the earlier model of using **Object** as the common type for all generic values, at least as those values are implemented inside the Java runtime system. The type parameters don't actually change the representation but instead provide the compiler with additional type information that it can use to ensure that types supplied by the client match the specifications imposed by the type parameters.

The easiest way to circumvent the restriction on creating arrays of parameterized values is to adopt the same strategy that Java uses internally. Although it is illegal to create an array of some parameter type **T**, it is perfectly legal to create an array of type **Object** and then assign values of type **T** to the elements of that array. As in the early versions of Java, this strategy compromises strong typing for the object array, but it is easy to encapsulate that problem inside a class that functions like an array from the client's point of view. The array-based implementations in this chapter all use the parameterized class **GenericArray<T>**, which appears in Figure 13-2. Inside the implementation, the elements of a **GenericArray** are stored as objects. From the client's point of view, the **GenericArray** class provides a strongly typed array-like structure that supports only three operations, specified by the methods **get**, **set**, and **size**. The constructor for **GenericArray** takes the number of elements in the array as a parameter and allocates that many spaces. Once created, the size of a **GenericArray** never changes, just as the length of a Java array remains fixed once it has been allocated.

The **GenericArray** class uses exactly the same representation strategy that the Java collection classes do. Like **GenericArray**, the library implementation of the **ArrayList** class creates an array of type **Object** and uses that array to store the actual elements. Moreover, just like the code in Figure 13-2, the library code uses the **@SuppressWarnings("unchecked")** annotation to ensure that the compiler does not issue a warning when it can't verify that the internal conversions maintain type safety. You don't worry about that problem when you use an **ArrayList**, and there is no more reason to worry about it for **GenericArray**. Moreover, once you have the **GenericArray** class, you can forget entirely about these details. From the client's perspective, the **GenericArray** class presents a strongly typed abstraction that lets you ignore one of Java's most frustrating restrictions.

The most important advantage of using the **GenericArray** class is that you can see its implementation and verify that the **get**, **put**, and **size** methods all run in constant time. Although you could use the library version of **ArrayList** to implement abstractions like stacks and queues, doing so would make it harder to assess the efficiency of the individual operations because the implementation is hidden behind an abstraction barrier.

FIGURE 13-2 Class to implement generic array operations without violating Java's restrictions

```java
/*
 * File: GenericArray.java
 * -----------------------
 * This class exists only to get around the limitations on arrays in
 * Java.  The GenericArray class is a parameterized type that acts like
 * an array in terms of its primitive operations, which are limited to
 * size, get, and put.  The size of a GenericArray object is fixed at the
 * time it is created.  All operations on a GenericArray can therefore be
 * guaranteed to operate in constant time.
 */

package edu.stanford.cs.javacs2.ch13;

public class GenericArray<T> {

/**
 * Allocates a GenericArray object with n elements.
 */

   public GenericArray(int n) {
      array = new Object[n];
   }

/**
 * Returns the length of the underlying array.
 */

   public int size() {
      return array.length;
   }

/**
 * Gets the element at index k.
 */

   @SuppressWarnings("unchecked")
   public T get(int k) {
      return (T) array[k];
   }

/**
 * Sets the element at index k to value.
 */

   public void set(int k, T value) {
      array[k] = value;
   }

/* Private instance variables */

   private Object[] array;

}
```

13.2 Implementing stacks

The simplest collection type of all is the **Stack** class. The behavior of the **Stack** class is defined by the six methods shown in Figure 13-3. As noted in Chapter 6, the **Stack** class predates the design of the Java Collection Framework and therefore does not fit as cleanly into Java's class hierarchy as the other collection classes. In particular, **Stack** is a concrete class instead of an interface in the way **Queue** and **List** are. Although this asymmetry reduces the overall elegance of the collection classes, it has the advantage of making **Stack** an ideal first example because it involves somewhat less complexity than the other classes.

Implementing stacks using an array structure

The standard implementation of the **Stack** class uses an array as its underlying representation and uses much the same overall strategy as the array implementation of the **EditorBuffer** in Chapter 12. As with the editor buffer, the only real complexity in the problem is allowing the stack to expand its internal capacity as necessary. The solution in this case is pretty much the same as it was in the earlier example: you simply allocate an array with some initial capacity and then double the capacity whenever you run out of space.

The code, however, requires some changes. It would be wonderful if you could allocate the initial array of elements using the code you saw in the **EditorBuffer** example, changing only the name of the type. The relevant line of code in the **ArrayBuffer** implementation was

```
array = new char[INITIAL_CAPACITY];
```

FIGURE 13-3 Methods exported by the **Stack** class

Constructor	
`Stack<T>()`	Creates an empty stack capable of holding values of the specified type.

Methods	
`size()`	Returns the number of elements currently on the stack.
`isEmpty()`	Returns **true** if the stack is empty.
`push(value)`	Pushes *value* on the stack so that it becomes the topmost element.
`pop()`	Pops the topmost value from the stack and returns it to the caller. Calling **pop** on an empty stack generates an error.
`peek()`	Returns the topmost value on the stack without removing it. Calling **peek** on an empty stack generates an error.
`clear()`	Removes all the elements from a stack.

which suggests the following line for the implementation of **ArrayStack<T>**:

```
array = new T[INITIAL_CAPACITY];
```

However, as the bug symbol seeks to remind you, this line is not legal in Java because it is illegal to create an array of a generic type. It is therefore necessary to use the **GenericArray** class introduced in Figure 13-2, as follows:

```
array = new GenericArray<T>(INITIAL_CAPACITY);
```

The instance variable **array** must be declared as a **GenericArray<T>**, and all operations on **array** must use the **get** and **set** methods instead of square brackets to indicate selection. That syntax is a little more cumbersome than the one you were able to use for characters in Chapter 12, but the idea is exactly the same. The code that uses this model to implement **Stack** appears in Figure 13-4.

FIGURE 13-4 Implementation of the **Stack** class using an array representation

```
/*
 * File: Stack.java
 * ------------------
 * This file simulates the Stack class from the java.util package.
 */

package edu.stanford.cs.javacs2.ch13;

import java.util.NoSuchElementException;

public class Stack<T> {

/**
 * Creates a new empty stack.
 */

   public Stack() {
      capacity = INITIAL_CAPACITY;
      array = new GenericArray<T>(capacity);
      count = 0;
   }

   public int size() {
      return count;
   }

   public boolean isEmpty() {
      return count == 0;
   }

   public void clear() {
      count = 0;
   }
```

FIGURE 13-4 **Implementation of the array-based stack (continued)**

```
/*
 * Implementation notes: push and pop
 * ----------------------------------------
 * These methods manipulate the contents of the underlying array.  The push
 * method checks the capacity; pop checks for an empty stack.
 */

   public void push(T value) {
      if (count == capacity) expandCapacity();
      array.set(count++, value);
   }

   public T pop() {
      if (count == 0) throw new NoSuchElementException("Stack is empty");
      return array.get(--count);
   }

   public T peek() {
      if (count == 0) throw new NoSuchElementException("Stack is empty");
      return array.get(count - 1);
   }

/*
 * Implementation notes: expandCapacity
 * ----------------------------------------
 * The expandCapacity method allocates a new array of twice the previous
 * size, copies the old elements to the new array, and then replaces the
 * old array with the new one.
 */

   private void expandCapacity() {
      capacity *= 2;
      GenericArray<T> newArray = new GenericArray<T>(capacity);
      for (int i = 0; i < count; i++) {
         newArray.set(i, array.get(i));
      }
      array = newArray;
   }

/* Constants */

   private static final int INITIAL_CAPACITY = 10;

/*
 * Private instance variables
 * ----------------------------------------
 * The elements in a Stack are stored in a GenericArray, which is necessary
 * to get around Java's prohibition on arrays of a generic type.
 */

   private GenericArray<T> array;    /* Array of elements in the stack    */
   private int capacity;             /* Allocated capacity of the array   */
   private int count;                /* Actual number of elements in use  */

}
```

Implementing stacks using a linked list

Although arrays are the most common underlying representation for stacks, it is also possible to implement stacks using linked lists by defining the **LinkedStack** class, which is similar to—but much simpler than—the **LinkedBuffer** class used in Chapter 12 to implement the editor buffer. The operations for a stack are so simple that you can dispense with the cursor reference and the strategy of using a dummy cell. All you need is a single linked list.

In the linked list representation, the conceptual representation for the empty stack is simply the **null** reference:

When you push a new element onto the stack, the element is simply added to the front of the linked-list chain. Thus, if you push the element e_1 onto an empty stack, that element is stored in a new cell that becomes the only link in the chain:

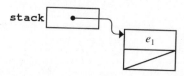

Pushing a new element onto the stack adds that element at the beginning of the chain. The steps involved are the same as those required to insert a character into a linked-list buffer. You first allocate a new cell, then enter the data, and, finally, update the link fields so that the new cell becomes the first element in the chain. Thus, if you push the element e_2 on the stack, you get the following configuration:

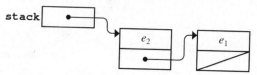

In the linked-list representation, the **pop** operation consists of removing the first cell in the chain and returning the value stored there. Thus, a **pop** operation from the stack shown in the preceding diagram returns e_2 and restores the previous state of the stack, as follows:

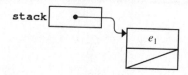

The complete code for the linked-list implementation of the **Stack** interface appears in Figure 13-5.

FIGURE 13-5 Implementation of the linked-list stack

```java
/*
 * File: LinkedStack.java
 * ------------------------
 * This file reimplements the Stack class using a linked list.
 */

package edu.stanford.cs.javacs2.ch13;

import java.util.NoSuchElementException;

public class LinkedStack<T> extends Stack<T> {

/**
 * Creates a new empty stack.
 */

   public LinkedStack() {
      clear();
   }

/*
 * Implementation notes: size, isEmpty
 * ------------------------------------
 * These methods use the count variable and therefore run in constant time.
 */

   @Override
   public int size() {
      return count;
   }

   @Override
   public boolean isEmpty() {
      return count == 0;
   }

   @Override
   public void clear() {
      start = null;
      count = 0;
   }

/*
 * Implementation notes: push
 * --------------------------
 * This method chains a new element onto the front of the list where it
 * becomes the top of the stack.
 */

   @Override
   public void push(T value) {
      Cell cp = new Cell();
      cp.value = value;
      cp.link = start;
      start = cp;
      count++;
```

FIGURE 13-5 Implementation of the linked-list stack (continued)

```
/*
 * Implementation notes: pop, peek
 * -------------------------------
 * These methods check for an empty stack and report an error if
 * there is no top element.
 */

    @Override
    public T pop() {
        if (count == 0) throw new NoSuchElementException("Stack is empty");
        T value = start.value;
        start = start.link;
        count--;
        return value;
    }

    @Override
    public T peek() {
        if (count == 0) throw new NoSuchElementException("Stack is empty");
        return start.value;
    }

/* Inner class that represents a cell in the linked list */

    private class Cell {
        T value;
        Cell link;
    }

/*
 * Private instance variables
 * --------------------------
 * The elements in the list-based stack are stored in a singly linked
 * list in which the top of the stack is always at the front of the list.
 * Including the count field allows the size method to run in constant time.
 *
 * The following diagram illustrates the structure of a stack containing
 * three elements -- A, B, and C -- pushed in that order:
 *
 *         +--------+        +--------+       +--------+       +--------+
 * start  |   o----+------>|   C    | +-->|   B    | +-->|   A    |
 *         +--------+        +--------+ |   +--------+ |   +--------+
 * count  |   3    |        |   o----+--+   |   o----+--+   |  null  |
 *         +--------+        +--------+       +--------+       +--------+
 */

    private Cell start;          /* First item in the linked list  */
    private int count;           /* Number of elements in the stack */

}
```

There are several aspects of the implementation in Figure 13-5 that are worth special mention. As in the linked-list implementation of the editor buffer, the implementation must define a type for each cell in the linked list, which is easiest to write as an inner class so that its details are entirely private to the **LinkedStack** implementation. The value in the cell type is specified by the type parameter **T**, so the definition of **Cell** (which can no longer be **static** because of the type parameter) looks like this:

```
private class Cell {
    T value;
    Cell link;
}
```

The implementation must keep track of the first cell in the list, which corresponds to the top of the stack. In the code in Figure 13-5, the reference to the first cell is stored in the instance variable **start**, as follows:

```
private Cell start;
```

In addition to the linked list itself, the implementation also declares an instance variable named **count**, which keeps track of the number of elements in the list. This variable is not strictly necessary, in the sense that it is always possible to determine the number of elements by cycling through the linked list and counting the number of elements. That strategy, however, requires $O(N)$ time. To ensure that the **size** method runs in constant time, the simplest approach is to keep track of the number of values in a separate instance variable.

The constructor is responsible for setting up the initial state of the object, which consists of an empty linked list and an element count of zero. Setting up an empty linked list and restoring the count to zero are precisely the functions of the **clear** method, which means that the constructor can simply call **clear** to produce the desired initial state.

The code for the **push** method illustrates the standard pattern for adding a new cell to the beginning of a linked list:

```
public void push(T value) {
    Cell cp = new Cell();
    cp.value = value;
    cp.link = start;
    start = cp;
    count++;
}
```

This pattern is sufficiently important that it is worth going through the steps in detail. Suppose, for example, that you are working with a `LinkedStack<String>` that already includes the strings `"A"` and `"B"`, pushed in that order. The current state of the `LinkedStack` data structure looks like this:

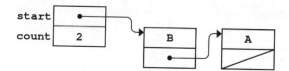

The first step in the **push** method creates a new cell and assigns a reference to the newly created cell to the local variable **cp**, which produces the following state:

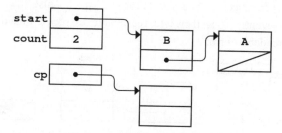

The next two statements assign values to the **value** and **link** components of the cell. The **value** is taken from the argument to the **push** method, and the **link** field gets a copy of the reference from **start**. If the call was **push("C")**, the state after setting these two fields would look like this:

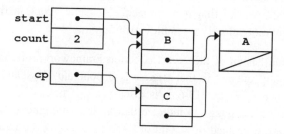

The next statement copies the reference from **cp** into **start**, as follows:

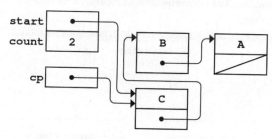

The final step in the execution of the **push** method is to increment the **count** field. After the method returns, the state of the **LinkedStack** looks like this:

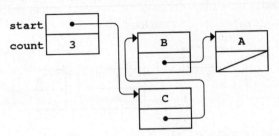

It's important to keep in mind that the structure of a linked list is determined entirely by the references. The layout on the page—just like the layout in memory—is irrelevant. It is therefore reasonable to recast this diagram in the following more readable form:

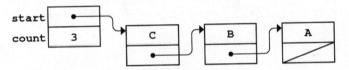

13.3 Implementing queues

As you know from Chapter 6, stacks and queues are extremely similar structures. Conceptually, the only difference between them is in the order in which elements are processed. A stack uses a last-in/first-out (LIFO) discipline in which the last item pushed is always the first item popped. A queue adopts a first-in/first-out (FIFO) model that more closely resembles a waiting line.

In terms of the design of the Java Collection Framework, the major difference between stacks and queues is that **Stack** is a concrete class and **Queue** is an interface, as shown in Figure 13-6. As discussed in Chapter 6, you can use the Universal Modeling Language to indicate that a class implements an interface by using a dashed arrow instead of a solid one and by marking the interface with the keyword **«interface»** above the interface name. The UML diagram for the **Queue** interface and the **ArrayQueue** and **LinkedQueue** classes that implement it therefore looks like this:

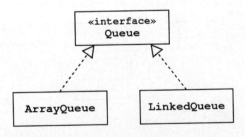

FIGURE 13-6 Interface for the queue abstraction

```
/*
 * File: Queue.java
 * ----------------
 * This file defines the interface for a class that implements a queue,
 * which is characterized by first-in/first-out (FIFO) behavior.
 */

package edu.stanford.cs.javacs2.ch13;

public interface Queue<T> {

/**
 * Returns the number of values in this queue.
 */

   public int size();

/**
 * Returns true if this queue contains no elements.
 */

   public boolean isEmpty();

/**
 * Removes all elements from this queue.
 */

   public void clear();

/**
 * Adds the specified value to the tail of this queue.
 */

   public void add(T value);

/**
 * Removes the first element from this queue and returns it.  This method
 * throws a NoSuchElementException if called on an empty queue.
 */

   public T remove();

/**
 * Returns the value of the first element in this queue without removing it.
 * This method throws a NoSuchElementException if called on an empty queue.
 */

   public T peek();

}
```

Implementing queues using arrays

In the array-based implementation of the stack, the fact that all operations were confined to one end of the underlying array made it possible to get away with a single variable `count` to mark the position into which the next value would be pushed. In a queue, however, you add elements at one end and remove them from the other. You thus need two instance variables for this purpose: an index variable named `head` that indicates the index position of the next item to be removed, and an index variable named `tail` that marks the first free slot. If you combine these two variables with the `GenericArray` and its capacity, the private instance variables for the `ArrayQueue` implementation look like this:

```
private GenericArray<T> array;
private int capacity;
private int head;
private int tail;
```

When the constructor creates an empty queue, it allocates some initial space to the array and keeps track of its capacity to avoid making frequent calls to `size`. In the initial queue, it is clear that the `tail` field should be 0 to indicate that the first data item should go at the beginning of the array, but what about the `head` field? For convenience, the usual strategy is to set the `head` field to 0 as well. When queues are defined in this way, having the `head` and `tail` fields be equal indicates that the queue is empty.

If you use this representation strategy, the `Queue` constructor looks like this:

```
public ArrayQueue() {
    capacity = INITIAL_CAPACITY;
    array = new GenericArray<T>(capacity);
    head = 0;
    tail = 0;
}
```

Although it is tempting to think that the **add** and **remove** methods will look almost exactly like their **push** and **pop** counterparts in the **Stack** class, you'll run into several problems if you try to copy the existing code. As is often the case in programming, it makes more sense to begin by drawing diagrams to make sure you understand exactly how the queue should operate before you turn to the implementation.

To get a sense of how this representation of a queue works, imagine that the queue represents a waiting line, similar to one in the simulation from Chapter 6. From time to time, a new customer arrives and is added to the queue. Customers waiting in line are periodically served at the head of the queue, after which they leave the waiting line entirely. How does the queue data structure respond to each of these operations?

Assuming that the queue is empty at the beginning, its internal structure looks like this:

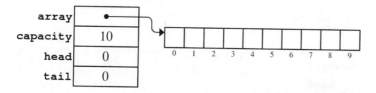

Suppose now that five customers arrive, indicated by the letters *A* through *E*. Those customers are added in order, which gives rise to the following configuration:

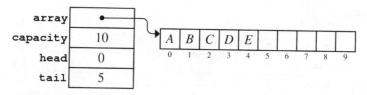

The value 0 in the **head** field indicates that the first customer in the queue is stored in position 0 of the array; the value 5 in **tail** indicates that the next customer will be placed in position 5. So far, so good. At this point, suppose that you alternately serve a customer at the beginning of the queue and then add a new customer to the end. For example, customer *A* is removed and customer *F* arrives, which leads to the following situation:

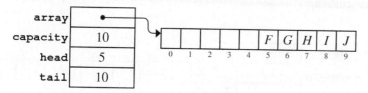

Imagine that you continue to serve one customer just before the next customer arrives and that this trend continues until customer *J* arrives. The internal structure of the queue then looks like this:

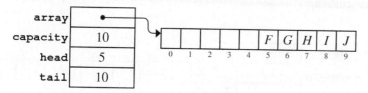

At this point, you've got a bit of a problem. There are only five customers in the queue, but you have used up all the available space. The `tail` field is pointing beyond the end of the array. On the other hand, you now have unused space at the beginning. Thus, instead of incrementing `tail` so that it indicates the nonexistent position 10, you can "wrap around" from the end of the array back to position 0, as follows:

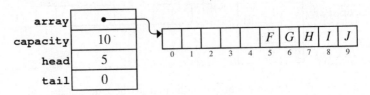

From this position, you have space to add customer *K* in position 0, which leads to the following configuration:

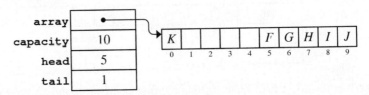

If you allow the elements in the queue to wrap around from the end of the array to the beginning, the active elements always extend from the **head** index up to the position immediately preceding the **tail** index, as illustrated in this diagram:

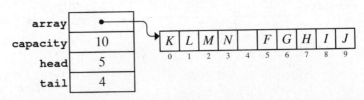

Because the ends of the array act as if they were joined together, programmers call this representation a *ring buffer.*

The only remaining issue you need to consider before you can write the code for **add** and **remove** is how to check whether the queue is completely full. Testing for a full queue is trickier than you might expect. To get a sense of where complications might arise, suppose that three more customers arrive before any additional customers are served. If you add the customers *L, M,* and *N,* the data structure looks like this:

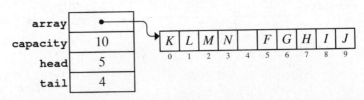

At this point, it appears that there is one extra space. What happens, though, if customer *O* arrives at this moment? If you follow the logic of the earlier **add** operations, you end up with the following configuration:

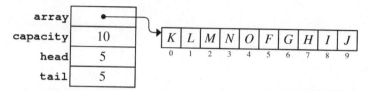

The queue array is now completely full. Unfortunately, whenever the **head** and **tail** fields have the same value, as they do in this diagram, the queue is considered to be empty. There is no way to tell from the contents of the queue structure itself which of the two conditions—empty or full—actually applies, because the data values look the same in each case. Although you can fix this problem by adopting a different definition for the empty queue and writing some special-case code, the simplest approach is to limit the number of elements in the queue to one less than the capacity and to expand the array whenever that limit is reached.

The code for the ring-buffer implementation of the **Queue** class appears in Figure 13-7. It is important to observe that the code does not explicitly test the array indices to see whether they wrap around from the end of the array to the beginning. Instead, the code makes use of the **%** operator to compute the correct index automatically. The technique of using remainders to reduce the result of a computation to a small, cyclical range of integers is an important mathematical technique called *modular arithmetic.*

Using modular arithmetic to calculate the indices would be easier if Java adopted its definition from mathematics. Sadly, programming languages tend to violate standard mathematical conventions when they apply the remainder operator to negative numbers. In Java, the expression **x % y** is defined so that the result always has the same sign as **x**, which means that you need to be careful if you are using modular arithmetic on values in which the first operand might be negative.

The implementation of the **size** method in Figure 13-7 offers an example of a calculation in which this need for caution arises. As long as the **tail** index is larger than the **head** index, you can determine the number of values in the queue by subtracting **head** from **tail**. In the ring-buffer implementation of a queue, it often happens that the value of **tail** is less than the value of **head**, which means that **tail** − **head** is negative. In that case, applying the **%** operator gives a negative result, which leads to an incorrect calculation of the number of values. The code for the **size** method in Figure 13-7 takes account of this possibility by adding **capacity** to **tail** − **head**, just to keep negative numbers out of the calculation.

FIGURE 13-7   Implementation of the array-based queue

```java
/*
 * File: ArrayQueue.java
 * ------------------------
 * This file implements the Queue abstraction using a ring buffer.
 */

package edu.stanford.cs.javacs2.ch13;

import java.util.NoSuchElementException;

public class ArrayQueue<T> implements Queue<T> {

/**
 * Creates a new empty queue.
 */

    public ArrayQueue() {
        capacity = INITIAL_CAPACITY;
        array = new GenericArray<T>(capacity);
        head = 0;
        tail = 0;
    }

    public int size() {
        return (tail + capacity - head) % capacity;
    }

    public boolean isEmpty() {
        return head == tail;
    }

    public void clear() {
        head = tail = 0;
    }

    public void add(T value) {
        if (size() == capacity - 1) expandCapacity();
        array.set(tail, value);
        tail = (tail + 1) % capacity;
    }

    public T remove() {
        if (isEmpty()) throw new NoSuchElementException("Queue is empty");
        T value = array.get(head);
        head = (head + 1) % capacity;
        return value;
    }

    public T peek() {
        if (isEmpty()) throw new NoSuchElementException("Queue is empty");
        return array.get(head);
    }
```

FIGURE 13-7 Implementation of the array-based queue (continued)

```
/*
 * Implementation notes: expandCapacity
 * -----------------------------------------
 * This private method doubles the size of the array whenever the old one
 * runs out of space.  To do so, expandCapacity allocates a new array,
 * copies the old elements to the new array, and then replaces the old
 * array with the new one.  Note that the queue capacity is reached when
 * there is still one unused element in the array.  If the queue is allowed
 * to fill completely, the head and tail indices have the same value, and
 * the queue appears empty.
 */

   private void expandCapacity() {
      GenericArray<T> newArray = new GenericArray<T>(2 * capacity);
      int count = size();
      for (int i = 0; i < count; i++) {
         newArray.set(i, array.get((head + i) % capacity));
      }
      head = 0;
      tail = count;
      capacity *= 2;
      array = newArray;
   }

/* Constants */

   private static final int INITIAL_CAPACITY = 10;

/*
 * Private instance variables
 * ----------------------------
 * In the ArrayQueue implementation, the elements are stored in successive
 * index positions in a GenericArray, just as they are in an ArrayStack.
 * What makes the queue structure more complex is the need to avoid
 * shifting elements as the queue expands and contracts.  In the array
 * model, this goal is achieved by keeping track of both the head and tail
 * indices.  The tail index increases by one each time an element is added,
 * and the head index increases by one each time an element is removed.
 * Each index therefore marches toward the end of the allocated array and
 * will eventually reach the end.  Rather than allocate new memory, this
 * implementation lets each index wrap around to the beginning as if the
 * ends of the array were joined to form a circle.  This representation
 * is called a ring buffer.
 */

   private GenericArray<T> array;   /* Array of elements in the queue   */
   private int capacity;            /* Allocated capacity of the array  */
   private int head;                /* Index of the first queue element */
   private int tail;                /* Index of the first free slot     */

}
```

Implementing queues using a linked list

The queue class also has a simple representation using list structure. If you adopt this approach, the elements of the queue are stored in a list beginning at the head of the queue and ending at the tail. To allow both **add** and **remove** to run in constant time, the **Queue** object must keep a reference to both ends of the queue. The private instance variables therefore look like this, assuming the same definition for the **Cell** class:

```
private Cell head;
private Cell tail;
private int count;
```

Here, for example, is a diagram of a queue containing the customers *A, B,* and *C:*

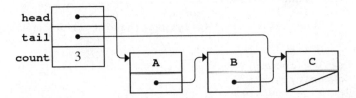

The code for the linked-list implementation of queues appears in Figure 13-8. On the whole, the code is reasonably straightforward, particularly if you use the linked-list implementation of stacks as a model. The diagram of the internal structure provides the essential insights you need to understand how to implement each of the queue operations. The **add** operation, for example, adds a new cell after the one marked by the **tail** field and then updates **tail** so that it continues to indicate the end of the list. The **remove** operation consists of removing the cell addressed by the **head** pointer and returning the value in that cell.

The only place where the implementation gets tricky is in the representation of the empty queue. The simplest approach is to indicate an empty queue by storing **null** in the **head** pointer, as follows:

The **add** implementation must check for the empty queue as a special case. If the **head** pointer is **null**, **add** must set both the **head** and **tail** pointers so that they point to the cell containing the new element. Thus, if you were to add customer *A* into an empty queue, the internal structure of the pointers at the end of the **add** operation would look like the diagram at the top of page 527.

FIGURE 13-8 Implementation of the list-based queue

```java
/*
 * File: LinkedQueue.java
 * ------------------------
 * This file implements the Queue interface using a linked list.
 */

package edu.stanford.cs.javacs2.ch13;

import java.util.NoSuchElementException;

public class LinkedQueue<T> implements Queue<T> {

/**
 * Creates a new empty queue.
 */

   public LinkedQueue() {
      head = tail = null;
      count = 0;
   }

   public int size() {
      return count;
   }

   public boolean isEmpty() {
      return count == 0;
   }

   public void clear() {
      head = tail = null;
      count = 0;
   }

/*
 * Implementation notes: add
 * ----------------------------
 * This method allocates a new list cell and chains it in at the tail of
 * the queue.  If the queue is currently empty, the new cell also becomes
 * the head of the queue.
 */

   public void add(T value) {
      Cell cp = new Cell();
      cp.value = value;
      cp.link = null;
      if (head == null) {
         head = cp;
      } else {
         tail.link = cp;
      }
      tail = cp;
      count++;
   }
```

FIGURE 13-8 Implementation of the list-based queue (continued)

```
/*
 * Implementation notes: remove, peek
 * -----------------------------------
 * These methods check for an empty queue and report an error if there is
 * no first element.  If the queue becomes empty, the remove method sets
 * both the head and tail variables to null.
 */

   public T remove() {
      if (isEmpty()) throw new NoSuchElementException("Queue is empty");
      T value = head.value;
      head = head.link;
      if (head == null) tail = null;
      count--;
      return value;
   }

   public T peek() {
      if (isEmpty()) throw new NoSuchElementException("Queue is empty");
      return head.value;
   }

/* Type that represents a cell in the linked list */

   private class Cell {
      T value;
      Cell link;
   }

/*
 * Private instance variables
 * --------------------------
 * The list-based queue uses a linked list to store the elements of the
 * queue.  To ensure that adding a new element to the tail of the queue
 * is fast, the data structure maintains a pointer to the last cell in
 * the queue as well as the first.  If the queue is empty, both head
 * and tail are set to null.
 *
 * The following diagram illustrates the structure of a queue containing
 * two elements, A and B.
 *
 *        +--------+       +--------+        +--------+
 * head |    o---+-------->|   A    | +--==>|   B    |
 *        +--------+       +--------+ | |    +--------+
 * tail |    o---+---+     |   o---+--+ |    |  null  |
 *        +--------+   |   +--------+   |    +--------+
 *                     |               |
 *                     +---------------+
 */

   private Cell head;         /* First cell in the queue           */
   private Cell tail;         /* Last cell in the queue            */
   private int count;         /* Number of elements in the queue */

}
```

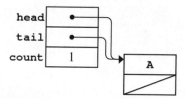

If you make another call to **add**, the **head** pointer is no longer **null**, which means that the implementation no longer has to perform the special-case action for the empty queue. Instead, the **add** implementation uses the **tail** pointer to find the end of the linked-list chain and adds the new cell at that point. For example, if you add customer *B* after customer *A*, the resulting structure looks like this:

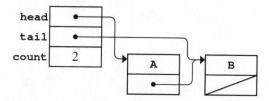

A similar special-case test is needed in the **remove** operation. When you remove the last element from the queue, the **tail** reference continues to point to a cell that has now been removed. The code for **remove** therefore checks to see if the queue becomes empty and, if so, sets the **tail** field to **null**.

◼ 13.4 Implementing lists

The **ArrayList** class introduced in Chapter 6 is another example of a linear structure that can be implemented in more than one way. The Java Collection Framework, for example, defines an **ArrayList** and a **LinkedList** class that both implement the **List** and **Collection** interface hierarchy, as follows:

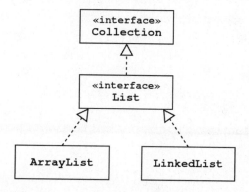

The **Collections** interface, which appears in Figure 13-9, exports the methods that are common to both lists and sets. The **List** interface in Figure 13-10 adds

FIGURE 13-9   The Collection interface

```
/*
 * File: Collection.java
 * ----------------------
 * This interface defines the operations shared by sets and lists.
 */

package edu.stanford.cs.javacs2.ch13;

import java.util.Iterator;

public interface Collection<T> extends Iterable<T> {

/**
 * Returns the number of values in this collection.
 */

   public int size();

/**
 * Returns true if this collection contains no elements.
 */

   public boolean isEmpty();

/**
 * Removes all elements from this collection.
 */

   public void clear();

/**
 * Adds the specified value to this collection.
 */

   public void add(T value);

/**
 * Removes the element with the specified value.
 */

   public void remove(T value);

/**
 * Returns true if the collection contains the specified value.
 */

   public boolean contains(T value);

/**
 * Returns an iterator for this collection.
 */

   public Iterator<T> iterator();

}
```

FIGURE 13-10 The `List` interface

```
/*
 * File: List.java
 * ----------------
 * This interface extends Collection to produce an indexable list.
 */

package edu.stanford.cs.javacs2.ch13;

public interface List<T> extends Collection<T> {

/**
 * Adds the specified value before index position k.
 */

    public void add(int k, T value);

/**
 * Removes the element at index position k.
 */

    public void remove(int k);

/**
 * Returns the first index at which the value appears, or -1 if not found.
 */

    public int indexOf(T value);

/**
 * Gets the element at index position k.
 */

    public T get(int k);

/**
 * Sets the element at index position k to value.
 */

    public void set(int k, T value);

}
```

those methods that are appropriate for sequential lists. For the most part, however, those operations are easy to implement and add nothing to your understanding beyond what you have already seen in this chapter and the **EditorBuffer** abstraction in Chapter 12. This chapter therefore focuses on the new features (most notably iteration) and leaves the rest of the code as an exercise.

The only method that is at all different from what you have already seen is the **iterator** method at the end of Figure 13-9. This method implements the interface

`Iterable<T>`, which is treated specially by Java. Any class that implements `Iterable<T>` can use the following pattern to cycle through the elements of the collection in turn:

```
for (T value : collection)
```

An iterator in Java implements the interface `Iterator<T>`, which is defined in the `java.util` package. The `Iterator<T>` interface specifies three methods: `hasNext`, `next`, and `remove`. The `hasNext` method returns `true` if the iterator has more elements. The `next` method returns the next element. The `remove` method is listed in the documentation as an "optional method" and often simply throws an `UnsupportedOperationException`.

Java interfaces are typically implemented by defining an inner class that keeps track of the current element. For example, Figure 13-11 shows the code for inner class `ArrayListIterator`, which implements the `Iterator<T>` interface for the `ArrayList` class.

FIGURE 13-11 Implementation of the nested iterator class for `ArrayList`

```java
private class ArrayListIterator implements Iterator<T> {

/* Creates a new iterator for this ArrayList */

    public ArrayListIterator() {
        currentIndex = 0;
    }

/* Returns true if there are more elements in the ArrayList */

    public boolean hasNext() {
        return currentIndex < count;
    }

/* Returns the next element in the ArrayList and advances the index */

    public T next() {
        if (!hasNext()) throw new NoSuchElementException("No next element");
        return array.get(currentIndex++);
    }

/* Unsupported operation defined by Iterator but not implemented here */

    public void remove() {
        throw new UnsupportedOperationException("remove not implemented");
    }

/* Private instance variables */

    private int currentIndex;    /* The index of the current element */

}
```

Since you haven't seen the complete code for the `ArrayList` class itself, understanding the code for `ArrayListIterator` requires making some educated guesses about the underlying representation. Like the `Stack` class presented in Figure 13-4, the `ArrayList` class maintains the following instance variables as its underlying representation:

```
private GenericArray<T> array;
private int capacity;
private int count;
```

The `ArrayListIterator` keeps track of the index of the current element in its own instance variable called `currentIndex`, which starts off at 0. The `hasNext` method can then test whether more elements exist by checking to see that this index is less than the total number of values, which is stored in `count`, as reflected in the following code:

```
public boolean hasNext() {
    return currentIndex < count;
}
```

The code for the `next` method is almost as straightforward:

```
public T next() {
    if (!hasNext()) throw new NoSuchElementException();
    return array.get(currentIndex++);
}
```

If there is no next element, `next` throws `NoSuchElementException` as required by the `Iterator` model. If there is a next element, `next` simply gets the current element from the array, incrementing the value of `currentIndex` as it does so.

These implementations depend on a property of inner classes in Java that you have not yet seen. The code for the `hasNext` and `next` methods refers not only to the instance variable of the `ArrayListIterator` class but also to the instance variables `count` and `array` defined by the `ArrayList` class itself. In Java, inner classes inherit the variables that are available at the time of the class definition, which makes it much easier to share information between a main class and the inner classes it defines. In computer science, the combination of a class definition and the variables available in its defining environment is called a ***closure.***

Defining an iterator for the `LinkedList` implementation of the `List` interface is equally straightforward. The underlying representation for a linked list consists of a sequence of cells chained together, where a reference to the first cell in the list is conventionally stored in a variable called `start`. All the `LinkedListIterator` class needs to do is keep track of the current cell.

The **ArrayList** and **LinkedList** classes are both included in the materials that accompany this chapter, but it is still worth trying to write these classes out from scratch to test your understanding.

13.5 Analysis of the doubling strategy

In every case, the array-based implementations of the linear structures presented in this chapter double the amount of space in the **GenericArray** whenever the data structure runs out of space. That strategy is not entirely arbitrary. If you chose instead to add some fixed number of elements to the array, it would no longer be reasonable to claim that the **Stack** and **ArrayQueue** classes have constant-time performance on average. This section walks through the underlying mathematics behind the decision to use the doubling strategy and is included entirely to illustrate how mathematical theory can be used in the design of algorithms. If your only concern is using these classes as a client, feel free to skip this section. If, however, you are interested in the connection of theory and practice, read on.

As you know from Chapter 11, the efficiency of an algorithm is traditionally expressed in terms of its computational complexity, which is a qualitative measure of how running time varies as a function of the size of the problem. For the **Stack** class, most of the methods run in constant time as a function of the current size of the stack. In fact, there is only one method for which the size of the stack makes any difference at all. Ordinarily, the **push** method simply adds a character to the next free slot in the **GenericAraay**, which requires only constant time. If, however, that array is full, the **expandCapacity** method has to copy its contents into a new array. Since this operation requires copying every element in the stack, **expandCapacity** requires linear time, which indicates that the computational complexity of the **push** method is $O(N)$ in the worst case.

Up to this point in the book, complexity analysis has focused on how a particular algorithm performs in the worst case. There is, however, an important characteristic that makes the **push** operation different from the other operations that arise in traditional complexity analysis: the worst case can't possibly happen every time. In particular, if pushing one item on the stack triggers an expansion that makes that particular call run in $O(N)$ time, the cost of pushing the next item is guaranteed to be $O(1)$ because the capacity has already been expanded. It therefore makes sense to distribute the cost of the expansion over all the **push** operations that benefit from it. This style of complexity measurement is called *amortized analysis.*

To make this process easier to understand, it is useful to compute the total cost of the **push** operation if it is repeated N times, where N is some large number. Every **push** operation incurs some cost whether or not the stack is expanded. If you represent that fixed cost using the Greek letter alpha (α), the total fixed cost of pushing N items is αN. Every so often, however, the implementation needs to expand the capacity of the internal array, which is a linear-time operation that costs some constant—indicated by the Greek letter beta (β)—times the number of characters on the stack.

In terms of the total running time across all N **push** operations, the worst-case situation arises when expansion is required on the very last cycle. In that case, the final **push** operation incurs an additional cost of βN. Given that `expandCapacity` always doubles the size of the array, the capacity also had to be expanded when the stack was half as large as N, a quarter as large as N, and so on. The total cost of pushing N items is therefore given by the following formula:

$$ \textit{total time} \ = \ \alpha N \ + \ \beta \left(N \ + \ \frac{N}{2} \ + \ \frac{N}{4} \ + \ \frac{N}{8} \ + \ \cdots \right) $$

The average time is simply this total divided by N, as follows:

$$ \textit{average time} \ = \ \alpha \ + \ \beta \left(1 \ + \ \frac{1}{2} \ + \ \frac{1}{4} \ + \ \frac{1}{8} \ + \ \cdots \right) $$

Although the sum inside the parentheses depends on N, the total can never be larger than 2, which means that the average time is bounded by the constant value $\alpha + 2\beta$ and is therefore $O(1)$.

Summary

In this chapter, you have learned how to use parameterized classes to define the generic containers corresponding to stacks, queues, and lists. Important points in this chapter include:

- Java supports polymorphism by specifying type parameters after the name of the class. By convention, type parameters are named using a single uppercase letter.

- Stacks can be implemented using a linked-list structure in addition to the more traditional array-based representation.

- The array-based implementation of queues is somewhat more complex than its stack counterpart. The traditional implementation uses a structure called a *ring buffer*, in which the elements logically wrap around from the end of the array to the beginning. Modular arithmetic makes it easy to implement the ring buffer concept.

- In the ring-buffer implementation used in this chapter, a queue is considered empty when its head and tail indices are the same. This representation strategy means that the maximum capacity of the queue is one element less than the allocated size of the array. Attempting to fill all the elements in the array makes a full queue indistinguishable from an empty one.

- Queues can also be represented using a linked list marked by two pointers, one to the head of the queue and another to the tail.

- Lists can easily be represented using either arrays or linked lists. In the array representation, inserting or removing elements requires shifting data in the array, which means that these operations typically require $O(N)$ time. In the linked-list implementation, selecting an element by its index requires $O(N)$ time.

Review questions

1. What convention does Java adopt for the names of type parameters?

2. Draw a diagram of the cells used to represent **s** after the following operations have been performed:

```
Stack<Character> s = new LinkedStack<Character>();
s.push('A');
s.push('B');
s.push('C');
```

3. If you use an array to store the underlying elements in a queue, what private instance variables do you need for the **Queue** class?

4. What is a *ring buffer*? How does the ring-buffer concept apply to queues?

5. How can you tell whether an array-based queue is empty? How can you tell whether it has reached its capacity?

6. Assuming that **INITIAL_CAPACITY** has the artificially small value of 3, draw a diagram showing the underlying representation of the array-based queue **q** after the following sequence of operations:

```
Queue<Character> q = new ArrayQueue<Character>();
q.add('A');
q.add('B');
q.remove();
q.add('C');
q.remove();
q.add('D');
q.add('E');
```

7. Explain how modular arithmetic is useful in the array-based implementation of queues.

8. Describe what is wrong with the following implementation of **size** for the array-based representation of queues:

```
public int size() {
    return (tail - head) % capacity;
}
```

9. Draw a diagram showing the internal structure of a linked-list queue after the computer finishes the set of operations in question 6.

10. How can you tell whether a linked-list queue is empty?

11. What interfaces are involved in the declaration of an *iterator?*

12. What is a *closure?*

13. The argument that the amortized complexity of the **push** operation is $O(1)$ depends on the claim that the sum of the series

$$1 + \frac{1}{2} + \frac{1}{4} + \frac{1}{8} + \cdots$$

can never exceed 2 no matter how many terms you include. In your own words, try to explain why. (If you have trouble, you might look up *Zeno's paradox* on the web and then giving this question another go.)

Exercises

1. Design and implement a parameterized class **Pair<T1,T2>** that represents a pair of values, the first of type **T1** and the second of type **T2**. The **Pair** class should export the following methods:

    - A default constructor that generates a pair whose values are the default values for the types **T1** and **T2**

    - A constructor **Pair(**v1, v2**)** that takes explicit values of the two types

    - A **toString** method that returns the string " [*v1*,*v2*] "

    - Getter methods **getFirst** and **getSecond** that return the stored values

2. If you were designing Java's collection classes from scratch, you would certainly make **Stack** an interface, just like **Queue** and **List**. You could then write two concrete implementations of **Stack**, as follows:

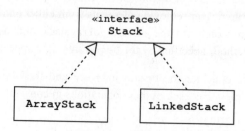

Write the code necessary to implement this interface-based design.

3. Develop a unit test for the **Stack** class that tests the operations exported by the **Stack** class using stacks with several different base types. Use your test program to validate both the **Stack** and the **ListStack** class.

4. Devise a similar unit test for the **Queue** interface.

5. Because the ring-buffer implementation of queues makes it impossible to tell the difference between an empty queue and one that is completely full, the implementation must increase the capacity when there is still one unused cell in the dynamic array. You can avoid this restriction by changing the internal representation so that the concrete structure of the queue keeps track of the number of elements in the queue instead of the index of the tail element. Given the index of the head element and the number of data values in the queue, you can easily calculate the tail index, which means that you don't need to store this value explicitly. Rewrite the array-based queue representation so that it uses this representation.

6. In exercise 4 from Chapter 6, you had the opportunity to write a function

```
void reverseQueue(Queue<String> queue)
```

that reverses the elements in the queue, working entirely from the client side. If you are the designer of a class, however, you could add this facility to the **Queue** interface and export it as one of its methods. For both the array- and list-based implementations of the queue, make all the changes necessary to export the method

```
void reverse();
```

that reverses the elements in the queue. In both cases, write the functions so that they use the original memory cells and do not allocate any additional storage.

7. The Java Collection Framework includes a number of collection classes beyond those described in Chapter 6. One of those is a **deque** (pronounced like *deck*) that stands for *double-ended queue*. The **Deque** interface includes methods for adding or removing elements from either end of a linear structure and therefore combines the features of a stack and a queue. The most important methods specified by the **Deque** interface appear in Figure 13-12.

Write the code for the **Deque** interface and then build an **ArrayDeque** class that implements each of these operations in constant time.

FIGURE 13-12 Methods defined by the `Deque` interface

`size()`	Returns the number of elements currently in the deque.
`isEmpty()`	Returns **true** if the deque is empty.
`addFirst(value)`	Adds *value* to the beginning of the deque.
`addLast(value)`	Adds *value* to the end of the deque.
`removeFirst()`	Removes and returns the first element in the deque.
`removeLast()`	Removes and returns the last element in the deque.
`getFirst()`	Returns the first element in the deque without removing it.
`getLast()`	Returns the last element in the deque without removing it.
`clear()`	Removes all the elements from the deque.

8. Implement a **LinkedDeque** class that implements the **Deque** interface from Figure 13-12. To ensure that all the methods operate in constant time, you should include both forward and backward links as described in the section on "Doubly linked lists" on page 492.

9. Although unit tests are important for long-term program maintenance, it is often useful, particularly during the development phase, to write test programs that allow you to enter commands interactively on the console. Each of the abstractions in this chapter includes a test program that does just that. For example, the following sample run illustrates the interactive stack test:

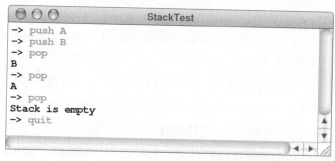

Even though the implementation of the **InteractiveTest** class that supports these tests uses features of Java that are beyond the scope of this text, you can still use it as a client. Drawing on the **StackTest** application as a model, write an interactive test for the **Deque** class from exercises 7 and 8.

10§. Complete the code for the **ArrayList** and **LinkedList** classes described in this chapter. Check your answers by comparing your implementation with the code that comes with this book.

11.   Design and implement a unit test for the **List** interface.

12.   In Java, the data type **long** is stored using 64 bits, which means that the largest positive value of type **long** is 9,223,372,036,854,775,807 or $2^{63} - 1$. While this number seems enormous, there are applications that require even larger integers. For example, if you were asked to compute the number of possible arrangements for a deck of 52 cards, you would need to calculate 52!, which works out to be

   80658175170943878571660636856403766975289505440883277824000000000000

If you are solving problems involving integer values on this scale (which come up often in cryptography, for example), you need a software package that provides *extended-precision arithmetic,* in which integers are represented in a form that allows them to grow dynamically.

   Although there are more efficient techniques for doing so, one strategy for implementing extended-precision arithmetic is to store the individual digits in a linked list. In such representations, it is conventional—mostly because doing so makes the arithmetic operators easier to implement—to arrange the list so that the units digit comes first, followed by the tens digit, then the hundreds digit, and so on. Thus, to represent the number 1729 as a linked list, you would arrange the cells in the following order:

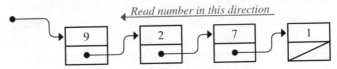

Read number in this direction

   Design and implement a class called **BigInt** that uses this representation to implement extended-precision arithmetic, at least for nonnegative values. At a minimum, your **BigInt** class should support the following operations:

   • A constructor that creates a **BigInt** from an **int** or from a string of digits

   • A **toString** method that converts a **BigInt** to a string

   • The methods **add** and **multiply** for addition and multiplication

You can implement the arithmetic operators by simulating what you do if you perform these calculations by hand. Addition, for example, requires you to keep track of the carries from one digit position to the next. Multiplication is a bit more challenging, but is still straightforward to implement if you find the right recursive decomposition.

   Use your **BigInt** class to generate a table showing the value of *n*! for all values of *n* between 0 and 52, inclusive.

Chapter 14
Maps

A map was a fine thing to study when you were disposed to think of something else . . .

— George Eliot, *Middlemarch,* 1874

One of the most useful data structures you have encountered in this book is the *map,* which implements an association between keys and values. Chapter 6 introduces two classes—**HashMap** and **TreeMap**—that implement the map idea. These two classes implement the same methods and can often be used interchangeably. The primary difference between these classes is the order in which keys are processed when you iterate over the elements. The **HashMap** class offers greater efficiency but iterates through the keys in a seemingly random order. The **TreeMap** class is slightly less efficient but has the advantage of iterating through the keys in their natural order.

The goal of the next two chapters is to look at how these two classes are implemented. This chapter focuses on the **HashMap** class, which makes it possible to find the value associated with a key in constant time. Chapter 15 then introduces the concept of a tree. Although trees have many other applications as well, they provide the underlying framework for the **TreeMap** class, which offers $O(\log N)$ performance while retaining the capability of processing the keys in order.

As you presumably discovered as you read through the code examples in Chapter 13, implementing a complete collection class can take a fair amount of code—so much so that the complexity of the full implementation can get in the way of understanding the structure of the algorithms used to implement the primitive operations for that class. To minimize this complexity, the next few sections implement a simpler interface called **StringMap** in which both the keys and the values are strings. As a further simplification, the **StringMap** interface exports only those methods that are essential to the map abstraction, which are **put** and **get**. The code for the **StringMap** interface appears in Figure 14-1.

14.1 Implementing maps using arrays

Before moving on to consider more efficient strategies, it is useful to start with a simple array-based implementation just to make sure that you understand how the **StringMap** class works. One particularly straightforward approach is to keep track of the key-value pairs in an **ArrayList**, each of whose elements is an inner class with the following definition:

```
private static class KeyValuePair {
    String key;
    String value;
};
```

Given that this type is intended to implement the **StringMap** class, both the **key** and the **value** field have type **String**. A generic implementation would use a similar structure—without the **static** keyword—in which the two instances of **String** are replaced by the type parameters **K** and **V**, as you saw in Chapter 13.

FIGURE 14-1 Simplified interface for the map abstraction

```
/*
 * File: StringMap.java
 * --------------------
 * This file defines the interface for a simplification of the Map class
 * in which the keys and values are always strings and the interface
 * specifies only the get and put methods.
 */

package edu.stanford.cs.javacs2.ch14;

public interface StringMap {

/**
 * Sets the binding of key to value.
 */

   public void put(String key, String value);

/**
 * Returns the value associated with key, or null if none exists.
 */

   public String get(String key);

}
```

The code to implement **StringMap** using an **ArrayList<KeyValuePair>**
appears in Figure 14-2 on the next page. The bindings for the keys are kept in an
instance variable called **bindings**. For the most part, the implementation in Figure
14-2 is entirely straightforward. The constructor simply creates an empty
ArrayList and assigns it to **bindings**. Given that both the **get** and **put** methods
must search for an existing key, it makes sense for those methods to delegate the
process of searching the **ArrayList** to a private method called **findKey**, which
looks like this:

```
        private int findCell(String key) {
           for (int i = 0; i < bindings.size(); i++) {
              if (bindings.get(i).key.equals(key)) return i;
           }
           return -1;
        }
```

This method returns the index at which a particular key appears in the list of keys
already included in **bindings**. If the key does not appear, **findKey** returns −1.
The use of the linear-search algorithm means that the **get** and **put** methods both
require $O(N)$ time.

FIGURE 14-2   Code for the array-based implementation of StringMap

```java
/*
 * File: ArrayStringMap.java
 * ---------------------------
 * This file implements the StringMap interface using an ArrayList of
 * key-value pairs.
 */

package edu.stanford.cs.javacs2.ch14;

import edu.stanford.cs.javacs2.ch13.ArrayList;

public class ArrayStringMap implements StringMap {

    public ArrayStringMap() {
        bindings = new ArrayList<KeyValuePair>();
    }

    public void put(String key, String value) {
        int index = findCell(key);
        if (index == -1) {
            KeyValuePair kvp = new KeyValuePair();
            kvp.key = key;
            kvp.value = value;
            bindings.add(kvp);
        } else {
            bindings.get(index).value = value;
        }
    }

    public String get(String key) {
        int index = findCell(key);
        return (index == -1) ? null : bindings.get(index).value;
    }

    private int findCell(String key) {
        for (int i = 0; i < bindings.size(); i++) {
            if (bindings.get(i).key.equals(key)) return i;
        }
        return -1;
    }

/* Inner class to represent a key-value pair */

    private static class KeyValuePair {
        String key;
        String value;
    }

/* Private instance variables */

    private ArrayList<KeyValuePair> bindings;

}
```

It is possible to improve the performance of the `get` method by keeping the keys in sorted order and applying the binary-search algorithm, which was introduced in Chapter 11. Binary search reduces the search time to $O(\log N)$, which represents a dramatic improvement over the $O(N)$ time required by linear search. Unfortunately, there is no obvious way to apply that same optimization to the `put` method. Although it is certainly possible to check whether the key already exists in the map—and even to determine exactly where a new key needs to be added—in $O(\log N)$ time, inserting the new key-value pair at that position requires shifting every subsequent entry forward. Thus, `put` requires $O(N)$ time, even in a sorted list.

◼ 14.2 Lookup tables

The map abstraction comes up so frequently in programming that it is worth investing significant effort into improving its performance. The implementation strategy described in the preceding section—storing the key-value pairs in sorted order in an array—offers $O(\log N)$ performance for the `get` operation and $O(N)$ performance for the `put` operation. It is possible to do much better.

When you are trying to optimize the performance of a data structure, it is often helpful to identify performance enhancements that work in some special case and then look for ways to apply those algorithmic improvements more generally. This section introduces a specific problem for which it is easy to find constant-time implementations of the `get` and `put` operations. It then goes on to explore how a similar technique might help in a more general context.

In 1963, the United States Postal Service introduced a set of two-letter codes for the individual states, districts, and territories of the United States. The codes for the 50 states appear in Figure 14-3. Although you might also want to translate in the opposite direction as well, this section considers only the problem of translating two-letter codes into state names. The data structure that you choose must therefore be able to represent a map from two-letter abbreviations to state names.

FIGURE 14-3 **USPS abbreviations for the 50 states**

AK Alaska	HI Hawaii	ME Maine	NJ New Jersey	SD South Dakota
AL Alabama	IA Iowa	MI Michigan	NM New Mexico	TN Tennessee
AR Arkansas	ID Idaho	MN Minnesota	NV Nevada	TX Texas
AZ Arizona	IL Illinois	MO Missouri	NY New York	UT Utah
CA California	IN Indiana	MS Mississippi	OH Ohio	VA Virginia
CO Colorado	KS Kansas	MT Montana	OK Oklahoma	VT Vermont
CT Connecticut	KY Kentucky	NC North Carolina	OR Oregon	WA Washington
DE Delaware	LA Louisiana	ND North Dakota	PA Pennsylvania	WI Wisconsin
FL Florida	MA Massachusetts	NE Nebraska	RI Rhode Island	WV West Virginia
GA Georgia	MD Maryland	NH New Hampshire	SC South Carolina	WY Wyoming

You could, of course, encode the translation table in a **StringMap** or, more generally, a **Map<String,String>**. If you look at this problem strictly from the client's point of view, however, the details of the implementation aren't particularly important. In this chapter, the goal is to identify new implementation strategies that allow maps to operate more efficiently. In this example, the important question to ask is whether the fact that the keys are two-letter strings makes it possible to design a more efficient implementation than was possible using the array-based strategy.

As it turns out, the two-character restriction on the keys makes it easy to reduce the complexity of the lookup operation to constant time. All you need to do is store the state names in a two-dimensional array in which the letters in the state abbreviation are used to compute the row and column indices. Tables of this sort are called *lookup tables.* The first nine columns of the lookup table for the state abbreviations appear in Figure 14-4.

FIGURE 14-4 **First nine columns of the state lookup table**

	A	B	C	D	E	F	G	H	I	
A										0
B										1
C	California									2
D					Delaware					3
E										4
F										5
G	Georgia								Hawaii	6
H										7
I	Iowa			Idaho						8
J										9
K										10
L	Louisiana								Michigan	11
M	Massachusetts			Maryland	Maine					12
N			North Carolina	North Dakota	Nebraska			New Hampshire		13
O								Ohio		14
P	Pennsylvania									15
Q									Rhode Island	16
R										17
S			South Carolina	South Dakota						18
T										19
U										20
V	Virginia								Wisconsin	21
W	Washington									22
X										23
Y										24
Z										25
	0	1	2	3	4	5	6	7	8	

To select an element from the array, you simply break the state abbreviation down into the two characters it contains, subtract the Unicode value of `'A'` from each character to get an index between 0 and 25, and then use these indices to select a row and column. Thus, given an array that contains the state abbreviations, all you have to do is look at the value in the appropriate row and column to find the state name. Figure 14-5 shows the `LetterPairMap` class, which implements the `StringMap` interface for this restricted set of two-letter keys.

FIGURE 14-5 Code to implement `StringMap` for keys consisting of two letters

```
/*
 * File: LetterPairMap.java
 * ---------------------------
 * This file defines the class LetterPairMap, which implements the StringMap
 * interface, but only for keys composed of two uppercase letters.  Given
 * these restrictions, the put and get methods run in constant time.
 */

package edu.stanford.cs.javacs2.ch14;

public class LetterPairMap implements StringMap {

    public LetterPairMap() {
        lookupTable = new String[26][26];
    }

    public void put(String key, String value) {
        checkKey(key);
        int row = key.charAt(0) - 'A';
        int col = key.charAt(1) - 'A';
        lookupTable[row][col] = value;
    }

    public String get(String key) {
        checkKey(key);
        int row = key.charAt(0) - 'A';
        int col = key.charAt(1) - 'A';
        return lookupTable[row][col];
    }

    private void checkKey(String key) {
        if (key.length() != 2 || !Character.isUpperCase(key.charAt(0)) ||
                                 !Character.isUpperCase(key.charAt(1))) {
            throw new IllegalArgumentException("Only two-letter keys allowed");
        }
    }
}
/* Private instance variables */

    private String[][] lookupTable;

}
```

The implementations of the **get** and **put** methods in the **LetterPairMap** class contain nothing that looks like the traditional process of searching an array. What happens instead is that the method performs simple arithmetic on the character codes and then looks up the answer in a two-dimensional array. There are no loops in the implementation or indeed any code that depends on the number of keys.

The reason that lookup tables are so efficient is that the key tells you immediately where to look for the answer. In the current application, however, the organization of the table depends on the fact that the keys always consist of two uppercase letters. If the keys could be arbitrary strings—as they are in the **StringMap** class—the lookup-table strategy would no longer apply, at least in its current form. The critical question is whether it is possible to generalize this strategy so that it applies to the more general case.

If you think about how this question applies to real-life applications, you may discover that you in fact use something akin to the lookup-table strategy when you search for words in a dictionary. If you were to apply the array-based map strategy to the dictionary-lookup problem, you would start at the first entry, go on to the second, and then the third, until you found the word. No one, of course, would apply this algorithm in a real dictionary of any significant size. But it is also unlikely that you would apply the $O(\log N)$ binary search algorithm, which consists of opening the dictionary exactly at the middle, deciding whether the word you're searching for appears in the first or second half, and then repeatedly applying this algorithm to smaller and smaller parts of the dictionary. In all likelihood, you would take advantage of the fact that many dictionaries have tabs along the side that indicate where the entries for each letter appear. You look for words starting with A in the A section, words starting with B in the B section, and so on. These tabs represent a lookup-table that gets you to the right section, thereby reducing the number of words through which you need to search.

At least for maps like **StringMap** that use strings as their key type, it is relatively straightforward to apply the same strategy. In a **StringMap**, each key begins with some character value, although that character is not necessarily a letter. If you want to simulate the strategy of using thumb tabs for every possible first character, you can divide the map into 65,536 independent lists of key-value pairs, one for each starting character. Whenever the client calls **put** or **get** with some key, the code can choose the appropriate list on the basis of the first character. If the characters used to form keys were uniformly distributed, this strategy would reduce the average search time by a factor of 65,536.

Unfortunately, keys in a map—like words in a dictionary—are not uniformly distributed. In the dictionary case, for example, many more words begin with C than with X. If you use a map in an application, it is likely that most of the 65,536 possible first characters never appear at all. As a result, some of the lists will remain empty, while others become quite long. The increase in efficiency you get by applying the first-character strategy therefore depends on how common the first character in the key happens to be.

On the other hand, there is no reason that you have to use only the first character of the key as you try to optimize the performance of the map. The first-character strategy is simply the closest analogue to what you do with a physical dictionary. What you need is a strategy in which the value of the key tells you where to find the location of the value, as it does in a lookup table. That idea is most elegantly implemented using a technique called *hashing,* which is described in the following section.

14.3 Hashing

The best way to improve the efficiency of the map implementation is to come up with a way of using the key to determine, at least fairly closely, where to look for the corresponding value. Choosing any obvious property of the key, such as its first character or even its first two characters, runs into the problem that keys are not equally distributed with respect to that property.

Given that you are using a computer, however, there is no reason that the property you use to locate the key has to be something easy for a *human* to figure out. To maintain the efficiency of the implementation, the only thing that matters is whether the property is easy for a *computer* to determine. Since computers are better at computation than humans are, allowing for algorithmic computation opens a much wider range of possibilities.

The computational strategy called **hashing** operates as follows:

1. Select a function *f* that transforms a key into an integer value, which is called the **hash code** of that key. The function that computes the hash code is called, naturally enough, a **hash function.** An implementation of the map abstraction that uses this strategy is conventionally called a **hash table.**

2. Use the hash code for a key to determine the starting point as you search for a matching key in the table.

Designing the data structure

The first step in implementing the **StringMap** class as a hash table is to design the data structure. Although other representations are possible, a common strategy is to use the hash code to compute an index into an array of linked lists, each of which holds all the key-value pairs corresponding to that hash code. Each of those linked lists is traditionally called a **bucket.** To find the key you're looking for, all you need to do is search through the list of key-value pairs in that bucket.

In most implementations of hashing, the number of possible hash codes is larger than the number of buckets. You can, however, convert an arbitrarily large hash code into a bucket number by taking the remainder of the absolute value of the hash code divided by the number of buckets. Thus, if the number of buckets is stored in the instance variable **nBuckets** and the method **hashCode** returns the hash code for a given key, you can compute the bucket number as follows:

```
int bucket = Math.abs(key.hashCode()) % nBuckets;
```

A bucket number represents an index into an array, each of whose elements is a pointer to the first cell in a linked list of key-value pairs. Colloquially, computer scientists say that a key **hashes to a bucket** if the hash function applied to the key returns that bucket number after applying the remainder operation. Thus, the common property that links all the keys in a single linked list is that they all hash to the same bucket. Having two or more different keys hash to the same bucket is called **collision.**

The reason that hashing works is that the hash function always returns the same value for any particular key. If a key hashes to bucket #17 when you call **put** to enter it into the hash table, that key will still hash to bucket #17 when you call **get** to find its value. Figure 14-6 shows the code for the **StringHashMap** class, which implements the **StringMap** interface using a hash table.

Understanding the hash function for strings

If you look carefully at the statement in the preceding section that calculates the bucket index, you will see that the **hashCode** method is applied directly to the key. For that to work, the **String** class in Java must implement a **hashCode** method. You're in luck. In Java, *every* object implements a **hashCode** method. The **hashCode** method is specified as part of the **Object** class. Individual classes can then override the standard definition of **hashCode** so that the value is appropriate to that type. For strings, the **hashCode** implementation is functionally equivalent to the following code:

```
public int hashCode() {
    int hc = 0;
    for (int i = 0; i < length(); i++) {
        hc = 31 * hc + charAt(i);
    }
    return hc;
}
```

FIGURE 14-6 Implementation of `StringMap` using a hash table

```
/*
 * File: HashStringMap.java
 * --------------------------------
 * This file implements the StringMap interface using a hash table.
 */

package edu.stanford.cs.javacs2.ch14;

public class HashStringMap implements StringMap {

/*
 * Implementation notes: constructor
 * ---------------------------------
 * The constructor creates the buckets array, in which each element is a
 * linked list of key-value pairs.
 */

   public HashStringMap() {
      nBuckets = INITIAL_BUCKET_COUNT;
      buckets = new Cell[nBuckets];
   }

/*
 * Implementation notes: get
 * ---------------------------
 * The get method calls findCell to search the linked list for the
 * matching key.  If no key is found, get returns null.
 */

   public String get(String key) {
      int bucket = Math.abs(key.hashCode()) % nBuckets;
      Cell cp = findCell(bucket, key);
      return (cp == null) ? null : cp.value;
   }

/*
 * Implementation notes: put
 * ---------------------------
 * If findCell can't find a matching key, the put method creates a new
 * cell and adds it to the front of the chain for that bucket.
 */

   public void put(String key, String value) {
      int bucket = Math.abs(key.hashCode()) % nBuckets;
      Cell cp = findCell(bucket, key);
      if (cp == null) {
         cp = new Cell();
         cp.key = key;
         cp.link = buckets[bucket];
         buckets[bucket] = cp;
      }
      cp.value = value;
   }
```

FIGURE 14-6 **Implementation of StringMap using a hash table (continued)**

```
/*
 * Implementation notes: findCell
 * ------------------------------
 * This private method looks for a key in the specified bucket chain to
 * find a matching key.  If the key is found, findCell returns it.  If
 * no match is found, findCell returns null.
 */

   private Cell findCell(int bucket, String key) {
      for (Cell cp = buckets[bucket]; cp != null; cp = cp.link) {
         if (cp.key.equals(key)) return cp;
      }
      return null;
   }

/* Inner class to represent a cell in the linked list */

   private static class Cell {
      String key;
      String value;
      Cell link;
   }

/* Constants */

   private static final int INITIAL_BUCKET_COUNT = 14;

/* Private instance variables */

   private Cell[] buckets;
   private int nBuckets;

}
```

The code for the **String** class implementation of **hashCode** is certainly a bit mysterious. It goes through the characters in the string and replaces the value of the variable **hc** with the constant 31 times the previous value of **hc**, plus the Unicode value of the current character. For example, the string **"AK"** has the hash code 2090, which is produced by the executing the following steps:

- Before the first cycle of the **for** loop, the variable **hc** is initialized to 0.

- The first cycle of the loop updates the value of **hc** by multiplying the initial value by 31 and then adding in the Unicode value of the character **'A'**, which is 65. The new value of **hc** is therefore $31 \times 0 + 65$, which is 65.

- The second cycle of the loop again multiplies **hc** by 31 and then adds in the Unicode value of **'K'**, which is 75. The value returned by the **hashCode** method is therefore $31 \times 65 + 75$, or 2090.

The specific details of the **hashCode** method can have a significant effect on the efficiency of the implementation. Consider, for example, what might happen if you used the following, somewhat simpler implementation that leaves out the step of multiplying the previous hash code by the constant 31:

```
public int hashCode() {
    for (int i = 0; i < length(); i++) {
        hc += charAt(i);
    }
    return hc;
}
```

This code is easier to understand, because all it does is add up the Unicode codes for the characters in the string. Unfortunately, writing **hashCode** in this way would almost certainly cause collisions if the keys happened to fall into certain patterns. The strategy of adding the Unicode values means that any keys whose letters were permutations of each other would collide. Thus, **cat** and **act** would hash to the same bucket. So would the keys **a3**, **b2**, and **c1**. If you were using this hash table in the context of a compiler, variable names that fit such patterns would all end up hashing to the same bucket.

Even though choosing a better hash function can reduce the number of collisions and thereby improve performance, it is important to recognize that the *correctness* of the algorithm is not affected by the collision rate. Implementations that use poorly designed hash functions run more slowly but continue to give correct results.

Tracing the hash table implementation

The easiest way to understand the implementation of the hash table in Figure 14-6 is to go through a simple example. The constructor creates a dynamic array and sets each element of the **buckets** array to **null**, which indicates an empty list. This structure can therefore be diagrammed as follows:

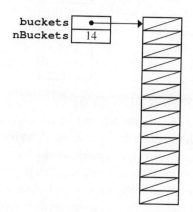

Suppose that the program then executes the call

```
stateMap.put("AK", "Alaska");
```

The first step in the code for **put** is to compute the bucket number for the key **"AK"**. As you saw on page 550, the result of invoking **hashCode** on **"AK"** is 2090. If you divide 2090 by the number of buckets and then take the remainder, you end up discovering that **"AK"** hashes to bucket #4. The **put** method therefore links the key **"AK"** into the list in bucket #4, which was initially empty. The result is therefore a linked list containing only the cell for Alaska, which looks like this:

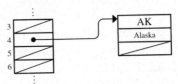

By much the same process, you can figure out that **"AL"** goes in bucket #5, which gives rise to the following diagram:

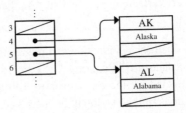

Eventually—particularly in a hash table with 14 buckets—a collision will occur. As an example, the key **"AZ"** also hashes to bucket #5. The code for **put** must then search through the chain beginning at index 0 for a matching key. Since **"AZ"** does not appear, **put** adds a new cell at the beginning of the chain, as follows:

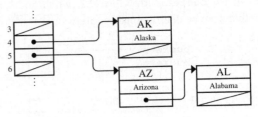

Figure 14-7 shows how the abbreviations for the 50 states fit into a table with 14 buckets. The abbreviations **AK, KS, ME, RI,** and **VT** all hash to bucket #0; **AL, MS, NY, OR, SC,** and **WA** all hash to bucket #1; and so on. Distributing the keys among the buckets means that **get** and **put** have a much shorter list to search. At the same time, arranging keys by their bucket number rather than the natural ordering of the key makes it hard to iterate through the keys in ascending order. Accomplishing that goal requires a new data structure called a *tree,* as described in Chapter 15.

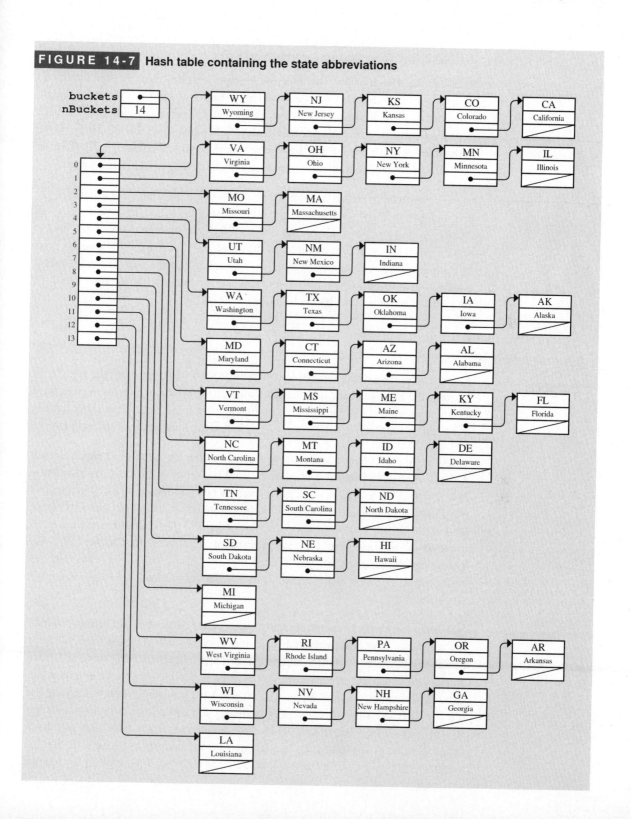

FIGURE 14-7 Hash table containing the state abbreviations

Adjusting the number of buckets

Although the design of the hash function is important, it is clear that the likelihood of collision also depends on the number of buckets. If the number is small, collisions occur more frequently. In particular, if there are more entries in the hash table than buckets, collisions are inevitable. Collisions affect the efficiency of the hash table because **put** and **get** have to search through longer chains. As the hash table fills up, the number of collisions rises, which in turn reduces performance.

It is important to remember that the goal of using a hash table is to optimize the **put** and **get** methods so that they run in constant time, at least in the average case. Achieving this goal requires that the linked-list chains emerging from each bucket remain short, which in turn implies that the number of buckets must always be large in comparison to the number of entries. Assuming that the hash function does a good job of distributing the keys evenly among the buckets, the average length of each bucket chain is given by the formula

$$\lambda = \frac{N_{\text{entries}}}{N_{\text{buckets}}}$$

For example, if the total number of entries in the table is three times the number of buckets, the average chain will contain three entries, which in turn means that three string comparisons will be required, on average, to find a key. This ratio, usually indicated by the Greek letter lambda (λ), is called the **load factor** of the hash table.

For good performance, you want to make sure that the value of λ remains small. Although the mathematical details are beyond the scope of this text, maintaining a load factor of 0.7 or less means that the average cost of looking up a key in a map is $O(1)$. Smaller load factors imply that there will be lots of empty buckets in the hash table array, which wastes a certain amount of space. Hash tables represent a good example of a time-space tradeoff, a concept introduced in Chapter 13. By increasing the amount of space used by the hash table, you can improve performance, but there is little advantage in reducing the load factor below the 0.7 threshold.

Unless the hashing algorithm is engineered for a particular application in which the number of keys is known in advance, it is impossible to choose a fixed value for **nBuckets** that works well for all clients. If a client keeps entering more and more entries into a map, the performance will eventually decline. If you want to maintain good performance, the best approach is to allow the implementation to increase the number of buckets dynamically. For example, you can design the implementation so that it allocates a larger hash table if the load factor in the table ever reaches a certain threshold. Unfortunately, if you increase the number of buckets, the bucket numbers all change, which means that the code to expand the table must reenter every key from the old table into the new one. This process is called *rehashing.* Although rehashing can be time-consuming, it is performed infrequently and therefore has minimal impact on the overall running time of the application. You will have a chance to implement the rehashing strategy in exercise 5.

Implementing your own hash functions

Whenever you implement a class that someone might reasonably want to use as a key, you have an obligation to implement a **hashCode** method for that class. When you do, it is important to keep the following criteria for an effective hash function in mind:

1. The **hashCode** method must always return the same code if it is called on the same object. This requirement is part of the essential character of the hashing strategy. The hash table implementation knows where to look for a particular key because its hash code determines where it goes. If that hash code is subject to change, the implementation might put it in one place and then look for it in another.

2. The implementation of **hashCode** must be consistent with the implementation of the **equals** method, because the hashing mechanism uses the **equals** method internally to compare keys. This condition is stronger than the first one, which says only that the hash code for a specific object should not change arbitrarily. This new requirement strengthens the first one by insisting that any two objects that are considered equal by the **equals** method must have the same hash code.

3. The **hashCode** method should avoid returning hash codes that lead to collisions. For example, it would not be ideal for the **String** class to use the internal code of the first character as its hash code. If it did, every string beginning with the same character would hash to the same bucket, which would dramatically reduce performance.

4. The **hashCode** method should be easy to compute. If you write a **hashCode** method that takes a long time to evaluate, you give up the primary advantage of hashing, which is that the hashing algorithm runs very quickly.

If you do find yourself implementing **hashCode** methods, you can adopt a simple strategy that helps you meet these criteria. In most cases, classes that you define include instance variables that specify the value of the object. To compute a hash code for the object as a whole, you can compute the hash code for each of its identifying components and then combine those pieces in some way that does not increase the odds of a collision. One strategy is to copy the model from Java's **String** class in which you include a constant multiplier in the formula that adds the individual components.

FIGURE 14-8   Implementation of equals and hashCode for the Rational class

```
/**
 * Returns the hash code for this rational number.
 *
 * @return The hashCode for this rational number
 */

   @Override
   public int hashCode() {
      return 31 * num + den;
   }
/**
 * Returns true if this rational number is equal to obj.
 *
 * @param obj The object with which this Rational is compared.
 * @return The value true if this rational number is equal to obj
 */

   @Override
   public boolean equals(Object obj) {
      if (!(obj instanceof Rational)) return false;
      Rational r = (Rational) obj;
      return (this.num == r.num) && (this.den == r.den);
   }
```

Figure 14-8 offers an illustration of how to add a **hashCode** method to an existing class, which in this case is the **Rational** class introduced in Chapter 7. The implementation of **hashCode** adopts the strategy outlined in the preceding paragraph: it multiplies the value of **num** by a small prime number (which is in fact the same constant used in the library implementation of **hashCode** for strings) and then adds in the value of **den**. The **equals** method allows you to determine whether two **Rational** numbers are equal, and the **hashCode** method allows you to use **Rational** objects as keys in a **hashMap**.

The code in Figure 14-8 also includes an implementation of the **equals** method, which overrides the definition of **equals** in the **Object** class. The code for **equals** begins by applying the **instanceof** operator to ensure that the argument value is also a **Rational** and, if so, uses a type cast to assign that value to the **Rational** variable **r**. Given that the **Rational** class ensures that the numerator and denominator are reduced to lowest terms, two **Rational** objects are equal if their **num** and **den** fields match.

The juxtaposition of the **hashCode** and **equals** methods in Figure 14-8 also makes it possible to emphasize a tremendously important point about class design in Java. The **equals** method is useful enough that you might have expected it to be part of the initial implementation of the **Rational** class in Chapter 7. The problem, however, is that overriding the **equals** method without also overriding the **hashCode** method often makes it impossible to use objects of that class as keys in a **HashMap**. You should therefore be sure to override these methods together as a pair. The original definition of **Rational** excluded **equals** because you were unprepared at that time to write the associated **hashCode** method.

14.4 Implementing the HashMap class

Up to now, the code examples in this chapter have implemented the **StringMap** interface rather than the more general **Map** interface shown in Figure 14-9. Completing the implementation requires making the following changes in the code:

- *Adding the missing methods.* The **Map** interface exports the additional methods **size**, **isEmpty**, **containsKey**, **remove**, **clear**, and **keySet**.

- *Generalizing the key and value types.* The **Map** interface uses the type parameters **K** and **V** to give clients more flexibility. Given that this change introduces a generic type, the implementation can no longer use a Java array for the buckets and must use the **GenericArray** class from Chapter 13.

The code for the **HashMap** class appears in Figure 14-10 on the next four pages.

FIGURE 14-9 Entries in the generic Map interface

```
/*
 * File: Map.java
 * ---------------
 * This file defines the interface for a class that implements a Map
 * that associates keys and values.
 */

package edu.stanford.cs.javacs2.ch14;

import java.util.Set;

public interface Map<K,V> {

    public int size();

    public boolean isEmpty();

    public void clear();

    public void put(K key, V value);

    public V get(K key);

    public boolean containsKey(K key);

    public void remove(K key);

    public Set<K> keySet();

}
```

FIGURE 14-10 Implementation of the `HashMap` class

```
/*
 * File: HashMap.java
 * --------------------
 * This file implements the Map interface using a hash table.
 */

package edu.stanford.cs.javacs2.ch14;

import edu.stanford.cs.javacs2.ch13.GenericArray;
import java.util.ArrayList;
import java.util.HashSet;
import java.util.Iterator;
import java.util.Set;

public class HashMap<K,V> implements Map<K,V> {

/*
 * Implementation notes: HashMap constructor
 * -----------------------------------------
 * The constructor creates a GenericArray to hold the linked lists that
 * store the key-value pairs for each bucket.  In the exercises, you will
 * have a chance to extend this class so that it expands the table when
 * the load factor becomes too high.
 */

   public HashMap() {
      nBuckets = INITIAL_BUCKET_COUNT;
      buckets = new GenericArray<Cell>(nBuckets);
      count = 0;
   }

/*
 * Implementation notes: size, isEmpty, clear
 * ------------------------------------------
 * These methods are simple to implement because the number of elements
 * is stored in the instance variable count.
 */

   public int size() {
      return count;
   }

   public boolean isEmpty() {
      return count == 0;
   }

   public void clear() {
      count = 0;
      for (int i = 0; i < nBuckets; i++) {
         buckets.set(i, null);
      }
   }
```

FIGURE 14-10 Implementation of the `HashMap` class (continued)

```
/*
 * Implementation notes: get, put, containsKey
 * --------------------------------------------
 * These methods all use a private method called findCell to find the key.
 */

   public V get(K key) {
      int bucket = Math.abs(key.hashCode()) % nBuckets;
      Cell cp = findCell(bucket, key);
      return (cp == null) ? null : cp.value;
   }

   public void put(K key, V value) {
      int bucket = Math.abs(key.hashCode()) % nBuckets;
      Cell cp = findCell(bucket, key);
      if (cp == null) {
         cp = new Cell();
         cp.key = key;
         cp.link = buckets.get(bucket);
         buckets.set(bucket, cp);
         count++;
      }
      cp.value = value;
   }

   public boolean containsKey(K key) {
      int bucket = Math.abs(key.hashCode()) % nBuckets;
      return findCell(bucket, key) != null;
   }

/*
 * Implementation notes: remove
 * -----------------------------
 * This method stores the cell before the target cell in the variable prev.
 */

   public void remove(K key) {
      int bucket = Math.abs(key.hashCode()) % nBuckets;
      Cell cp = buckets.get(bucket);
      Cell prev = null;
      while (cp != null && !cp.key.equals(key)) {
         prev = cp;
         cp = cp.link;
      }
      if (cp != null) {
         if (prev == null) {
            buckets.set(bucket, cp.link);
         } else {
            prev.link = cp.link;
         }
         count--;
      }
   }
```

FIGURE 14-10   Implementation of the `HashMap` class (continued)

```
/*
 * Implementation notes: keySet
 * -------------------------------
 * This method assembles the set by iterating through each bucket chain.
 */

   public Set<K> keySet() {
      Set<K> keys = new HashSet<K>();
      for (int i = 0; i < buckets.size(); i++) {
         for (Cell cp = buckets.get(i); cp != null; cp = cp.link) {
            keys.add(cp.key);
         }
      }
      return keys;
   }

/*
 * Implementation notes: keyIterator
 * -----------------------------------
 * This method is not part of the HashMap interface but is exported here to
 * allow the HashSet class to implement an iterator.  The code builds an
 * ArrayList containing the keys and then returns the ArrayList iterator.
 */

   public Iterator<K> keyIterator() {
      ArrayList<K> keys = new ArrayList<K>();
      for (int i = 0; i < buckets.size(); i++) {
         for (Cell cp = buckets.get(i); cp != null; cp = cp.link) {
            keys.add(cp.key);
         }
      }
      return keys.iterator();
   }

/*
 * Implementation notes: findCell
 * -----------------------------------
 * This private method looks for a key in the specified bucket chain to
 * find a matching key.  If the key is found, findCell returns it.  If
 * no match is found, findCell returns null.
 */

   private Cell findCell(int bucket, K key) {
      Cell cp = buckets.get(bucket);
      while (cp != null && !cp.key.equals(key)) {
         cp = cp.link;
      }
      return cp;
   }
```

☞

FIGURE 14-10 Implementation of the `HashMap` class (continued)

```
/* Inner class for a cell in the linked lists for the bucket chains */

    private class Cell {
        K key;
        V value;
        Cell link;
    }

/* Constants */

    private static final int INITIAL_BUCKET_COUNT = 7;

/* Private instance variables */

    private GenericArray<Cell> buckets;
    private int nBuckets;
    private int count;

}
```

If you look closely at the code for the `HashMap` class, you will discover that the implementation exports a public method called `keyIterator` that is not part of the `Map` interface. This method is used by the `HashSet` class in Chapter 16.

 ## Summary

This chapter has focused on a variety of strategies for implementing the basic operations provided by the library version of the `HashMap` class. The `Map` class itself—which makes it possible to iterate through the keys in ascending order—requires a more complex data structure called a *tree,* which is the subject of Chapter 15.

Important points in this chapter include:

- It is possible to implement the basic map operations by storing key-value pairs in a array. Keeping the array in sorted order makes it possible for **get** to run in $O(\log N)$ time, even though **put** remains $O(N)$.

- Specific applications may make it possible to implement map operations using a lookup table in which both **get** and **put** run in $O(1)$ time.

- Maps can be implemented very efficiently using a strategy called *hashing,* in which keys are converted to an integer that determines where the implementation should look for the result.

- A common implementation of the hashing algorithm is to allocate a dynamic array of *buckets,* each of which contains a linked list of the keys that hash to that bucket. As long as the ratio of the number of entries to the number of buckets does not exceed about 0.7, the **get** and **put** methods operate in $O(1)$ time on average. Maintaining this performance as the number of entries grows requires periodic *rehashing* to increase the number of buckets.

- The detailed design of a hash function is subtle and requires mathematical analysis to achieve optimum performance. Even so, any hash function that delivers the same integer value whenever two keys are equal will ensure correct results.

Review questions

1. For the array-based implementation of maps, what algorithmic strategy does the chapter suggest for reducing the cost of the **get** method to $O(\log N)$ time?

2. If you implement the strategy suggested in the preceding question, why does the **put** method still require $O(N)$ time?

3. What is a *lookup table?* In what cases is the use of lookup tables appropriate?

4. What disadvantages would you expect from using the Unicode value of the first character in a key as its hash code?

5. What is meant by the term *bucket* in the implementation of a hash table?

6. What is a *collision?*

7. Explain the operation of the **findCell** method in the implementation of the hash-table version of the **StringHashMap** class shown in Figure 14-6.

8. Suppose that some lazy programmer in your employ has defined a new class and included the following **hashCode** method:

```
public int hashCode() {
    return 42;
}
```

Would applications written using this implementation work correctly?

9. In tracing through the code that enters state abbreviations into a map with 14 buckets, the text notes that the entries for **"AZ"** and **"AK"** collide in bucket #5. Assuming that new entries are added in alphabetical order by the state abbreviation, what is the next collision that occurs? You should be able to figure out the answer simply by looking over the diagram in Figure 14-7.

10. What time-space tradeoffs arise in the implementation of a hash table?

11. What is meant by the term *load factor?*

12. What is the approximate threshold for the load factor that ensures that the average performance of the **HashMap** class will remain $O(1)$?

13. What is meant by the term *rehashing?*

▮▮▮ Exercises

1. Modify the code in Figure 14-2 so that **put** always keeps the keys in sorted order in the array. Change the implementation of the private **findKey** method so that it uses binary search to find the key in $O(\log N)$ time.

2. Starting with the code for **ArrayStringMap** in Figure 14-2, add the methods needed to implement the full **Map<String,String>** interface.

3. Although using such a cumbersome notation presumably made mathematics more difficult, the Romans wrote numbers using letters to stand for various multiples of 5 and 10. The characters used to encode Roman numerals have the following values:

I	→	1
V	→	5
X	→	10
L	→	50
C	→	100
D	→	500
M	→	1000

    Design a lookup table that makes it possible to determine the value of each letter in a single array selection. Use this table to implement a method

    ```
    int romanToDecimal(String str)
    ```

    that translates a string containing a Roman numeral into its numeric form.

    To compute the value of a Roman numeral, you ordinarily add the values corresponding to each letter to a running total. There is, however, one exception to this rule: If the value of a letter is less than that of the following one, its value should be subtracted from the total instead of added. For example, the Roman numeral string

    MCMLXIX

    corresponds to

    $$1000 - 100 + 1000 + 50 + 10 - 1 + 10$$

or 1969. The C and the I are subtracted rather than added because those letters precede a letter with a larger value.

4. Starting with the code for **HashStringMap** in Figure 14-6, add the methods needed to implement the full **Map<String,String>** interface.

5. Extend the implementation of the **HashStringMap** class from Figure 14-6 so that the array of buckets expands dynamically. Your implementation should keep track of the load factor for the hash table and perform a rehashing operation if the load factor exceeds the limit indicated by a constant defined as follows:

```
private static final double REHASH_THRESHOLD = 0.7;
```

6. Write a program to evaluate the performance of the hashing algorithm by adding a **displayHashTableStatistics** method to the **HashStringMap** class. This method should report the number of items, the number of buckets, and the load factor, along with the mean and standard deviation of the lengths of the bucket chains. The mean is equivalent to the traditional average. The standard deviation is a measure of how much the individual values tend to differ from the mean. The formula for calculating the standard deviation of the lengths of the chains is

$$\sqrt{\frac{\sum_{i=1}^{N}(len_{ave} - len_i)^2}{N}}$$

where N is the number of buckets, len_i is the length of bucket chain i, and len_{ave} is the average chain length. If the hash function is working well, the standard deviation should be relatively small in comparison to the mean, particularly as the number of symbols increases.

7. In certain applications, it is useful to extend the map abstraction so that you can insert a temporary definition for a key, hiding any previous value associated with that key. Later in the program, you can delete the temporary definition, restoring the next most recent one. For example, you could use such a mechanism to capture the effect of local variables, which come into existence when a method is called and disappear again when the method returns.

Add such a facility to the **HashStringMap** class you implemented in exercise 5 by defining the method

```
void add(String key, String value)
```

Because the **get** and **put** methods always find the first entry in the linked list, you can ensure that **add** hides the previous definitions simply by adding each new entry at the beginning of the list for a particular hash bucket. Moreover, as long as the implementation of **remove** deletes only the first occurrence of a symbol from its hash chain, you can use **remove** to delete the most recently inserted definition for a key, restoring the definition of the key that appears next in the chain.

To make the problem a little simpler, your implementation of **size** should return the number of key-value pairs rather than the number of keys. Thus, if you add a new definition for a key on top of an existing one, the size of the map increases by one.

8. In the **EnglishWords.txt** lexicon, the words *hierarch* and *crinolines* both have the same hash code, which happens to be –1732884796. Write a program to find the other two pairs of English words that share the same hash code.

9. Implement **hashCode** and **equals** methods for the **Point** type introduced in section 7.2.

10. Although the bucket-chaining approach described in the text works well in practice, other strategies exist for resolving collisions in hash tables. In the early days of computing—when memories were small enough that the cost of introducing extra pointers was taken seriously—hash tables often used a more memory-efficient strategy called **open addressing,** in which the key-value pairs are stored directly in the array, like this:

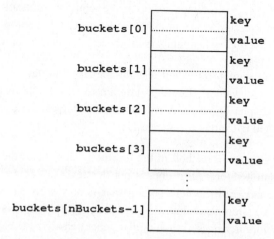

For example, if a key hashes to bucket #2, the open-addressing strategy tries to put that key and its value directly into the entry at **buckets[2]**.

The problem with this approach is that **buckets[2]** may already be assigned to another key that hashes to the same bucket. The simplest approach to dealing with collisions of this sort is to store each new key in the first free cell at or after its expected hash position. Thus, if a key hashes to bucket #2, the **put** and **get** methods first try to find or insert the key in **buckets[2]**. If that entry is filled with a different key, however, these methods move on to try **buckets[3]**, continuing the process until they find an empty entry or an entry with a matching key. As in the ring-buffer implementation of queues in Chapter 13, if the index advances past the end of the array, it should wrap around back to the beginning. This strategy for resolving collisions is called *linear probing.*

Reimplement the **StringMap** class so that it uses open addressing with linear probing. For this exercise, your implementation should simply throw a runtime exception if the client adds a key to a hash table that is already full.

11. One of the difficult aspects of the open-addressing model with linear probing as defined in exercise 10 is that using it makes deleting keys tricky. If you have previously resolved a collision by skipping over an earlier entry, deleting that entry creates a hole that makes it impossible to find any previously entered key that would have been stored in that space had it been available. Think about strategies that you might use to avoid this problem and then implement the methods **size**, **isEmpty**, **clear**, **containsKey**, **remove**, and **keySet** so that the class implements the interface **Map<String,String>**.

12. Extend your solution to exercise 11 so that it expands the array dynamically whenever the load factor exceeds the constant **REHASH_THRESHOLD**, as defined in exercise 5. As in that exercise, you will need to rebuild the entire table because the bucket numbers for the keys change when you rehash.

13. Design and implement a unit test for the **Map** interface that uses strings for both keys and values. Use this program to test the **HashMap** code included with the chapter and the implementations of **Map<String,String>** that you have created in exercises 2, 4, and 12.

14§. The **keyIterator** method in the **HashMap** class takes the easy approach to building an iterator. All it does is put the keys into an **ArrayList** and then use the **iterator** implementation that comes with the **ArrayList** class. Iterators that store the values first and then cycle through the stored values are called *offline iterators.* Iterators that generate each new value as it is needed are called *online iterators.*

Using the **ArrayListIterator** class on page 530 as a model, rewrite **keyIterator** so that it produces an online iterator.

Chapter 15
Trees

I like trees because they seem more resigned to the way they have to live than other things do.

— Willa Cather, *O Pioneers!*, 1913

As you have seen in several earlier chapters, linked lists make it possible to represent an ordered collection of values without using arrays. The link fields associated with each cell form a linear chain that defines the underlying order. Although linked lists require more memory space than arrays and are less efficient for operations such as selecting a value at a particular index position, they have the advantage that insertion and deletion operations can be performed in constant time.

The use of references to define the ordering relationship among a set of values is considerably more powerful than the earlier linked-list examples suggest and is by no means limited to creating linear structures. In this chapter, you will learn about a data structure that uses references to model hierarchical relationships. That structure is called a *tree*, which is defined to be a collection of individual entries called *nodes* for which the following properties hold:

- As long as the tree contains any nodes at all, there is a specific node called the *root* that forms the top of a hierarchy.

- Every other node is connected to the root by a unique line of descent.

Tree-structured hierarchies occur in many contexts outside of computer science. The most familiar example is the family tree, which appears in the next section. Other examples include

- *Game trees.* The game trees introduced in the section on "The minimax algorithm" in Chapter 10 have a branching pattern that is typical of trees. The current position is the root of the tree; the branches lead to positions that might occur later in the game.

- *Biological classifications.* The classification system for living organisms, which was developed in the eighteenth century by the Swedish botanist Carl Linnaeus, is structured as a tree. The root of the tree is all living things. The classification system then branches to form separate kingdoms, of which animals and plants are the most familiar. From there, the hierarchy continues down through several additional levels until it defines an individual species.

- *Organizational charts.* Many businesses are structured so that each employee reports to a single supervisor, thereby forming a tree that extends up to the company president, who represents the root.

- *Directory hierarchies.* On most modern computers, files are stored in directories that form a tree. There is a top-level directory that represents the root, which can contain files along with other directories. Those directories may contain subdirectories, which gives rise to the hierarchical structure representative of trees.

15.1 Family trees

Family trees provide a convenient way to represent the lines of descent from a single individual through a series of generations. For example, the diagram in Figure 15-1 shows the family tree of the House of Normandy, which ruled England after the accession of William I at the Battle of Hastings in 1066. The structure of the diagram fits the definition of a tree from the preceding section. William I is the root of the tree, and all other individuals in the chart are connected to William I through a unique line of descent.

Terminology used to describe trees

The family tree in Figure 15-1 makes it easy to introduce the terminology computer scientists use to describe tree structures. Each node in a tree may have several *children,* but only a single *parent* in the tree. For trees, the words *ancestor* and *descendant* have the same meaning as they do in English. The line of descent through Henry I and Matilda shows that Henry II is a descendant of William I, which in turn implies that William I is an ancestor of Henry II. Similarly, two nodes that share the same parent, such as Robert and Adela, are called *siblings.*

Although most of the terms used to describe trees come directly from the family-tree analogue, others—like the word *root*—come from the botanical metaphor instead. At the opposite end of the tree from the root, there are nodes that have no children, which are called *leaves.* Nodes that are neither the root nor a leaf are called *interior nodes.* For example, in Figure 15-1, Robert, William II, Stephen, William, and Henry II represent leaf nodes; Adela, Henry I, and Matilda represent interior nodes. The *height* of a nonempty tree is defined to be the length of the longest path from the root to a leaf. Thus, the height of the tree shown in Figure 15-1 is 3, because that is the length of the path from William I to Henry II, which is longer than any other path from the root. By convention, the height of an empty tree is defined to be −1.

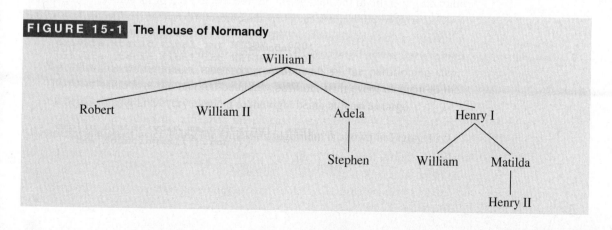

FIGURE 15-1 **The House of Normandy**

The recursive nature of a tree

One of the most important things to notice about any tree is that the same branching pattern occurs at every level of the decomposition. If you take any node in a tree together with all its descendants, the result fits the definition of a tree. For example, if you extract the portion of Figure 15-1 descending from Henry I, you get the following tree:

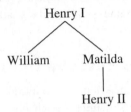

A tree formed by extracting a node and its descendants from an existing tree is called a *subtree* of the original one. The tree in this diagram, for example, is the subtree rooted at Henry I.

The fact that each node in a tree can be considered the root of its own subtree underscores the recursive nature of tree structures. If you think about trees from a recursive perspective, a tree is simply a node and a set—possibly empty, as in the case of a leaf node—of attached subtrees. The recursive character of trees is fundamental to their underlying representation as well as to most algorithms that operate on trees.

Representing family trees in Java

In order to represent a tree in Java, you need some way to model the hierarchical relationships among the data values. In most cases, the easiest way to represent the parent/child relationship is to include object references in the parent, one for each child. If you use this strategy, each node is an object that contains—in addition to other data specific to the node itself—references to each of its children. In general, it works well to think about nodes as the objects themselves and to the tree as the reference to the node object. This definition is mutually recursive even in its English conception because of the following relationship:

- Trees are references to node objects.

- Nodes are objects that contain trees.

You can use this recursive insight to design a structure suitable for storing the data in a family tree such as the one shown in Figure 15-1. Each node consists of the name of a person and a list of references to its children. If you store the child references in an **ArrayList**, a node has the following form as a nested Java class:

```
class FamilyTreeNode {
   String name;
   ArrayList<FamilyTreeNode> children;
};
```

A family tree is simply the reference to the node at the root of the tree.

A diagram showing the internal representation of the royal family tree appears in Figure 15-2. To keep the figure neat and orderly, Figure 15-2 represents the children as if they were stored in a five-element array; in fact, the **children** field is an **ArrayList** that grows to accommodate any number of children. You will have a chance to explore other strategies for storing the children, such as keeping them in a linked list rather than an **ArrayList**, in the exercises at the end of this chapter.

15.2 Binary search trees

Although it is possible to illustrate tree algorithms using family trees, it is more effective to do so in a simpler environment that applies more directly to programming. Although the family-tree example provides a framework for introducing the terminology used to describe trees, it suffers in practice from the complication that each node can have an arbitrary number of children. In many

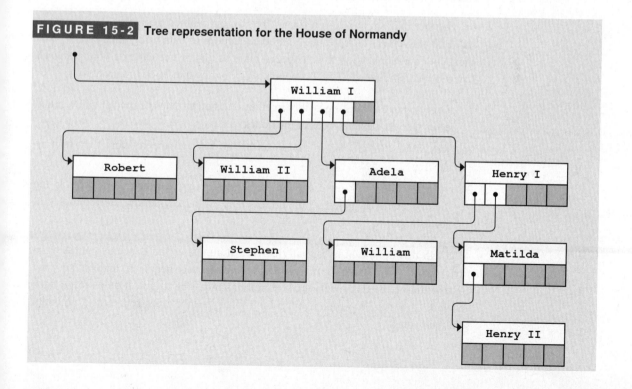

FIGURE 15-2 **Tree representation for the House of Normandy**

programming contexts, it is reasonable to restrict the number of children to make the resulting trees easier to implement.

One of the most important subclasses of trees—which has many practical applications—is a **binary tree,** which is defined to be a tree in which the following additional properties hold:

- Each node in the tree has at most two children.
- Every node except the root is designated as either a **left child** or a **right child** of its parent.

The second condition emphasizes the fact that child nodes in a binary tree are ordered with respect to their parents. For example, the binary trees

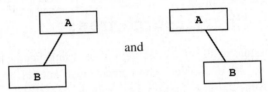

and

are different trees, even though they consist of the same nodes. In both cases, the node labeled **B** is a child of the root node labeled **A**, but it is a left child in the first tree and a right child in the second.

The fact that the nodes in a binary tree have a defined geometrical relationship makes it convenient to represent ordered collections of data using binary trees. The most common application uses a special class of binary tree called a **binary search tree**—often abbreviated to **BST**—which is defined by the following properties:

1. Every node contains—possibly in addition to other data—a special value called a *key* that defines the order of the nodes.
2. Key values are *unique,* in the sense that no key can appear more than once in the tree.
3. At every node in the tree, the key value must be greater than all the keys in the subtree rooted at its left child and less than all the keys in the subtree rooted at its right child.

Although this definition is formally correct, it almost certainly seems confusing at first glance. To make sense of the definition and begin to understand why constructing a tree that meets these conditions might be useful, it helps to go back and look at a specific problem for which binary search trees represent a potential solution strategy.

The motivation behind binary search trees

In Chapter 14, one of the strategies proposed for representing maps—before the hashing algorithm made other options seem far less attractive—was to store the key-value pairs in an array. This strategy has a useful computational property: if you keep the keys in sorted order, you can write an implementation of **get** that runs in $O(\log N)$ time. All you need to do is employ the binary search algorithm, which was introduced in Chapter 8. Unfortunately, the array representation does not offer any equally efficient way to code the **put** method. Although **put** can use binary search to determine where any new key fits into the array, maintaining the sorted order requires $O(N)$ time because each subsequent array element must be shifted to make room for the new entry.

This problem brings to mind a similar situation that arose in Chapter 12. When the editor buffer was implemented using arrays, inserting a new character was a linear-time operation. In that case, the solution was to replace the array with a linked list. Is it possible that a similar strategy would improve the performance of **put** for the map? After all, inserting a new element into a linked list—as long as you have a reference to the cell prior to the insertion point—is a constant-time operation.

The trouble with linked lists is that they do not support the binary search algorithm in any efficient way. Binary search depends on being able to find the middle element in constant time. In an array, finding the middle element is easy. In a linked list, the only way to do so is to iterate through the links in the first half of the list.

To get a more concrete sense of why linked lists have this limitation, suppose that you have a linked list containing the names of Walt Disney's seven dwarves:

→ Bashful → Doc → Dopey → Grumpy → Happy → Sleepy → Sneezy

The elements in this list appear in lexicographic order, which is the order imposed by their internal character codes.

Given a linked list of this sort, you can easily find the first element, because the initial reference gives you its address. From there, you can follow the link to find the second element. On the other hand, there is no easy way to locate the element that occurs halfway through the sequence. To do so, you have to walk through each cell in the chain, counting up to $N/2$. This operation requires linear time, which completely negates the efficiency advantage of binary search. If binary search is to offer any improvement in efficiency, the data structure must enable you to find the middle element quickly.

Although doing so might at first seem silly, it is useful to consider what happens if you simply point at the middle of the list instead of the beginning:

Bashful → Doc → Dopey → Grumpy → Happy → Sleepy → Sneezy

In this diagram, you have no problem at all finding the middle element. It's immediately accessible through the reference that points directly to Grumpy. The problem, however, is that you've thrown away the first half of the list. The references in the structure provide access to Grumpy and any name that follows it in the chain, but there is no longer any way to reach Bashful, Doc, and Dopey.

If you think about the situation from Grumpy's point of view, the general outline of the solution becomes clear. What you need is to have two chains emanating from the Grumpy cell: one that consists of cells whose names precede Grumpy and another for cells whose names follow Grumpy in the alphabet. In the conceptual diagram, all you need to do is reverse the arrows:

Bashful ← Doc ← Dopey ← Grumpy → Happy → Sleepy → Sneezy

Each of the strings is now accessible, and you can easily divide the entire list in half.

At this point, you need to apply the same strategy recursively. The binary search algorithm requires you to find the middle of not only the original list but its sublists as well. You therefore need to restructure the lists that precede and follow Grumpy, using the same decomposition strategy. Every cell points in two directions: to the midpoint of the list that precedes it and to the midpoint of the list that follows it. Applying this process transforms the original list into the following binary tree:

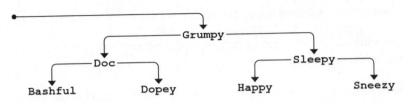

The most important feature of this particular style of binary tree is that it is ordered. For any particular node in the tree, the string it contains must follow all the strings in the subtree descending to the left and precede all strings in the subtree to the right. In this example, Grumpy comes after Doc, Bashful, and Dopey but before Sleepy, Happy, and Sneezy. The same rule applies at each level, so the node containing Doc comes after the Bashful node but before the Dopey node.

The formal definition of a binary search tree, which appears at the end of the preceding section, ensures that every node in the tree obeys this ordering rule.

Finding nodes in a binary search tree

The fundamental advantage of a binary search tree is that you can use the binary search algorithm to find a particular node. Suppose, for example, that you are looking for the node containing the string **Happy** in the tree diagram shown at the end of the preceding section. The first step is to compare **Happy** with **Grumpy**, which appears at the root of the tree. Since **Happy** comes after **Grumpy** in lexicographic order, you know that the **Happy** node, if it exists, must be in the right subtree. The next step, therefore, is to compare **Happy** and **Sleepy**. In this case, **Happy** comes before **Sleepy** and must therefore be in the left subtree of this node. That subtree consists of a single node, which contains the correct name.

Because trees are recursive structures, it is easy to code the search algorithm in its recursive form. For concreteness, let's suppose that the type definition for **BSTNode** looks like this:

```
private static class BSTNode {
   String key;
   BSTNode left, right;
};
```

Given this definition, you can easily write a method **findNode** that implements the binary search algorithm, as follows:

```
private BSTNode findNode(BSTNode node, String key) {
   if (node == null) return null;
   int cmp = key.compareTo(node.key);
   if (cmp == 0) return node;
   if (cmp < 0) {
      return findNode(node.left, key);
   } else {
      return findNode(node.right, key);
   }
}
```

If the tree is empty, it can't possibly contain the desired node, so **findNode** returns the value **null** as a sentinel indicating that the key cannot be found. If the tree is not equal to **null**, the implementation calls **compareTo** to see how the desired key compares to the key in the current node. If the two are equal, **findNode** returns a reference to the current node. If the keys are different, **findNode** proceeds recursively, looking in either the left or the right subtree depending on the result of the key comparison.

Inserting new nodes in a binary search tree

The next question to consider is how to create a binary search tree in the first place. The simplest approach is to begin with an empty tree and then call an `insertNode` method to insert new keys into the tree, one at a time. As each new key is inserted, it is important to maintain the ordering relationship among the nodes of the tree. To make sure the `findNode` method continues to work, the code for `insertNode` must use binary search to identify the correct insertion point.

As with `findNode`, the code for `insertNode` can proceed recursively starting at the root of the tree. At each node, `insertNode` must compare the new key to the key in the current node. If the new key precedes the existing one, the new key belongs in the left subtree. Conversely, if the new key follows the one in the current node, it belongs in the right subtree. Eventually, the process will encounter a `null` subtree that represents the point in the tree where the new node needs to be added. At this point, the `insertNode` implementation must replace the `null` reference with a new node initialized to contain a copy of the key.

The code for `insertNode`, however, is a bit tricky. The difficulty comes from the fact that `insertNode` must be able to change the value of the binary search tree by adding a new node. Since all parameters in Java are copied from the caller, you couldn't write a private method for which the call would look like this:

        insertNode(node, key);

The problem with this call is that there is no way in which the `insertNode` method can change the value of `node`.

The usual strategy for solving this problem in Java is to have the `insertNode` method return the updated tree that results from inserting the new node. A typical call to `insertNode` therefore looks like this:

        node = insertNode(node, key);

The effect of this statement is to insert the key into the tree rooted at `node` and then to assign the result of that insertion back into the variable `node`. The `insertTree` method therefore has the following prototype:

        private BSTNode insertNode(BSTNode node, String key)

Once you understand the prototype for the `insertNode` method, writing the code is not particularly hard. The implementation has the following form:

```
private BSTNode insertNode(BSTNode node, String key) {
   if (node == null) {
      node = new BSTNode();
      node.key = key;
      node.left = node.right = null;
   } else {
      int cmp = key.compareTo(node.key);
      if (cmp < 0) {
         node.left = insertNode(node.left, key);
      } else if (cmp > 0) {
         node.right = insertNode(node.right, key);
      }
   }
   return node;
}
```

If `node` is `null`, `insertNode` creates a new node, initializes its fields, and then replaces the `null` reference in the existing structure with a reference to the new node. If `node` is not `null`, `insertNode` compares the new key with the one stored in that node. If the keys match, the key is already in the tree and no further operations are required. If not, `insertNode` uses the result of the comparison to determine whether to insert the key in the left or the right subtree and then makes the appropriate recursive call.

Because the code for `insertNode` seems complicated until you've seen it work, it makes sense to go through the process of inserting a few keys in some detail. Suppose, for example, that you have declared and initialized an empty tree as follows:

```
BSTNode dwarfTree = null;
```

This statement creates a local variable `dwarfTree` and initializes it to `null`, as illustrated by the following diagram:

dwarfTree

What happens if you then call

```
dwarfTree = insertNode(dwarfTree, "Grumpy");
```

starting with this initial configuration in which `dwarfTree` is empty? In the frame for `insertNode`, the variable `node` is a copy of the variable `dwarfTree`, which means it has the value `null`. When `node` is `null`, the code for `insertNode` executes the first code block in the `if` statement, which begins with the line

```
node = new BSTNode();
```

This line allocates a new node and assigns it to **node**, which creates the following picture:

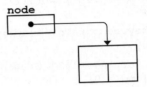

The remaining statements initialize the fields in the new node, copying the key **Grumpy** and initializing each of the subtree references to **null**, as follows: When **insertNode** returns, the tree looks like this:

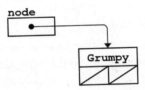

This structure correctly represents the binary search tree containing the single node **Grumpy**. When **insertNode** returns, that tree is assigned to **dwarfTree**, thereby completing the insertion in the context of the caller:

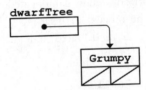

Suppose that you now make the following call:

```
dwarfTree = insertNode(dwarfTree, "Sleepy");
```

As before, the initial call copies the value of **dwarfTree** into the parameter **node**, like this:

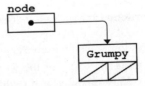

This time, however, the value of the tree **node** is no longer **null**. Because **Sleepy** comes after **Grumpy** in lexicographical order, the code for **insertNode** continues with the following recursive call:

```
node.right = insertNode(node.right, key);
```

This call creates a new stack frame in which the value of **node.right** is copied into the parameter **node**. Since this value is **null**, the implementation of **insertNode** again creates a new node and initializes its fields like this:

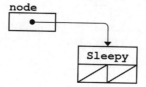

When **insertNode** returns, this value is assigned to the cell **node.right** in the calling frame, which results in the following diagram:

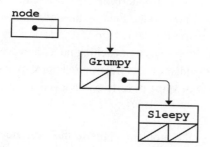

When this call to **insertNode** returns, it again assigns this value to **dwarfTree**, which gives rise to the following picture:

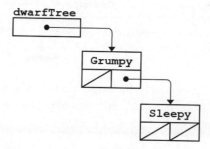

Additional calls to **insertNode** will create additional nodes and insert them into the structure in a way that preserves the ordering constraint required for binary search trees. For example, if you insert the names of the five remaining dwarves in the order **Doc**, **Bashful**, **Dopey**, **Happy**, and **Sneezy**, you end up with the binary search tree shown in Figure 15-3.

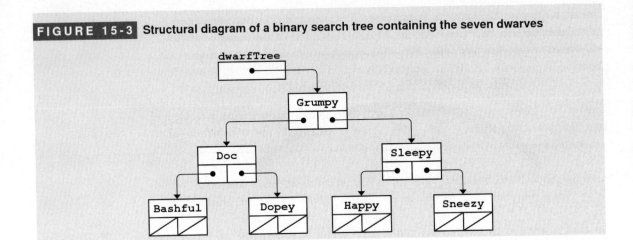

FIGURE 15-3 Structural diagram of a binary search tree containing the seven dwarves

Removing nodes

The operation of removing a node from a binary search tree is more complicated than that of inserting a new node. Finding the node to be removed is the easy part. All you need to do is use the same binary-search strategy that you use to locate a particular key. Once you find the matching node, however, you have to remove it from the tree without violating the ordering relationship that defines a binary search tree. Depending on where the node to be removed appears in the tree, removing it can get rather tricky.

To get a sense of the problem, suppose that you are working with the binary search tree containing the names of the seven dwarves:

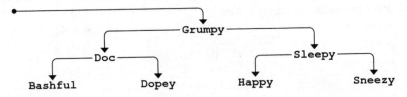

Removing **Sneezy** (presumably for creating an unhealthy work environment) is easy. All you have to do is replace the reference to the **Sneezy** node with a **null** reference, which produces the following tree:

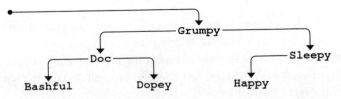

Starting from this configuration, it is also relatively easy to remove **Sleepy** (who has trouble staying awake on the job). If either child of the node you want to remove is **null**, all you have to do is replace it with its non-**null** child, like this:

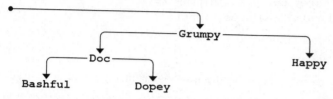

A problem arises, however, if you try to remove a node with both a left and a right child. Suppose, for example, that you instead want to remove **Grumpy** (for failure to whistle while working) from the original tree containing all seven dwarves. If you simply remove the **Grumpy** node, you're left with two partial search trees, one rooted at **Doc** and one rooted at **Sleepy**, as follows:

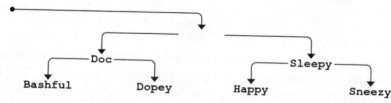

At this point, what you would like to do is find a node that can be inserted into the empty space left behind by the removal of the **Grumpy** node. To ensure that the resulting tree remains a binary search tree, there are only two nodes you can use: the rightmost node in the left subtree and the leftmost node in the right subtree. These two nodes work equally well. For example, if you choose the rightmost node in the left subtree, you get the **Dopey** node, which is guaranteed to be larger than anything else in the left subtree but smaller than the values in the right subtree. To complete the removal, all you have to do is replace the **Dopey** node with its left child—which may be **null**, as it is in this example—and then move the **Dopey** node into the deleted spot. The resulting picture looks like this:

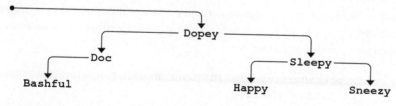

Tree traversals

The structure of a binary search tree makes it easy to go through the nodes of the tree in the order specified by the keys. For example, you can use the following method to display the keys in a binary search tree in lexicographic order:

```
void displayTree(BSTNode node) {
    if (node != null) {
        displayTree(node.left);
        System.out.println(node.key);
        displayTree(node.right);
    }
}
```

Thus, if you call `displayTree` on the tree shown in Figure 15-3, you get the following output:

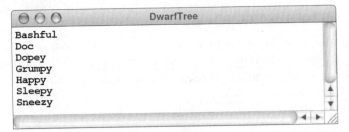

At each recursive level, `displayTree` checks to see whether the tree is empty. If it is, `displayTree` has no work to do. If not, the ordering of the recursive calls ensures that the output appears in the correct order. The first recursive call displays the keys that precede the current node, which appear in the left subtree. Displaying the nodes in the left subtree before the current one therefore maintains the correct order. Similarly, it is important to display the key from the current node before making the last recursive call, which displays the keys that follow the current node.

The process of going through the nodes of a tree and performing some operation at each node is called *traversing* or *walking* the tree. In many cases, you will want to traverse a tree in the order imposed by the keys, as in the `displayTree` example. This approach, which consists of processing the current node between the recursive calls to the left and right subtrees, is called an *inorder traversal*. There are, however, two other types of tree traversals that occur frequently in the context of binary trees, which are called *preorder* and *postorder* traversals. In the preorder traversal, the current node is processed before traversing either of its subtrees, as illustrated by the following code:

```
void preorderTraversal(BSTNode node) {
    if (node != null) {
        System.out.println(node.key);
        preorderTraversal(node.left);
        preorderTraversal(node.right);
    }
}
```

Given the tree from Figure 15-3, the preorder traversal prints the nodes in the order shown in the following sample run:

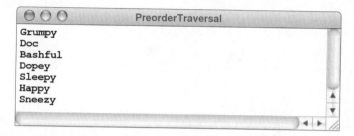

In the postorder traversal, the subtrees are processed first, followed by the current node. The code to display nodes in a postorder traversal is

```
void postorderTraversal(BSTNode node) {
   if (node != null) {
      postorderTraversal(node.left);
      postorderTraversal(node.right);
      System.out.println(node.key);
   }
}
```

Running this method on the binary search tree containing the seven dwarves produces the following output:

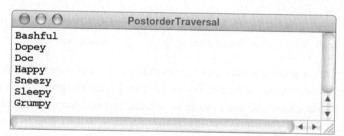

15.3 Balanced trees

Although the recursive strategy used to implement **insertNode** guarantees that the nodes are organized as a legal binary search tree, the structure of the tree depends on the order in which the nodes are inserted. The tree in Figure 15-3, for example, was generated by inserting the names of the dwarves in this order:

> **Grumpy, Sleepy, Doc, Bashful, Dopey, Happy, Sneezy**

Suppose that you had instead entered the names of the dwarves in alphabetical order. The first call to **insertNode** would insert **Bashful** at the root of the tree.

FIGURE 15-4 Unbalanced binary search tree

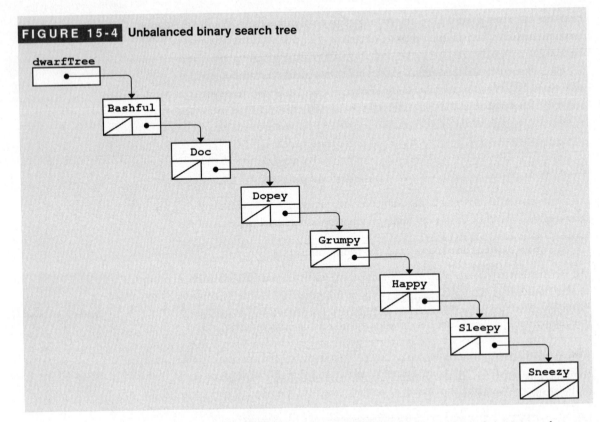

Subsequent calls would insert **Doc** after **Bashful**, **Dopey** after **Doc**, and so on, appending each new node to the **right** chain of the previous one.

The resulting figure, which is shown in Figure 15-4, looks more like a linked list than a tree. Nonetheless, the tree in Figure 15-4 maintains the property that the key field in any node follows all the keys in its left subtree and precedes all the keys in its right subtree. It therefore fits the definition of a binary search tree, so the **findNode** method will operate correctly. The running time of the **findNode** algorithm, however, is proportional to the height of the tree, which means that the structure of the tree can have a significant impact on the algorithmic performance. If a binary search tree is shaped like the one shown in Figure 15-3, the time required to find a key in the tree will be $O(\log N)$. On the other hand, if the tree is shaped like the one in Figure 15-4, the running time will deteriorate to $O(N)$.

The binary search algorithm used to implement **findNode** achieves its ideal performance only if the left and right subtrees have roughly the same height at each level of the tree. Trees in which this property holds—such as the tree in Figure 15-3—are said to be **balanced.** More formally, a binary tree is defined to be balanced if, at each node, the heights of the left and right subtrees differ by at most one. To illustrate this definition of a balanced binary tree, each of the tree diagrams in the top row of Figure 15-5 shows a balanced arrangement of a tree with seven nodes. The diagrams in the bottom row represent unbalanced arrangements. In each diagram, the nodes at which the balanced-tree definition fails are shown as open circles. In the leftmost unbalanced tree, for example, the left subtree of the root node has height 2 while the right subtree has height 0. In the remaining two examples, the root node is unbalanced because it has an unbalanced child.

The first diagram in Figure 15-5 is optimally balanced in the sense that the heights of the two subtrees at each node are equal. Such an arrangement is possible, however, only if the number of nodes is one less than a power of two. If the number of nodes does not meet this condition, there will be some point in the tree where the heights of the subtrees differ to some extent. By allowing the heights of the subtrees to differ by one, the definition of a balanced tree provides some flexibility in the structure of a tree without adversely affecting its computational performance.

FIGURE 15-5   Examples of balanced and unbalanced binary trees

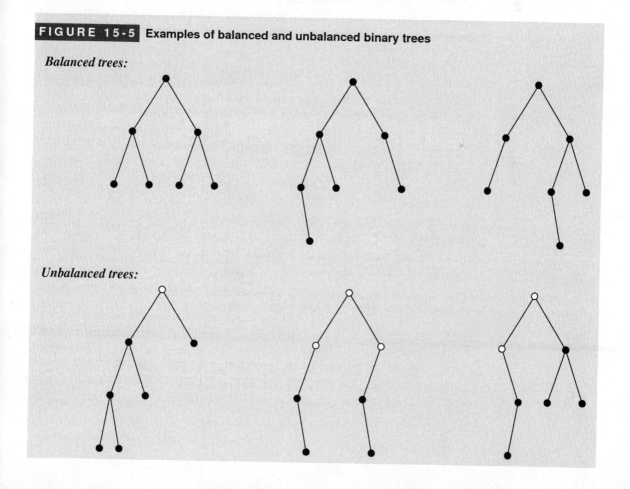

Balanced trees:

Unbalanced trees:

Tree-balancing strategies

Binary search trees are useful in practice only if it is possible to avoid the worst-case behavior associated with unbalanced trees. As trees become unbalanced, the `findNode` and `insertNode` operations become linear in their running time. If the performance of binary trees deteriorates to $O(N)$, you might as well use a sorted array to store the values. With a sorted array, it requires $O(\log N)$ time to implement `findNode` and $O(N)$ time to implement `insertNode`. From a computational perspective, an array-based representation is likely to outperform one based on unbalanced trees, as well as being considerably easier to write.

What makes binary search trees useful as a programming tool is the fact that you can keep them balanced as you build them. The basic idea is to extend the implementation of `insertNode` so that while inserting new nodes it keeps track of whether the tree is balanced. If the tree ever gets out of balance, `insertNode` must rearrange the nodes in the tree so that the balance is restored, without disturbing the ordering relationships that make the tree a binary search tree. Assuming that it is possible to rearrange a tree in time proportional to its height, both `findNode` and `insertNode` can be implemented in $O(\log N)$ time.

Algorithms for maintaining balance in a binary tree have been studied extensively in computer science. The algorithms used today to implement balanced binary trees are the product of decades of theoretical research in computer science. Most of these algorithms, however, are difficult to explain without reviewing mathematical results beyond the scope of this text. To demonstrate that such algorithms are indeed possible, the next few sections present one of the first tree-balancing algorithms, which was published in 1962 by the Russian mathematicians Georgii Adelson-Velskii and Evgenii Landis and which has since been known by the initials AVL. Although the AVL algorithm has been largely replaced in practice by more sophisticated techniques, it has the advantage of being considerably easier to explain than most current algorithms. Moreover, the operations used to implement the basic strategy reappear in many other algorithms, which makes the AVL algorithm a useful foundation for more modern techniques.

Visualizing the AVL algorithm

Before you attempt to understand the implementation of the AVL algorithm in detail, it helps to follow through the process of inserting nodes into a binary search tree to see what can go wrong and, if possible, what steps you can take to fix any problems that arise. Let's imagine that you want to create a binary search tree in which the nodes contain the symbols for the chemical elements. For example, the first six elements are

H   (Hydrogen)
He   (Helium)
Li   (Lithium)
Be   (Beryllium)
B   (Boron)
C   (Carbon)

What happens if you insert the chemical symbols for these elements in the indicated order, which is how these elements appear in the periodic table? The first insertion is easy because the tree is initially empty. The node containing the symbol H becomes the root of the tree. If you call **insertNode** on the symbol He, the new node will be added after the node containing H, because He comes after H in lexicographic order. Thus, the first two nodes in the tree are arranged like this:

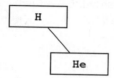

To keep track of whether the tree is balanced, the AVL algorithm associates an integer with each node, which is simply the height of the right subtree minus the height of the left subtree. This value is called the *balance factor* of the node. In the simple tree that contains the symbols for the first two elements, the balance factors, which are shown here in the upper right corner of each node, look like this:

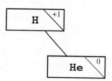

So far, the tree is balanced because none of the nodes has a balance factor whose absolute value is greater than 1. That situation changes, however, when you add the next element. If you follow the standard insertion algorithm, adding Li results in the following configuration:

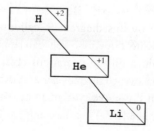

Here, the root node is out of balance because its right subtree has height 1 and its empty left subtree has (by definition) height −1, so the heights differ by two.

To fix the imbalance, you need to restructure the tree. For this set of nodes, there is only one balanced configuration in which the nodes are correctly ordered with respect to each other. That tree has **He** at the root, with **H** and **Li** in the left and right subtrees, as follows:

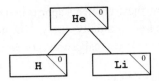

This tree is once again balanced, but an important question remains: how do you know what operations to perform in order to restore the balance in a tree?

Single rotations

The fundamental insight behind the AVL strategy is that you can always restore balance to a tree by a simple rearrangement of the nodes. If you think about what steps were necessary to correct the imbalance in the preceding example, it is clear that the **He** node moves upward to become the root while **H** moves downward to become its child. To a certain extent, the transformation has the characteristic of rotating the **H** and **He** nodes one position to the left, like this:

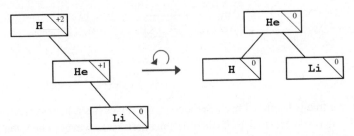

The two nodes involved in the rotation operation are called the *axis* of the rotation. In the example consisting of the elements **H**, **He**, and **Li**, the rotation was performed around the **H-He** axis. Because this operation moves nodes to the left, the operation illustrated by this diagram is called a *left rotation.* If a tree is out of balance in the opposite direction, you can apply a symmetric operation called a *right rotation,* in which all the operations are simply reversed. For example, the symbols for the next two elements—**Be** and **B**—each get added at the left edge of the tree. To rebalance the tree, you must perform a right rotation around the **Be-H** axis, as illustrated in the following diagram:

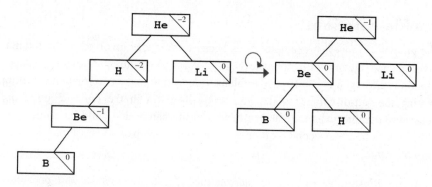

Unfortunately, simple rotation operations are not always sufficient to restore balance to a tree. Consider, for example, what happens when you add **c** to the tree. Before you perform any balancing operations, the tree looks like this:

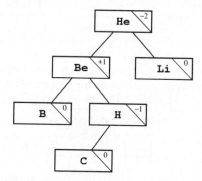

The **He** node at the root of the tree is out of balance. If you try to correct the imbalance by rotating the tree to the right around the **Be-He** axis, you get the following tree:

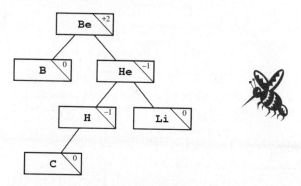

After the rotation, the tree is just as unbalanced as it was before. The only difference is that the root node is now unbalanced in the opposite direction.

Double rotations

The problem in this last example arises because the nodes involved in the rotation have balance factors with opposite signs. When this situation occurs, a single rotation is not enough. To fix the problem, you need to make two rotations. Before rotating the out-of-balance node, you rotate its child in the opposite direction. Rotating the child gives the balance factors in the parent and child the same sign, which means that the second rotation will succeed. This pair of operations is called a *double rotation.*

As an illustration of the double-rotation operation, consider the preceding unbalanced tree of elements just after the symbol **C** has been added. The first step is to rotate the tree to the left around the **Be-H** axis, like this:

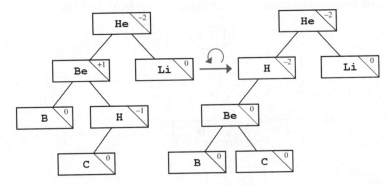

The resulting tree is still out of balance at the root node, but the **H** and **He** nodes now have balance factors that share the same sign. In this configuration, a single rotation to the right around the **H-He** axis restores balance to the tree, as follows:

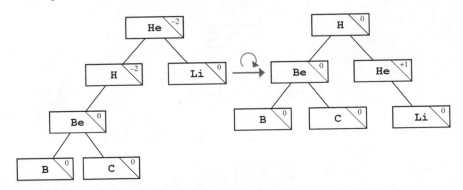

The rotation operations for AVL trees are illustrated in Figure 15-6, which shows how these operations work even in trees with arbitrarily large subtrees, which are represented by the gray triangles in the figure.

FIGURE 15-6 **Rotation operations in an AVL tree**

Single rotation

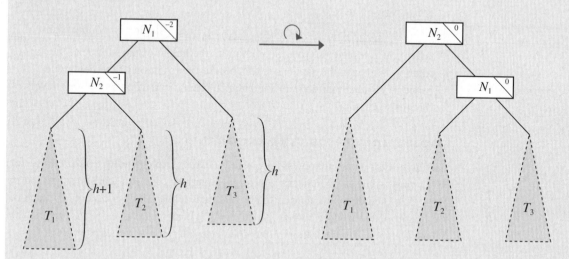

Double rotation

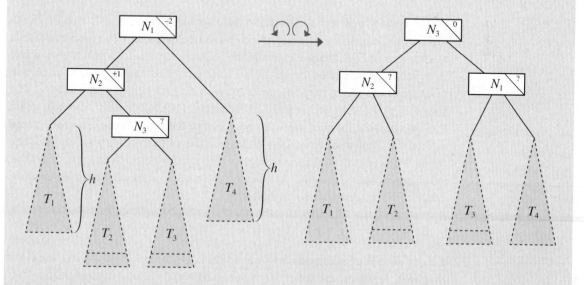

Note: At least one of the subtrees T_2 and T_3 must have height h; the other can have height h or $h-1$. The balance factors in the final nodes will need to be adjusted to take account of any difference in height.

In their paper describing these trees, Adelson-Velskii and Landis demonstrate the following properties of their tree-balancing algorithm, both of which are suggested (but by no means formally proved) by the diagrams in Figure 15-6:

- If you insert a new node into an AVL tree, you can always restore its balance by performing at most one operation, which is either a single or a double rotation.

- After you complete the rotation operation, the height of the subtree at the axis of rotation is always the same as it was before the insertion of the new node. This property ensures that none of the balance factors change at any higher levels of the tree.

Implementing the AVL algorithm

Although the process involves quite a few details, implementing `insertNode` for AVL trees is not as difficult as you might imagine. The first change you need to make is to include a new field in the node structure that allows you to keep track of the height of the subtree rooted at that node, which makes it easy to compute the balance factors. The definition of the node class therefore changes as follows:

```
class AVLNode {
    String key;
    int height;
    AVLNode left, right;
};
```

The updated code for `insertNode` itself appears in Figure 15-7, along with the various helper methods necessary to keep the tree balanced. The private methods `fixHeight` and `getHeight` maintain the height in each node, which is always one more than the maximum height of its children. The `fixLeftImbalance` and `fixRightImbalance` methods are called whenever the heights of the children of a node differ by two in one direction or the other. (The heights can't differ by more than two because the tree was in balance before the call to `insertNode`.) These methods are similar, differing only in the direction of the rotation. The same is true for the `rotateLeft` and `rotateRight` methods, which perform a single rotation in the appropriate direction. All four of these helper methods return the updated tree, just as the `insertNode` method does.

Using the code for the AVL algorithm shown in Figure 15-7 ensures that the binary search tree remains in balance as new nodes are added. As a result, both `findNode` and `insertNode` will run in $O(\log N)$ time. Even without the AVL extension, however, the code will continue to work. The advantage of the AVL strategy is that it guarantees $O(\log N)$ performance, at some cost in the complexity of the code.

FIGURE 15-7 Code to insert a node into an AVL tree

```
/*
 * Enters the key into the tree and returns the updated tree.  The usual
 * pattern for using this method assigns the result back to the tree, as
 * follows:
 *
 *     node = insertNode(node, key);
 */

   private AVLNode insertNode(AVLNode node, String key) {
      if (node == null) {
         node = new AVLNode();
         node.key = key;
         node.height = 0;
         node.left = node.right = null;
      } else {
         int cmp = key.compareTo(node.key);
         if (cmp < 0) {
            node.left = insertNode(node.left, key);
         } else if (cmp > 0) {
            node.right = insertNode(node.right, key);
         }
         fixHeight(node);
         int bf = getHeight(node.right) - getHeight(node.left);
         if (bf == -2) {
            node = fixLeftImbalance(node);
         } else if (bf == +2) {
            node = fixRightImbalance(node);
         }
      }
      return node;
   }

/*
 * Recomputes the height in the top node of the specified tree, assuming
 * that the heights of all subtrees are stored correctly.
 */

   private void fixHeight(AVLNode node) {
      if (node != null) {
         node.height = Math.max(getHeight(node.left),
                                    getHeight(node.right)) + 1;
      }
   }

/*
 * Returns the height of the specified tree.  The special case check is
 * necessary to define the height of the empty tree as -1.
 */

   private int getHeight(AVLNode node) {
      return (node == null) ? -1 : node.height;
   }
```

FIGURE 15-7 Code to insert a node into an AVL tree (continued)

```
/*
 * Restores the balance to a tree that has a longer subtree on the left.
 * Like insertNode, fixLeftImbalance returns the updated tree.
 */

   private AVLNode fixLeftImbalance(AVLNode node) {
      AVLNode child = node.left;
      if (getHeight(child.right) > getHeight(child.left)) {
         node.left = rotateLeft(child);
      }
      return rotateRight(node);
   }

/*
 * Restores the balance to a tree that has a longer subtree on the right.
 * Like insertNode, fixRightImbalance returns the updated tree.
 */

   private AVLNode fixRightImbalance(AVLNode node) {
      AVLNode child = node.right;
      if (getHeight(child.left) > getHeight(child.right)) {
         node.right = rotateRight(child);
      }
      return rotateLeft(node);
   }

/*
 * Performs a single left rotation around the specified node and its right
 * child, returning the updated tree.
 */

   private AVLNode rotateLeft(AVLNode node) {
      AVLNode child = node.right;
      node.right = child.left;
      child.left = node;
      fixHeight(node);
      fixHeight(child);
      return child;
   }

/*
 * Performs a single right rotation around the specified node and its left
 * child, returning the updated tree.
 */

   private AVLNode rotateRight(AVLNode node) {
      AVLNode child = node.left;
      node.left = child.right;
      child.right = node;
      fixHeight(node);
      fixHeight(child);
      return child;
   }
```

15.4 Implementing maps using BSTs

As its name suggests, the **TreeMap** class in the Java Collection Framework uses a binary search tree as its underlying representation. This implementation strategy means that the **get** and **put** methods run in $O(\log N)$ time, which is slightly less efficient than the $O(1)$ average running time offered by the hash table strategy. In practice, that difference is not all that important. The graph of $O(\log N)$ grows extremely slowly and is much closer to $O(1)$ than it is to $O(N)$. The ability to process keys in order is usually worth the modest additional cost.

The hard parts of implementing **TreeMap** are almost entirely in the code for the binary search trees themselves, which you have already seen in this chapter. Completing the **TreeMap** implementation requires only a few additional tasks:

- The code must use templates to parameterize the key and value types.
- The node structure must include a value field along with the key.
- The code must implement the methods in the **Map** interface.

These changes are implemented in the code shown in Figure 15-8.

Although updating the node structure to use template parameters is reasonably straightforward, it is not quite as easy as it might at first appear. Judging from the implementation of the **HashMap** class in Chapter 14, one is tempted simply to add the type parameters **K** and **V** to the class definition, as follows:

```
public class TreeMap<K,V>
```

The problem with this simple approach is that the **TreeMap** class requires that the keys be ordered. In particular, the code for **findNode** and **insertNode** assumes that it is possible to call the **compareTo** method to compare two keys. In the absence of more specific information, the compiler can't know whether it is legal to call this method on values of type **K**.

To fix this problem, you need to specify restrictions on the type parameter **K** to ensure that it supports comparison. In Java, the **compareTo** method is specified by the interface **Comparable<K>**, which means that you need to indicate that the type **K**—whatever it is—must at least implement the **compareTo** method.

Fortunately, Java makes it possible to add qualifications to a type parameter that enable the compiler to check that the type has the desired properties. If, for example, you wanted to insist that the type **K**, whatever it is, implements the interface **Comparable<K>**, you could do so by writing

```
K extends Comparable<K>
```

FIGURE 15-8   Code to implement the TreeMap class

```java
/*
 * File: TreeMap.java
 * --------------------
 * This file implements the Map interface using a binary search tree.
 * The code is simple enough that detailed comments are not required.
 */

package edu.stanford.cs.javacs2.ch15;

import edu.stanford.cs.javacs2.ch14.Map;
import java.util.ArrayList;
import java.util.Collection;
import java.util.Iterator;
import java.util.Set;
import java.util.TreeSet;

public class TreeMap<K extends Comparable<? super K>,V> implements Map<K,V> {

    public TreeMap() {
        clear();
    }

    public int size() {
        return count;
    }

    public boolean isEmpty() {
        return count == 0;
    }

    public void clear() {
        root = null;
        count = 0;
    }

    public V get(K key) {
        TreeMapNode np = findNode(root, key);
        return (np == null) ? null : np.value;
    }

    public void put(K key, V value) {
        root = insertNode(root, key, value);
    }

    public boolean containsKey(K key) {
        return findNode(root, key) != null;
    }

    public void remove(K key) {
        root = removeNode(root, key);
    }
```

FIGURE 15-8 Code to implement the `TreeMap` class (continued)

```
/*
 * Implementation notes: keySet and keyIterator
 * ------------------------------------------------
 * These methods call addKeysInOrder to perform an inorder walk.  Lists and
 * sets implement the Collection interface in Java, so the code is shared.
 */

   public Set<K> keySet() {
      Set<K> keys = new TreeSet<K>();
      addKeysInOrder(root, keys);
      return keys;
   }

   public Iterator<K> keyIterator() {
      ArrayList<K> keys = new ArrayList<K>();
      addKeysInOrder(root, keys);
      return keys.iterator();
   }

   private void addKeysInOrder(TreeMapNode t, Collection<K> keys) {
      if (t != null) {
         addKeysInOrder(t.left, keys);
         keys.add(t.key);
         addKeysInOrder(t.right, keys);
      }
   }
}
```

> *The implementation of the BST goes here.*

```
/* Inner class defining a node in the tree */

   private class TreeMapNode {
      K key;
      V value;
      int height;
      TreeMapNode left, right;
   }

/* Private instance variables */

   private TreeMapNode root;
   private int count;

}
```

as the type parameter. Armed with this new piece of Java syntax, you might then
try to write the **TreeMap** header line like this:

```
public class TreeMap<K extends Comparable<K>,V>
```

Although this version of the header line is closer to what you want, it still falls short of the optimal definition. The problem with this new header line is that it overly restrictive. It isn't actually necessary for `K` to implement `Comparable<K>`. It is enough for `K` to implement the `compareTo` function for some class that includes `K` as a subclass. The restriction you want—and the one you will usually want when you want to make sure that a type supports comparison—is the following header line:

```
public class TreeMap<K extends Comparable<? super K>,V>
```

The type specification

```
K extends Comparable<? super K>
```

indicates that `K` must implement the `Comparable` interface in `K`'s superclass chain.

Adding a value to the node type is simply a matter of adding a new field to the class definition. If you use the AVL model, you can define `TreeMapNode` like this:

```
private class TreeMapNode {
    K key;
    V value;
    int height;
    TreeMapNode left, right;
}
```

15.5 Partially ordered trees

Trees come up in many other programming contexts. One particularly useful application arises in the implementation of *priority queues,* where the order in which elements are removed depends on the natural order of the items imposed by its comparison function. Java's `PriorityQueue` class, which is part of the Java Collections Framework in the `java.util` package, follows conventional English usage in that lower priority values come earlier in the queue. For example, if you were using a priority queue of integers, priority 1 would come before priority 2.

Priority queues are usually implemented using a data structure called a *partially ordered tree,* in which the following properties hold:

1. The tree is a binary tree in that each node has at most two children. It is not, however, a binary search tree, which has different ordering rules.

2. The nodes of the tree are arranged in a pattern as close to that of a completely symmetrical tree as possible. Thus, the number of nodes along any path in the

tree can never differ by more than one. Moreover, the bottom level must be filled in a strictly left-to-right order.

3.   Each node contains a key that is always less than or equal to the key in its children. Thus, the smallest key in the tree is always at the root.

As an example, the following diagram shows a partially ordered tree with four nodes, each of which contains a numeric key:

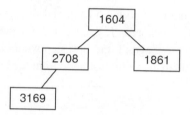

The second level of the tree is completely filled, and the third level is in the process of being filled from left to right, as required by the second property of partially ordered trees. The third property holds because the key in each node is always less than the keys in its children.

Suppose that you want to add a node with the key 2193. It is clear where the new node goes. The requirement that the lowest level of the tree be filled from left to right dictates that the new node be added at the following position:

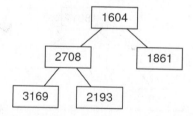

This diagram, however, violates the third property of partially ordered trees, because the key 2193 is smaller than the 2708 in its parent. To fix the problem, you begin by exchanging the keys in those nodes, like this:

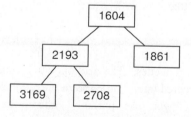

In general, it is possible that the newly inserted key would have to be exchanged with its parent in a cascading sequence of changes proceeding up through the levels of the tree. In this specific case, the process of exchanging keys stops here because 2193 is greater than 1604. In any event, the structure of the tree guarantees that these exchanges will never require more than $O(\log N)$ time.

The structure of the partially ordered tree means that the smallest value in the tree is always at the root. Removing the root node, however, takes a little more work because you have to arrange for the node that actually disappears to be the rightmost node in the bottom level. The standard approach is to replace the key in the root with the key in the node to be deleted and then swap keys down the tree until the ordering property is restored. If you wanted, for example, to delete the root node from the preceding tree diagram, the first step would be to replace the key in the root node with the 2708 in the rightmost node from the lowest level, as follows:

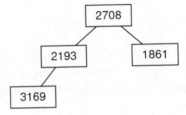

Then, because the nodes of the tree no longer have correctly ordered keys, you would need to exchange the key 2708 with the smaller of the two keys in its children, like this:

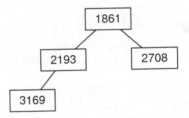

Although a single interchange is enough to restore the ordering property of the tree in this example, the general process of finding the correct position for the key that was moved into the root position might require you to swap that element through each of the levels in the tree. As with insertion, deleting the smallest key requires $O(\log N)$ time.

The operations that define the partially ordered tree are precisely the ones you need to implement priority queues. The **add** operation consists of inserting a new node into the partially ordered tree. The **remove** operation consists of removing the lowest value. Thus, if you use partially ordered trees as the underlying representation, you can implement the priority queue package so that it runs in $O(\log N)$ time.

Although you can implement partially ordered trees by using references, most implementations of priority queues employ an array-based structure called a *heap,* which simulates the operation of a partially ordered tree. (The terminology is confusing at first, because the heap data structure bears no relationship to the pool of unused memory available for dynamic allocation, which is also referred to by the word *heap.*) The implementation strategy used in a heap depends on the property that you can store the nodes in a partially ordered tree of size N in the first N elements of an array simply by numbering the nodes, level by level, from left to right.

As an example, the partially ordered tree

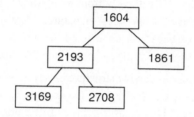

can be represented as the following heap:

1604	2193	1861	3169	2708			...
0	1	2	3	4	5	6	

The heap organization makes it simple to implement tree operations, because parent and child nodes always appear at an easily computed position. For example, given a node at index position **k**, you can find the indices of its parent and children using the following expressions:

`parentIndex(k)`	*is always given by*	`(k - 1) / 2`
`leftChildIndex(k)`	*is always given by*	`2 * k + 1`
`rightChildIndex(k)`	*is always given by*	`2 * k + 2`

The division operator in the calculation of **parentIndex** is the standard integer division operator from Java. Thus, the parent of the node at index position 4 in the array appears at position 1 in the array, because the result of evaluating the expression **(4 - 1) / 2** is 1.

A heap-based implementation of the **PriorityQueue** class is included in the materials that accompany this chapter. Even so, writing the code that maintains the ordering of the heap as new items are added and removed from the queue makes an excellent exercise. Remember that the elements of a priority queue must be comparable, which means that the class header line should look like this:

```
public class PriorityQueue<T extends Comparable<? super T>>
```

▮ Summary

In this chapter, you have been introduced to the concept of *trees,* which are hierarchical collections of nodes that have the following properties:

- There is a single node at the top that forms the root of the hierarchy.

- Every node in the tree is connected to the root by a unique line of descent.

  Important points in this chapter include:

- Many of the terms used to describe trees, such as *parent, child, ancestor, descendant,* and *sibling,* come directly from family trees. Other terms, including *root* and *leaf,* are derived from trees in nature. These metaphors make the terminology used for trees easy to understand because the words have the same interpretation in computer science that they do in more familiar contexts.

- Trees have a well-defined recursive structure because every node in a tree is the root of a subtree. Thus, a tree consists of a node together with its set of children, each of which is a tree. This recursive structure is reflected in the underlying representation for a tree, which is defined as a reference to a node; a node, in turn, is an object that contains trees.

- Binary trees are a subclass of trees in which nodes have at most two children and every node except the root is designated as either a left child or a right child of its parent.

- If a binary tree is organized so that every node in the tree contains a key field that follows all the keys in its left subtree and precedes all the keys in its right subtree, that tree is called a *binary search tree.* As its name implies, the structure of a binary search tree permits the use of the binary search algorithm, which makes it possible to find individual keys more efficiently. Because the keys are ordered, it is always possible to determine whether the key you're searching for appears in the left or right subtree of any particular node.

- Using recursion makes it easy to step through the nodes in a binary search tree, which is called *traversing* or *walking* the tree. There are several types of traversals, depending on the order in which the nodes are processed. If the key in each node is processed before the recursive calls to process the subtrees, the result is a *preorder* traversal. Processing each node after both recursive calls gives rise to a *postorder* traversal. Processing the current node between the two recursive calls represents an *inorder* traversal. In a binary search tree, the inorder traversal has the useful property that the keys are processed in order.

- Depending on the order in which nodes are inserted, given the same set of keys, binary search trees can have radically different structures. If the branches of the tree differ substantially in height, the tree is said to be unbalanced, which reduces its efficiency. By using techniques such as the AVL algorithm described in this chapter, you can keep a tree in balance as new nodes are added.

- Priority queues can be implemented efficiently using a data structure called a *heap,* which is based on a special class of binary tree called a *partially ordered tree.* If you use this representation, both the **add** and the **remove** operations run in $O(\log N)$ time.

Review questions

1. What two conditions must be satisfied for a collection of nodes to be a tree?

2. Give at least four real-world examples that involve tree structures.

3. Define the terms *parent, child, ancestor, descendant,* and *sibling* as they apply to trees.

4. The family tree for the House of Tudor, which ruled England in Shakespeare's time, is shown in Figure 15-9. Identify the root, leaf, and interior nodes. What is the height of this tree?

5. What is it about trees that makes them recursive?

6. Diagram the internal structure of the tree shown in Figure 15-9 when it is represented using the type **FamilyTreeNode**.

7. What is the defining property of a binary search tree?

FIGURE 15-9 **The House of Tudor**

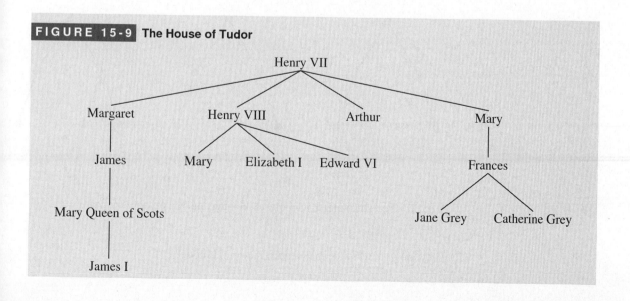

8. What strategy is used by the **insertNode** method to ensure that the code can change the root of the tree?

9. In *The Hobbit* by J. R. R. Tolkien, 13 dwarves arrive at the house of Bilbo Baggins in the following order: **Dwalin, Balin, Kili, Fili, Dori, Nori, Ori, Oin, Gloin, Bifur, Bofur, Bombur,** and **Thorin**. Diagram the binary search tree that results from inserting these names into an empty tree.

10. Given the tree you created to answer the preceding question, what key comparisons are made if you call **findNode** on the name **Bombur**?

11. Write down the preorder, inorder, and postorder traversals of the binary search tree you created for question 9.

12. One of the three standard traversal orders—preorder, inorder, or postorder—does not depend on the order in which the nodes are inserted into the tree. Which one is it?

13. What is the standard definition of the *height* of a binary tree? Under this definition, what is the height of a binary tree that contains a single node? What about the empty binary tree that is just a **null** pointer?

14. What does it mean for a binary tree to be balanced?

15. True or false: If a binary search tree becomes unbalanced, the algorithms used in the methods **findNode** and **insertNode** will fail to work correctly.

16. For each of the following tree structures, indicate whether the tree is balanced:

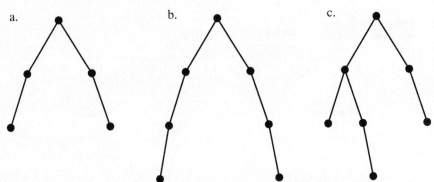

a.   b.   c.

For any tree structure that is out of balance, indicate which nodes are out of balance.

17. How do you calculate the balance factor of a node?

18. Fill in the balance factors for each node in the following binary search tree:

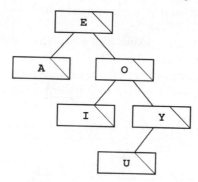

19. What do the letters *AVL* stand for?

20. If you use the AVL balancing strategy, what rotation operation must you apply to the tree in question 18 to restore its balanced configuration? What is the structure of the resulting tree, including the updated balance factors?

21. True or false: When you insert a new node into a balanced binary tree, you can always correct any resulting imbalance by performing one operation, which will be either a single or a double rotation.

22. As shown in the section on "Visualizing the AVL idea," inserting the symbols for the first six elements into an AVL tree results in the following configuration:

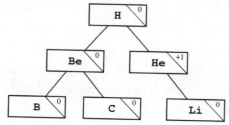

Show what happens to the tree as you add the symbols for the next six elements:

N	(Nitrogen)
O	(Oxygen)
F	(Fluorine)
Ne	(Neon)
Na	(Sodium)
Mg	(Magnesium)

23. Describe in detail what happens during a call to `insertNode`.

24. What strategy does the text suggest to avoid having a binary search tree become disconnected if you remove an interior node?

25. Suppose that you are working with a partially ordered tree that contains the following data:

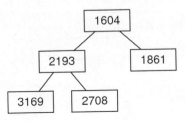

Show the state of the partially ordered tree after insertion of the key 1521.

26. What is the relationship between heaps and partially ordered trees?

▮▮▮ Exercises

1. Working from the definition of **FamilyTreeNode** given in the section entitled "Representing family trees in Java," write a method

   FamilyTreeNode readFamilyTree(String filename)

   that reads in a family tree from a data file whose name is supplied as the argument to the call.   The first line of the file should contain a name corresponding to the root of the tree.   All subsequent lines in the data file should have the following form:

   child:*parent*

   where *child* is the name of the new individual being entered and *parent* is the name of that child's parent, which must appear earlier in the data file.   For example, if the file **Normandy.txt** contains the lines

   ```
   Normandy.txt
   William I
   Robert:William I
   William II:William I
   Adela:William I
   Henry I:William I
   Stephen:Adela
   William:Henry I
   Matilda:Henry I
   Henry II:Matilda
   ```

   calling **readFamilyTree("Normandy.txt")** should return the family-tree structure shown in Figure 15-2.

2. Add a `displayFamilyTree` method to the `FamilyTreeNode` class that displays all the individuals in the family tree. To record the hierarchy of the tree, the output of your method should indent each generation so that the name of each child appears two spaces to the right of the corresponding parent, as shown in the following sample run:

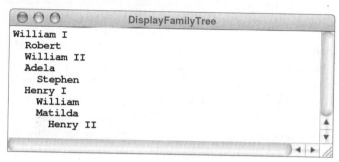

```
DisplayFamilyTree
William I
  Robert
  William II
  Adela
    Stephen
  Henry I
    William
    Matilda
      Henry II
```

3. As defined in the chapter, the `FamilyTreeNode` structure uses an `ArrayList` to store the children. Another possibility is to include an extra reference in these nodes that will allow them to form a linked list of the children. Thus, in this design, each node in the tree needs to contain only two references: one to its eldest child and one to its next younger sibling. A diagram of the House of Normandy that uses this representation appears in Figure 15-10. In each node, the reference on the left always points down to a child; the reference on the right indicates the next sibling in the same generation. Thus, the eldest child of William I is Robert, which you discover

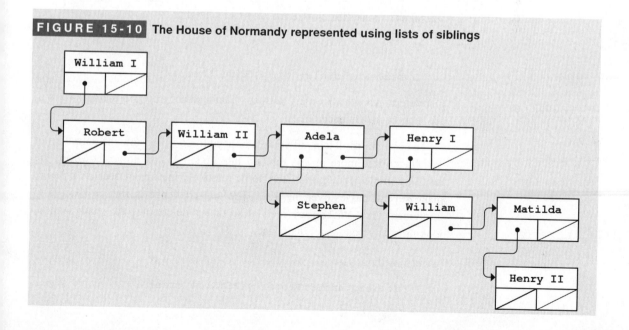

FIGURE 15-10 **The House of Normandy represented using lists of siblings**

by following the link at the left of the diagram. The remaining children are linked together through the link cells shown at the right of the node diagram. The chain of children ends at Henry I, which has the value `null` in its next-sibling link.

Using the linked design this diagram illustrates, write new definitions of `FamilyTreeNode`, `readFamilyTree`, and `displayFamilyTree`.

4. In exercise 3, the changes you made to the `FamilyTreeNode` structure forced you to rewrite the methods `readFamilyTree` and `displayFamilyTree` because those methods depend on the internal representation. If the family tree were instead represented as an interface that remains constant despite any changes in representation, you could avoid much of this recoding. Design a new data structure that allows you to implement the family tree operations using more than one underlying implementation strategy. Test your design by implementing both the design from the chapter and the linked-list model from exercise 3. Your new data-structure design should also allow the client to find the parent of any node in the family tree.

5. Using the interface you designed for exercise 4, write a method called `findCommonAncestor` that takes two individuals in a family tree and returns the closest ancestor shared by those individuals.

6. Using the definition of `BSTNode` from section 15.2, write a method

```
int getHeight(BSTNode tree)
```

that takes a binary search tree and returns its height.

7. Write a method

```
boolean isBalanced(BSTNode tree)
```

that determines whether a given tree is balanced according to the definition in the section on "Balanced trees."

To solve this problem, all you really need to do is translate the definition of a balanced tree more or less directly into code. If you do so, however, the resulting implementation is likely to be relatively inefficient because it has to make several passes over the tree. The real challenge in this problem is to implement the `isBalanced` method so that it determines the result without looking at any node more than once.

8. Write a method

```
boolean hasBSTProperty(BSTNode tree)
```

that takes a tree and determines whether it maintains the fundamental property that defines a binary search tree: that the key in each node follows every key in its left subtree and precedes every key in its right subtree.

9. When implementing a binary search tree, an important efficiency concern is taking care that the tree remains balanced to ensure logarithmic performance for insertion and lookup. Unfortunately, strategies that continually make minor rearrangements to rebalance the tree often end up spending too much time on those operations. An alternative strategy is to let the client determine whether a problem exists and, if so, rebalance the tree all at once.

   One reasonably efficient strategy for rebalancing a tree is to transfer the nodes into a sorted `ArrayList` and then reconstruct an optimally balanced tree from that `ArrayList`. If you adopt this approach, you can implement a rebalancing operation for the `BSTNode` type by decomposing the problem into two phases, as follows:

   1. Perform an inorder walk on the tree, adding the nodes to an `ArrayList`.
   2. Recreate the tree by choosing the element closest to the middle of the `ArrayList` as the root, and then rebuilding each child recursively from the left and right subarrays on each side of the root.

   Implement a method

   ```
   BSTNode rebalance(BSTNode root)
   ```

   that uses this approach to return a balanced tree containing the same nodes as `root`. Your method should not create or destroy any nodes but simply reorder the ones from the original tree.

10§. The discussion of the AVL algorithm in the text offers a strategy for inserting a node but does not cover the symmetric process of removing a node, which also requires rebalancing the tree. As it turns out, the rebalancing operations are similar. Removing a node either may have no effect on the height of a tree or may shorten it by one. If a tree gets shorter, the balance factor in its parent node changes. If the parent node is then unbalanced, it is possible to rebalance the tree at that point by performing either a single or a double rotation.

   Implement a method

   ```
   AVLNode removeNode(AVLNode node, String key)
   ```

   that removes the node containing `key` from the tree while keeping the underlying AVL tree balanced. Think carefully about the various cases that can arise and make sure that your implementation handles each case correctly.

FIGURE 15-11 Morse code tree

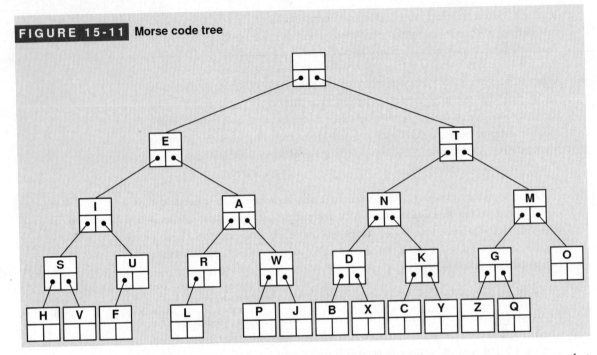

11. In exercise 8 from Chapter 6, you had the opportunity to write a program that translated messages from Morse code to the equivalent English letters. That exercise encouraged you to use a map to store the translation tables, but there are other ways to approach the problem. You can, for example, think of the Morse encodings as a binary tree in which dots take you to the left and dashes take you to the right. In this formulation, the letters in the Morse code table have the structure shown in Figure 15-11. As an example, you can reach the letter **L** by starting at the root and then following a sequence of links in the order left-right-left-left, which tells you that the Morse code for **L** is •■••.

Design a data structure to store the tree from Figure 15-11 and then write a method **getMorseCodeLetter**(*code*) that uses the tree to find the letter that corresponds to the Morse code string given by *code*.

12. The implementation of binary search trees given in the chapter—in which adding a node requires assigning the result of an insertion function back to the variable containing the tree—appears here because it is the conventional strategy for representing binary search trees in Java, and you are therefore likely to see this technique elsewhere. You can, however, simplify the code by adopting a representation with two inner classes instead of one. The **Tree** class contains a single element, which is a **Node**; the **Node** class contains the key, a **Tree** to the left, and a **Tree** to the right. Rewrite the **BST** class using this two-level representation.

13. In practice, the AVL algorithm is unattractive because it spends too much time maintaining perfect balance. If you allow trees to become somewhat more unbalanced—but still keep the heights relatively similar—you can reduce the balancing overhead significantly. One strategy that offers greater efficiency is **red-black trees,** which take their name from the fact that every node in the tree is assigned a color, either red or black. A binary search tree is a legal red-black tree if all three of the following properties hold:

1. The root node is black.

2. The parent of every red node is black.

3. All paths from the root to a leaf contain the same number of black nodes.

These properties ensure that the longest path from the root to a leaf can never be more than twice the length of the shortest path. Given the rules, you know that every such path has the same number of black nodes, which means that the shortest possible path is composed entirely of black nodes, and the longest has black and red nodes alternating down the chain. Although this condition is less strict than the definition of a balanced tree used in the AVL algorithm, it is sufficient to guarantee that the operations of finding and inserting new nodes both run in logarithmic time.

The key to making red-black trees work is finding an insertion algorithm that allows you to add new nodes while maintaining the conditions that define red-black trees. The algorithm has much in common with the AVL algorithm and uses the same rotation operations. The first step is to insert the new node using the standard insertion algorithm. The new node always replaces a `null` entry at some point in the tree. If the node is the first node entered into the tree, it becomes the root and is therefore colored black. In all other cases, the new node must initially be colored red to avoid violating the rule that every path from the root to a leaf must contain the same number of black nodes.

As long as the parent of the new node is black, the tree as a whole remains a legal red-black tree. The problem arises if the parent node is also red, which means that the tree violates the second condition, which requires that every red node have a black parent. In this case, you need to restructure the tree to restore the red-black condition. Depending on the relationship of the red-red pair to the remaining nodes in the tree, you can eliminate the problem by performing one of the following operations, as illustrated in Figure 15-12:

1. A single rotation followed by a recoloring that leaves the top node black

2. A double rotation followed by a recoloring that leaves the top node black

3. A simple change in node colors that leaves the top node red and may therefore require further restructuring at a higher level in the tree

FIGURE 15-12 Rotation operations in a red-black tree

Case 1: N_4 is black (or nonexistent); N_1 and N_2 are out of balance in the same direction.

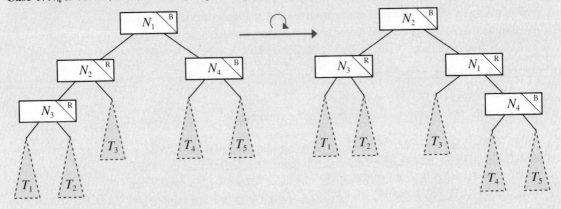

Case 2: N_4 is black (or nonexistent); N_1 and N_2 are out of balance in opposite directions.

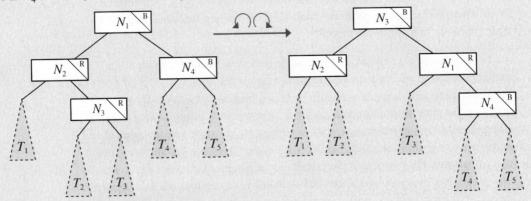

Case 3: N_4 is red; the relative balance of N_1 and N_2 doesn't matter.

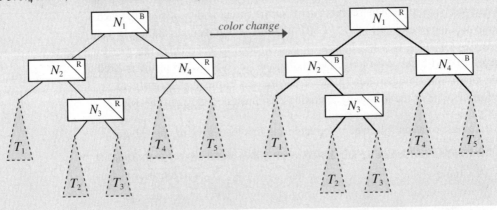

Implement a `RedBlackTree` class that uses this structure to maintain balance in a binary search tree. Your code need be responsible only for inserting nodes; implementing removal is much more difficult and is likely to generate more frustration than insight.

When you are debugging your program, you will find it helpful to implement a method that displays the structure of the tree, including the colors of the nodes, which are not revealed to the client. This method should also check to see that the rules for forming red-black trees are maintained as the tree changes.

14. The heap data structure forms a natural basis for a sorting algorithm that always runs in $O(N \log N)$ time. In this algorithm, which is called *heapsort*, all you do is enter each value into a heap and then take the items out of the heap from smallest to largest. Use this strategy to write a heapsort implementation of the method

```
void sort(String[] array)
```

15§. Write the necessary code to implement the `PriorityQueue` class using the heap data structure discussed in section 15.5.

16. Trees have many applications beyond those listed in this chapter. For example, trees can be used to implement a lexicon, which was introduced in Chapter 7. The resulting structure, first developed by Edward Fredkin in 1960, is called a *trie*. (Over time, the pronunciation of this word has evolved to the point that it is now pronounced like *try*, even though the name comes from the central letters of *retrieval*.) The trie-based implementation of a lexicon, while somewhat inefficient in its use of space, makes it possible for you to determine whether a word is in the lexicon more quickly than you can with a hash table.

At one level, a trie is simply a tree in which each node branches in as many as 26 ways, one for each possible letter of the alphabet. When you use a trie to represent a lexicon, the words are stored implicitly in the structure of the tree and represented as a succession of links moving downward from the root. The root of the tree corresponds to the empty string, and each successive level of the tree corresponds to the subset of the entire word list formed by adding one more letter to the string represented by its parent. For example, the *A* link descending from the root leads to the subtree containing all the words beginning with *A*, the *B* link from that node leads to the subtree containing all the words beginning with *AB*, and so forth. Each node is also marked with a flag indicating whether the substring that ends at that particular point is a legitimate word.

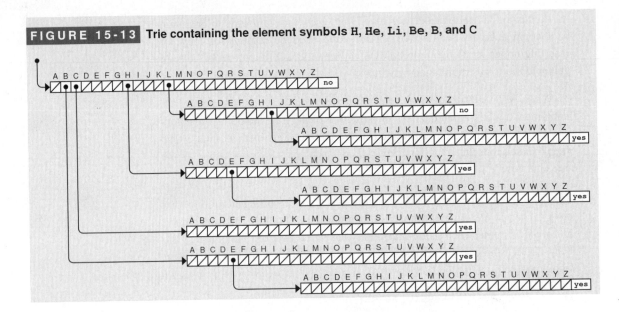

FIGURE 15-13 Trie containing the element symbols H, He, Li, Be, B, and C

The structure of a trie is much easier to understand by example than by definition. Figure 15-13 shows a trie containing the symbols for the first six elements—**H**, **He**, **Li**, **Be**, **B**, and **C**. The root of the tree corresponds to the empty string, which is not a legal symbol, as indicated by the designation **no** in the field at the extreme right end of the structure. The link labeled **B** from the node at the root of the trie descends to a node corresponding to the string **"B"**. The rightmost field of this node contains **yes**, which indicates that the string **"B"** is a complete symbol in its own right. From this node, the link labeled **E** leads to a new node, which indicates that the string **"BE"** is a legal symbol as well. The **null** references in the trie indicate that no legal symbols appear in the subtree beginning with that substring and therefore make it possible to terminate the search process.

Reimplement the **Lexicon** class from Chapter 8 so that it uses a trie as its internal representation.

17§. Exercise 14 in Chapter 14 introduced the distinction between offline and online iterators. If you're up for an interesting challenge, implement an online version of the **keyIterator** method in the **TreeMap** class. When you deliver the keys in order using an online iterator, however, you can no longer rely on the magic of recursion, because the iterator needs to operate sequentially, one step at a time. The code for the **TreeMap** iterator must therefore perform all the bookkeeping that occurs automatically when you implement the inorder walk recursively. Keeping track of that state will require you to maintain a stack of as-yet-unvisited nodes.

Chapter 16
Sets

We are an ambitious set, aren't we?

— Louisa May Alcott, *Little Women,* 1868

Sets are important in computer science for several reasons. As a practical matter, sets are useful in writing applications, particularly those in which you need to keep track of the objects you have already seen. Putting an object in a set after checking whether it is already present makes it easy to avoid processing the same object twice. In addition, understanding the underlying mathematical theory of sets makes it much easier for you to use them effectively in your programs. Moreover, sets provide an excellent illustration of how to build new classes from existing ones. The implementations of the `HashSet` and `TreeSet` classes presented in this chapter are easy to write because you already have the code for `HashMap` and `TreeMap`.

16.1 Sets as a mathematical abstraction

In all likelihood, you have already encountered sets at some point in your study of mathematics. In general terms, it is easiest to think of a *set* as an unordered collection of distinct elements. For example, the days of the week form a set of seven elements that can be written as follows:

{ Sunday, Monday, Tuesday, Wednesday, Thursday, Friday, Saturday }

The individual elements appear in this order only because it is conventional. If the names were in a different order, it would still be the same set. A set, however, never contains multiple copies of the same element.

The set of weekdays is a *finite set* because it contains a finite number of elements. In mathematics, there are also *infinite sets,* such as the set of all integers. In a computer system, sets are usually finite, even if they correspond to infinite sets in mathematics. For example, the set of integers that a computer can represent in a variable of type `int` is finite because the hardware imposes a limit on the range of integer values.

To understand the fundamental operations on sets, it is important to have a few sets to use as a foundation. In keeping with mathematical convention, this text uses the following symbols to refer to the indicated sets:

∅	The *empty set,* which contains no elements
Z	The set of all integers
N	The set of *natural numbers,* ordinarily defined in computer science as 0, 1, 2, 3, . . .
R	The set of all real numbers

In mathematics, sets are most often written using a single uppercase letter. Sets whose membership is defined—like **N**, **Z**, and **R**—are denoted using boldface letters. Names that refer to some unspecified set are written using italic letters, such as *S* and *T*.

Membership

The fundamental property that defines a set is that of ***membership,*** which has the same intuitive meaning in mathematics that it does in English. Mathematicians express membership symbolically using the notation $x \in S$, which indicates that the value x is an element of the set S. For example, given the sets defined in the preceding section, the following statements are true:

$$17 \in \mathbf{N} \qquad\qquad -4 \in \mathbf{Z} \qquad\qquad \pi \in \mathbf{R}$$

Conversely, the notation $x \notin S$ indicates that x is *not* an element of S. For example, $-4 \notin \mathbf{N}$, because the set of natural numbers does not include the negative integers.

The membership of a set is typically specified in one of the two following ways:

- ***Specification by enumeration.*** Defining a set by enumeration is simply a matter of listing its elements. By convention, the elements in the list are enclosed in curly braces and separated by commas. For example, the set **D** of single-digit natural numbers can be defined by enumeration as follows:

  $$\mathbf{D} = \{0, 1, 2, 3, 4, 5, 6, 7, 8, 9\}$$

- ***Specification by rule.*** You can also define a set by expressing a rule that distinguishes the members of that set. In most cases, the rule is divided into two parts: a larger set that provides the potential candidates and some conditional expression that identifies the elements that should be selected for inclusion. For example, the set **D** from the preceding example can also be defined this way:

  $$\mathbf{D} = \{x \mid x \in \mathbf{N} \text{ and } x < 10\}$$

If you read this definition aloud, it comes out sounding like this: "**D** is defined to be the set of all elements x such that x is a natural number and x is less than 10."

Set operations

Mathematical set theory defines several operations on sets, of which the following are the most important:

- ***Union.*** The union of two sets is written as $A \cup B$ and consists of all elements belonging to the set A, the set B, or both.

  $$\{1, 3, 5, 7, 9\} \cup \{2, 4, 6, 8\} = \{1, 2, 3, 4, 5, 6, 7, 8, 9\}$$
  $$\{1, 2, 4, 8\} \cup \{2, 3, 5, 7\} = \{1, 2, 3, 4, 5, 7, 8\}$$
  $$\{2, 3\} \cup \{1, 2, 3, 4\} = \{1, 2, 3, 4\}$$

- ***Intersection.*** The intersection of two sets is written as $A \cap B$ and consists of the elements belonging to both A and B.

$$\{1, 3, 5, 7, 9\} \cap \{2, 4, 6, 8\} = \varnothing$$
$$\{1, 2, 4, 8\} \cap \{2, 3, 5, 7\} = \{2\}$$
$$\{2, 3\} \cap \{1, 2, 3, 4\} = \{2, 3\}$$

- **Set difference.** The difference of two sets is written as $A - B$ and consists of the elements belonging to A except for those that are also contained in B.

$$\{1, 3, 5, 7, 9\} - \{2, 4, 6, 8\} = \{1, 3, 5, 7, 9\}$$
$$\{1, 2, 4, 8\} - \{2, 3, 5, 7\} = \{1, 4, 8\}$$
$$\{2, 3\} - \{1, 2, 3, 4\} = \varnothing$$

In addition to set-producing operations like union and intersection, the mathematical theory of sets also defines several operations that determine whether some property holds between two sets. Operations that test a particular property are the mathematical equivalent of predicate methods and are usually called ***relations.*** The most important relations on sets are the following:

- ***Equality.*** The sets A and B are equal if they have the same elements. The equality relation for sets is indicated by the standard equal sign used to denote equality in other mathematical contexts. Thus, the notation $A = B$ indicates that the sets A and B contain the same elements.

- ***Subset.*** The subset relation is written as $A \subseteq B$ and is true if all the elements of A are also elements of B. For example, the set $\{2, 3, 5, 7\}$ is a subset of the set $\{1, 2, 3, 4, 5, 6, 7, 8, 9\}$. Similarly, the set **N** of natural numbers is a subset of the set **Z** of integers. From the definition, it is clear that every set is a subset of itself. Mathematicians use the notation $A \subset B$ to indicate that A is a ***proper subset*** of B, which means that the subset relation holds but that the sets are not equal.

Set operations are often illustrated by drawing ***Venn diagrams,*** which are named for the British logician John Venn (1834–1923). In a Venn diagram, the individual sets are represented as geometric figures that overlap to indicate regions in which they share elements. For example, the results of the set operations union, intersection, and set difference are indicated by the shaded regions in the following Venn diagrams:

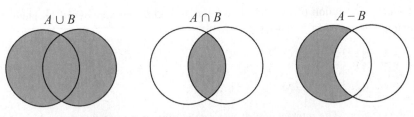

Set identities

One of the useful bits of knowledge you can derive from mathematical set theory is that the union, intersection, and difference operations are related to each other in various ways. These relationships are usually expressed as *identities,* which are rules indicating that two expressions are invariably equal. In this text, identities are written in the form

$$lhs \equiv rhs$$

which means that the set expressions *lhs* and *rhs* are equal by definition and can therefore be substituted for one another. The most common set identities are shown in Figure 16-1.

You can get a sense of how these identities work by drawing Venn diagrams to represent individual stages in the computation. Figure 16-2, for example, verifies the first of De Morgan's laws listed in Figure 16-1, which are named after the British mathematician Augustus De Morgan, who first formalized these identities. The shaded areas represent the value of each subexpression in the identity. The fact that the Venn diagrams along the right edge of Figure 16-2 have the same shaded region demonstrates that the set $A - (B \cup C)$ is the same as the set $(A - B) \cap (A - C)$.

What may still be unclear is why you as a programmer might ever need to learn rules that at first seem so complex and arcane. Mathematical techniques are important to computer science for several reasons. For one thing, theoretical knowledge is useful in its own right because it deepens your understanding of the foundations of computing. Moreover, this type of theoretical knowledge often has direct application to programming practice. By relying on data structures whose

---

FIGURE 16-1 Fundamental set identities

$S \cup S \equiv S$ $S \cap S \equiv S$	Idempotence
$A \cup (A \cap B) \equiv A$ $A \cap (A \cup B) \equiv A$	Absorption
$A \cup B \equiv B \cup A$ $A \cap B \equiv B \cap A$	Commutative laws
$A \cup (B \cup C) \equiv (A \cup B) \cup C$ $A \cap (B \cap C) \equiv (A \cap B) \cap C$	Associative laws
$A \cup (B \cap C) \equiv (A \cup B) \cap (A \cup C)$ $A \cap (B \cup C) \equiv (A \cap B) \cup (A \cap C)$	Distributive laws
$A - (B \cap C) \equiv (A - B) \cup (A - C)$ $A - (B \cup C) \equiv (A - B) \cap (A - C)$	De Morgan's laws

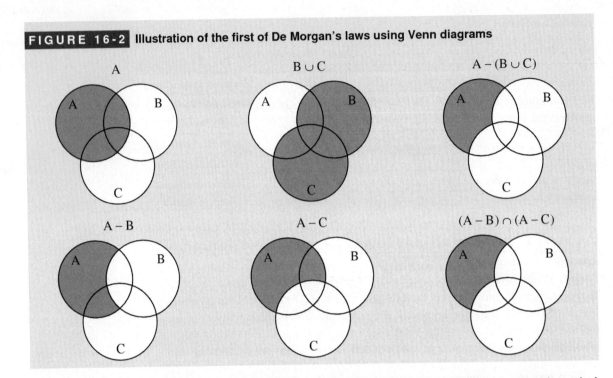

FIGURE 16-2 Illustration of the first of De Morgan's laws using Venn diagrams

mathematical properties are well established, you can use the theoretical underpinnings of those structures to your advantage. For example, if you write a program that uses sets as an abstract type, you may be able to simplify your code by applying one of the standard set identities from Figure 16-1. The justification for making that simplification comes from the abstract theory of sets. Choosing to use sets as a programming abstraction, as opposed to designing some less formal structure of your own, makes it easier for you to apply theory to practice.

16.2 Implementation strategies for sets

As you know from Chapter 7, Java provides two concrete implementations of the **Set** interface—**HashSet** and **TreeSet**—which differ primarily in their iteration order. The **HashSet** class uses a hash table to store the keys, which means that a **HashSet** offers $O(1)$ performance but offers no facility to iterate through the elements in order. The **TreeSet** class offers $O(\log N)$ performance but makes it easy to iterate through the elements of the set in sorted order.

As it happens, both the **TreeSet** and **HashSet** models are easy to implement in Java, as long as you make use of the classes you have already built. The code for the **TreeSet** class, for example, fits on a single page, as shown in Figure 16-3, simply because every operation translates directly into a map operation.

FIGURE 16-3 Implementation of the `TreeSet` class using a `TreeMap` representation

```java
/*
 * File: TreeSet.java
 * --------------------
 * This file implements the TreeSet class using an underlying TreeMap.
 * Every method body is one line long because TreeSet can simply forward
 * the operation to the underlying TreeMap.
 */

package edu.stanford.cs.javacs2.ch16;

import edu.stanford.cs.javacs2.ch15.TreeMap;
import java.util.Iterator;

public class TreeSet<T extends Comparable<? super T>> implements Set<T> {

   public TreeSet() {
      map = new TreeMap<T,Boolean>();
   }

   public int size() {
      return map.size();
   }

   public boolean isEmpty() {
      return map.isEmpty();
   }

   public void clear() {
      map.clear();
   }

   public void add(T value) {
      map.put(value, true);
   }

   public void remove(T value) {
      map.remove(value);
   }

   public boolean contains(T value) {
      return map.containsKey(value);
   }

   public Iterator<T> iterator() {
      return map.keyIterator();
   }

/* Private instance variables */

   private TreeMap<T,Boolean> map;

}
```

The fundamental insight you need to develop a simple implementation is that a set can be implemented as a map in which you ignore the associated value. A set contains an element if the underlying map contains that element as a key. The **Map** interface, of course, requires a value type, but you can supply any type you want. The code in Figure 16-3 uses the Boolean value **true** as the value for each key in the map to suggest the idea that a particular element is either present or absent from the set.

When you define one abstraction in terms of another—as in the current strategy that implements a set using a map—the resulting abstraction is said to be *layered.* Layered abstractions have a number of advantages. For one thing, they are usually easy to implement because much of the work can be relegated to the existing, lower-level interface.

■ 16.3 Extending the set model

Although you have been using the **HashSet** and **TreeSet** classes ever since Chapter 6, those classes are not as powerful as they might be. In particular, the standard implementations of the **Set** interface don't implement the high-level set operations described in section 16.1. Including those high-level methods as part of an extended **Set** class makes it easier to understand set-based algorithms, largely because having those operations often makes the code look almost exactly like the algorithmic descriptions. This fact becomes particularly relevant in the discussion of graphs in Chapter 17. Graph algorithms are the most important—not to mention the most intellectually captivating—algorithms you will learn about from this book, and it is easier to understand graph algorithms if you have access to high-level operations.

Figure 16-4 shows a new **XSet** class, which represents an extended version of the **TreeSet** class. The **XSet** class offers the following extensions over the simpler **TreeSet** model:

- A simplified constructor that supports creating a new set by listing the elements
- A constructor that produces an **XSet** by copying the elements of an existing set
- High-level methods like union, intersection, set difference, subset, and equality
- A **compareTo** method that makes sets comparable

The simplified constructor uses the variadic parameter syntax introduced in Chapter 5 to create a set from the list of arguments. For example, if you want to create a set of the odd digits, you can use the following declaration:

```
XSet<Integer> odds = new XSet<Integer>(1, 3, 5, 7, 9);
```

FIGURE 16-4 **Implementation of the extended XSet class**

```java
/*
 * File: XSet.java
 * ---------------
 * This file exports the extended XSet class.
 */

package edu.stanford.cs.javacs2.ch16;

import java.util.Iterator;

public class XSet<T extends Comparable<? super T>> extends TreeSet<T>
                      implements Comparable<XSet<T>> {

/**
 * Creates an empty XSet.
 */

   public XSet() {
      /* Empty */
   }

/**
 * Creates an XSet containing the values supplied as arguments.
 */

   @SuppressWarnings("unchecked")
   public XSet(T... args) {
      for (T value : args) {
         add(value);
      }
   }

/**
 * Creates an XSet containing the values from the argument set.
 */

   public XSet(Set<T> set) {
      for (T value : set) {
         add(value);
      }
   }

/**
 * Converts the set to its string representation.
 */

   public String toString() {
      String str = "";
      for (T value : this) {
         if (!str.isEmpty()) str += ", ";
         str += value.toString();
      }
      return "{" + str + "}";
   }
```

FIGURE 16-4   Implementation of the extended XSet class (continued)

```java
/**
 * Creates a new set that is the union of this set and s2.
 */

   public XSet<T> union(Set<T> s2) {
      XSet<T> result = new XSet<T>();
      for (T value : this) {
         result.add(value);
      }
      for (T value : s2) {
         result.add(value);
      }
      return result;
   }

/**
 * Creates a new set that is the intersection of this set and s2.
 */

   public XSet<T> intersect(Set<T> s2) {
      XSet<T> result = new XSet<T>();
      for (T value : this) {
         if (s2.contains(value)) result.add(value);
      }
      return result;
   }

/**
 * Creates a new set that is the set difference of this set and s2.
 */

   public XSet<T> subtract(Set<T> s2) {
      XSet<T> result = new XSet<T>();
      for (T value : this) {
         if (!s2.contains(value)) result.add(value);
      }
      return result;
   }

/**
 * Returns true if this set is a subset of s2.
 */

   public boolean isSubsetOf(Set<T> s2) {
      for (T value : this) {
         if (!s2.contains(value)) return false;
      }
      return true;
   }
```

FIGURE 16-4 Implementation of the extended XSet class (continued)

```java
/**
 * Returns true if obj is an XSet and this set is equal to obj.
 */

   @SuppressWarnings("unchecked")
   public boolean equals(Object obj) {
      try {
         XSet<T> s2 = (XSet<T>) obj;
         return s2.isSubsetOf(this) && this.isSubsetOf(s2);
      } catch (ClassCastException ex) {
         return false;
      }
   }

/**
 * Returns a hash code based on the elements of the set.
 */

   public int hashCode() {
      int hc = 0;
      for (T value : this) {
         hc += value.hashCode();
      }
      return hc;
   }

/**
 * Compares this set to the set s2, returning a negative value if this
 * set is less than s2, a positive value if this set is greater than s2,
 * and 0 if the two sets contain the same elements.  Sets are compared
 * first by their length and then by their elements in iterator order.
 */

   public int compareTo(XSet<T> s2) {
      int cmp = this.size() - s2.size();
      if (cmp != 0) return cmp;
      Iterator<T> it1 = this.iterator();
      Iterator<T> it2 = s2.iterator();
      while (it1.hasNext() || it2.hasNext()) {
         T v1 = it1.next();
         T v2 = it2.next();
         cmp = v1.compareTo(v2);
         if (cmp != 0) return cmp;
      }
      if (it1.hasNext()) return +1;
      if (it2.hasNext()) return -1;
      return 0;
   }

}
```

The code for the high-level set primitives is in most cases just what you would expect. The code for **intersect**, for example, looks like this:

```
public XSet<T> intersect(Set<T> s) {
    XSet<T> result = new XSet<T>();
    for (T value : this) {
        if (s.contains(value)) result.add(value);
    }
    return result;
}
```

The method begins by constructing a new **XSet** called **result** that is initially empty. The **for** loop then iterates over the contents of the current set and adds those elements to **result** only if they also appear in the set **s**.

The only implementation that might seem surprising is the code for **equals**, which implements the equality relation for sets. The complexity in the code comes from the definition of **equals** in the **Object** class, which declares its parameter as an **Object**. To override the standard definition of **equals**, you need to match this signature. Unfortunately, Java's restrictions on generic types make it impossible to test whether the set passed to **equals** has the same element type as the current set without using unsafe operations. As in the implementation of the **GenericArray** class, the code in Figure 16-4 uses **@SuppressWarnings("unchecked")** to keep the compiler quiet about this potential breach of type safety, along with a similar annotation in the variadic constructor. The library implementations of the set classes, of course, have to do exactly the same thing. It is also important to observe that the **XSet** class overrides the **hashCode** method. As noted in Chapter 14, it is good programming practice to override **hashCode** whenever you overload **equals**.

The **compareTo** method is included in the **XSet** class to enable the creation of sets of sets. The **XSet** class requires its element type to implement **Comparable**, and defining a **compareTo** method accomplishes that goal. The implementation first compares the sets by size. If the sizes are the same, **compareTo** looks at the sets element by element. As soon as a difference is found, **compareTo** returns the result of the element comparison. If the elements are equal throughout the entire contents of both sets, **compareTo** returns 0.

Suppose, for example, that you have declared two three-element sets as follows:

```
XSet<Integer> s1 = new XSet<Integer>(1, 2, 3);
XSet<Integer> s2 = new XSet<Integer>(1, 3, 5);
```

Calling **s1.compareTo(s2)** returns a negative value because 2 is less than 3 in the second element position.

16.4 Optimizing sets of small integers

The implementation strategy in the preceding section works for any value type. That implementation, however, can be improved substantially for sets whose values are represented internally as small integers, such as enumeration types or the ASCII portion of the Unicode character set.

Characteristic vectors

Suppose for the moment that you are working with a set whose elements always lie between 0 and **RANGE_SIZE** $- 1$, where **RANGE_SIZE** is a constant that specifies the size of the range to which element values are restricted. You can represent such sets efficiently using an array of Boolean values. The value at index position k in the array indicates whether the integer k is in the set. For example, if **elements[4]** has the value **true**, then 4 is in the set represented by the Boolean array **elements**. Similarly, if **elements[5]** is **false**, then 5 is not an element of that set.

Boolean arrays in which the elements indicate whether the corresponding index is a member of some set are called ***characteristic vectors.*** The following examples illustrate how the characteristic-vector strategy can be used to represent the indicated sets, assuming that **RANGE_SIZE** has the value 10:

$\varnothing$

F	F	F	F	F	F	F	F	F	F
0	1	2	3	4	5	6	7	8	9

$\{1, 3, 5, 7, 9\}$

F	T	F	T	F	T	F	T	F	T
0	1	2	3	4	5	6	7	8	9

$\{2, 3, 5, 7\}$

F	F	T	T	F	T	F	T	F	F
0	1	2	3	4	5	6	7	8	9

The advantage of using characteristic vectors is that doing so makes it possible to implement the operations **add**, **remove**, and **contains** in constant time. For example, to add the element k to a set, all you have to do is set the element at index position k in the characteristic vector to **true**. Similarly, testing membership is simply a matter of selecting the appropriate element in the array.

Packed arrays of bits

Even though characteristic vectors allow highly efficient implementations in terms of their running time, storing characteristic vectors as explicit arrays can require a large amount of memory, particularly if **RANGE_SIZE** is large. To reduce the storage requirements, you can pack the elements of the characteristic vector into machine words so that the representation uses every bit in the underlying representation. Since Java defines the data type `int` to be 32 bits long, you can store 32 elements of a characteristic vector in a single value of type `int`, since each element of the characteristic vector requires only one bit of information. Moreover, if **RANGE_SIZE** is 256, you can store all 256 bits needed for a characteristic vector in an array of eight values of type `int`.

To understand how characteristic vectors can be packed into an array of machine words, imagine that you want to represent the integer set consisting of the ASCII code for the alphabetic characters. That set consists of the 26 uppercase letters with codes between 65 and 90 and the 26 lowercase letters with codes between 97 and 122. It can therefore be encoded as the following characteristic vector:

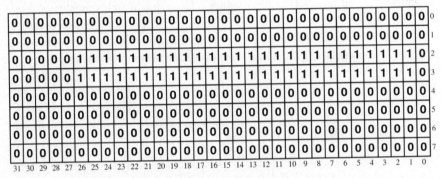

If you want to find the bit that corresponds to a particular integer value, the simplest approach is to use integer division and modular arithmetic. For example, suppose that you want to locate the bit corresponding to the character `'X'`, which has 88 as its ASCII code. The row number of the desired bit is 2, because there are 32 bits in each row and 88 / 32 is 2 according to the standard definition of integer division. Similarly, in row 2, you find the entry for `'X'` at bit number 24, which is the remainder of 88 divided by 32. Thus, the bit in the characteristic vector corresponding to the character `'X'` is the one highlighted in this diagram:

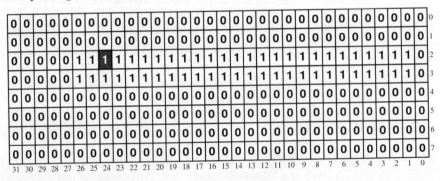

The fact that the highlighted bit is a **1** indicates that `'X'` is a member of the set.

Bitwise operators

In order to write code that works with arrays of bits stored in this tightly packed form, you need to learn how to use the low-level operators that Java provides for manipulating the bits in a memory word. These operators, which are listed in Figure 16-5, are called *bitwise operators.* They take values of any scalar type and interpret them as sequences of bits that correspond to their underlying representation at the hardware level.

To illustrate the behavior of the bitwise operators, it's useful to consider a specific example. Suppose that the variables **x** and **y** have been declared as 16-bit values of type **short**, as follows:

```
short x = 0x002A;
short y = 0xFFF3;
```

If you convert the initial values from hexadecimal to binary notation as described in Chapter 5, you can easily determine that the bit patterns for the variables **x** and **y** look like this:

x `0 0 0 0 0 0 0 0 0 0 1 0 1 0 1 0`

y `1 1 1 1 1 1 1 1 1 1 1 1 0 0 1 1`

The **&**, **|**, and **^** operators each apply the logical operation specified in Figure 16-5 to each bit position in the operand words. The **&** operator, for example, produces a result that has a **1** bit only in positions in which both operands have a **1** bit. Thus, if you apply the **&** operator to the bit patterns in **x** and **y**, you get this result:

x & y `0 0 0 0 0 0 0 0 0 0 1 0 0 0 1 0`

FIGURE 16-5 Bitwise operators in Java

x **&** *y*	Logical AND. The result has a **1** bit in positions where both *x* and *y* have a **1** bit.
x **|** *y*	Logical OR. The result has a **1** bit in positions where either *x* or *y* has a **1** bit.
x **^** *y*	Logical XOR. The result has a **1** bit in positions where the bits in *x* and *y* differ.
~*x*	Logical NOT. The result has a **1** bit where x has a **0** bit, and vice versa.
x **<<** *n*	Left shift. The bits in *x* are shifted left *n* positions, always shifting in a **0**.
x **>>** *n*	Right shift. The bits in *x* are shifted right *n* positions, preserving the sign bit.
x **>>>** *n*	Unsigned right shift. The bits in *x* are shifted right *n* positions, always shifting in a **0**.

The | and ^ operators produce the following results:

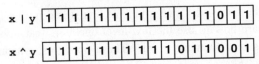

The ~ operator is a unary operator that reverses the state of every bit in its operand. For example, if you apply the ~ operator to the bit pattern in **x**, the result looks like this:

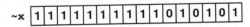

In programming, applying the ~ operation is called *taking the complement* of the single operand that follows the operator.

The operator **<<** shifts the bits in its left operand the number of positions specified by the right operand, filling in **0** bits at the right. Thus, the expression **x << 1** produces a new value in which every bit in the value of **x** is shifted one position to the left, as follows:

x << 1 | 0 | 0 | 0 | 0 | 0 | 0 | 0 | 0 | 1 | 0 | 1 | 0 | 1 | 0 | 0 |

The **>>** and **>>>** operators both shift their left operand to the right, but differ with regard to how new bits are filled in on the left. The **>>** operator performs what is called an *arithmetic shift,* which preserves the sign of the original value. Given that **y** contains the value

y | 1 | 1 | 1 | 1 | 1 | 1 | 1 | 1 | 1 | 1 | 1 | 0 | 0 | 1 | 1 |

the expression **y >> 2** produces a value in which the bits in **y** have been shifted two positions to the right. The new bit shifted in is always the same as the first bit in the original value, which has the effect of preserving the sign of the integer value:

y >> 2 | 1 | 1 | 1 | 1 | 1 | 1 | 1 | 1 | 1 | 1 | 1 | 1 | 1 | 0 | 0 |

The operator **>>>** performs a *logical shift,* in which the new bits shifted in at the left are always **0**. Thus, starting with the original value of **y**, evaluating the expression **y >>> 2** produces the following result:

Implementing characteristic vectors

The bitwise operators introduced in the preceding section make it possible to implement operations on characteristic vectors in an extremely efficient way. If you want to test the state of an individual bit in a characteristic vector, all you have to do is create a value that has a **1** bit in the desired position and **0** bits everywhere else. Such a value is called a *mask* because you can use it to hide all the other bits in the word. If you apply the **&** operator to the word in the characteristic vector that contains the bit you're trying to find and the mask that corresponds to the correct bit position, all the other bits in that word will be stripped away, leaving you with a value that reflects the state of the desired bit.

To understand how this strategy works, it helps to consider the underlying representation of a characteristic vector in more detail. A characteristic vector is simply an array of integer words in which the total number of bits is equal to the range size. The number of words needed can therefore be calculated using the following sequence of constant definitions:

```
private static final int RANGE_SIZE = 256;
private static final int BITS_PER_WORD = 32;
private static final int CVEC_WORDS =
                        RANGE_SIZE / BITS_PER_WORD;
```

The characteristic vector **cv** can then be declared and initialized as follows:

```
private int[] cv = new int[CVEC_WORDS];
```

Given these definitions, you can test a specific bit in a characteristic vector by using the method **testBit**, which has the following implementation:

```
private boolean testBit(int k) {
   if (k < 0 || k >= RANGE_SIZE) {
      throw new RuntimeException("Index out of range");
   }
   return (cv[k / BITS_PER_WORD] & createMask(k)) != 0;
}
```

The final line of this method calls the method **createMask**, which has the following definition:

```
private int createMask(int k) {
   return 1 << k % BITS_PER_WORD;
}
```

Suppose, for example, that you call **testBit(cv, 'X')**, where **cv** is bound to the characteristic vector corresponding to the set of all alphabetic characters. As discussed in the section on "Packed arrays of bits" earlier in the chapter, that characteristic vector looks like this:

The method **testBit** begins by choosing the appropriate word in the characteristic vector by evaluating the expression

```
cv[k / BITS_PER_WORD];
```

The subscript expression **k / BITS_PER_WORD** determines the index of the word in the characteristic vector that contains the kth bit in the entire structure. Because the character **'X'** has the ASCII value 88 and **BITS_PER_WORD** is 32, the subscript expression selects the word at index position 2, which consists of the following bits:

The method **createMask(k)** produces a mask that contains a **1** bit in the appropriate position. If **k**, for example, has the value 88, **k % BITS_PER_WORD** is 24, which means that the mask value consists of the value 1 shifted left 24 bit positions, as follows:

Because the mask has only a single **1** bit, the **&** operation in the code for **testBit** will return a nonzero value if and only if the corresponding bit in the characteristic vector is a **1**. If the characteristic vector contained a 0 in that bit position, there would be no bits common to both the vector and the mask, which means that the **&** operation would return a word containing only **0** bits. A word composed entirely of **0** bits has the integer value 0.

The strategy of using a mask also makes it easy to manipulate the state of individual bits in the characteristic vector. By convention, assigning the value **1** to a specific bit is called *setting* that bit; assigning the value **0** is called *clearing* the bit. You can set a particular bit in a word by applying the logical OR operation to the old value of that word and a mask containing the desired bit. You can clear a bit by applying the logical AND operation to the old value of the word and the complement of the mask. These operations are illustrated by the following definitions of the methods `setBit` and `clearBit`:

```
    private void setBit(int k) {
        if (k < 0 || k >= RANGE_SIZE) {
            throw new RuntimeException("Index out of range");
        }
        cv[k / BITS_PER_WORD] |= createMask(k);
    }

    private void clearBit(int k) {
        if (k < 0 || k >= RANGE_SIZE) {
            throw new RuntimeException("Index out of range");
        }
        cv[k / BITS_PER_WORD] &= ~createMask(k);
    }
```

Defining a `CharSet` class

You can use the `testBit`, `setBit`, and `clearBit` operations from the preceding section to create a `CharSet` class that implements the operations from the extended `XSet` class extremely efficiently in terms of both space and time. The code for the `CharSet` class appears in Figure 16-6, which extends over the next four pages. Fortunately, none of that implementation is particularly complicated. The basic set operations like `add`, `remove`, and `contains` are simple one-line calls to the appropriate bit-manipulation method, as defined in the preceding section.

The use of characteristic vectors also increases the efficiency of the high-level operations of union, intersection, and set difference because it is possible to compute each word in the new characteristic vector using a single application of the appropriate bitwise operator. As an example, the union of two sets consists of all elements that belong to either of its arguments. If you translate this idea into the realm of characteristic vectors, it is easy to see that any word in the characteristic vector of the set $A \cup B$ can be computed by applying the logical OR operation to the corresponding words in the characteristic vectors for those sets. The result of the logical OR operation has a **1** bit in those positions in which either of its operands has a **1** bit, which is exactly what you want to compute the union. The code for the `union` method therefore looks like this:

```
    public CharSet union(CharSet s) {
        CharSet result = new CharSet();
        for (int i = 0; i < CVEC_WORDS; i++) {
            result.cv[i] = this.cv[i] | s.cv[i];
        }
        return result;
    }
```

FIGURE 16-6 Implementation of the CharSet class

```java
/*
 * File: CharSet.java
 * --------------------
 * This file offers an efficient implementation of sets whose elements
 * are ASCII characters.
 */

package edu.stanford.cs.javacs2.ch16;

public class CharSet {

/**
 * Creates an empty CharSet.
 */

   public CharSet() {
      /* Empty */
   }

/**
 * Creates a CharSet containing the characters contained in the string.
 */

   public CharSet(String str) {
      for (int i = 0; i < str.length(); i++) {
         add(str.charAt(i));
      }
   }

/**
 * Returns the number of values in this set.
 */

   public int size() {
      int n = 0;
      for (int i = 0; i < RANGE_SIZE; i++) {
         if (testBit(i)) n++;
      }
      return n;
   }

/**
 * Returns true if this set contains no elements.
 */

   public boolean isEmpty() {
      for (int i = 0; i < CVEC_WORDS; i++) {
         if (cv[i] != 0) return false;
      }
      return true;
   }
```

FIGURE 16-6 Implementation of the `CharSet` class (continued)

```java
/**
 * Removes all elements from this set.
 */

   public void clear() {
      for (int i = 0; i < CVEC_WORDS; i++) {
         cv[i] = 0;
      }
   }

/**
 * Adds the specified character to the set if it is not already present.
 */

   public void add(char ch) {
      setBit(ch);
   }

/**
 * Removes the specified character from the set, if necessary.
 */

   public void remove(char ch) {
      clearBit(ch);
   }

/**
 * Returns true if the set contains the character ch.
 */

   public boolean contains(char ch) {
      return testBit(ch);
   }

/**
 * Creates a new set which is the union of this set and the set s.
 */

   public CharSet union(CharSet s) {
      CharSet result = new CharSet();
      for (int i = 0; i < CVEC_WORDS; i++) {
         result.cv[i] = this.cv[i] | s.cv[i];
      }
      return result;
   }
```

FIGURE 16-6   Implementation of the CharSet class (continued)

```java
/**
 * Creates a new set which is the intersection of this set and the set s.
 */

   public CharSet intersect(CharSet s) {
      CharSet result = new CharSet();
      for (int i = 0; i < CVEC_WORDS; i++) {
         result.cv[i] = this.cv[i] & s.cv[i];
      }
      return result;
   }

/**
 * Creates a new set which is the set difference of this set and the set s.
 */

   public CharSet subtract(CharSet s) {
      CharSet result = new CharSet();
      for (int i = 0; i < CVEC_WORDS; i++) {
         result.cv[i] = this.cv[i] & ~s.cv[i];
      }
      return result;
   }

/*
 * Overrides the toString method to support printing of CharSet values.
 */

   @Override
   public String toString() {
      String str = "";
      for (int i = 0; i < RANGE_SIZE; i++) {
         if (testBit(i)) {
            if (!str.isEmpty()) str += ", ";
            str += (char) i;
         }
      }
      return "{" + str + "}";
   }

/*
 * Tests whether the specified bit is set in the characteristic vector.
 */

   private boolean testBit(int k) {
      if (k < 0 || k >= RANGE_SIZE) {
         throw new RuntimeException("Index out of range");
      }
      return (cv[k / BITS_PER_WORD] & createMask(k)) != 0;
   }
```

☞

FIGURE 16-6 Implementation of the `CharSet` class (continued)

```
/*
 * Sets the specified bit in the characteristic vector.
 */

   private void setBit(int k) {
      if (k < 0 || k >= RANGE_SIZE) {
         throw new RuntimeException("Index out of range");
      }
      cv[k / BITS_PER_WORD] |= createMask(k);
   }

/*
 * Clears the specified bit in the characteristic vector.
 */

   private void clearBit(int k) {
      if (k < 0 || k >= RANGE_SIZE) {
         throw new RuntimeException("Index out of range");
      }
      cv[k / BITS_PER_WORD] &= ~createMask(k);
   }

/*
 * Creates the mask for bit k.
 */

   private int createMask(int k) {
      return 1 << k % BITS_PER_WORD;
   }

/* Constants */

   private static final int RANGE_SIZE = 256;
   private static final int BITS_PER_WORD = 32;
   private static final int CVEC_WORDS = RANGE_SIZE / BITS_PER_WORD;

/* Private instance variables */

   private int[] cv = new int[CVEC_WORDS];

}
```

Summary

In this chapter, you have learned about sets, which are important to computer science as both a theoretical and a practical abstraction. The fact that sets have a well-developed mathematical foundation, rather than making them too abstract to be useful, increases their utility as a programming tool. Because of that theoretical foundation, you can count on sets to exhibit certain properties and obey specific

FIGURE 16-7	Summary of the mathematical notation for sets	

Empty set	∅	The set containing no elements
Membership	$x \in S$	True if x is an element of S
Nonmembership	$x \notin S$	True if x is not an element of S
Equality	$A = B$	True if A and B contain exactly the same elements
Subset	$A \subseteq B$	True if all elements in A are also in B
Proper subset	$A \subset B$	True if A is a subset of B but the sets are not equal
Union	$A \cup B$	The set of elements in A, B, or both
Intersection	$A \cap B$	The set of elements in both A and B
Set difference	$A - B$	The set of elements in A that are not also in B

rules. By coding your algorithms in terms of sets, you can build on that theoretical base to write programs that are easier to understand.

Important points in this chapter include:

- A set is an unordered collection of distinct elements. The set operations used in this book appear in Figure 16-7, along with their mathematical symbols.

- Interactions among the various set operators are often easier to understand if you keep in mind certain identities which indicate that two set expressions are invariably equal. Using these identities can also improve your programming practice, because they provide you with tools to simplify set operations appearing in your code.

- The set class is straightforward to implement because much of it can be layered on top of the **Map** abstraction, using either the tree-based or the hash-based representation.

- Sets of integers can be implemented very efficiently using arrays of Boolean data called *characteristic vectors*. If you use the bitwise operators provided by Java, you can pack characteristic vectors into a small number of machine words and perform such set operations as union and intersection on many elements of the vector at a time.

Review questions

1. True or false: The elements of a set are unordered, so the set {3, 2, 1} and the set {1, 2, 3} represent the same set.

2. True or false: A set can contain multiple copies of the same element.

3. What sets are denoted by each of the following symbols: ∅, **Z**, **N**, and **R**?

4. What do the symbols ∈ and ∉ mean?

5. Use an enumeration to specify the elements of the following set:

$$\{x \mid x \in \mathbf{N} \ \text{and} \ x \le 100 \ \text{and} \ \sqrt{x} \in \mathbf{N}\}$$

6. Write a rule-based definition for the following set:

    $$\{0, 9, 18, 27, 36, 45, 54, 63, 72, 81\}$$

7. What are the mathematical symbols for the operations union, intersection, and set difference?

8. Evaluate the following set expressions:

    a. $\{a, b, c\} \cup \{a, c, e\}$
    b. $\{a, b, c\} \cap \{a, c, e\}$
    c. $\{a, b, c\} - \{a, c, e\}$
    d. $(\{a, b, c\} - \{a, c, e\}) \cup (\{a, b, c\} - \{a, c, e\})$

9. What is the difference between a subset and a proper subset?

10. Give an example of an infinite set that is a proper subset of some other infinite set.

11. For each of the following set operations, draw Venn diagrams whose shaded regions illustrate the contents of the specified set expression:

    a. $A \cup (B \cap C)$
    b. $(A - C) \cap (B - C)$
    c. $(A - B) \cup (B - A)$
    d. $(A \cup B) - (A \cap B)$

12. Write set expressions that describe the shaded region in each of the following Venn diagrams:

    a.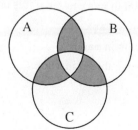

    b.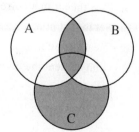

13. Draw Venn diagrams illustrating each of the identities in Figure 16-1.

14. The general implementation of the **TreeSet** class uses a data structure from an earlier chapter to represent the elements of a set. What is that structure? What properties make that structure useful for this purpose?

15. What is a characteristic vector?

16. What restrictions must be placed on a set in order to use characteristic vectors as an implementation strategy?

17. Assuming that **RANGE_SIZE** has the value 10, diagram the characteristic vector for the set {1, 4, 9}.

18. Suppose that the variables **x** and **y** are of type **short** and contain the following bit patterns:

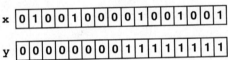

Expressing your answer as a sequence of bits, compute the value of each of the following expressions:

a. x & y

b. x | y

c. x ^ y

d. x ^ x

e. ~x

f.   x & ~y

g.   ~x & ~y

h.   y >> 4

i.   x << 3

j.   (x >> 8) & y

19. Express the values of **x** and **y** from the preceding exercise as constants using hexadecimal notation.

20. Suppose that the variables **x** and **mask** are both declared to be of type **int**, and that the value of **mask** contains a single **1** bit in some position. What expressions would you use to implement the following operations:

a. Test the bit in **x** corresponding to the bit in **mask** to see if it is nonzero.

b. Set the bit in **x** corresponding to the bit in **mask**.

c. Clear the bit in **x** corresponding to the bit in **mask**.

d. Complement the bit in **x** corresponding to the bit in **mask**.

 **Exercises**

1§. Figure 16-3 shows how the **TreeSet** class can be implemented as a nested class using **TreeMap** as its underlying representation. Write the corresponding nested implementation of **HashSet** using the **HashMap** class.

2. To make it easier to write programs that use the **XSet** class, it would be useful if there were some way to read in a set from the user. Write a method

   XSet<Integer> parseIntegerSet(String line)

   that interprets the value of line as a set of integers enclosed in curly braces with the individual elements separated by commas.

3. Write a simple test program that uses the **parseIntegerSet** from the preceding exercise to read in two sets of integers and then display the result of calling the union, intersection, and set difference operators on those sets. A sample run of the program might look like this:

   ```
   ⬤ ⬤ ⬤              SetOperations
   Enter s1: {1, 3, 5, 7, 9}
   Enter s2: {2, 3, 5, 7}
   s1.union(s2) = {1, 2, 3, 5, 7, 9}
   s1.intersect(s2) = {3, 5, 7}
   s1.subtract(s2) = {1, 9}
   ```

4. Write a method

   XSet<Integer> createPrimeSet(int max)

   that returns a set of the prime numbers between 2 and **max**. A number N is prime if it has exactly two divisors, which are always 1 and the number N itself. Checking for primality, however, doesn't require you to try every possible divisor. The only numbers you need to check are the prime numbers between 2 and the square root of N. As it tests whether a number is prime, your code should make use of the fact that all potential factors must be in the set of primes you have already constructed.

5. Write a method

   XSet<XSet<String>> createPowerSet(XSet<String> set)

   that returns that returns the *power set* of the **set**, which is defined as the set of all subsets of a given set. For example, if **set** is the set {a, b, c}, calling **createPowerSet(s)** should return the following set:

   {{}, {a}, {b}, {c}, {a, b}, {a, c}, {b, c}, {a, b, c}}

6. Write a program that implements the following procedure:

    - Read in two strings, each of which represents a sequence of bits. These strings must consist only of the characters 0 and 1 and must not be longer than 16 characters.

    - Convert each of these strings into a value of type `int` with the same internal pattern of bits. Assume that the variables used to store the converted result are named `x` and `y`.

    - Display the value of each of the following expressions as a sequence of 16 bits: `x & y`, `x | y`, `x ^ y`, `~y`, `x & ~y`.

    The operation of this program is illustrated by the following sample run:

    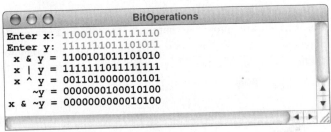

    ```
    ┌─────────────────────────────────────────┐
    │ ● ● ●              BitOperations         │
    ├─────────────────────────────────────────┤
    │ Enter x: 1100101011111110                │
    │ Enter y: 1111111011101011                │
    │  x & y = 1100101011101010                │
    │  x | y = 1111111011111111                │
    │  x ^ y = 0011010000010101                │
    │     ~y = 0000000100010100                │
    │ x & ~y = 0000000000010100                │
    └─────────────────────────────────────────┘
    ```

7. One of the easiest ways to implement the character-classification methods like `Character.isDigit` and `Character.isUpperCase` is to use the bitwise operators. The strategy is to use specific bit positions in a word to indicate properties that a character might have. For example, imagine that the three bits at the right end of a word are used to indicate whether a character is a digit, a lowercase letter, or an uppercase letter, as shown in this diagram:

    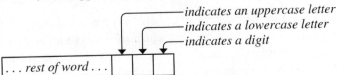

    indicates an uppercase letter
    indicates a lowercase letter
    indicates a digit

    . . . *rest of word* . . .

    If you create an array consisting of 256 of these words—one for each character in the ASCII subset of the character range—you can implement the static methods from the `Character` class so that each operates by selecting the appropriate array element, applying one of the bitwise operators, and testing the result. Use this strategy to implement each of the static methods in the `Character` class listed in Figure 3-3 on page 108.

8. The `CharSet` class shown in Figure 16-6 is missing the methods `equals`, `hashCode`, and `iterator`. Complete the implementation of `CharSet` by defining those methods.

Chapter 17
Graphs

So I draw the world together link by link:
Yea, from Delos up to Limerick and back!

— Rudyard Kipling, "The Song of the Banjo," 1894

Many structures in the real world consist of a set of values connected by a set of links. Such a structure is called a *graph.* Common examples of graphs include cities connected by highways, web pages connected by hyperlinks, and courses in a college curriculum connected by prerequisites. Programmers typically refer to the individual elements—such as the cities, web pages, and courses—as *nodes* and the interconnections—the highways, hyperlinks, and prerequisites—as *arcs,* although mathematicians tend to use the terms *vertex* and *edge,* respectively, instead.

Because they consist of nodes connected by a set of links, graphs are similar to trees, which were introduced in Chapter 15. In fact, the only difference is that there are fewer restrictions on the structure of the connections in a graph than there are in a tree. The arcs in a graph, for example, often form cyclical patterns. In a tree, cyclical patterns are illegal because of the requirement that every node must be linked to the root by a unique line of descent. Because trees have restrictions that do not apply to graphs, graphs are a more general type that includes trees as a subset. Thus, every tree is a graph, but there are some graphs that are not trees.

In this chapter, you will learn about graphs from both a practical and a theoretical perspective. Learning to work with graphs as a programming tool is useful because they come up in a surprising number of contexts. Mastering the theory is extremely valuable as well, because doing so often makes it possible to find much more efficient solutions to problems with considerable practical importance.

■ 17.1 The structure of a graph

The easiest way to get a sense of the structure of a graph is to consider a simple example. Suppose that you work for a small airline that serves 10 major cities in the United States with the routes shown in Figure 17-1. The labeled circles represent cities and constitute the nodes of the graph. The lines between the cities represent airline routes and constitute the arcs.

Although graphs are often used to represent geographical relationships, it is important to keep in mind that the graph is defined purely in terms of the nodes and connecting arcs. The layout is unimportant to the abstract concept of a graph. For example, the following diagram represents the same graph as Figure 17-1:

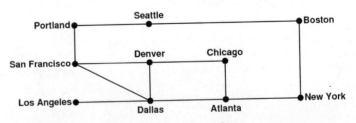

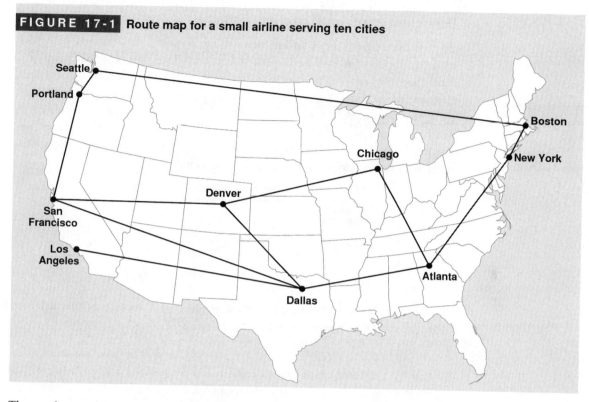

FIGURE 17-1 Route map for a small airline serving ten cities

The nodes representing the cities are no longer in the correct positions geographically, but the connections remain the same.

You can go one step further and eliminate the geometrical relationships altogether. Mathematicians use the tools of set theory to define a graph as the combination of two sets, which are typically called *V* and *E* after the mathematical terms *vertex* and *edge*. The airline graph, for example, consists of the following sets:

V = { Atlanta, Boston, Chicago, Dallas, Denver, Los Angeles,
        New York, Portland, San Francisco, Seattle }

E = { Atlanta↔Chicago, Atlanta↔Dallas, Atlanta↔New York,
        Boston↔New York, Boston↔Seattle, Chicago↔Denver,
        Dallas↔Denver, Dallas↔Los Angeles, Dallas↔San Francisco,
        Denver↔San Francisco, Portland↔San Francisco,
        Portland↔Seattle }

Beyond underscoring the connections between graphs and mathematics, defining a graph in terms of sets also simplifies the implementation, because the **Set** class already implements many of the necessary operations.

Directed and undirected graphs

Because the diagram gives no indication to the contrary, the arcs in Figure 17-1 represent flights that operate in both directions. Thus, the fact that there is a connection between Atlanta and Chicago implies that there is also one between Chicago and Atlanta. A graph in which every connection runs both ways is called an **undirected graph.** In many cases, it makes sense to use **directed graphs,** in which each arc has a direction. For example, if your airline operates a plane from San Francisco to Dallas but has the plane stop in Denver on the return flight, that piece of the route map will look like this in a directed graph:

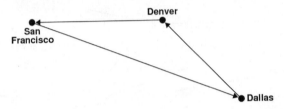

The diagrams in this text represent directed graphs only if the arcs include an arrow indicating their direction. If the arrows are missing—as they are in the airline graph in Figure 17-1—you can assume the graph is undirected.

Arcs in a directed graph are specified using the notation *start→finish,* where *start* and *finish* are the nodes on each side of the directed arc. Thus, the triangular route shown in the preceding diagram consists of the following arcs:

> **San Francisco →Dallas**
> **Dallas →Denver**
> **Denver → San Francisco**

Although arcs in an undirected graph are often written using a double-headed arrow, you don't actually need a separate symbol. If a graph contains an undirected arc, you can always represent it as a pair of directed arcs. For example, if a graph contains a bidirectional arc **Portland↔Seattle**, you can represent that fact by including both **Portland→ Seattle** and **Seattle→Portland** in the set of arcs. Because it is always possible to simulate undirected graphs using directed ones, most graph packages—including the ones introduced in this chapter—define a single graph type that supports directed graphs. If you want to define an undirected graph, all you have to do is create two arcs for every connection, one in each direction.

Paths and cycles

The arcs in a graph represent direct connections, which correspond to nonstop flights in the airline example. The fact that the arc **San Francisco → New York** does not exist in the example graph does not mean that you cannot travel between those cities on this airline. If you want to fly from San Francisco to New York, you can use any of the following routes:

> San Francisco → Dallas → Atlanta → New York
> San Francisco → Denver → Chicago → Atlanta → New York
> San Francisco → Portland → Seattle → Boston → New York

A sequence of arcs that allow you to move from one node to another is called a *path.* A path that begins and ends at the same node, such as the path

> Dallas → Atlanta → Chicago → Denver → Dallas

is called a *cycle.* A *simple path* is a path that contains no duplicated nodes. Similarly, a *simple cycle* is a cycle that has no duplicated nodes other than the common node that appears at the beginning and the end.

Nodes in a graph that are connected directly by an arc are called *neighbors.* If you count the number of neighbors for a particular node, that number is called the *degree* of that node. In the airline graph, for example, **Dallas** has degree 4 because it has direct connections to four cities: **Atlanta, Denver, Los Angeles,** and **San Francisco.** By contrast, **Los Angeles**, has degree 1 because it connects only to **Dallas**. In the case of directed graphs, it is useful to differentiate the concepts of *in-degree,* which indicates the number of arcs coming into that node, and *out-degree,* which indicates the number of arcs leaving that node.

Connectivity

An undirected graph is *connected* if there is a path from each node to every other node. For example, the airline graph in Figure 17-1 is connected according to this rule. The definition of a graph, however, does not require that all nodes be connected in a single unit. For example, the graph

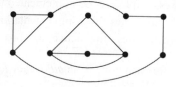

is an example of an unconnected graph, because no path links the cluster of four nodes in the interior of the diagram to any of the other nodes.

Given any unconnected graph, you can always decompose it into a unique set of subgraphs in which each subgraph is connected, but no arcs lead from one subgraph to another. These subgraphs are called the *connected components* of the graph. The connected components of the preceding graph diagram look like this:

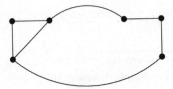

For directed graphs, the concept of connectivity is somewhat more complicated. If a directed graph contains a path connecting every pair of nodes, the graph is **strongly connected.** A directed graph is **weakly connected** if eliminating the directions on the arcs creates a connected graph. For example, the graph

is not strongly connected because you cannot travel from the node on the lower right to the node on the upper left moving only in the directions specified by the arcs. On the other hand, the graph is weakly connected because the undirected graph formed by eliminating the arrows is a connected graph. If you reverse the direction of the top arc, the resulting graph

is strongly connected.

17.2 Representation strategies

Like most abstract structures, graphs can be implemented in several different ways. The primary feature that differentiates these implementations is the strategy used to represent connections between nodes. In practice, the most common strategies are:

- Storing the connections for each node in an *adjacency list*
- Storing the connections for the entire graph in an *adjacency matrix*
- Storing the connections for each node as a *set of arcs*

These representation strategies are described in greater detail in the sections that follow.

Representing connections using an adjacency list

The simplest way to represent connections in a graph is to store within the data structure for each node a list of the nodes to which it is connected. This structure is called an *adjacency list.* For example, in the now-familiar airline graph

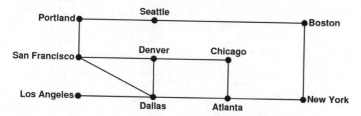

the adjacency lists for each node look like this:

Atlanta	→	**(Chicago, Dallas, New York)**
Boston	→	**(New York, Seattle)**
Chicago	→	**(Atlanta, Denver)**
Dallas	→	**(Atlanta, Denver, Los Angeles)**
Denver	→	**(Chicago, Dallas, San Francisco)**
Los Angeles	→	**(Dallas)**
New York	→	**(Atlanta, Boston)**
Portland	→	**(San Francisco, Seattle)**
San Francisco	→	**(Dallas, Denver, Portland)**
Seattle	→	**(Boston, Portland)**

Representing connections using an adjacency matrix

Although lists provide a convenient way to represent the connections in a graph, they can be inefficient when an operation requires searching through the list of arcs associated with a node. For example, if you use the adjacency list representation, determining whether two nodes are connected requires $O(D)$ time, where D represents the degree of the originating node. If the nodes in a graph all have a small number of neighbors, the cost of searching through this list is small. If, however, the nodes in a graph tend to have a large number of neighbors, the cost becomes more significant.

If efficiency becomes a concern, you can reduce the cost of checking for connections to constant time by representing the arcs in a two-dimensional array called an *adjacency matrix* that shows which nodes are connected. The adjacency matrix for the airline graph looks like this:

	Atlanta	Boston	Chicago	Dallas	Denver	Los Angeles	New York	Portland	San Francisco	Seattle
Atlanta			✕	✕			✕			
Boston							✕			✕
Chicago	✕				✕					
Dallas	✕				✕	✕			✕	
Denver			✕	✕					✕	
Los Angeles				✕						
New York	✕	✕								
Portland									✕	✕
San Francisco				✕	✕			✕		
Seattle		✕						✕		

For an undirected graph of this sort, the adjacency matrix is **symmetric,** which means that the entries match when they are reflected across the main diagonal, which is shown in the figure as a dotted line.

To use the adjacency matrix approach, you must associate each node with an index number that specifies the column or row number in the table corresponding to that node. As part of the concrete structure for the graph, the implementation needs to allocate a two-dimensional array with one row and one column for each node in the graph. The elements of the array are Boolean values. If the entry in `matrix[`*start*`]` `[`*finish*`]` is `true`, there is an arc *start*→*finish* in the graph.

In terms of execution time, using an adjacency matrix is considerably faster than using an adjacency list. On the other hand, a matrix requires $O(N^2)$ storage space, where N is the number of nodes. For most graphs, the adjacency list representation tends to be more efficient in terms of space, although some graphs violate this principle. In the adjacency list representation, each node has a list of connections, which, in the worst case, will be D_{max} entries long, where D_{max} is the maximum degree of any node in the graph, which is therefore the maximum number of arcs emanating from a single node. The space cost for adjacency lists is therefore $O(N \times D_{max})$. If most of the nodes are connected to each other, D_{max} will be relatively close to N, which means that the cost of representing connections is comparable for the two approaches. If, on the other hand, the graph contains many nodes but relatively few interconnections, the adjacency list representation can save a considerable amount of space.

Although the dividing line is never precisely defined, graphs for which the value of D_{max} is small in comparison to N are said to be **sparse.** Graphs in which D_{max} is comparable to N are considered **dense.** Often, the algorithms and representation strategies you use for graphs depend on whether you expect those graphs to be sparse or dense. The analysis in the preceding paragraph, for example, indicates that the list representation is likely to be more appropriate for sparse graphs; if you are working with dense graphs, the matrix representation may well be a better choice.

Representing connections using a set of arcs

The motivation behind the third strategy for representing connections in a graph comes from the mathematical formulation of a graph as a set of nodes coupled with a set of arcs. If you were content to store no information with each node other than its name, you could define a graph as a pair of sets, as follows:

```
class StringBasedGraph {
   Set<String> nodes;
   Set<String> arcs;
};
```

The set of nodes contains the names of every node in the graph. The set of arcs contains pairs of node names connected in some way that makes it easy to separate the node names representing the beginning and end of each arc.

The primary advantages of this representation are its conceptual simplicity and the fact that it mirrors so precisely the mathematical definition. The set-based representation does, however, have two important limitations. First, finding the neighbors for any particular node requires going through every arc in the entire graph. Second, most applications need to associate additional data with the individual nodes and arcs. For example, many graph algorithms assign a numeric value to each of the arcs that indicates the **cost** of traversing that arc, which may or may not refer to actual monetary cost. In Figure 17-2, for example, each arc in the airline graph is labeled with the distance in miles between the endpoints. You could use this information to implement a frequent-flier program that assigns points to travelers on the basis of the distance flown.

Fortunately, neither of these problems is particularly difficult to solve. Iterating over the nodes and arcs in a graph is easy if you represent them using a collection class that supports iteration. You can, moreover, incorporate additional data into a graph by using classes to represent the nodes and arcs.

Given the fact that Java is an object-oriented language, you would expect that graphs, nodes, and arcs would be represented as objects, with a new class definition for each level of the hierarchy. Moreover, the fact that different applications need to associate different data with the nodes and arcs suggests that clients should be

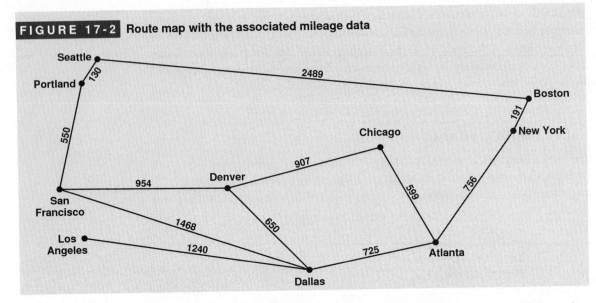

FIGURE 17-2 Route map with the associated mileage data

able to extend the node and arc classes so that they can add whatever information they need. That design is certainly appropriate for graphs, as you will discover later in this chapter. The following section adopts the conceptually simpler strategy of defining **Graph**, **Node**, and **Arc** classes without any concern for how clients might extend those classes. You will learn how to generalize these classes in section 17.6.

17.3 A set-based graph abstraction

This section outlines the design of a graph package in which the three levels of the hierarchy—the graph as a whole, the individual nodes, and the arcs that connect those nodes—are represented using Java classes called **Graph**, **Node**, and **Arc**. Of these, the **Node** and **Arc** classes are the easiest to define. The **Node** class stores the name of the node along with a set of the arcs that extend from that node. The **Arc** class contains the references to the node at which the arc starts and the node at which it finishes. The **Arc** class also contains a numeric value representing the cost of traversing that arc.

The definitions of the **Node** and **Arc** classes for this simple model of a graph appear in Figures 17-3 and 17-4. Since these definitions are intended as a rough draft that focuses attention on the basic structure of the code, the comments have been kept to a minimum so that you can see each class on a single page. Most of the methods are simple getters and setters. The only methods that involve any complexity are the **compareTo** methods in each class. Nodes are compared by their names; arcs are compared first by their start node, then by their finish node, and finally by their cost.

FIGURE 17-3 Definition of a simple Node class

```java
/*
 * File: Node.java
 * ----------------
 * This file exports the basic Node class, which contains only the minimal
 * information necessary to implement the Graph abstraction.  Clients that
 * want to extend nodes should use the GenericNode class instead.
 */

package edu.stanford.cs.javacs2.ch17;

import edu.stanford.cs.javacs2.ch16.XSet;

public class Node implements Comparable<Node> {

   public Node(String name) {
      this.name = name;
      arcs = new XSet<Arc>();
   }

   public String getName() {
      return name;
   }

   public XSet<Arc> getArcs() {
      return arcs;
   }

   public void addArc(Arc arc) {
      arcs.add(arc);
   }

   public boolean isConnectedTo(Node n2) {
      for (Arc arc : arcs) {
         if (arc.getFinish() == n2) return true;
      }
      return false;
   }

   public int compareTo(Node n2) {
      return name.compareTo(n2.getName());
   }

   public String toString() {
      return name;
   }

/* Private instance variables */

   private String name;
   private XSet<Arc> arcs;

}
```

FIGURE 17-4 Definition of a simple Arc class

```java
/*
 * File: Arc.java
 * ----------------
 * This file exports the basic Arc class, which contains only the minimal
 * information necessary to implement the Graph abstraction.  Clients that
 * want to extend arcs should use the GenericArc class instead.
 */

package edu.stanford.cs.javacs2.ch17;

public class Arc implements Comparable<Arc> {

   public Arc(Node start, Node finish) {
      this(start, finish, 0);
   }

   public Arc(Node start, Node finish, double cost) {
      this.start = start;
      this.finish = finish;
      this.cost = cost;
   }

   public Node getStart() {
      return start;
   }

   public Node getFinish() {
      return finish;
   }

   public double getCost() {
      return cost;
   }

   public int compareTo(Arc a2) {
      if (this == a2) return 0;
      int cmp = start.compareTo(a2.getStart());
      if (cmp != 0) return cmp;
      cmp = finish.compareTo(a2.getFinish());
      if (cmp != 0) return cmp;
      if (cost < a2.cost) return -1;
      if (cost > a2.cost) return 1;
      return a2.hashCode() - hashCode();
   }

   public String toString() {
      return start + "->" + finish;
   }

/* Private instance variables */

   private Node start;
   private Node finish;
   private double cost;

}
```

If you look at the code for the **Node** and **Arc** classes in Figures 17-3 and 17-4, you will notice that the definitions are mutually recursive. Every **Node** contains a set of values of type **Arc**, and every **Arc** contains two values of type **Node**. In contrast to many other languages, Java has no problem working with recursive types. Like all objects in Java, the values of type **Node** and **Arc** are represented as references, which are stored internally as the address of the actual value in memory. Each element of the set stored in the variable **arcs** inside the **Node** class is simply a reference to some **Arc** object. Similarly, the **start** and **finish** fields inside each of the **Arc** values is a reference to a **Node**.

Defining graphs in terms of sets has many advantages. In particular, this strategy means that the data structure closely parallels the mathematical formulation of a graph, which is defined in terms of sets. The layered approach also has significant advantages in terms of simplifying the implementation. For example, defining graphs in terms of sets eliminates the need to define a separate iteration facility for graphs, because sets already support iteration. For example, the code for **isConnectedTo** in the **Node** class can use iteration over the set of arcs, as follows:

```
public boolean isConnectedTo(Node n2) {
   for (Arc arc : arcs) {
      if (arc.getFinish() == n2) return true;
   }
   return false;
}
```

In addition to simplifying the process of iteration, defining graphs in terms of the **XSet** class from Chapter 16 means that clients can easily apply higher-level set operations like union and intersection. Theoretical computer scientists often formulate graph algorithms in terms of these operations, and having them available to clients often makes those algorithms easier to code.

The code for the **Graph** class itself appears in Figure 17-5 on the next two pages. This version of **Graph** maintains three instance variables. The first two—a set of nodes and a set of arcs—follow directly from the mathematical definition of a graph. The **nodeMap** variable is a map that associates node names with the actual **Node** objects. Having that map, which is available to the client through the **getNode** method, makes it much easier to write applications that use graphs.

This implementation of **Graph** in Figure 17-5 exports a minimal set of methods, just enough to write some of the most important graph algorithms. Once you have seen how those algorithms work in the context of the simple version of **Graph**, it will then be possible to go back and add additional features to the graph abstraction.

FIGURE 17-5 Definition of a simple Graph class

```
/*
 * File: Graph.java
 * ------------------
 * This file exports a class that represents graphs consisting of nodes
 * and arcs.  Clients that want to extend the node and arc types should
 * use the GenericGraph class instead.
 */

package edu.stanford.cs.javacs2.ch17;

import edu.stanford.cs.javacs2.ch14.HashMap;
import edu.stanford.cs.javacs2.ch16.XSet;

public class Graph {

/**
 * Creates an empty Graph object.
 */

   public Graph() {
      nodes = new XSet<Node>();
      arcs = new XSet<Arc>();
      nodeMap = new HashMap<String,Node>();
   }

/**
 * Returns the number of nodes in the graph.
 */

   public int size() {
      return nodes.size();
   }

/**
 * Returns true if the graph is empty.
 */

   public boolean isEmpty() {
      return nodes.isEmpty();
   }

/**
 * Removes all nodes and arcs from the graph.
 */

   public void clear() {
      nodes.clear();
      arcs.clear();
      nodeMap.clear();
   }
```

FIGURE 17-5   Definition of a simple Graph class (continued)

```
/**
 * Adds a new node to the graph.
 */

    public void addNode(Node node) {
        nodes.add(node);
        nodeMap.put(node.getName(), node);
    }

/**
 * Looks up a node in the name table attached to the graph and returns it.
 * If no node with the specified name exists, getNode returns null.
 */

    public Node getNode(String name) {
        return nodeMap.get(name);
    }

/*
 * Adds an arc to the graph.
 */

    public void addArc(Arc arc) {
        arc.getStart().getArcs().add(arc);
        arcs.add(arc);
    }

/**
 * Returns the set of all nodes in the graph.
 */

    public XSet<Node> getNodeSet() {
        return nodes;
    }

/**
 * Returns the set of all arcs in the graph.
 */

    public XSet<Arc> getArcSet() {
        return arcs;
    }
```

The methods for loading and saving files are left as an exercise.

```
    private XSet<Node> nodes;               /* The set of nodes in the graph */
    private XSet<Arc> arcs;                 /* The set of arcs in the graph  */
    private HashMap<String,Node> nodeMap;   /* Map from names to nodes       */

};
```

To give you an example of how you might use the **Graph** class, the code in Figure 17-6 uses several helper methods to create the airline graph from Figure 17-1 and then prints the names of the cities that can be reached in one step. A sample run of the **AirlineGraph** program looks like this:

```
Atlanta -> Chicago, Dallas, New York
Boston -> New York, Seattle
Chicago -> Atlanta, Denver
Dallas -> Atlanta, Denver, Los Angeles, San Francisco
Denver -> Chicago, Dallas, San Francisco
Los Angeles -> Dallas
New York -> Atlanta, Boston
Portland -> San Francisco, Seattle
San Francisco -> Dallas, Denver, Portland
Seattle -> Boston, Portland
```

FIGURE 17-6 Program to create the airline graph

```java
/*
 * File: AirlineGraph.java
 * ------------------------
 * This program displays the structure of the airline graph.
 */

package edu.stanford.cs.javacs2.ch17;

public class AirlineGraph {

    public void run() {
        Graph airline = createGraph();
        printAdjacencyLists(airline);
    }

/*
 * Prints the adjacency list for each city in the graph.
 */

    private void printAdjacencyLists(Graph g) {
        for (Node node : g.getNodeSet()) {
            System.out.print(node.getName() + " -> ");
            boolean first = true;
            for (Arc arc : node.getArcs()) {
                if (!first) System.out.print(", ");
                System.out.print(arc.getFinish().getName());
                first = false;
            }
            System.out.println();
        }
    }
```

FIGURE 17-6 Program to create the airline graph (continued)

```
/*
 * Creates an airline graph containing the flight data from Figure 17-2.
 * Real applications would almost certainly read the data from a file.
 */

   public Graph createGraph() {
      Graph airline = new Graph();
      addFlight(airline, "Atlanta", "Chicago", 599);
      addFlight(airline, "Atlanta", "Dallas", 725);
      addFlight(airline, "Atlanta", "New York", 756);
      addFlight(airline, "Boston", "New York", 191);
      addFlight(airline, "Boston", "Seattle", 2489);
      addFlight(airline, "Chicago", "Denver", 907);
      addFlight(airline, "Dallas", "Denver", 650);
      addFlight(airline, "Dallas", "Los Angeles", 1240);
      addFlight(airline, "Dallas", "San Francisco", 1468);
      addFlight(airline, "Denver", "San Francisco", 954);
      addFlight(airline, "Portland", "San Francisco", 550);
      addFlight(airline, "Portland", "Seattle", 130);
      return airline;
   }

/*
 * Adds an arc in each direction between the cities c1 and c2.
 */

   private void addFlight(Graph airline, String c1, String c2, int miles) {
      Node n1 = airline.getNode(c1);
      if (n1 == null) airline.addNode(n1 = new Node(c1));
      Node n2 = airline.getNode(c2);
      if (n2 == null) airline.addNode(n2 = new Node(c2));
      Arc arc = new Arc(n1, n2, miles);
      airline.addArc(arc);
      arc = new Arc(n2, n1, miles);
      airline.addArc(arc);
   }

/* Main program */

   public static void main(String[] args) {
      new AirlineGraph().run();
   }

}
```

17.4 Graph traversals

As you saw in the preceding example, it is easy to cycle through the nodes in a graph, as long as you are content to process the nodes in the order imposed by the set abstraction. Many graph algorithms, however, require you to process the nodes in an order that takes the connections into account. Such algorithms typically start at some node and then advance from node to node by moving along the arcs, performing some operation on each node. The precise nature of the operation depends on the algorithm, but the process of performing that operation—whatever it is—is called *visiting* the node. The process of visiting each node in a graph by moving along its arcs is called *traversing* the graph.

In Chapter 15, you learned that several traversal strategies exist for trees, of which the most important are preorder, postorder, and inorder traversals. Like trees, graphs also support more than one traversal strategy. For graphs, the two fundamental traversal algorithms are *depth-first search* and *breadth-first search,* which the next two sections describe.

Each of the graph-traversal methods takes two parameters: the starting node and an object that implements the **Visitor** interface shown in Figure 17-7. This interface supports an important programming model called the *visitor pattern.* As you can see from the definition, all **Visitor<T>** objects implement a **visit**

FIGURE 17-7 Definition of the **Visitor** interface

```
/*
 * File: Visitor.java
 * ---------------------
 * This interface defines the behavior of classes that can serve as
 * visitors for nodes in a graph.
 */

package edu.stanford.cs.javacs2.ch17;

public interface Visitor<T> {

/**
 * Performs an operation on the specified node as part of the visitor
 * pattern.
 *
 * @param obj The object to be visited
 */

   public void visit(T obj);

}
```

method that takes a single argument of type **T**. The implementation of the **visit** method depends on the application. For the test programs, the **visit** method simply prints the name of the node, as follows:

```
public void visit(Node node) {
    System.out.println("Visiting " + node.getName());
}
```

The goal of a traversal is to apply the **Visitor** method once—and only once—to every node in the order specified by the traversal. Because graphs often have multiple paths that lead to the same node, ensuring that nodes are not revisited requires additional bookkeeping. The implementations of the traversal algorithms use a set called **visited** to record which nodes have been processed. If the traversal finds a node that is in the **visited** set, that node has already been visited.

Depth-first search

The *depth-first search* algorithm for traversing a graph is similar to the preorder traversal of trees and has the same recursive structure. The only additional complication is that graphs can contain cycles. As a result, it is essential to keep track of the nodes that have already been visited. The code that implements depth-first search starting at a particular node appears in Figure 17-8.

FIGURE 17-8 Code to execute a depth-first search

```
/*
 * Initiates a depth-first search beginning at the specified node, calling
 * the visit method provided by the Visitor object at each one.
 */

    private void depthFirstSearch(Node node, Visitor<Node> visitor) {
        XSet<Node> visited = new XSet<Node>();
        dfs(node, visitor, visited);
    }

/*
 * Executes a depth-first search beginning at the specified node that
 * avoids revisiting any nodes in the visited set. If visitor is
 * non-null, its visit method is applied to each node.
 */

    private void dfs(Node node, Visitor<Node> visitor, XSet<Node> visited) {
        if (visited.contains(node)) return;
        if (visitor != null) visitor.visit(node);
        visited.add(node);
        for (Arc arc : node.getArcs()) {
            dfs(arc.getFinish(), visitor, visited);
        }
    }
```

In this implementation, **depthFirstSearch** is a wrapper method whose only purpose is to introduce the **visited** set used to keep track of nodes that have already been processed. The **dfs** method visits the current node and then calls itself recursively for each node directly accessible from the current one.

The depth-first strategy is most easily understood by tracing its operation in the context of a simple example, such as the airline graph introduced at the beginning of the chapter:

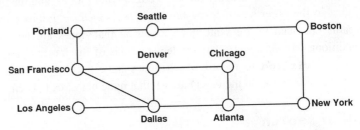

In this rendering of the graph, the nodes are drawn as open circles to indicate that they have not yet been visited. As the algorithm proceeds, each of these circles is marked with a number recording the order in which that node was processed.

Suppose that you initiate the depth-first search by making the following call:

```
depthFirstSearch(airline.getNode("San Francisco"));
```

The call to the **depthFirstSearch** method itself creates an empty **visited** set and then hands control off to the recursive **dfs** method. The first call visits the **San Francisco** node, which is recorded in the diagram as follows:

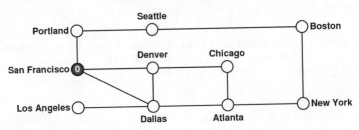

The code then makes several recursive calls to **dfs**, one for each cycle of the loop

```
for (Arc arc : node.getArcs()) {
    dfs(arc.getFinish(), visitor, visited);
}
```

The order in which these calls occur depends on the order in which the **for** statement steps through the arcs, which is defined by the **compareTo** methods in the **Node** and **Arc** classes. Since these comparison methods specify that the **for** loop will process the nodes in alphabetical order, the first cycle of the loop calls **dfs** with the **Dallas** node, which leads to the following state:

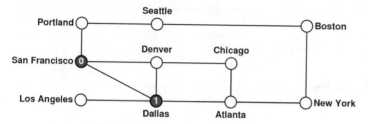

Given the way the code is written, the program must complete the entire call involving the **Dallas** node before it considers the other possible routes leaving the **San Francisco** node. The next node to be visited is therefore the city reachable from **Dallas** that appears first alphabetically, which is **Atlanta**:

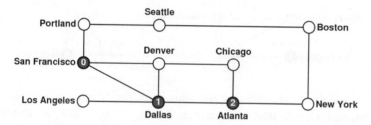

The overall effect of the depth-first search algorithm is to explore a single path in the graph as far as possible before backtracking to complete the exploration of paths at higher levels. From the **Atlanta** node, the process will continue to follow the path by choosing the starting point that appears first in the alphabetical list of neighbors. The depth-first exploration therefore continues with the nodes **Chicago** and **Denver**, which results in the following situation:

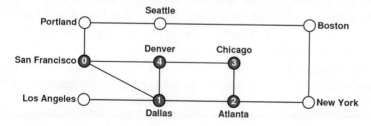

At this point in the process, forward progress becomes impossible. Every one of the connections from the **Denver** node has already been visited and therefore returns immediately. The recursive process therefore returns to **Chicago**, where it also finds no connections to unexplored territory. The recursive backtracking process then returns to **Atlanta**, where it can now pick up where it left off and explore the

New York link. As always, the depth-first algorithm explores this path as far as it can, which leads to the following configuration:

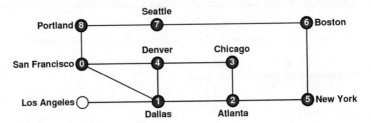

From here, the process will back up all the way to the **Dallas** node, from which it can pick up **Los Angeles**:

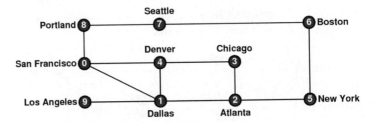

If you think about the depth-first algorithm in relation to other algorithms you've seen, you will realize that its operation is exactly the same as that of the maze-solving algorithm in Chapter 10. In that algorithm, it was necessary to mark squares along the path to avoid cycling forever around a loop in the maze. The marks in the maze are therefore analogous to the nodes in the **visited** set in the depth-first search implementation.

Breadth-first search

Although depth-first search has many important uses, the strategy has drawbacks that make it inappropriate for certain applications. The biggest problem with the depth-first approach is that it explores an entire path beginning at one neighbor before it goes back and looks at the other nearby neighbors. If you were trying to discover the shortest path between two nodes in a large graph, using depth-first search would take you all the way to the far reaches of the graph, even if your destination were one step away along a different path.

The *breadth-first search* algorithm gets around this problem by visiting each node in an order determined by how close it is to the starting node, measured in terms of the number of arcs along the shortest possible path. When you measure distance by counting arcs, each arc constitutes one *hop.* Thus, the essence of breadth-first search is that you visit the starting node first, then the nodes that are one hop away, followed by the nodes two hops away, and so on.

To get a more concrete sense of this algorithm, suppose that you want to apply a breadth-first traversal to the airline graph, again starting at the **San Francisco** node. The first phase of the algorithm simply visits the starting node:

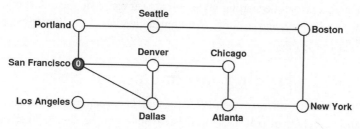

The next phase visits the nodes that are one hop away, as follows:

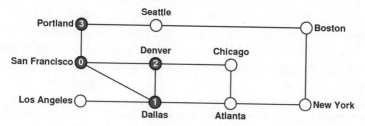

From here, the algorithm goes on to explore the nodes that are two hops away:

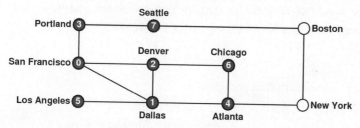

In the final phase, the algorithm completes its exploration of the graph by visiting the nodes that are three hops from the start:

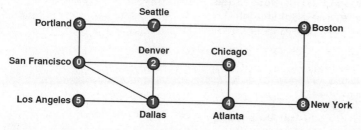

The easiest way to implement the breadth-first algorithm is to use a queue of unprocessed nodes. At each step in the process, you add the neighbors of the current node to the queue. Because the queue is processed in order, all nodes that are one hop away from the starting node will appear earlier in the queue than nodes that are two hops away, and so forth. An implementation of this strategy appears in Figure 17-9.

17.5 Finding minimum-cost paths

Because graphs arise in many applications that have commercial importance, a considerable amount of research has been invested in developing effective algorithms for solving graph-related problems. Of these problems, one of the most interesting is that of finding a path in a graph from one node to another that has the smallest possible cost when evaluated according to some metric. This metric need not be economic. Although you might be interested in finding the least expensive path between two nodes for certain applications, you can use the same algorithm to find a path with the shortest overall distance, the smallest number of hops, or the least travel time.

As a concrete example, suppose that you want to find the path from San Francisco to Boston that has the shortest total distance, as computed by the mileage values shown on the arcs in Figure 17-2. Is it better to go through Portland and Seattle, or should you instead go through Dallas, Atlanta, and New York? Or is there perhaps some less obvious route that is shorter still?

FIGURE 17-9 Code to execute a breadth-first search

```
/*
 * Initiates a breadth-first search beginning at the specified node,
 * calling the visit method provided by the Visitor object at each one.
 */

private void breadthFirstSearch(Node node, Visitor<Node> visitor) {
    XSet<Node> visited = new XSet<Node>();
    Queue<Node> queue = new ArrayQueue<Node>();
    queue.add(node);
    while (!queue.isEmpty()) {
        node = queue.remove();
        if (!visited.contains(node)) {
            visitor.visit(node);
            visited.add(node);
            for (Arc arc : node.getArcs()) {
                queue.add(arc.getFinish());
            }
        }
    }
}
```

With graphs as simple as the route map of this tiny airline, it is easy to compute the answer just by adding up the length of the arcs along all possible paths. As the graph grows larger, however, this approach can become unworkable. In general, the number of paths between two nodes in a graph grows in an exponential fashion, which means that the running time of the explore-all-paths approach is $O(2^N)$. As you know from the discussion of computational complexity in Chapter 11, problems whose solutions require exponential running time are considered to be intractable. If you want to find the minimum-cost path through a graph in a reasonable time, it is essential to use a more efficient algorithm.

The most commonly used algorithm for finding minimum-cost paths was discovered by Edsger W. Dijkstra in 1959. Dijkstra's algorithm for finding minimum-cost paths is a particular example of a class of algorithms called *greedy algorithms,* in which you find the overall answer by making a series of locally optimal decisions. Greedy algorithms do not work for every problem, but are quite useful in solving the problem of finding the minimum-cost path.

At its essence, the core of Dijkstra's algorithm for finding the path whose arcs have the minimum total cost can be expressed as follows: explore all paths from the starting node in order of increasing total path cost until you encounter a path that takes you to your destination. This path must be the best one, because you have already explored all paths beginning at the starting node that have a lower cost.

Dijkstra's algorithm is easier to implement if you start by defining a **Path** class that maintains a sequence of arcs. One possible strategy, of course, is to use an **ArrayList<Arc>** for this purpose, but there are advantages to encapsulating the list of arcs inside a separate class. For one thing, you can include the necessary checks in the **Path** class to ensure that the path is not disconnected, in the sense that each new arc starts at the node at which the previous one ended. In addition, the class can keep track of the total cost of the path so that it isn't necessary to add up the arc costs every time you need this information. Most importantly, however, you can define **Path** as an immutable class that never changes after it is created, but instead can be extended to form entirely new paths that include additional arcs. The primary advantage of using an immutable **Path** class is that doing so sidesteps the question of whether you need to copy a path during the execution of the algorithm, as you will see later in this section.

Figure 17-10 shows an implementation of an immutable **Path** class which also defines a **compareTo** method that compares two paths on the basis of their total length. Having **Path** implement the **Comparable<Path>** interface means that you can store paths in a priority queue so that shorter paths come before longer ones.

Implementation of the Path class

```java
/*
 * File: Path.java
 * ------------------
 * This file exports the Path class, which consists of a sequence of Arc
 * objects.  The Path class is immutable in that paths are never changed
 * once they are constructed.  Clients instead use the extend method to
 * create new paths that contain an additional arc.
 */

package edu.stanford.cs.javacs2.ch17;

import edu.stanford.cs.javacs2.ch13.ArrayList;
import java.util.Iterator;

public class Path implements Comparable<Path>, Iterable<Arc> {

    public Path() {
        arcs = new ArrayList<Arc>();
        totalCost = 0;
    }

/**
 * Creates a new path that has the same arcs as the current one, but
 * includes the new arc at the end.  Note that this method leaves the
 * current path unchanged.
 */

    public Path extend(Arc arc) {
        if (!isEmpty() && getFinish() != arc.getStart()) {
            throw new RuntimeException("Arcs are disconnected");
        }
        Path path = new Path();
        for (Arc a : this.arcs) {
            path.arcs.add(a);
        }
        path.arcs.add(arc);
        path.totalCost = this.totalCost + arc.getCost();
        return path;
    }

/**
 * Returns true if this path is empty.
 */

    public boolean isEmpty() {
        return arcs.isEmpty();
    }

/**
 * Gets the total cost of this path.
 */

    public double getCost() {
        return totalCost;
    }
```

FIGURE 17-10 Implementation of the `Path` class (continued)

```java
/**
 * Gets the starting node of this path.
 */

    public Node getStart() {
        if (arcs.isEmpty()) throw new RuntimeException("Path is empty");
        return arcs.get(0).getStart();
    }

/**
 * Gets the finish node of this path.
 */

    public Node getFinish() {
        if (arcs.isEmpty()) throw new RuntimeException("Path is empty");
        return arcs.get(arcs.size() - 1).getFinish();
    }

/**
 * Converts the path to a string.
 */

    public String toString() {
        if (arcs.isEmpty()) return "empty";
        String str = arcs.get(0).getStart().getName();
        for (Arc arc : arcs) {
            str += " -> " + arc.getFinish().getName();
        }
        return str;
    }

/**
 * Compares this path to p2 based on the total cost.
 */

    public int compareTo(Path p2) {
        return (int) Math.signum(this.totalCost - p2.totalCost);
    }

/**
 * Returns an iterator over the arcs in the path.
 */

    public Iterator<Arc> iterator() {
        return arcs.iterator();
    }

/* Private instance variables */

    private ArrayList<Arc> arcs;
    private double totalCost;

}
```

Once you have the `Path` class, Dijkstra's algorithm becomes relatively easy to code, as shown in the `findMinimumPath` method in Figure 17-11. This method takes two nodes and returns the minimum-cost path between them, or `null` if no connecting path exists.

The code for `findMinimumPath` makes more sense if you think about the data structures it uses. The implementation declares three local variables, as follows:

- The variable `path` keeps track of the minimum path as a `Path` object
- The variable `queue` is a priority queue of paths, which are ordered so that paths are processed in order of increasing cost.
- The variable `fixed` is a map that associates each node name with the minimum cost of reaching that node, as soon as that cost becomes known. Whenever you remove a path from the priority queue, you know that the path must show the cheapest route to its final node, unless that cost is already fixed. By storing the distance in a map, you can keep track of the costs you already know.

The operation of `findMinimumPath` is illustrated in Figure 17-12, which shows the steps involved in computing the minimum-cost path from San Francisco to Boston in the airline graph from Figure 17-2.

FIGURE 17-11 Implementation of Dijkstra's algorithm for finding the minimum-cost path

```
/*
 * Finds the minimum-cost path between start and finish using Dijkstra's
 * algorithm, which keeps track of the shortest paths in a priority
 * queue.  The method returns a Path object, or null if no path exists.
 */

    private Path findMinimumPath(Node start, Node finish) {
        Path path = new Path();
        PriorityQueue<Path> queue = new PriorityQueue<Path>();
        HashMap<String,Double> fixed = new HashMap<String,Double>();
        while (start != finish) {
            if (!fixed.containsKey(start.getName())) {
                fixed.put(start.getName(), path.getCost());
                for (Arc arc : start.getArcs()) {
                    if (!fixed.containsKey(arc.getFinish().getName())) {
                        queue.add(path.extend(arc));
                    }
                }
            }
            if (queue.isEmpty()) return null;
            path = queue.remove();
            start = path.getFinish();
        }
        return path;
    }
```

FIGURE 17-12 Steps in the execution of Dijkstra's algorithm

Fix the distance to **San Francisco** at 0.
Process the arcs out of **San Francisco (Dallas, Denver, Portland)**.
    Enqueue the path: **San Francisco → Dallas** (1468).
    Enqueue the path: **San Francisco → Denver** (954).
    Enqueue the path: **San Francisco → Portland** (550).
Dequeue the shortest path: **San Francisco → Portland** (550).
Fix the distance to **Portland** at 550.
Process the arcs out of **Portland (San Francisco, Seattle)**.
    Ignore **San Francisco** because its distance is known.
    Enqueue the path: **San Francisco → Portland → Seattle** (680).
Dequeue the shortest path: **San Francisco → Portland → Seattle** (680).
Fix the distance to **Seattle** at 680.
Process the arcs out of **Seattle (Boston, Portland)**.
    Enqueue the path: **San Francisco → Portland → Seattle → Boston** (3169).
    Ignore **Portland** because its distance is known.
Dequeue the shortest path: **San Francisco → Denver** (954).
Fix the distance to **Denver** at 954.
Process the arcs out of **Denver (Chicago, Dallas, San Francisco)**.
    Ignore **San Francisco** because its distance is known.
    Enqueue the path: **San Francisco → Denver → Chicago** (1861).
    Enqueue the path: **San Francisco → Denver → Dallas** (1604).
Dequeue the shortest path: **San Francisco → Dallas** (1468).
Fix the distance to **Dallas** at 1468.
Process the arcs out of **Dallas (Atlanta, Denver, Los Angeles, San Francisco)**.
    Ignore **Denver** and **San Francisco** because their distances are known.
    Enqueue the path: **San Francisco → Dallas → Atlanta** (2193).
    Enqueue the path: **San Francisco → Dallas → Los Angeles** (2708).
Dequeue the shortest path: **San Francisco → Denver → Dallas** (1604).
Ignore **Dallas** because its distance is known.
Dequeue the shortest path: **San Francisco → Denver → Chicago** (1861).
Fix the distance to **Chicago** at 1861.
Process the arcs out of **Chicago (Atlanta, Denver)**.
    Ignore **Denver** because its distance is known.
    Enqueue the path: **San Francisco → Denver → Chicago → Atlanta** (2460).
Dequeue the shortest path: **San Francisco → Dallas → Atlanta** (2193).
Fix the distance to **Atlanta** at 2193.
Process the arcs out of **Atlanta (Chicago, Dallas, New York)**.
    Ignore **Chicago** and **Dallas** because their distances are known.
    Enqueue the path: **San Francisco → Dallas → Atlanta → New York** (2949).
Dequeue the shortest path: **San Francisco → Denver → Chicago → Atlanta** (2460).
Ignore **Atlanta** because its distance is known.
Dequeue the shortest path: **San Francisco → Dallas → Los Angeles** (2708).
Fix the distance to **Los Angeles** at 2708.
Process the arcs out of **Los Angeles (Dallas)**.
    Ignore **Dallas** because its distance is known.
Dequeue the shortest path: **San Francisco → Dallas → Atlanta → New York** (2949).
Fix the distance to **New York** at 2949.
Process the arcs out of **New York (Atlanta, Boston)**.
    Ignore **Atlanta** because its distance is known.
    Enqueue the path: **San Francisco → Dallas → Atlanta → New York → Boston** (3140).
Dequeue the shortest path: **San Francisco → Dallas → Atlanta → New York → Boston** (3140).

As you read through the implementation of Dijkstra's algorithm, it is useful to keep the following points in mind:

- *Paths are explored in order of the total distance rather than the number of hops.* Thus, the connections beginning with **San Francisco** → **Portland** → **Seattle** are explored before those of either **San Francisco** → **Denver** or **San Francisco** → **Dallas**, because the total distance is shorter.

- *The distance to a node is fixed when a path is removed from the priority queue, not when it is added.* The first path to Boston added to the priority queue is the one that goes through Portland and Seattle, which is not the shortest path. The total distance along the path **San Francisco** → **Portland** → **Seattle** → **Boston** is 3169. Because the minimum is 3140, the **San Francisco** → **Portland** → **Seattle** → **Boston** path is still in the priority queue when the algorithm finishes its operation.

- *The arcs from each node are scanned at most once.* The inner loop of the algorithm is executed only when the distance to that node is fixed, which happens once for each node. As a result, the total number of cycles executed within the inner loop is the product of the number of nodes and the maximum number of arcs leading from a node. A complete analysis of Dijkstra's algorithm is beyond the scope of this text, but the running time is $O(M \log N)$, where N is the number of nodes and M is either N or the number of arcs, whichever is larger.

■ 17.6 Generalizing the Graph class

The **Graph**, **Node**, and **Arc** classes defined earlier in this chapter are not as general as one would like. For applications that are more sophisticated than the ones you have seen so far, it is almost certain that clients will want to add additional fields to the **Node** and **Arc** classes. For example, if you want to display the graph on the screen, you will need to include the x and y coordinates of each node as part of the data stored with the **Node** class. Similarly, if you want to draw arcs in different colors, you will want to include a **color** field in the **Arc** class definition.

Even with the classes you have already seen, there is nothing that prevents you from defining subclasses that contain the necessary fields. For example, you could use the code in Figure 17-13 to define the nested subclasses **AirlineNode** and **AirlineArc** that include these additional fields. The problem with this approach is that the **Graph** class—along with the **Node** and **Graph** classes themselves—uses the original **Node** and **Arc** classes rather than their extended counterparts. As a result, any method calls that return values of type **Node** or **Arc** need type casts before the result can be assigned to a variable declared as an **AirlineNode** or **AirlineArc**. For example, if you have a graph **g** containing these extended classes and wanted to

> **FIGURE 17-13** Defining extensions of the Node and Arc classes
>
> ```
> /* Inner class for a node containing the screen location */
>     private static class AirlineNode extends Node {
>
>         public AirlineNode(String name, double x, double y) {
>             super(name);
>             this.x = x;
>             this.y = y;
>         }
>
>         private double x;
>         private double y;
>
>     }
>
> /* Inner class for an arc containing color information */
>     private static class AirlineArc extends Arc {
>
>         public AirlineArc(AirlineNode start, AirlineNode finish, Color color) {
>             super(start, finish);
>             this.color = color;
>         }
>
>         private Color color;
>
>     }
> ```

find the `AirlineNode` whose name is `Portland`, you would need to use the following declaration:

```
AirlineNode city = (AirlineNode) g.getNode("Portland");
```

Unfortunately, remembering to use the required type casts is tedious and does nothing to help the readability of the code.

Using parameterized types in the graph abstraction

The best way to eliminate the need for type casts is to define the classes that make up the graph abstraction so that they take the actual types used for nodes and arcs as type parameters. This section introduces four new classes—`GenericGraph<N,A>`, `GenericNode<N,A>`, `GenericArc<N,A>`, and `GenericPath<N,A>`—each of which represents a generalization of a class you have already seen. The type parameters `N` and `A` in these class names stand for the node and arc types actually in use.

Writing the template definitions, however, is not as simple as it might at first appear. You can't, for example, use the following header line to define the parameterized version of `GenericGraph`:

```
public class GenericGraph<N,A>
```

That definition would allow the replacements for **N** and **A** to be any Java classes. To make the graph abstraction work, **N** must be a subclass of `GenericNode`, and **A** must be a subclass of `GenericArc`. Since those classes are themselves parameterized, the header line you need for `GenericGraph` looks like this:

```
public class GenericGraph<N extends GenericNode<N,A>,
                          A extends GenericArc<N,A>>
```

The same pattern applies for the definitions of `GenericNode`, `GenericArc`, and `GenericPath`. Once you have written the correct header lines, the rest of the code changes very little. All you need to do is substitute the appropriate type parameter name at every point in which the concrete types **Node** and **Arc** appear in the earlier implementation.

Adding additional operations

If you want to make the parameterized version of the graph abstraction as useful as possible, it makes sense to define additional methods beyond the ones included in the `Graph` class from Figure 17-5. Some of those methods might make using the classes more convenient. For example, you could overload the methods that take nodes as parameters so that the client could pass the names of those nodes instead. Other extensions include adding algorithmic methods like depth- and breadth-first searches (implemented by the methods **dfs** and **bfs**) and Dijkstra's algorithm (implemented as **findMinimumPath**). Figure 17-14 lists the methods exported by the `GenericGraph` class, as it is defined in the code examples for this chapter.

▮ 17.7 Algorithms for searching the web

As noted in the introduction to this chapter, the web is a graph in which the nodes are the individual pages and the arcs are the hyperlinks that take you from one page to another. In contrast to the graphs you have seen in this chapter, the graph for the web is huge. The number of pages on the web runs well into the billions, and the number of links is larger still.

In order to find something useful in that vast collection of pages, most people use a search engine to produce a list of the pages most likely to be of interest. Typical search engines operate by scanning the entire web—this process is called *crawling* and is carried out by many computers working in parallel—and then using

FIGURE 17-14 Methods exported by the `GenericGraph` class

Constructor

`GenericGraph<N,A>()`	Creates an empty graph with no nodes and no arcs.

Methods

`size()`	Returns the number of nodes in the graph.
`isEmpty()`	Returns **true** if the graph contains no nodes.
`clear()`	Removes all the nodes and arcs from the graph.
`addNode`(*node*)	Adds the node to the graph.
`removeNode`(*name*) `removeNode`(*node*)	Removes a node from the graph, along with all arcs involving that node.
`getNode`(*name*)	Returns the node associated with *name*. If no node exists with the specified name, `getNode` returns **null**.
`addArc`(s_1, s_2) `addArc`(n_1, n_2) `addArc`(*arc*)	Adds an arc to the graph connecting the two nodes. The first two forms add an arc connecting the specified nodes; the third form adds an arc constructed by the client.
`removeArc`(s_1, s_2) `removeArc`(n_1, n_2) `removeArc`(*arc*)	Removes any arcs connecting the specified nodes.
`getNodeSet()`	Returns the set of all nodes in a graph.
`getArcSet()`	Returns the set of all arcs in a graph.
`getNeighbors`(*name*) `getNeighbors`(*node*)	Returns the set of all nodes that are neighbors of the current node, in the sense that there is an arc from the specified node to the neighbor.
`bfs`(n_1, *visitor*) `bfs`(n_1, n_2, *visitor*)	Conducts a breadth-first search starting at node n_1, calling the **visit** method from *visitor* on each node. If n_2 is specified, the search stops when that node has been visited.
`dfs`(n_1, *visitor*) `dfs`(n_1, n_2, *visitor*)	Conducts a depth-first search starting at node n_1, calling the **visit** method from *visitor* on each node. If n_2 is specified, the search stops when that node has been visited.
`findMinimumPath`(n_1, n_2)	Finds the minimum-cost path from n_1 to n_2 using Dijkstra's algorithm. This method returns a `GenericPath` object, or **null** if no path exists.
`load`(*file*)	Loads the contents of the file into the graph.
`save`(*file*)	Saves the contents of the graph to the file.

that information to create an index indicating which pages contain a particular word or phrase. Given the scale of the web, however, the index alone is not sufficient. Unless the query terms are extremely specific, the list of all pages containing those terms will be unmanageably long. Search engines must therefore sort their results so pages that appear early in the list are the ones most likely to be of interest.

Coming up with an algorithm to rank the importance of each page is the primary challenge in designing an effective search engine.

The Google PageRank algorithm

The best-known strategy for sorting web pages is Google's **PageRank algorithm,** which assigns each page a value that reflects the importance of that page based on the structure of the web graph as a whole. Although the name suggests the idea of ranking web pages, PageRank is in fact named after Larry Page, who designed the algorithm together with Google cofounder Sergey Brin while both were graduate students at Stanford University.

At one level, the idea behind the PageRank algorithm is simply that a page becomes more important if other pages link to it. In a sense, each page on the web represents an endorsement of the importance of the pages to which it links. All links, however, do not confer the same level of endorsement. A link from a page that is recognized as authoritative carries more weight than a link coming from a less credible source. This observation suggests a minor reformulation of the earlier characterization of importance: a page becomes more important if *important* pages link to it.

The fact that the importance of a page varies along with the importance of the pages that link to it suggests that the ranking of a page will fluctuate up and down as the rankings of other pages change. The PageRank algorithm therefore proceeds as a series of successive approximations. At the beginning, all pages are given equal weight. In subsequent iterations, the ranking of each page is used to adjust the rankings of the pages to which it points. Eventually, this process converges to a stable point in which the ranking of each page provides a measure of its importance as determined by the link structure of the web.

Another way to describe the effect of the PageRank algorithm is that the final ranking of each page represents the probability of reaching that page by following links on the web at random. Processes that proceed by making random choices without regard to previous decisions are called **Markov processes** after the Russian mathematician Andrei Markov (1856–1922) who was among the first to analyze their mathematical properties.

A tiny example of the PageRank calculation

Given that the actual web is too large to serve as an effective instructional example, it makes sense to start with a much smaller example. The diagram in Figure 17-15 shows the graph of a tiny web consisting of five pages, identified by the letters **A**, **B**, **C**, **D**, and **E**. The arcs in the graph represent the links between pages. For example, page **A** links to each of the other pages, while page **B** links only to page **E**.

FIGURE 17-15 Graph of a five-page web in which each page has equal probability

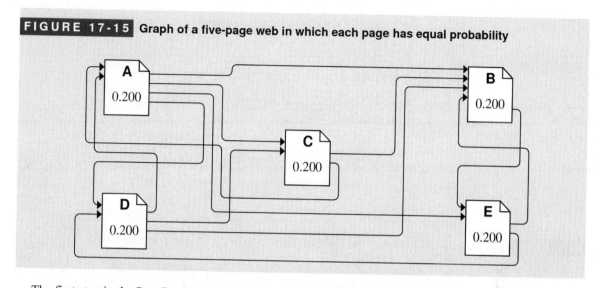

The first step in the PageRank algorithm is to assign each page an initial ranking that is simply the probability of choosing that page at random out of the entire collection of pages. There are five pages in this example, so the chance that any particular page gets chosen at random is one in five. This chance corresponds to a mathematical probability of 0.2, which appears at the bottom of each page.

On each of its iterations, the PageRank algorithm updates the probabilities assigned to each of the pages by computing the likelihood that the user reaches that page after following a random link from the end of the preceding cycle. For example, if you happen to be at node **A**, you have a choice to visit any of the other four nodes, because **A** has links to all of them. If you choose a link at random, you will go to node **B** a quarter of the time, node **C** a quarter of the time, and so on for nodes **D** and **E**. What happens, however, if you find yourself at node **B**? Given that there is only one link out of node **B**, any user who chooses a link from **B** will invariably end up at node **E**.

You can use this calculation to determine the likelihood of being at any node after following a random link. The are two ways, for example, to reach node **A** after following a link. You could have started at node **C** and chosen the link back to **A**, which was one of two links on the page. Alternatively, you could have started at node **D**, but in this case you had to be lucky enough to choose the link to **A** from three possibilities rather than two. The probability of reaching node **A** after following one random link is therefore one-half times the chance of being at **C** plus one-third times the chance of being at **D**. If you express this calculation as a formula using primed letters to indicate probabilities on the next cycle, the result looks like this:

$$\mathbf{A}' = \tfrac{1}{2}\mathbf{C} + \tfrac{1}{3}\mathbf{D}$$

A similar analysis yields the following formulas for the other pages in the graph:

$$B' = \tfrac{1}{4}A + \tfrac{1}{2}C + \tfrac{1}{3}D + \tfrac{1}{2}E$$
$$C' = \tfrac{1}{4}A + \tfrac{1}{3}D$$
$$D' = \tfrac{1}{4}A + \tfrac{1}{2}E$$
$$E' = \tfrac{1}{4}A + B$$

Each iteration of the PageRank algorithm replaces the probabilities for the pages **A, B, C, D**, and **E** with the values **A′, B′, C′, D′**, and **E′** computed by these formulae. The results of executing the first two iterations are shown in Figure 17-16.

FIGURE 17-16 **Probabilities after the first two iterations of the PageRank algorithm**

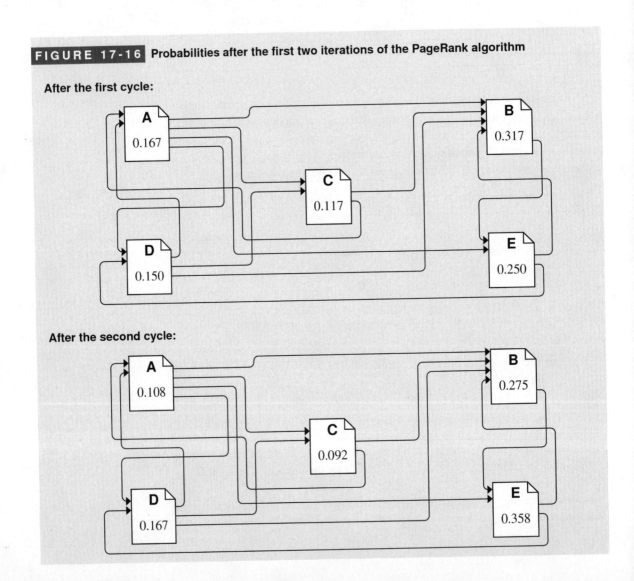

After the first cycle:

After the second cycle:

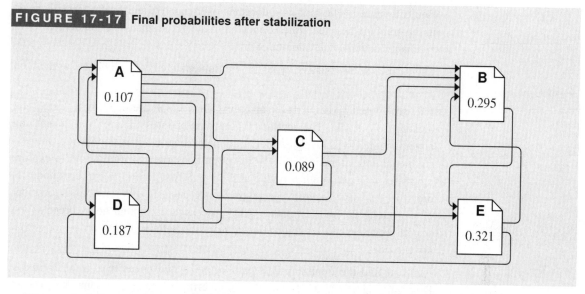

FIGURE 17-17 Final probabilities after stabilization

The wonderful thing about most Markov processes that arise in the real world is that the probabilities tend to stabilize after a relatively modest number of iterations. Figure 17-17 shows the probabilities for these five pages after 16 iterations, at which point the probabilities no longer change in the first three decimal places. These values, therefore, indicate the probability that a random web surfer ends up on that particular page, which is the essence of the PageRank idea.

Summary

This chapter has introduced you to the idea of a graph, which is defined as a set of nodes linked together by a set of arcs that connect individual pairs of nodes. Like sets, graphs are not only important as a theoretical abstraction, but also as a tool for solving practical problems that arise in many application domains. For example, graph algorithms are useful in studying the properties of connected structures ranging from the Internet to large-scale transportation systems.

Important points in this chapter include:

- Graphs may be either directed or undirected. The arcs in a directed graph run in one direction only, so the existence of an arc $n_1 \rightarrow n_2$ does not imply the existence of an arc $n_2 \rightarrow n_1$. You can represent undirected graphs using directed graphs in which the connected pairs of nodes are linked by two arcs, one in each direction.

- You can adopt any of several strategies to represent the connections in a graph. One common approach is to construct an adjacency list, in which the data structure for each node contains a list of the connected nodes. You can also use an adjacency matrix, which stores the connections in a two-dimensional array of

Boolean values. The rows and columns of the matrix are indexed by the nodes in the graph; if two nodes are connected in the graph, the corresponding entry in the matrix contains the value **true**.

- The **Graph**, **Node**, and **Arc** types can be implemented easily by layering them on top of sets.

- The two most important traversal orders for a graph are depth-first search and breadth-first search. The depth-first algorithm chooses one arc from the starting node and then recursively explores all paths beginning with that arc until no additional nodes remain. Only at that point does the algorithm return to explore other arcs from the original node. The breadth-first algorithm explores nodes in order of their distance from the original node, measured in terms of the number of arcs along the shortest path. After processing the initial node, breadth-first search processes all the neighbors of that node before moving on to nodes that are two hops away.

- You can find the minimum-cost path between two nodes in a graph by using Dijkstra's algorithm, which is vastly more efficient than the exponential strategy of comparing the cost of all possible paths. Dijkstra's algorithm is an example of a larger class of algorithms called *greedy algorithms,* which select the locally best option at any decision point.

- You can increase the generality of the graph abstraction by using parameterized types to define specific classes for the nodes and arcs. This model is built into the **GenericGraph** class, whose methods are listed in Figure 17-14.

- Google's PageRank algorithm illustrates the enormous importance of graph algorithms in practice.

Review questions

1. What is a graph?

2. True or false: Trees are a subset of graphs, which form a more general class.

3. What is the difference between a directed and an undirected graph?

4. If you are using a graph package that supports only directed graphs, how can you represent an undirected graph?

5. Define the following terms as they apply to graphs: *path, cycle, simple path, simple cycle.*

6. What is relationship between the terms *neighbor* and *degree?*

7. What is the difference between a strongly connected and a weakly connected graph?

8. True or false: The term *weakly connected* has no practical relevance to undirected graphs because all such graphs are automatically strongly connected if they are connected at all.

9. What terms do mathematicians often use in place of the words *node* and *arc?*

10. Suppose that the computer science offerings at some university consists of eight courses with the following prerequisite structure:

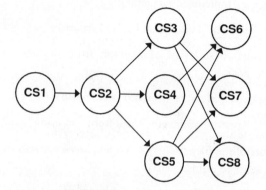

Using the mathematical formulation for graphs described in this chapter, define this graph as a pair of sets.

11. Draw a diagram showing the adjacency list representation of the graph in the preceding question.

12. Given the prerequisite graph shown in question 10, what are the contents of the corresponding adjacency matrix?

13. What is the difference between a sparse and a dense graph?

14. If you were asked to choose the underlying representation of a graph for a particular application, what factors would you consider in deciding whether to use adjacency lists or adjacency matrices in the implementation?

15. What are the two most common traversal strategies for graphs?

16. Write down both the depth-first and the breadth-first traversal of the airline graph in Figure 17-1, starting from Atlanta. Remember that iteration over nodes and arcs always occurs in alphabetical order.

17. What is a greedy algorithm?

18. Explain the operation of Dijkstra's algorithm for finding minimum-cost paths.

19. Show the contents of the priority queue at each step of the trace of Dijkstra's algorithm shown in Figure 17-12.

20. Using Figure 17-12 as a model, trace the execution of Dijkstra's algorithm to find the minimum-cost path from Portland to Atlanta.

Exercises

1§. Although these definitions are included in the code supplied with this chapter, it is instructive to implement the method

```
public void load(String filename)
```

that reads a text description of a graph from the specified file and the symmetric method

```
public void save(String filename)
```

that writes the structure of the graph in a form that is compatible with **load**.

The format of the files used by **load** and **save** consists of lines that can be in any of these three forms:

x	Defines a node with name *x*
x - *y*	Defines the bidirectional arc $x \leftrightarrow y$
x -> *y*	Defines the directional arc $x \rightarrow y$

The names *x* and *y* are arbitrary strings that do not contain a hyphen. The two connection formats also allow the user to specify the cost of the arc by enclosing a number in parentheses at the end of the line. If no parenthesized value appears, the cost of the arc should be initialized to 0. The definition of the graph ends with a blank line or the end of the file.

New nodes are defined whenever a new name appears in the data file. Thus, if every node is connected to some other node, it is sufficient to include only the arcs in the data file, because defining an arc automatically defines the nodes at its endpoints. If you need to represent a graph containing isolated nodes, you must specify the names of those nodes on separate lines.

When reading in an arc, your implementation should discard leading and trailing spaces from the node names, but retain internal spaces. The line

```
San Francisco - Denver (954)
```

should define nodes with the names `"San Francisco"` and `"Denver"`, and then create connections in each direction, so that both arcs have a cost of 954.

As an example, calling **load** on the following data file would produce the airline graph that appears in the chapter as Figure 17-2:

AirlineGraph.txt

```
Atlanta - Chicago (599)
Atlanta - Dallas (725)
Atlanta - New York (756)
Boston - New York (191)
Boston - Seattle (2489)
Chicago - Denver (907)
Dallas - Denver (650)
Dallas - Los Angeles (1240)
Dallas - San Francisco (1468)
Denver - San Francisco (954)
Portland - Seattle (130)
Portland - San Francisco (550)
```

For the most part, the implementation of the **save** method is easier than that of **load**. The only tricky parts of the **save** implementation are making sure that the output includes nodes that contain no outgoing arcs and using the undirected syntax if the graph contains arcs in both directions between two nodes.

2. Eliminate the recursion from the implementation of **depthFirstSearch** in Figure 17-8 by using a stack to store the unexplored nodes. At the beginning of the algorithm, you simply push the starting node on the stack. Then, until the stack is empty, you repeat the following operations:

    1. Pop the topmost node from the stack.
    2. Visit that node.
    3. Push its neighbors on the stack

3. Take your solution from the preceding exercise and replace the stack with a queue. Describe the traversal order implemented by the resulting code.

4. Write a method

        boolean pathExists(Node n1, Node n2)

    that returns **true** if there is a path in the graph between the nodes **n1** and **n2**. Implement this method by using depth-first search to traverse the graph from **n1**; if you encounter **n2** along the way, then a path exists. Reimplement your method so that it uses breadth-first search instead. In a large graph, which implementation is likely to be more appropriate?

5. Write a method

       int hopCount(Node n1, Node n2)

   that returns the number of hops in the shortest path between the nodes **n1** and **n2**. If **n1** and **n2** are the same node, **hopCount** should return 0; if no path exists, **hopCount** should return −1. This method is easily implemented using breadth-first search.

6. Write a method

       Path bfsPath(Node n1, Node n2)

   that uses breadth-first search to find a path between the nodes **n1** and **n2** that has the shortest possible hop count. There may be many such paths, and your program is free to return any minimal path. If there is no path between **n1** and **n2** your function should return **null**.

7. A *word ladder* is a puzzle invented by Lewis Carroll in which the goal is to convert one word into another by changing one letter at a time, subject to the additional constraint that at each step the sequence of letters must still form a valid word. For example, here is a word ladder connecting **code** to **data**.

   code → **core** → **care** → **dare** → **date** → **data**

   That word ladder, however, is not the shortest possible one. Although the words are a little less familiar, the following ladder is one step shorter:

   code → **cade** → **cate** → **date** → **data**

   Your job in this problem is to write a program that finds a minimal word ladder between two words, which turns out to be easy if you use breadth-first search. The first step in the process is to construct a graph in which the nodes are the English words that are exactly four letters long. The arcs in the graph connect nodes that differ by a single letter, which makes them eligible for inclusion in a word ladder. The following diagram shows a small part of the graph of four-letter English words that includes all the words that are no more than two hops away from **chug**:

Once you have the graph, finding a word ladder is simply a matter of applying the **bfsPath** method you wrote for the preceding exercise.

Write a program that reads in two words from the user and finds a word ladder that connects them. A sample run of your program might look like this:

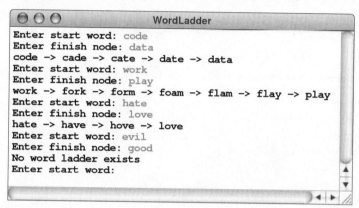

```
⊖ ○ ○                    WordLadder
Enter start word: code
Enter finish node: data
code -> cade -> cate -> date -> data
Enter start word: work
Enter finish node: play
work -> fork -> form -> foam -> flam -> flay -> play
Enter start word: hate
Enter finish node: love
hate -> have -> hove -> love
Enter start word: evil
Enter finish node: good
No word ladder exists
Enter start word:
```

8. When you use Facebook, the site will often make suggestions of new friends by scanning its database to find people to whom you are connected by some friendship path. To illustrate this process, imagine that one tiny part of the Facebook friend database consists of the graph shown in Figure 17-18, in which the arcs trace the friendship relation. For example, the arcs leading out of the highlighted **Eric** node near the left side of the graph show that I am friends with **Keith**, **Lauren**, and **Mehran**. Given this graph, Facebook would presumably suggest that I become friends with **Olivia** because she is directly connected to all three of my current friends. Facebook might also suggest that I might want to become friends with **Hannah**, because **Hannah** and I have two mutual friends: **Keith** and **Mehran**.

Write a method

```
void suggestFriends(Graph g, Node start)
```

that prints three (or fewer if there aren't three possibilities) suggested friends for the person at the specified starting node. The suggestions should be sorted in descending order by the number of friends the person at the starting node has in common with each suggested candidate.

For example, if **friends** is initialized to the graph in Figure 17-18, calling

```
suggestFriends(friends, friends.getNode("Eric"));
```

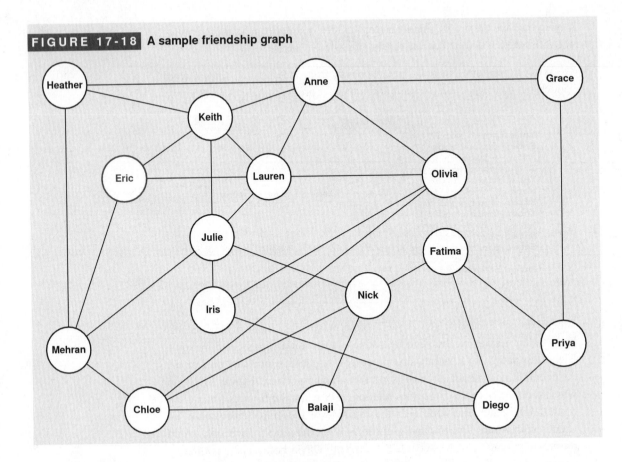

FIGURE 17-18 A sample friendship graph

should generate output that looks like this:

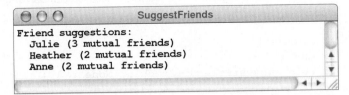

It might seem that one way to implement this problem would be to iterate over all nodes in the graph and count the number of mutual connections. The problem with this approach is that the Facebook friendship graph is *huge*. In this problem, you must therefore work only in the neighborhood of the initial node. You can certainly look at friends of friends, but not at completely unrelated parts of the graph.

9. Design and implement a method that calculates the *diameter* of a graph, which is the maximum of the shortest path lengths between any two nodes in the graph. In the friend graph shown in Figure 17-18, the diameter is 4 because

that is the maximum distance between any two nodes. If the graph is disconnected, your method should return −1. (For an interesting application of graph diameter, look up "Six Degrees of Kevin Bacon" on the web.)

10. Several important graph algorithms operate on a special class of graphs in which the nodes can be divided into two sets in such a way that all the arcs connect nodes in different sets, with none of the arcs running between nodes in the same set. Such graphs are said to be *bipartite*. Write a method

    ```
    boolean isBipartite(Graph g);
    ```

    that takes a graph and returns **true** if it has the bipartite property.

11. A *dominating set* of a graph is a subset of the nodes such that those nodes along with their immediate neighbors constitute all graph nodes. That is, every node in the graph is either in the dominating set or is a neighbor of a node in the dominating set. In the graph diagrammed below—in which each node is labeled with the number of neighbors to facilitate tracing the algorithm—the filled-in nodes constitute a dominating set for the graph. Other dominating sets are also possible.

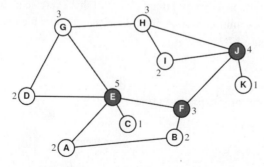

    Ideally, you would like to be able to find the smallest possible dominating set, but that is known to be a computationally difficult task—too expensive for most graphs. The following algorithm usually finds a relatively small dominating set, even though it does not always produce the optimal result:

    1. Start with an empty set *S*.

    2. Consider each graph node in order of decreasing degree. In other words, you want to start with the node that has the most neighbors and then work down through the nodes with fewer neighbors. If two or more nodes have the same degree, you can process them in any order.

    3. If the node you chose in step 2 is not redundant, add it to *S*. A node is *redundant* if it and all its neighbors are neighbors of a node already in *S*.

    4. Continue until *S* dominates the entire graph.

Write a method

```
XSet<Node> findDominatingSet(Graph g)
```

that uses this algorithm to find a small dominating set for the graph **g**.

12. Suppose that you are working for a company that is building a new cable system that connects 10 large cities in the San Francisco Bay area. Your preliminary research has provided you with cost estimates for laying new cable lines along a variety of possible routes. Those routes and their associated costs are shown in the graph on the left side of Figure 17-19. Your job is to find the most economical way to lay new cables so that all the cities are connected through some path.

To minimize the cost, one of the things you need to avoid is laying a cable that forms a cycle in the graph. Such a cable would be unnecessary, because there must be another path connecting the cities. The remaining graph, given that it has no cycles, forms a tree. A tree that links all the nodes of a graph is called a *spanning tree.* The spanning tree in which the total cost associated with the arcs is as small as possible is called a *minimum spanning tree.* The cable-network problem described earlier in this exercise is therefore equivalent to finding the minimum spanning tree of the graph, which is shown in the right side of Figure 17-19.

FIGURE 17-19 **A graph and its minimum spanning tree**

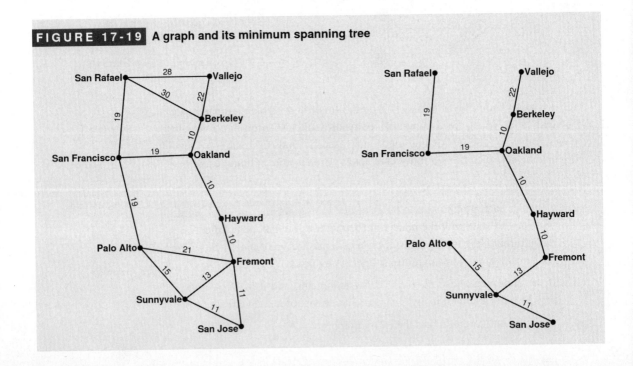

There are many algorithms in the literature for finding a minimum spanning tree. One of the simplest was devised by Joseph Kruskal in 1956. In Kruskal's algorithm, all you do is consider the arcs in the graph in order of increasing cost. If the nodes at the endpoints of the arc are unconnected, then you include this arc as part of the spanning tree. If, however, a path already exists between the two nodes in the new graph, you ignore the arc entirely. The steps in the construction of the minimum spanning tree for the graph in Figure 17-19 are shown in the following sample run:

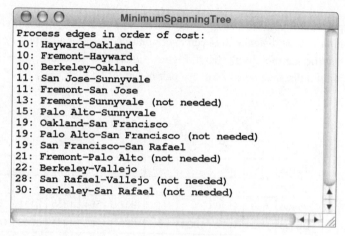

Using the **pathExists** method from exercise 4 to determine whether two nodes are connected by a path, write a method

```
Graph findMinimumSpanningTree(Graph g)
```

that implements Kruskal's algorithm to find the minimum spanning tree. The method should return a new graph whose nodes have the same names as those in **g** but that includes only the arcs from the minimum spanning tree.

13. Exercise 12 suggests that you use **pathExists** to determine whether an arc is needed in the minimum spanning tree. Although this strategy is easy to code, it is not particularly efficient because it requires searching the graph for each step of the process. A much more efficient approach is to maintain a record of the connected regions of the graph as you go. To implement this process, the easiest approach is to use sets to record the connected components of the new graph as you create it. Initially, each node in the new graph is part of a set that contains only that node. Adding arcs to the graph creates new connections that merge those sets together. Implementing this strategy requires you to design a data structure that supports the following operations:

- Find the set that contains a particular node.

- Merge two existing sets to produce the union of the two.

In computer science, this process is called the ***union-find algorithm.***

Reimplement Kruskal's algorithm so that it uses the union-find algorithm. As you go through the arcs in order of increasing cost, you simply check the sets to which the endpoints belong. If they are part of different sets, you need to merge those sets and add the arc to the new graph. If the endpoints of the arc belong to the same set, then there must already be a path that connects the two, and you can leave it out of the spanning tree.

14. Suppose that you have been assigned the task of creating a chart showing the minimum-cost distance between every pair of nodes in a graph. For example, given the airline graph from Figure 17-2, the following table shows the minimum distance between every pair of cities:

	Atlanta	Boston	Chicago	Dallas	Denver	Los Angeles	New York	Portland	San Francisco	Seattle
Atlanta	0	947	599	725	1375	1965	756	2743	2193	2873
Boston	947	0	1546	1672	2322	2912	191	2619	3140	2489
Chicago	599	1546	0	1324	907	2564	1355	2411	1861	2541
Dallas	725	1672	1324	0	650	1240	1481	2018	1468	2148
Denver	1375	2322	907	650	0	1890	2131	1504	954	1634
Los Angeles	1965	2912	2564	1240	1890	0	2721	3258	2708	3388
New York	756	191	1355	1481	2131	2721	0	2810	2949	2680
Portland	2743	2619	2411	2018	1504	3258	2810	0	550	130
San Francisco	2193	3140	1861	1468	954	2708	2949	550	0	680
Seattle	2873	2489	2541	2148	1634	3388	2680	130	680	0

You could, of course, apply Dijkstra's algorithm to find the minimum-cost path between every pair of nodes, but there are more efficient strategies if your goal is to find the complete set of shortest paths.

The most widely used algorithm for finding all shortest paths in a graph is called the ***Floyd–Warshall algorithm*** after its independent inventors Robert Floyd and Stephen Warshall. That algorithm operates by setting up an initial matrix of distances and then adjusting the distance values through successive refinement. The initial contents of the matrix are 0 for every node to itself, the cost of the arc for every pair of nodes that are directly connected, and infinity (the constant `Double.POSITIVE_INFINITY` in Java) everywhere else. For the airline graph, the initial version of the matrix looks like this:

0	∞	599	725	∞	∞	756	∞	∞	∞
∞	0	∞	∞	∞	∞	191	∞	∞	2489
599	∞	0	∞	907	∞	∞	∞	∞	∞
725	∞	∞	0	650	1240	∞	∞	1468	∞
∞	∞	907	650	0	∞	∞	∞	954	∞
∞	∞	∞	1240	∞	0	∞	∞	∞	∞
756	191	∞	∞	∞	∞	0	∞	∞	∞
∞	∞	∞	∞	∞	∞	∞	0	550	130
∞	∞	∞	1468	954	∞	∞	550	0	∞
∞	2489	∞	∞	∞	∞	∞	130	∞	0

From here, the Floyd–Warshall algorithm makes a series of passes over the matrix. On each cycle, the algorithm determines the length of the shortest path using only nodes with indices in the range between 0 and k, where k is the cycle count.

Assuming that the matrix is stored in an **nxn** array called **table**, the Floyd–Warshall algorithm looks like this in pseudocode form:

```
for (int k = 0; k < n; k++) {
   for (int i = 0; i < n; i++) {
      for (int j = 0; j < n; j++) {
         If going through node k gives a shorter path, update table_i,j.
      }
   }
}
```

The essence of the code in the innermost loop is to check whether it is possible to improve an existing path from node i to node j by going through node k.

Write a method

```
double[][] mileageChart(Graph g)
```

that uses Floyd–Warshall to compute the complete matrix of shortest paths.

15. Graph algorithms are often well suited to distributed implementations in which processing is performed at each node in the graph. In particular, such algorithms are used to find optimal transmission routes in a computer network. As an example, the following graph shows the first 10 nodes in the ARPANET, which was the forerunner of the modern Internet:

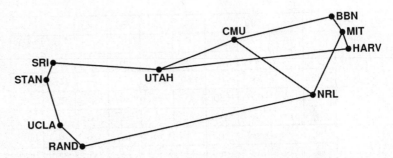

Each node in the early ARPANET consisted of a small computer called an *Interface Message Processor,* or *IMP.* As part of the network's operation, each IMP sent messages to its neighbors indicating the number of hops from that node to every other node. By monitoring the messages coming in, each IMP could quickly develop routing information about the network as a whole.

To make this idea more concrete, imagine that every IMP maintains a map showing the hop count to every node. When the network is up and running, the map in the Stanford node (**STAN**) should have the following associations:

4	3	3	4	3	2	1	0	1	2
BBN	CMU	HARV	MIT	NRL	RAND	SRI	STAN	UCLA	UTAH

The interesting question, however, is not what the map contains but rather how the network computes and maintains this information. When a node is restarted, it has no knowledge of the complete network. In fact, the only piece of data the Stanford node can figure out on its own is that its own entry is 0 hops away.

The routing algorithm then proceeds by letting each node send all the information it has to its neighbors. The Stanford IMP, for example, sends the fact that it is 0 hops away from **STAN** to SRI and UCLA. When those nodes receive this information, they each know that they can get to **STAN** in one hop by sending a message along their link to **STAN**. In general, whenever any node gets a routing array from its neighbor, all it has to do is go through each of the known entries in the incoming array and replace the corresponding entry in its own array with the incoming value plus one, unless its own entry is already smaller. In a very short time, the routing arrays throughout the entire network will have the correct information.

Write a program that uses the graph package to simulate the calculations of this routing algorithm on a network of nodes.

16. Implement the PageRank algorithm as it is described in this chapter. Each node in the web should extend **GenericNode** and maintain the information about the current rank of that page.

Chapter 18
Expression Trees

We have nothing to fear and a great deal to learn from trees.
— Marcel Proust, *Pleasures and Regrets,* 1896

Inheritance hierarchies can be combined with trees in many useful ways. For programmers, this combination is easiest to see in the strategies that compilers use to represent the structure of programs. By exploring this topic in some detail, you will learn quite a bit, not only about trees, but also about the compilation process itself. Understanding how compilers work removes some of the mystery surrounding programming and makes it easier to understand the programming process as a whole.

Unfortunately, designing a complete compiler is too complex to serve as a useful illustration. Commercial compilers require many person-years of programming, done by teams of programmers, much of which is beyond the scope of this text. Even so, it is possible for you to get a sense of how they work—and of how trees fit into the process—by adopting the following strategies to simplify the process:

- *Building an interpreter instead of a compiler.* As described in Chapter 1, a compiler translates a program into machine-language instructions that the computer can then execute directly. Although it has much in common with a compiler, an ***interpreter*** never actually translates the source code into machine language but simply performs the operations necessary to achieve the effect of the compiled program. Interpreters are generally easier to write, although they have the disadvantage that interpreted programs tend to run much more slowly than their compiled counterparts.

- *Focusing only on the problem of evaluating arithmetic expressions.* A full-scale language translator for a modern programming language must be able to process statements, method calls, type definitions, and many other language constructs. Most of the fundamental techniques used in language translation, however, are illustrated by the seemingly simple task of translating arithmetic expressions.

- *Restricting the types used in expressions to integers.* Modern programming languages allow expressions to manipulate data of many different types. In this chapter, all data values are assumed to be of type **int**, which simplifies the structure of the interpreter.

■■■ 18.1 Overview of the interpreter

The goal of this chapter is to explore the representation of arithmetic expressions by implementing a simple application that repeatedly executes the following steps:

1. Read an expression entered by the user into a tree-structured internal form.

2. Evaluate the expression tree to compute its value.

3. Print the result of the evaluation.

This iterated process is called a ***read-eval-print loop.***

At the highest level of abstraction, the structure of the read-eval-print interpreter is easy to implement and appears in Figure 18-1. In this implementation, the operation of reading an expression and converting it to its internal form has also been decomposed into three phases, as follows:

1. **Input.** The input phase consists of reading in a line of text from the user, which is implemented by calling the `nextLine` method from the `Scanner` class.

2. **Lexical analysis.** The lexical analysis phase consists of dividing the input line into individual units called *tokens,* each of which represents a single logical

---

FIGURE 18-1   **Top-level class for the expression interpreter**

```java
/*
 * File: Interpreter.java
 * ---------------------------
 * This program simulates the top level of an expression interpreter.  The
 * program reads an expression, evaluates it, and then displays the result.
 */

package edu.stanford.cs.javacs2.ch18;

import edu.stanford.cs.console.Console;
import edu.stanford.cs.console.SystemConsole;

public class Interpreter {

    public void run() {
        EvaluationContext context = new EvaluationContext();
        ExpParser parser = new ExpParser();
        Console console = new SystemConsole();
        while (true) {
            try {
                String line = console.nextLine("=> ");
                if (line.equals("quit")) break;
                parser.setInput(line);
                Expression exp = parser.parseExp();
                int value = exp.eval(context);
                console.println(value);
            } catch (RuntimeException ex) {
                console.println("Error: " + ex.getMessage());
            }
        }
    }

/* Main program */

    public static void main(String[] args) {
        new Interpreter().run();
    }

}
```

entity, such as an integer constant, an operator, or a variable name. The interpreter uses the **TokenScanner** class to accomplish this phase of the process.

3. *Parsing.* The final phase in the process of reading an expression consists of reading the tokens from the **TokenScanner** and determining whether those tokens represent a legal expression and, if so, what the structure of that expression is.

A sample run of the read-eval-print interpreter might look like this:

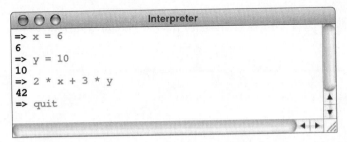

As the sample run makes clear, the interpreter allows assignment to variables and adheres to Java's precedence conventions by evaluating multiplication before addition.

The heart of the implementation is the **Expression** class, which represents an arithmetic expression. Even before you look at the code for the **Expression** class, you can make reasonable inferences about its structure from looking at the code for the interpreter. You know, first of all, that **Expression** objects are produced by the **parseExp** method in the **ExpParser** class. You can also infer from the code that the **Expression** class has a method called **eval**, even though you don't know the details of that operation. That, of course, is how it should be. As a client of the **Expression** class, you are less concerned with how expressions are implemented than you are with how to use them. As a client, you need to think of the **Expression** class as an abstract data type. The underlying details become important only when you need to understand the implementation.

Another thing you should notice from Figure 18-1 is that the **eval** method takes a parameter called **context**, which is an object of type **EvaluationContext**. The primary purpose of the **EvaluationContext** parameter is to maintain a *symbol table,* which keeps track of what value is currently assigned to each variable name. As you might expect, the code for the **EvaluationContext** class uses a map to implement these associations. That fact, however, is an implementation detail. The methods in the **EvaluationContext** class frame the operations of the symbol table in terms that make sense in the context of a programming language.

18.2 The structure of expressions

Before you can complete the implementation of the interpreter, you need to understand what expressions are and how they can be represented as objects. As is often the case when you are thinking about a programming abstraction, it helps to begin with the insights you have acquired about expressions from your experience as a Java programmer. For example, you know that the lines

```
0
2 * 11
3 * (a + b + c)
x = x + 1
```

represent legal expressions in Java. At the same time, you also know that the lines

```
2 * (x - y
17 k
```

are not expressions. The first has unbalanced parentheses, and the second is missing an operator. An important part of understanding expressions is articulating what constitutes an expression so that you can differentiate legal expressions from malformed ones.

A recursive definition of expressions

As it happens, the best way to define the structure of a legal expression is to adopt a recursive perspective. A sequence of symbols is an expression if it has one of the following forms:

1. An integer constant
2. A variable name
3. An expression enclosed in parentheses
4. A sequence of two expressions separated by an operator

The first two possibilities represent the simple cases. The last two possibilities define an expression recursively in terms of simpler expressions.

To see how you might apply this recursive definition, consider the following sequence of symbols:

```
y = 3 * (x + 1)
```

Does this sequence constitute an expression? You know from experience that the answer is yes, but you can use the recursive definition of an expression to justify that answer. The integer constants 3 and 1 are expressions according to rule #1. Similarly, the variable names **x** and **y** are expressions as specified by rule #2. Thus, you already know that the expressions marked by the symbol *exp* in the following diagram are expressions, as defined by the simple-case rules:

$$
\begin{array}{cccccccc}
exp & & exp & & exp & & exp \\
| & & | & & | & & | \\
\text{y} & = & 3 & * & (& \text{x} & + & 1 &)
\end{array}
$$

At this point, you can start to apply the recursive rules. Given that **x** and **1** are both expressions, you can tell that the string of symbols **x + 1** is an expression by applying rule #4, because it consists of two expressions separated by an operator. You can record this observation in the diagram by adding a new expression marker tied to the parts of the expression that match the rule, as shown:

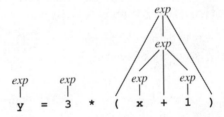

The parenthesized quantity can now be identified as an expression according to rule #3, which results in the following diagram:

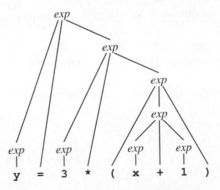

By applying rule #4 two more times to take care of the remaining operators, you can show that the entire set of characters is indeed an expression, as follows:

As you can see, this diagram forms a tree. A tree that demonstrates how the input symbols fit the syntactic rules of a programming language is called a ***parse tree.***

Ambiguity

Generating a parse tree from a sequence of symbols requires a certain amount of caution. Given the four rules for expressions outlined in the preceding section, it is possible to generate more than one parse tree for the expression

```
y = 3 * (x + 1)
```

Although the tree structure shown at the end of the last section presumably represents what the programmer intended, it is just as valid to argue that `y = 3` is an expression according to rule #4, and that the entire expression therefore consists of the expression `y = 3`, followed by a multiplication sign, followed by the expression `(x + 1)`. This argument ultimately reaches the same conclusion about whether the input line represents an expression, but generates a different parse tree. Both parse trees are shown in Figure 18-2. The parse tree on the left is the one generated in the preceding section and corresponds to what the expression presumably means. The parse tree on the right represents a legal application of the expression rules but is unlikely to reflect the programmer's intent.

The problem with the second parse tree is that it ignores the precedence rule that multiplication should be performed before assignment. The recursive definition of an expression indicates only that a sequence of two expressions separated by an operator is an expression; it says nothing about the relative precedence of the various operators and therefore admits both the intended and unintended interpretations. Because it allows multiple interpretations of the same string, the informal definition of *expression* given in the preceding section is said to be ***ambiguous.*** To resolve the ambiguity, the parsing algorithm must include some mechanism for determining the order in which operators are applied.

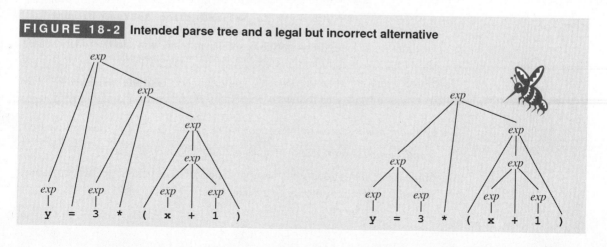

FIGURE 18-2 Intended parse tree and a legal but incorrect alternative

The question of how to resolve the ambiguity in an expression is discussed in the section on "Parsing an expression" later in this chapter. At the moment, the point of introducing parse trees is to provide some insight into how you might represent an expression as a data structure. To this end, it is important to note that the parse trees in Figure 18-2 are not ambiguous. The structure of each tree explicitly represents the structure of a valid expression. The ambiguity exists only in deciding how to generate the parse tree from the input string. Once you have the correct parse tree, its structure contains everything you need to understand the order of the operators.

Expression trees

In fact, parse trees contain more information than you need in the evaluation phase. Parentheses are useful in determining how to generate the parse tree but play no role in the evaluation of an expression once its structure is known. If your concern is simply to find the value of an expression, you do not need to include parentheses within the structure. This observation allows you to simplify a complete parse tree into an abstract structure called an ***expression tree*** that is more appropriate for the evaluation phase. In the expression tree, nodes in the parse tree that represent parenthesized subexpressions are eliminated. Moreover, it is convenient to drop the *exp* labels from the tree and instead mark each node in the tree with the appropriate operator symbol. For example, the intended interpretation of the expression

```
y = 3 * (x + 1)
```

corresponds to the following expression tree:

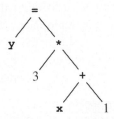

The structure of an expression tree is similar in many ways to the binary search tree from Chapter 15, but there are also some important differences. In the binary search tree, every node has the same structure. In an expression tree, there are three different types of nodes, as follows:

1. ***Constant nodes*** represent integer constants, such as 3 and 1 in the example tree.

2. ***Identifier nodes*** represent the names of variables, such as **x** and **y**.

3. ***Compound nodes*** represent the application of an operator to two operands, each of which is an arbitrary expression tree.

Each of these node types corresponds to one of the rules in the recursive formulation of an expression. The definition of the **Expression** class itself must make it possible for clients to work with expression nodes of all three types. Similarly, the underlying implementation must somehow make it possible for different expression types to coexist within the tree.

To represent such a structure, you need to define a representation for expressions that allows them to have different structures depending on their type. An integer expression, for example, must include the value of the integer as part of its internal structure. An identifier expression must include the name of the identifier. A compound expression must include the operator along with the left and right subexpressions. Defining a single abstract type that allows expressions to represent these different underlying structures requires you to implement a class hierarchy in which a general **Expression** class becomes the superclass for three subclasses, one for each of the expression types.

Creating an inheritance hierarchy is an appropriate way to represent the different types of expression trees. The top of the hierarchy is occupied by the **Expression** class, which specifies the features that are common to each of the expression types. The **Expression** class has three subclasses—**ConstantExp**, **IdentifierExp**, and **CompoundExp**—one for each expression type. The definition of the abstract **Expression** class itself appears in Figure 18-3. As is typical for a class hierarchy, several methods are defined at the level of the **Expression** class but implemented individually for each subclass.

Every **Expression** object implements the following methods:

- The **eval** method determines the value of the expression, which is always an integer in this version of the interpreter. For constant expressions, **eval** simply returns the value of the constant. For identifier expressions, **eval** determines the value by looking up the identifier name in the symbol table. For compound expressions, **eval** begins by calling itself recursively on the left and right subexpressions and then applying the appropriate operator.

- The **toString** method—which overrides the **toString** method specified by the **Object** class—converts an expression into a string that makes the structure explicit by adding parentheses around every subexpression, even if those parentheses are not required. Although the **toString** method is not used in the interpreter, it will almost certainly prove useful in debugging.

As a convenience, the **Expression** class also exports a set of getter methods that return various parts of the expression structure. Defining these methods at the **Expression** level streamlines the code by eliminating the need for type casts.

FIGURE 18-3 Implementation of the Expression class

```
/*
 * File: Expression.java
 * -----------------------
 * This file exports the Expression class, which is the root of the
 * expression hierarchy.
 */

package edu.stanford.cs.javacs2.ch18;

/**
 * This abstract class represents the highest level in the expression
 * hierarchy.  Every Expression object is an instance of one of the
 * concrete subclasses, which are ConstantExp, IdentifierExp, and
 * CompoundExp.
 */

public abstract class Expression {

/**
 * Evaluates this expression in the specified evaluation context.
 *
 * @param context The evaluation context
 * @return The result of evaluating the expression
 */

    public abstract int eval(EvaluationContext context);

/**
 * Converts the expression to a string.
 *
 * @return The string form of the expression
 */

    @Override
    public String toString() {
        throw new RuntimeException("No override for the toString method");
    }

/*
 * Implementation notes: getter methods
 * -------------------------------------
 * The remaining methods are implemented at lower levels of the expression
 * hierarchy but exported from the Expression class as a convenience.  These
 * methods throw exceptions if they are called on the wrong expression type.
 */
```

FIGURE 18-3 Implementation of the Expression class (continued)

```java
/**
 * Returns the value of a ConstantExp.
 *
 * @return The value of the constant
 */

  public int getValue() {
     throw new RuntimeException("getValue: Illegal expression type");
  }
/**
 * Returns the name of an IdentifierExp.
 *
 * @return The name of the identifier
 */

  public String getName() {
     throw new RuntimeException("getName: Illegal expression type");
  }
/**
 * Returns the operator field of a CompoundExp.
 *
 * @return The operator field of a compound
 */

  public String getOperator() {
     throw new RuntimeException("getOperator: Illegal expression type");
  }
/**
 * Returns the left hand side of a CompoundExp.
 *
 * @return The left hand side of a compound
 */

  public Expression getLHS() {
     throw new RuntimeException("getLHS: Illegal expression type");
  }
/**
 * Returns the right hand side of a CompoundExp.
 *
 * @return The right hand side of a compound
 */

  public Expression getRHS() {
     throw new RuntimeException("getRHS: Illegal expression type");
  }
}
```

All **Expression** objects are immutable, which means that any **Expression** object, once created, will never change. Although clients are free to embed existing expressions in larger ones, the interface offers no facilities for changing the components of an existing expression. Using an immutable type to represent expressions helps enforce the separation between the implementation of the **Expression** class and its clients. Because clients are prohibited from making changes in the underlying representation, they are unable to change the internal structure in a way that violates the requirements for expression trees.

Another important advantage of defining **Expression** as an immutable class is that it is possible for many different expressions to share common parts of the structure. Since no client can change any of the components of an **Expression** or any of its subclasses, there is no danger that one part of the program will make changes to one expression that end up affecting others. The exercises include several applications in which the ability to share the expression structure simplifies the code significantly.

Implementing the Expression subclasses

The abstract **Expression** class declares no instance variables. This design makes sense because no data values are common to all node types. Each specific subclass has its own unique storage requirements—an integer node needs to store an integer constant, a compound node stores references to its subexpressions, and so on. Each subclass declares the specific data members that are required for its particular expression type. Each subclass also defines its own constructor whose arguments provide the information needed to represent an expression of that type. To create a constant expression, for example, you need to specify the value of the integer. To construct a compound expression, you need to provide the operator and the left and right subexpressions.

The three expression subclasses are implemented in Figure 18-4. Each subclass definition follows a common pattern. Each subclass defines a constructor that takes the arguments specified by its interface and uses those arguments to initialize the appropriate instance variables. The implementations of the **toString** and getter methods then follow directly from the structure of that subclass.

The implementation of **eval** differs significantly for each expression type. The value of a constant expression is the value of the integer stored in that node. The value of an identifier expression comes from the symbol table in the evaluation context. The value of a compound expression requires a recursive computation. Each compound expression consists of an operator and two subexpressions. For the arithmetic operators (+, −, *, and /), **eval** uses recursion to evaluate the left and right subexpressions and then applies the appropriate operation.

FIGURE 18-4 Implementation of the Expression subclasses

```java
/*
 * File: ConstantExp.java
 * ------------------------
 * This file exports the ConstantExp subclass.
 */

package edu.stanford.cs.javacs2.ch18;

public class ConstantExp extends Expression {

/**
 * Creates a new ConstantExp with the specified value.
 *
 * @param value The value of the constant
 */

   public ConstantExp(int value) {
      this.value = value;
   }

/* Evaluates a constant expression, which simply returns its value */

   @Override
   public int eval(EvaluationContext context) {
      return value;
   }

/* Converts the expression to a string */

   @Override
   public String toString() {
      return Integer.toString(value);
   }

/* Gets the value in this node */

   @Override
   public int getValue() {
      return value;
   }

/* Private instance variables */

   private int value;

}
```

FIGURE 18-4 Implementation of the Expression subclasses (continued)

```java
/*
 * File: IdentifierExp.java
 * --------------------------
 * This file exports the IdentifierExp subclass.
 */

package edu.stanford.cs.javacs2.ch18;

public class IdentifierExp extends Expression {

/**
 * Creates a new IdentifierExp with the specified name.
 */

   public IdentifierExp(String name) {
      this.name = name;
   }

/* Evaluates the identifier by looking it up in the evaluation context */

   @Override
   public int eval(EvaluationContext context) {
      if (!context.isDefined(name)) {
         throw new RuntimeException(name + " is undefined");
      }
      return context.getValue(name);
   }

/* Converts the expression to a string */

   @Override
   public String toString() {
      return name;
   }

   @Override
   public String getName() {
      return name;
   }

/* Private instance variables */

   private String name;

}
```

FIGURE 18-4 Implementation of the `Expression` subclasses (continued)

```java
/*
 * File: CompoundExp.java
 * -----------------------
 * This file exports the CompoundExp subclass, which is used to represent
 * expressions consisting of an operator joining two operands.
 */

package edu.stanford.cs.javacs2.ch18;

public class CompoundExp extends Expression {

/**
 * Creates a new CompoundExp from an operator and the expressions for the
 * left and right operands.
 *
 * @param op The operator
 * @param lhs The expression to the left of the operator
 * @param rhs The expression to the right of the operator
 */

   public CompoundExp(String op, Expression lhs, Expression rhs) {
      this.op = op;
      this.lhs = lhs;
      this.rhs = rhs;
   }

/* Evaluates a compound expression recursively */

   @Override
   public int eval(EvaluationContext context) {
      int right = rhs.eval(context);
      if (op.equals("=")) {
         context.setValue(lhs.getName(), right);
         return right;
      }
      int left = lhs.eval(context);
      if (op.equals("+")) return left + right;
      if (op.equals("-")) return left - right;
      if (op.equals("*")) return left * right;
      if (op.equals("/")) return left / right;
      throw new RuntimeException("Illegal operator");
   }

/* Converts the expression to a string */

   @Override
   public String toString() {
      return '(' + lhs.toString() + ' ' + op + ' ' + rhs.toString() + ')';
   }
```

FIGURE 18-4 **Implementation of the Expression subclasses (continued)**

```
/* Gets the operator field */

   @Override
   public String getOperator() {
      return op;
   }

/* Gets the left subexpression */

   @Override
   public Expression getLHS() {
      return lhs;
   }

/* Gets the right subexpression */

   @Override
   public Expression getRHS() {
      return rhs;
   }

/* Private instance variables */

   private String op;
   private Expression lhs;
   private Expression rhs;

}
```

The assignment operator (=), however, represents a special case. The left-hand side of an assignment expression is an identifier, which is *not* evaluated. Instead, `eval` updates the symbol table by assigning the value of the right-hand side to the identifier that appears to the left of the assignment operator. To make sure that the interpreter has access to the variables defined during execution, `eval` takes an `EvaluationContext` parameter, which is passed down through all recursive calls. The `EvaluationContext` class is implemented as a simple wrapper on the `HashMap` class, as shown in Figure 18-5.

Diagramming expressions

A useful way to reinforce your understanding of how `Expression` objects are stored is to diagram how the concrete structure is represented inside the computer's memory. The representation of an `Expression` object depends on its specific subclass. You can diagram the structure of an expression tree by considering the three classes independently. The diagrams in this section include the subclass name to make it easier to tell the types apart even though the expression type is not explicitly stored in the instance variables of the class.

FIGURE 18-5 The EvaluationContext class

```
/*
 * File: EvaluationContext.java
 * --------------------------------
 * This file exports the EvaluationContext class, which maintains the
 * information necessary to support expression evaluation.
 */

package edu.stanford.cs.javacs2.ch18;

import edu.stanford.cs.javacs2.ch14.HashMap;

public class EvaluationContext {

/* Creates a new evaluation context with no variable bindings */

   public EvaluationContext() {
      symbolTable = new HashMap<String,Integer>();
   }

/* Sets the value of the variable var */

   public void setValue(String var, int value) {
      symbolTable.put(var, value);
   }

/* Gets the value of the variable var */

   public int getValue(String var) {
      return symbolTable.get(var);
   }

/* Returns true if the variable var is defined */

   public boolean isDefined(String var) {
      return symbolTable.containsKey(var);
   }

/* Private instance variables */

   private HashMap<String,Integer> symbolTable;

}
```

A `ConstantExp` object simply stores an integer value, shown here as it would exist for the integer 3:

ConstantExp
3

An **IdentifierExp** stores a variable name, illustrated here for the variable **x**:

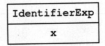

A **CompoundExp** stores the operator along with the left and right subexpressions:

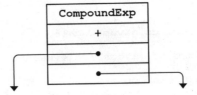

Because compound nodes contain subexpressions that can themselves be compound nodes, expression trees can grow to an arbitrary level of complexity. Figure 18-6 illustrates the internal data structure for the expression

y = 3 * (x + 1)

which includes three operators and therefore requires three compound nodes.

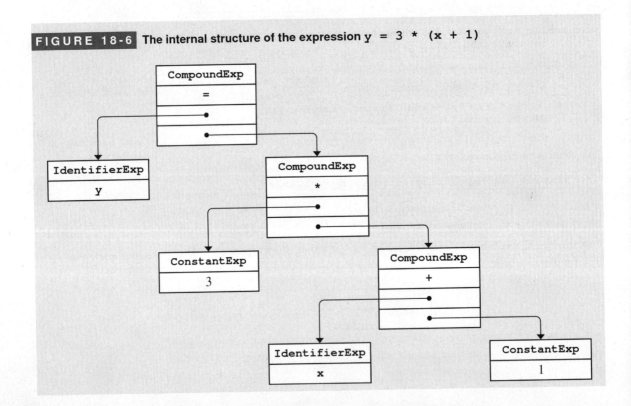

FIGURE 18-6 The internal structure of the expression y = 3 * (x + 1)

Tracing the evaluation process

It's worth going through at least one example of what happens when you call **eval**. If you call **eval** on the expression

```
y = 3 * (x + 1)
```

with an **EvaluationContext** in which the variable **x** is bound to 13, the first call to **eval** uses the code from **CompoundExp** and creates the following frame:

```
public int eval(EvaluationContext context) {
☞   int right = rhs.eval(context);
    if (op.equals("=")) {
        context.setValue(lhs.getName(), right);
        return right;
    }
    int left = lhs.eval(context);
    if (op.equals("+")) return left + right;
    if (op.equals("-")) return left - right;
    if (op.equals("*")) return left * right;
    if (op.equals("/")) return left / right;
    throw new RuntimeException("Illegal operator");
}
```

left	right	context
		<x=13>

From here, the code makes a recursive call to **eval** on the right subexpression, which is again a **CompoundExp**. This call adds a new stack frame, as follows:

```
public int eval(EvaluationContext context) {
  public int eval(EvaluationContext context) {
  ☞   int right = rhs.eval(context);
      if (op.equals("=")) {
          context.setValue(lhs.getName(), right);
          return right;
      }
      int left = lhs.eval(context);
      if (op.equals("+")) return left + right;
      if (op.equals("-")) return left - right;
      if (op.equals("*")) return left * right;
      if (op.equals("/")) return left / right;
      throw new RuntimeException("Illegal operator");
  }
```

left	right	context
		<x=13>

The expression is simpler, but this situation is very much the same as in the earlier call. The right subexpression is again a **CompoundExp**, so this call produces yet another stack frame, like this:

```
public int eval(EvaluationContext context) {
  public int eval(EvaluationContext context) {
    public int eval(EvaluationContext context) {
☞     int right = rhs.eval(context);
      if (op.equals("=")) {
        context.setValue(lhs.getName(), right);
        return right;
      }
      int left = lhs.eval(context);
      if (op.equals("+")) return left + right;
      if (op.equals("-")) return left - right;
      if (op.equals("*")) return left * right;                    this
      if (op.equals("/")) return left / right;
      throw new RuntimeException("Illegal operator");
    }
                          left    right    context
                                           <x=13>
```

At this point, the code still calls for the evaluation of the right subexpression, but that expression is now a **ConstantExp**. The call is therefore routed to the **eval** method in the **ConstantExp** class, which simply returns the value. Given that this situation represents a simple case of the recursion, it should be easy enough to skip over the details and simply assign the value 1 to the local variable **right** in this stack frame, giving rise to the following stack configuration:

```
public int eval(EvaluationContext context) {
  public int eval(EvaluationContext context) {
    public int eval(EvaluationContext context) {
      int right = rhs.eval(context);
      if (op.equals("=")) {
        context.setValue(lhs.getName(), right);
        return right;
      }
☞     int left = lhs.eval(context);
      if (op.equals("+")) return left + right;
      if (op.equals("-")) return left - right;
      if (op.equals("*")) return left * right;                    this
      if (op.equals("/")) return left / right;
      throw new RuntimeException("Illegal operator");
    }
                          left    right    context
                                  1        <x=13>
```

The next step is to evaluate the left subexpression, which is again a simple case. This time the call goes to the **eval** method in **IdentifierExp**, which returns the value of the variable **x**, as it appears in the evaluation context. Copying that value into **left** leads to the following state:

```
public int eval(EvaluationContext context) {
   public int eval(EvaluationContext context) {
      public int eval(EvaluationContext context) {
         int right = rhs.eval(context);
         if (op.equals("=")) {
            context.setValue(lhs.getName(), right);
            return right;
         }
         int left = lhs.eval(context);
☞       if (op.equals("+")) return left + right;
         if (op.equals("-")) return left - right;
         if (op.equals("*")) return left * right;
         if (op.equals("/")) return left / right;
         throw new RuntimeException("Illegal operator");
      }
```

	left	right	context
	13	1	<x=13>

this

From here, the code for the evaluator uses the operator in the current expression to determine what operation to apply. Here, the operator in the current node is **+**, so the code returns the value of **left + right**, which is 14. Returning from this stack frame restores the previous one, which was waiting to assign the return value to the variable **right**, as follows:

```
public int eval(EvaluationContext context) {
   public int eval(EvaluationContext context) {
      int right = rhs.eval(context);
      if (op.equals("=")) {
         context.setValue(lhs.getName(), right);
         return right;
      }
☞    int left = lhs.eval(context);
      if (op.equals("+")) return left + right;
      if (op.equals("-")) return left - right;
      if (op.equals("*")) return left * right;
      if (op.equals("/")) return left / right;
      throw new RuntimeException("Illegal operator");
   }
```

	left	right	context
		14	<x=13>

this

From here, the code evaluates the left subexpression, which is the constant 3, and then applies the operator ***** to the values 3 and 14, which returns 42 to the previous level:

```
public int eval(EvaluationContext context) {
    int right = rhs.eval(context);
    if (op.equals("=")) {
        context.setValue(lhs.getName(), right);
        return right;
    }
    int left = lhs.eval(context);
    if (op.equals("+")) return left + right;
    if (op.equals("-")) return left - right;
    if (op.equals("*")) return left * right;
    if (op.equals("/")) return left / right;
    throw new RuntimeException("Illegal operator");
}
```

	left	right	context
		42	<x=13>

This time, the operator is indeed an equal sign, which signifies assignment. Instead of evaluating the left subexpression, the code simply assigns the value of **right** to the name, thereby adding a binding of **y** to 42 in the evaluation context. The **eval** method then returns the assigned value to complete the process.

18.3 Parsing an expression

The problem of building the appropriate parse tree from a stream of tokens is not an easy one. To a large extent, the underlying theory necessary to build an efficient parser lies beyond the scope of this text. Even so, it is possible to make some headway on the problem and write a parser that works for the limited case of arithmetic expressions.

Parsing and grammars

In the field of computer science, parsing is one of the areas in which it is easiest to see the profound impact of theory on practice. In the early days of programming languages, programmers implemented the parsing phase of a compiler without thinking very hard about the nature of the process. As a result, early parsing programs were difficult to write and even harder to debug. In the 1960s, however, computer scientists studied parsing from a more theoretical perspective, which has dramatically reduced the complexity of designing and implementing new programming languages. Today, a computer scientist who has taken a course on compilers can write a parser for a programming language with very little work. In fact, most parsers can be generated automatically from a simple specification of the language for which they are intended.

The essential theoretical insight necessary to simplify parsing is actually borrowed from linguistics. Like human languages, programming languages have rules of syntax that define the grammatical structure of the language. Moreover, because programming languages are much more regular in structure than human languages, it is usually easy to describe the syntactic structure of a programming language in a precise form called a *grammar.* In the context of a programming language, a grammar consists of a set of rules that show how a particular language construct can be derived from simpler ones.

If you start with the English rules for formulating expressions, it is not hard to write a grammar for the simple expressions used in this chapter. Partly because it simplifies things a little, it helps to incorporate into the parser the notion of a *term* as any single unit that can appear as an operand to a larger expression. For example, constants and variables are clearly terms. Moreover, an expression in parentheses acts as a single unit and can therefore also be regarded as a term. Thus, a term always has one of the following forms:

- An integer constant

- A variable

- An expression in parentheses

An expression is then either of the following:

- A term

- Two expressions separated by an operator

This informal definition can be translated directly into the following grammar, presented in what programmers call *BNF,* which stands for Backus–Naur Form, named after its inventors John Backus and Peter Naur:

$$E \;\rightarrow\; T \qquad\qquad T \;\rightarrow\; \textit{integer}$$
$$E \;\rightarrow\; E \; \textit{op} \; E \qquad\qquad T \;\rightarrow\; \textit{identifier}$$
$$T \;\rightarrow\; (\; E \;)$$

In the grammar, uppercase letters like E and T are called *nonterminal symbols* and stand for an abstract linguistic class, such as an expression or a term. The specific punctuation marks and the italicized words represent the *terminal symbols,* which are those that appear in the token stream. Explicit terminal symbols, such as the parentheses in the last rule, must appear in the input exactly as written. The italicized words represent placeholders for tokens that fit their general description. Thus, the notation *integer* stands for any string of digits returned by the scanner as a token. Each terminal corresponds to exactly one token in the scanner stream. Nonterminals typically correspond to a sequence of tokens.

Taking precedence into account

Like the informal rules for defining expressions presented in the section on "A recursive definition of expressions" earlier in the chapter, grammars can be used to generate parse trees. Just like those rules, this grammar is ambiguous as written and can generate several different parse trees for the same sequence of tokens. Once again, the problem is that the grammar does not take into account how tightly each operator binds to its operands. Generating the correct parse tree from an ambiguous grammar therefore requires the parser to have access to the precedence information.

The easiest way to specify precedence is to assign each operator a numeric value that indicates its precedence, with higher precedence values corresponding to operators that bind more tightly to their operands. The precedence values can easily be saved in a **Map<String, Integer>** in which the keys are the operator names and the values are the precedence numbers.

Recursive-descent parsers

Most parsers today are created automatically from a grammar for the language through the use of programs called *parser generators.* For simple grammars, however, it is not difficult to implement a parser by hand. The general strategy is to write a method that is responsible for reading each of the nonterminal symbols in the grammar. The expression grammar uses the nonterminals E and T, which suggests that the parser needs the methods **readE** and **readT**. Each of these methods takes read tokens from the scanner. By checking those tokens against the rules of the grammar, it is usually possible—at least for simple grammars—to determine which rule to apply, particularly if the **readE** method has access to the current precedence level.

The implementation of the parser module appears in Figure 18-7. As you can easily see from the code, the **readE** and **readT** methods are mutually recursive. When the **readE** method needs to read a term, it does so by calling **readT**. Similarly, when **readT** needs to read an expression enclosed in parentheses, it calls **readE** to accomplish that task. Parsers that use mutually recursive methods in this fashion are called *recursive-descent parsers.*

As the mutual recursion proceeds, the **readE** and **readT** methods build up the expression tree by calling the constructors for the appropriate expression class. For example, if **readT** discovers an integer token, it can allocate a **ConstantExp** node that contains that value. This expression tree is then returned up the chain of recursive calls through the return value of these methods.

FIGURE 18-7 Implementation of the expression parser

```java
/*
 * File: ExpParser.java
 * ----------------------
 * This file exports a simple recursive-descent parser for expressions.
 */

package edu.stanford.cs.javacs2.ch18;

import edu.stanford.cs.javacs2.ch14.HashMap;
import edu.stanford.cs.javacs2.ch14.Map;
import edu.stanford.cs.tokenscanner.TokenScanner;

public class ExpParser {

/**
 * Creates a new expression parser.
 */

   public ExpParser() {
      scanner = createTokenScanner();
      precedenceTable = createPrecedenceTable();
   }

/**
 * Sets the input for the parser to be the specified string.
 *
 * @param str The input string for parsing.
 */

   public void setInput(String str) {
      scanner.setInput(str);
   }

/**
 * Parses the next expression from the scanner.
 *
 * @return The parsed representation of the input
 */

   public Expression parseExp() {
      Expression exp = readE(0);
      if (scanner.hasMoreTokens()) {
         String token = scanner.nextToken();
         throw new RuntimeException("Unexpected token \"" + token + "\"");
      }
      return exp;
   }
```

FIGURE 18-7 Implementation of the expression parser (continued)

```java
/**
 * Reads an expression starting at the specified precedence level.
 *
 * @param prec The current precedence level
 * @return The parsed expression
 */

   public Expression readE(int prec) {
      Expression exp = readT();
      String token;
      while (true) {
         token = scanner.nextToken();
         int tprec = precedence(token);
         if (tprec <= prec) break;
         Expression rhs = readE(tprec);
         exp = new CompoundExp(token, exp, rhs);
      }
      scanner.saveToken(token);
      return exp;
   }

/*
 * Scans a term, which is either an integer, an identifier, or a
 * parenthesized subexpression.
 *
 * @return The parsed term
 */

   public Expression readT() {
      String token = scanner.nextToken();
      if (token.isEmpty()) throw new RuntimeException("Illegal expression");
      if (Character.isLetter(token.charAt(0))) {
         return new IdentifierExp(token);
      }
      if (Character.isDigit(token.charAt(0))) {
         return new ConstantExp(Integer.parseInt(token));
      }
      if (!token.equals("(")) {
         throw new RuntimeException("Unexpected token \"" + token + "\"");
      }
      Expression exp = readE(0);
      token = scanner.nextToken();
      if (!token.equals(")")) {
         throw new RuntimeException("Unbalanced parentheses");
      }
      return exp;
   }
```

FIGURE 18-7 Implementation of the expression parser (continued)

```java
/**
 * Returns the precedence of the operator.  If the operator is not defined,
 * its precedence is 0.
 *
 * @param token The operator token
 * @return The numeric precedence value or 0 if token is not an operator
 */

   public int precedence(String token) {
      Integer prec = precedenceTable.get(token);
      return (prec == null) ? 0 : prec;
   }

/*
 * Creates the TokenScanner for this parser.  Subclasses can override
 * this method to change the characteristics of the scanner.
 */

   public TokenScanner createTokenScanner() {
      TokenScanner scanner = new TokenScanner();
      scanner.ignoreWhitespace();
      return scanner;
   }

/*
 * Creates the precedence table for this parser.  Subclasses can override
 * this method to add new operators to the parser.
 */

   public Map<String,Integer> createPrecedenceTable() {
      Map<String,Integer> map = new HashMap<String,Integer>();
      map.put("=", 1);
      map.put("+", 2);
      map.put("-", 2);
      map.put("*", 3);
      map.put("/", 3);
      return map;
   }

/* Private instance variables */

   private TokenScanner scanner;
   private Map<String,Integer> precedenceTable;

}
```

The only complex part of the parser implementation is the code for **readE**, which needs to take precedence into account. As long as the precedence of the operators it encounters is greater than the current precedence provided by its caller, **readE** can create a compound expression node from the subexpressions to the left and right of the operator, after which it can loop back to check the next operator. When **readE** encounters the end of the input or an operator whose precedence is less than or equal to the current precedence, it returns to the next higher level in the chain of **readE** calls, where the prevailing precedence is lower. Before doing so, **readE** must put the as-yet-unprocessed operator token back into the scanner input stream so that it can be read again at the appropriate level. This task is accomplished by calling the **saveToken** method in the **TokenScanner** class.

In my experience, it is nearly impossible to understand the code for **readE** without walking through at least one example. The rest of this section traces what happens if you call **readE(0)** when the scanner contains the string

```
odd = 2 * n + 1
```

In this expression, the multiplication is performed first, followed by the addition, and then finally by the assignment. The interesting question is how the parser determines this ordering and assembles the appropriate expression tree.

The process of parsing this expression is too complicated to trace one line at a time. A more practical approach is to show the execution history at a few interesting points along the way. In the initial call to **readE**, the code reads the first term and the token that follows it, which is the assignment operator. The = operator has a precedence value of 1, which is greater than the prevailing precedence of 0. The code therefore reaches the following point in the first **readE** call:

```
Expression readE (int prec) {
    Expression exp = readT();
    String token;
    while (true) {
        token = scanner.nextToken();
        int tprec = precedence(token);
        if (tprec <= prec) break;
☞      Expression rhs = readE(tprec);
        exp = new CompoundExp(token, exp, rhs);
    }
    scanner.saveToken(token);
    return exp;
}
```

scanner	prec	tprec	token	exp	rhs
odd = 2 * n + 1	0	1	"="	odd	

From here, the parser needs to read the right operand of the assignment operator, which requires a recursive call to **readE**. This call proceeds similarly, but with a new precedence value of 1. Execution of the call soon reaches the following state:

```
Expression readE (int prec) {
  Expression readE (int prec) {
    Expression exp = readT();
    String token;
    while (true) {
      token = scanner.nextToken();
      int tprec = precedence(token);
      if (tprec <= prec) break;
☞    Expression rhs = readE(tprec);
      exp = new CompoundExp(token, exp, rhs);
    }
    scanner.saveToken(token);                    exp      rhs
    return exp;
  }                                             ┌────┐  ┌────┐
                                                │ 2  │  │    │
  scanner          prec   tprec   token         └────┘  └────┘
  ┌──────────────┐ ┌────┐ ┌────┐ ┌────┐
  │ odd = 2 * n̂ + 1│ │ 1  │ │ 3  │ │"*"│
  └──────────────┘ └────┘ └────┘ └────┘
}
```

This level of the process is concerned only with reading the subexpression starting with the token **2**. The stack frame underneath the current one keeps track of what the parser was doing prior to making the recursive call.

At this point, the parser makes yet another recursive call to **readE**, passing in the precedence of the * operator, which has the value 3. On this call, however, the precedence of the + operator that comes next in the token stream is less than the current precedence, which causes the loop to exit at the following point:

```
Expression readE (int prec) {
  Expression readE (int prec) {
    Expression readE (int prec) {
      Expression exp = readT();
      String token;
      while (true) {
        token = scanner.nextToken();
        int tprec = precedence(token);
        if (tprec <= prec) break;
        Expression rhs = readE(tprec);
        exp = new CompoundExp(token, exp, rhs);
      }
☞    scanner.saveToken(token);                   exp      rhs
      return exp;
    }                                            ┌────┐  ┌────┐
                                                 │ n  │  │    │
    scanner          prec   tprec   token        └────┘  └────┘
    ┌──────────────┐ ┌────┐ ┌────┐ ┌────┐
    │ odd = 2 * n +̂ 1│ │ 3  │ │ 2  │ │"+"│
    └──────────────┘ └────┘ └────┘ └────┘
  }
```

The parser saves the **+** operator in the token stream and returns the identifier expression **n** to the point at which the most recent call occurred. The result of the **readE** call is assigned to the variable **rhs**, as follows:

```
Expression readE(int prec) {
  Expression readE(int prec) {
    Expression exp = readT();
    String token;
    while (true) {
        token = scanner.nextToken();
        int tprec = precedence(token);
        if (tprec <= prec) break;
        Expression rhs = readE(tprec);
     ☞ exp = new CompoundExp(token, exp, rhs);
    }
    scanner.saveToken(token);
    return exp;
  }
}
```

scanner	prec	tprec	token	exp	rhs
odd = 2 * n ^+ 1	1	3	"*"	2	n

From here, the parser creates a new compound expression by combining **exp** and **rhs**. That value is not yet returned as the value from this level but is instead assigned to the variable **exp**. The parser then makes another pass through the **while** loop in which it reads the **+** token a second time. On this cycle, the precedence of **+** is greater than the precedence set by the assignment operator. The execution therefore reaches the following state:

```
Expression readE(int prec) {
  Expression readE(int prec) {
    Expression exp = readT();
    String token;
    while (true) {
        token = scanner.nextToken();
        int tprec = precedence(token);
        if (tprec <= prec) break;
     ☞ Expression rhs = readE(tprec);
        exp = new CompoundExp(token, exp, rhs);
    }
    scanner.saveToken(token);
    return exp;
  }
}
```

scanner	prec	tprec	token	exp	rhs
odd = 2 * n +^1	1	2	"+"	2 * n	

Although you can go through the steps in detail if you need to, you should be able to apply the recursive leap of faith by now. The scanner contains a single token, which is the integer 1. Given that you've already watched the parser read the integer 2, you should be able to skip ahead to the next line in the execution:

```
Expression readE(int prec) {
  Expression readE(int prec) {
    Expression exp = readT();
    String token;
    while (true) {
      token = scanner.nextToken();
      int tprec = precedence(token);
      if (tprec <= prec) break;
      Expression rhs = readE(tprec);
☞    exp = new CompoundExp(token, exp, rhs);
    }
    scanner.saveToken(token);
    return exp;
  }
```

scanner	prec	tprec	token
odd = 2 * n + 1	1	3	"+"

exp: 2 * n   rhs: 1

The parser again assembles the values of **exp** and **rhs** into a new compound expression and cycles back for another iteration of the **while** loop.

On the next iteration, **token** is the empty string marking the end of the token stream. The empty string is not a legal operator, so the **precedence** method returns the value 0, which is less than the prevailing precedence at this level. The parser therefore exits from the **while** loop, which leads to the following configuration:

```
Expression readE(int prec) {
  Expression readE(int prec) {
    Expression exp = readT();
    String token;
    while (true) {
      token = scanner.nextToken();
      int tprec = precedence(token);
      if (tprec <= prec) break;
      Expression rhs = readE(tprec);
      exp = new CompoundExp(token, exp, rhs);
    }
    scanner.saveToken(token);
☞  return exp;
  }
```

scanner	prec	tprec	token
odd = 2 * n + 1	1	0	""

exp: (2 * n) + 1   rhs:

When control returns to the first **readE** call, all the necessary information is now in place, as follows:

```
Expression readE(int prec) {
    Expression exp = readT();
    String token;
    while (true) {
        token = scanner.nextToken();
        int tprec = precedence(token);
        if (tprec <= prec) break;
        Expression rhs = readE(tprec);
        exp = new CompoundExp(token, exp, rhs);
    }
    scanner.saveToken(token);
    return exp;
}
```

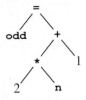

scanner	prec	tprec	token	exp	rhs
odd = 2 * n + 1	0	1	"="	odd	

All **readE** has to do is create the new compound and—after reading the empty token one more time—return the final version of the expression tree to **parseExp**:

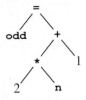

▮▮ Summary

In this chapter, you have learned how to represent expressions in Java and, in the process, gotten a brief glimpse of how compiler writers can use inheritance hierarchies to represent arithmetic expressions.

Important points in this chapter include:

- Expressions in a programming language have a recursive structure. There are simple expressions, which consist of constants and variable names. More complex expressions combine simpler subexpressions into larger units, forming a hierarchical structure that can be represented as a tree.

- Inheritance makes it easy to define a class hierarchy to represent the nodes of an expression tree.

- The process of reading an expression from the user can be divided into the phases of *input, lexical analysis,* and *parsing.* The input phase is the simplest and consists of reading a string from the user. Lexical analysis involves breaking a string into component tokens in a fashion similar to that used in the **TokenScanner** class from Chapter 7. Parsing consists of translating the collection of tokens returned from the lexical analysis phase into its internal representation, following a set of syntactic rules called a *grammar*.

- For many grammars, it is possible to solve the parsing problem using a strategy called *recursive descent*. In a recursive-descent parser, the rules of the grammar are encoded as a set of mutually recursive methods.

- Once parsed, expression trees can be manipulated recursively in much the same way as the trees in Chapter 16. In the context of the interpreter, one of the most important operations is evaluating an expression tree, which consists of walking the tree recursively to determine its value.

Review questions

1. What is the difference between an *interpreter* and a *compiler?*

2. What is a *read-eval-print loop?*

3. What are the three phases involved in reading an expression?

4. Identify which of the following lines constitutes an expression according to the definition used in this chapter:

   a.   `(((0)))`

   b.   `2x + 3y`

   c.   `x - (y * (x / y))`

   d.   `-y`

   e.   `x = (y = 2 * x - 3 * y)`

   f.   `10 - 9 + 8 / 7 * 6 - 5 + 4 * 3 / 2 - 1`

5. For each of the legal expressions in the preceding question, draw a parse tree that reflects the standard precedence assumptions of mathematics.

6. Of the legal expressions in question 4, which ones are ambiguous with respect to the simple recursive definition of expressions?

7. What are the differences between parse trees and expression trees?

8. What are the three types of expressions that can occur in an expression tree?

9. What are the public methods of the **Expression** class?

10. Using Figure 18-6 as a model, draw a complete structure diagram for the following expression:

       `y = (x + 1) / (x - 2)`

11. Why are grammars useful in translating programming languages?

12. What do the letters in *BNF* stand for?

13. In a grammar, what is the difference between a *terminal symbol* and a *nonterminal symbol?*

14. What is a *recursive-descent parser?*

15. What is the significance of the argument to **readE** in the implementation of the parser?

16. If you look at the definition of **readT** in Figure 18-7, you will see that the method body does not contain any calls to **readT**. Is **readT** a recursive method?

17. In the implementation of the **CompoundExp** subclass, why is the = operator handled differently from the arithmetic operators?

Exercises

1. Make the necessary changes to the interpreter introduced in section 18.3 so that expressions can include the remainder operator %, which has the same precedence as * and /.

2. In the expression interpreter introduced in section 18.3, every operator is a binary operator in the sense that it takes two operands, one on each side. Most programming languages also allow unary operators that take a single operand. Make the changes to the interpreter necessary to support the unary – operator.

3. Make the changes you would need to have the interpreter work with values of type **double** and **String** in addition to type **int**. When an operator is applied to values of different types, your interpreter should interpret those operators as Java does. Thus, the + operator should signify concatenation if either or both operands are strings.

   To implement this change, you will need to write new versions of most of the files in this package, changing the type name **int** into a new **ExpValue** class that has a subclass for each of the supported value types.

4. Add the relational operators (==, !=, <, <=, >, >=) and Boolean types to the interpreter you created for exercise 3.

5. Using the **Expression** hierarchy as it appears in Figure 18-4, write a method

```
void listVariables(Expression exp)
```

that prints the variable names in that expression. The variables should appear in alphabetical order with one variable name per line. For example, if you enter the expression

```
3 * x * x - 4 * x - 2 * a + y
```

calling **listVariables** should produce the following output:

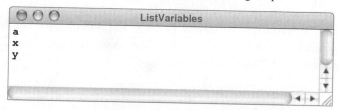

6. In mathematics, there are several common procedures that require you to replace all instances of a variable in a formula with some other variable. Without changing any of the expression classes, write a method

```
Expression changeVariable(Expression exp,
                          String oldName,
                          String newName)
```

that returns a new expression which is the same as **exp** except that every occurrence of the identifier **oldName** is replaced with **newName**. For example, if **exp** is the expression

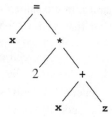

calling

```
Expression newExp = changeVariable(exp, "x", "y");
```

will assign the following expression tree to **newExp**:

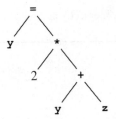

7. Write a program that reads expressions from the user in their standard mathematical form and then displays those same expressions using reverse Polish notation, in which the operators follow the operands to which they apply. (Reverse Polish notation, or RPN, was introduced in the discussion of the calculator application in Chapter 6.) Your program should be able to duplicate the following sample run:

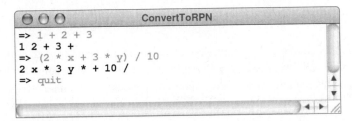

8. Write a method

   ```
   boolean expMatch(Expression e1, Expression e2);
   ```

   that returns **true** if **e1** and **e2** are matching expressions, which means that they have exactly the same structure, the same operators, the same constants, and the same identifier names, in the same order. If there are any differences at any level of the expression tree, your method should return **false**.

9. After it parses an expression, a commercial compiler typically looks for ways to simplify that expression so that it can be computed more efficiently. This process is part of a more general technique called *optimization*, in which the compiler seeks to make the code it generates as efficient as possible. One common technique used in the optimization process is *constant folding*, which consists of identifying subexpressions that are composed entirely of constants and replacing them with their value. For example, if a compiler encounters the expression

   ```
   days = 24 * 60 * 60 * sec
   ```

   there is no point in generating code to perform the first two multiplications when the program is executed. The value of the subexpression **24 * 60 * 60** is constant and might as well be replaced by its value (86400) before the compiler actually starts to generate code.

Write a method `foldConstants(exp)` that takes an expression and returns a new expression in which all subexpressions composed entirely of constants are replaced by the computed value.

10. The process of turning the internal representation of an expression back into its text form is generally called ***unparsing*** the expression. Extend the `ExpParser` class so that is exports a method `unparse(exp)` that returns a string form of the expression `exp` in its standard mathematical form. Unlike the `toString` method in the `Expression` class, parentheses should appear in the string only if they are required by the precedence rules. Thus, the expression

```
y = 3 * (x + 1)
```

should be unparsed as

```
y = 3 * (x + 1)
```

and not as the fully parenthesized form returned by `toString`, which is

```
(y = (3 * (x + 1)))
```

11. Although the interpreter program that appears in this chapter is considerably easier to implement than a complete compiler, it is possible to get a sense of how a compiler works by defining one for a simplified computer system called a ***stack machine.*** A stack machine performs operations on an internal stack, which is maintained by the hardware, in much the same fashion as the Reverse Polish calculator from Chapter 6. For the hypothetical stack machine used in this problem, the available instructions appear in Figure 18-8.

FIGURE 18-8 **Instructions implemented by the stack machine**

LOAD #*n*	Pushes the constant *n* on the stack.
LOAD *var*	Pushes the value of the variable *var* on the stack.
STORE *var*	Stores the top stack value in *var* without actually popping it.
DISPLAY	Pops the stack and displays the result.
ADD SUB MUL DIV	These instructions pop the top two values from the stack and apply the indicated operation, pushing the final result back on the stack. The top value is the right operand; the next one down is the left.

Write a method

```
void compile(BufferedReader rd, PrintWriter wr)
```

that reads expressions from **rd** and writes to **wr** a sequence of instructions for the stack machine that have the same effect as entering those lines in the interpreter. For example, if the file opened as **rd** contains

```
x = 7
y = 5
2 * x + 3 * y
```

calling **compile(rd, wr)** should write a file containing the following code:

```
LOAD #7
STORE x
DISPLAY
LOAD #5
STORE y
DISPLAY
LOAD #2
LOAD x
MUL
LOAD #3
LOAD y
MUL
ADD
DISPLAY
```

12. Using tree structures to represent expressions makes it possible to perform sophisticated mathematical operations. For example, it is not hard to write a method that differentiates an expression by applying the standard rules from calculus. The most common rules for differentiating an arithmetic expression are shown in Figure 18-9.

FIGURE 18-9 Standard formulas for differentiation

$x' = 1$

$c' = 0$

$(u + v)' = u' + v'$

$(u - v)' = u' - v'$

$(uv)' = uv' + vu'$

$(u / v)' = \dfrac{uv' - vu'}{v^2}$

where:

x is the variable used as the basis for the differentiation

c is a constant or variable that does not depend on x

u and v are arbitrary expressions

Write a recursive method `differentiate(exp, var)` that uses the rules in Figure 18-9 to find the derivative of `exp` with respect to the variable `var`. The result of `differentiate` is an `Expression` that you can use in any context. You could, for example, evaluate that expression or pass it to `differentiate` to calculate the second derivative.

13. Extend the expression interpreter so that it supports sets of integers as a separate value type. When they are used with sets as arguments, the operators `+`, `*`, and `-` should compute the union, intersection, and set difference, respectively. Sets are specified in the traditional way, which means that you need to extend the grammar used by the parser to support braces that enclose a comma-separated list of expressions. A sample run of the program might look like this:

```
                        SetInterpreter
=> odds = {9, 7, 5, 3, 1}
{1, 3, 5, 7, 9}
=> evens = {0, 2, 2 * 2, 3 * 2, 2 * 2 * 2}
{0, 2, 4, 6, 8}
=> primes = {2, 3, 5, 7}
{2, 3, 5, 7}
=> odds + evens
{0, 1, 2, 3, 4, 5, 6, 7, 8, 9}
=> odds * evens
{}
=> primes - evens
{3, 5, 7}
```

Note that expressions involving integers are still legal and can be used in any expression context, including the values used to specify the elements of a set.

14.
> *[Paul] Allen rushed to the dorm to find Bill Gates. They had to do a BASIC for this machine. They had to. If they didn't, the revolution would start without them.*
>
> —Stephen Manes and Paul Andrews, *Gates*, 1994

Expand the power of the interpreter by turning it into a simple programming language along the lines of the BASIC language developed in the mid-1960s by John Kemeny and Thomas Kurtz. In BASIC, programs consist of lines beginning with a number that determines the order of execution. Each line contains a statement chosen from those in Figure 18-10. The line numbers determine the order in which the statements are executed but also provide a simple framework for editing the program. If you need to add a line between two existing ones, you can give it a line number that falls between the existing ones. You can replace a line simply by reentering a new version.

FIGURE 18-10 Simple statements in the BASIC language

LET *var* = *exp*	Assigns the value of *exp* to the variable *var*.
INPUT *var*	Requests an input value from the user and assigns it to *var*.
PRINT *exp*	Prints the value of *exp* on the console.
GOTO *line*	Jumps to the specified line number and continues execution from there.
IF *e₁ op e₂* **THEN** *line*	Transfers control to the specified line number if the specified test is true. The operator may be any of the standard relational operators.
END	Marks the end of the program.

Entering the **RUN** command in place of a statement runs the program, starting with the lowest numbered line and continuing until the program reaches the **END** statement marking the end of the program. As an example, the following session prints the powers of 2 less than 500:

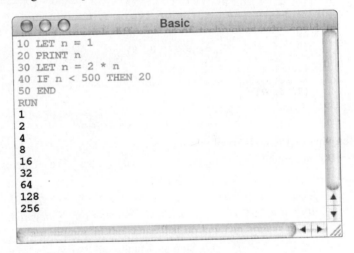

```
                            Basic
10 LET n = 1
20 PRINT n
30 LET n = 2 * n
40 IF n < 500 THEN 20
50 END
RUN
1
2
4
8
16
32
64
128
256
```

Chapter 19
Using Functions as Data

To live is to function.
— Oliver Wendell Holmes, Jr., radio address, 1931

In the programming you have done up to this point, the concepts of functions and data structures have remained relatively separate. Functions provide the means for representing an algorithm; data structures allow you to organize the information to which those algorithms are applied. Functions, which object-oriented languages generally call *methods,* have been part of the algorithmic structure, not part of the data structure. Being able to use functions as data values, however, often makes it much easier to design effective interfaces, because this facility allows clients to specify operations as well as data.

Throughout its history, Java has been evolving to make it easier to think of functions as data objects. From the very beginning, Java has made it possible to use objects to implement some of the techniques that make programming with functional data so powerful. Objects, after all, encapsulate data and behavior, which means that you can use an object to specify a particular behavior simply by defining the appropriate method. However, that strategy is not as flexible as programmers would like, particularly if those programmers are familiar with the *functional programming paradigm,* a style of programming that emphasizes the application of functions to data and avoids the use of assignment and other operations that change the program's state. Over time, Java has become more compatible with this style of programming, particularly with the release of Java 8 in early 2014. Java 8 introduces a new feature called a *lambda expression,* which is an abstraction that supports functional programming using a model derived from the *lambda calculus,* a mathematical model for computation developed by Alonzo Church in 1936. This chapter explores several different strategies—up to and including lambda expressions—that make it possible to use functional programming in Java.

19.1 Interactive programs

To some extent, many of the programs in this book can be classified as interactive, in the sense that they require input from the user. At the same time, reading input using the `Scanner` class offers a rather different model of interactivity than what most users expect from modern applications. In the programs you have seen so far, the user has the opportunity to provide input to the program only at certain well-defined points in its execution history, most commonly when the program calls a method like `nextInt` and then waits for a response. This style of interaction is called *synchronous,* because user input is synchronized with the program operation. Modern user interfaces, by contrast, are *asynchronous,* in that they allow the user to intercede at any point, typically by employing the mouse or the keyboard to trigger a particular action. Actions that occur asynchronously with respect to the program's operation, such as clicking the mouse or typing on the keyboard, are generically referred to as *events.* Interactive programs that operate by responding to these events are said to be *event-driven.*

The Java event model

Before it makes sense to look at any event-driven programs, it is important for you to understand the underlying conceptual model. In Java, every event is associated with an object that provides information about the nature of the event. Although Java supports many kinds of events, this chapter focuses on the **MouseEvent** class, which can serve as a model for other event types that work in a similar way. Each **MouseEvent** object represents an action taken with the mouse, such as moving or dragging it from one position to another or clicking the mouse button. Because different event objects contain different information, the methods that apply to each event class depend on the particular requirements of that type. A **MouseEvent**, for example, exports the methods **getX** and **getY** to determine the mouse position.

In the Java event model, event objects do not themselves perform any actions. What happens instead is that events are delivered to some other object that is charged with responding to that particular type of event. Such objects are called *listeners.* As you might expect, there are different kinds of listeners that correspond to different types of events. Java defines two listener types that respond to mouse events: **MouseListener** and **MouseMotionListener**. The first event is generated for relatively infrequent events like pushing a mouse button. The second occurs much more often and is generated every time the mouse moves. If you don't need to track mouse motion, it is more efficient to define only a **MouseListener**.

Unlike events, the various listener types are not implemented as classes in Java. Instead, each listener type is defined as an interface that specifies a set of methods. Any class that supplies definitions for those methods can declare that it implements that interface by including the name of the interface in an **implements** clause as part of the class header. The methods required for both the **MouseListener** and the **MouseMotionListener** interfaces appear in Figure 19-1.

FIGURE 19-1 Methods specified by MouseListener and MouseMotionListener

MouseListener interface

`mouseClicked(e)`	Generated when the mouse is clicked on a single location.
`mouseEntered(e)`	Generated when the mouse enters the component.
`mouseExited(e)`	Generated when the mouse leaves the component.
`mousePressed(e)`	Generated when the mouse button is pressed.
`mouseReleased(e)`	Generated when the mouse button is released.

MouseMotionListener interface

`mouseMoved(e)`	Generated when the mouse moves with the button up.
`mouseDragged(e)`	Generated when the mouse moves with the button down.

All the event classes and listener interfaces that are part of Java's Abstract Windowing Toolkit are defined in the **java.awt.event** packages   For convenience, that package also defines a class called **MouseAdapter**, which provides empty implementations for all the methods in both the **MouseListener** and **MouseMotionListener** interfaces. Classes that extend **MouseAdapter** can therefore override particular methods in the listener models and rely on the default behavior to ignore any other events.

Applications don't receive events unless they ask for them by adding a listener to the graphics component in which they occur. For programs that use the graphics package described in Chapter 8, the component that needs to receive the events is the **GCanvas** that is stored inside the **GWindow** frame. Thus, if the variable **gw** contains a reference to the graphics window, you can listen for mouse events in that canvas by calling

> **gw.getCanvas().addMouseListener(***listener***);**

where *listener* is any object that implements the **MouseListener** interface.

Simple event-driven applications

The principles described in the preceding section are illustrated by the **DrawDots** application in Figure 19-2 on the next page. This program begins by creating an empty **GWindow** and then having its associated **GCanvas** listen for mouse events. Most mouse events occuring in the window are ignored because they are defined as empty methods in the **MouseAdapter** class that **DrawDots** extends. If, however, the user clicks the mouse button, that click generates a call to the **mouseClicked** method, which is overridden in this class with the following definition:

```
public void mouseClicked(MouseEvent e) {
    double r = DOT_RADIUS;
    GOval dot = new GOval(e.getX() - r, e.getY() - r,
                            2 * r, 2 * r);
    dot.setFilled(true);
    gw.add(dot);
}
```

This method creates a circular **GOval** whose center is at the coordinates of the mouse click and whose radius is specified by the value of the constant **DOT_RADIUS**. The call to **setFilled** marks the **GOval** as filled, and the final statement adds the **GOval** to the graphics window. Adding the **GOval** triggers a repaint request for the window, which then draws the **GOval** at the desired position. The process of adding dots to the window is repeatable. Clicking the mouse again creates a new **GOval** and adds it to the window, where it joins its predecessor in the list of objects to be displayed.

FIGURE 19-2 Code for the DrawDots program

```
/*
 * File: DrawDots.java
 * ---------------------
 * This program draws a dot everywhere the user clicks the mouse.
 */

package edu.stanford.cs.javacs2.ch19;

import edu.stanford.cs.javacs2.ch8.GOval;
import edu.stanford.cs.javacs2.ch8.GWindow;
import java.awt.event.MouseAdapter;
import java.awt.event.MouseEvent;

public class DrawDots extends MouseAdapter {

    public void run() {
        gw = new GWindow(WIDTH, HEIGHT);
        gw.getGCanvas().addMouseListener(this);
    }

/* Called on a mouse click to create a new dot */

    @Override
    public void mouseClicked(MouseEvent e) {
        double r = DOT_RADIUS;
        GOval dot = new GOval(e.getX() - r, e.getY() - r, 2 * r, 2 * r);
        dot.setFilled(true);
        gw.add(dot);
    }

/* Constants */

    private static final double WIDTH = 500;
    private static final double HEIGHT = 300;
    private static final double DOT_RADIUS = 4;

/* Private instance variables */

    private GWindow gw;

/* Main program */

    public static void main(String[] args) {
        new DrawDots().run();
    }

}
```

The **DrawDots** application responds only to the **mouseClicked** event and ignores everything else. Figure 19-3 shows a slightly more sophisticated example that tracks mouse motion so that the user can draw lines on the graphics window. Pressing the mouse button down creates a new **GLine**. Dragging the mouse to another location changes the endpoint of the line as the mouse moves.

FIGURE 19-3   Code for the DrawLines program

```
/*
 * File: DrawLines.java
 * ----------------------
 * This program allows users to draw lines on the graphics window by
 * clicking and dragging with the mouse.
 */

package edu.stanford.cs.javacs2.ch19;

import edu.stanford.cs.javacs2.ch8.GCanvas;
import edu.stanford.cs.javacs2.ch8.GLine;
import edu.stanford.cs.javacs2.ch8.GWindow;
import java.awt.event.MouseAdapter;
import java.awt.event.MouseEvent;

public class DrawLines extends MouseAdapter {

    public void run() {
        gw = new GWindow(WIDTH, HEIGHT);
        GCanvas gc = gw.getGCanvas();
        gc.addMouseListener(this);
        gc.addMouseMotionListener(this);
    }

/* Called on mouse press to create a new line */

    @Override
    public void mousePressed(MouseEvent e) {
        line = new GLine(e.getX(), e.getY(), e.getX(), e.getY());
        gw.add(line);
    }

/* Called on mouse drag to reset the endpoint */

    @Override
    public void mouseDragged(MouseEvent e) {
        line.setEndPoint(e.getX(), e.getY());
    }

/* Constants */

    private static final int WIDTH = 500;
    private static final int HEIGHT = 300;

/* Private instance variables */

    private GWindow gw;
    private GLine line;

/* Main program */

    public static void main(String[] args) {
        new DrawLines().run();
    }

}
```

By adopting this strategy, the **DrawLines** program operates—at least for straight lines—the way commercial figure-drawing applications do. To create a line on the canvas, you press the mouse at its starting point. From there, you hold the mouse button down and drag the mouse to the other endpoint. As you do so, the line keeps itself updated on the canvas so that it connects the starting point with the current position of the mouse.

As an example, suppose that you press the mouse button somewhere on the screen and then drag the mouse rightward an inch, holding the button down. What you'd like to see is the following picture:

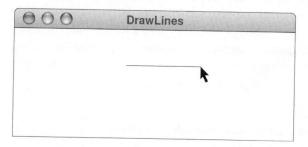

If you then move the mouse downward without releasing the button, the displayed line will track the mouse, so that you might see the following picture:

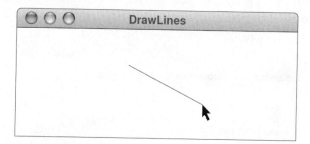

When you release the mouse, the line stays where it is. If you then press the mouse button again on that same point, you can go ahead and draw an additional line segment by dragging the mouse to the endpoint of the new line, as follows:

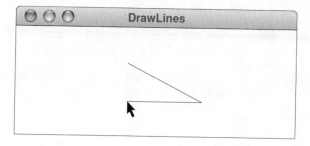

Alternatively, you could move the mouse to an entirely new location and draw a disconnected line in some other part of the canvas.

While you are dragging the line with the mouse, the line that joins the initial point and the current mouse position will stretch, contract, and change direction. Because the effect is what you would expect if you joined the initial point and the mouse cursor with a stretchy elastic line, this technique is called *rubber-banding.*

Anonymous inner classes

One of the first features that the Java designers added to streamline the process of specifying a functional response was *anonymous inner classes,* which are the same as other inner classes except that they lack a name and are instantiated only at one point in the program. Like other inner classes, anonymous inner classes have access to the variables visible in the environment in which the class is declared. The usual syntax for creating an object of an inner class looks like this:

new *class* **() {**
>   *definitions that override behavior in the class*
}

The instance generated by **new** is not that of the specified class but instead of an anonymous subclass in which the new definitions override those in the original. This technique is illustrated in Figure 19-4, which reimplements the **DrawDots** application using an anonymous inner class as the listener.

FIGURE 19-4 **Code for DrawDots using an anonymous inner class**

```
/*
 * This version of the run method uses an anonymous inner class to
 * specify the response to the mouseClicked event.
 */

    public void run() {
        gw = new GWindow(WIDTH, HEIGHT);
        gw.getGCanvas().addMouseListener(
            new MouseAdapter() {
                public void mouseClicked(MouseEvent e) {
                    double r = DOT_RADIUS;
                    GOval dot = new GOval(e.getX() - r, e.getY() - r,
                                          2 * r, 2 * r);
                    dot.setFilled(true);
                    gw.add(dot);
                }
            }
        );
    }
```

19.2 Command dispatch tables

Testing is essential to software development. Along with the unit tests described in Chapter 7, it is often useful to create interactive tests that let you, as the developer, play around with the package and test individual methods. Interactive test programs are particularly valuable during debugging because they allow you to execute a sequence of commands and check whether everything works correctly.

The code supplied with this book includes interactive test programs for many of the utility classes that illustrate this technique. In most cases, these test programs implement a console-based interactive test in which the user types in commands, usually with the same names as the methods exported by the class being tested. The test program then executes those commands and displays the result. As an example, the programs for Chapter 13 include a **StackTest** application that tests the standard implementation of the **Stack** class. That program might produce the following sample run, which tests each of the exported operations:

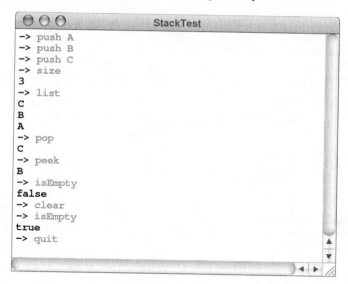

The goal of the sections that follow is to explore several possible strategies for implementing test programs of this sort. The details of the stack operations are not the focus here. The central question is how to move from a command name like **"push"**, **"size"**, or **"list"** to the code that implements that operation. This process is called *command dispatch.*

Command dispatch using cascading `if` statements

The simplest strategy for implementing a command dispatch is to use a series of `if-else` statements that explicitly compares the name entered by the user with the name of each possible command. That strategy is implemented in Figure 19-5.

FIGURE 19-5 Code for the interactive `StackTest` program using `if` statements

```
/*
 * File: StackTestUsingIfStatements.java
 * ----------------------------------------
 * This program implements an interactive test for the Stack abstraction.
 */

package edu.stanford.cs.javacs2.ch19;

import edu.stanford.cs.console.Console;
import edu.stanford.cs.console.SystemConsole;
import edu.stanford.cs.javacs2.ch13.Stack;
import edu.stanford.cs.javacs2.ch7.TokenScanner;

public class StackTestUsingIfStatements {

    public void run() {
        Console console = new SystemConsole();
        stack = new Stack<String>();
        scanner = new TokenScanner();
        scanner.ignoreWhitespace();
        while (true) {
            String line = console.nextLine("-> ");
            scanner.setInput(line);
            if (scanner.hasMoreTokens()) dispatch(scanner.nextToken());
        }
    }

/* Calls the appropriate method based on the command name */

    private void dispatch(String name) {
        if (name.equals("push")) {
            pushCommand();
        } else if (name.equals("pop")) {
            popCommand();
        } else if (name.equals("clear")) {
            clearCommand();
        } else if (name.equals("peek")) {
            peekCommand();
        } else if (name.equals("size")) {
            sizeCommand();
        } else if (name.equals("isEmpty")) {
            isEmptyCommand();
        } else if (name.equals("list")) {
            listCommand();
        } else if (name.equals("quit")) {
            quitCommand();
        } else {
            System.out.println("Unknown command: " + name);
        }
    }
```

FIGURE 19-5 Code for the interactive `StackTest` program using `if` statements (continued)

```
/* Command methods for each of the test commands */

    private void pushCommand() {
        stack.push(scanner.nextToken());
    }

    private void popCommand() {
        System.out.println(stack.pop());
    }

    private void clearCommand() {
        stack.clear();
    }

    private void peekCommand() {
        System.out.println(stack.peek());
    }

    private void sizeCommand() {
        System.out.println(stack.size());
    }

    private void isEmptyCommand() {
        System.out.println(stack.isEmpty());
    }

    private void listCommand() {
        Stack<String> save = new Stack<String>();
        while (!stack.isEmpty()) {
            System.out.println(stack.peek());
            save.push(stack.pop());
        }
        while (!save.isEmpty()) {
            stack.push(save.pop());
        }
    }

    private void quitCommand() {
        System.exit(0);
    }

/* Private instance variables */

    private Stack<String> stack;
    private TokenScanner scanner;

/* Main program */

    public static void main(String[] args) {
        new StackTestUsingIfStatements().run();
    }

}
```

The **run** method in Figure 19-5 creates a **TokenScanner** and uses it to scan the first token on the input line, which is the command name. It then calls **dispatch**, which goes through a long series of **if** tests looking for a command with that name. If it finds one, **dispatch** calls the associated method. If not, **dispatch** prints a message indicating that the command is undefined. Although this strategy gets the job done, it is by no means elegant. The code for the **dispatch** method will grow larger and larger as more commands are added to the test suite, making the program much harder to read.

Command dispatch using a command table

For all intents and purposes, the **dispatch** method introduced in Figure 19-5 is implementing a map operation. The key is the command name. The value is the command that should be executed if the user enters that command. Many languages define references to methods so that they behave just like any other data value, which means that you can store a reference to the implementing method directly in the map. Unfortunately, Java is not one of those languages.

The traditional strategy for solving this problem in Java is to declare an interface that defines the operations any command must support. For instance, in the command-dispatch example, you have to be able to execute a command. That fact suggests that an appropriate interface description would look like this:

```
interface Command {
    public void execute();
}
```

Any object which includes an **execute** method that takes no arguments and returns no result can be marked as a **Command**. You could then define implementing classes for each of the possible commands. For example, you could define the command that lists the contents of the stack using an explicit inner class as follows:

```
class ListCommand implements Command {
    public void execute() {
        listCommand();
    }
}
```

Defining **ListCommand** as an inner class within the **StackTest** application means that it has access to the private methods and variables declared in that scope.

If you declared a **HashMap<String,Command>** called **commands**, you could then associate the string **"list"** with the **ListCommand** action by calling

```
commands.put("list", new ListCommand());
```

Alternatively, you could avoid having to define a new class for each command by using anonymous inner classes as shown in the code Figure 19-6. In either case, the code for **dispatch** would look like this:

```
private void dispatch(String name) {
   Command cmd = commands.get(name);
   if (cmd == null) {
      System.out.println("Unknown command: " + name);
   } else {
      cmd.execute();
   }
}
```

FIGURE 19-6 Code to initialize a command table using anonymous inner classes

```
private void initCommandTable() {
   commands = new HashMap<String,Command>();
   commands.put("push",
                new Command() {
                   public void execute() { pushCommand(); }
                });
   commands.put("pop",
                new Command() {
                   public void execute() { popCommand(); }
                });
   commands.put("peek",
                new Command() {
                   public void execute() { peekCommand(); }
                });
   commands.put("size",
                new Command() {
                   public void execute() { sizeCommand(); }
                });
   commands.put("isEmpty",
                new Command() {
                   public void execute() { isEmptyCommand(); }
                });
   commands.put("clear",
                new Command() {
                   public void execute() { clearCommand(); }
                });
   commands.put("list",
                new Command() {
                   public void execute() { listCommand(); }
                });
   commands.put("quit",
                new Command() {
                   public void execute() { quitCommand(); }
                });
}
```

Implementing command dispatch using lambdas

Aesthetically, however, the code to initialize the command table in Figure 19-6 leaves a lot to be desired. Each of the calls to **put** is spread across four lines that are a nightmare to indent in any readable way. If writing functional code in Java introduces this much complexity, the functional programming paradigm is unlikely to win many adherents.

Fortunately, Java 8 introduces a new language feature called a *lambda expression* that makes this code much easier to read. Lambda expressions are defined in the following section, but you can get a feel for their importance by looking at how they simplify the command dispatch problem. Instead of the jumbled mass of code in Figure 19-6, Java 8 allows you to rewrite the **initCommandTable** method in the much simpler form shown in Figure 19-7. Nothing else in the program changes. The next section introduces the tools you need to achieve this substantial reduction in the size of the code.

▦ 19.3 Lambda expressions

A lambda expression is a concise representation of a function that shows how a list of arguments is transformed into a result. The name comes from the Greek letter λ, which Alonzo Church used as the function-producing operator in his lambda calculus. My Stanford colleague, the late John McCarthy, incorporated the lambda calculus into the programming language Lisp in 1960. Because of its generality, the lambda calculus adds considerable expressive programming power, and it has since been incorporated into many other languages.

Syntax of lambda expressions in Java

In Java, lambda expressions have the form

> (*argument list*) -> *result*

FIGURE 19-7 Code to initialize a command table using lambda expressions

```
private void initCommandTable() {
    commands = new HashMap<String,Command>();
    commands.put("push", () -> pushCommand());
    commands.put("pop", () -> popCommand());
    commands.put("peek", () -> peekCommand());
    commands.put("size", () -> sizeCommand());
    commands.put("isEmpty", () -> isEmptyCommand());
    commands.put("clear", () -> clearCommand());
    commands.put("list", () -> listCommand());
    commands.put("quit", () -> quitCommand());
}
```

where *argument list* is a list of parameter declarations similar to that in a method declaration and *result* is an expression indicating the result. Lambda expressions support several simplifications that promote ease of use, including the following:

- It is usually possible to omit the parameter types from the argument list, since Java is able to infer those types from the context. For example, if you want to specify a lambda expression for computing the length of the hypotenuse of a triangle with edges **z** and **y**, you can either use the fully specified expression

  ```
  (double x, double y) -> Math.sqrt(x * x + y * y)
  ```

  or simplify this expression to

  ```
  (x, y) -> Math.sqrt(x * x + y * y)
  ```

- If there is only one parameter, you can omit the parentheses around the argument list. Thus, a lambda expression that squares its argument can be written as

  ```
  x -> x * x
  ```

- If you need to include more code, the *result* specification can be a block of statements enclosed in curly braces. You can, however, omit the braces if the body is a call to a method whose result type is **void**. For example, the lambda expressions in Figure 19-6 all look something like this:

  ```
  () -> pushCommand()
  ```

  This syntax specifies a lambda expression that takes no arguments and whose result consists of calling the **pushCommand** method, even though that method does not return a result.

Functional interfaces

In Java, lambda expressions are closely linked to the idea of a ***functional interface,*** which is any interface that specifies precisely one method. The **Command** interface in the code for the command dispatch application is a functional interface because its definition specifies only the **execute** method. Similarly, the interface

```
interface DoubleFunction {
    public double apply(double x);
}
```

specifies a functional interface whose **apply** method takes a **double** and returns a **double**. In this way, the **DoubleFunction** interface represents the type space of all functions that map one floating-point number into another. Most of the static methods in the **Math** class—**Math.sqrt**, **Math.sin**, **Math.cos**, and so forth—have this form.

Some functional interfaces are so common that Java 8 introduced a new package called **java.util.function** that exports them. Although this package defines dozens of such interfaces, this chapter will stick to the five listed in Figure 19-8, all of which take type parameters. The interface **Function<T,U>** encompasses all functions that take one parameter. For example, the **DoubleFunction** interface shown on the preceding page is compatible with **Function<Double,Double>** or **UnaryOperator<Double>**. The examples in this chapter work with lambda expressions that are traditionally characterized as functions and therefore use **Function<Double,Double>** to refer to this function type. By contrast, several of the exercises ask you to work with operators, in which case the names that include **Operator** seem more appropriate.

If you have a modern version of Java, you can assign a lambda expression to a compatible functional interface, either in an explicit assignment statement or as an argument to a method. For example, the statement

```
commands.put("push", () -> pushCommand());
```

passes the lambda expression **() -> pushCommand()** to the **put** method for a map declared as a **HashMap<String,Command>**. Since the compiler knows that the second argument to **put** should be a **Command**, it checks to see whether the argument is compatible with that type. Given that the single method that defines **Command** as a functional interface takes no arguments and returns no result, Java is happy to accept the lambda expression **() -> pushCommand()**, which also takes no arguments and returns no result.

A simple application of lambda functions

Lambda functions are useful in a wide variety of applications, particularly after you become familiar with the idea. As a simple example, suppose that you want to design a method that allows you to list all the English words that fit a certain form, but that allows greater generality than the programs in Chapter 6 which list the two- and seven-letter English words. Imagine, for example, that you have filled in

---

FIGURE 19-8   Selected interfaces in the **java.util.function** package

Function<T,U>	Classes including an **apply** method that maps **T** to **U**.
Predicate<T>	Classes including a **test** method that maps **T** to **boolean**.
Consumer<T>	Classes including an **accept** procedure that takes a **T**.
UnaryOperator<T>	Classes including an **apply** method that maps **T** to **T**.
BinaryOperator<T>	Classes including an **apply** method that maps two **T** values to a **T**.

most of a crossword puzzle and are looking for a ten-letter word that starts with
"th" and ends with "y". If the word is stored in the variable s, the test you need to
apply is

```
s.length() == 10 && s.startsWith("th") && s.endsWith("y")
```

Although you could include this test as part of the method that looks through the
English lexicon, it would be better if the client could pass any such test in the form
of a method that takes a string and returns a Boolean value indicating whether that
string passes the selection test. Such methods are compatible with the functional
interface **Predicate<String>** in **java.util.function**. You can therefore
implement the following method, which takes a lexicon and a lambda expression:

```
private void listMatchingWords(Lexicon lexicon,
                                    Predicate<String> fn) {
    for (String word : lexicon) {
        if (fn.test(word)) System.out.println(word);
    }
}
```

Once you have implemented this function, calling

```
listMatchingWords(new Lexicon("EnglishWords.txt"),
                s -> s.length() == 10 &&
                s.startsWith("th") &&
                s.endsWith("y"));
```

produces the following output:

19.4 Plotting a function

Of the many contexts in which passing a functional value makes sense, one of the
most natural is an application that plots a client-specified function in the graphics
window. Suppose, for example, that you want to write a **PlotFunction** program
that plots the value of some function $f(x)$ for values of x in a specified range, where
f is some function supplied by the client. For example, if f is the trigonometric
sine function, you would like your program to produce a sample run like this:

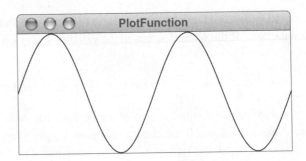

The graphical output shows only the shape of the graph and does not indicate any units along the *x*- and *y*-axes. In this diagram, the values of *x* vary from -2π to 2π, and the values of *y* extend from −1 to 1. The **plot** function needs to include these ranges as parameters, which means that the call looks something like this:

```
plot(gw, x -> Math.sin(x), -2 * Math.PI, 2 * Math.PI,
                           -1, 1);
```

The first parameter is the graphics window. The second parameter is the lambda expression corresponding to the function you want to plot. In this example, the function is the trigonometric function **sin** from the **Math** class.

If **plot** is designed in a general way, however, it should be possible to plot a different function by changing the second argument. For example, the call

```
plot(gw, x -> Math.sqrt(x), 0, 4, 0, 2);
```

should plot the **Math.sqrt** function on a graph that extends from 0 to 4 along the *x*-axis and from 0 to 2 along the *y*-axis, as follows:

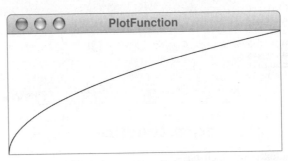

In order for a call to **plot** to make sense, the second argument must implement the functional interface **Function<Double,Double>**. The header line for **plot** therefore looks like this:

```
void plot(GWindow gw, Function<Double,Double> fn,
          double xMin, double xMax,
          double yMin, double yMax)
```

FIGURE 19-9 **Implementation of the `plot` function**

```
/**
 * Plots the specified function on the graphics window.
 *
 * @param gw The graphics window
 * @param fn A lambda expression that implements Function<Double,Double>
 * @param minX The minimum x value at the left edge of the window
 * @param maxX The maximum x value at the right edge of the window
 * @param minY The minimum x value at the bottom of the window
 * @param maxY The maximum x value at the top of the window
 */
    private void plot(GWindow gw, Function<Double,Double> fn,
                      double minX, double maxX,
                      double minY, double maxY) {
        double dx = (maxX - minX) / WIDTH;
        double sx0 = 0;
        double sy0 = HEIGHT - (fn.apply(minX) - minY) / (maxY - minY) * HEIGHT;
        for (int i = 1; i < WIDTH; i++) {
            double x = minX + i * dx;
            double y = fn.apply(x);
            double sx1 = (x - minX) / (maxX - minX) * WIDTH;
            double sy1 = HEIGHT - (y - minY) / (maxY - minY) * HEIGHT;
            gw.add(new GLine(sx0, sy0, sx1, sy1));
            sx0 = sx1;
            sy0 = sy1;
        }
    }
```

The implementation of **plot** appears in Figure 19-9. The code for **plot** cycles through each pixel coordinate across the graphics window, transforming each *x* coordinate into the corresponding position in the interval between **minX** and **maxX**. For example, the point halfway across the window corresponds to the value halfway between **minX** and **maxX**. The program then applies the functional value **fn** to compute the value of *y,* as follows:

```
        double y = fn.apply(x);
```

The final step consists of converting the *y* value to the appropriate vertical position on the screen by scaling this value with respect to **minY** and **maxY**. This operation is essentially the inverse of the transformation to derive the value of *x.* The only difference is that the *y*-axis on the screen is inverted from the traditional Cartesian coordinate plane, which makes it necessary to subtract the computed value from the height of the graphics window.

The **plot** method creates the graphical output by drawing a series of line segments using the **GLine** class. The method begins by computing the coordinates of the point at the left edge of the window, storing the result in the variables **sx0** and **sy0**. From there it computes the coordinates of the curve one pixel farther to the right, storing these coordinates in the variables **sx1** and **sy1**. The graphics library call then connects these points with a call to

```
gw.drawLine(sx0, sy0, sx1, sy1);
```

Each additional cycle of the loop connects the current point to its predecessor. This process has the effect of approximating the graph of the function by connecting a sequence of line segments, each of which extends one pixel in the *x* direction.

Although the **plot** function in Figure 19-9 is probably too primitive to be used in a practical application, it offers an example of how treating functions as data values can be useful in an application.

◼ 19.5 Mapping functions

No matter whether they are implemented as traditional objects or as lambda expressions, functional interfaces provide another strategy for iterating over the elements of a collection. Classes that support this behavior typically export a method called **map** that applies a function to each element of the collection. For example, if **list** were an instance of a collection class that supported the **map** operation, you could print every element of **list** on the console by calling

```
list.map(x -> System.out.println(x));
```

Methods like **map** that allow you to call a function on every element in a collection are called *mapping functions.*

A **map** method of the sort described in the preceding section is easy to add to the existing collection classes by extension. For example, the **MappableList<T>** class in Figure 19-10 extends **ArrayList<T>** by adding three methods that implement mapping functions. The **map** method takes a **Consumer<T>** and applies the consumer method to every element in the list. For example, given the mapping functions defined in Figure 19-10, you could, for example, print every element in a **MappableList<String>** called **names** like this:

```
names.map(s -> System.out.println(s));
```

The **mapList** method takes a **Function<T,T>** and returns a **MappableList<T>** created by applying the client-specified function to every element in the original list. Thus, if **digits** is a **MappableList<Integer>** containing the integers from 0 to 9, calling

```
System.out.println(digits.mapList(n -> n * n));
```

prints a list containing the values 0, 1, 4, 9, 16, 25, 36, 49, 64, and 81.

FIGURE 19-10   Extended list class that supports mapping functions

```java
/*
 * File: MappableList.java
 * -------------------------
 * This file exports a list that supports mapping operations.
 */

package edu.stanford.cs.javacs2.ch19;

import java.util.ArrayList;

/**
 * This class extends the ArrayList class by adding mapping functions.
 */

public class MappableList<T> extends ArrayList<T> {

/**
 * Applies the function fn to every element in the list.
 *
 * @param fn A lambda expression matching Consumer<T>
 */

   public void map(Consumer<T> fn) {
      for (T value : this) {
         fn.accept(value);
      }
   }

/**
 * Creates a new MappableList<T> by applying fn to every element of this one.
 *
 * @param fn A lambda expression matching Function<T,T>
 */

   public MappableList<T> mapList(Function<T,T> fn) {
      MappableList<T> list = new MappableList<T>();
      for (T value : this) {
         list.add(fn.apply(value));
      }
      return list;
   }

/**
 * Applies reduce to the result of applying map to each element.
 *
 * @param map A lambda expression matching Function<T,T>
 * @param reduce A lambda expression matching Consumer<T>
 */

   public void mapReduce(Function<T,T> map, Consumer<T> reduce) {
      for (T value : this) {
         reduce.accept(map.apply(value));
      }
   }

}
```

The final method in the **MappableList** class is

```
void mapReduce(Function<T,T> map, Consumer<T> reduce)
```

which takes the values produced by the **map** operation and applies the **reduce** operation to those results. For example, you could compute the sum of the squares of the integers in **digits** using the following code, where **sum** is an instance variable in the defining class:

```
sum = 0;
digits.mapReduce(d -> d * d, n -> { sum += n; });
```

The effect of these statements is identical to that of the following iterative code:

```
sum = 0;
for (int d : digits) {
   sum += d * d;
}
```

The primary difference between **mapReduce** and its iterative counterpart is that **mapReduce** hides the details of the underlying computational process. As long as the **mapReduce** method makes no guarantees about the order in which the map operation is applied to the elements in the list, the implementation of **mapReduce** is free to avoid iteration and adopt a different approach.

The **mapReduce** method in the **MappableList** class represents an extremely simple implementation of the *MapReduce* programming model, which is a framework originally developed by Google to process massive amounts of data. As in the **mapReduce** method, the MapReduce model operates in two phases. There is a *map* operation that is applied to every element in a collection—which could potentially involve millions or even billions of data items—and a *reduce* operation that performs some summary computation on the results of applying the map. To make that computation feasible, real implementations of the MapReduce model divide the work into individual pieces that can be performed simultaneously on many different machines.

The MapReduce model is much easier to describe in functional programming terms than in the more traditional imperative style. Even if the techniques needed to distribute computation across many servers are beyond the scope of this book, thinking about how functional interfaces enable you to implement a simple version of the model will help you understand the basics of computing with big data.

Summary

This chapter has explored several methods for treating functions and methods as data objects in Java. Important concepts in this chapter include:

- Events in Java are represented as objects whose components specify the precise nature of the event. A **MouseEvent**, for example, responds to **getX** and **getY**.

- Applications respond to events by declaring *listeners* that implement an interface containing methods associated with a particular event type. For mouse events, Java uses two different listener interfaces. The **MouseListener** interface specifies conditions that happen relatively infrequently, such as pressing the mouse button. By contrast, the **MouseMotionListener** interface responds to moving or dragging the mouse, which generates new events as the mouse moves.

- Java supports several strategies for implementing a command dispatch, including testing explicitly for each command with cascading **if** statements and using a map to associate each name with an object that implements that command.

- Java 8 introduces the concept of *lambda expressions,* which have the syntax

  (argument list) -> *result*

  signifying a function that maps the arguments into a particular result. Lambda expressions make it possible to specify behavior in a much more streamlined form than that traditionally supported by Java.

- A *functional interface* is an interface that specifies exactly one method. Lambda expressions may be passed or assigned to any variable whose declaration marks it as matching a compatible functional interface.

- The **java.util.function** package declares several functional interfaces, including the five used in this chapter: **Function<T,U>**, **Predicate<T>**, **Consumer<T>**, **UnaryOperator<T>**, and **BinaryOperator<T>**.

- A *mapping function* applies a client-specified callback function to every element of a collection. Mapping functions can therefore be used in many of the same contexts as iterators or the range-based **for** loop.

- Lambda expressions—and the functional programming paradigm that supports them—have widespread application in programming. In particular, this paradigm makes it much easier to define coding models that work for "big data," including the MapReduce model originally developed at Google.

 ## Review questions

1. Define the terms *event* and *event-driven.*

2. What is an *event listener?*

3. In what package are the graphical event and listener classes defined?

4. What two interfaces does the Java event model use for responding to mouse events? What is the reason for defining two interfaces instead of one?

5. What is the purpose of the **MouseAdapter** class?

6. What is meant by the term *rubber-banding?*

7. What is an *anonymous inner class?*

8. What are the types of the keys and values in the map used to implement the command-dispatch process?

9. What roles did the mathematician Alonzo Church and the computer scientist John McCarthy play in the development of the lambda-expression model?

10. What is the syntactic pattern for a lambda expression in Java?

11. What simplifications does Java support for particular types of lambda expressions?

12. Write a lambda expression that returns the average of two values, *x* and *y*.

13. How many methods does a functional interface specify?

14. What five interfaces from the **java.util.function** package are used in this chapter?

15. What functional interface from **java.util.function** best matches the lambda expression:

        (int n) -> n % 2 == 0

16. How would you code **Consumer<T>** as a complete Java interface?

17. What lambda expression would you pass to **listMatchingWords** to list all words that begin and end with the same letter?

18. Describe the role of each of the six arguments to the **plot** function as defined in this chapter?

19. What is a *mapping function?*

20. Describe the two phases in the MapReduce computational model.

Exercises

1. Modify the **DrawDots** program so that clicking the mouse draws a small **X** every time you click the mouse. The **X**, which consists of two **GLine** objects, should be positioned so that the intersection appears at the point at which the mouse was clicked.

2. Use the **GOval**, **GLine**, and **GRect** classes to create a cartoon drawing of a face that looks like this:

Once you have this picture, add a **MouseMotionListener** to the program so that the pupils in the eyes follow the cursor position. For example, if you move the cursor to the lower right side of the screen, the pupils should shift so that they appear to be looking at that point, as follows:

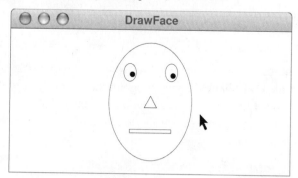

Although it doesn't matter much when the cursor is outside the face, it is important to compute the position of the pupil independently for each eye. If you move the mouse between the eyes, for example, the pupils should point in opposite directions so that the face appears cross-eyed.

3. In addition to line drawings of the sort generated by the **DrawLines** program, interactive drawing programs allow you to add other shapes to the canvas. In a typical drawing application, you create a rectangle by pressing the mouse at one corner and then dragging it to the opposite corner. For example, if you

press the mouse at the location in the left diagram and then drag it to the position in which you see it in the right diagram, the program creates the rectangle shown:

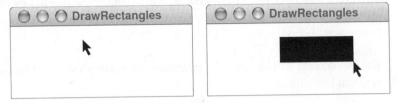

The rectangle grows as you drag the mouse. When you release the mouse button, the rectangle is complete and stays where it is. You can then go back and add more rectangles in the same way.

Although the code for this exercise is quite short, there is one important consideration that you will need to take into account. In the example above, the initial mouse click is in the upper left corner of the rectangle. Your program, however, has to work just as well if you drag the mouse in some other direction besides to the right and down. For example, you should also be able to draw a rectangle by dragging to the left, as shown in the following illustration:

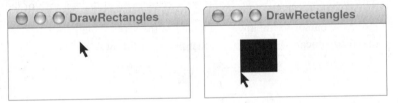

4. Using the **DrawLines** and **DrawRectangles** programs as a starting point, create a more elaborate drawing program that displays an onscreen menu of five shapes—a filled rectangle, an outlined rectangle, a filled oval, an outlined oval, and a straight line—along the left side of the canvas, as shown in the following diagram:

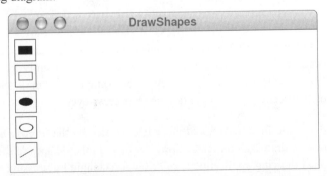

Clicking on one of the squares in the menu chooses that shape as a drawing tool. Thus, if you click on the filled oval in the middle of the menu area, your program should draw filled ovals. Clicking and dragging outside the menu should draw the currently selected shape.

5. Extend the **DrawShapes** application from the preceding exercise so that the left sidebar also includes a palette of colors, one for each of Java's predefined color names. Clicking on one of the colors sets the current color for the application, so that subsequent shapes are drawn in that color.

6. Extend the **DrawShapes** application from exercises 4 and 5 so that clicking on an existing shape drags that shape around the screen. To do so, you will have to store the dimensions of each shape so that you can test whether the mouse click occurs inside a shape the user has already drawn.

7. Write a program to play the classic arcade game of Breakout, which was developed in 1976 by Steve Wozniak, who would later become one of the founders of Apple. In Breakout, your goal is to clear a collection of bricks by hitting each of them with a bouncing ball.

    The initial configuration of the Breakout game appears in the leftmost diagram in Figure 19-11. The colored rectangles in the top part of the screen are bricks, two rows each of red, orange, yellow, green, and blue. The slightly larger rectangle at the bottom is the paddle. The paddle is in a fixed position in the vertical dimension, but moves back and forth across the screen along with the mouse until it reaches the edge of its space.

FIGURE 19-11 Selected configurations in the Breakout game

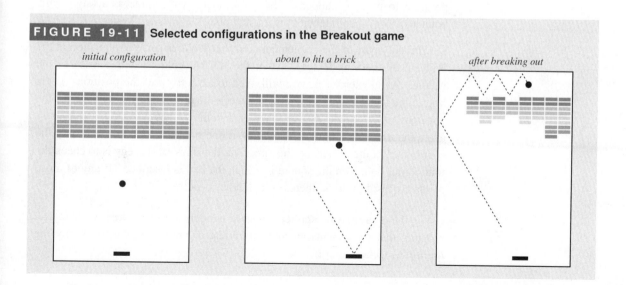

initial configuration   *about to hit a brick*   *after breaking out*

A complete Breakout game consists of three turns. On each turn, a ball is launched from the center of the window toward the bottom of the screen at a random angle. That ball bounces off the paddle and the walls of the world. Thus, after two bounces—one off the paddle and one off the right wall—the ball might have the trajectory shown in the middle diagram.

As you can see from the middle diagram, the ball is about to collide with one of the bricks on the bottom row. When that happens, the ball bounces just as it does on any other collision, but the brick disappears (which you can accomplish even in the simplified graphics library by painting it white). The play continues in this way until one of the following conditions occurs:

- The ball hits the lower wall, which means that you must have missed it with the paddle. In this case, the turn ends and the next ball is served, assuming that you have not already exhausted your allotment of three turns. If you have, the game ends in a loss.

- The last brick is eliminated. In this case, the game ends immediately, and you can retire victorious.

After all the bricks in a particular column have been cleared, a path will open to the top wall, as shown in the rightmost diagram in Figure 19-11. When this delightful situation occurs, the ball will often bounce back and forth several times between the top wall and the upper line of bricks without the user ever having to worry about hitting the ball with the paddle. This condition is called "breaking out."

It is important to note that, even though breaking out is a very exciting part of the player's experience, you don't have to do anything special in your program to make it happen. The game operates the same as always: balls bounce off walls, collide with bricks, and obey the laws of physics.

The only part of the implementation that requires some explanation is the problem of checking to see whether the ball has collided with a brick or the paddle. As in exercise 6, you will need to keep track of the positions of the bricks in a suitable data structure and check the position of the ball against the positions of the bricks to see whether a collision has occurred. Moreover, given that the ball is not a single point, it doesn't work well to check only the coordinates of the center. In this program, the simplest strategy is to check the four corner points on the square in which the ball is inscribed. If any of those points are inside a brick, then a collision has occurred.

8. Using the **StackTest** application as a model, create an **ArrayListTest** program that implements an interactive test of the methods exported by the **ArrayList** class.

9.   Extend the `plot` method from Figure 19-9 so that it takes an additional `Color` parameter, which controls the color of the line. Use this extended `plot` method to create a graph showing the growth curves of the most common complexity classes—constant, logarithmic, linear, $N \log N$, quadratic, and exponential—each in a different color. If you use an x range of 1 to 15 and a y range of 0 to 50, the graph looks like this:

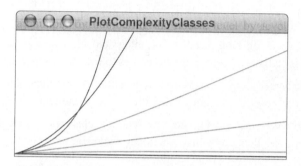

10. In the expression evaluator presented in Chapter 18, the `eval` method for the `CompoundExp` class contains the following chain of `if` statements:

```
if (op.equals("+")) return left + right;
if (op.equals("-")) return left - right;
if (op.equals("*")) return left * right;
if (op.equals("/")) return left / right;
```

As in the command dispatch example earlier in this chapter, it is possible to replace this code with a dispatch table that calls the function appropriate to the name of the operator.

Recode the expression evaluator using lambda expressions so that adding a new operator requires only one line of code, as in the following example:

```
defineOperator("+", 1, (x,y) -> x + y);
```

This call indicates that the operator `+` should have precedence 1 and should return the sum of its arguments, as indicated by the lambda expression.

11. You can also use lambda expressions to maintain a map of mathematical functions by name. For example, if you start with the declaration

```
HashMap<String,Function<Double,Double>> fnTable =
    new HashMap<String,Function<Double,Double>>();
```

you can then store functions under their conventional names simply by adding entries to `fnTable`. For example, the following lines add entries for the trigonometric `sin` and `cos` functions:

```
fnTable.put("sin", x -> Math.sin(x));
fnTable.put("cos", x -> Math.cos(x));
```

Use this technique to add a few mathematical functions to the expression interpreter. This change requires you to make several extensions to the existing framework, as follows:

- The interpreter must use real numbers rather than integers in its computation, as described in exercise 2 from Chapter 18.

- The function table needs to be integrated into the **EvaluationContext** class so that the interpreter has access to the functions by name.

- The parser module needs to include a new grammatical rule for expressions that represents a function call with a single argument.

- The **eval** method for the new function class must look up the function name and then apply that function to the result of evaluating the argument.

Your implementation should allow functions to be combined and nested just as in Java. For example, if your interpreter defines the functions **sqrt**, **sin**, and **cos**, your program should be able to produce the following sample run:

```
FunctionInterpreter
=> sqrt(2)
1.4142135623730951
=> sqrt(sqrt(sqrt(256)))
2.0
=> cos(0)
1.0
=> PI = 3.1415926535897936
3.1415926535897936
=> sin(PI / 2)
1.0
=> sin(PI / 6)
0.5
=> x = 5
5
=> y = 12
12
=> sqrt(x * x + y * y)
13.0
```

12. Starting with the extended version of the **Expression** class you implemented in exercise 11, define a new class called **ExpFunction** that implements **Function<Double,Double>**. The constructor for the **ExpFunction** class should take a string and create an object whose **apply** method carries out the following steps:

- Create an **EvaluationContext** that defines the mathematical functions.

- Create a binding for **x** whose value is the argument to **apply**.

- Parse the string into an expression.
- Evaluate the expression in the **EvaluationContext** where **x** is bound.

For example, if you execute the declaration

```
ExpFunction fn = new ExpFunction("2 * x + 3");
```

the result should be a function that you can apply to a **double** value. Thus, if you call **fn.apply(7.0)**, the result should be 17.0, which is the value of the expression **2 * x + 3** after binding **x** to 7.0 in the **EvaluationContext**.

13. In its current design, the **plot** function takes six arguments: the graphics window, the lambda expression to be plotted, and two pairs of values indicating the range of the plot in both the x and the y dimension. You can eliminate the last two parameters by having **plot** compute the limits of the y range from the displayed valued. All you need to do is execute the computation twice, once to find the minimum and maximum values of the function and once to plot the function using those values as the limits of the range. Write an overloaded version of the **plot** method that uses this strategy to compute the y limits automatically.

14. Combine the **ExpFunction** facility from exercise 12 with the **plot** method from exercise 13 so that the function argument can be any expression string involving the variable **x**. For example, after making these extensions to the **plot** function, you should be able to call

```
plot(gw, "sin(x)", -2 * Math.PI, 2 * Math.PI, 1, 1)
```

to produce the sine wave plot shown at the top of page 750. The string expression, however, can use any of the facilities recognized by the expression parser, thereby allowing you to plot more complicated functions, as illustrated by the following call:

```
plot(gw, "sin(2 * x) + cos(3 * x)", -Math.PI, Math.PI)
```

This call parses the expression **sin(2 * x) + cos(3 * x)** and then generates the following plot:

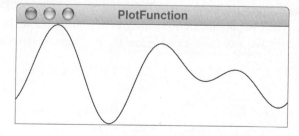

15. In calculus, the ***definite integral*** of a function is defined to be the area bounded horizontally by two specified limits and vertically by the *x*-axis and the value of the function. For example, the definite integral of the trigonometric sine function in the range 0 to π is the area of the shaded region in the following diagram:

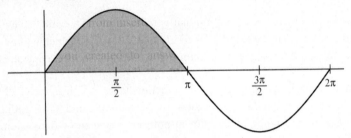

You can compute an approximation of this area by adding the areas of small rectangles of a fixed width, where the height is given by the value of the function at the midpoint of the rectangle:

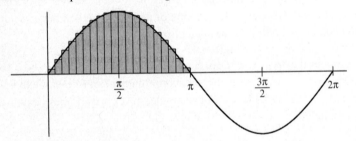

Design the prototype and write the code for an **integrate** method that approximates the definite integral by summing the areas of the rectangles. For example, to calculate the area of the shaded region in the earlier example, the client would write

```
integrate(x -> Math.sin(x), 0, Math.PI, 20);
```

The last argument is the number of rectangles into which the area gets divided; the larger this value, the more accurate the approximation.

Note that any region that falls below the *x*-axis is treated as negative area. Thus, if you compute the definite integral of **sin** from 0 to 2π, the result will be 0 because the areas above and below the axis cancel each other out.

Index